RECENT POLITICAL THOUGHT

THE CENTURY
POLITICAL SCIENCE SERIES

Edited by FREDERIC A. OGG, *University of Wisconsin*

———

Frederic A. Ogg and P. Orman Ray, INTRODUCTION TO AMERICAN GOVERNMENT, Seventh Edition, and ESSENTIALS OF AMERICAN GOVERNMENT, Fourth Edition.

L. Vaughan Howard and Hugh A. Bone, CURRENT AMERICAN GOVERNMENT (in preparation).

Robert S. Rankin, READINGS IN AMERICAN GOVERNMENT.

Walter F. Dodd, STATE GOVERNMENT IN THE UNITED STATES.

Thomas H. Reed, MUNICIPAL GOVERNMENT IN THE UNITED STATES.

Lent D. Upson, THE PRACTICE OF MUNICIPAL ADMINISTRATION.

John A. Fairlie and Charles M. Kneier, COUNTY GOVERNMENT AND ADMINISTRATION.

Joseph P. Chamberlain, LEGISLATIVE PROCESSES: NATIONAL AND STATE.

Edward M. Sait, AMERICAN PARTIES AND ELECTIONS, Third Edition.

Andrew C. McLaughlin, CONSTITUTIONAL HISTORY OF THE UNITED STATES

John M. Mathews, AMERICAN FOREIGN RELATIONS: CONDUCT AND POLICIES.

Graham H. Stuart, LATIN AMERICA AND THE UNITED STATES, Fourth Edition.

Pitman B. Potter, INTRODUCTION TO THE STUDY OF INTERNATIONAL ORGANIZATION.

Charles G. Fenwick, INTERNATIONAL LAW.

Herbert Adams Gibbons, INTRODUCTION TO WORLD POLITICS.

Frank M. Russell, THEORIES OF INTERNATIONAL RELATIONS.

William Anderson (ed.), LOCAL GOVERNMENT IN EUROPE.

Harold S. Quigley, JAPANESE GOVERNMENT AND POLITICS.

Edward M. Sait, POLITICAL INSTITUTIONS: A PREFACE.

W. F. Willoughby, THE GOVERNMENT OF MODERN STATES.

Francis W. Coker, RECENT POLITICAL THOUGHT.

Raymond G. Gettell, HISTORY OF POLITICAL THOUGHT and HISTORY OF AMERICAN POLITICAL THOUGHT.

J. Mark Jacobson, THE DEVELOPMENT OF AMERICAN POLITICAL THOUGHT.

Anna Haddow, POLITICAL SCIENCE IN AMERICAN COLLEGES AND UNIVERSITIES, 1636-1900.

RECENT POLITICAL THOUGHT

BY

FRANCIS W. COKER

COWLES PROFESSOR OF GOVERNMENT
YALE UNIVERSITY

KENNETH DOUGLAS McRAE

D. APPLETON–CENTURY COMPANY
INCORPORATED
NEW YORK   LONDON

PREFACE

THIS book is a review of dominant political ideas, as set forth in theoretical writings and active social movements, during the period from about the middle of the nineteenth century to the present day. Although chapters and sections are for the most part arranged topically rather than chronologically, some attempt is made to show the progression of ideas within each field. The author has persistently sought to maintain some sort of impartial attitude in the exposition of the doctrines; but his own theoretical preconceptions have possibly colored his critical interpretation at many points.

Compression of the matter into a single volume has presented many difficult problems of selection. No writers have been omitted on the ground merely that they were not primarily students of government. Accordingly there are included at various points certain psychologists, sociologists, economists, jurists, journalists, who have approached political ideas from neighboring fields of observation. What may be a notable defect of the work in this connection is the lack of a separate chapter devoted to a consideration of psychological discussions of political behavior, as exemplified in the writings of Walter Bagehot, Graham Wallas, and John Dewey and as recently summarized by Charles E. Merriam, C. H. Driver, and others. The author made a start toward a special description of these approaches but was confronted by so much variety in the prevalent psychological theories that it seemed impossible to give, in brief space, any clear account of the varying political orientations of the theories. Limitations of space have also excluded any treatment of the studies by Stuart A. Rice, Floyd H. Allport, and others who are attempting to devise exact numerical measurements of political behavior as a means of testing and clarifying our political beliefs.

The author desires to express grateful acknowledgment for the many helpful criticisms he has received, particularly from Henry R. Spencer and Walter J. Shepard of Ohio State University; George H. Sabine of Cornell University; C. H. Driver of King's College, London; George Vernadsky of Yale University; Frederic A. Ogg of the University of Wisconsin, editor of the series in which this book appears; and Carlton C. Rodee, August O. Spain, David Fellman, and Ewing G. Simpson, Cowles Fellows in Government in Yale University.

v

CONTENTS

CONTENTS

CONTENTS

CHAPTER I

THE MID-NINETEENTH CENTURY HERITAGE OF POLITICAL IDEAS

THE SCOPE OF POLITICAL THEORY

EVERY community—however remote from the centers of civilization its habitat may be and however primitive its culture—is organized politically—in however rudimentary form. Moreover, in all regions to-day allegiance to the political organization of the community is normally all-inclusive and compulsive. Each individual, whether he likes it or not, is a member of some state. He may in some cases—partly, at least, at his discretion—terminate membership in one state, but only by acquiring it in another. He may by his conduct forfeit some of the privileges of citizenship; but his citizenship remains. He may manifest very little interest in the business of his state; but he remains, none the less, on the one hand a beneficiary of its services and on the other hand subject to definite, formal modifications of his conduct and social relationships as a consequence of the power which the state exercises. The state is *sui generis* in these respects. No other social organization is so universal and so comprehensive in its membership.

The state is as old as recorded history; and political theory is as old as the state. It is sometimes said that systematic political theory appeared first among the Greeks of about the fifth century B. C. This is true in one sense: in writings available to us from periods previous to that time, we find little explicit discussion of what we now regard as the major questions of political theory. So we make the rough generalization that ancient Oriental writers were not given to systematic reflection on political questions; we say that they were inclined to accept the political arrangements of their time as sufficiently sanctioned by religion or tradition, that their theoretical writings were generally concerned only with such metaphysical subjects as the nature of reality or the soul of man, or that their political discussions related only to questions concerning the personal virtues and vices of rulers and subjects. But some sort of political theory has existed even among the

1

most primitive peoples, as well as among the despotisms of the most ancient civilizations. The formulas *sic volo jubeo* or *Deus vult* have never been adequate, either theoretically or practically, as explanations of the prerogatives claimed by political rulers. The wielders of power always have to give some general justification of the demands they make upon the loyalty and obedience of their subjects.

The universality and permanence of political authority would seem to create a presumption that the state satisfies some unique and constant needs of men. Some have denied this. Since the earliest times of political speculation, there have been men who have denied the social and moral legitimacy of political authority. This doctrine we call anarchism; and it has had devoted and intelligent exponents both in antiquity and in modern times—writers who have ably expressed their faith that man's naturally rational and social impulses constitute, when they are not distorted by artificial encroachments of organized coercive authority, the surest guarantee we can have for a just and peaceful social life.

The doctrine of anarchism, however, has never had numerous adherents. In all ages the great majority of political writers have accepted the state as an indispensable institution of social life; but there has never been agreement among them as to just what are the benefits we may properly expect to derive from political organization or as to the proper place to draw the line between governmental control and individual freedom. Some writers have associated political action with the baser or weaker sides of human nature, assigning to the state a relatively undignified place in society and attempting to accommodate its structure and action to man's defects rather than to his virtues: the fifth century Church Father, St. Augustine, held that the state was made necessary only by the sins of man; and the eighteenth century Anglo-American rationalist, Thomas Paine, argued that government is "produced by our weaknesses" and "even in its best state is but a necessary evil." Others in various ages have greatly exalted the position and functions of the state: Greek philosophers of the fourth and third centuries B.C. believed that the state contributed, in greater degree than any other social institution, to the realization of the finer and nobler capacities of man; early nineteenth century German philosophers also glorified political institutions, Hegel characterizing the state as "the advance of God in the world"; and we shall find contemporary instances of a similar exaltation of political authority.

There have been wide varieties of opinion not only as to the part we should expect political action to play in the life of man, but also as to how the state should be organized and as to the kinds and degrees of authority and power it must be accorded in order that it may play that part effectively and equitably. Why do we have the state? What are the things that it can do better than individuals acting alone, or than other, smaller, social groups which individuals enter and leave more spontaneously and informally? What spheres of individual or social life is it incompetent to enter? Who should control political life? What relation should the state, in its organization and activity, bear to the ideas and sentiments of the people or to the economic structure of the community? When political government and its forms and activities are studied not simply as facts to be described and compared, or judged in reference to their immediate and temporary effects, but as facts to be understood and appraised in relation to the constant needs, desires, and opinions of men—then we have political theory.

Political theory has not flourished equally or in the same forms in all ages. The practical social problems which the scholars of a particular age seek to solve, in terms of relatively general and permanent truths, are set mainly by the peculiar experiences of that age; the form and content of their solutions are influenced both by those experiences and by the general intellectual temper of the times. In the vigorous cultural and political life of the Greek city-states of the fifth and fourth centuries B. C., great philosophers elaborately explored political questions that we still consider to be of basic significance and in categories that we still widely accept. With the disappearance of the independent Greek states under Roman domination, reflective interests of writers centered more generally on the individual rather than government. Both Stoic and Epicurean philosophers of that age argued that if man were only persuaded to live in obedience to the good reason, sense of justice and broad human sympathy, or intelligent self-interest, with which Nature had endowed him, then the forms of his political relations would be of relatively little importance to him. Jurists and essayists of the Roman Republic and Empire supplied valuable expositions of the logical and practical phases of their systems of law and administration; in their more philosophical writings on political questions, however, they copied in the main the speculations of the Greeks. Throughout most of the Middle Ages the state (as we use the term) played a smaller part than other social institutions—e.g., the Church and organized vocational groups—in controlling man's social relations; and prior to the twelfth century there was little in the way of philosophical inquiry into political matters. Frequently in this period debates arose out of conflicting claims by temporal and ecclesiastical rulers; but the argument was generally in the form of an appeal to authority—the Bible, the Pope, the Church Fathers—or to precedents, accepted by both sides but in conflicting interpretations. With the reinvigoration of practical political life and the revival of general humanistic interests in the later Middle Ages, there reappeared a broader, somewhat more rationalistic, and in some respects more empirical, discussion of the nature of political organization and action, and this has continued constantly during the seven succeeding centuries.

Our political reasoning to-day has certain roots that connect it peculiarly with the latter half of the eighteenth century. In the first place, a "scientific" attitude towards social institutions took somewhat definite form at that time. Under the influence of the great progress in the natural sciences, philosophers maintained that natural laws of human society could be discovered by intelligent men, not mainly by an introspective analysis of the human mind, but by systematic observation of the ways in which men live and act in actual societies. Secondly, the wide extension of man's control over physical nature, made possible by the great mechanical inventions of that era, gave impetus to the idea that man could in large measure control also the forms and activities of his institutional life by intelligently applying the permanent social laws to immediate social problems. Thirdly, the mechanical inventions brought on changes in the economic structure of society which have influenced all later political theorizing. A new industrial "middle class" appeared, and with its strengthening economic position in society it soon successfully asserted its claims to political power, so that an increasing number of citizens were actually participating in political discussion. The industrial revolution also—massing large bodies of wage-workers into cities and placing peculiar difficulties in the way of healthy, comfortable, and orderly living conditions—precipitated, on the one hand, new problems for the new middle-class democracy to solve, and, on the other hand, led in time to efforts by the working-men themselves to obtain their share of self-government, within or without the political structure of society. Finally, still another intellectual attitude of the eighteenth century has influenced the course of later political theory. "Romanticism" entered into the scientific and practical rationalism of that age, partly tempering and partly confirming it. Philosophers pictured an ideal order of society and manifested their clear faith in the power of man's conscious endeavors, inspired by his spiritual vision but guided by his reason, to move steadily towards a political goal satisfying the noblest aspirations of normal men. These eighteenth century "revolutions"—rational, mechanical, political, and romantic—determine the problems as well as the form and content of much of our contemporary social theory.

We cannot name a decade or half-century, or an episode or movement, or some school of doctrine or group of authors, and say that in any of these "recent" political thought has its origin. However, we recognize certain ideas as especially prominent in discussions and practical movements of to-day. Though their roots are set deeply in the past, yet in their recent developments they have assumed somewhat new phases. This book is devoted to a description of what seem, to the writer, to be the more significant developments in political thought during the last three quarters of a century. The exposition will perhaps be made clearer if we first review briefly some conceptions that were familiar in the earlier half of the nineteenth century, concerning the ever-recurring questions as to the rational basis of political authority, the proper line between governmental control and individual freedom, the proper location of political power, and the spheres of economic and social life that can be properly placed under that power. The aim here is not to summarize all the significant doctrines of that period, but rather to give sketches of typical ideas that were particularly prominent and influential in the mid-nineteenth century and that in many instances have remained, in some form or other, as assumptions or convictions in various fields of recent and contemporary political reasoning.

IDEAS ON THE LOCATION OF POLITICAL AUTHORITY

Every political theory has some explicit or implicit doctrine as to where ultimate control over the power which governing agencies exert ought to be located. We still debate the relative merits of monarchy, aristocracy, and democracy. The validity of these terms is now frequently challenged, on the ground that actual governments cannot generally be sharply distinguished in such fashion. A monarch, for example, always depends upon the support of aristocratic groups and is always variously limited by them; and both monarchs and aristocrats take some account of popular beliefs and prejudices, and the possibilities of an insurrection always set bounds to their powers. In democracies, on the other hand, the people as a whole do not actually rule: most of the inhabitants in nominally democratic states have been (until very recent times) outside the pale of "the people," considered politically; and even in states that now accord formal political rights to the adult citizens generally, the exercise of actual governing power is variously controlled by minority groups. Despite these necessary qualifications, the traditional terms have some validity in indicating the ideal forms of state conceived by those who are attacking or defending some existing organization of authority, or the ideas which the writers have in mind as to the natural or prevailing tendencies in the actual location of political power.

The arguments over the question as to whether the one ablest individual, or the most capable and virtuous minority, or the general body of citizens should, or does, rule were hardly different a century ago from those we find in the classics of ancient Greece, or indeed, as we shall see, from most of what is said in the contemporary controversy.

In every age there have been some who have held that the unity and orderliness essential in any stable political society can be secured only where supreme authority is vested in a single ruler. The idea that this unified rulership must be vested in a hereditary king, exercising an authority unlimited by any other secular body, reached, in modern times, its high point in the seventeenth century, and was exemplified notably in the claims somewhat effectively asserted by James I in England and Louis XIV in France. This principle of absolute monarchy was greatly weakened, but by no means extinguished, by the English revolutions of that century. The French Revolution in the late eighteenth century and the wave of popular revolutionary doctrine that spread over continental Europe during the two succeeding decades, seemed again to have swept away the foundations of any sort of monarchic system. Yet after the final victory of the alliance of the great monarchies of Europe over Jacobin and Napoleonic France, the royalist principle reappeared with great practical vigor on the Continent. When the restored Bourbon monarch proclaimed a constitution for France in 1814, he put it forth as a voluntary grant; and the constitution affirmed that "all authority in France resides in the person of the King." Similar claims for royal supremacy appeared in the constitutions of the German states and in the pronouncements of German rulers and ministers.

The French and German royalist writers of the early nineteenth century argued that monarchy is the only natural, rational, and efficient form of state, because it is the most conducive to unity and constancy in political policy and to the preservation of the national culture.[1] In France the Count de Maistre and the Marquis de Bonald represented rule by a single person as the form approved by God, and as indeed inevitable, whatever the formal declarations of a constitution might be. A single human will, they maintained, is the determining factor in any "national" decision; so that the only choice before a people is between, on the one hand, government by a formally recognized sovereign, known to all, and possessed of an ability to rule gained by inheritance and experience, and, on the other hand, government by frequently changing dictators or popular demagogues, acquiring their supremacy through the operation of fictitious and temporary forces. The German theorists (e.g., Hegel and Friedrich J. Stahl) admitted ideas of constitutionalism into their systems and acknowledged a vague sort of ultimate sovereignty of the general will or of the common moral sense of the community; but they ascribed only negative or consultative functions to elected assemblies and made a hereditary king the highest exponent of the general will.

Few of the royalist writers, however, attributed absolute powers to kings; and the main issue in theoretical discussions of the early nineteenth century was whether some aristocratic group or "the people" was the proper despositary of ultimate political authority.

We find in that period the still familiar attitudes of scorn or apprehension for governments that rest on popular discussion and decision. French publicists—notably François Guizot and Alexis de Tocqueville —set forth, in specific detail, the practical dangers of majority tyranny inherent in any government based on a broad suffrage.[2] English writers made eloquent appeals for a return to the aristocratic order of the past. Edmund Burke, at the time of the French Revolution, had urged his countrymen to reject the "barbarous philosophy" of eighteenth century rationalist and revolutionary equalitarianism—a philosophy "destitute of all taste and eloquence," the "offspring of cold hearts and muddy understandings," in which "all the decent drapery of life is torn off"

---

[1] See W. A. Dunning, *Political Theories from Rousseau to Spencer*, Ch. 5, Secs. 3 and 4.

[2] Guizot (1787–1874), *Histoire des origines du gouvernement représentatif* (1821–1822), English translation (1852). De Tocqueville (1805–1859), *De la démocratie en Amérique* (1835), English translation (1863, etc.).

and "a king is but a man, a queen is but a woman." [3] He upheld the values of rank and social privilege in insuring the preservation of good manners, heroic enterprise, orderly living, respectful subservience of the humble to their betters, and generous guardianship of the common by the noble. "The sad conclusion," said Thomas Carlyle, half a century later, "which all experience, wherever it has been tried, is fatally making good, appears to be, That Parliaments, admirable as Advising Bodies, and likely to be in future universally useful in that capacity, are, as Ruling and Sovereign Bodies, not useful, but useless or worse. That a Sovereign with 900 or with 658 heads, all set to talk against each other in the presence of 34 or 27 or 18 millions, cannot do the work of sovereignty at all; but is smitten with eternal incompetence for that function by the law of Nature itself. Such alas, is the sad conclusion; and in England, and wherever else it is tried, a sad experience will rapidly make it good." [4] He maintained that government by an intelligent and benevolent aristocracy was ordained by universal laws of nature and was demonstrable as best both by human reason and by observation of the actual futility of all attempts to reach stable political decisions in public debate. "Surely," he said, "of all 'rights of man,' this right of the ignorant man to be guided by the wiser, to be, gently or forcibly, held in the true course by him, is the indisputablest. Nature herself ordains it from the first; Society struggles toward perfection by enforcing and accomplishing it more and more. . . . In Rome and Athens, as elsewhere, if we look practically, we shall find that it was not by loud voting and debating of many, but by wise insight and ordering of a few that the work was done. So is it ever, so will it ever be." [5]

German metaphysicians and jurists supplied more philosophic statements of a positive aristocratic doctrine. Most profound and distinctive was the reasoning of Hegel, who argued that the state has of its very essence an aristocratic constitution: hereditary rulers and politically privileged classes are as indispensable parts of a state as are the directing brain and soul in a normal human being. [6] He admitted that a constitution must reflect the political character of the nation and that a

---

[3] *Reflections on the Revolution in France* (1790), in *Works* (Boston, 1865–1867), pp. 233–362, at p. 333.
[4] *Latter-Day Pamphlets* (1849), Vol. XX in *The Works of Thomas Carlyle* (Centenary ed., 1899–   ), at pp. 226–227.
[5] *Chartism* (1839) in Vol. IV of his *Critical and Miscellaneous Essays*, 5 vols. (Centenary ed.), Vols. XXVI–XXX at pp. 157–159.
[6] *Grundlinien der Philosophie des Rechts* (1821), translated by S. W. Dyde as *The Philosophy of Right*, Secs. 275 ff.

government must serve the interests and obey ultimately the will of the people; but deputies chosen by the people can have no understanding of either the true interest or the actual will of the people. Even in so-called democracies, he argued, the political summits are always occupied by a few individuals, who arrive at such positions, not because they represent the average quality of the individuals composing the nation or because they reflect prevailing popular ideas, but because they possess qualities that mark them off from the rest of the people and know how to maintain their independence of public opinion, however passionately expressed. Thus in every state the men who dominate politically are those who can see and execute the implicit, or the "real" or "rational," will of the people—as distinguished from the explicit and apparent will of the majority. The true statesman represents the popular will in the sense that he does things the people would want done if they possessed the knowledge, insight, and experience which he has; as a physician, who prescribes things distasteful to and opposed by his patient, yet represents, in such action, the real will of his patient to get well. "He who tells the time what it wills and means and then brings it to completion is the great man of the time. . . . Who does not learn to despise public opinion, which is one thing in one place and another in another, will never achieve anything great." [7]

The aristocratic argument was often then, as now, given an economic cast. The records of political debate and correspondence in England reveal a widely held idea that government must be controlled by the small group of wealthy landowners. Not only tenants and laborers, but also manufacturers, merchants, and professional men, it was said, lacked that fixed stake in the general prosperity, and that inherited familiarity with the traditions, of a country, possessed by the nobility and landed gentry. "The bulk and weight of the House of Commons," said Lord North, ought to be "the country gentlemen," for they "are the best and most respectable objects of the confidence of the people." [8] Carlyle looked to both landholders and to "captains of industry" (a term he seems to have invented) for the wise, practical, and benevolent direction of affairs: political direction through their supremacy in the chief legislative and executive organs of the government; economic direction through the paternalistic control they should be allowed to exercise over the common men in farms and factories. "The Leaders of Industry,"

[7] *The Philosophy of Right,* Sec. 318, p. 325.
[8] William Cobbett, *Parliamentary History of England,* Vol. XXV, Col. 461.

he said, "if Industry is ever to be led, are virtually the Captains of the World! If there be no nobleness in them, there will never be an Aristocracy more." [9] It was often argued likewise, in the early nineteenth century constitutional conventions of the American commonwealths, that fitness to share in public power presupposes the possession of a fair amount of wealth, on the general ground that a man should not take part in the management of public affairs until he has demonstrated his capacity in the management of private affairs; or that a man of fortune has greater stake and interest in the sound management of public affairs than a property-less or poor man can have.

These defenders of aristocracy, in the mid-nineteenth century, were opposing an apparently strong democratic trend, in practice and theory. The movement of economic forces (the rise of the factory system and the concentration of industrial populations) brought to the forefront problems of practical administration (in dealing with irregular employment, urban sanitation, bad living conditions among industrial workers, and rising prices) with which the traditional aristocratic groups showed themselves unable to deal competently. Economic changes were also increasing the opportunities of middle-class groups to make effective demands for representation in government. France in 1830 and England in 1832 accorded voting rights to these groups, and the American commonwealths were changing their constitutions in order to establish substantially an adult, male, citizenship suffrage. Although the mid-century revolutions in Europe were suppressed, yet the periods of reaction that followed were, in most of the states, brief; and the movement for democratizing representative assemblies and enlarging their powers was well under way and soon showed itself to be irresistible.

Political theory also played an important part in the democratic movement. The advocacy of democracy was set forth, then as now, partly in terms of a theory of original and natural human rights and partly in terms of a conception of empirically proved utility.[10] According to the former theory—familiar since Milton's *Tenure of Kings and Magistrates* and the Levellers' pamphlets in mid-seventeenth century England, and given its most classic statement in Rousseau's *Contrat Social* and the American and French revolutionary declarations in the next century—man is naturally and, therefore, rightfully a free, self-determining being; as a

---

[9] *Past and Present* (1843), Vol. X of *Works* (Centenary ed.), at p. 271. "Captains of Industry" is the title of Bk. IV, Ch. 13.

[10] For references to accounts of the natural-rights and utilitarian doctrines, see notes 23 and 25, *infra* pp. 22 and 23.

member of society he must retain that freedom if he is to remain fully a man; accordingly the only doctrine that can reconcile his subjection to political government with his natural freedom is the doctrine that subjects him to the authority of the community alone. It is illogical to conceive of a rational man submitting to the direction of some particular person or group within the community. Thus the state must be regarded as founded upon a voluntary association of free and equal persons. Although these persons, by combining into a political society, form an authoritative organization to which each becomes a subject, yet (to follow roughly the phrases of Rousseau) each remains free in the sense that he has subordinated himself only to an authority in the exercise of which he has a share equal to that of every other member of the community; the individual gives himself up to no single person or group, but to the whole people; so he receives back as much as he gives; he becomes politically subject only to the degree that he becomes politically sovereign.

Utilitarian doctrine agreed with the natural-rights doctrine in the belief that the qualities in which men differ are of less significance than those which they have in common. Its defense of democracy, however, was in terms not of absolute right but of the beneficial results that spring from popular participation in government. Equality in political privilege should be maintained, not because men are born with equal rights but because in an equal exercise of political privileges they become more efficient agents of happiness for themselves and others. Men have a natural right to self-government only in the sense that experience and common reason show that freedom is an essential element of happiness and that natural self-interest is the best security against oppressive or negligent political action. Democracy is government by those who have a greater awareness of and a greater concern for the interests of all the members of the community. It is, therefore, best adapted to serve both freedom and happiness. Where government is controlled by the general body of citizens, it is least likely to establish unreasonable restraints upon individual conduct and most likely to be impartial in the determination and enforcement of whatever restrictions experience shows it is necessary to impose.

IDEAS ON THE PROVINCE OF GOVERNMENT

What are the limitations that a government may properly impose upon the free action of individuals? Prevailing ethical and economic doctrines of the early nineteenth century, largely a heritage from the seventeenth and eighteenth centuries, pointed generally to conclusions of governmental non-interference. Natural-rights philosophers, utilitarian reformers, and economic theorists contrasted liberty with government, regarded governmental control as in some way going against the nature of man or the natural social order, posited a sort of antagonism between the citizen and his state, and argued that extensive governmental activity was an obstacle to the increase of human happiness and to the development of the highest types of individual character. A basic idea in writings of all three groups goes back at least to the later seventeenth century (found notably in the works of the metaphysician and political philosopher, John Locke); it is that laws of nature, discoverable by human reason, govern the social relations of men, and political societies are rationally formed only for the purpose of sustaining these laws and so are limited by them.

The doctrine of natural rights holds that man in political society is entitled to exercise the rights with which he is born, so long as he does not aggressively interfere with an equally free exercise of the same rights by other members of society. According to this doctrine, men deliberately create a state only for the purpose of protecting rights which they have independently of the state. In all that a government does, therefore, it must respect these rights, if it is to attain its legitimate authority. Each individual owes to his state only those services and self-denials that are necessary for the conservation of the rights of individuals generally. The individualist creed of the utilitarians was also based upon a conception of rules of action which men normally follow and which human reason perceives and approves. The rules, in this doctrine, are rules, not of right, but of self-interest. The doctrine considers man as acting always under the impulse of a desire to obtain pleasure or avoid pain and regards this universal impulse as supplying the only key to the test of rightness. Each man, the argument proceeds, is the safest judge of his own happiness, so that if left to himself, freed from "unnecessary" public or private interference, he will choose the course of action that best promotes his happiness; moreover, in intelligently pursuing his own well-being he advances best the well-being of others, for his reason perceives that the happiness of his neighbors is the surest guaranty for his own. So all are benefited by a policy of non-interference.

The new discipline of political economy adopted and fortified with ideas of its own these doctrines of rationalized social laws, of natural rights recognized by human reason, of happiness as the test of right, and of the natural identity of the egoistic and altruistic interests of man. The "Physiocrats," beginning with the work of Quesnay in 1763, are generally considered to be the founders of the modern science of economics.[11] This French school opposed the prevailing "mercantilism"—which advocated a policy of active governmental regulation and protection of industry and commerce as a means of increasing the national wealth and power—by their notions of a "natural order" of society in which an enlightened self-interest realizes best both private and the public welfare. Their scientific system was purely deductive—dealing with *a priori* laws, simple, clear to the disciplined mind, universal in application. Moreover, they regarded private property, and freedom in the transactions traditionally associated with it, as the most obvious and essential phenomena of a naturally and logically ordered society. Accordingly they considered a governmental policy good to the extent that it respected private property, permitted free competition everywhere, and recognized an absolute equality of all individuals before the law—an equality which, they believed, without disapproval, led inevitably to wide and irremediable variations in economic condition among the members of society.

It is particularly from the influence of the more comprehensive and detailed works of the "classical" political economy (beginning with Adam Smith's *Wealth of Nations* in 1776 and dominant in economic writings throughout the Western world during the first half of the nineteenth century) that the creed of *laisser-faire* came to be the authoritative doctrine in most discussions of the scope of governmental activity.[12] The writers of this school took over from the Physiocrats the doctrine that natural economic principles fixed private property and free competition as the essential features of a rational economic system, integrated this doctrine with the prevailing utilitarian ethics, and showed how the natural economic and ethical principles should work normally in a capitalist system.

[11] Cf. Henry Higgs, *The Physiocrats* (1897) ; Georges Weulerrse, *Le mouvement physiocratique en France de 1756 à 1770* (1910).

[12] The classical economic doctrine appears, with varying qualifications and applications, most notably in the writings of Smith, Thomas Robert Malthus, David Ricardo, John Stuart Mill (in his earlier writings), and J. E. Cairnes in England; Jean Baptiste Say in France; J. H. von Thünen and Karl Heinrich Rau in Germany; and Henry C. Carey in the United States. Cf. Lewis H. Haney, *History of Economic Thought*, Chs. X–XVII; Gide and Rist, *History of Economic Doctrines*, Bk. I, Chs. II, III, and Bk. III.

Thus the classical economists assumed, first, a natural economic man—self-seeking, intelligent and well-informed in pursuing his interest, constantly desirous and able to buy goods and services in the cheapest and sell them in the dearest markets; and second, a natural economic order, in which the relations among individuals are controlled by laws as universal and permanent and as unchangeable by human effort as the laws of the physical universe. They recognized that in actual society other motives and conditions enter to disturb the perfect working of the fundamental and permanent laws; but they maintained that these "disturbing" and "temporary" deviations should not be allowed to obscure the overwhelming force of the laws; and they held that the phenomena of an existing industrial society should be judged principally according to standards supplied by conceptions of the natural economic man living in the natural economic order. Some of the classical economists saw in the practical operation of these laws unhappy consequences for large numbers of individuals. They qualified the broad conception of identity of interests and recognized that the normal working of the natural laws often creates antagonisms of interest between certain groups, e.g., between capitalists and working-men, as a result of the fact that, in general, profits tend to rise as wages decrease and to decrease as wages rise. Others endeavored to show that the laws work normally for the good of all: the interests of different individuals, however superficially antagonistic, are 'fundamentally harmonious; although in specific relations—as those of wage-earner to employer, or renter to landlord—immediate interests might conflict, yet broadly and in the long run the interests of the several groups are fundamentally the same; each in pursuing his own welfare, without considering that of others, would best discover and achieve his own good and at the same time serve best the interests of the whole community. Both "dismal" and "optimistic" economists were united in the general idea that, whether the natural economic laws were harmful or useful, man had nothing to do but accept them and adapt his conduct to them; neither legislation nor, in most cases, organized voluntary effort could improve results.

None of the classical economists held absolutely to the principle of non-interference in economic affairs. They admitted legal limitation of the rate of interest, compulsory education, and governmental administration of postal communication and of various public works. On other questions of governmental policy, however, they held generally to the principle that freedom of exchange and association, for both property-owners and wage-earners, offers the better solution for the problems of an industrial society. The general rule of *laisser-faire* is well indicated in the following paragraph from the *Wealth of Nations:*

All systems either of preference or of restraint, therefore, being thus completely taken away, the obvious and simple system of natural liberty establishes itself of its own accord. Every man, as long as he does not violate the laws of justice, is left perfectly free to pursue his own interest his own way, and to bring both his industry and capital into competition with those of any other man, or order of men. The sovereign is completely discharged from a duty, in the attempting to perform which he must always be exposed to innumerable delusions, and for the proper performance of which no human wisdom or knowledge could ever be sufficient: the duty of superintending the industry of private people, and of directing it towards the employments most suitable to the interest of the society. According to the system of natural liberty, the sovereign has only three duties to attend to; three duties of great importance, indeed, but plain and intelligible to common understandings: first, the duty of protecting the society from the violence and invasion of other independent societies; secondly, the duty of protecting, as far as possible, every member of the society from the injustices or oppression of every other member of it, or the duty of establishing an exact administration of justice; and thirdly, the duty of erecting and maintaining certain public works and certain public institutions, which it can never be for the interest of any individual, or small number of individuals, to erect and maintain, because the profit could never repay the expense to any individual or small number of individuals, though it may frequently do much more than repay it to a great society.[13]

There were, on the other hand, many publicists of the period who found that the doctrine of *laisser-faire* left room for, and even required, a program of extensive governmental activity—particularly in a situation where the mistakes of past governmental intervention had created artificial conditions of inequality and restraint. Thus in England the "Philosophical Radicals," mainly utilitarians, were active and aggressive reformers. They worked diligently for legislation that would make profound changes in the system of political representation, in the economic policy of government, and in the traditional laws of crime and judicial procedure.[14] Existing laws, they held, denied to the ordinary man his proper participation in public affairs and imposed unnecessary

---

[13] Adam Smith, *Wealth of Nations,* near the end of Bk. IV, Ch. IX.
[14] For accounts of the individualistic ideas of utilitarians, see the references in note 25, *infra,* p. 23; and for an account of the legislative reforms in England under

fetters upon his movements and activities in pursuing his welfare and vindicating his rights. Privilege and class distinction prevailed throughout the whole political organization; legislative and administrative officers, in both central and local governing bodies, were selected by processes in which the great mass of the people had no part. The laws of political representation, crime, civil justice, and trade circumscribed manifoldly the free movements of peaceful and competent persons and made inequitable differentiations of various sorts between rich and poor, landholder and tenant, landed gentleman and tradesman or manufacturer, Anglican and Catholic or dissenter, employer and wage-earner. Lawmakers and publicists were generally unawake or insensitive to those abuses and were disposed to regard traditional legal and political institutions as immutable. The Radicals regarded it as their task, therefore, to overcome the forces of tradition and vested interest and to arouse public and private opinion from ignorance and complacency in the face of the inequities and absurdities of an inherited legal system. In successfully promoting legislation to remove many of these burdens and discriminations—by liberalizing the suffrage, making Catholics and dissenters eligible to public office, mitigating the harshness and ending the oppressive discrimination of the criminal laws, and removing barriers to freedom of trade and association—they remained true to their doctrine of individualism. They sought only the governmental intervention that was necessary for abolishing the restraints which past legislation and judicial action had established and for thus restoring to ordinary men their freedom of action in taking care of themselves.

Other reforming groups went further. They threw overboard the basic assumptions of individualism and treated social evils as largely manmade and as capable of being in considerable measure removed by a courageous application of the moral authority of the Church and a vigorous and positive assertion of the powers of political government. Generally these groups developed no "scientific" doctrine upon which to base a logically arranged collectivist program; that was to come later in the century. They were simply repelled by their vision of the wretched consequences of *laisser-faire* in actual life. Parliamentary reports and popular pamphlets gave detailed and vivid pictures of the arduous and unsanitary conditions under which multitudes of working people lived

the inspiration of utilitarian leadership, see A. V. Dicey, *Law and Opinion in England* (second edition, 1914), pp. 184–210.

in that rapidly developing industrial era. Popular agitators—such as Michael Sadler, Richard Oastler, William Cobbett, and John Fielder— were warmly supported, in their efforts for reform through governmental interference, by famous literary persons—Robert Southey, Thomas Arnold, Carlyle, and Mrs. Gaskell—who made fervid appeals to the humanitarian sentiments of a Christian and civilized nation and expressed their emphatic distrust of the dogmas that tolerated suffering among so many British citizens.[15] To say that whatever goes on in existing economic relations must go on, and that, in the face of whatever consequences, the only proper social policy is to "button your pocket and stand still," was, declared Carlyle, a principle which he would "by no manner of means believe in, but pronounce at all fit times to be false, heretical and damnable, if ever aught was!"[16] The revelations, protests, and appeals had much influence in promoting the enactment of legislation limiting the employment of women and children and imposing various requirements to protect the safety and health of factory workers generally.

Other repudiations of the individualist creeds are seen in the writings and activities of those who advocated socialist ideas of one sort or another. Socialism in its present-day comprehensive and systematic forms has its definite origin principally in the works of Karl Marx, in the middle of the nineteenth century. Many of the basic economic doctrines of Marxian socialism, however, are to be found in writings several decades earlier—notably in the works of William Thompson, Thomas Hodgskin, John Gray, John Francis Bray, and other British writers.[17] These men set forth fully the doctrine that wage-workers, in fields, factories and mines, are the real producers of wealth, most of which is unjustly taken away from them by employers, traders, and other nonproducers; and they proposed collectivist schemes—a state monopoly of the services of marketing and banking, a currency system based on time units of labor, voluntary coöperative societies—in order either to insure an exchange of goods on the basis of the quantities of labor em-

---

[15] Dicey, *op cit.*, pp. 214–240.

[16] *Chartism* (see *supra*, p. 8, n. 5), p. 131.

[17] See William Thompson (d. 1833), *Inquiry into the Principles of the Distribution of Wealth Most Conducive to Happiness* (1824); Thomas Hodgskin (1787–1869), *The Natural and Artificial Right of Property Contrasted* (1832); John Gray (1799–1850?), *A Lecture on Human Happiness* (1825) and *Social Systems* (1831); John Francis Bray (1809–1895), *Labour's Wrongs and Labour's Remedy* (1828–1839). See also generally, Max Beer, *History of British Socialism* (1919), Vol. I, Pt. II, Ch. VII.

ployed in producing them or to secure generally an equitable distribution of wealth among those who create it.

More influential on immediate practical efforts were the "Utopian" and "Christian" socialists. These reformers challenged the psychological and ethical assumptions upon which the current defenses of private property rested, and showed the inhumane and "unnatural" consequences of unrestrained competition. They looked for relief, however, not, as the Marxists, to the revolutionary or other aggressive action of oppressed groups organized to avail themselves of the benefits of a natural evolution of society, but to the deliberate and pacific efforts of men inspired by feelings of benevolence and justice.

"Utopian socialist" is the term applied particularly to Count Henri de Saint-Simon, Charles Fourier, and Étienne Cabet in France, and Robert Owen in England. These men regarded poverty as the principal source of the ills of society and private property as the chief cause of poverty. Saint-Simon and Fourier made elaborate analyses of the emotional and rational qualities of man and gave somewhat realistic descriptions of the ways in which these qualities showed themselves in the actual life of a society where the traditional moral code and the whole legal order accorded a particularly privileged position to private property. They believed that the changes they desired could be achieved through appeals to the reason and sense of justice of influential members of the community. The details of their schemes differed considerably. They did not look at all to revolutionary action, nor primarily to political action, for bringing about the changes. They sought rather to set up select communities, in which principles of justice, benevolence, and intelligence would rule and from the example of which the whole of society would be gradually converted to their ideals. They attracted many devoted followers, including talented and distinguished persons, from various walks of life, who attempted, for several decades after the death of their masters, to propagate and apply their teachings. Most of the experimental communities and coöperative associations founded by these disciples soon failed. However, their basic doctrine—that if coöperation were substituted for competition as the mainspring of economic activity, most social evils would disappear—survives in later collectivist creeds. It was also the basic doctrine of the Christian socialists.[18]

---

[18] Many of the communities were established in the United States, chiefly by followers of Fourier. On the whole movement, cf. H. W. Laidler, *History of*

The term "Christian socialism" was first used in connection with a movement originating in England in the middle of the century; but the essential ideas which the terms denote have been expressed by prominent Christians, of various sects and in various countries, since the beginning of the modern industrial era.[19] The general doctrine is that no one, facing conditions as they actually are in an industrial civilization, can reconcile a policy of unregulated competition with the doctrines of Christianity. The prevailing economic creed, it was said, advises men to deal with one another as rivals and puts its approval upon those who outdistance their fellows in the pursuit of success; whereas Christ invited men to live together as brothers and co-laborers and taught that the rich should not be looked upon as the peculiarly successful members of society. Priests and others urged the Church to recognize both the dignity of human labor and the social responsibility of property and to see that the principles of Christianity were reflected in the laws of the state.

During the French Revolution, several clubs had been formed with the object of making the Revolution a movement for the achievement of a communist order based on Christ's teachings of universal brotherhood. Saint-Simon, a few decades later, called upon the Pope to use his great authority in aiding the realization of an ideal society based on coöperation among all who in any way contributed their labors to the production of useful things; some of Saint-Simon's most influential followers emphasized the religious aspect of his doctrine. In the second quarter of the century, French clergymen were energetic in their efforts to bring the Catholic Church into support of legislation restricting child labor, protecting adult labor from excessive hours, supplying public aid to the poor and afflicted, limiting profits, establishing minimum wages, and providing free education. Felicité Robert de Lamennais—distinguished priest and philosophical writer, often called the founder of Christian socialism in France—wrote moving descriptions of the miseries of the poor and diligently sought to persuade the Church to associate itself in the work of organizing working-men so that they might release themselves from the yoke of dependence upon selfish landlords

Socialist Thought (1927), Chs. VII–XII; J. O. Hertzler, *History of Utopian Thought* (1923), Ch. V; Morris Hillquit, *History of Socialism in the United States* (1910), pp. 2–148; G. B. Lockwood, *The New Harmony Movement* (1905); G. D. H. Cole, *The Life of Robert Owen* (second ed., 1930).

[19] For general accounts of Christian socialism, see R. T. Ely, *French and German Socialism in Modern Times*, Ch. XVI; M. Kaufman, *Christian Socialism*, (1888).

and employers. His chief work, *Words of a Believer,* was of great influence in spreading socialism among the workers and in arousing sympathy for them among their fellow-citizens in other walks of life.[20]

The Christian socialist movement in England was led by two famous
literary clergymen of the Church of England—Charles Kingsley and
Frederick Denison Maurice—and by a lawyer, J. M. Ludlow.[21] These
men, in their efforts to apply Christian ethics to the reform of social conditions, accepted considerable parts of the program of the newly emerging proletarian socialism. They regarded the latter in general as a natural outgrowth of Christianity and described their own movement as an
effort to socialize Christianity and Christianize socialism. They repudiated the notion that Christianity has no direct concern with political and
economic questions or with the problem of setting up just and healthy
modes of social life in this everyday world. The miracles, parables, and
sermons of Christ, they said, show that His supreme interest was not in
formal creeds and rituals but rather in seeing that the ordinary man was
housed, clothed, fed, protected from distress, and enabled to live a
temperate and decent life. The interest of the true Christian cannot
be altogether other-worldly; he must be concerned with establishing a
righteous and happy society on earth and must use his influence to see
that his government takes positive steps to that end.

The mid-nineteenth century English Christian socialists devoted their
practical efforts specifically to the tasks of educating industrial workers
—through meetings, conferences, free night schools, and cheap periodicals—and aiding them in forming coöperative producers' associations.
The leaders had no comprehensive ideas on political questions, and only
slight contacts with the growing trade-union movement; and their periodicals and associations soon failed. Their activities and writings, however, were influential in promoting a general movement for coöperation
among working-men and also in securing the enactment of laws to
facilitate the organization of coöperative societies.

The movement to interest the Christian Church in organized efforts
to make the Gospel an active factor in guiding business and political

[20] Lamennais (1782–1854), *Paroles d'un croyant* (1834).
[21] See C. E. Raven, *Christian Socialism, 1848–1854* (1920); J. E. Barker,
British Socialism (1908), Ch. 28. Also the following Fabian Tracts (in *Fabian
Tracts, Nos. 1 to 212, Published by the Fabian Society from 1884 to 1924* (1924):
No. 78, "Socialism and the Teaching of Christ," by Rev. John Clifford (1897);
No. 133, "Socialism and Christianity," by Rev. Percy Dearmer (1907), new ed.,
1919; No. 174, "Charles Kingsley and Christian Socialism," by Colwyn E. Vul-
liamy (1914).

life appeared in various forms of practical and theoretical expression in other European countries and in the United States; and it has continued into the present. The organizations of to-day do not generally employ the name of socialism, and they differ, in several aspects of their theory, both from earlier Christian socialists and among themselves. All, however, work in various ways for social and economic legislation as a means of carrying out their conceptions of the teachings of Christ.[22]

THE CRITERIA OF POLITICAL THEORY

A doctrine concerning the right location of political supremacy or the proper sphere of governmental activity has ordinarily some logical relation to a theory of the rational or moral basis of political authority in general. A system of political doctrines sets up, or else assumes, some universal criterion for judging the reasonableness or justice of any given governmental organization or policy. When certain powers are ascribed to a state over its subjects, or when rights are asserted for citizens over or against their government, there has to be some sort of a theoretical standard by which to appraise the soundness of the claims.

Two standards of political judgment pervaded the political writing of the eighteenth and early nineteenth centuries; they are found in the natural-rights and utilitarian doctrines to which we have already alluded; and they are variously involved, explicitly or implicitly, in political discussions of to-day, appearing sometimes as opposing, more often as concurring, ideas.

The basic idea among all the natural-rights theorists is that the standard of judgment must be outside the state and its history, and that the foundation and justification for all legal privileges and obligations can be found only in eternal and universal principles of justice and truth. In other words, there are elements in a man's life that are independent of and logically prior to his position as a member of political society and too important to be submitted to political authority. A man's natural rights are as essential parts of him as are his sensory organs. They are not derived from and are not modifiable by laws of the state; and they are valid for all normal men, however men may

---

[22] In the middle of the century there was a Catholic movement led by Bishop von Ketteler and a Protestant movement led by Pastor Todt and Dr. Stocker; a Belgian movement was led by Professor Huet. See C. Périn, *Le socialisme chrétien* (1886): F. S. Nitti, *Catholic Socialism* (1895).

differ in other respects. States also may properly differ from one another only as to the ways in which they protect rights, not as to the rights which they ought to protect. Accordingly, that government is best which bests protects the rights an individual possesses independent of government.[23]

The doctrine of natural rights has had, in explication and application, somewhat indefinite and wavering meanings. One element of confusion arises from the fact that the writers frequently identify rights which they think ought to exist with rights which, they assert, do exist, or with rights which they assume to have existed at some earlier, more natural, era, and to have been subsequently destroyed by the mistaken devices of man. In general, the theory rests upon a discrimination in political matters between that which is essential, spontaneous, and self-evident and that which is artificial or accidental. Some formulations of the doctrine have described, or evidently presupposed, the actual existence, at some time in the past, of a "state of nature"—a condition of society when men lived together without any sort of political organization; and the doctrine almost necessarily postulates some sort of picture of the situation in which men would be without the restraint or aid which organized government supplies.

Generally the exponents of this doctrine have not attempted to prove the theory or to show what there is in the nature of man that requires us to regard certain claims made in his behalf as claims not to be denied by society. They have variously held the source of natural rights to be in God or Nature, state of nature or custom, universal reason, or some sense of right and justice divinely or naturally implanted in the mind or conscience of man. Even when the several writers agree in defining the standard of natural right, they often disagree sharply in indicating the specific rights that are guaranteed by that standard. This diversity in applying the general theory to concrete rights appears notably in the writings of Americans in the late eighteenth and early nineteenth centuries.[24] Most of the American exponents of the natural-rights doctrine believed that men were by nature "equal and free"; a minority, however, held that men are naturally distributed into various "orders" according to their differences in political competence. Some maintained that slavery was "against natural right" and a "daring infringement on

[23] For general expositions of the modern idea of natural rights, see D. G. Ritchie, *Natural Rights* (1895); A. R. Lord, *Principles of Politics* (1921), Ch. IX.

[24] See Benjamin F. Wright, Jr., *American Interpretations of Natural Law* (1931).

the law of nature"; others argued that slavery was ordained by nature for the good both of society in general and of the slaves in particular. Universal suffrage and majority rule were said to be demanded by natural right—or to be violations of it; natural right was held to affirm —or to deny—property as a qualification for voting. Most of the theorists agreed that men are endowed by nature with rights to worship, express and publish opinions, freely acquire and exchange goods, enter into contracts and associations with other men, and avail themselves of certain traditional guarantees of fair trial before the courts. They generally held also that political authority rests rightfully only on the consent of those who are restrained by the authority and that the persons who possess the attributes (variously described) which naturally qualify them to speak politically for the entire citizenry have also the right to change the form and location of political authority whenever they deliberately decide that unassailable natural rights are being persistently violated by the existing wielders of authority.

The utilitarians likewise found their standard of judgment outside the state, and in the interests of individual men.[25] They held the measure of right, in politics as in everything else, to be utility—i.e., human welfare or happiness. The idea of happiness as a test of right was familiar as a general ethical doctrine in the eighteenth century, when it appeared in opposition to doctrines that founded their ideas of right and wrong on divine revelation or that made their appeals to abstract principles of reason or right, or to the dictates of human conscience. Happiness, according to the utilitarian doctrine, has no meaning except in reference to the feelings of individual men. "The happiness of a people," said William Paley, "is made up of the happiness of single persons." Moreover, with the later utilitarians—notably Jeremy Bentham, James and John Stuart Mill, George Grote, and Alexander Bain—the proof of the happiness is to be found chiefly in experience. Conduct is to be appraised morally by its observed results in terms of the pleasures and pains experienced by large numbers of individuals. Accordingly, that government is best which, in its organization and activity, is most effective in increasing the net total of pleasures for the largest possible number of persons.

Political utilitarianism arose partly as a criticism of the doctrine of

[25] For historical and critical reviews of political utilitarianism, see Leslie Stephen, *The English Utilitarians*, 3 vols. (1900); Elie Halévy, *The Growth of Philosophic Radicalism*, translated by Mary Morris (1928); W. L. Davidson, *Political Thought in England: the Utilitarians from Bentham to J. S. Mill* (1916).

natural rights. The assertion that men are self-evidently endowed by God or nature with certain specifiable rights, was regarded by the utilitarians as a mere metaphysical assumption, not verifiable or realizable under any conditions. Especially in England the conception of the state as an implement of the general welfare superseded the doctrine of the state as an institution for safeguarding natural rights. In the doctrine of Bentham the nature of man is the foundation of political authority only in the sense that man naturally, in all he does, is determined by pain and pleasure. It is these two springs of action that supply our standards of right and wrong in any sphere of human conduct. The sense of obligation to submit to political authority is created by a conception of the efficiency of political action in promoting the greatest happiness of the greatest number. Political authority, under the utilitarian theory, is not limited by claims of individual rights which impede it. The end of all political activity is neither, on the one hand, the safeguarding of natural rights nor, on the other hand, the advancement of the strength of the state or the prestige of the nation; the end is the promotion of general happiness—meaning the happiness of all members of the community.

It is not suggested, however, that the doctrines of natural rights and utilitarianism appeared generally as sharply opposed to one another. On the contrary, they are, in many of their assumptions, closely interrelated. Thus Bentham's utilitarianism involves a calculus of pains and pleasures based on the explicit hypothesis that "everybody is to count for one and nobody is to count for more than one"—which implies that there must be no system of social or political privileges; yet such a system might conceivably realize best the greatest sum of happiness, except for the assumption that men are, by nature, equally entitled to happiness. On the other hand, a natural-rights theory generally finds its content in utilitarian principles, naming as rights the comforts, conveniences, and securities that men generally and therefore "naturally" demand. Both theories take their content from the experiences of human personality, and in application they frequently arrive at the same kind of reforms.

In both natural-rights and utilitarian theories, moreover, political society is regarded as something consciously and voluntarily established by human beings. The state is an institution which men set up for the sake of security or convenience and which they can reorganize at will. When a government ceases to fulfil the purposes for which it was established, it can be remodeled with reference solely to the ideas and desires of the citizens of the day. The state, existing solely as a creation of its citizens, has no independent character of its own. Men can make and remake it, and devise new and untried institutions in place of old and established ones, in order better to protect rights or increase happiness.

Against such attitudes of eighteenth century rationalism, persisting into the nineteenth century, there were several lines of theoretical reaction—all aiming to displace the citizen from his assumed position of ultimate priority to the state, all seeking to find the ground of existence of political society and the principles of its development in forces superior to, or at least apart from, human will.[26] Some writers, such as Burke in England and the Count de Maistre and other supporters of the old régime in France, revived earlier conceptions of the state as divinely sanctioned and guided; they maintained that certain political institutions—the Crown, for example, or an hereditary upper legislative chamber—were sacred and unassailable, divinely approved through the sanction given by the Pope, God's representative on earth.

Others found the independent position for political authority in the nature of the state itself. The state, they said, is an organism and as such is independent of human will and invention because it follows the laws of its own life and evolution. Some writers set forth this organic character of political society in literal biologic terms, ascribing to the state all the essential properties that differentiate plants and animals from inanimate objects. In describing the structure and functioning of governments, they drew up detailed analogies between states and the higher sorts of animals: they discussed the state's nutritive and circulatory systems and indicated the political organs that perform the functions of the brain, the heart, the muscles, and the nerve fibers. There were also organismic theories of a more philosophic kind, which sought to demonstrate the state's organic character not by indicating specific analogies in structure and functions between the state and an animal but by showing in a more general way the independent origin and organic unity of the state. Each state, they argued, comes into existence independently of the conscious efforts of the people who compose it, and its

[26] For general accounts of the reactions from eighteenth-century political rationalism, see W. A. Dunning, *Political Theories from Rousseau to Spencer*, Ch. V; R. G. Gettell, *History of Political Thought*, Ch. XX; Alfred Cobbam, *Edmund Burke and the Revolt against the Eighteenth Century* (1931); F. J. C. Hearnshaw, ed., *Social and Political Ideas of Some Representative Thinkers of the Age of Reaction and Reconstruction* (1932), Chs. I–IV.

subsequent evolution is largely independent of human will. It has a will and consciousness of its own, and each individual, by virtue of his citizenship, surrenders a part of his moral and intellectual individuality to this common mind. The state's organic unity is revealed in its general structure and action: its component elements are distributed into functionally differentiated parts, so that the parts are interdependent, and the unity and vigor of the whole are essential to the existence and activity of the parts. Like any other organism, it develops in constant dependence upon its environment, so that the nature of its development depends upon the native qualities of its citizens and the characteristics of its physical habitat; but the principal factors in its genesis and evolution are to be found within itself. Thus the state is in an important sense its own end, or else it is the vital structure of an integral national community; in either case, to regard it primarily as an instrument in the service of any number of its citizens is false and pernicious.[27]

This more abstractly organismic theory of political society is in some essential ways similar to conservative doctrines that make their explicit appeal to "history." Law and government in any given state, according to ideas current in the early nineteenth century (typified in the writings of Burke in England and Friedrich von Savigny in Germany), are the products of a slow evolution through many generations of human beings. Each state has a life of its own, independent of the men who come and go. England or Prussia has a destiny and well-being apart from the aims and achievements of the individuals who make up the English or Prussian nation in any generation. Burke indeed put forward also the notion of a divine sanction of the state; he regarded that sanction, however, as revealed not in decrees of a church but in certain "facts" shown by the records of history to be of a permanent character. Any statesman, he said, must respect this divinely sanctioned, natural growth of the state, regardless of whatever clamors for change are made on grounds of the natural right or convenience of any number of individuals. If the institution of private property is shown by the

---

[27] The organismic conception of political society was taken over by some mid-nineteenth century French, German, and English sociologists—notably Auguste Comte, René Worms, Alfred Fouillée, Paul von Lilienfeld, Albert Schäffle, and Herbert Spencer; but it has no longer, in either its pseudo-biologic or its more metaphysical form, any significant place in political theory. Cf. F. W. Coker, *Organismic Theories of the State* (1910). For a recent interesting, but ineffective, effort to revive the conception, see Henry Jones Ford, *The Natural History of the State* (1915).

records of the past to be a constant feature in the evolution of a given nation, the present generation acts irrationally, immorally, atheistically, if it attempts to destroy or radically transform that institution. Thus in England, Burke maintained, the citizens of the day must accept and revere the now inevitable hierarchy of "an inheritable Crown, an inheritable peerage, a House of Commons and a people inheriting privileges, franchises, and liberties from a long line of ancestors." Man can apply his small mind usefully only in seeking to understand, appreciate, and adapt his life to his inherited institutions, which represent the accumulated wisdom of the ages. If he attempts to change them substantially, he will destroy them and will then be unable to reconstruct them. "When ancient opinions and rules of life are taken away . . . we have no compass to govern us, nor can we know distinctly to what port we steer." [28]

This is the typical attitude of political conservatism, illustrated in Burke's dictum that "prescription is the most solid of all titles, not only to property, but to that which is to secure that property, the government." It is the attitude that prevailed among British jurists of the early nineteenth century, who, in opposing the projects of legal reform advocated by utilitarians and the Philosophical Radicals, appealed to rules of common law that had come down "from a time whereof the memory of man runneth not to the contrary" and so had acquired "their binding power, and the force of law, by long and immemorial usage." [29]

The political progressives of a century ago had also their philosophy of history, running counter to the conservative apotheosis of tradition and established authority. Reformers of that period found in the records of history proofs of the possibility of continuous and beneficent change. A belief in the perfectibility of man, or in an orderly movement of society towards an ever fuller realization of humanly conceived ideals, was a characteristic phase of a general philosophical conception of "progress" as a "law" of human existence. The conception received its most elaborate statement in the late eighteenth century—notably in the work of the Marquis de Condorcet. This French philosopher reviewed the history of mankind in order to show the successive stages in the ascent of civilized man and society and he predicted the future course of progress towards a condition in which there would be no imperfections in human nature and no inequalities in opportunity

---

[28] *Appeal from the New to the Old Whigs* (1791), in *Works* (1865–1867), III, 334.

[29] Sir William Blackstone, *Commentaries on the Laws of England* (1765), Vol. I, Bk. I, p. 64 in Sharswood ed. (1872).

among men.[30] In this view, which was widely accepted in the early nineteenth century, it is irrational and "unhistorical" to hold one generation bound by the action of its predecessors; to restrain mankind by the prescription of tradition is to try to go against both "nature" and history. Somewhat visionary expressions of this faith in the future appear in the romantic projects of the Utopian Socialists; and also in the poems of Shelley; the earlier poems of Wordsworth, Coleridge, and Southey; and the essays of Carlyle.

The idea of "progress" was a characteristic notion in the doctrines of the mid-nineteenth century founders of sociology—notably, Auguste Comte and Herbert Spencer, who sought to discover and formulate the laws that determine or reveal the upward course of social evolution.[31] Thus Spencer maintained that the evolution of human society is a phase of mankind's "mighty movement towards perfection," and that the development proceeds in accordance with laws of a general evolution under the sway of which everything (inanimate and animate) in the universe is in process of continual change from uniformity and simplicity to diversity and complexity. Spencer also, and others following him, as we shall see, drew special political conclusions from the laws, then newly formulated, of the evolution of plants and animals.[32] This sociological doctrine, conceiving social change (generally regarded as beneficent) as "natural," represented it as predominantly automatic, proceeding independently of man's direction. But the idea of Condorcet —that human progress is a conscious and active movement and that each generation has in considerable measure the power to determine the forms and workings of its own institutions—was more widely prevalent, and it is a characteristic idea in modern political theory.

In our political discussions to-day, when we seek some basic theoretic position to support or attack a proposed arrangement in governmental structure or policy, we still make use of criteria that were familiar in the writings of the early nineteenth century. We argue variously as to the natural rights or the happiness of individual men. We deduce conclu-

[30] Condorcet (1743–1794), *Esquisse d'un tableau des progrès de l'esprit humain* (1795), in *Œuvres* (1847–1849), Vol. VI; translation (anonymous) *Outlines of an Historical View of the Human Mind* (1795).

[31] Comte (1798–1857), *Cours de philosophie positive* (1830–1842; fourth ed. 1877), Vol. 4, Lect. 51; translation by Harriet Martineau, *The Positive Philosophy* (1853). Spencer (1820–1903), *Principles of Sociology* (1876–1880), Vol. I, pt. i, and *passim*.

[32] See *infra*, pp. 393 ff.

sions from conceptions of the nature of human society in general or the history of a particular political community. We consider the nature of man in terms now of his "primitive" characteristics and now of his potentialities for development toward an "ideal" to be attained in the future. In some instances we add new criteria derived from attempts to study contemporary man through the techniques of the new sciences of biology and psychology. We derive varying conclusions, it will be seen, from any of the criteria. We still have all manner of ideas on the relations of state authority to private right and individual welfare, and also opposing attitudes of conservatism and reformism in our ideas as to the possibilities and methods of political change.

Some writers still regard the individual as less important than the corporate community, describe the state as a means of maintaining the supremacy of national interests over the interests of any number of citizens, and consider the conduct of public agencies as not amenable to the criteria of right and wrong we apply to private conduct. There are contemporary writers who appear to be distrustful of all political innovation and to be uneasy over any sort of experimentation with social institutions. If these conservatives accept the idea of change, they incline to the position that the period of change has come to a close; or, they believe, the change is so gradual and so predetermined in its course by past events that there is little or no place for deliberate human effort in shaping it; they look upon man's past, not as merely conditioning, but as generally preventing, all conscious transformation of the institutional life of a community.

Others to-day, on the other hand, regard a political community as (in the words of Paley again) "only a collection of the citizens who compose it." They hold that only men, not states or nations, have rights and interests and that in order to protect these interests it may be necessary to change existing social institutions by organized human efforts. Whether or not they accept the idea of a "law" of social progress, they are inclined to Bentham's position that "antiquity is no reason"; that, in fact, the antiquity of an institution is often the very feature that disqualifies it, making its meaning obscure to present-day understandings and rendering it practically unsuitable for the needs of the present. In any case, these writers maintain, there is nothing in the nature of man or in the history of human society that compels us to pay blind respect to traditional forms or mystic dogmas which disguise vested privileges and inherited injustices.

Indeed all schools of political thought—authoritarian or liberal, collectivistic or individualistic, conservative or reformist—agree that there is room somewhere for the fruitful use of human reason in choosing wise and avoiding unwise courses of political action; all assume that man, by taking thought, can in some manner play an effective part in the "mighty movement" of human society. Moreover, as in earlier times, so now, there are widely varying ideas as to just how we may, by discovering correct ways of organizing our political relations, rectify the path of human development, accelerate its pace, or at any rate, best accommodate ourselves to its inevitable course.

SELECT BIBLIOGRAPHY

GENERAL SURVEYS OF THE HISTORY AND LITERATURE OF POLITICAL THOUGHT

Burns, C. Delisle, *Political Ideals* (New York and London, 1915).

Dunning, William A., *Political Theories, Ancient and Medieval* (New York, 1902).

——————, *Political Theories from Luther to Montesquieu* (New York, 1905).

——————, *Political Theories from Rousseau to Spencer* (New York, 1920).

Engelmann, Géza, *Meisterwerke der Staatsphilosophie* (Berlin and Leipsic, 1923).

——————, *Political Philosophy from Plato to Jeremy Bentham,* translated by Karl Frederick Geiser, with introductions by Oscar Jászi (New York and London, 1927). A translation of the *Meisterwerke der Staatsphilosophie.*

Gettell, R. G., *History of Political Thought* (New York, 1924).

Janet, Paul, *Histoire de la science politique dans ses rapports avec la morale,* 2 vols. (third ed., Paris, 1887).

Laski, H. J., *Political Thought in England from Locke to Bentham* (London and New York, 1920).

McIlwain, Charles H., *The Growth of Political Thought in the West, from the Greeks to the End of the Middle Ages* (New York, 1932).

Mohl, Robert von, *Die Geschichte und Literatur der Staatswissenschaften,* 3 vols. (Erlangen, 1855–1858).

Morris, C. R., and Mary, *A History of Political Ideas* (New York and London, 1924).

Murray, R. H., *The History of Political Science* (Cambridge, Eng., and New York, 1926).

Pollock, Sir Frederic, *History of the Science of Politics* (London, 1890).

Vaughan, C. E., *Studies in the History of Political Thought Before and After Rousseau*, 2 vols. (London and New York, 1925).

GENERAL WORKS IN RECENT AND CONTEMPORARY POLITICAL THOUGHT

Barker, Ernest, *Political Thought in England from Herbert Spencer to the Present Day* (New York, 1915).

Brown, Ivor, *English Political Theory* (London, 1920).

Davidson, William L., *Political Thought in England: the Utilitarians from Bentham to J. S. Mill* (New York and London, 1916).

Dunning, William A., *Political Theories from Rousseau to Spencer* (New York, 1920).

Elliott, W. Y., *The Pragmatic Revolt in Politics* (New York, 1928).

Gettell, R. G., *History of American Political Thought* (New York, 1928).

Halévy, Élie, *The Growth of Philosophic Radicalism* (New York, 1928), a translation by Mary Morris, of his *Formation du radicalisme*, 3 vols. (Paris, 1901–1903).

Hearnshaw, F. J. C., ed., *The Social and Political Ideas of Some Representative Thinkers of the Victorian Age* (London, etc., 1933).

Hocking, William Ernest, *Man and the State* (New Haven, 1926).

Holcombe, A. N., *The Foundations of the Modern Commonwealth* (New York, 1923).

Jacobson, J. Mark, *The Development of American Political Thought: a Documentary History* (New York and London, 1932).

Joad, C. E. M., *Modern Political Theory* (Oxford, 1924).

Laski, H. J. *A Grammar of Politics* (New Haven, 1925).

McIver, R. M., *The Modern State* (Oxford, 1926).

Merriam, Charles E., *American Political Ideas* (New York, 1920).

Merriam, Charles E., and Barnes, Harry E., eds., *A History of Political Theories: Recent Times* (New York, 1924).

Mosca, Gaetano, *Elementi di scienza politica* (second ed., Turin, 1923).

——————, *Teorica dei governi e governo parlamentare* (second ed., Milan, 1925).

Parrington, Vernon L., *Main Currents in American Thought*, 3 vols. (New York, 1927–1930).

Randall, John Herman, *The Making of the Modern Mind* (Boston and New York, 1926).

Rockow, Lewis, *Contemporary Political Thought in England* (New York, 1925).

Ruggiero, Guido de, *The History of European Liberalism*, translated by R. G. Collingwood (New York and London, 1927).

Soltau, Roger, *French Political Thought in the Nineteenth Century* (New Haven, 1931).

Vorländer, Karl, *Von Machiavelli bis Lenin: neuzeitliche Staats-und Gesellschaftstheorien* (Leipsic, 1926).

Wright, Benjamin F., Jr., *American Interpretations of Natural Law* (Cambridge, Mass., 1931).

PART I

SOCIALISTIC DOCTRINES

CHAPTER II

KARL MARX

THE most difficult of all the problems confronting social philosophers is that of determining (to use the words of Edmund Burke) "what the state ought to take upon itself to direct by public wisdom, and what it ought to leave, with as little interference as possible, to individual freedom." [1] There is no clear theoretical line of division. The whole problem is usually debated with reference to some particular field of activity; and a given school of theorists, we shall see, may exalt social control over the individual in certain phases of his life and disparage it in others. There are creeds, however, that, in most matters under debate, take their stand for a relatively wide range of political control. They direct attention to the social causes and consequences of the normal activities of men; and they hold generally that the essential significance of an individual consists principally in his relations to the community, or to some social group in which he falls naturally in pursuing his most important needs and aspirations. These creeds differ in the degrees of rigidity with which they would subordinate individual to community or group ends and in the particular spheres of life in which they would chiefly enforce the subordination.

In all schools of recent political doctrine, an important place is given to the state's functions in relation to private property; and the recent "collectivist" creeds apply their general philosophy mainly to economic affairs. They contend that the merchant, manufacturer, or farmer is not an isolated creator of wealth and that any single producer's ability to exercise his economic talents fruitfully, for himself or for others, is dependent upon the labors of millions of others and also upon some sort of coöperative maintenance of an orderly and enlightened social life. We apply the general term "socialist" to the doctrines that stand for a relatively rapid and sweeping economic collectivism.

[1] *Works* (Boston, ninth ed., 1889), V, 166.

The term is not precise.[2] There is no sharp and certain line of division between socialists and non-socialists. Many recent writers, outside any recognized school of socialists, observing industrial changes since the middle of the seventeenth century, are impressed with the fact that, despite the great increase in quantities of commodities produced, a great majority of the people go through life at or very near a mere subsistence level, while a very small minority are able to live lavishly; they believe that this condition is due in considerable measure to the ways in which productive capital is administered by private owners, and they hold that the condition may be remedied in part by collectively imposed limits on the range of private ownership.

A complete history of socialist doctrine would have a broad range, including authors and projects widely separated in time and character. It would describe the economic ideas of certain early Christian writers, the social experiments of some medieval Christian sects, and most of the "utopias" of medieval and modern writers. It would give an account of the doctrine of the medieval Christian Church in reference to private property. That doctrine regarded common ownership as the original (and, therefore, the "natural") as well as the ideal economic system; it accepted private ownership of property as an existing institution, resulting unhappily from man's avarice; but it accepted the institution subject to important conditions—namely, that the property, though privately owned, be used for the good of the community or, more specifically, that the rights of all members of the community to have their proper needs satisfied out of the abundance of the earth's produce be fully recognized.[3]

In the preceding chapter we gave some indication of the socialist and closely related doctrines of the earlier nineteenth century. The wide differences and bitter disputes among the several socialist groups to-day do not indicate that they are not united in certain fundamental doctrines.[4] Every broad system of ideas—philosophical, theo-

---

[2] On the origins (apparently in the fourth decade of the nineteenth century) of the terms "socialist" and "socialism," cf. *The Oxford Dictionary,* and also Alexandre Zévaès, "De l'origine des mots: socialisme, communisme, collectivisme," *Revue mondiale,* CXCI, (1929), 7–14.

[3] See A. J. Carlyle, "The Theory of Property in Medieval Theology," in *Property: Its Duties and Rights* (1914; new ed., 1915), pp. 117–132.

[4] For collections of recent definitions of socialism, see the following: W. D. P. Bliss, *Handbook of Socialism* (1907); John Martin, "An Attempt to Define Socialism," *American Economic Association Bulletin,* I (1911), 347–354; Dan Griffiths, *What is Socialism: a Symposium* (1924). The last-named book contains 261 brief definitions.

logical, ethical, or political—shows similar varieties and conflicts in its particular forms. Certainly "socialism," as a name for a doctrinal system, has a signification no more uncertain or fluctuating than "individualism," "democracy," or "Christianity." The several schools of socialists differ considerably in their programs of action, but they agree in certain of their theoretical assumptions and also in their general aim; all seek to secure, through some substantial limitations on the private ownership of property, a fairer and practically more satisfactory apportionment of wealth and economic opportunity. What further unity and also what variety there is among socialists to-day we shall attempt to see in the immediately succeeding chapters.

Socialism since the middle of the nineteenth century has been concerned mainly, although not exclusively, with the interests of hand-laborers in an industrial society; its policy has been developed chiefly in connection with organized movements of urban wage-earners. The doctrinal origins of this "proletarian" socialism are to be found principally in the utterances and activities of three able Germans—Ferdinand Lassalle (1815–1864), Karl Marx (1818–1883), and Friedrich Engels (1820–1895). None of these men was a wage-earner or a member of a wage-earning family. Lassalle was the son of wealthy Jewish parents, who intended him to follow a business career; and he had many aristocratic associations. He devoted his brief life, however, chiefly to radical political writing and agitation; he was the first to set forth, for socialist purposes, the doctrine of an "iron law of wages," and one of the first to advocate using government as the principal instrumentality in furthering the organized activities of working-men. Perhaps his chief achievement for socialism was his work in organizing (the year before his death) the General Association of German Workers (*Allgemeiner deutsche Arbeiterverein*), which a few years later became the German Social Democratic party—longest-lived and (until within the last decade and a half) strongest of socialist political parties.[5] Marx was of a middle-class family in comfortable circumstances; his father, a Jew converted to Christianity when Marx was six years of age, held an important office in the Prussian civil service. Engels, who became famous chiefly as friend, collaborator, benefactor, and interpreter of Marx, was the son of pious Protestants. His father was a wealthy manufacturer in Prussia,

[5] On Lassalle, see Harry W. Laidler, *History of Socialist Thought* (1927), Ch. XIX; Thomas Kirkup, *History of Socialism* (fifth ed., 1913), Chs. V, VI; Eduard Bernstein, *Ferdinand Lassalle, eine Würdigung des Lehrers und Kämpfers* (1919).

and Engels himself, for nearly a score of years, held an important position in a manufacturing firm in which his father was interested, in Manchester, England.[6]

Marx is regarded as the founder, with Engels, of a "scientific" socialism for a working-men's movement. As a youth, he displayed signs of intellectual brilliance and achieved distinction in his university studies at Bonn and Berlin, his chief interests being in history, jurisprudence, and philosophy—especially the Hegelian philosophy then predominant in the German universities. He married into the petty nobility, became interested in politics, and entered actively as a journalist into the liberal movements then stirring hopefully in Germany. In his very early manhood, however, he reached the definite conclusion that effective remedies for social and political ills could be devised by neither abstract reasoning nor the imaginative fashioning of fine social ideals, for the appropriate remedies at any given time depended upon the special, basic conditions of a then existing social order. Accordingly he set himself to a searching study of modern industrial society. He considered the progress of mechanical invention, the resulting development of the capitalist system with its special rules for fixing prices and wages, and the accompanying segregation of the whole people into two opposing classes— the owners of the machines and raw materials of production against all others, the latter able to maintain their existence only by laboring with these machines and materials under conditions set by the former. He soon arrived at the main tenets of his socialism and spent the rest of his life in efforts to elaborate their theoretical and historical foundation and persuade the workers of Europe to adopt and apply them.[7]

For half a dozen years, Marx carried on his editorial and organizing activities successively in Cologne, Paris, Brussels, and Cologne again. These shifts of residence were caused mainly by expulsions and suppressions imposed upon him because of his bold criticism of the policies of the governmental authorities. His residence in Paris and Brussels brought him into intimate contact with leading radicals and socialists of the day, notably: Cabet, utopian communist; Proudhon, philosophical anarchist;

[6] See Karl Kautsky, *Friedrich Engels* (1895), translated by A. M. Simons, (1899); Gustav Mayer, *Friedrich Engels*, 2 vols. (1920–1933).

[7] The following are good critical biographies of Marx: Achille Loria, *Karl Marx*, translated from the Italian by Eden and Cedar Paul (1920); F. Mehring, *Karl Marx: Geschichte seines Lebens* (1918; fourth ed., 1923); D. Ryazanoff, *Karl Marx and Friedrich Engels*, translated by J. Kunitz (1927); Otto Rühle, *Karl Marx: His Life and Work*, translated by Eden and Cedar Paul (1929); John Spargo, *Karl Marx: His Life and His Work* (new ed., 1910).

Bakunin, communist anarchist; Heine, radical poet; Wolff, secretary to the revolutionary patriot, Mazzini; and Engels. Marx moved to London in 1849 and lived there for the remaining thirty-four years of his life, most of the time in extreme poverty. His life was in many ways that of a quiet scholar, having little contact with practical affairs. He was, however, the moving spirit in the formation of the first socialist "International" in 1864, and he remained thereafter in every way the dominant personality of the socialist movement. From his secluded home in London, he maintained throughout life—by means of theoretical writings and practical guidance, through conferences and correspondence—his unique position as leader of socialist thought and action in Western Europe. His predominant influence continued after his death. Even after the lasting socialist schisms produced by the World War, a leading American socialist asserted: "Marxism is still the avowed creed of all contending [socialist] camps, each claiming strict adherence to the doctrine of the theoretical founder of the modern socialist movement and charging its opponents with a palpable departure from them." [8]

MARX'S SCIENCE OF SOCIALISM

The books, pamphlets, articles, and addresses of Marx were written during three decades, from the early forties to the early seventies. Through them all his historical, economic, and political ideas remained fairly consistent. His basic conceptions of economic determinism, of labor as the source of value, of the progressive decay of capitalism, and of the program for a socialist revolution were set forth in the forties, notably in the following forms: an article, in criticism of Hegel's philosophy of law, appearing in a review, called *Deutsch-französische Jahrbücher*, published in 1844 by Marx and Arnold Ruge, philosopher and radical political writer, and suspended after one issue; [9] a brief book, *Misère de la philosophie*, published in 1847, written as a polemic against the economic ideas of Proudhon, moderate French anarchist; and the *Communist Manifesto*, issued in 1848.

The *Manifesto* was prepared for a "League of Communists"—a society of exiled working-men, organized early in 1847 chiefly through the efforts of Marx and Engels, whose lifelong friendship and coöperation

[8] Morris Hillquit, *From Marx to Lenin* (1921), p. 6.
[9] For a reprint of the article see D. Ryazanoff, ed., *Karl Marx und Friedrich Engels, Historisch-kritische Gesant-Ausgabe, Werke, Schriften, Briefe* (1927–1931), I, 607–621.

had begun two years earlier.[10] Similar societies, pursuing generally the
policy of secret propaganda and intrigue, had been formed in Paris, London, and other European cities during the preceding decade; and efforts
had been made to unite them. The insurrectionary plans of these societies were mainly in the French tradition, dating back to the schemes
of François Baboeuf in the time of the Revolution; and from this source,
as well as from the utopian socialists, they drew their ideas of working-
men's republics, resting on a common ownership of all goods. Now in
the middle forties the leaders of the societies were turning to Marx's
conception of a workers' movement planned deliberately in the light of
history and accommodated to the existing stage of economic development. Late in 1847 the new league commissioned Marx to draw up a
declaration of principles and a program of action. Assisted by Engels,
he promptly executed the commission; and the "Manifest der Kommunisten" was issued from a London printing office early in 1848. The
word "Communist" was deliberately chosen, Engels explained, in order
to distinguish their doctrine from the visionary sort of socialism then
associated with the names of Owen, Fourier, and other "respectable
middle-class" reformers. The *Manifesto* is the most widely read of all
socialist documents and has been translated into almost every civilized
tongue of to-day. It contains the clearest and most compact statement
of Marx's conceptions of the past struggles between economic classes,
the modern bourgeois-proletarian conflict, the inevitable movement of
present-day capitalism towards its own destruction, and the program
of action working-men must adopt in order to fit in their efforts with
the actual march of events.

Marx's more systematic statement of his economic doctrines appeared
first in his *Contribution to the Critique of Political Economy* (*Zur Kritik
der politischen Oekonomie,* originally published in 1859). He gave a
clear epitome of these doctrines in an address delivered in 1865,
published posthumously under the title, *Value, Price, and Profit.* He
then devoted himself to setting forth in elaborate detail an historical and
critical examination of the whole system of capitalist economy. The

<hr>

[10] For accounts of the origin of the *Communist Manifesto,* see the prefaces
by Engels in later editions, and also the following: D. Ryazanoff, *The Communist
Manifesto* (1930), pp. 1–24; Karl Grünberg, *Die Londoner kommunistische Zeit-
schrift und andere Urkunden aus den Jahren, 1847–1848* (1921). The volume by
Ryazanoff reproduces the several prefaces to the *Manifesto* and contains extensive
"explanatory notes," made up for the most part of quotations from other works of
Marx and Engels. Handy editions of the *Manifesto* are published by the Rand
School of Social Science, New York, and by Charles H. Kerr & Co., Chicago.

results of these labors appear in the three ponderous volumes of *Das Kapital,* often called the "Gospel" or "Bible" of socialists. This work displays considerable historical and psychological insight and contains a wealth of factual detail; it presents an unusual combination of abstract theory and realistic observation. Only the first volume, appearing in 1867, was arranged for publication by Marx himself; the other two were published posthumously (in 1885 and 1894), arranged by Engels from notes and chapters (some complete, others incomplete) among the manuscripts left by Marx.

In these historical and economic discussions, Marx professed to be proceeding objectively and inductively; and in many of the details of his exposition he lived up to that claim. Yet all of his writings were dominated by a clearly preconceived purpose of attacking the existing economic and political order. Despite this propagandist motive, which at times he confessed, he supplied his followers with only the brief and broad outlines of a program of action. He was attempting to reveal to manual laborers their actual place in modern society—what part they played in the capitalist system, how they had got into their lowly position, why it was economically impossible for their position to be raised by willing help from above, and yet how help from above was inevitably coming to them. He was concerned in showing wage-earners why they should, and could successfully, unite in overthrowing the present economic order, rather than specifically how they should go about it.

Marx's principal doctrines were not new; but he greatly amplified and systematized older ideas, putting them into new and effective combinations. The innovations of his socialist system are to be found partly in its distinctively proletarian class appeal and in its call for organized political action by wage-workers, but also in its thorough attempt to relate socialist practice to a carefully wrought historical and economic theory and in its synthesis of the evolutionary and revolutionary phases of socialist action. He attempted to show that a socialist program, however radical and violent, must be based upon a systematic interpretation of social evolution and a critical analysis of the existing system of production and exchange. More specifically, his design was to show how a socialist community is to be built upon capitalist foundations.

A central point in Marx's explanation of the evolution and social consequences of capitalism is his doctrine of surplus value, which he based upon the labor theory of value. The latter theory holds that in the long run the exchange value of a commodity depends upon the amount of labor expended upon its production, and it was a familiar doctrine, among both conservative and radical theorists long before Marx's time.[11] It was in the main an English doctrine, stated by Sir William Petty in the seventeenth century, and later emphasized and variously qualified by some of the most famous of the classical economists—notably Adam Smith and David Ricardo.

The eighteenth century "Mercantilists" had made the distinction between "natural" and "artificial" value, the former indicating the "intrinsic utility" of commodities, the latter indicating their "purchasing-power" or "exchange value," derived chiefly from the toil it takes to produce them. Adam Smith emphasized this distinction, generally treated "cost of production" as the cause of exchange value, and generally represented labor as the exclusive or primary element in cost of production. In some passages he was evidently treating labor as specifically the "measure" rather than the "cause" of exchange values, meaning that the ordinary worth of price of a thing is to be determined by discovering the amount of labor "commonly employed in acquiring or producing it." In some passages, moreover, he stated the labor theory of value as applicable only in the conditions of a primitive society. In other passages, however, he seemed to regard the theory as valid also in civilized society, and he appeared at times to confuse the conceptions of cause of value and measure of value. He never made an unequivocal choice between a general cost-of-production theory and a purely labor theory of value.[12] Ricardo admitted that certain articles had exchange values due to scarcity, as in the case of rare works of art or wines "made from grapes grown only in a particular soil"; but he excluded these objects from his further consideration of value because they constituted so small a part of the commodities subject to daily exchange. For most commodities, he maintained, the quantity of labor required to produce them regulates their normal exchange values. He admitted also the existence of differences in the qualities—the intensity and skill—of labor but held them to be ordinarily of no importance in determining exchange values. He argued, finally, that the profits that

[11] Marx himself, in *Theorien über den Mehrwert* (published posthumously, 1905–1910), has given one of the fullest and clearest accounts of the history of the labor theory of value. See also Gide and Rist, *History of Economic Doctrines*, pp. 75–93, 141–152, and *passim;* Lewis H. Haney, *History of Economic Thought* (rev. ed., 1920), Chs. X–XII; Albert C. Whitaker, *History and Criticism of the Labor Theory of Value* (1904), Chs. II–V.

[12] Smith's discussion of value appears in *The Wealth of Nations* (first ed., 1776), especially Bk. I, Chs. I, V–VII.

rightly go to capital create no modification in the relations between labor and value because profits are payments for "stored-up" labor; capital represents the labor spent "on all those implements or machines required to give effect to the particular labour to which they were applied." [13]

Certain British writers, in the third quarter of the nineteenth century, argued, we have seen, that since "labor produces all wealth" the laborers have "the right to the whole produce of labor." Marx quoted freely from these proletarian exponents of the labor value theory. The classical economists drew no such socialistic conclusion from that theory. They were thinking of the labor of artisan-owners or of labor generally without differentiation of wage-earners from those who invested their savings in productive industrial activity. They were looking at the problem of the distribution of wealth from the point of view of manufacturers and traders as against land-owners. They defended private ownership of industrial property; they regarded private capital as essential to the welfare and progress of mankind. Their abstract theory of value arose out of a picture of a condition (vanished before their time—if it ever existed) in which individuals freely produced commodities by self-directed efforts and freely exchanged them. When those who exchange commodities are the same as those who make them, each individual, producing primarily for himself and then offering for exchange the commodities which he does not need for himself, will value his surplus product by the labor it costs him to make it. Many passages in the works of the classical economists made it appear, however, that they regarded their abstract theory as a practical statement of the actual way in which prices operate in the conditions of modern capitalist economy.[14]

Marx took over the labor theory of value and used it for his own purposes.[15] He admitted many of the orthodox qualifications but gen-

[13] For Ricardo's views on value, see his *Principles of Political Economy and Taxation* (first ed., 1817), especially Chs. I, IV, XX, XXI.

[14] See especially Smith, *Wealth of Nations*, Ch. V, and Ricardo, *Principles of Political Economy*, Ch. I.

[15] See his *Capital*, especially Vol. I, Chs. I–XXII, *Value, Price, and Profit*, and *Contribution to the Critique of Political Economy*. For critical discussions of Marx's theories of value, cf. A. D. Lindsay, *Karl Marx's Capital* (1925), Chs. III and IV; O. D. Skelton, *Socialism: A Critical Analysis* (1911), Ch. VI; Thorstein Veblen, "The Socialist Economics of Karl Marx and His Followers," *Quarterly Journal of Economics*, XX (1906), 575–595; XXI (1906), 299–322; Sidney Hook, *Towards the Understanding of Karl Marx* (1933), Ch. XIV. W. H. Emmett, *The Marxian Economic Handbook and Glossary* (1925) is a useful abstract of the first

erally ignored them when he wished to point to practical conclusions. Obviously, Marx explained, the "use-value"—the usefulness or desira-bility—of an article is independent of the amount of labor applied to it; air and water are useful although no labor is spent upon them. When objects have exchange values, however, it is because labor has had to be applied to them in order to render them useful or available for use; and the rate of such values will depend upon the amount of the required labor. The proportions in which two commodities, say corn and iron, will exchange for one another can be determined only by a measurement in terms of some property they have in common; and the thing they have in common is not their chemical content or any other "natural, intrinsic," quality but the human labor that has been put into them. "If then we leave out of consideration the use-value of commodities, they have only one common property left, that of being products of labor." A "useful article, therefore, has value only because human labor in the abstract has been embodied or materialized in it. How, then, is the magnitude of this value to be measured? Plainly by the quantity of the value-creating substance, the labor, contained in the article. The quantity of labor, however, is measured by its duration, and labor-time in its turn finds its standard in weeks, days, and hours." "We see then that which determines the magnitude of the value of any article is the amount of labor socially necessary, or the labor-time socially necessary, for its production. Each individual commodity, in this connection, is to be con-sidered as an average sample of its class. . . . The value of one com-modity is to the value of any other, as the labor-time necessary for the production of the one is to that necessary for the production of the other." [16]

Marx's theory of value is primarily a statement of what commodities are "worth": the real worth of a commodity is determined by the amount of socially useful labor that has been put into its production. From this doctrine of labor as the only productive element in the creation of wealth Marx proceeds to his discussion of surplus value. Writers before

volume of *Capital*. See also the titles by Böhm-Bawerk, Boudin, Fischer, Kautsky, and Oppenheimer, listed *infra*, pp. 63–65.

On the connection between Marx and the earlier proletarian exponents (mainly in England and notably Thomas Hodgskin) of the labor value theory, see Carl Koepp, *Das Verhältnis der Mehrwerttheorien von Karl Marx und Thomas Hodgskin* (1911); and Sidney and Beatrice Webb, *The History of Trade Unionism* (1920 ed.), pp. 142 and 147. The Webbs describe Marx as "Hodgskin's illustrious disciple."

[16] *Capital*, translated by Samuel Moore and Edward Aveling, I (1909), 44, 45, 46.

Marx had, in varying forms, set forth conceptions of values created by laborers above what were returned to them in wages. The eighteenth century "Physiocrats" had introduced the idea of a "net product" derived from agricultural production, which, they argued, yields more than enough to pay the price for use of the land and to supply the needs of agricultural workers. Ricardo suggested that the profits of industry are mainly dependent upon the surplus which laborers produce over what they are paid. A distinguished German economist, J. H. von Thünen, contended repeatedly that labor receives less than its fair share of the values it helps to create.[17] Other writers went further and maintained explicitly that the whole of what owners of capital receive—in the forms of rent, interest, and profits—comes from the surplus values produced by laborers; this idea appeared in the writings of early nineteenth century utopian socialists, of agrarian socialists in Ireland and Great Britain, and again in the work of Karl Rodbertus and Proudhon just before Marx's earliest discussions of value.

Marx's doctrine of surplus value is definitely related to the conception of subsistence wages, also familiar in the works of orthodox economists. Some of the Physiocrats maintained that a laborer normally receives enough to live on and no more; Adam Smith argued that under normal conditions wages tend to keep at that point; and British economists of the early nineteenth century, notably Ricardo, formulated the same idea in more absolute and precise terms.[18] The general theory of a subsistence wage is that the laborer is paid the price which his labor commands as itself a commodity and that this price tends, under the laws of the market, to be the amount that ensures a continued supply of that human commodity; wages, in other words, tend to be the equivalent of the bare means of subsistence for the laborer and his family.

Marx greatly elaborated the idea of surplus value. As did slaves and serfs in earlier ages, so now wage-earners supply services for which they receive no return and which constitute the values appropriated by property-owners. The capitalist owns the tools and materials upon which alone labor can be performed. Laborers own only their ability to work, which they must sell to the property-owner at a price sufficient merely to enable them to obtain enough to keep themselves and their families alive. Perhaps the most effective parts of Marx's writings are those in

[17] In *Der isolirte Staat* (1826, third ed., 1875), II, 38 ff. See Lewis Haney, *History of Economic Thought*, Ch. XVII, *passim*.
[18] Smith, *Wealth of Nations*, Bk. I, Ch. VIII. Ricardo, *Principles of Political Economy*, Ch. V.

which he describes the efforts of capitalists, under the dominance of their inevitable need for profits, to exploit the laborer's time and strength in order to increase surplus values; and also the parts in which he depicts, with abundant citation of historical records and official reports, the miserable living conditions that result. His conclusion is that the only way to put an end to the conditions is to destroy all opportunity for private rents, interest, and profits; and that this result can be achieved only under a socialist régime, where collective capital will replace private capital, both capitalists and wage-earners disappear, and all persons become coöperating producers.

As already indicated, Marx undertook to show that a collectivist régime would grow out of the competitive régime of capitalism as the latter grew out of serfdom and feudalism, and as they in turn grew out of a social order resting on slavery. This conception of the advent of socialism is part of Marx's general theory of history. In part Marx followed the prevailing trend in the historical writing of his time. History, according to the view prevalent since the late seventeenth century, is a process of continuous, regular change in some sort of an inherently rational manner. Social institutions, like all the other phenomena of the universe, are properly to be explained as manifestations of general, "natural," laws. If the designs of God control the whole process of change, the control is exercised only in ways that are constant and ascertainable by the mind of man.

Marx accepted this idea of history as a continuous and logical evolution, but he gave it a special interpretation. He showed specifically the influence of Hegel, of whose writings he had been a thorough and critical student, but rejected what he considered to be the most basic idea in Hegel's philosophy of history. History, according to Hegel, is the realization of the "Absolute Idea"—"Reason," "Freedom," "God," the "World Spirit"—which works itself out, in both inanimate nature and the life of man, according to absolutely necessary laws. Man in all that he does, helps, unintentionally and unconsciously, in the process of realization. Thus, according to Hegel, "ideas" are predominant in the movement of history, and they exist apart from reality and experience, which they create. Marx, in explaining his own theory, represented ideas as only the creatures or reflections of experience. Hegel attached great importance to the influence, in history, of the ideals of great religious systems—Judaism, Confucianism, Mohammedanism, Buddhism, Christianity—each embodying some partial manifestation of the "World Spirit";

whereas Marx regarded all creeds and rituals as consequences rather than causes in the major movements of history. "My dialectic method," said Marx, "is not only different from the Hegelian, but is its direct opposite. To Hegel, the life-process of the human brain, i.e., the process of thinking, which, under the name of 'the Idea,' he even transforms into an independent subject, is the demiurgos of the real world, and the real world is only the external, phenomenal form of 'the Idea.' With me, on the contrary, the ideal is nothing else than the material world reflected by the human mind, and translated into forms of thought." [19]

Thus Marx contrasted his materialistic to Hegel's idealistic interpretation of history. Marx's materialism, however, is not an application of the old philosophical idea that mental and spiritual phenomena are in reality nothing but physical phenomena. The significant element in his historical materialism is the doctrine of economic determinism.[20] And this is not a contention that man in all that he does is determined by motives of economic or material self-interest. Marx did not believe that you could explain a social system by analyzing the motives under which men act. The real forces that control historical development in all its phases are to be found in the limitations upon the behavior of man— acting under the impulsion of whatever motives—created by the economic position he occupies in society. The practical methods of production (tools, machines, processes) and the physical and cultural conditions of production (topography, fertility, climate, historical influences) create certain "relations" of production (landlord and tenant, lord and vassal, property-owner and wage-laborer); and it is these relations of production (*Produktions-verhältnisse*) that chiefly determine the whole cultural order of an epoch—its moral, religious, social, and political in-

---

[19] *Capital*, Marx's Preface, I, 25, of the Moore and Aveling translation; and cf. *Die heilige Familie* (1845), *passim*.

[20] Marx set forth his theory of history most effectively in the following works: *Die deutsche Ideologie*, written in 1846 and published posthumously, in *Karl Marx, Friedrich Engels, historisch-kritische Gesamt-Ausgabe*, ed. by D. Ryazanoff, 11 vols. (1927–1931), Vol. I, 5, esp. pp. 7–67, 211–219; *Poverty of Philosophy; Contribution to the Critique of Political Economy; Capital*. For critical interpretations of Marx's economic determinism, see Mandell M. Bober, *Marx's Interpretation of History* (1927); F. J. C. Hearnshaw, *Survey of Socialism*, (1928), pp. 230–241; Eduard Heiman, "Der Sozialismus als sittliche Idee und die materialistische Geschichtstheorie," *Archiv für Sozialwissenschaft und Sozialpolitik*, LII (1924), 139–176; Sidney Hook, *Towards the Understanding of Karl Marx*, Chs. XI–XVI, and appendix; H. J. Laski, *Karl Marx: an Essay* (1922); A. D. Lindsay, *Karl Marx's Capital;* Franz Oppenheimer, *Das Grundgesetz der Marxschen Gesellschaftslehre* (1903); O. D. Skelton, *Socialism: a Critical Analysis* (1911), Ch. V. See also the titles by Croce, Cunow, Engels, Kautsky, Kraus, Labriola, Loria, Sée, Seligman, Turgeon, and Woltman, listed *infra*, pp. 64–65.

stitutions and ideas. Social changes, transformations in religious dogmas and conventional moral standards, political revolutions, are mainly the results of alterations of economic relations brought on by changing methods of production and distribution. Moreover, this substratum of society is never stable; it is in a constant state of change, developing towards a point at which social institutions become unfitted to their economic foundations. Any fundamental incongruity between these two situations—the economic relations created by the prevailing methods of production and exchange, on the one hand, and the cultural and political order, on the other hand—produces a social crisis, escape from which comes only through a revolution bringing on a new social superstructure in harmony with the new economic relations. And ideas as well as institutions are "relative" to the particular economic situation. The rules of social life are not made by men's creeds. The process is just the opposite. Prevailing moral, religious, economic, and political doctrines and ideals are in large part determined by the "interests" (not necessarily the "self-interest") of those who hold them; they are the notions that fit in peculiarly with the economic conditions of the social group to which their adherents belong. In other words, the ordinary man—in his political ideas, moral precepts, or assumptions as to general economic efficiency— cannot transcend the limitations upon his thought and judgment fixed by the economic position of his group in the social order of the time.

Marx found the most important manifestation of economic determinism to be in the constant presence of opposing economic classes.[21] In any age, he maintained, the differing modes of acquiring means of existence divide men into separate groups and create within each group a special group consciousness. All social change has been determined chiefly by the economic class struggles that have pervaded history since the break up of tribal community organization. The history of humanity is largely the history of class conflict. Every system of production has given rise to two principal, mutually hostile, classes—the exploiters and the exploited, the owners and the toilers—, the character of the contending classes being determined by the particular character of the prevailing mode of production and exchange.

Marx borrowed from Hegel the conception of history as the evolution of humanity through conflict. Hegel arrived at this phase of his philos-

---

[21] The doctrine of class struggle is stated most succinctly in the *Communist Manifesto*, but it dominates all Marx's writings.

ophy of history through the application of a "dialectic" which he took over from Fichte. The latter depicted the reasoning process as a succession of three stages—thesis, synthesis, and antithesis: every logical conclusion (synthesis) is a derivation from two opposite notions (thesis and antithesis); reasoning is the act of discovering hypotheses for reconciling truths which apparently, and in part actually, contradict one another. This logic, Hegel maintained, reveals itself in the evolution of human institutions; for reason governs the world, and the process of history is necessarily a rational process. Thus the orderly evolution of thought and culture is a movement in which one partially valid trend is being constantly met by an opposite, equally one-sided trend, their conflict being gradually resolved in a combination that comprises the valid elements of the opposing currents. Each reconciliation is only temporary; for its underlying principle will suffer an overemphasis that will raise a contradiction to itself, so that a new solution will be required. The process of thesis, antithesis, and synthesis goes on.[22]

As Marx turned the theory of value, developed by classical economists in defense of capitalism, into a criticism of these systems, so he turned the ideas of Hegel, arch-theorist of conservatism and political aristocracy, into other theoretical foundations for his revolutionary socialism. The progress of history through conflict of contradictory half-truths becomes with Marx a progress through struggles of hostile classes differentiated by their economic conditions: the principle of private property and capitalism develops inevitably the opposite principle of proletarian, socialist dictatorship. Marx was mainly concerned in showing the application of his general historical doctrine to the past and future evolution of the capitalist era and in indicating especially the ways in which the needs of such an order of society determined the legal and governmental arrangements of the nineteenth century. The major portions of his formal writings are devoted less to an exposition of socialist policy than to an explanation of the evolution and degeneration of capitalism—showing its origin, analyzing its characteristic features, appraising its strength and weakness, predicting its future course.

To find in the contrasts and struggles between social groups the clue

---

[22] Hegel's lectures on history were delivered during the last decade of his life and were published posthumously as *Philosophie der Geschichte,* edited by Edward Gans (1837), Vol. IX in *Werke* (1832–1845); translation by J. Sibree (1852), *The Philosophy of History.* Hegel's dialectic is set forth in his *Wissenschaft der Logik,* 3 vols. (1812–1816), Vols. III–V in *Werke.*

to the interpretation of history was not new with Marx. His contribution was to center attention upon a single source of class antagonism—
namely, difference in economic status. At every stage of history, he
argued, the cultural and political position of any social group depends
upon the nature of its function in the production of economic goods;
and in every society the class that is able to control the methods and
amounts of production, to determine how the economic demands of the
time are to be supplied, will govern that society. And it will, by economic
necessity, govern oppressively. It cannot properly execute the tasks to
which it is committed by the assumptions upon which the validity of its
economic position rests, except by exploiting the other economic classes.
The latter, on the other hand, cannot survive unless they, by their resistance, put limits to that exploitation. All history reveals this struggle
of the economic under dogs against their masters: slaves against free-
men, plebeians against patricians, serfs against barons, journeymen
against guildsmen, bourgeoisie against the landed aristocracy.

The "democratic" revolutions from the seventeenth to the early nineteenth centuries were, according to Marx, the characteristic incidents of
the last-named struggle. The bourgeoisie finally triumphed; and recent
economic and social developments show the distinctive features of a
bourgeoisie society: machine industry and the factory system, separating
owners and workers; congestion of population in cities; large-scale production and the development of international trade; *laisser-faire* in
domestic governmental policy, imperialism in foreign affairs. These
conditions, which have promoted and confirmed the victory of industrial
capitalism over landlordism, have also engendered the existing conflict
between bourgeoisie and proletariat. This conflict is, in some phases,
simpler than the class antagonisms in the more highly stratified societies
of earlier times. It is between two clearly opposed groups—owners of
the instruments and raw materials of production, and wage-earners dependent for their lives on their use of those instruments and materials.

Marx proceeded to show that the natural, logical incidents in this
conflict lead to a new—and final—reconciliation. The inevitable trend
of development in the existing economic system is in the direction of a
constantly greater intensification of the inexorable warfare between the
owners of industrial property and the property-less workers. At the same
time the trend is towards the overthrow of capitalism. Capitalism constantly generates the seeds of its own destruction. The instruments which
the owners use to enlarge their profits and rents are the instruments

which, when perfected, fall inevitably into the hands of the workers, to be used by them to demolish the whole capitalist system.

Marx developed that prognosis in concrete detail.[23] In the first place, the tendency under capitalist production is towards large-scale production and monopoly. As a result of this tendency—manifested in the formation of partnerships, joint-stock companies, and corporations—wealth becomes concentrated in fewer and fewer hands, so that smaller capitalists are more and more crowded out and pushed down into the proletarian class. Thus along with the increase in great capitalist fortunes the number of capitalists decreases, while the working-class gains in numbers. Secondly, the tendency is towards local concentration. Large-scale production necessitates the bringing together of thousands of workers into small areas, and by these contacts they become more fully conscious of their common hardships and needs; their class consciousness is strengthened and their means of coöperation facilitated. In the third place, the tendency of capitalist production is towards the attainment of ever wider fields for markets. This requires a high development of the means of communication among different parts of the industrial world; and this, in turn, facilitates intercommunication among the workers distributed throughout the industrial world. Fourthly, the capitalist system produces recurring economic crises. The laborers, who constitute the great body of consumers, are paid enough to purchase only a very limited portion of what they produce; the products accumulate and crises of extreme overproduction take place. The recurring crises, becoming more acute as capitalism develops, make the domination of capitalists more insecure; and the means which the latter adopt to avoid the crises—such as acquiring new markets—only pave the way for severer and more extensive crises and destroy the means whereby they may be prevented. Finally, the tendency under capitalism is towards a steady increase in the misery, ignorance, and dependency of the workers; and this aggravates their hostility and discontent. Throughout the whole process, capitalism, while always increasing the number of the property-less, is always, by its development of labor-saving machinery, reducing the number of laborers that it needs; in other words, it constantly cuts down

[23] Marx's ideas of the future course of capitalism appear best in the *Communist Manifesto* and in various parts of *Capital*. For critical discussion of those ideas, cf. the following: Harry W. Laidler, *Socialism in Thought and Action* (1920), pp. 80–117; Franz Oppenheimer, *Das Grundgesetz der Marxschen Gesellschaftslehre*, Ch. XII; O. D. Skelton, *Socialism: A Critical Analysis*, Ch. VII; Peter von Struve, "Die Marxsche Theorie der sozialen Entwickelung," *Archiv für Sozialwissenschaft und Sozialpolitik*, XIV (1899), 658–704.

the number of those who are able to purchase its constantly increasing products.

Thus the capitalist system enlarges the number of workers, brings them together into compact groups, makes them class conscious, supplies them with means of intercommunication and coöperation on a world-wide scale, reduces their purchasing power, and by increasingly exploiting them arouses them to organized resistance. Capitalists, acting persistently in pursuit of their own natural needs and in vindication of a system dependent upon the maintenance of profits, are all the time creating conditions which stimulate and strengthen the natural efforts of workers in preparing for a system that will fit the needs of a workingman's society.

MARX'S PROGRAM OF ACTION

We see, then, that Marx's socialism is a theory of economic value, maintaining that the exchange values of commodities result from, or are measured by, the efforts of those who have applied their labor to the commodities. It is a theory of social causation in general, maintaining that all important social and political phenomena are to be explained principally in terms of the contemporary economic phenomena. Finally, it bases all social and political development upon the natural conflicts of interest between economic classes; it forecasts the natural course of the future struggle, indicating the successive changes in position of the classes —changes that will occur without premeditation and as the consequences of changing conditions of production and of constant readjustments of strategy by the contending groups, each pursuing only its immediate needs.

Marx's socialism, on the other hand, is a constructive plan for deliberate political action. Marx was not a fatalist. Men, he held, suffer inevitably the influences of their economic environment but not passively; they react positively to these influences; and they can to a significant degree, although acting always under normal economic pressures of the time, change the environment. In Marx's discussion of socialist policy, his historical determinism is far from absolute. He regarded it as the business of the social philosopher not only to explain what human society is but also to show how, and within what limits, it can be changed. Although capitalism proceeds naturally to its own destruction, it does not create socialism. In other words, capitalism inevitably prepares the way for, but does not inevitably lead into, socialism. Deliberate, intelligent, and informed action is needed for the achievement of socialism.[24]

Marx's ideas of economic determinism, surplus value, the class struggle, and the process of past and future social evolution and revolution supply the logical foundation of his system of practical socialism— his justification of his program. If the whole social order is determined by the relations of production, then the evils of an existing social order can be remedied only by a change in these relations. If, under the existing system, the private owners of capital are obtaining—in the forms of rent, interest, and profits—the greater part of that which labor alone produces, then private ownership of capital should be abolished and a system of production and distribution established under which there can be no private rents, interest, or profits. If the inevitable trend under the capitalist system is towards an intensification which develops into a weakening and destruction of the system, then the workers, in using the means at hand to put themselves in position to dislodge and supplant capitalists in the control of the instruments of production, are simply falling in with the natural trend of events—going with the actual course of social evolution, not against it. Thus the logic and movement of facts indicate to the workers their program of action.

Marx's most direct and explicit sketch of a political program appears in a few pages of the *Communist Manifesto*. The fuller picture has to be made up by inferences from his observations on critical events occurring during his lifetime. The occasions for his most important political comments were the revolutionary attempts in France in 1848, the Paris Commune of 1871, and the adoption of a platform by the German Social Democratic party at Gotha in 1875. The discussion of the events of 1848 is contained in *Class Struggles in France* and *The Eighteenth Brumaire of Louis Bonaparte*. The former appeared first in 1850, in the form of articles in the *Neue Rheinische Zeitung* (a monthly edited by Marx and Engels and in existence for only six months), and was published in book form posthumously by Engels; the latter is a brief book, first published in 1852. The analysis of the Paris Commune is set forth in *The Civil War in France*, published in London in 1871. The comments on the Gotha program, mainly an adverse criticism, were written as marginal notes on a manuscript of the program

[24] Cf. on this point Otto Rühle, *Karl Marx* (1929), *passim*, and Sidney Hook, *Towards the Understanding of Karl Marx*, pp. 31 ff., 83 ff. and Chs. XI–XIII.

and were first published a quarter of a century later, in the socialist journal—*Die Neue Zeit*.[25]

The function of a socialist program, Marx held, is to show wage-workers how to convert their potential into an actual superiority or how to prepare themselves for transforming an automatic economic struggle into a consciously designed political struggle. The first step in such a program is to "win the battle of democracy." The workers must organize as an oppressed class and raise themselves "to the position of ruling class." The wage-earners in each country should form a political party and seek, through ordinary electioneering methods, to become the majority party in the electorate and in the national parliament. In a country where the group in control of government persists in maintaining constitutional barriers, supported by military force, to deny to a proletarian majority its rightful title to political control, the workers will have to resort to organized force. Having acquired control, peacefully or by violence, they must then make their supremacy secure; and this is to be accomplished through the familiar devices of an advanced democracy: universal suffrage; a direct popular election and recall of principal political officials—legislative, executive, and judicial; an "armed people," in place of a standing army; free public education; payment of political officers (and this is the only distinctively socialist feature in the political scheme) at the rate of wages for manual workers.[26]

After the workers have securely established their political supremacy they must enter upon their major task of socializing capital. The process must be gradual, but it will involve, in the beginning, "despotic inroads on the rights of property." The destruction of capitalism cannot be accomplished in one comprehensive stroke. Accompanying a transfer, "by degrees," of the instrumentalities of production from private to state ownership, there must be various governmental measures for improving the physical and intellectual welfare of those workers who, in the transitional period, remain under private employment, and also for diminishing the economic power of the remaining capitalists. The particular steps cannot be the same in all states. For the "most advanced countries," the immediate measures, according to the program of the *Communist Manifesto*, are the following: abolition of private ownership of land; centralization of the means of transport and communication in the hands of the state; establishment of a state monopoly of credit and banking;

---

[25] For editions of these works, see the list on pp. 62–63 *infra*.
[26] See *The Civil War in France, passim*.

abrogation of rights of inheritance; heavily progressive income taxation; prohibition of child labor in factories; enforcement of an equal liability of all to work. These measures are to be followed by a gradual extension of public ownership in other fields of production.

In the *Manifesto* this program of gradual social reform is set forth as something to be begun only after the organized workers acquire control of the state. Later utterances and acts of Marx show that he was willing for socialists to lend aid to piecemeal encroachments upon private capital, imposed before the acquisition of control, in instances where such measures, although enacted by non-socialists, tend to strengthen the workers economically and politically. In his inaugural address before the organization meeting of the International Workingmen's Association in 1864, he characterized the British ten-hours act of 1847 as a measure of great moral and economic benefit to the workers. Resolutions prepared by him for the 1866 congress of the Association included proposals for immediate legislation limiting the hours of labor for women and children and for tax reforms to lighten the workers' cost of living. Generally he was opposed to detailed and doctrinaire statements of policy; for, he held, they tend to hamper the comprehensive coöperation of workers in building up a powerful proletarian movement. The workers, he said in 1871, "have no ready-made Utopias to introduce by order of the people. They know that in order to work out their own emancipation, and along with it that higher form to which society is irresistibly tending, by its own economic agencies, they will have to pass through long struggles, through a series of historic processes, transforming circumstances and men." [27] Four years later he wrote, in commenting on the Gotha program of the German Social Democratic party: "Every step of real movement is more important than a dozen programs." [28]

Popular comments on socialism frequently give chief attention to what is supposed to be its main tenet—namely, that wealth must be distributed equally among the members of society. But this is not to be found in the doctrine of Marx. "Popular socialism," he said in his criticism of the Gotha program, "has followed the bourgeois economists . . . in treating distribution as independent of the means of production and, therefore, in representing socialism as principally concerned with distribution." The methods of distribution, he continued,

---

[27] *Civil War in France* (Charles H. Kerr & Co. edition), p. 50.
[28] "Zur Kritik des sozialdemokratischen Parteiprograms," edited by Engels, in *Die Neue Zeit*, IX (1890–1891), no. 18, 561–575, at p. 562

vary according to the stage of historical development and the general productive organization of the community. "When the means of production become the common property of workers, there will follow as a matter of course, a distribution of the means of consumption different from the method to-day." Under a régime of socialism, a part of the product will have to be reserved for replacement and expansion of the means of production, for general administrative expenses, for insurance against the chances of natural misfortune, and for provision for the common physical and cultural needs of the community and relief of those unable to work. The remainder can then be used to pay the workers severally according to the amount and quality of their labors. But this principle of rewarding individuals according to their supposed deserts smacks of bourgeois morality and will be abandoned when socialism has attained its goal. "In a higher phase of communist society, when the degenerating subordination of individuals to the division of labor has disappeared, and therewith also the opposition between intellectual and manual labor; when labor has become, not merely a means of life, but itself the biggest need of life; when, with the development of all the faculties of the individual, the productive forces have correspondingly increased and all the springs of social wealth flow more abundantly— then only can the limited horizon of bourgeois right be crossed and society inscribe upon its banners: 'Each according to his abilities; to each according to his needs.' " [29]

As to many other questions concerning the tactics of socialism—the methods of expropriating capitalists, of selecting and assigning the working personnel, and of determining the quantity and quality of products —Marx either ignored them or deliberately withheld his opinion, on the ground that such practical problems might, under varying conditions of time and place, be variously solved, although always in conformity to socialist principles.

Thus Marx's program is both evolutionary and revolutionary. It conceives a socialist society evolving gradually out of a capitalist society, as the result of a natural and progressive degeneration of the latter. Socialism appears only when the processes of transformation of the economic order of society have prepared the way for it. Revolution is timely only when an existing economic system has lost its validity. A nation can be made into a socialist society only after it has passed through the contradictory capitalist stage. Even after society comes to be dominated

[29] *Die Neue Zeit*, pp. 567, 568.

by the socialist ideal, the full realization of the ideal can be attained only by slow stages. But Marx's socialism is also a revolutionary creed. Here again the association of Marx's ideas with previous movements appears. The way for his aggressive socialism was prepared not only by earlier developments in economic theory but also by the activities of proletarian groups in various European countries. The practical antecedents of Marx's program are found not in the idealistic communities established by followers of Saint-Simon, Fourier, and Cabet but in the more militant enterprises set in motion among the disgruntled workers themselves. There had been, for example, a French revolutionary-communistic current, which, appearing during the French Revolution in conspiratory movements led by Baboeuf, was revived in the eighteen twenties by Buonarroti [30] and in the thirties by other insurrectionary leaders. Similar movements sprang up in Belgium and Germany in the next decade. In the thirties and forties, preparations for the revolutionary aspects of Marxism can be found both in the Chartist movement in England, with its agitation for political reforms through workers' mass demonstrations, and in the radical efforts of trade-unionists, in England and elsewhere, to elevate the workers' position by means of prolonged and hard-fought strikes. Through such activities the workers in Europe were acquiring experience in coöperative, self-reliant action and were developing traditions of a working-class revolution.

It can also be said, more generally, that the tendency of industrial development since the later eighteenth century was to concentrate the workers into populous centers, make them conscious of their common problems, and drive them into concerted efforts to change forcibly the social conditions under which they were forced to live and work. They formed insurrectionary societies in order to obtain elementary rights of association and discussion, which the existing social régimes prevented them from acquiring by peaceful means. Both Marx and Engels were born in the Rhine province of Prussia, where the influences of the French Revolution remained; Jacobin societies had been formed there and many German residents had been volunteers in the military forces of the Revolution. The local revolutionary tradition was still strong in the period of the youth of Marx and Engels.[31] These two, we have seen, prepared the *Manifesto* for a secret society that included within

---

[30] François Noel Baboeuf (1764–1797), communist agitator, guillotined for the conspiracy which he organized against the Directory in 1796; Filippo Buonarroti (1761–1837), Italian political agitator, associated with Baboeuf's conspiracy.

[31] D. Ryazanoff, *Karl Marx and Friedrich Engels,* Ch. II.

its membership many advocates of revolutionary force. "Communists," the *Manifesto* asserted accordingly; "openly declare that their ends can be attained only by the forcible overthrow of all existing conditions. Let the ruling classes tremble at a Communistic revolution!" The *Manifesto* also suggested that the Communists of Germany should, after the French manner of 1793 and 1830, coöperate with the bourgeoisie in a revolutionary fight for the overthrow of autocracy. It went on to say that victory in such a revolution should be regarded as "but the prelude to an immediately following proletarian revolution" against the bourgeoisie. Marx also advocated revolutionary action in connection with the political movements of 1848 in France and Germany; he urged all liberal and radical citizens to refuse to pay taxes and to offer armed resistance to efforts of the government to collect the taxes by force. During the early years of his sojourn in London, he indicated on several occasions his approval of projects to revive the physically menacing measures of the Chartists.[32]

Thus Marx's earlier program gave an important place to insurrectionary methods. Moreover, his socialism is revolutionary in the sense that it insists upon the irreconcilable antagonism between labor and capital, has no respect for vested interests incompatible with its ideal, and is ready to take any step towards its goal when the conditions are propitious; it will not be restrained by considerations of formal or traditional legitimacy. It has been pointed out, however, that the experiences of the revolutionists in the struggles of 1848 and 1849 and the recent changes in industrial conditions, political methods, and military technique contributed in various ways to disclose to the radical leaders of that time the unavailability or futility of armed resistance by minority groups. Moreover, Marx acknowledged (in 1850) that there was no likelihood that workers, however numerous, could be moved to resistance at times when prosperity prevails "within the framework of bourgeois conditions." A socialist revolution, he said, can take place only in periods when "the modern forces of production and the bourgeois forces of production are in antagonism—brought into antagonism by the miseries of a numerous proletariat." [33] His prevailing attitude, in most of his later utterances, appears to be one of skepticism concerning secret, conspiratory activities and of confidence in the efficacy of

---

[32] Cf. Franz Mehring, *Aus dem literarischen Nachlass von Karl Marx, Friedrich Engels und Ferdinand Lassalle* (1902, fourth ed. 1923), *passim.*
[33] Quoted in Otto Rühle, *Karl Marx*, p. 172.

education, agitation, coöperation, organization, and political-party activity, as the better means whereby working-men can reach the political maturity and strength that will enable them to grasp control of political machinery at the appropriate time.

It is impossible, however, to formulate from Marx's various and sometimes vague discussions of the methods of acquiring supremacy any precise and consistent statement that can be offered as an entirely faithful representation of his views. He generally recognized that the means for securing political power might differ at different times and in different countries; the method might be direct economic action at one time and place, a revolution at another, and slow achievement of political predominance at another. His attitude was generally pragmatic. He would advocate organized violence where conditions indicated that socialists could obtain political supremacy in that way. However, the "forcible overthrow of all existing social conditions" would not necessarily, or even ordinarily, be through physical force but rather through the attainment of a political majority by legitimate means, followed by the gradual expropriation of capitalist owners through political, though not necessarily formally or traditionally legal, measures. The method of forcible rebellion is permissible where the circumstances are such as to make that method necessary and probably successful. But certainly assassination and incendiarism are not what Marx had in mind in speaking of "revolution" and "forcible overthrow" of the capitalist system. He opposed, on the one hand, an untimely revolution and, on the other hand, all attempts, even through legitimate means, to establish a socialist régime before the conditions were ripe. "Even," he said, "when a society has got upon the right track by bold leaps, for the discovery of the natural laws of its development . . . it can neither clear, nor remove by legal enactments, the obstacles offered by the successive phases of its normal development." [34]

When Marx approved devices of direct action, industrial or violent, he approved them only as auxiliary to the main project of capturing political supremacy for the workers when economic developments had made them a majority. He was not an orthodox democrat, however. Political democracy was only a detail, although an important detail, in his social scheme. He held to the position taken in his earlier writings, where he repudiated the "democratic-republican institutions" designed

[34] Marx's Preface to Vol. I of *Das Kapital*. See *Capital,* Moore and Aveling translation, pp. 14–15.

"as the means, not to remove the two extremes—Capital and Wage-slavery—but in order to weaken their antagonism and transform them into a harmonious whole." Such a transformation, he maintained, could not be accomplished "within the boundaries of the small traders' class with their vague idea of popular sovereignty." [35] Control of surplus value by those who created it held the first place in all his theory. In other words, Marx was not interested in political democracy except when it appeared as a part of an organized proletarian movement and as a preparation for a thoroughgoing socialization of wealth.

Marx, however, advocated organized political activity by the workers and accepted the state as the indispensable organization through which the socialist ideal of the proletariatization of capital would be achieved. He thought of the state, moreover, not as a voluntary association of community coöperation but as a compulsive, force-employing organization and indeed as inevitably an instrument of domination of one class over others. On two occasions (in 1850 and 1875) he spoke of a "class" or "revolutionary" "dictatorship of the proletariat" in designating the socialist régime that would "immediately" succeed the abolition of "bourgeois dictatorship" and constitute the "political transition period" "between the capitalist and communist systems of society." [36] But dictatorship, in Marx's doctrine, obviously cannot be understood in the sense of absolute governmental authority, exercised by a single person or by any number of persons, resting solely on force and not bound by laws of any sort. It can be understood only in the sense of authority exercised by a new politically sovereign class over a dislodged, formerly sovereign, class; and as a régime not bound by laws that had obtained under the régime which it has, by lawful or unlawful means, displaced. [37]

Although Marx opposed doctrinairism and was willing to make many compromises in tactics, he never abandoned the position, taken early in his life, that emancipation for the workers would come only through a complete political and economic transformation of existing national

---

[35] *Eighteenth Brumaire of Louis Bonaparte,* translated by Daniel De Leon (third ed., 1913), p. 52.

[36] *Class Struggles in France,* pp. 170, 174. *On the Gotha Program,* ed. by Daniel De Leon (1922), p. 48.

[37] For a discussion of Marx's ideas, in reference to the Russian-Communist conception of a proletarian dictatorship, see *infra,* Ch. VI, pp. 174–177.

societies; through a dissolution, gradual or sudden, peaceful or forcible, of existing political relations, and a re-creation in the form of a society established on radically different principles of production, distribution, and control. Class-antagonism remained persistently the foundation of both the evolutionary and the revolutionary aspects of his doctrine, the central point in both his theoretical and his practical teaching. Finally, however, although Marx believed that the workers must obtain control of the state and use its power to dispossess the capitalists, he maintained also that the state would ultimately disappear; because, when it had been used to accomplish fully the ultimate objectives of socialism, its authority and power would no longer be needed. The proximate goal of socialist activity is the centralization of all instruments of production in the hands of a state controlled by the organized proletariat or in the hands of the proletariat organized as a state. The ultimate goal is the condition in which all class warfare, all authority of one group over another, will have disappeared since the circumstances which create hostile or competing classes will have disappeared.[38] Under this view, the class antagonisms of a given time arise not from any essentially malevolent dispositions in men but from necessities of economic self-preservation imposed by the special conditions of an existing system of production and exchange. The complete application of socialism, said Marx and Engels, will allay all class antagonisms. The dialectic of thesis and antithesis will be resolved in a final synthesis. Through socialism mankind will make the ascent "from the kingdom of necessity to the kingdom of freedom." [39]

Marx's writings revolved mainly around questions of economic and historical theory and around practical problems of economic and political tactics. But his ultimate interest was in liberated and cultivated individuals. Fairer and more productive economic arrangements are necessary, he believed, in order that every man may have the time and opportunity for "free development, intellectual and social." The goal of Marx's socialism—like the goal of most other political creeds, radical or conservative—is "a society in which the full and free development of every individual forms the ruling principle." [40]

[38] See the *Communist Manifesto*.
[39] Friedrich Engels, *Socialism, Utopian and Scientific,* Kerr ed. (1908), p. 135.
[40] *Capital,* Moore and Aveling translation, I, 581, 649.

SELECT BIBLIOGRAPHY

BIBLIOGRAPHIES OF SOCIALISM

Drahn, E., *Führer durch das Schriftum des deutschen Sozialismus* (Berlin, 1911).

——————, *Marx-Bibliographie* (second ed., Berlin, 1923).

Kerr, C. H., *What to Read on Socialism* (Chicago, 1910).

Laidler, Harry W., *Socialism in Thought and Action* (New York, 1920), pp. 511–518.

Rappoport, A. S., *A Dictionary of Socialism* (London, 1924), pp. 227–263.

Skelton, O. D., *Socialism: a Critical Analysis* (Boston and New York, 1911), pp. 313–322.

Stammhammer, Josef, *Bibliographie des Sozialismus und Kommunismus*, 3 vols. (Jena, 1893, 1900, 1909).

Zimand, Savel, *Modern Social Movements: Descriptive Summaries and Bibliographies* (New York, 1921), pp. 143–183.

HISTORIES OF SOCIALISM

Adler, Georg, *Geschichte des Sozialismus und Kommunismus von Plato bis zur Gegenwart* (Leipsic, 1899).

Hertzler, Joyce O., *The History of Utopian Thought* (New York, 1923).

Kirkup, Thomas, *History of Socialism*, fifth ed., revised and enlarged by E. R. Pease (London, 1913).

Laidler, Harry W., *A History of Socialist Thought* (New York, 1927).

Mumford, Lewis, *The Story of Utopias* (New York, 1922).

Villegardelle, François, *Histoire des idées sociales avant la révolution française* (Paris, 1846).

WORKS OF KARL MARX (ARRANGED CHRONOLOGICALLY)

Deutsch-französische Jahrbücher (1844), articles reprinted in *Karl Marx und Friedrich Engels, Historisch-kritische Gesamt-Ausgabe, Werke, Schriften, Briefe*, ed. by D. Ryazanoff, 11 vols. (Frankfort, 1927–1931), I, 607–621.

Die heilige Familie, oder Kritik der kritischen Kritik (with Friedrich Engels, Frankfort, 1845).

Misère de la philosophie: Réponse à la philosophie de la misère de Proudhon (Paris and Brussels, 1847; later editions, 1896, etc.).

Poverty of Philosophy, translated by H. Quelch (Chicago, 1910).

The Communist Manifesto (1848).

Die Klassenkämpfe in Frankreich, 1848 bis 1850, appearing as magazine articles in 1849 and 1850, published posthumously by Friedrich Engels (Berlin, 1895, etc.).

The Class Struggles in France, translated by Henry Kuhn (New York, 1924).

Der achtzehnte Brumaire des Louis Bonaparte (New York, 1852; third ed., Hamburg, 1885).

The Eighteenth Brumaire of Louis Bonaparte, translated by Daniel De Leon (New York, 1897; third ed., Chicago, 1913).

Zur Kritik der politischen Oekonomie (Berlin, 1859; Stuttgart, 1897).

A Contribution to the Critique of Political Economy, translated from the second German edition by N. I. Stone (New York and London, 1904).

Die Inauguraladdresse der internationalen Arbeiterassociation (1862; Berlin, 1922).

Value, Price, and Profit (1865); ed. by Eleanor Marx Aveling (Chicago, 1913).

Das Kapital: Kritik der politischen Oekonomie, 3 vols. (Hamburg, 1867, 1885, 1894).

Capital: A Critique of Political Economy, translated from the third German edition by Samuel Moore and Edward Aveling, edited by Friedrich Engels; revised from the fourth German edition by Ernest Untermann, 3 vols. (Chicago and London, 1909–1913).

The Civil War in France (1871), translated from the German by E. Belfort Bax (Chicago, 1912).

Zur Kritik des sozialdemokratischen Parteiprograms (1875), in *Die Neue Zeit,* IX (1890–1891), 561–575.

The Gotha Program, translated by Daniel De Leon (New York, 1922).

Theorien über den Mehrwert, 3 vols., posthumous (Stuttgart, 1905–1910).

Aus dem literarischen Nachlass von Karl Marx, Friedrich Engels und Ferdinand Lassalle, posthumous, ed. by Franz Mehring, 4 vols. (second ed., Stuttgart, 1913).

Karl Marx, Friedrich Engels: historisch-kritische Gesamt-Ausgabe, Werke, Schrifte, Briefe, posthumous, ed. by D. Ryazanoff, 11 vols. (Frankfort, 1927–1931).

CRITICAL EXPOSITIONS OF THE DOCTRINES OF MARX

Adler, Max, *Marx als Denker* (Berlin, 1908).

Aveling, Edward B., *The Student's Marx* (London, 1892; fourth ed., 1902).

Bober, Mandell M., *Karl Marx's Interpretation of History* (Cambridge, Mass., 1927).

Böhm-Bawerk, Eugen von, *Zum Abschluss des Marxschen Systems* (Berlin, 1896).

    Karl Marx and the Close of His System, translated by Alice M. Macdonald (London and New York, 1898).

Boudin, Louis B., *Theoretical System of Karl Marx* (Chicago, 1907).

Burns, C. Deslisle, *The Principles of Revolution: a Study in Ideals* (New York, 1921).

Chang, Sherman H., *The Marxian Theory of the State* (Philadelphia, 1931).

Croce, Benedetto, *Historical Materialism and the Economics of Karl Marx,* translated by C. M. Meredith (London and New York, 1907).

Cunow, Heinrich, *Die Marxsche Geschichts-, Gesellschafts- und Staatstheorie* (Berlin, 1920–1921).

Eastman, Max, *Marx, Lenin, and the Science of Revolution* (London, 1926), Pt. I.

Emmett, W. H., *The Marxian Economic Handbook and Glossary* (New York, 1925).

Engels, Friedrich, *Die Entwickelung des Sozialismus von der Utopie zur Wissenschaft,* fourth edition (Berlin, 1891).

   Socialism, Utopian and Scientific, translated by Edward Aveling (New York, 1892).

Fischer, Paul, *Die Marxsche Werththeorie* (Berlin, 1889).

Gray, J. L., "Karl Marx and Social Philosophy," Ch. VI in F. J. C. Hearnshaw, ed., *The Social and Political Ideas of Some Representative Thinkers of the Victorian Age* (London, 1933).

Hearnshaw, F. J. C., *A Survey of Socialism* (London, 1928), Ch. VII.

Heiman, Eduard, "Der Sozialismus als sittliche Idee und die materialistische Geschichtstheorie," *Archiv für Sozialwissenschaft und Sozialpolitik,* LII (1924), 139–176.

Hillquit, Morris, *Socialism in Theory and Practice* (New York, 1909).

Hook, Sidney, *Towards the Understanding of Karl Marx* (New York, 1933).

Kautsky, Karl, *Karl Marx's oekonomische Lehren* (Stuttgart, 1894; twelfth ed., 1908).

——————, *The Economic Doctrines of Karl Marx,* translated by H. J. Stenning (London, 1925).

——————, *Das Erfurter Programm* (Stuttgart, eighth ed., 1907).

——————, *The Class Struggle,* translation of *Das Erfurter Programm,* by W. E. Bohn (Chicago, 1910).

——————, *Ethik und die materialistische Geschichtsauffassung* (Stuttgart, 1906).

——————, *Ethics and the Materialist Conception of History,* translated by J. B. Askew (Chicago, 1907).

Korsch, Karl, *Marxismus und Philosophie* (second ed., Leipsic, 1930).

Kraus, Emil, *Die geschichtliche Grundlagen des Sozialismus; eine Einführung in der Materialist-Geschichts-Theorie* (Karlsruhe, 1922).

Labriola, Antonio, *Essays on the Materialistic Conception of History,* translated by C. H. Kerr (Chicago, 1912).

Laidler, Harry W., *Socialism in Thought and Action* (New York, 1920).

Laski, Harold J., *Karl Marx: an Essay* (London, 1922).

Lenin, N., "The Materialistic Interpretation of History and Karl Marx," *Labour Monthly*, IV (1923), 265–268.

Lindsay, A. D., *Karl Marx's Capital* (London, 1925).

Loria, Achille, *Economic Foundations of Society*, translated from the second French edition by L. M. Keasbey (London, 1899).

Oppenheimer, Franz, *Das Grundgesetz der Marxschen Gesellschaftslehre* (Berlin, 1903; Jena, 1926, a reprint).

Pareto, Vilfredo, *Introduction aux systèmes socialistes*, 2 vols., second ed. (Paris, 1926), vol. II, Ch. XIV and pp. 397–468.

Plekhanov, G., *Fundamental Problems of Marxism*, translated by Eden and Cedar Paul (London, 1929).

Ryazanoff, D., *Karl Marx and Friedrich Engels* (New York, 1927).

Rühle, Otto, *Karl Marx: His Life and Work* (New York, 1929).

Sachs, A. S., *Basic Principles of Scientific Socialism* (New York, 1925).

Sée, Henri, *The Economic Interpretation of History*, translated by M. M. Knight (New York, 1929).

Seligman, E. R. A., *Economic Interpretation of History*, second revised edition (New York, 1922), Ch. III.

Skelton, O. D., *Socialism: a Critical Analysis* (Boston and New York, 1911).

Spargo, John, *Socialism: a Summary and Interpretation of Socialist Principles*, second revised edition (New York, 1918).

Spargo, John and Arner, G. B. L., *Elements of Socialism* (New York, 1912).

Struve, Peter von, "Die Marxsche Theorie der sozialen Entwickelung," *Archiv für Soziale Gesetzgebung und Statistik*, vol. XIV (1899), pp. 658–704.

Turgeon, Charles, *La conception materialiste de l'histoire*, Vols. II–III (1908–1909, 1911, 1912) of *Travaux juridiques et économiques de l'Université de Rennes*.

Veblen, Thorstein, "The Socialist Economics of Karl Marx and His Followers," *Quarterly Journal of Economics*, XX (1906), 575–595, and XXI (1906), 299–322.

Woltmann, Ludwig, *Der historische Materialismus* (Düsseldorf, 1900).

CHAPTER III

THE SOCIALIST MOVEMENT AND THE ORTHODOX FOLLOWERS OF MARX: BEFORE THE WORLD WAR

SINCE Marx's death, the great majority of professed socialists—those active in party politics as well as the theorists and propagandists—have been his professed followers. There have been wide divergencies of opinion among them, however, as to what true Marxism is, as a plan of action. This is not strange. Marx's various instructions and suggestions for a socialist program are not easily unified into a logically consistent system. They are scattered through a number of his books, pamphlets, and letters, widely differentiated as to time and occasion. Some of the statements were deliberately elaborated in the seclusion of his study, remote from the exigencies of practical policy. Others were called forth by demands from his followers for guidance in meeting some immediate emergency in political maneuverings. Neither he nor his collaborators ever prepared a *résumé* of his political proposals.

Marx's direct influence on the practical movement of socialism was exercised chiefly through his part in the activities of the "International Association of Workingmen," founded in 1864.[1] This association was formed in London through the joint initiative of English trade-unionists, leaders of radical labor groups in France, and political refugees from other Continental countries. Later known as the "First International,", it was in existence for twelve years. It was not created primarily for the promotion of socialism or any other doctrine. It was designed rather as a medium through which the working-men of the several countries could interchange ideas and coöperate more effectively in formulating their grievances and asserting their rights. Marx assisted at the initial meeting, which, after rejecting plans proposed by other leaders, accepted

[1] For brief accounts of the history and achievements of the First International, see the following: M. Beer, *History of British Socialism*, II (1920), 213–333; Lewis L. Lorwin, *Labor and Internationalism* (1929), Ch. II; R. W. Postgate, *The Workers' International* (1920), Ch. I; John Spargo, *Karl Marx: His Life and Work* (new ed., 1910), Ch. XI. For more extensive and original accounts, cf. the works by Guillaumme, Jaeckh, and Longuet, cited in the bibliographical list, pp. 82–83, *infra.*

unanimously a declaration of principles and rules prepared by him; and he was thenceforth its most influential member. The Association, however, was never thoroughly in accord. Its leaders were alike in looking forward to an ultimate emancipation of oppressed workers, to be effected through a substantial transformation of the existing industrial system; and they generally agreed that only a consolidated effort of the workers themselves could achieve this goal. But the Association did not commit itself to any distinctly socialist declaration until 1867, when, in a congress at Lausanne, it adopted a resolution advocating governmental ownership of the means of transportation and communication. This was followed in the immediately succeeding congresses by resolutions calling for the socialization of landed property.

The rapid disintegration of the "First International" after 1870 was due to a number of converging factors. The Franco-Prussian war evoked nationalist animosities between French and German members. British trade-unionists, appeased and encouraged by their increase in political power, from the franchise-reform legislation of 1867, and by their general improvement in living conditions, were becoming less inclined to follow the more aggressive methods of economic and political struggle favored by the Continental sections. There was also a diminishing interest among some of the German groups, who were preoccupied with the conventional political activities of their rising Social Democratic party. Moreover, the governments of France and several other countries imposed rigid restrictions upon the Association's activities because of its supposed connection with the revolutionary Paris Commune of 1871—a connection charged against the Association by its antagonists and boastfully claimed for it by some of its members but probably of no great significance in fact. Added to and greatly aggravating these factors of disruption was the sharp and bitter conflict of doctrine and personality between Marx and the anarchist leader, Michael Bakunin. The latter opposed the centralizing, authoritarian program of Marx and urged a withdrawal altogether from political action.[2] At the Congress at The Hague, in 1872, the Association, after a heated debate, expelled Bakunin and his numerous followers. At the same time it voted to move the headquarters of its council from London to New York. Marx desired this latter change in order to release the International from Bakunin's intrigues and to relieve himself from further responsibility for it, as he was then in ill health. At a final and slimly attended con-

[2] See pp. 202–207, 218, *infra*.

gress in Philadelphia in 1876, the Association voted its own dissolution.

Although the First International, in its brief existence, was weakened both by governmental interference and by internal conflicts of opinion, it accomplished much for the progress of organized socialism. It brought working-men's representatives together in larger numbers and from a wider area than ever before, and it greatly strengthened the feeling of a community of interest among workers of the different nations. On several occasions it facilitated an exchange of practical help across natural boundaries in times of strikes, and its discussions served in many ways to clarify the problems with which socialists would have to deal in formulating the policies for a working-men's movement.

This exchange of opinions in the congresses of the First International gave great impetus and support to the formation of socialist parties in the various countries. In the seventies and eighties strong parties of this character were formed in France, Belgium, and the Scandinavian countries, and weaker parties in some of the states of Southern Europe and in the United States. By the close of the century there were socialist parties in every European state outside the industrially backward Balkan countries; there were also strong labor parties with considerable socialist membership in Great Britain and Australia. By the beginning of the World War, a labor party with socialist leanings had been formed in South Africa; and small socialist parties had been established in Canada, China, Japan, and several of the Balkan and South American countries.[3]

In the meantime the socialist parties had, in 1889, formed a new international association, which was in existence until the disruption of the socialist ranks in the World War. This "Second International" held its meetings at irregular intervals of two or three years in various European cities, and, in 1900, set up in Brussels a permanent administrative office—the International Socialist Bureau. The Bureau, composed of three representatives from each national section, arranged the congresses, and its staff served as a clearing-house of information and advice in the furtherance of labor and socialist activities in the various countries. The Second International, however, was only a loose federation of autonomous parties. Normally, each party was free to

[3] For sketches of the development of socialist party organization and policy in the several countries, see the following: Thomas Kirkup, *History of Socialism*, Chs. IX and XII; O. D. Skelton, *Socialism: a Critical Analysis* (1911), Ch. IX; John Spargo and G. B. L. Arner, *Elements of Socialism* (1912), pp. 255–368.

pursue independently the course of action suited to its peculiar aims and needs. The socialists had nowhere any powerful center of control over action or opinion.[4]

As already indicated, the various parties and their leaders were generally united in their allegiance to Marx, but they often differed in interpreting his ideas. The most persistent line of division was between those who laid stress upon the revolutionary phases of Marx's doctrine and those who directed attention to his "science" of socialist evolution and his proposals for immediate constructive measures. These main groups came to be known as the "orthodox," or "revolutionary," socialists, and the "revisionists"; the former maintaining that socialists can reach their goal only through incessant and uncompromising warfare against the bourgeoisie; the latter arguing that since, as Marx showed, capitalist society tends to evolve towards the socialist goal, socialists can confirm and accelerate this tendency by supporting reforms which lack any revolutionary appearance and which often are best obtainable through compromise and coöperation with non-socialists.[5] It is not possible, of course, to separate the socialists into rival schools sharply differentiated according to the revolutionary or reformist character of their views. Each group has disclosed numerous shades of doctrinairism and opportunism; here, as elsewhere in political and social movements, there is considerable shifting of position. Orthodox socialists have sometimes committed themselves to opportunist policies and acquiesced in compromise with anti-socialists, and revisionists have on occasions felt the necessity of proclaiming the ultimately revolutionary character of their aims. In general, however, the revisionists, in their practical policy, appeared to be less closely related to the Marxists than to socialists who based their programs on theories not derived, for the most part, from Marx. Accordingly, the revisionist policy will be considered in the account (in the immediately succeeding chapter) of socialist creeds

[4] For accounts of the Second International, cf. the following: Thomas Kirkup, *History of Socialism*, Ch. XIII; Lewis L. Lorwin, *Labor and Internationalism*, Ch. III; R. W. Postgate, *The Workers' International*, Ch. II; John Spargo, *Karl Marx: His Life and Work*, Ch. XII; William E. Walling and H. W. Laidler, *The Socialism of Today* (1916), Pt. I, Ch. I.

[5] The following contain useful summaries of the issues between orthodox and opportunist groups, as revealed both in treatises by socialist authors and in the programs and tactics of socialist parties: R. C. K. Ensor, *Modern Socialism as Set Forth by Socialists in Their Speeches, Writings, and Programmes* (third ed., rev. and enl., 1910); Michel Ralea, *L'idée de révolution dans les doctrines socialistes* (1923), Pt. III, Ch. II; William E. Walling, *Socialism As It Is* (1912).

that generally repudiate the doctrines of class war and revolution and adopt explicitly the orderly coöperative devices of political democracy as the means for establishing a socialist society.

After the death of Engels in 1895, Karl Kautsky was, until the transformations created by the World War, the foremost theorist of Marxian socialism. He was the doctrinal leader of the orthodox wing of the German Social Democratic party, and a voluminous writer of books and articles. In 1885 he established the leading German socialist review—*Die Neue Zeit*—and was its editor until 1917. Others who have been in the socialist front ranks as authoritative interpreters of Marx are Franz Mehring, William Liebknecht, Rudolf Hilferding, and Rosa Luxemburg, in Germany; Jules Guesde in France; H. M. Hyndman in England; George Plekhanov in Russia; and Daniel De Leon in the United States.[6]

Some of these orthodox socialists admitted doubts as to the validity of Marx's theory of value and suggested that the theory was not an essential part of socialist doctrine. But they generally held wholeheartedly to the materialistic interpretation of history and defended, against Eduard Bernstein's criticism, Marx's prophecies as to the future development of capitalism. Kautsky, it is true, accepted the evidences adduced by Bernstein to show that, since Marx first made his prophecy, the workers in the leading industrial countries were becoming better off economically rather than more miserable. Nevertheless, he contended that Marx's prophecy was substantially vindicated by the grievous situation of workers in industrially backward regions, as in Russia and Italy, and in newly exploited territories, such as the Balkans; by the extended employment of women and children in civilized countries; and by the increasing monotony of the workers' labors everywhere, due to the perfecting of the machine system.[7] In other words, Kautsky con-

[6] Important orthodox socialists in the field of practical politics were, besides those mentioned above, Victor Adler in Austria, August Bebel in Germany, and J. K. Hardie in England. For titles of the works of leading theorists of orthodox socialism, cf. the bibliographical list, pp. 83–84, *infra*. Their ideas were also set forth in numerous articles in socialist periodicals—notably *Die Neue Zeit* (weekly, Stuttgart), *Vorwaerts* (daily, Berlin), *Humanité* (daily, Paris), *The Socialist Review* (monthly, London), and the *International Socialist Review* (published in Chicago from 1900 to 1918). Since the World War, *Humanité* has become an organ of communism in its contemporary Russian form.

[7] Karl Kautsky, *Bernstein und das sozialdemokratische Programm* (1899), pp. 114–128.

tended, if the workers' situation is considered broadly and relatively, it appears to be becoming steadily worse.

Accordingly, the orthodox socialists maintained that the most essential features of modern society are still the points which divide classes rather than those which unite them; and the classes cannot effectively coöperate. Any significant change in the relative positions of the classes must come, said De Leon, not through reform—a mere "change of externals"—but only through a "change from within"—a revolution, "peaceful or bloody, the peacefulness or bloodiness of it cuts no figure whatever in the essence of the question." [8] The interests of capitalists and wage-earners, said Kautsky, are irreconcilable, and the tendency is towards an intensification of class divisions. Kautsky maintained also that the transfer of the conflict from the economic to the political field had ended all hope that existing society could be gradually transformed from a capitalist into either a democratic or a proletarian society.[9] Thus a socialist party must always be a revolutionary organization of the working class. "Those who repudiate political revolution as the principal means of social transformation or wish to confine this to such measures as have been granted by the ruling class" are not socialists, but "social reformers." "We Socialists," said De Leon, "are not Reformers; we are Revolutionists." "Goodnaturedness and sentimentality," said Liebknecht, "have no place in politics." "On the ground of the class struggle we are invincible; if we leave it we are lost, because we are no longer socialists." We must obtain power by conquering our enemies, not by compromising with them.[10]

The orthodox Marxians did not mean that socialists should be incessantly engaged in concocting uprisings; nor did they ordinarily contend that a revolution is a project which can be instituted in the present or in the near future with any hope of success. Engels, the orthodox, united with Bernstein, the revisionist, in combating the violent spirit developing among the rank and file of German socialists in the eighties; both advised socialists to confine themselves at that time to orderly, legal, parliamentary activity.[11] Other orthodox socialists preached ab-

[8] *Reform or Revolution* (1896), pp. 2, 11.
[9] *The Road to Power*, a translation (1909) of *Weg zum Macht* (1909), p. 101.
[10] Kautsky, *The Social Revolution*, a translation (1909) of *Die soziale Revolution* (1902), p. 9. De Leon, *Reform or Revolution*, p. 3. William Liebknecht, *No Compromise, No Political Trading*, pp. 48, 55.
[11] Cf. Friedrich Engels' introduction to the 1894 edition of Karl Marx's *Klassenkämpfe in Frankreich*.

stention from premature revolutionary attempts as well as from irrelevant reformist compromises. The socialist revolution can be accomplished only when the workers are strong enough, in numbers and
organization, for a successful assault upon capitalism. Accordingly,
socialists must not be diverted from the main tasks of the present—
organization, education, propaganda—in preparing for the final political
conquest, which may or may not take the form of a violent insurrection.

The orthodox socialists recognized fully that the complex subdivision
of labor demanded by modern industry requires an organizing and directing authority, in order to insure a harmonious working together of
the variously interdependent individuals and groups.[12] They pointed
out the need for order and discipline in all social action; and the
state had an indispensable and enduring place in their system. They
would, therefore, have the proletariat strive in every way to obtain
universal suffrage and the other political expedients indispensable to an
effective exercise of the vote. The German Social Democratic party was
organized in order to take advantage of the manhood suffrage established by the legislation of 1867. At first, it is true, Liebknecht and
other party leaders advised a very cautious and limited employment of
political means—urging socialists in the Reichstag to use their positions
as forums for protest, agitation, and propaganda, rather than to try to
secure legislation favorable to the workers. The party soon abandoned
this negative attitude, however, and the resolutions of its annual congresses permitted, and later commanded, political activity of a positive,
practical character.

The disputes between orthodox and revisionist socialists centered
mainly around questions of parliamentary strategy. Should socialists in
parliament support labor legislation of immediate benefit to workers,
when the legislation is offered by non-socialists seeking socialist co-
operation? Should they endorse proposed extensions of public ownership under a government controlled by defenders of the capitalist system? Should they accept office in a non-socialist ministry or lend their
votes of confidence to keep in office a liberally inclined ministry, when
such support appeared to be necessary in order to save that ministry
from being supplanted by a reactionary group? In case of the outbreak
of a war in which the national existence of a capitalist-controlled state
is endangered, should a socialist acknowledge the superior obligations

[12] De Leon, *Reform or Revolution*, pp. 17–18.

of proletarian solidarity and refuse to take part in the war, or should he, recognizing his political citizenship, acknowledge an obligation to defend his state and accept membership in its armies?

The conflicts of opinion occasioned by these practical questions can be briefly indicated.

The orthodox socialist was inclined to disparage immediate reforms: to regard them as, in many cases, dangerous to the cause of socialism and as, in any case, of only secondary importance. He pointed to the policy laid down in the *Communist Manifesto*—that steps for the betterment of the working class and the undermining of capitalism were to be taken only after the proletariat had achieved their conquest of political power. The attitude towards any given capitalist-conceded reform must be determined by the bearing of the concession upon the larger, ultimate program of socialism. Accordingly, a socialist should support labor legislation only where the measures tended not merely to bring increased physical comforts to wage-earners but also to improve their position relatively to that of the capitalists, and only where the measures were based upon socialist principles.[13] Thus orthodox French socialists condemned the reformist Jaurès for supporting the government's project for old-age pensions, because the pension fund was to be made up in part from compulsory contributions from the workers.

The orthodox socialists argued generally that reforms obtained in a non-socialist society are in no case to be regarded as "instalments" of socialism. Increasing governmental control over industry in a non-socialistic society is generally accompanied, they contended, by an increasing capitalists' control over government. Changes made under such conditions rarely result in securing for the worker any increasing proportion of the benefits of the changes. Moreover, reforms of the existing system tend to soften the antagonism between classes and to weaken the workers' belief in the desirability and feasibility of revolution.

This attitude of non-coöperation was frequently made explicit in reference to the question of "state socialism." The orthodox position was that government ownership in itself is not socialism and may not be even a step in that direction. Socialism involves a fundamental alteration of the relation of workers to the instruments and materials with which they work. A change from private to state ownership will not bring about that transformation unless the state itself is fundamentally transformed. "The economic activity of the modern state," said

[13] Kautsky, *The Social Revolution*, p. 66 ff.

Kautsky, "is the natural starting point of the development that leads to Coöperative Commonwealth. It does not, however, follow that every nationalization of an economic function or of an industry is a step toward the Coöperative Commonwealth, and that the latter could be the result of a general nationalization of all industries without any change in the character of the state." [14] The orthodox socialists were inclined to regard with peculiar skepticism the extension of public ownership of local utilities. They contended that the rapid growth of "municipal socialism" in the latter decades of the nineteenth century—a development which many revisionists pointed to as unmistakable evidence of the advance of socialism—had little relation to the ultimate overthrow of the capitalist order. Even where public ownership is set up by city governments controlled by socialists, no essential part of a revolutionary program is accomplished as long as the power of taxation remains in the hands of central authorities controlled by non-socialists.

The orthodox socialists often argued that in many instances nationalization weakens rather than strengthens the position of the workers. "Who is less free than the state employee?" exclaimed Jules Guesde in 1883.[15] He is only another wage-worker, subject to the economic and industrial power of a powerful bourgeois organization. The modern state, said Engels, "is essentially a capitalist machine, the state of the capitalists, the ideal personification of the total national capital. The more it proceeds to taking over of productive forces, the more it actually becomes the national capitalist, the more citizens does it exploit. The workers remain wage-workers—proletarians. The capitalist relation is not done away with." [16]

On the question of a general political collaboration with sympathetic non-socialists, the orthodox position was as follows: However appropriate or necessary it may be for socialists to vote for particular measures or reform, they must never accept office in a non-socialist ministry or approve the annual budget, except in extraordinary emergencies—when, for example, the supplanting of a progressive by a reactionary ministry might threaten the very existence of a socialist party. The majority of the socialists in the German Reichstag, on all occasions prior to the World War, refused their support to the government in votes on questions of confidence and on the budget. The French social-

---

[14] *The Class Struggle,* translation (1910) of *Das Erfurter Programm* (eighth ed., 1907), p. 109.
[15] Quoted by Émile Vandervelde, *Le socialisme contra l'état* (1918), p. liii.
[16] Friedrich Engels, *Socialism, Utopian and Scientific* (1892), pp. 71–72.

ists refused to combine with the Radical parties in opposition to the militarist and monarchical Boulanger movement in 1889. The orthodox leaders often argued that socialists should not help to correct blunders and injustices of the Church, army, and state, under the existing order; they should rather welcome such manifestations of incompetence, regarding them as indicative of the approaching collapse of the existing order. When Jaurès, in 1899, proposed that French socialists approve the entrance of Alexandre Millerand, a socialist, into the progressive ministry of Waldeck-Rousseau, Guesde and his followers declared such action would be an utter abandonment of the class war. Guesde carried the matter to the Second International, and the question was vigorously and eloquently debated at the congresses of 1900 and 1904, Jaurès and Émile Vandervelde (of Belgium) leading the defense of the revisionist position and Guesde and Bebel arguing for the orthodox side. The former congress adopted a resolution, framed by Kautsky, characterizing the acceptance of a cabinet position by a socialist as a "dangerous experiment," to be made use of "only if it is agreed upon by the party as a whole, and on the understanding that the socialist minister is, and remains, representative of this party"; and the latter congress adopted a similar resolution, declaring that socialists "can accept participation in government in a capitalist country only under very exceptional and critical circumstances." [17] This position was not abandoned by any subsequent congress of the Second International; it was confirmed by congresses of the French and German parties. When, in 1906, Aristide Briand, who had been a socialist leader in parliament for over a decade, accepted the portfolio of public instruction and worship in the Sarrien ministry, he was promptly expelled from the recently formed "union" of French socialist groups.

On the question as to whether the obligations of proletarian solidarity should obliterate all nationalist obligations, the socialist position was never clear; and the divisions of opinion cut across the line between the orthodox and the revisionist. The variations and vacillations in socialist policy following the outbreak of the World War gave rise to a number of studies by socialist writers who canvassed the evidences as to the traditional theory and practice of the followers of Marx in their attitude to patriotism and war.[18] These accounts point, on the one

[17] *Comte rendu sténographique . . . du cinquième Congrès socialiste international . . . 1900* (Paris, 1901), pp. 99–170. The Kautsky resolution is on pp. 101–102.

[18] W. E. Walling, *The Socialists and The War* (1915), Pt. I, Louis B. Boudin,

hand, to socialist assertions that appear to deny unqualifiedly any patriotic obligation. Thus the *Communist Manifesto* asserted that "the proletariat has no Fatherland"; and Gustave Hervé declared, over a half-century later: "The Fatherland is the Fatherland of the ruling classes; it does not concern the proletariat." The writers show, on the other hand, that the prevailing socialist attitude was never essentially antinationalist. Orthodox socialists were not generally opposed to patriotism in the sense of devotion to one's native land. Said Bebel, in the international congress of 1907: "Hervé's thought that it is all the same for the proletariat whether France belongs to Germany, or Germany belongs to France, is absurd." And Jaurès, a revisionist but one of the most extreme of the antimilitarists, said on the same occasion: "Hervéism . . . is dying out. Hervé wishes to destroy the Fatherland. We wish to socialize the Fatherland for the benefit of the proletariat, by the transformation of the means of production into the property of all. For the nation is a treasure house of human genius and progress. And it would be a bad service to the proletariat to destroy this treasure of human culture." [19] Marx himself had written a letter to the German Social Democrats approving their participation in the Franco-Prussian war, "in so far as and so long as it limits itself to the defence of Germany." A later party manifesto explained their position as follows: "So long as the measures of Napoleon threatened Germany it was our duty as Germans to defend the independence of the Fatherland. Such a defensive war does not exclude offensive measures. It includes, as does every war, the necessity of forcing the enemy to accept peace." [20] After the flight of Louis Napoleon and the setting up of a provisional republican government in France, the German Socialists demanded peace and condemned the transformation of a defensive war against French militarism and imperialism into a predatory war for German territorial aggrandizement. When the question of war credits was before the Reichstag in 1870, Bebel had abstained from voting. Thirty-six years later, however, in a congress of the Second International, he opposed the French proposal for an international general strike and insurrection in case of a declaration of war and spoke in justification of

Socialism and War (1915), Chs. V–VI. Cf. also B. J. Hovde, "Socialistic Theories of Imperialism Prior to the Great War," *Journal of Political Economy*, XXXVI (1928), 569–591.

[19] *Internationalen Sozialisten-Kongress zu Stuttgart . . . 1907*, p. 89. See Walling, *Socialists and the War*, Ch. III.

[20] Walling, *Socialists and the War*, p. 9.

defensive wars, which, he contended, could without difficulty be differentiated from aggressive wars. In the 1914 congress of the French socialists, three weeks before the outbreak of the World War, the orthodox Compère-Morel asserted: "We must declare that we will use all means to prevent a war of aggression and also that we will use all means for the defence of our country." [21]

Socialists, it is true, have looked upon hostility between nations as one of the greatest impediments to the development of socialism. They have regarded the international organization of the proletariat as one of the most effective means of promoting socialism within the several countries. Some sort of political and economic federation among the leading states they have postulated as a prerequisite to the full realization of the socialist ideal. One of the counts in their indictment of capitalism is that it leads to economic rivalry between nations—particularly, to competitive efforts for the acquisition of colonies and spheres of influence.[22] Correspondingly, socialists have held that the advance of socialism within the several countries promotes the elimination of international hostility. The *Communist Manifesto* argued that the ending of the exploitation of some individuals by others within the several nations would put an end to the exploitation of one nation by another. Marx, in his inaugural address before the First International in 1864, laid it down as the duty of all workers to "vindicate the simple laws of morality and justice that ought to govern the inter-relations of private individuals as well as the intercourse of nations."

At national conventions of socialist parties and at the congresses of the Second International, some of the most prolonged debates were evoked by resolutions designed to declare the socialist position on war and formulate the proper means of action in support of that position.[23] In times of peace, the socialist parties uniformly opposed the military measures of their governments. They directed their members in parliament to vote against grants of money for the army and navy and urged socialists to avoid military service as far as possible. The International congress of 1907 declared unanimously that "the congress regards it as the duty of all working-men, and particularly of their representatives in the parliaments . . . to oppose all naval and military armaments

---

[21] Walling, *Socialists and the War,* p. 59.

[22] The same idea was epitomized by President Wilson in an address on September 5, 1919, when he said that "the seed of war in the modern world is industrial and commercial rivalry."

[23] Cf. L. R. Boudin, *Socialism and War,* p. 186 ff.

and to refuse funds for their upkeep." [24] This peace-time stand of socialists, in voting against parliamentary grants for military and naval armaments, is to be explained partly by their opposition to the capitalist
groups controlling the governments, and partly by their belief that
large military armaments promote international hostility and that the
wars for which governments prepare are aggressive wars for capitalist rather than patriotic aims. In the 1910 congress, the socialists, adopting again the resolution of 1907, added declarations favoring compulsory
arbitration of international disputes, the initiation of movements towards "ultimately complete disarmament," the abolition of secret
diplomacy, and an international guarantee of the independence of all
nations.

Several of the leaders from both orthodox and revisionist camps made
attempts from time to time to commit the socialists to a more insurrectionary and spectacular means of preventing imperialist wars—which
they assumed any future wars would be. Their plan was to persuade the
socialist parties to declare that, in the event of the outbreak of war,
they would thwart the military action by joining in an international
general strike. The First International had, in 1868, approved this plan;
and Ferdinand Nieuwenhuis, a revolutionary socialist from Holland,
had unsuccessfully proposed it in the 1891 congress of the Second International. Later advocates included revolutionary socialists, such as
Hervé and Edouard Vaillant; and reformists, such as Jaurès, Ramsay
MacDonald, and J. Keir Hardie. The most vigorous opposition came
from the orthodox leaders, Liebknecht, Bebel, and Guesde. The plan
was rejected by immense majorities in 1891 and 1893; but in 1907,
the last occasion upon which it was voted upon by the International,
it was defeated by only a slight majority. The proposal was introduced
again in 1910; but, after prolonged discussion, the congress adopted a
motion presented by Vandervelde, directing the International Socialist
Bureau to circularize the national sections and make a report on the
matter at a congress planned to be held in 1914. Meanwhile the plan had
been approved by the Independent Labour party and the Labour party
in Great Britain and by the French Socialist Party. The French party,
in its 1914 congress, passed the following resolution, which was advocated by Jaurès, Vaillant, and Marcel Sembat, and opposed by the
orthodox Guesde and Compère-Morel: "The French Party considers
the spontaneous general strike of the workers of all countries, combined

[24] *Internationalen Sozialisten-Kongress zu Stuttgart . . . 1907*, p. 86.

with anti-war propaganda among the masses, as the most workable of all means in the hands of the workers to prevent war and to force international arbitration of the dispute." [25]

Despite these evidences of an anti-imperialist and antimilitarist attitude, there is nowhere to be found any authoritative and explicitly uncompromising socialist declaration against war. The Second International's latest declaration, in a resolution adopted at Stuttgart in 1907, and reaffirmed at Copenhagen in 1910, became famous as a result of the subsequent conduct of socialists during the World War. The resolution repeated the familiar socialist explanation of war as the product of unreasonable national prejudices and of capitalist competition for markets; it characterized war as the chief obstacle to the highest aim of socialism—namely, "the creation of an economic order on a socialist basis, which shall express the solidarity of all nations." It asserted the inability of the congress to prescribe to the working classes any one set mode of action: efforts to prevent the occurrence or continuation of war must necessarily be different in different lands and times. The resolution then concluded as follows:

If war threatens to break out it is the duty of the working class in the countries concerned, and of their parliamentary representatives, with the help of the International Socialist Bureau as a means of coördinating their action, to use every effort to prevent war by all the means which seem to them most appropriate, having regard to the sharpness of the class war and to the general political situation.

Should war none the less break out, their duty is to intervene to bring it promptly to an end, and with all their energies to use the political and economic crises created by the war to rouse the masses of the people from their slumbers, and to hasten the fall of capitalist domination.[26]

This resolution, drafted by Rosa Luxemburg, Lenin, and Martov, was "consciously designed," says a socialist writer, "to cover up some of the socialist differences connected with war," and defined only "that relatively restricted area of common ground" on which most socialists could stand.[27] We shall see later whether, when war broke out in 1914, the common ground was restricted enough.[28]

[25] Walling, *Socialists and the War*, p. 55.
[26] *Internationalen Sozialisten-Kongress zu Stuttgart*, p. 102.
[27] William E. Walling, *Socialists and the War*, p. 25.
[28] *Infra*, p. 122 ff.

The orthodox socialists were not able to hold consistently to a policy of non-coöperation with the several national governments even in matters of domestic, peace-time policy. Thus the French socialists followed Jaurès in support of the liberal Combes ministry in the latter's program for separating church and state and secularizing the schools. Even under Guesde's leadership, the party programs contained demands for labor legislation, to be enacted by existing parliaments. The program adopted by the German Social Democratic party at Erfurt in 1891, and thenceforth accepted as the authoritative statement of its creed, formulated demands for immediate realization. These were the familiar demands of liberal groups everywhere: the eight-hour day, restrictions on the labor of women and children, and social insurance in its various forms. In the following years, this party—forgetting its theory that reliance upon such measures was unnecessary or futile or destructive of socialist faith, and influenced by the practical necessity of winning and maintaining the allegiance of working-men generally—gave steadily increasing attention to "social legislation"; and its representatives in the *Reichstag* frequently introduced, or cordially supported, bills designed to secure political, financial, and economic reforms within the existing state.

Thus, despite the disparagement of revisionism as a policy for socialists, the orthodox leaders defended socialist votes supporting labor legislations and public ownership proposed by liberal ministries. Measures of this sort, they conceded, do unsettle foundation stones of the capitalist structure and weaken the reactionary groups who defend that structure; in such cases the socialist coöperation, they said, is in accord with revolutionary doctrine. Kautsky approved support of much of the reform legislation enacted by conservative German governments. What differentiates a socialist party from other parties, he said, "is the totality of its practical demands and the goals towards which these point. The eight-hour day, for example, is in itself no revolutionary demand; it is such within the frame-work of a socialist program, where it is a means for lifting up the working class and for contributing to its political and social maturity and to its capacity to take the work of liberation and reconstruction into its own hands. The same eight-hour day may be a conservative demand within the frame-work of the program of a social-reformist party, which is subject to the illusion that it can, by concessions, reconcile the working-class to the existing social order. . . . What holds political parties together, when they have great historical tasks to accomplish . . . is their ultimate aims, not their momentary demands." [29]

The resolutions of the international congresses and the programs of the parties reveal an agreement both as to the ultimate goal of socialist action—namely, the transfer to society of the ownership of the instruments of production, distribution, and exchange—and also as to the general means for attaining that goal—namely, conquest of political power by the organized working-class. The several factions were also in general agreement as to the specific political and economic changes to be obtained in the immediate present: universal suffrage, protective labor legislation, encouragement and support of the economic conflict carried on by trade-unions, legislative guarantee of the right of workers to organize and strike, and restriction of the imperialist and militarist policies of national governments. Thus, in the early twentieth century, a common opposition to basic economic principles of the existing governments, held together, in the Second International, the revolutionary Russian Bolsheviks, the nominally revolutionary but practically compromising German Social Democrats and orthodox French socialists, the frankly revisionist British and Belgian Laborites, and the pacific and intellectual Fabians. The International Socialist Bureau included moderate reformists, such as Ramsay MacDonald, Jaurès, and Branting of Sweden; leading exponents of socialist orthodoxy, such as Kautsky and De Leon; and the violently militant Raskowski of Russia and Rosa Luxemburg of Germany.

The orthodox theorists continued to insist upon the sharp differentiation of true socialists from democrats and liberals. The march of socialism, they maintained, cannot in all its stages be a gradual progression, under democratic auspices, from a capitalist to a proletarian state. There must be somewhere in the transformation an upheaval, a revolutionary act of some sort. Democracy is not sufficient, and it cannot "make possible a peaceable, revolutionless development" or avert "the overthrow of present society." [30] However, despite these orthodox professions, the prevailing trend in the development of the practical socialist policy before the World War, was in a reformist, democratic direction. The socialist politicians were becoming more tolerant of the existing state and more conscious of national, as distinguished from

[29] *Parlamentarismus und Demokratie* (fourth ed., 1922), p. 133.
[30] Kautsky, *Social Revolution,* p. 65, and *The Road to Power,* p. 101.

class, interests and divisions. The socialists maintained a sufficient aloofness from other parties to save themselves from the designation of merely liberal democrats; but they had become too much preoccupied with present-day reforms, obtained through traditional methods and from existing governments, to be regarded as revolutionary socialists. Indeed the general doctrines underlying the practical policies of the socialist parties are to be found chiefly in the writings, not of Marx, but of other socialists who claimed to have a broader social philosophy, and frankly acknowledged their constant predilection for democratic, pacific, and piecemeal methods of action.

SELECT BIBLIOGAPHY

DEVELOPMENT OF SOCIALIST ORGANIZATION AND POLICY

Bebel, August, *Die Sozialdemokratie im deutschen Reichstag, 1871–1893* (Berlin, 1907–1909).

Bericht über den vierten internationalen Sozialisten-Congress in London . . . 1896, in *Volkswirtschaftliche Zeitfragen,* XIX (Berlin, 1897).

Boudin, Louis B., *Socialism and War* (New York, 1916), Chs. V–VI.

Comte rendu sténographique non officiel . . . du cinquième Congrès socialiste international . . . 1900 (Paris, 1901).

Ensor, R. C. K., *Modern Socialism as Set Forth by Socialists in Their Speeches, Writings and Programmes* (third ed., rev. & enl. New York, 1910).

Guillaume, James, *L'Internationale: documents et souvenirs 1864–1878* (Paris, 1905–1910).

Hillquit, Morris, *History of Socialism in the United States* (New York and London, 1903).

Hovde, B. J., "Socialistic Theories of Imperialism Prior to the Great War," *Journal of Political Economy,* XXXVI (1928), 569–591.

Internationalen Sozialisten-Kongress zu Stuttgart . . . 1907 (Berlin, 1907).

Internationalen Sozialisten-Kongress zu Kopenhagen . . . 1910 (Berlin, 1910).

Jaeckh, Gustav, *Die Internationale: eine Denkschrift zur vierzigjährigen Gründung der Internationale Arbeiter-assoziation* (Leipsic, 1904).

Kirkup, Thomas, *A History of Socialism* (fifth ed., London, 1913), Chs. VIII and XIII.

Lipinski, Richard, *Die Sozialdemokratie von ihren Anfängen bis zur Gegenwart,* 2 vols. (1927–1928).

Longuet, Jean, *Le mouvement socialiste internationale* (Paris, 1913).

Lorwin, Lewis L., *Labor and Internationalism* (New York, 1929), Chs. II and III.

Louis, Paul, *Histoire du socialisme en France de la révolution à nos jours* (Paris, 1925).

Mehring, Franz, *Zur Geschichte der deutschen Soziale-demokratie* (fourth ed., Stuttgart, 1909).

Menger, Anton, *The Right to the Whole Produce of Labour,* translated by M. E. Tanner (London and New York, 1899), chs. X–XIV.

Orth, S. P., *Socialism and Democracy in Europe* (New York, 1913).

Postgate, R. W., *The Workers' International* (London and New York (1920).

Ralea, Michel, *L'idée de révolution dans les doctrines socialistes: étude sur l'évolution de la tactique révolutionnaire* (Paris, 1923), Pt. III, Ch. II.

Shadwell, A., *The Socialist Movement, 1824–1924,* 2 vols. (London, 1925).

Skelton, O. D., *Socialism: a Critical Analysis* (Boston and New York, 1911), Ch. IX.

Sombart, Werner, *Socialism and the Social Movement,* translated from sixth German edition by M. Epstein (London and New York, 1909).

————, *Der proletarische Sozialismus,* tenth rev. ed. of *Sozialismus und soziale Bewegung im 19 Jahrhundert,* of which the immediately preceding work is a translation, 2 vols. (Jena, 1924).

Spargo, John, *Karl Marx: His Life and His Work* (New York, 1910), Chs. XI–XII.

Spargo, John, and Arner, G. B. L., *Elements of Socialism* (New York, 1912), pp. 255–315.

Tawney, R. H., *The British Labor Movement* (New Haven, 1925).

Walling, W. E., *Socialism as It Is: a Survey of the World-Wide Revolutionary Movement* (New York, 1912).

————, *The Socialists and the War* (New York, 1915), Pt. I.

Webb, Sidney, *Socialism in England* (second ed., London and New York, 1893).

Weill, Georges, *Histoire du mouvement social en France 1852–1924* (third ed., rev. & enl. Paris, 1924).

Zévaès, Alexandre, *Histoire des partis socialistes en France,* 11 vols. in 3 parts, (Paris, 1911–1912).

ORTHODOX DISCIPLES OF MARX

Boudin, Louis B., *Theoretical System of Karl Marx* (Chicago, 1907).

De Leon, Daniel, *Reform or Revolution,* an address delivered at Boston in 1896 (New York, 1920).

Engels, Friedrich, *Socialism, Utopian and Scientific,* translated by Edward Aveling (New York, 1892).

Guesde, Jules, *Le Socialisme au jour le jour* (Paris, 1899).

————, *Questions d'hier et d'aujourd'hui* (Paris, 1911).

————, *Essai de catéchisme socialiste* (Brussels, 1878).

Hilferding, Rudolf, *Die Finanzkapital* (Vienna, 1910; reprint 1927).

Hyndman, H. M., *England for All* (London, 1881).

Kautsky, Karl, *Das Erfurter Programm* (Stuttgart, 1892., eighth ed., 1907).

——————, *The Class Struggle*, translation of *Das Erfurter Programm* by William E. Bohn (Chicago, 1910).

——————, *Parlamentarismus und Demokratie* (Stuttgart, 1922), fourth ed., of *Der Parlamentarismus, die Volksgesetzgebung und die Sozialdemokratie* (1893).

——————, *Bernstein und das sozialdemokratische Programm* (Stuttgart, 1899).

——————, *Die soziale Revolution* (Berlin, 1902).

——————, *The Social Revolution*, translated by A. M. and May W. Simons (Chicago, 1903).

——————, *Der Weg zum Macht* (Berlin, 1909).

——————, *The Road to Power*, translated by A. M. Simons (Chicago, 1909).

Liebknecht, Wilhelm, *Was die Sozialdemokraten sind und was sie Wollen* (Chemnitz, 1894).

——————, *Socialism: What It Is and What It Seeks to Accomplish*, translated by May W. Simons (Chicago, 1897).

——————, *No Compromise, No Political Trading*, a pamphlet written in 1899, translated by A. M. Simons and Marcus Hitch (Chicago, 1918).

Luxemburg, Rosa, *Sozial Reform oder Revolution* (Leipsic, 1899).

Plekhanov, G., *Anarchismus und Sozialismus* (Berlin, 1894).

——————, *Anarchism and Socialism*, translated by Eleanor Marx Aveling (Chicago, 1908).

Rubinow, I. M., *Was Marx Wrong?* (New York, 1914).

CHAPTER IV

DEMOCRATIC AND EVOLUTIONARY SOCIALISTS

ORTHODOX Marxians, we have seen, have constantly insisted upon the class character of their socialism and upon their revolutionary aims. They have accepted the state as an indispensable agency of socialist change and have admitted the practical necessity of utilizing the instrumentalities of modern democracy—voting, party campaigns, parliamentary debate. But they have also maintained that existing society is fundamentally hostile to the interests of wage-workers and that the transfer of the class conflict from the economic to the political field offers no hope that a capitalist society can, through the normal activities of a democratic state, be gradually transformed into a proletarian society. "Democracy alone cannot destroy class antagonisms or make unnecessary the final overthrow of present society." [1] Socialism in this sense is a revolutionary doctrine for wage-earners, who are to use the agencies of the democratic state only as means of preparing for the revolution.

With other socialists, democracy is no more a means to socialism than socialism a means to democracy; the two are regarded as co-ordinate factors in a comprehensive movement to create a social condition in which all individuals find equal opportunity to utilize and enjoy their native faculties—so far as any community action can bring about that equality. Socialism, in this general sense, stands for an extensive control over the basic means of wealth and culture—a control to be exercised not by some class within the community but by the community itself and to be built up gradually and in orderly forms. This democratic and evolutionary sort of socialism has had great vogue among contemporaries and successors of Marx, some of whom drew their first inspiration from Marx, or were greatly influenced by him, while others derived their ideas principally from other sources.

ACADEMIC STATE SOCIALISTS

Most professional economists in the early and middle nineteenth century adhered to the dogmas of *laisser-faire*. Their maxims were that

[1] Karl Kautsky, *Road to Power*, p. 101.

capital naturally flows into its most remunerative investment, that un-regulated competition reduces prices to the level of cost of production, that wages cannot safely rise above the minimum of cost of subsistence, and, more generally, that every individual in pursuing his own private interest, without restraint or aid from his government, contributes best to both his own and the public welfare. There were, however, always respectable dissenters from this position. From the time of Adam Smith on, the orthodox principles have been assailed with increasing emphasis.[2]

A systematic and thoroughgoing criticism of the orthodox position is found in the writings, appearing chiefly in the eighth decade of the century, of a group of German professors of political economy—notably Professors Adolf Wagner (1835–1917), Gustav Schmoller (1838–1917), Lujo Brentano (1844–1931), Adolf Held (1844–1880), Lorenz von Stein (1852–1890), and Albert Schaeffle (1831–1903).[3] Some of these men, joined by several laymen and public officials, formed in the early seventies, a "Union for Social Politics" (*Verein für Sozialpolitik*) for the discussion and elaboration of their ideas of a realistic and social-ized science of economics. They were derisively called "Katheder Sozial-ister"—that is, "professorial" or "academic" socialists or "socialists of the chair." They accepted the designation; and the terms passed into general use as names for those who advocate moderate extensions of governmental ownership and control to be set up by existing govern-ments, enlightened and inspired by learned and high-minded students of economic affairs.

[2] Challenges appear, in somewhat limited and tentative form, in the early nine-teenth century writings of the Swiss historian and economist, J. C. L. Sismondi (1773–1842), and the German economist, Friedrich List (1789–1846). In the mid-century they appear more extensively, combined with positive suggestions for col-lectivist policies, in the works of Karl Rodbertus (1805–1875) in Germany and of Charles B. Dupont-White (1807–1878) in France. Cf. Charles Gide and Charles Rist, *History of Economic Doctrines*, Bk. III, Chs. I and IV; Bk. IV, Ch. II, Sec. II; Lewis H. Haney, *History of Economic Thought* (rev. ed., 1926) Chs. XIX, XX, and pp. 436–441.

[3] Best among the original statements of the ideas of the academic socialists are the following: Gustav Schmoller, *Ueber einige Grundfragen des Rechts und der Volkswirtschaft* (1875); "Die Gerechtigkeit in der Volkswirtschaft," *Schmoller's Jahrbuch für Gesetzgebung, Verwaltung und Volkswirtschaft*, V (1881), 19–54, and a translation of the latter, by Ludwig von Haller and Carl L. Schultz—"The Idea of Justice in Political Economy," *Annals of the American Academy of Political and Social Science*, IV (1894), 697–737; Adolf Wagner, *Rede über die soziale Frage* (1872), and *Grundlegung der politischen Oekonomie* (1876; third ed. 3 vols. 1892–1893), Bk. VII. Cf. the following: R. T. Ely, *French and German So-cialism*, Ch. XV; Charles Gide and Charles Rist, *op. cit.*, Bk. IV, Ch. II, Sec. III; Lewis H. Haney, *op. cit.*, pp. 577–579; Harry W. Laidler, *History of Socialist Thought*, pp. 669–675.

These German economists criticized the abstract, *a priori* approach of orthodox political economy. They challenged the assumption that a free play of natural law and individual self-interest brings about a distribution of social advantages apportioned according to the merits and efforts of the several individuals. A science of economics should draw its conclusions chiefly from data supplied by history and observation. Recent experience, they maintained, shows that the most important social question is the problem not of production but of distribution and that extensive intervention by government is necessary for a solution of the problem. Their doctrine, though realistic in method, was explicitly ethical in its objectives. Political economy, as they understood it, had practical, moral aims: to show how principles of justice could actually control the distribution of wealth and how individual selfishness could be subordinated to the interests of the community. They believed that their economic ethics had a realistic basis. The modern state, they maintained, had evolved as the natural expression of a cultural, moral, spiritual solidarity—manifested in a sameness of language, manners, and institutions and transcending the economic differences among individuals and classes within a national community. It was essentially fallacious, therefore, to follow either the classical economist, who contrasted the artificial and coercive action of the state to the free and spontaneous action of individuals, or the Marxian, who pictured the democratic state as representative only of property owners.

A democratic state, the academic socialists believed, represents the whole nation in its best aspects, and it is more competent than any other social institution to deal sympathetically and effectively with the complex interests of modern industrial society. Its natural function is to limit and supplement individual activity by promoting the material interests of a nation and by vindicating national ideals of benevolence and fair play; it aids the weak, suppresses abuses by the strong, and provides those cultural facilities which the efforts of individuals and smaller associations are unable to provide. Existing states in civilized countries already assume these tasks. They take care of the dependent, limit the labor of women and children, enforce temperance, protect the public health, supply education and postal communication, and conserve natural resources. Moreover, the actual tendencies in private economic life—the development of large-scale industry and the consequent centralization of industrial management—indicate the natural extension of public economic activity in the future: national governments will provide directly those services that are of a peculiarly essential and permanent character and that require a unified administration—roads, railway transportation, banking, and social insurance; municipalities will supply light, water, heat and other local utilities; other governmental agencies will intervene to adjust differences between employers and employes; taxation will be increasingly used as a means of bringing about a better distribution of wealth. The academic socialists did not proscribe rents, profits, or interest, nor advocate the abolition of the wage system. They believed that the state should, on proper occasions, limit profits in order to secure fairer relations between income and effort, and that it should establish minimum rates of wages in order to secure more humane conditions of existence for wage-earners. They did not regard it as possible to establish hard and fast lines for defining the spheres of activity that belong to the individual and the state, respectively. They were content to let experience be the guide in showing where increased governmental intervention inhibits, and where it sustains, individual initiative and the common well-being.

THE LAND TAXERS

The socialism we call democratic involves the idea of a socialist policy based upon the doctrine that the community has certain predominant rights over economic goods because it creates and safeguards their values. An important factor in the development of this doctrine has been the conception of the social foundation of land values. The latter conception was set forth by several French writers of the eighteenth century and has been persistently agitated for a century and a half in Great Britain, where the narrow concentration of the ownership of land in both rural and urban communities has given the idea a peculiarly practical significance. The British exponents of the conception, in the late eighteenth and early nineteenth centuries, set forth both the state-of-nature doctrine that, prior to political society, all men had equal access to the land, and the ethical doctrine that the utilities of land are not made by human efforts; in either case, it was said, there is no justification for the proprietary titles claimed by the landed aristocrats of to-day. They made also the practical argument that land, like light, air, and water, is an essential requirement of human existence, and its possession by idle owners is the chief cause of the miseries suffered by the toiling masses. Some of these writers proposed that the government, as representative of the community, take over the ownership of the land and rent it out at moderate rates, the income from the rents to be the only or chief source of public revenue. Others made more moderate suggestions, retaining private ownership of land and proposing a governmental limitation of rents and special taxes on land. Thomas Paine—the Anglo-American strangely celebrated in American opinion as an uncompromising opponent of any sort of governmental control of private economic affairs—held that "land is the common property of the human race"; and he proposed a ten per cent inheritance tax on landed estates, the revenue to be expended for popular education, aid to the defective, and old-age pensions.[4]

Herbert Spencer, perhaps the most renowned of nineteenth century individualists, pronounced in his first book—*Social Statics*, published in 1850—as unqualified a condemnation of private land-ownership as can be found anywhere. In that work, after setting forth his "first principle" for "the law of right social relationships"—his doctrine of "equal freedom"—he devoted a chapter to a discussion of the application of that principle to "The Right to the Use of the Earth." [5] The chapter begins as follows:

Given a race of beings having like claims to pursue the objects of their desires—given a world adapted to the gratification of those desires—a world into which such beings are similarly born, and it unadvoidably follows that they have equal rights to the use of this world. For if each of them 'has freedom to do all that he wills provided that he infringes not the equal freedom of any other,' then each of them is free to use the earth for the satisfaction of his wants, provided he allows all others the same liberty. And conversely, it is manifest that no one, or part of them, may use the earth in such a way as to prevent the rest from similarly using it; seeing that to do this is to assume greater freedom than the rest, and consequently to break the law.

Equity, therefore, does not permit property in land. For if *one* portion of the earth's surface may justly become the possession of an individual, and

---

[4] Exponents of the ideas indicated above include the Abbé Gabriel de Mably (1709–1785) in France, Jean de Colins (1793–1859) in Belgium, Thomas Paine (1737–1809), and a number of British writers—notably the following: William Ogilvie (1736–1813), a learned and well-to-do classical scholar, professor of "humanity" at Aberdeen University; Thomas Spence (1750–1814), a vigorous lecturer and pamphleteer, who served several terms in prison; and Patrick Dove (1815–1893), philosophical writer and lecturer. Cf. M. Beer, *History of British Socialism*, II, 237–245; Morrison Davidson, *Precursors of Henry George: Ogilvie, Spence, Paine, Dove* (1899). For Paine's ideas see his *Agrarian Justice* (1795–1796).

[5] Herbert Spencer, *Social Statics*, Ch. IX, in the edition of 1850 and other editions before 1892.

may be held by him for his sole use and benefit, as a thing to which he has an exclusive right, then *other* portions of the earth's surface may be so held; and eventually the *whole* of the earth's surface may be so held; and our planet may thus lapse altogether into private hands. Observe now the dilemma to which this leads. Supposing the entire habitable globe to be so enclosed, it follows that if the landowners have a valid right to its surface, all who are not landowners have no right at all to its surface. Hence, such can exist on the earth by sufferance only. They are all trespassers. Save by the permission of the lords of the soil, they can have no room for the soles of their feet. Nay, should the others think fit to deny them a resting-place, these landless men might equitably be expelled from the earth altogether. If, then, the assumption that land can be held as property involves that the whole globe may become the private domain of a part of its inhabitants; and if, by consequence, the rest of its inhabitants can then exercise their faculties—can then exist even— only by consent of the landowners; it is manifest, that an exclusive possession of the soil necessitates an infringement of the law of equal freedom. For, men who cannot 'live and move and have their being' without the leave of others, cannot be equally free with those others.

Spencer then went on to argue that all existing titles derived originally from "violence, fraud, the prerogative of force, the claims of superior cunning"; that "Time" and "immemorial possession" could not change a "wrong" into a "right "; and that consequently "the right of mankind at large to the earth's surface is still valid, all deeds, customs, and laws notwithstanding." He concluded the chapter as follows:

Briefly reviewing the argument, we see that the right of each man to the use of the earth, limited only by the like rights of his fellow-men, is immediately deducible from the law of equal freedom. We see that the maintenance of this right necessarily forbids private property in land. On examination all existing titles to such property turn out to be invalid; those founded on reclamation inclusive. It appears that not even an equal apportionment of the earth amongst its inhabitants could generate a legitimate proprietorship. We find that if pushed to its ultimate consequences, a claim to exclusive possession of the soil involves a landowning despotism. We further find that such a claim is constantly denied by the enactments of our legislature. And we find lastly, that the theory of the co-heirship of all men to the soil, is consistent with the highest civilization; and that, however difficult it may be to embody that theory in fact, Equity sternly commands it to be done.

Whatever is "theoretically just" should as far as possible, Spencer then contended, be made just in application. He proposed therefore, that "society" should, after paying existing landowners for their "inseparable improvements," resume its rightful ownership and then lease the land to individuals, each paying in return "a stated amount of the produce he obtains from that soil." [6]

These statements were later a source of extreme embarrassment to Spencer, in his uncompromising opposition to all socialism and to any governmental "interference" in private economic affairs. In the course of a prolonged and bitter controversy, in the eighties, he sought to explain away his earlier position by arguing that, since the present owners had acquired their titles by valid means and since the whole system of private land-tenure rested on universal and long-standing custom among civilized peoples, any attempt to abrogate or qualify existing titles would produce "disastrous" consequences to society.[7] In his "abridged and revised" edition of the Social Statics, published in 1892, he omitted the chapter on the right to the use of the earth, and thus withdrew himself from the discussion of that difficult question.

It is in the works of John Stuart Mill, in the third quarter of the century, that we find the clearest, and probably the most practically influential, statement of the theory of the unearned increment of land values, and he added a specific proposal for the special taxation of these values. Mill's idea is a development of the Ricardian theory of rent. According to this theory, the rent of any given piece of land is due primarily to the superior natural advantages (of soil and site) that piece holds over the worst lands—the lands that are least worth cultivating. The progress of civilization enhances these differences between the worst lands and all better lands; and the landowner obtains the benefits of the differences in the rents he receives. Thus rent is a sum paid to owners for the use of original powers of the soil. Ricardo made no proposal to meet this illogical situation, except that of free competition and free international trade. Mill's conclusions from the Ricardian theory can be best stated in his own words:

Suppose there is a kind of income which constantly tends to increase, without any exertion or sacrifice on the part of the owners; those owners con-

---

[6] Social Statics, p. 128 of the 1850 edition.
[7] For a full account of the controversy, with quotations from Spencer's earlier views and his later letters of explanation, see Henry George, A Perplexed Philosopher: Being an Examination of Mr. Spencer's Various Utterances on the Land Question, with Some Incidental References to his Synthetic Philosophy (1892), VII of The Writings of Henry George (1898-1901). See especially Spencer's letter to the London Times, Nov. 7, 1889, on pp. 74-77 of A Perplexed Philosopher.

stituting a class in the community, whom the natural course of things progressively enriches, consistently with complete passiveness on their own part. In such a case it would be no violation of the principles on which private property is grounded, if the state should appropriate this increase of wealth, or part of it, as it arises. This would not properly be taking anything from anybody; it would merely be applying an accession of wealth, created by circumstances, to the benefit of society instead of allowing it to become an unearned appendage to the riches of a particular class. This is actually the case with rent. The ordinary progress of a society which increases in wealth, is at all times tending to augment the incomes of landlords. They grow richer, as it were, in their sleep, without working, risking, or economizing. What claim have they, on the general principle of social justice, to the accession of riches? In what way would they have been wronged if society had, from the beginning, reserved the right of taxing the spontaneous increase of rent, to the highest amount required by financial exigencies?

Mill proposed a tax to restore gradually to society the values it had created. "The first step should be a valuation of all land in the country. The present value of land should be exempted from the tax; but after an interval had elapsed, during which society had increased in population and capital, a rough estimate might be made of the spontaneous increase which had accrued to rent since the valuation was made"; and a tax should then be laid on this increase in value.[8]

The idea of achieving fundamental social reforms through the abolition of all taxes save a tax on land is associated particularly with the name of an American, Henry George.[9] In his exposition of the peculiar nature of land value, George contributed no new ideas. His distinction and influence rest partly upon the vigor and eloquence with which he described the social evils resulting from private land-ownership and partly upon the clear emphasis he put upon a single remedy for those evils. He restated the old idea that men are born into the world with

[8] John Stuart Mill, *Principles of Political Economy* (first ed., 1848; seventh ed., 1871), Bk. II, Ch. II, Sec. VI.
[9] George was born in San Francisco in 1838 and died in New York City in 1897. He was first a newspaper writer, later a traveler, lecturer, and author. He was an unsuccessful candidate for mayor of New York City in 1886. He was a candidate for the same office in 1897, but he died during the campaign. His single-tax doctrines were set forth first in a book published in 1871, under the title, *Our Land and Land Policy* (in *Writings of Henry George,* 1898–1901, Vol. IX). The ideas were developed more fully in his famous *Progress and Poverty,* published in 1879 (*ibid.,* Vols. I–II). The most important of his other works are perhaps *The Land Question* (1881, *ibid.,* Vol. IV) and *A Perplexed Philosopher* (1892, *ibid.,* Vol. VI).

equal rights—including the right of equal access to land, which is the original and most essential source of the means of human existence. The custom under which a limited number of people have been allowed to acquire exclusive possession of land is simply a blunder of modern civilization—irrational in its origin and harmful in its practical results. The value of land is in large measure created by the community and rises as the population of a community grows and as the demands created by the needs and desires of the people multiply. Moreover, the community determines the value not only by creating the demands for land and its products but also by supplying the conveniences of trade and the guarantees of orderly living which make it possible for the products to be collected, sold, and transformed into salable commodities. The basic and constant cause of present-day social evils—unemployment, low wages, bad housing, low standards of living—is to be found not in over-population, over-production, and economic crises but in the ownership of the land by a small minority, who are able, by virtue of that ownership, to determine the conditions under which the great majority, whose lives and labors increase the land's value, are permitted to work, build, or live upon the land.

George held the basic problem of modern civilization to be this: How can the people resume their natural rights to the land or recover the values that their lives and labors create? A simple and natural means would be to permit each member of the community to take possession of whatever amount of land he needed and could effectively utilize. Such a means, however, is available only in countries that are still in the initial stages of cultivation. In settled regions, where private land-ownership has become a fixed part of the whole fabric of social life, the only method is to abolish all taxes on industry and its products and establish instead a single tax, falling solely upon land values, irrespective of the values of improvements. This tax should be speedily pushed up to an amount equivalent to the whole value of the economic rent. In that way the development of industry and trade would be relieved of the impediments that most existing taxes create. More important, the tax would "compel every individual controlling natural opportunities to utilize them by employment of labor or abandonment to others," thus increasing the opportunities for work. George believed that these changes should be achieved only through the methods of political democracy: not through moral suasion or voluntary coöperation, nor through political revolution or trade-union action, but through educating the electorate to elect to legislative bodies the men who would enact measures incorporating the proposed scheme of taxation.

The single-tax doctrine has been variously attacked by well-known economists on the grounds that the value of land is no more a gift of nature or a creation of the community than are the values of buildings or movable articles; or that it is impossible to separate values produced by owners from values socially or naturally created; or that present titles of land are now vested rights, the owners having acquired their titles in good faith under rules long accepted as valid by the community. So, it is said: Not only the soil's fertility and resources or the land's elevation but also the clay in a building's bricks and the wood in its timbers are supplied by nature; land is not the only commodity whose supply is limited; every valuable commodity derives its value in large part from the needs and desires of the members of society and from the securities and conveniences which organized society provides; the distinctions in value derived from varying relations of the community to differing tracts of land do not exist, or, if they exist, are not measurable.[10]

The idea that the value of land is in a special degree socially created survives, however; and not only in the lively discussion and propaganda conducted by thoroughgoing disciples of Henry George,[11] but also in theoretical writings and in practical schemes of taxation that do not incorporate fully the single-tax doctrine. Many contemporary economists hold that since the rent of bare land is peculiarly a social product,

---

[10] For typical examples of adverse criticisms by professional economists, see E. R. A. Seligman, *Essays on Taxation* (ninth ed., 1921), Ch. III; Merlin H. Hunter, *Outlines of Public Finance* (1921), Ch. XVI; and, in briefer space, C. C. Plehn, *Introduction to Public Finance* (fourth ed., 1921), pp. 84–89; and F. R. Fairchild, *Essentials of Economics* (1923), pp. 524–527.

[11] Some of the best-known advocates of the single-tax doctrine of Henry George have been the following: Charles B. Fillebrowne (1842–1917), New England manufacturer; Joseph Fels (1854–1914), wealthy Philadelphia merchant; Thomas L. Johnson (1854–1911), inventor, capitalist, member of the city council and later, for six years, mayor, of Cleveland; and Henry George, Jr. (1862–1916), biographer and editor of the works of his father, and member of Congress from 1911 to 1915; Lewis F. Post (1849–1928), lawyer, editor, author, and Assistant-Secretary of Labor of the United States, 1913–1921; William S. U'Ren (1859–1929), of Oregon, former member of the State legislature and active in movements for direct legislation and municipal reform. Among living single-tax propagandists the following are important: Dr. Frederick C. Howe, former member of the Cleveland city council and of the Ohio senate, and commissioner of immigration for the Port of New York, 1914–1919; Lewis J. Johnson, professor of civil engineering at Harvard University; Charles D. Hennessy, former member of the New Jersey senate and president of the International Union for Land Value Taxation and Free Trade. For titles of works by several of these men, see the list, p. 119, *infra*.

society may justly, and with benefit to the community, set up a policy of special taxation of rents. They propose an increased taxation of land values, with commensurate reductions in the taxes on improvements and personal property. In this way, they argue, lands would be more promptly and cheaply devoted to the uses for which they are fitted for supplying needs of the community; tax burdens on successful enterprise could be mitigated; and net incomes would be more equitably apportioned to variations in diligence, thrift, and forethought.[12] It is now widely maintained, moreover, that in all taxation a distinction should be made between wealth obtained by individual enterprise and that proceeding from luck or from the growth and prosperity of the community. Accordingly, in taxing incomes, it is common to fix lower rates for "earned" incomes (chiefly salaries and wages) than for incomes from rents, interests, and profits. Indeed, as we shall see, the conception of community-created values has a still wider application and is offered to justify not only a differential taxation but also extensive programs of social legislation and public ownership as the means for recapturing socially created values.

The principle of a special tax on land values has been put into practical operation in various parts of the world. Its most extensive use is to be found in regions where it was first adopted at a time of an unusually rapid increase in population—notably in Western Canada and Australasia, where it was initiated in the early seventies (before the appearance of *Progress and Poverty*), and in many German cities, beginning in the first decade of the twentieth century. There are other scattered and limited instances of its use, as in Denmark, since 1922, and in the cities of Pittsburgh and Scranton in the United States.[13]

As already indicated, it is in England that the land-value tax has been most widely and continuously advocated. In 1870, John Stuart Mill took the lead in forming a Land Tenure Reform Association,

---

[12] See Harry Gunnison Brown, *Economic Science and the Common Welfare* (1923), Pt. II, Ch. VI, and "Land Rent as a Function of Population Growth," *Journal of Political Economy*, XXXIV (1926), 274–288; H. J. Davenport, "Theoretical Issues in the Single Tax," *American Economic Review*, VII (1917), 1–10. Cf. George R. Geiger, *The Philosophy of Henry George* (1933), pp. 467–475.

[13] In these cities, under an enabling act of the Pennsylvania legislature, in 1913, the tax rate on improvements has been gradually reduced to one-half the rate on land.

On the recent practice of land-value taxation, see Yetta Scheftel, *The Taxation of Land Values* (1916); George R. Geiger, *The Philosophy of Henry George*, Ch. VIII; A. N. Young, *The Single Tax Movement in the United States* (1916); Robert M. Haig, *Exemption of Improvements from Taxation in Canada and the United States* (1915).

committed to that project and to other measures for recapturing unearned land values for the community; the association included among
its members distinguished publicists of varied interests,[14] and some
leaders of the socialist and labor groups joined actively in the movement. Forty years later, the land tax received one of its most interesting
trials in the famous "Lloyd George Budget" of 1909, enacted into law
in 1910. This law contained, among other taxes differentiating between
earned and unearned wealth, a 20 per cent tax on increases in land
values not due to improvements made by the owner, a 2 per cent tax
on undeveloped lands, and a 5 per cent tax on mining royalties. The
Liberal and Labour supporters of the budget—notably Mr. Lloyd
George himself, Premier Asquith, and Messrs. Philip Snowden, Winston
Churchill, and Hilaire Belloc—stated plainly the ideas of Mill and
Henry George. Mr. Lloyd George spoke of the recent "enormous increase in the value of urban land and of mineral property" due not
to any "expenditure of capital or thought on the part of the ground
owner" but solely to the "energy and enterprise of the community." [15]
His proposals gave rise to the most extended and bitter constitutional
conflict in England since 1832. Conservatives, notably among the Lords,
denounced the budget as "confiscation of property," "based on class
hatred," "a social and political revolution of the first magnitude," a
"plunge into socialism," initiating a course of action which, if not
promptly checked, would lead to "the end of all—the negation of faith,
of family, of religion, property, of Monarchy, of Empire." [16]

The British land taxes of 1910 were repealed in 1920; this came
about partly as a necessary concession to the Conservative majority
in the Liberal-Conservative coalition, then in control of Parliament,
and partly as a result of the practical difficulties that had been experienced in carrying out the system of valuation. A preponderant opinion
in the Liberal party has, however, continued to support the principle

[14] Notably John Morley, liberal writer and statesman; Professor J. E. Cairnes,
economist; and Sir Alfred Russel Wallace, naturalist and philosopher, who wrote
a book advocating the nationalization of land.
   For the program of the Land Tenure Reform Association, see J. S. Mill, *Dis-
sertations and Discussions*, V (1874–1880), 225–226; and for Mill's explanation,
ibid., pp. 226–284. For other organizations, see Sidney Webb, *Socialism in England*,
pp. 56–60.
   [15] *Parliamentary Debates*, fifth series, Vol. 4 (1909), Col. 532. For speeches of
the others see *ibid.*, Col. 843–854, 967–974, 1072–1096; and for a general summary
of the arguments on both sides, see *Annual Register*, 1909, *passim*.
   [16] See *Parliamentary Debates, Lords*, Vol. IV (1909), Col. 430–1342; and the
London *Times*, June 22, 1909, p. 8 and September 11, 1909, pp. 7–8.

of a tax on land values, and the Labour party has stood committed to it since the origin of the party in 1900. The Labour cabinet revived the issue in 1931. The budget of that year contained clauses imposing an annual tax of one penny in the pound on the value of land (excluding agricultural land), the tax to begin in the fiscal year 1933–1934; a preparatory valuation of the land to be completed in the intervening period was provided for. The Chancellor of the Exchequer, Mr. Snowden, set forth the familiar argument in support of the tax. "Every increase in population," he said, "every expansion of industry, every scientific development, every improvement in transportation, all expenditure of public money, indeed every child born, adds to the rent of the land. Rent enters into the price of every article produced and into every public service." [17] On this occasion the opposing arguments were mainly of a practical sort. Conservatives complained that the present owners of land were already specially taxed and that there was no practical scheme for ascertaining fairly the changing values of land. They made no charge that the proposed tax was revolutionary in nature or inherently monstrous.[18]

It is not possible to allocate among George and the other land-taxers the exact portions of influence on the spread of the idea in theoretical writing and practical application. It is generally agreed that George exercised a strong influence on the movements of socialism and land reform in England since the early eighties. His *Progress and Poverty,* first published in 1879, enjoyed an immediate and wide circulation in Great Britain. He visited that country in 1882, lecturing in the principal cities of England and Ireland, and he aroused great enthusiasm for his views. Two years later Sidney Webb wrote: "Little as Mr. Henry George intended it, there can be no doubt that it was the enormous circulation of his 'Progress and Poverty,' which gave the touch which caused all the seething influences to crystallize into a popular socialist movement. The optimistic and confident tone of the book, and the irresistible force of its popularization of Ricardo's Law of Rent, sounded

[17] *Parliamentary Debates,* fifth series, Vol. 252 (1931), Col. 48. For the full debate in the Commons, see *ibid.,* Col. 47–168, 405–523.

[18] Mr. Snowden's land-tax scheme was enacted into law in the summer of 1931. In the following December, however, Mr. Neville Chamberlain, Conservative Chancellor of the Exchequer in the "National" Cabinet, announced in the House of Commons, with cheers from the Conservative benches, that the preparatory land valuation was suspended, for economy's sake, and "without prejudice to the merits of the plan." Indefinite postponement of the valuation, however, meant indefinite postponement of the tax.

the dominant 'note' of the English Socialist party of to-day. Adherents of Mr. George's views gathered into little propagandist societies, and gradually developed, in many cases, into complete socialists."[19] Said Prof. J. A. Hobson in 1897: "The real importance of Henry George is derived from the fact that he was able to drive an abstract notion, that of economic rent, into the minds of a large number of 'practical' men, and to generate therefrom a socialist movement"; and "Henry George may be considered to have exercised a more directly powerful formative and educational influence over English radicalism of the last fifteen years than any other man."[20] George Bernard Shaw wrote a few years later: "When I was swept into the great Socialist revival of 1883, I found that five-sixths of those who were swept in with me had been converted by Henry George."[21]

The union between single-taxers and British socialists did not, however, last long. George persistently declared his opposition to socialism, regarding the abolition of private property, in things other than land, as incompatible with the development of individual initiative and enterprise and also as unnecessary, since a destruction of land monopoly would be sufficient in itself for the elimination of all social ills, in so far as collective action could eliminate them.[22] The socialists, on the other hand, challenged George's basic hypothesis—that property in land is the only form of property whose value is not created by the owners—and they regarded his remedy as entirely inadequate. Land, they argued, is not the only source of unearned wealth, and nationalization of rent, without a socialization of other basic means of production, would not end the exploitation of laborers and would secure only a narrowly limited redistribution of wealth.[23]

THE FABIAN SOCIALISTS

A general conception of community-created values is a characteristic feature of the particular sort of socialism that has had greatest vogue

---

[19] *Socialism in England*, p. 21.

[20] "The Influence of Henry George in England," *Fortnightly Review*, LXVIII (1897), 836–837, 844.

[21] Archibald Henderson, *Bernard Shaw, Playboy and Prophet* (1932), p. 150, quoting from a letter of Shaw to Hamlin Garland, Jan. 24, 1905.

[22] *Progress and Poverty*, p. 317. Cf. also Louis F. Post, *What is the Single Tax?* (1926), pp. 27–30.

[23] See E. R. Pease, *History of the Fabian Society* (rev. ed., 1925), p. 21., and cf. George R. Geiger, *The Philosophy of Henry George*, Ch. V.

in England. From the end of the Chartist movement in 1848, to the early eighties, there was little active socialism of any sort in England. English working-men, it is true, participated in the organization of the International Workingmen's Association in 1864, and London was the seat of the Association during its more vigorous years and also the home of its leader, Marx, during the last thirty years of his life. But British socialism was not effectively allied with the labor movement until the beginning of the twentieth century. There are several probable explanations for this relative tardiness and weakness of aggressive socialism in England. It has been suggested that national characteristics and historical experiences combined to create a predominantly individualistic attitude and a practical and compromising disposition among Englishmen.[24] A better explanation can perhaps be found in that English working-men, better paid than their Continental neighbors, had freer rights of speech and association, and were, therefore, less radically dissatisfied with existing conditions.

In the early eighties, however, several socialist movements got under way in England. Various events and circumstances supplied the preparation and incentives for this: the extension of the elective franchise to industrial workers, by the act of 1867, followed by popular disappointment over its effects upon the government's policy in dealing with urgent problems of taxation and industrial regulation; the financial depression of the seventies; the agitation of the land question; the spread of Marx's doctrines in England, through the publication of translations of his works; the attacks, by eminent English economists, upon the traditional doctrine of *laisser-faire*. Several organizations, active in the propagation of socialist ideas of one sort or another, were formed. The more important of these are the Social Democratic Federation, the Socialist League, the Independent Labour Party,[25] and the Fabian Society.

The Social Democratic Federation, original Marxian body in England, was formed in 1881, chiefly through the efforts of H. M. Hyndman; William Morris, the artist and poet; Helen Taylor, step-daughter of John Stuart Mill; E. Belfort Bax, poet, philosopher, and historian

[24] Cf. O. D. Skelton, *Socialism: a Critical Analysis,* pp. 282–285.
[25] For accounts of the Social Democratic Federation, Socialist League, and Independent Labour Party, cf. the following: M. Beer, *History of British Socialism,* Vol. II, Ch. XIII; Harry W. Laidler, *History of Socialist Thought,* Ch. XVII; Sidney Webb, *Socialism in England,* Ch. III; Godfrey Elton, *"England Arise!" A Study of the Pioneering Days of the Labour Movement* (1931), *passim.*

of socialism; Edward Aveling and his wife, Eleanor Marx Aveling, youngest daughter of Marx.[26] This organization, although repeatedly asserting its belief that an "energetic class war" is the only effective means for the attainment of the socialist goal, has never made clear what forms it would have the class war assume; in its later statements of objectives it has approached the democratic-socialist ideal of collective ownership in the interest of the whole community. It has suffered secessions from both right and left, because it has never succeeded in achieving such an accommodation between theoretical doctrine and practical program as to satisfy either the uncompromising Marxists or the reforming state-socialists. It played a part of some importance in disseminating information on socialism and in furthering the later movement for the political organization of socialists; but its membership has always been small, and its influence to-day is relatively insignificant.

The Socialist League was a small and short-lived organization, founded in 1884 by Morris, Bax, the Avelings, and others who withdrew from the Social Democratic Federation, partly because of personal discords and partly because of differences in doctrine. There was never any effective unity in the League: some favored, others opposed, parliamentary action; some were definitely anarchistic in their opinions, while others regarded anarchism as futile. Morris' attitude was one of opposition both to organized anarchism and to reformism. His view was that the proper task for socialists was that of preaching their ideals until a sufficient number of converts are obtained to make discussion of immediate policies and methods a timely occupation. The members of the League were never over a few hundred. Morris withdrew in 1889, and visionary anarchists were then in control until the disintegration of the League a few years later.[27]

Neither the Social Democratic Federation nor the Socialist League made the political phase of socialism paramount, and neither of the major political parties in England made the interests of the workers

[26] The original name of the organization was "Democratic Federation," the present name being adopted in 1884; in the same year it established its periodical, *Justice*, which it still issues.

[27] The periodical of the Socialist League was *The Commonweal*, first a monthly, later a weekly. William Morris was the first editor. The publication expired in 1894. Among important works written by founders of the league, the following are the more significant: William Morris (1839–1896), *A Dream of John Ball* (1888), *Signs of Change* (1888), and *News from Nowhere* (1890). Cf. *The Collected Works of William Morris*, 24 vols. (1910–1915); E. Belfort Bax, *The Religion of Socialism*, (1887, third rev. ed., 1891); William Morris and E. Belfort Bax, *Socialism: Its Growth and Outcome* (1893).

paramount. There were a few local political associations of working-men, but when they achieved any success in elections they usually became closely affiliated with the Liberal party. There was a growing conviction among some of the trade-union leaders that the workers needed a national party for independent political action on socialist lines. In 1893 representatives of local labor parties in Scotland and the north of England joined with others from the Social Democratic Federation and the Fabian Society, to form the Independent Labour Party. Among the early leaders of this party were J. Keir Hardie, a self-educated, mystically minded Scottish miner, who had been an active trade-unionist from early youth; J. Bruce Glasier, an architect and designer, interested in the idealistic, humanitarian phases of socialism; Tom Mann, a trade-union leader; and the now famous statesmen, J. Ramsay Mac-Donald and Philip Snowden—both men of lowly origin who rose gradually to the highest offices in the government of England. The party has been less doctrinaire and more disposed to compromise than the earlier socialist organizations but more aggressively socialist than the Fabian Society. It took a leading part in the formation, in 1900, of the British Labour party, and supplied most of the leaders of that party. When spokesmen for the Independent Labour group have undertaken to set forth the case for a general socialist program, their theoretical position has been essentially similar, until very recently, to that of the "revisionists" of Continental Europe, to be considered below.

The Fabian Society was established in January, 1884, by a small group of intellectuals who had been meeting together for several years for the study and discussion of current problems of social ethics.[28] They were highly educated men and women, widely read in the works of classical political economy and the recent literature of land-taxation and socialism. They were influenced particularly by the doctrines of Henry George, the various British interpretations of Marx, and the developing collectivism in John Stuart Mill's exposition of his individualist doctrine. George Bernard Shaw joined the society in September, 1884, and Sidney Webb the following year; these two became the most active and influential members of the Society.[29] The objects of the Fabians

[28] For a record of the Fabian Society, cf. the following: Edward R. Pease, *History of the Fabian Society* (rev. ed., 1925); George Bernard Shaw, *The Fabian Society: Its Early History, Fabian Society Tracts*, No. 41 (1892); Archibald Henderson, *Bernard Shaw, Playboy and Prophet*, Chs. XVII–XXII.

[29] Other distinguished men and women who have been members are: Professor Graham Wallas, H. G. Wells, Annie Besant, Mrs. Sidney Webb (Beatrice

have been to spread the socialist doctrine, as they understand it, throughout the educated middle class and to persuade the national and local governments of Great Britain to put the doctrine gradually into practical operation.

The original Fabians pledged themselves only to this general basis of agreement: "The members of the Society assert that the Competitive system assures the happiness and comfort of the few at the expense of the suffering of the many and that Society must be reconstituted in such a manner as to secure the general welfare and happiness." In a manifesto prepared by Shaw and adopted in September, 1884, just after he joined, the Society committed itself somewhat more explicitly to socialism, advocating that "the Land" should be nationalized "in some form," and that "the State should compete with all its might in every department of production." [30] The Society's participation in practical politics was at first devoted to efforts to "permeate" the established parties, particularly the Liberal party, with the Fabian ideas; later its members spoke in political campaigns, and the Society took part in the founding of both the Independent Labour party and the Labour party. Its characteristic work, however, has been in its efforts—through books, pamphlets, tracts, and lectures—to set forth the ethical and scientific justification of a socialist policy definitely related to the economic and social facts of present-day Britain, and to show how, from time to time, particular parts of a moderately socialistic program can be realized in specific legislative and administrative measures. In other words, the Fabians, said Shaw, "agreed to give up the delightful ease of revolutionary heroics and to take to the hard work of practical reform on ordinary parliamentary lines." [31]

Potter), William Clarke, Sydney Olivier, Sir Chiozza Money, Rev. Stewart Headlam, J. Campbell, J. R. MacDonald, and, more recently, Emil Davies, and Professors Harold Laski, R. H. Tawney, Herman Finer, and Leonard Woolf. The London society, of a few thousand members, has always been its main center of activity. In its earlier years local branches, chiefly of working-men, existed in the provincial towns; most of these dissolved when socialist working-men aligned themselves with the Independent Labour party. Later branches were established in the universities, and these exist to-day. The name of the society is explained by its motto: "For the right moment you must wait as the Fabians did when warring against Hannibal, though many censured his delays; but when the time comes you must strike hard, as Fabius did, or your waiting will be in vain and fruitless."

[30] E. R. Pease, *op. cit.*, pp. 32, 42.

[31] In 1912 the society established the Fabian Research Department, which in 1916 was transformed into the Labour Research Department, under the joint control of the Fabian Society and British labor bodies. This organization has through various committees conducted extensive investigations into doctrines and experi-

In their theoretical writings the Fabians followed the Marxian tradition of establishing historical and economic foundations for their socialist creed; but the materials they took from history and economics are not those used by Marx. History, they maintained, supplies an explanation for the socialism of to-day not by proving that economic conditions dominate everything but by revealing a steady movement towards democracy and socialism, in both practice and theory. All history shows that society is not static; recent history shows the incompatibility of either political aristocracy or economic individualism with the conditions of nineteenth century civilization.

Sidney Webb set forth in some detail the Fabian idea that history constantly demonstrates both "the irresistible progress of democracy" and the "almost continuous progress of socialism." [32] As to the former, he pointed out that, in England, middle-class suffrage superseded aristocratic suffrage in the early nineteenth century and that later legislation had enfranchised other classes, so that in his day democracy had entered fully into the political world. Meanwhile, he maintained, industrial changes had brought on a somewhat similar transformation of the economic world: the development of the factory system was gradually eliminating the purely personal element in the management of industrial property, and joint-stock and corporate enterprises were largely replacing individual management. The owners of property, his argument continued, are no longer, as they were under the domestic system of production, managers of the business to which they devote their property. The capitalist is now mainly not an entrepreneur or superintendent of an industry, but a mere investor in business—a "rent or interest receiver." Management and ownership have been separated. Large-scale business has destroyed individual responsibility and free competition. The growth of unrestrained capitalism has, therefore, put an end to economic individualism. Modern society, if it is to preserve any democracy or

ments in collectivism, syndicalism, trade-unionism, coöperation, and state and municipal socialism, and has issued publications embodying results of the investigations.

The following are the most important sources for Fabian theory: *Fabian Essays in Socialism*, by George Bernard Shaw, Sidney Webb, William Clarke, Sydney Olivier, Annie Besant, Graham Wallas, and Hubert Bland (1905); *The Fabian Society Tracts, 1884 to 1924*, Nos. 1 to 212 (1924), a bound volume of tracts (excluding those out of print or withdrawn). The tracts are brief pamphlets; some of them are general expositions of Fabian doctrine; others discuss a special theory, such as the basis of land values; others relate to particular projects of reform, such as the control of monopolies, or the minimum wage.

[32] See his essay on "The Historical Basis of Socialism," in the *Fabian Essays in Socialism*.

freedom in the economic world, is confronted by these alternatives: either dissolve large-scale industry and thereby destroy also the advantages which the latter creates in the way of checking waste, facilitating transportation, and reducing overhead costs; or else control, or absorb, these economically necessary concentrations by a gradual extension of governmental ownership or regulation of industry. Society has progressively adopted the latter alternative. Moreover, this collectivist development of practical policy is reflected in the prevailing trend in economic thought. Each succeeding edition of Mill's *Political Economy,* the most widely read economic text of its time, shows a further step away from the individualistic assumptions of Smith and Ricardo. Thus, Webb concluded, socialism as a fact having become a part of the constitution of modern society, it is the function of socialist doctrine to explain that fact.

The Fabians found in a theory of value their rational or ethical explanation for this developing socialization in thought and practice. They rejected, however, the labor-value doctrines of both the classical economists and Marx. They regarded value as the creation of society rather than of laborers.[33] Their doctrine was influenced both by the Ricardian theory of rent and the single-tax doctrine, and it is an extension of each. Under the Ricardian theory, as we have seen, the rent of any given piece of land is in general the equivalent of its superior advantages—in site, fertility, or resources—over the worst available land at the time. The landowner, under a system of unrestrained private ownership, retains the revenue which these advantages produce, even though they are not due to his efforts or talents. The Fabians extended this interpretation to other differential values—to values in the form of incomes from movable capital. They showed that under the unregulated competitive system a capitalist, in manufacture or trade as well as in land, retains the superior yield of his capital, which is due not to his superior ability or service but to the location of his business, the general increase in population, or the growing prosperity of the people. Bernard Shaw, discussing the indebtedness of the Fabians to Henry George, explained that the latter's single-tax arguments led British socialists into the advocacy of a "total industrial reconstruction. . . . We outgrew Progress and Poverty in many respects."[34]

Fabians and Marxians were in full agreement that investment alone

---

[33] Cf. Bernard Shaw's "Economic Basis of Socialism," in the *Fabian Essays.*
[34] Archibald Henderson, *Bernard Shaw, Playboy and Prophet,* p. 150.

confers no valid title to income. In so far as the existing system of production and distribution engenders a conflict of interest within society, the conflict, according to Fabians, is not between those who work for wages and those who employ wage-workers; it is rather between the community, on the one hand, and those who grow rich through investment, on the other hand. "The individuals or class who possess social power have at all times, consciously or unconsciously, made use of that power in such way as to leave the great majority of their fellows practically nothing beyond the means of subsistence according to the current living standard. The additional product, determined by the relative differences in productive efficiency of the different sites, soils, capitals, and forms of skill above the margin of cultivation, has gone to those exercising control over these valuable but scarce factors. This struggle to secure surplus of 'economic rent' is the key to the confused history of European progress and the underlying unconscious motive of all revolutions." [35]

Thus the object of socialism, as the Fabians conceived it, is to obtain for all members of society the values which society creates; and this object is to be achieved by gradually transferring land and industrial capital to the community, while making the state more fully representative of the community. The Fabians sought to explain the implications of tendencies already in action and to show how such tendencies can be safely and beneficially broadened and accelerated. They did not seek to draw wage-earners into a distinct class in order to make them, in a new form of society, supreme over other groups. "We have never advanced the smallest pretension to represent the working-classes of this country"; the Society "steadfastly discountenances all schemes for securing to any person, or any group of persons, the entire product of their labor." [36] Its object is to transfer ownership, not to the workers, but to society.[37] The transfer must be effected gradually, applied at any given time only to such industries as can then be successfully administered by the community; and, though without full compensation, yet with such relief to the expropriated individuals as may seem fair to the representatives of the community in the political parliament.

The Fabians were highly confident of the fairness and effectiveness of action by the state—the nineteenth century democratic state of

[35] "English Progress Towards Social Democracy," *Fabian Tract, No. 15* (not in the bound volume).
[36] "Report on Fabian Policy," *Fabian Tract, No. 70* (not in the bound volume).
[37] "Socialism: True and False," by Sidney Webb, *Fabian Society Tracts*, No. 51 (1894).

Western Europe and America. This state is "the representative and trustee of the people," "their guardian, their man of business, their manager, their secretary, even their stockholder." The existing state can, in these capacities, be made, without radical transformation, "if not absolutely perfect, at least trustworthy." [38] Changes are needed in the way of broadening the suffrage, securing a better trained civil service, and equalizing educational opportunities. Beyond such improvements, no fundamental innovations in political machinery are necessary. If the citizens of a democracy will simply make adequate use of powers they now possess, they can, through their national, provincial, and municipal governments, bring about gradually the appropriation by the community of all forms of economic rent from both land and industrial capital.

The Fabians appraised specific policies in reference to their probable consequences in promoting the widest possible distribution of physical well-being and cultural opportunity. Their practical influence has been principally in the field of domestic policy. They have devised concrete measures—and strongly fortified them, factually and logically—for diffusing more equitably the advantages of modern industrial civilization by raising the economic and civic status of wage-earners and paring down the fortunes of property-owners. The chief factor of their strength has been their skill in working out definite and workable schemes for immediate application by way of: (1) "social legislation"—shorter hours; safeguards against unemployment; minimum standards for health, safety, and wages; improved educational opportunities; (2) public ownership, national or municipal, of public utilities and natural monopolies; and (3) taxation of inheritances, ground rents, and investment incomes. It is perhaps in the latter two fields that they have exerted their most distinctive influence. Their tracts and lectures helped greatly in promoting the rapid expansion of municipal socialism in England and Scotland, and in forming the public opinion that supported the national government when it turned to new methods of taxing wealth—imposing relatively high rates on incomes from investment, taking heavy tolls from inherited estates, and (in the Finance Act of 1910) imposing special taxes on unused lands and the unearned increment in the values of used lands.

Their relations to the Labour party have been closer since the World War. Sidney Webb prepared the new constitution and program of the

[38] "The Outlook of Socialism," by Hubert Bland, in the *Fabian Essays*.

party in 1918 (*Labour and the New Social Order*), which broadened the membership but definitely committed the party to socialism. Five members of the Society, including two authors—Sidney Webb and Sydney Olivier—of the original *Fabian Essays,* were members of the first British Labour cabinet, in 1924.[39] In fact the Labour party has committed itself so thoroughly to the Fabian program, that the activities of the Society appear now to be devoted more preponderantly than even before to factual research and theoretical discussion.

It may be said generally that the Fabian socialists have contributed more to practice than to theory. The diligence and intelligence with which they have assembled and explained facts about the actual economic and social conditions of Great Britain have contributed substantially to the success with which national and local governments in that country have gradually and cautiously put into actual operation a very moderate sort of socialism.

REVISIONIST AND REFORMIST SOCIALISTS OF CONTINENTAL EUROPE

On the European Continent, the principles of this moderate and practical socialism, in the quarter of a century preceding the World War, are revealed somewhat typically in the utterances and activities of Eduard Bernstein in Germany, Jean Jaurès in France, Edouard Anseele in Belgium, Leonida Bissolati in Italy, M. Tugan-Baronowsky in Russia, and Karl Branting in Sweden,[40] and also in the platforms and tactics of such parties as the Belgian Labor party, the Social Democratic parties of the South German states, the Independent Labour party of Great Britain, the Broussists and Independent Socialists of France, and, at various times, the Italian Socialist party. The underlying doctrines

---

[39] Sidney Webb, President of the Board of Trade; Lord Olivier, Secretary for India; Noel Buxton, President of the Board of Agriculture; Arthur Henderson, Home Secretary; Lord Thomson, Secretary for Air. Four other Fabians held secondary ministerial positions. Moreover, Prime Minister MacDonald and Chancellor of the Exchequer Snowden, former members of the Society, were still in agreement with the Fabians on matters of domestic policy. Webb served as Secretary of State for Dominion Affairs and for the Colonies, in the second Labour cabinet, in 1931.

[40] Others of this group are Anton Menger (1841–1906) of Austria, Prof. Werner Sombart (1864–   ), Georg von Vollmar (1850–1922) and Eduard David (1863–   ) of Germany, and Peter Struve of Russia. The still more moderate position of the post-war reformist socialism is to be sketched in Chapter V, *infra,* pp. 129–140.

of this reformist socialism are set forth most fully in the writings of Bernstein, Jaurès, and Tugan-Baronowsky.[41]

Revisionists, as well as the stricter Marxists, regarded socialism as mainly a doctrine and program for the working class. Both sought to find the policy that would serve best the interest of working-men in improving their physical, economic, and cultural well-being, and strengthening their political position. The disputes between the two groups arose chiefly out of their opposing ideas as to the present economic situation of the wage-earners, the tendencies under way towards a change in that position, and the political tactics a socialist party should pursue in order to enable the workers to take full advantage of the actual movement of events.

The heresy of revisionism in Germany appeared first in a series of articles by Bernstein, published between 1896 and 1898 in *Die Neue Zeit*, under the title of "Probleme des Sozialismus." The controversy which these articles evoked, with Kautsky as chief protagonist for the orthodox group, led to the publication in 1899 of Bernstein's *Voraussetzungen des Sozialismus*,[42] in which he assailed some of the major tenets of the Marxian system, notably its theory of value and its interpretation of history.

In criticizing Marx's theory of value, Bernstein pointed out the confusion arising from an apparent shift of ground in the third volume of *Das Kapital*. In this later volume, market value is represented as equal to cost of production, including average profit; whereas in the earlier volume exchange value is represented as measured solely by the amount of necessary labor used in production. The earlier view survives in the third volume only in the form of a contention that the social value of the total of commodities is equivalent to the total labor time used in their production and that the excess of total product over total wages represents the total social surplus created by labor and wrongfully withheld from it. Bernstein held, however, that any theory of labor-

---

[41] Their important works are the following: Eduard Bernstein, *Die Voraussetzungen des Sozialismus und die Aufgabe des Sozial-demokratie* (1899), translated by Edith C. Harvey under the title, *Evolutionary Socialism* (1909); Jean Jaurès, *Études socialistes* (1902), translated by Mildred Minturn under the title, *Studies in Socialism* (1906); M. Tugan-Baronowsky, *Theoretische Grundlagen des Marxismus* (1905), *Modern Socialism: Its Historical Development*, translated from the Russian by M. I. Redmount (1910).

Cf. Max Eastman, *Marx, Lenin, and the Science of Revolution* (London, 1926), Pt. II, Ch. IX; Harry W. Laidler, *History of Socialist Thought*, Ch. XX; Werner Sombart, *Socialism and the Social Movement;* W. E. Walling, *Socialism As It Is*, especially Pt. II, Chs. I–IV; Pt. III, Ch. I.

[42] Cf. the immediately preceding note.

created value is untenable as a basis for discovering a just system of distribution.[43] "The theory of value gives a norm for the justice or injustice of the partition of the product of labor just as little as does the atomic theory for the beauty or ugliness of a piece of sculpture. We meet indeed today the best placed workers just in those trades with a very high rate of surplus value, the most infamously ground-down workers in those with a very low rate. A scientific basis for socialism or communism cannot be supported on the fact only that the wage worker does not receive the full value of the product of his work."

Revisionists in general followed Bernstein in rejecting Marx's theory of value—in so far as the theory involves the principle that the exchange value of commodities is measured solely by the efforts of wage-earners and that the surplus value absorbed by the capitalists is measurable only by the excess of what laborers produce over what they receive. But they did not reject the contention that there is a surplus value or that the surplus represents generally the excess of what capitalists receive for the sale of commodities over what they contribute to the value of those commodities. And they held to the belief that the effort of capitalists to increase the surplus supplies the propelling force in the natural development of capitalism and creates an exploitation of wage-earners.

In criticizing the materialistic conception of history, Bernstein undertook to discredit the current interpretation of Marx's views as to the degree of necessity in historical evolution and as to the predominance of economic factors in that evolution. He held that, with the developing intelligence and insight of mankind, individuals and nations acquire increased freedom in shaping their progress. He contended generally that intellectual or ideal factors operate as coördinate causes with economic factors in determining the course of history.[44]

The most definite issue between Bernstein and the orthodox Marxians arose out of his challenge of Marx's prophecy as to the future irresistible movement through which capitalism, under the laws of its own growth and disintegration, would lead to socialism. In refuting that prophecy, Bernstein argued, with an abundance of supporting statistics, that small-scale industries were not disappearing; that concentration into large industries through the corporate form of organization tended to diffuse rather than concentrate the ownership of wealth; that the num-

[43] *Evolutionary Socialism*, p. 39; cf. pp. 28 ff.
[44] *Ibid.*, pp. 6–18.

ber of owners of capital was thus increasing rather than diminishing; that the increase in total production was enlarging the *per capita* wealth and thereby mitigating, absolutely and relatively, the misery of the wage-earners; and that, with the extension of markets and improved forms of credit, commercial crises were becoming less frequent and less severe, and the likelihood of a universal and fatal crash was becoming more remote.

In short, the proletariat is not increasing in numbers and is not becoming the homogeneous and united group that the orthodox Marxian visualized. Diversities in interests, sharp contrasts in social and economic status, significant differences in political ideas are found among the various groups that make up the great unprivileged majority in any modern country. It is, therefore, futile to expect the elevation of this majority to come about through a revolution establishing a dictatorship of a class-conscious proletariat. The working-men must be content slowly to acquire a capacity for economic and political supremacy, through whatever training they can obtain in the institutions of democracy and in the agencies of industrial self-government. They must utilize the advantages which democratic government is supplying to them in the way of improving their own position and limiting the capitalist autocracy. They must, moreover, regard as indispensable the coöperation of those among the bourgeoisie (like the proletariat, a highly composite group), who, if not repelled by an antagonistic attitude on the part of the workers, are disposed to make common cause with them in restricting capitalist exploitation and abolishing political privileges.

Jaurès also rejected the Marxian prophecy. Agreeing with Bernstein, he maintained that, since Marx made his prophecy, the prevailing tendency had been for the proletariat to rise rather than sink economically; that an approach to utter impoverishment would decrease rather than increase the ability of the workers to supplant the capitalists; and that economic crises, although demonstrating and confirming the chaotic tendency of the capitalist system, could do little to develop any other economic system to take its place.

Bernstein and other revisionists held faithfully, however, to certain basic economic and evolutionary doctrines of Marx and contended that such doctrines constituted all that was essential in Marx's theoretical system. A capitalist society, they said, does mercilessly exploit the great majority of working-men, constantly allowing them to receive less than they contribute to the production of values; it does tend to under-

mine itself, by producing more than the underpaid majority can purchase; and these conditions do foment class antagonisms, so that a
violent insurrection by the under class may, under certain circumstances, be the only way out of class conflict. Accordingly, they contended, although the tendency has been towards an increase in the
relative numbers of owners of capital and towards an elevation of the
workers' actual wages, there is no chance, under a system of private
ownership, for a majority of the workers to reach the positions of luxury and ease flaunted by the wealthy minority; and the improved
economic condition of working-men generally tends to strengthen, not
weaken, both their desire to achieve their full rights and their ability
to work effectively for that achievement—whether through revolutionary or through peaceful means.

Thus although the revisionists advocated coöperation of wage-earners
with sympathetic groups outside, they nevertheless agreed that economic
inequalities supply the explanation and justification of socialism. They
accepted the class character of socialism, in the sense that socialism is
a movement devoted to vindicating essential rights of workers and to
improving their material and social condition, and also in the sense that
the workers find their natural place only in socialist parties. "No one,"
said Bernstein, "has questioned the necessity for the working classes to
gain the control of government." The formation of a proletarian socialist
party is the indispensable first step toward democracy.[45] Jaurès insisted that society is divided, by the present form of property-holding,
into two antagonistic classes: the first class living mainly by its ownership of property; the second living only by its work, dependent for
that work upon the utilization of the property owned by the first class,
and having no share in determining in what manner and to what ends its
work is to be employed. The main task of socialism is to break down
this supremacy of one class over another. "All difference of class must
be abolished by transferring to the whole body of citizens, the organized
community, the ownership of the means of production and of life which
today, in the hands of a single class, is a power of exploitation and
oppression."[46]

Most revisionists claimed, therefore, to be revolutionists as well as
reformists. Bernstein admitted that where political democracy did
not exist and the propertied interests were entrenched in control, revo-

[45] *Evolutionary Socialism*, pp. xiv–xvi and *passim*.
[46] *Studies in Socialism*, pp. 3–9.

lution might be the only means whereby a non-propertied popular majority could make themselves political masters. Jaurès approved the use of the general strike as means in a general socialist movement, and he agreed that, in the case of persistent refusal of reforms by a callous capitalistic régime, a violent general strike might be the workers' "final and desperate recourse." [47]

Such expressions, however, appear to be nothing more than claims to an ultimate right of revolution explicit or implicit in almost any political creed, radical or conservative. Jaurès generally repudiated all methods which require a violent rupture with the existing institutions of a democratic society. He rejected specifically the Marxian hypothesis of a proletarian political revolution to be engrafted upon a bourgeois revolution and of an economic cataclysm demolishing capitalism. In so far as the proletariat lie in wait for such a revolution, they become incapable of reaping any benefits from bourgeois movements. "It is not by the collapse of the capitalistic bourgeoisie but by the invigoration of the proletariat, that the communist order will gradually install itself in our society." [48] Bernstein accepted the right of revolution only in the general sense of an imprescriptible right, "as little touched if we place ourselves on the path of reform as the right of self-defense is done away with when we make laws to regulate our personal and property disputes." [49] In one of the earliest expressions of his views he argued that the excesses of the Blanquists were responsible for the collapse of the French working-men's uprising of 1848. And the theme of one of his latest works is the contention that the German revolution of 1918 was made unproductive of substantial socialist progress by the activities of extremists—Karl Liebknecht, Rosa Luxemburg, and the Spartacists and revolutionary communists. [50]

Thus the revisionist policy, like the policy of the Fabians, is that of achieving the socialist goal through utilizing the agencies of the existing state. The modern socialist movement is regarded as a part of the modern democratic movement. "Without a certain amount of democratic institutions and traditions," said Bernstein, "the socialist doctrine of the present time would not indeed be possible. There would, indeed, be a workers' movement, but no social democracy. The modern socialist movement—and also its theoretic explanation—is actually the product

[47] *Studies in Socialism*, p. 128.
[48] *Ibid.*, pp. 168–169.
[49] *Evolutionary Socialism*, p. 197.
[50] *Die deutsche Revolution* (1921), esp. Chs. VIII, XII, XIII.

of the great French Revolution and of the conceptions of right which through it gained general acceptance in the wages and labor movement." Democracy and socialism are not mutually antagonistic; the former is a condition of the latter. Democracy "is not only the means but also the substance of socialism." The democrat or liberal should be regarded as the natural ally, or the unconscious agent, of the socialist. Bernstein urged the German Social Democratic party to offer itself for "what it is in reality—a democratic, socialistic party of reform." [51]

For all practical purposes socialism, to the revisionist, meant state restriction upon private capitalism: the restriction might take the form of governmental interference with the property rights of private owners, or the setting up state ownership in place of private ownership for a given section of capital. Jaurès—in debates in parliament and the socialist congresses and in his journal, *L'Humanité*—argued earnestly for both reform legislation and nationalization. Programs which the French socialists (e.g., in 1902) adopted under his leadership included demands for universal suffrage, proportional representation, the initiative, referendum and recall, secularization of the schools, removal of the legal disabilities of women, progressive taxation, social insurance, protection of labor, regulation of industry, and international peace. Bernstein pointed out that, whatever the professions of the orthodox socialists in Germany, their practice conformed to his view of the function of a socialist party: in the Reichstag they worked for the establishment of compulsory arbitration of trade disputes; in the cities they formed alliances with middle-class democrats for the promotion of municipal ownership; in private industry they united with trade-unionists in setting up coöperative stores. "Everywhere there is action for reform, action for social progress, action for the victory of democracy." [52]

As long as socialists are in a minority they can, according to the revisionists, work for such reforms only by coöperating with parties that are willing to go farthest in granting the instalments of socialism. They should support a progressive ministry if their support is necessary to prevent the triumph of a conservative or reactionary group; and it may be proper for socialists to accept office in a progressive cabinet. In the famous debate, at the congress of the Second International in 1904, on the question as to whether socialists should be allowed to join with non-socialist parties in progressive cabinets, Jaurès stated his position as

[51] *Evolutionary Socialism*, pp. 166, 197,
[52] *Ibid.*, p. 192.

follows: The orthodox group "is right in saying that socialism must be carried on by a class organization, independent in its end and action and devoted to the complete transformation of the capitalist system with the object of abolishing all exploitation and restoring to the collective workers all the fruits of their labor. All our reforms must have for their revolutionary object the emancipation of oppressed and exploited labor. But you must recognize that socialism must make its appeal to all the forces of democracy if it is to accomplish immediate reforms. We must not cease to grasp and to utilize democratic evolution to further proletarian evolution wherever it has need of such assistance." [53] He held that it was foolish to reject coöperation with other parties which were willing to promote such reforms. Fear of such coöperation implied distrust of the proletariat—a belief that it would "compromise itself and lose itself through its collaboration with democracy."

The action of the French party in rejecting Jaurès' proposal to permit the entry of socialists into a liberal ministry cost them the loss of some of their ablest parliamentary and propagandist leaders—notably Alexandre Millerand, Aristide Briand, and René Viviani. These men had been members of a group known as "Independent Socialists," who were so much interested in the attainment of reforms made available by circumstances of the moment that they strove to avoid any rigid formulation of dogma or policy. Their program was stated in a speech delivered by Millerand at a gathering of leaders of various socialist factions at Saint Mandé, in 1896, following the socialist successes in municipal elections of that year. Millerand accepted the Marxian doctrine that capitalist society is carrying itself towards its own doom and that collectivism is setting itself up as an unpremeditated part of the advance of capitalism. The task of socialists, he went on to say, is simply to take advantage, in intelligent fashion, of that normal and gradual development. He thus defined socialism as the "necessary and progressive substitution of social property for capitalist property." The "necessary and sufficient" parts of a socialist program are: "(a) state intervention to transfer from the capitalist domain to the national domain the various categories of the means of production and exchange, as fast as they become ripe for social appropriation; (b) the conquest of public power by means of universal suffrage; (c) the international understanding of the workers." [54]

[53] Quoted from the official report of the congress by William E. Walling, and others, *The Socialism of Today* (1916), pp. 16–17.
[54] See "The Saint-Mandé Programme, by A. Millerand," in R. C. K. Ensor,

The other socialist groups in France were held loosely together, until the outbreak of the World War, under the political leadership of the conciliatory Jaurès. They accepted the doctrinal declarations of the orthodox Guesde and held consistently to the orthodox policy of non-acceptance of ministerial posts, but they followed the parliamentary leadership of Jaurès in supporting legislative measures of piecemeal economic and political reform, put forth by non-socialist ministries. On some occasions also they were persuaded, by Jaurès' logic and eloquence, that flagrant social injustice of any sort, as in the persecution of Dreyfus, should move socialists to action; and they generally agreed that it was of grave concern to socialists to join with others in thwarting domestic attempts to overthrow republican government.

The underlying ethical philosophy of this moderate and conciliatory policy of contemporary socialism was perhaps best set forth by two earlier writers—César de Paepe, a Belgian, and Benoît Malon, a Frenchman—who were less actively connected with the practical movement of socialism and less well known than most of the men whom we have particularly considered. De Paepe and Malon based their socialist views frankly upon considerations of right and justice, gave emphasis to the spiritual aims of socialism, and urged the importance of the moral betterment of the proletariat. They sought to differentiate their attitude from what they regarded as the materialism and selfishness of Marxism. They deprecated Marx's dominant appeal to economic motives and class-consciousness. Their doctrine was sometimes called "integral socialism" (which is the title of one of Malon's books); for they represented socialism as a creed not for the proletariat alone but for all humanity; as inspired by visions of spiritual as well as economic goals, aiming at a conciliation rather than an antagonism of classes, seeking benefits for all who suffer hardship, and demanding the coöperation of liberal elements among all groups—aristocrats, intellectuals, bourgeoisie, proletariat. Altruism, benevolence, and coöperation are key words in their writings.[55]

The revisionists, like the Fabians, showed the influence of Marx's scientific and synthetic treatment of socialism. A socialist policy, they

Modern Socialism as Set Forth by Socialists in Their Speeches, Writings, and Programmes (third ed., 1910), pp. 49–55.

[55] De Paepe (1842–1890), *Examen de quelques questions socialistes* (1866), *Collectivisme et services publics* (1892); Malon (1841–1893), *Le Socialisme integral* (1891).

agreed, must be elaborated in the light of general social and economic facts, which are in historic flux. They also accepted in part the implications of Marx's doctrine of class war; they admitted that a socialist policy cannot overlook the existing social stratification based on economic differences. But they deprecated the Marxist emphasis on revolutionary means for destroying that stratification. They regarded socialism as part of the whole modern evolution of society—an important phase of a movement, begun in the eighteenth century and advanced continually since then—through which political, social, and economic rights had been successively asserted and attained. Sudden upheavals had marked some of the stages, but they were no more the essential characteristics of the movement than the slower and quieter advances.

Thus the revisionists sought generally to steer a midway course between mere democratic reformism and an exclusively revolutionary, class-war socialism. They held, on the one hand, that political democracy alone would not eliminate class antagonisms and, on the other hand, that a class war alone would not establish socialism. The normal path must be one of negotiation and compromise. The ultimate goal of the revisionists is that of all socialists; but just because the completed changes which its attainment will involve are so sweeping, complex, and remote, the only effective plan for socialists to-day is to work for the partial changes that can be introduced as economic and political conditions permit. If immediate reforms, offered or conceded by non-socialist governments, narrow the field of private ownership or improve the economic and social condition of wage-workers, they should be regarded as "installments of socialism" and as significant steps towards the disappearance of the capitalist régime.

THE "NATIONALISM" OF FABIANS AND REVISIONISTS

There was little or no antinationalism in the social outlook of the Fabian and revisionist socialists. They desired to make each national government a more efficient instrument in promoting human welfare. Thus the Fabians admitted no claims of "right"—by any traditionally privileged group at home or by any backward race elsewhere—that stood in the way of the discharge of world obligations resting upon civilized nations under democratic control. With all their opposition to landlordism and industrial capitalism, they had no objection to an efficient and benevolent imperialism; they sought not to defeat but rather to socialize the colonial and international policy of the British Empire. Socialists, they said, should, approvingly or disapprovingly, recognize the fact that the world is on the point of being partitioned among the great powers; small groups of international traders and bankers will exploit this situation to their own advantage, if socialists and liberals are merely negative antimilitarists and anti-imperialists. Fabians must "accept the Empire," point out its opportunities and responsibilities, and show how to make its imperial policy efficient and socialistic. They should persuade the imperial government to concede to the "white inhabitants" of South Africa "a free constitution and responsible government within the Empire." They should stand also for a liberal policy in India, urging the government to provide the opportunities of Western secondary education "for natives capable of it"; they should extend "the Indianization of the higher grades of the civil service"; develop "the germs of self-government" in the native and provincial councils "under the guidance of the British Raj"; and expend funds generously in studying and remedying industrial and social ills in that region.[56] But they should not seek to restrict imperial policy by the outmoded assumption of Liberals that each race has some "inherent right to have its own government and work out its own policy, unfettered by any consideration of the effect of their independence on other races, or on the world at large." [57] Indeed, both Webb and Shaw appeared to be of the opinion that the division of the Western world into relatively large political and economic units tended to promote the major objectives of Fabian socialism.

Accordingly, it was also a part of Fabian policy to work for the "application of Socialism to foreign trade." The benefits of this trade must be spread to all members of the nation; but there must first be ample benefits to be spread. The old Liberal policy of "Peace, Retrenchment, and Reform" can create, under the economic conditions of the late nineteenth century, no new opportunities of well-being for any group. England needs an expert, aggressive, businesslike consular service, in order to "bring the power, the information, and the organization of the Empire to the help of the individual trader." [58] If British foreign trade is

[56] Bernard Shaw, ed., *Fabianism and the Empire: a Manifesto by the Fabian Society* (1900).

For a bitter attack on this attitude see L. T. Hobhouse, *Democracy and Reaction* (1904), Ch. II and *passim*.

[57] Sidney Webb, "Lord Rosebery's Escape from Houndsditch," *Nineteenth Century*, L (1901), 366–386.

[58] Bernard Shaw, *Fabianism and the Empire*, p. 12.

not prosperous, it cannot be the means of bringing prosperity to the masses of British citizens and subjects.

"National efficiency," indeed, came to be a slogan for Fabians— efficiency for the people of all classes and in all parts of the Empire, it is true; but an efficiency to be obtained only through intelligent, benevolent, strong, hard-headed control by the Mother Country. "Virility in government" must be maintained and devoted to the "raising of an Imperial race." [59] The Fabian leaders became intolerant of premature appeals to an idealistic internationalism that might divert the nation from its imperial duty. After the outbreak of the South African War, they persuaded the Society to agree—by a narrow majority, following a heated debate—to abandon all further opposition to the war policy of the government. In 1914, a majority of the Fabians split away from the Independent Labour party and followed the Labour party in supporting British participation in the World War.[60]

German and French Revisionists repudiated the antinationalist doctrine of the *Communist Manifesto*. Bernstein argued that workingmen, having been endowed with political privileges, have a legitimate concern in the defense of national interests. Socialists should work for popular control of foreign policy and for international conciliation; but they may defend national rights, and they may, under proper conditions, even support colonial expansion—in order to strengthen pacific and democratic against autocratic and imperialistic nations. Jaurès, accepting the national democratic state as an indispensable agency in the attainment of socialism, proclaimed, on several occasions, the loyalty of French socialists to the French Republic.

SELECT BIBLIOGRAPHY

THE ACADEMIC SOCIALISTS

Schmoller, Gustav, *Ueber einige Grundfragen des Rechts und der Volkswirtschaft* (Jena, 1875).

――――――, "Die Gerechtigkeit in der Volkswirtschaft," *Schmoller's Jahrbuch für Gesetzgebung, Verwaltung und Volkswirtschaft im deutschen Reich*, V (1881), 19–54.

――――――, "The Idea of Justice in Political Economy" (a translation of

---

[59] Sidney Webb, "Lord Rosebery's Escape from Houndsditch," p. 386.

[60] The stand in the Boer War cost the Society the loss of fifteen active members, including Mr. and Mrs. Ramsay MacDonald. In 1914, Mr. and Mrs. Philip Snowden and several other prominent members withdrew from the Society.

the foregoing by Ludwig von Haller and Carl L. Schutz), *Annals of the American Academy of Political and Social Science*, IV (1894), 697–737.

Wagner, Adolf, *Rede über die soziale Frage* (Berlin, 1872).

——————, *Grundlegung der politischen Oekonomie*, 3 vols. (Leipsic, 1876, third ed., 1892–1893), Bk. VII.

Ely, Richard T., *French and German Socialism* (New York and London, 1883), Ch. XV.

Gide, Charles, and Rist, Charles, *History of Economic Doctrines,* translation from rev. and enl. ed. of 1913 (Boston, New York, etc. n.d.) Bk. II, Chs. I and IV; Bk. IV, Ch. II.

Haney, Lewis H., *History of Economic Thought* (revised ed. New York, 1926), Chs. XIX, XX, and pp. 436–441, 577–579.

Laidler, Harry W., *History of Socialist Thought* (New York, 1927), pp. 669–675.

THE SINGLE TAXERS

George, Henry, *Progress and Poverty* (1879) in *The Writings of Henry George, Memorial Edition*, 10 vols., (New York, 1898–1901), Vols. I–II.

——————, *Our Land and Land Policy* (1871), *ibid.,* Vol. IX.

——————, *The Land Question* (1881), *ibid.,* Vol. IV.

——————, *A Perplexed Philosopher* (1892), *ibid.,* Vol. IV.

Fels, Mary, *Joseph Fels: His Life and Work* (New York, 1916).

Fillebrown, C. B., *The ABC of Taxation, with Boston Object Lessons, Private Property in Land, and Other Essays and Addresses* (New York, 1909).

——————, *Principles of Natural Taxation* (Chicago, 1917).

George, Henry, Jr., *The Life of Henry George* (New York, 1900).

Hirsch, Max, *Democracy versus Socialism* (New York and London, 1901), pp. 345–463.

Howe, F. C., *Privilege and Democracy in America* (New York, 1910).

Post, Louis F., *What Is the Single Tax?* (New York, 1926).

——————, *The Prophet of San Francisco: Personal Memoirs and Interpretations of Henry George* (New York, 1931).

Bullock, E. D., ed., *Selected Articles on the Single Tax* (second ed., New York, 1917).

Douglas, Paul H., "The Single Tax," in C. E. Merriam and H. E. Barnes, *Political Theories, Recent Times* (New York, 1924), pp. 246–254.

Geiger, George R., *The Philosophy of Henry George* (New York, 1933).

Scheftel, Yetta, *The Taxation of Land Values: A Study of Certain Discriminatory Taxes on Land* (Boston, 1916).

Young, A. N., *The Single Tax Movement in the United States* (Princeton, 1916).

THE FABIAN SOCIALISTS

Fabian Essays in Socialism, by G. Bernard Shaw, Sidney Webb, William
    Clarke, Sydney Olivier, Annie Besant, Graham Wallas, and Hubert
    Bland (London, 1889; Boston, 1909; London, 1920).

Fabian Tracts, Nos. 1– to 212, *1884–1924* (London, 1924).

Finer, Herman, *Representative Government and a Parliament of Industry*
    (London, 1923).

Gordon, Alban, *Social Insurance: What It Is and What It Might Be* (London,
    1924).

Shaw, George Bernard, ed., *Fabianism and the Empire: a Manifesto by the
    Fabian Society* (London, 1900).

——————, *"The Fabian Society: Its Early History,"* Fabian Tract No. 41,
    (London, 1892).

Webb, Sidney, and Webb, Beatrice, *The Decay of Capitalist Civilization* (Lon-
    don, 1923).

Webb, Sidney, "Lord Rosebery's Escape from Houndsditch," *Nineteenth Cen-
    tury*, L (1901), 366–386.

Henderson, Archibald, *Bernard Shaw, Playboy and Prophet* (New York and
    London, 1932), Chs. XVII–XXVI.

Laidler, Harry W., *History of Socialist Thought*, Chs. XVII, XVIII.

Pease, Edward R., *History of the Fabian Society* (London, 1916); rev. ed.
    1925).

THE REVISIONISTS AND REFORMISTS

Bernstein, Eduard, *Die Voraussetzungen des Sozialismus und die Aufgabe des
    Sozialdemokratie* (Stuttgart, 1899).

——————, *Evolutionary Socialism*, translated by Edith C. Harvey (Lon-
    don, 1909).

Ensor, R. C. K., *Modern Socialism as Set Forth by Socialists in Their Speeches,
    Writings, and Programmes* (first ed., 1903; third ed., rev. and enl. New
    York, 1910).

Jaurès, Jean, *Études socialistes* (Paris, 1902).

——————, *Studies in Socialism*, translated by Mildred Minturn (New
    York and London, 1906).

——————, *Pages choisis* (Paris, 1922).

MacDonald, J. Ramsay, *Socialism and Government* (London, 1909).

——————, *Socialism and Society* (London, 1905).

Malon, Benoît, *Le socialisme integral* (second ed., Paris, 1891).

Paepe, César de, *Collectivisme et services publics* (Paris, 1892).

Simkhovitch, V. Y., *Marxism versus Socialism* (New York, 1913).

Struve, Peter, "Die Marxsche Theorie der sozialen Entwickelung," *Archiv für soziale Gesetzgebung und Statistik*, XIV (1899), 658–704.

Tugan-Baranovsky, M., *Theoretische Grundlagen des Marxismus* (Leipsic, 1905).

———————, *Modern Socialism: Its Historical Development,* translated from the Russian by M. I. Redmount (London, 1910).

Wells, H. G., *New Worlds for Old* (New York, 1908).

Wells, H. G. and others, *Socialism and the Great State* (New York and London, 1912).

Eastman, Max, *Marx, Lenin, and the Science of Revolution* (London, 1926) Pt. II, Ch. IX.

Hecker, Julius F., *Russian Sociology: a Contribution to the History of Sociological Thought and Theory* (New York, 1915), Ch. II.

Kautsky, Karl, *Bernstein und das sozial demokratische Programm: eine Antikritik* (Stuttgart, 1899).

Laidler, Harry W., *History of Socialist Thought*, Ch. XX.

Soltau, Roger, *French Political Thought in the Nineteenth Century* (New Haven, 1931), Ch. XIII, Sec. III.

Sombart, Werner, *Socialism and the Social Movement,* translated from the sixth German edition by Mordecai Epstein (London and New York, 1909).

Sternberg, Fritz. *The Marxisthe Theorie der sozialen Entwicklung, Wyng. W. pp. 11.* (Reprint, Leipzig, etc., XIV. (1900), 653-704.

Tugan-Baranowsky, M. *Theoretische Grundlagen des Marxismus* (Leipzig, 1905).

Untermann, Ernest. *Marxian Economics* (Chicago, 1907).

Untermann, Ernest. *Die logischen Mängel des engeren Marxismus* (Munich, 1910).

Wells, H. G., *A and G* various other. *The New Worlds for Old* (1908).

Wells, H. G., and others. *Socialism and the Great State* (New York and London, 1912).

Wolfe, A. B. *Conservatism, Radicalism, and Scientific Method* (New York, 1923).

Woltmann, Ludwig. *Der historische Materialismus* (Düsseldorf, 1900).

CHAPTER V

SOCIALISM SINCE 1914

THE SOCIALISTS AND THE WORLD WAR

THE Second International, as we have seen, was a coöperative league of socialist parties. It was never an organization for the formulation of a coherent socialist doctrine. Socialists in the several countries needed some means of international coöperation for the promotion of their efforts to improve the standards of living and to strengthen the political position of wage-earners; the International supplied this need. The parties associated in it were more interested in unity of action than in consistency of doctrine; and they were generally able to serve the former end by shirking consideration of the latter. This practical unity was disrupted by the outbreak of the World War.

The disruption was occasioned by the varying positions assumed by the several parties on the immediate question as to whether socialists should strive to maintain an international working-class unity by refusing to support the war or should sacrifice loyalty to their class and defend the integrity and prestige of their several nations. The inability to agree on this question is not unusual. No man is very clear as to the full implications of a profession of unqualified loyalty, either to an economic class or to an established political authority; nor does he act consistently in the matter. A thoroughgoing believer in the capitalist system may rank his allegiance to this system above his patriotism. If his country is controlled by radical socialists, he may refuse to support his government, in either peace or war, and particularly in a war which he may believe to be designed to extend radical socialism into other lands. Many French and American patriots have regarded with sympathy and admiration the post-war Russian *émigré*, even when he is disloyal to the constituted government of his native land.

The outbreak of the World War created a several-fold division within the socialist ranks. There was the separation within each party into pro-war and anti-war sections; there was the hostility between pro-war socialists of the Allied Powers and pro-war socialists of the Central Powers; and socialist parties of the neutral countries pursued varying courses in their efforts towards reconciliation.[1] In most of the belligerent countries, there were, in the days immediately preceding and just following the beginning of the war, emphatic anti-war pronouncements by the socialists. Party proclamations, editorials, and mass meetings denounced the war as the unhappy consequence of imperialistic policies pursued by the great European states. After a few days, however, there were sudden and sweeping changes in the socialist position. In Germany, Austria, France, and Belgium (the countries in which political socialism was strongest) large majorities in the official socialist parties supported their governments and voted for war loans; minority socialists in Russia and England took a similar stand. In France, Jules Guesde and Marcel Sembat, both of whom had, for a long time, emphatically opposed coöperation with non-socialist ministries, now promptly accepted positions in the French war cabinet; they were joined, a few months later, by Albert Thomas. Émile Vandervelde resigned his position as president of the Executive Committee of the International Bureau of the Second International, in order to take office in the Belgian ministry. In 1915, Arthur Henderson, in England, and Bissolati, in Italy, joined the coalition cabinets of their respective countries.

Thus a majority of socialists in the belligerent countries came quickly to the position that the war was an inevitable exercise of a legitimate right of self-defense, a fight for political liberty, sure to lead to "an honorable and lasting peace." [2] They were persuaded that they were fighting not so much for military victory or the glorification of their country as for great idealistic and international aims—the ending of imperialism and war. Said the German Social Democratic party, in its manifesto of August fourth, explaining its position in voting for the war loan:

Now we are only too surely confronted by the fact that war is upon us and that we are menaced by the terror of foreign invasion. The problem before

[1] Cf. the following: William E. Walling, *Socialists and the War*, Pts. II–IV; H. W. Laidler, "The European War and Socialism," *Intercollegiate Socialist*, III (1914), 3–11; "Excerpts from Socialist War Manifestoes," *ibid.*, pp. 12–15; Emily G. Balch, *Approaches to the Great Settlement* (1918), Ch. IV; A. W. Humphrey, *International Socialism and the War* (1915); Lewis L. Lorwin, *Labor and Internationalism* (1929), Ch. VI; Jean Maxe, *De Zimmerwald au Bolchevisme* (1920); Alexander Trachtenberg, *The American Socialists and the War* (1917).
[2] Walling, *Socialists and the War*, p. 292.

us now is not the relative advisability of war or peace, but a consideration of just what steps must be taken for the protection of our country. . . . . We take our stand upon the doctrine basic to the international labor movement, which at all times has recognized the right of every people to national independence and national defence, and at the same time we condemn all war for conquest.[3]

A joint manifesto prepared by French and Belgian socialists reviewed recent relations between Germany and other European countries, and then declared as follows:

These facts, which we submit to the judgment of the international prole-tariat, suffice to establish from which side aggression came, from which side war was sought. . . . It was not with the idea of aggression, it was not even because it had sentiments of ill will and hostility that our government resolved to go to war. We have every certainty of defending the independence and autonomy of our nation against German imperialism. . . . It is with the certainty of supporting the principle of liberty, the right of the people to dispose of themselves, that the French and Belgian socialists suffer the hard necessity of war.[4]

Pro-war socialists in Great Britain declared that victory for the Central Powers would mean the spread of military despotism and lead to further wars of conquest. The Belgian socialists, said Vandervelde, were agreed that the war, on the Allied side, was a fight not only for the independence of Belgium but also against Prussian militarism and "for the, freedom and civilization of Europe," and that victory by the Allies would supply a great impulse "to all democratic institutions." [5]

From the beginning of the war the Independent Labour party of Great Britain, and the major socialist parties of the United States, Italy, and Russia (both Bolsheviks and Mensheviks), and small socialist minorities in France, Germany, and Austria, opposed the war and challenged the aims of the political leaders responsible for its conduct. They denied that their governments were fighting for democracy or civilization. They viewed the war as a consequence of mutual jealousies of increasing power among the several national plutocracies. The alignments of the nations, they held, were determined by international engagements that had no reference to the promotion of liberal aims, and

---

[3] *Socialists and the War*, pp. 143–144.
[4] *Ibid.*, p. 177.
[5] Report of an interview with M. Vandervelde, by H. W. Laidler, "The European War and Socialism," *Intercollegiate Socialist*, III (1914), 7.

the conduct of the war proved that militarism had not changed its character. Support of the warring governments was, therefore, an abandonment of socialism. Late in 1915, the British Independent Labour party unanimously adopted the following resolution:

The Conference is of the opinion that it is the duty of the Socialists of all countries to determine once and for all that the Socialist parties shall in the future refuse to support any government in any war, whatever the war may be, even if the war be conducted in the name of self-defence.[6]

Notable among the socialist leaders in radical opposition to the war were Keir Hardie, J. Ramsay MacDonald, and Philip Snowden in Great Britain; Karl Liebknecht (son of the late orthodox leader), Rosa Luxemburg, and Clara Zetkin in Germany; Friedrich Adler and Rudolf Hilferding in Austria; A. Merrheim, Fernand Loriot, and Marcel Cachin in France. They carried on various forms of anti-war agitation at home and made persistent efforts to reëstablish international coöperation among socialists in the hostile countries. Their efforts led to the peace conferences in 1915 and 1916, at Zimmerwald and Kienthal, Switzerland.

In several of the countries intermediate socialist groups, steering between unchallenging coöperation and uncompromising opposition, strove to mitigate international prejudices and to prevent the war from becoming a purely chauvinist struggle. In Germany, this group included both Kautsky and Bernstein, leaders respectively of the orthodox and revisionist wings of German socialism, and also Hugo Haase, who had been parliamentary leader of the Social Democrats at the outbreak of the war; out of this group there was formed in 1917 the Independent Social Democratic party. In France, the intermediate group was led by Jean Longuet, son-in-law of Marx. In Belgium, Edouard Anseele, member of the International Bureau at the outbreak of the war, maintained in the columns of his newspaper this intermediate position. These men were chiefly concerned that socialists in the belligerent countries should preserve such an independent position in relation to their governments as to make it easier for them to take a stand of protest if the war aims should become aggressive in character. They participated in movements, inaugurated in the neutral countries (by socialists and others), for the formulation of reasonable peace aims. Out of these efforts came the

[6] *American Labor Yearbook,* 1916, p. 187.

Stockholm conference of 1917 and also the London conference of 1918 —with its famous memorandum on war aims, drawn up mainly by members of the Fabian Society and the Labour party of Great Britain.[7] Meanwhile many socialists among the factions supporting the war had become critical of the programs of their governments and were making demands for moderate and negotiated terms of peace. When the Peace Conference met in January, 1919, most socialists in the victorious countries were in definite opposition to their governments, holding that the latter were pursuing predominantly imperialistic aims in the treaty negotiations.

In the early post-war years, there were efforts, in both neutral and belligerent countries, to reconsolidate the socialist movement by reuniting the factions created by the war. The socialist current at that time seemed to be running in three main channels. In a movement to restore the old Second International, socialists from some twenty countries met at Geneva, in July, 1920; and under the leadership of British Labourites (chiefly Fabians), supported by representatives of the majority factions of the German and Swedish Social Democratic parties and the Belgian Socialist party, they adopted a moderate program of practical socialism. The Geneva group sought to define its position in clear differentiation from that of the Bolsheviks. It repudiated violence and dictatorship, asserted its faith in democracy, laid stress upon "the inevitable gradualness" of the process of socialization, rejected confiscation as a method of socialization, and adopted a definition of the term "labor" so as to include independent handicraftsmen and intellectual and managerial workers as well as ordinary wage-earners.

The majority of socialists held aloof from this movement to reëstablish the old International. They believed that the impotence of that body had been proved by its failure either to check the outbreak of the war or to influence the peace negotiations. Moreover, it was controlled by socialists who had forsaken the Marxian tradition by committing themselves after the war to a program of pure reformism. This opposing majority was itself soon split into two sections. On the one hand, there was the group led by the Russian Bolsheviks. Its activities had begun

---

[7] For accounts of the above-mentioned conferences, cf. Emily G. Balch, *Approaches to the Great Settlement*, Ch. VII. The memorandum on war aims demanded the ending of imperialism, approved the principle of self-determination, and urged a limitation of armaments and the establishment of a league of nations and other agencies for peaceable settlement of international disputes and for the promotion of progressive social legislation and international coöperation generally.

in the Zimmerwald movement, which, however, soon lost its pacific character and became a militant attack upon capitalism. It was soon taken over entirely by the Bolsheviks and culminated in the organization in March, 1919, of the "Third International." On the other hand, there were socialists who were dissatisfied with the national patriotism and mild revisionism of the reconstituted Second International and at the same time distrustful of the insurrectionary creed and dictatorial methods of the Bolsheviks. This intermediate group formed at Vienna, in February, 1921, an "International Working Union of Socialist Parties," designed only as a temporary center of action for a reunion of the various factions. The dominant parties in this group were the British Independent Labour party, the French Socialist party (led by Longuet and Renaudel), and the German Independents; they drew support from Swiss and Austrian socialists and from the Mensheviks and Socialist Revolutionaries of Russia.

Thus there were, for a brief period, three international organizations of socialists: the "Right"—the extremely revisionist wing of the old Second International, with headquarters at Geneva; the "Center"—the International Working Union of Socialist Parties, at Vienna; and the "Left"—the Bolshevik or Communist International, at Moscow. Resolutions of these internationals disclosed varying combinations and permutations of old socialist dogmas. The Second International now dropped, the other two retained, the conception of inevitable class warfare, the Third giving shrill emphasis to it. The Second repudiated violence as a method of achieving political power, while the Vienna association recognized it as a supplementary means for getting rid of capitalist control, and the Moscow group put its main faith in violence. The Geneva Right declared for the "community" as the proper source of economic and political power; the Vienna Center looked forward to a "proletarian majority," which, by virtue of the political strength of numbers, would secure control, first of political and then of economic power; the Moscow Left demanded an immediate revolution to establish a "dictatorship of the proletariat." The Geneva group was silent on the issue of national patriotism; the Vienna and Moscow groups explicitly denied all patriotic obligations. The Second International spoke of coöperation with all parties in the work of economic and political reform and of gradual nationalization with compensation; the other two reaffirmed the orthodox policies of political non-coöperation and of nationalization by confiscation.

The activity of the Vienna International reflected the efforts of moderate socialists to reconsolidate the political movement of labor, in order to save it from wreckage on either the rocks of communist violence or the shoals of political opportunism. During 1922, it took the lead in a scheme to unite the three rival sections into a single international, committed to an explicitly socialist but not predominantly revolutionary program and organized in a form that would restore the pre-war autonomy of the several national parties. The Bolsheviks were unwilling to surrender either their revolutionary program or their highly centralized organization. Differences between the Second and Vienna organizations were gradually compromised, and in May, 1923, at a joint congress in Hamburg, with delegates from thirty countries, a new International was formed under the title of "Labor and Socialist International." The practical object of this organization, as stated in its constitution, was "to unify the activities of the affiliated parties, to arrange economic action, and to bring about the entire unification of the international labor and socialist movement on the basis of this constitution." The parties affiliated with this International were reëstablished generally along the pre-war lines, with programs calling for the capture of governmental control through political, preferably peaceful, methods and rejecting both the Bolshevik emphasis upon insurrection and the opportunist alliance with bourgeois parties. Thus, since 1923, there have been two important political international associations of socialists—the Labor and Socialist International and the Third (Communist) International. Each has branches in most of the countries of Europe, as well as in the United States and some of the Latin-American countries.[8]

The recent programs of the national socialist parties and the resolutions of the international congresses are of significance as indications of trends

---

[8] See the following: *Conference of the Executive Committee of the Three Organizations: the Second and Third Internationals and the Vienna Union . . . Berlin . . . 1922* (London, 1922); *Reports and Proceedings . . . of the . . . Labour and Socialist International* (Zurich, 1923, 1925, 1928, 1932).

The L.S.I. has been strongest politically in Sweden, Austria, Belgium, Denmark and Finland; in 1932, the Socialists numbered 45, 44, 41, 35, and 33 percent, respectively, of the members of the parliaments of these countries; in the same year they held between 20 and 25 percent of the parliamentary membership in Switzerland, Luxembourg, The Netherlands, Estonia, Germany, Latvia, France and Czechoslovakia, and a small representation in half a dozen or more other countries. The Communists, besides their 100 percent membership in the Russian government, had 17 percent of the parliamentary seats in the German Republic, slightly over 10 percent in Czechoslovakia and Latvia, and under 5 percent in Sweden, France and a few other countries.

of contemporary socialist thought.[9] The war and its after-effects did not so much create new sorts of division as reveal already existing divergencies in doctrine and sentiment. Socialism is not now, as it has not been in the past, a thoroughly unified body of doctrine that can be defined in a single, coherent set of dogmas or that can find clear expression in a single international organization. Some socialists continue to conceive socialism as a peaceful, national policy; others look upon it almost exclusively as a weapon of class war. This division creates clashes, both as to the proper policies for socialists in a capitalist society and as to the proper structure for a socialist commonwealth. Many men calling themselves socialists find it impossible to associate themselves with any organization of socialists.

LIBERAL TRENDS IN CONTEMPORARY SOCIALISM

The stronger parties in the new Labor and Socialist International have recently shared in controlling their national governments, and their political success has made it more than ever difficult for them to maintain a theoretically consistent program. Their spokesmen become silent on first principles—on the maxims which Marx, Engels, and, in his earlier years, Kautsky, held to be the rigid precepts of socialism. Their socialism becomes less doctrinaire, more conciliatory and experimental. They lose their faith that the world can be saved by impressive manifestoes.

Thus socialists of Western Europe have been taking the lead in the practical, constructive work of maintaining peace in international relations and of preserving democracy and advancing economic reforms in internal governmental policy. At Weimar in 1919, socialists took the lead in drafting the constitution of the new German Republic; one of their leaders became the first president of the Republic; and they subsequently coöperated with bourgeois groups, liberal and conservative, in several coalition cabinets. The program upon which independent and majority socialists joined, in 1922, to form the "United Social Democratic Party of Germany," proclaimed the defense of the Republic to be the chief

---

[9] Cf. Emil Frankel, "Present-day Tendencies in the German Socialist Movement," *Journal of Political Economy*, XXXIII (1925), 60–80; H. B. Usher, "Socialism: Dogmatic and Empirical," *Contemporary Review*, CXXX (1926), 161–167; Émile Vandervelde, "Ten Years of Socialism in Europe," *Foreign Affairs*, III (1925), 556–566.

aim of their union; and the party regarded itself as a chief pillar of the state—a stabilizing, not in any sense a revolutionary, force. The French socialists have modified their pre-war policy of non-coöperation. In the elections of 1924 the Socialist party entered into a coalition with the strongest liberal party in France—the "Radical Socialists"—in order to defeat the "nationalist bloc" of Premier Poincaré and President Millerand, and thereby promote a more conciliatory foreign policy. This coalition resulted in the triumph of a left bloc in the election and caused the resignation of Poincaré and Millerand. Although the socialist leaders declined to accept portfolios in the Herriot cabinet, the party voted, by a large majority, to give their parliamentary support as long as the government continued to pursue a liberal policy in domestic and foreign affairs. In Sweden, Karl Branting (leader, from 1907 until his death in 1925, of the moderately socialist Labor party of that country), held office, in 1919, with three other socialists, in a coalition cabinet of Liberals and Socialists.[10] Otto Bauer and Karl Renner, in Austria; Vandervelde, Huysmans, and Anseele, in Belgium; and socialists in Czechoslovakia, Denmark, Estonia, Finland, Latvia, and Lithuania have held important posts in the cabinets of their countries.

These socialist parties have broadened their programs in order to win the suffrages of trade-unionists, small tradesmen, and middle-class consumers. Their platforms contain the familiar declarations for an ultimate socialization of all wealth, but are concerned mainly with specifying the first steps towards that goal and with describing the piecemeal measures to improve the workers' lot and pare down inequalities of wealth in a capitalist society. They stand for a gradual nationalization of "key" industries essential to the common life of society—mines, railways, electric power, local utilities, and large landholdings. They demand a shortened work-day for workers in private industry; a minimum wage to provide a living income; governmental insurance against the needs of old age, sickness, unemployment, and maternity; and a legal limitation of home rents. For the benefit of the community generally, they advocate public control of banking and credit, an extension of the cultural and benevolent services of government, and a transfer of tax burdens from the necessities of life to capital and its profits, through sharply graduated taxes on incomes and inheritances. This is very much

10 Later he was premier three times (in 1920–1921, 1921–1923, and 1924–1925) in all-socialist cabinets.

like the program of the Fabians, and of contemporary liberals and
"empirical collectivists" in other countries.[11]

The most notable attempts to set forth general theoretical principles,
underlying this moderate and flexible program for post-war socialists,
have been made by Otto Bauer and Karl Kautsky in Austria; Werner
Sombart and Heinrich Stroebel in Germany; Hendrik de Man in Belgium; J. B. Glasier, Ramsay MacDonald, H. N. Brailsford, and
G. D. H. Cole in Great Britain; and Norman Thomas in the United
States.[12] These men declare their goal to be the suppression of a predominantly competitive by a predominantly collectivist system; but
they place studious emphasis upon the gradualness, peaceableness, reasonableness, constructiveness, and efficiency of a socialist movement
towards that goal. Socialism, they say, is to come about through a
natural evolution of society, as Marx explained. Moreover, the evolution,
as Marx also understood, will be one in which "mutations," as well as
minute variations in social forms, occur and in which human will and
intelligence play a significant part in determining how the several
social groups adjust themselves to these substantial social changes.
They regard other Marxian dogmas, however, as misrepresentative both
of human motives and of social conditions. His program, they say,
relying principally upon economic motives and class antagonisms and
looking forward to an exclusively proletarian conquest of political power,
followed by a general socialization of industrial property, is an artificial simplification of the pressing problem of finding an efficient, stable,

---

[11] Cf. *supra*, pp. 98–107, and *infra*, Ch. XX.
Some moderate socialists in England and the United States have advocated a
rapid and radical means for redistributing wealth and transforming a capitalist into
a socialist régime. It is the "capital levy"—a tax, running up to a rate of over 50
per cent on large fortunes, laid, once for all, on the net total wealth of individuals,
with exemptions high enough to avoid, on the one hand, severe changes in living
standards for any but the most spendthrifty of existing property-owners and, on
the other hand, the practical difficulties of administering a levy on small fortunes;
the tax to be paid in instalments and in the form of cash, governmental securities
(to be immediately retired), or other approved securities (to be either sold on the
open market or held as a means of gaining control of the industries concerned).
Cf. Hugh Dalton, *The Capital Levy Explained* (1923); Norman Thomas, *The Socialist Cure for a Sick Society* (1932).
[12] For titles of the works of these and other theoretical spokesmen for contemporary revisionist socialism, see the list on pp. 143–144, *infra*. See also the contemporary socialist periodicals, especially the following: the *New Leader*, a weekly
published in London and owned by the Independent Labour party; the *Socialist
Review*, a monthly published also in London; *Die Gesellschaft*, a Berlin monthly,
edited by Dr. Rudolf Hilferding; *La nouvelle revue socialiste*, a Paris monthly
founded in 1925 and edited by Jean Longuet.

and morally satisfying adjustment of human relations in the actual conditions of contemporary society. Their program is one of "socialism by stages": one step at a time; no new step to be taken until the preceding step has been approved by practical results; each advance to be achieved with the least possible upsetting of established institutions, and with public assent; the whole process to be in the interest not of any one class but of all. Let socialization start with those services from which the competitive and experimental features have largely disappeared and which are already subject to extensive control by public authority. As experience is gained in these fields, let socialization be extended further. There must be no violent revolution and no actual confiscation of property. Kautsky is willing to allow a reasonable payment "to those who have kept their undertakings in a state of efficiency." He suggests that the money to be paid for the properties taken over by government should be raised from taxes on large incomes and inheritances and that payments to the former owners should be in the form of public bonds bearing interest equal in total amount "to the total former profits of the socialized undertakings." [13]

Both practical and theoretical socialists, outside of Russia, have become not only more moderate but also more eclectic in their programs. They have borrowed policies both from allied theoretical systems, such as guild socialism and syndicalism, and from various practical schemes for a joint control of industry by workers and owners.[14] Their plans for public ownership now attempt to distinguish political and economic aspects of the problem and to differentiate the location of administrative direction from that of ownership. They admit that centralized, bureaucratic administration is, in many cases, unsuited to the present stage of industrial development. Industries, they say, are to be socialized rather than nationalized. "Nobody," says Otto Bauer, "manages industrial undertakings worse than the state. For this reason we Social Democrats have never advocated the nationalization of industry, but always its socialization." [15] Recent socialist schemes for the administration of state-owned enterprises give an important place to trade-unions and professional associations, at least to the extent of inviting their coöperation by way of complaint and suggestion. Some of the plans

---

[13] Karl Kautsky, *The Labour Revolution* (1925), pp. 141, 155. Cf. H. W. Laidler, *History of Socialist Thought*, pp. 589–590.

[14] Cf. *infra*, Ch. VIII and Ch. IX.

[15] *Weg zum Sozialismus* (1921), p. 10. Cf. Norman Thomas, *America's Way Out* (1931), Ch. X.

go further and provide specifically for semi-autonomous boards for the management of state-owned enterprises. The boards are to be made up in such manner as to prevent them from serving the special interests or reflecting the prejudices of any limited group, whether of bureaucrats, consumers, producers, or proletarians. Thus an industry that is to be thoroughly "nationalized" would be put under the management of a board representing the following major groups, each having its legitimate and distinctive interest in the fair and efficient operation of the enterprise: all those who work in the enterprise—manual laborers, technicians, and managers; those who consume the products or directly use the services of the enterprise; and the government, as guardian of the interests of the community as a whole.[16] However, although these socialist schemes assign to the composite boards a considerable range of initiative and discretion in selecting shop officials and business managers, regulating working conditions, and fixing wages and prices, and although they accord to the community or government only a minority voice in the boards, they do not set up a system of syndicalism or of industrial self-government. For each board obtains its powers only by delegation from organs of the state, and these central political bodies define the social ends that are to be served by the boards and the general standards that are to be maintained in prices and wages; they reserve also the authority to modify or revoke any of the delegated powers. The contemporary socialist remains a state socialist.

In their conception of the democratic structure and liberal aims of the socialist state, these moderate socialists are carrying forward generally the revisionist trend of pre-war socialism; and their program of state-ownership hardly differs from that of the democratic "liberal" of to-day.[17] Perhaps their most significant contribution to socialist doctrine is to be found in their critical discussion of the psychological and ethical assumptions they hold to be dominant in both traditional individualism and orthodox Marxism.

The classical economic doctrine of *laisser-faire* is wrong, they maintain, both in its hypothesis that economic self-interest can be served adequately by the competing efforts of individuals and in its belief that a satisfaction of that interest satisfies the most basic impulses of human nature and supplies the motives that move man to his noblest and most useful endeavors. Everyday experience refutes the assumption that

---

[16] Heinrich Stroebel, *Sozialisierung—Ihre Wege und Voraussetzungen* (1921).
[17] See *infra,* Ch. XX.

only the prospect of unlimited personal gain in material possessions is adequate to hold men to the persistent and difficult labors necessary for supplying the needs of society. Scientists, inventors, explorers, artists, physicians, teachers, soldiers, statesmen, bankers, business entrepreneurs, willingly submit themselves to toils and deprivations that bring them little in the way of added means of physical comfort and security for themselves or their dependents; they work for other rewards—fame, a good conscience, self-respect, self-expression, the satisfaction of some creative impulse, or the fulfilment of a sympathetic desire to relieve others from discomfort or oppression.[18]

Moreover, the contemporary socialist argument proceeds, everyday experience shows not only that other motives than economic self-interest control the conduct of normal men but also that, even when men seek their own economic benefit, they pursue collectivist methods. The creed of economic individualism fails practically in serving its own ends. Private capitalists coöperate rather than compete among themselves, and they appeal for outside aid. They combine their properties into great trusts, which, if efficiently managed and not overcapitalized, yield definite advantages by reducing overhead costs and eliminating other wastes of competition; but these benefits go, under private ownership, mainly to the capitalists and hardly at all to the workers or to the community whose needs and virtues make the advantages ample and secure. Employers not only unite in arrangements that put them in position to exploit wage-earners and consumers but they also call upon the government for help—demanding subsidies, tariffs, and other public aids for the protection and enlargement of their profits, at home and abroad. Thus under the domination of a so-called creed of *laisser-faire* we have a property-owners' collectivism, protected and encouraged by the intervention of the state.[19]

Marxism, these socialists hold, is superior to capitalism in that it shapes its theory and program in reference to the material needs of a relatively large proportion of the members of the community. But it is still too narrow in its interpretation of human interests and motives. Accordingly, Marx was wrong, both in his prophecy of the actual course of social change and in his exposition of the underlying factors of change. The concentration of wealth has not proceeded to the extent he predicted;

[18] Cf. H. N. Brailsford, *Socialism for Today* (1925), Ch. XII.
[19] Cf. *infra* Ch. XX.

and where there has been concentration, it has not produced the consequences he expected. Small owners do not disappear from the capitalist system; and large owners do not increasingly exploit their employes. Many employers become less hostile to high wages and to improved conditions of labor and even admit a limited participation by the workers in the management of industry. In these and other ways, capitalism socializes itself constructively and positively, developing into socialism through a process not of increasing opposition but of increasing adaptation to the conditions that show its own inadequacy and inequity. If society is now on a higher plane—industrially and morally —than it was a century ago, if we are making any advance towards more humane conditions of living for ordinary men, the change has come about principally through the progressive application of psychological and moral principles opposed both to Marxian socialism and classical individualism. But the progress has been needlessly slow. There is no excuse for "poverty and unemployment in the midst of potential plenty."

What we need then, according to these socialists, is a new psychology and ethics of socialism. The basic error of Marxism is in its over-emphasis on economic determinism. Although economic conditions have their influence, other factors have profound effects in determining the culture, philosophy, and politics of an age. The great social and political transformations of the past did not arise out of conflicts of material interests alone. Men have fought as violently over differences in religious doctrine as over their conflicting economic claims. Racial, cultural, and religious factors have competed with, or transformed, or even overcome, economic factors in determining the alliances and enmities between nations. Economic affiliations and antagonisms cannot explain the opposition between Ulster and South Ireland, or the rivalries among the Balkan states, or the support accorded by majorities of wage-earners to their several governments in the World War. Much of a man's political conduct is determined by his nationalist instincts or habits, or by his religious feelings, or by his pride of social position, or by his neighborhood prejudices, or by his sense of fair play. In all phases of the life of men in society, there is action and reaction: economic conditions produce effects in moral, religious, and political creeds and the forms of social organization; but these latter act upon, even when they are adapting themselves to, the economic conditions.

This psychological and ethical criticism of the Marxian doctrine has been set forth most explicitly and elaborately by the Belgian social-ist, Hendrik de Man.[20] His new conception of socialism, de Man ex-plains, grew largely out of his reflections on his own experiences in the pre-war labor movement in Belgium, where he had been a propa-gandist of Marxism. That experience "rubbed the corners off" his social-ist orthodoxy, by showing him that working-men have no overwhelming sense of a solidarity of interest or opinion with other working-men who make up some world-wide or nation-wide class of workers. They act normally under the pressure of the immediate needs of self-preservation. They are capable of acting, when occasions present themselves, under the impulsion of a sense of wider moral and spiritual ends to be served by their lives—provided only that this higher aim is set effectively in their moral consciousness; and this latter is the task of the social phi-losopher. The outbreak of the World War, de Man avers, shook his Marxist faith to its foundations. How could millions of socialists abandon their alleged working-men's class consciousness, as well as their anti-militarism and internationalism, and feel it their duty to take up arms against their fellows? The answer is that Marxism supplied them with no idealistic appeal strong enough to overcome either their concern for the immediate security of themselves and their dependents nor their somewhat broader sentiments of national solidarity. "Marxism failed to disclose to socialists the way that could lead them to fulfill their duty to humanity." [21]

Marx, de Man explains, was a victim of the social philosophy of his time. He accepted its narrow rationalism and attempted to transfer the principles of mechanical causality from the physical to the moral and social world. Like the classical economists and biological sociologists, he assumed that a rational concern for one's own welfare supplied the sole, or most habitual, guide to human conduct. As the economists explained the competitive industrial system, so Marx explained his socialist system, on the basis of this assumption. Common economic interests, he said, made working-men a social class, and the class conflict that arose from the opposite interests of workers and owners supplied the sole reason for a socialist movement and the sole guide for its policy. But economic in-terests, de Man maintains, cannot create a working-men's class or sustain a working-men's socialist movement. There is no common bond of

[20] See especially his *Zur Psychologie des Sozialismus* (1926). There was a revised edition in 1927, and the work has been translated into French—*Au delà du Marx-isme* (1927), and into English—*The Psychology of Socialism* (1929).
[21] *Zur Psychologie des Sozialismus*, Preface.

economic interest that completely unites the workers and puts them persistently in opposition to property-owners. On the contrary, economic considerations often create divisions among wage-earners and unite them with their employers. As vendors of labor, working-men are competitors: they compete individually among themselves for the same jobs; group rivalries range skilled against unskilled workers, journeymen against immigrant laborers, and employers and employes combine in arrangements to maintain high profits and high wages. Economic motives lead workers to forsake their fellows. They aspire to rise to the ranks of the petty bourgeoisie, and so they become patriotic. When, on the other hand, they coöperate in an aggressive movement against capitalism they do so less under the impulsion of economic conditions than from their common moral revulsion against a system that seems to them to be unjust and ugly.

Socialism, de Man acknowledges, does have certain immediate economic objectives. There is a moral justification for the Marxian economic philosophy of social evolution and even for the feelings of violent envy and hate his creed of class struggle engenders. The Marxian doctrine, although far below the level of the Christian creed of universal brotherhood and benevolence, is on a higher plane than the physical submissiveness and spiritual degradation to which a complacent individualism holds the workers. Marx's bitter appeal to the material interests of the workers did arouse them to sporadic threats of violence which led to some improvement in their social status. "The resentment of a class has been an indispensable means of procuring for millions of men better and healthier conditions of living, and, by reducing their working hours, new possibilities of cultural enjoyment." [22] The practical service of socialism is to improve the material welfare of the masses, to relieve them from the fear of hunger and unemployment and thus make them free and safe in yielding to nobler moral impulses and devoting their efforts to intellectual satisfactions. "Ordinary mortals must have money before they can despise it or, at any rate, free themselves from obsession with it. The masses must attain a certain minimum of physical well-being before they can be expected to renounce their belief in the identity of wealth and happiness." [23]

Thus, according to de Man, the underlying defect of Marxism is not that it recognized the importance of material factors but that it stops

[22] *Zur Psychologie des Sozialismus,* p. 371.
[23] *Ibid.,* p. 373.

with the satisfaction of the economic motive. "The most tragic feature of the destiny of the working masses is not their material poverty in itself; it is that this poverty condemns them to an impoverishment of the spirit. Anxiety about a job, social dependency, inhibition of their finest constructive impulses by joyless and undignified labor; it is these things I mean when I speak of the inhibition of higher wants by the non-satisfaction of lower wants." [24] Marxism believes that a mere transformation of the economic institutions under which these conditions exist is sufficient in itself to elevate the moral and cultural plane of living for ordinary men. But when the workers raise themselves to a ruling position in society and then use their political power to dispossess existing property-owners, what guarantee is there that they will not administer the public property selfishly, the workers of one country ignoring the interests of workers in other parts of the world, or one group in control of government exploiting other groups? There is no change in principle, in passing from private to public ownership or from control by "laborers" to control by "owners," unless the change is accompanied by a transformation in the springs of human conduct. If socialism is to be something radically different from private capitalism, it must be revolutionary not in the sense that it pursues disorderly or insurrectionary methods but in the sense that it is a movement towards a society that acts according to moral and psychological principles fundamentally antagonistic to the principles operative in an existing capitalist society. This sort of socialism is scientific, in the sense that it is founded upon a realistic analysis of human impulses and motives and of the forms of their expression; it considers the actual consequences that flow from the expression of the several impulses, and thereby shows how lower can be overcome by higher motives that lead to permanent human satisfactions. It is based upon a "psychological hypothesis . . . that human motives are alterable, in their ethical quality, through a sublimation of the baser instincts." [25]

This idea that socialism stands on a higher psychological and ethical plane than capitalism is implicit in most statements of socialist doctrine to-day. The chief values of a socialist system are found in the better opportunities it will afford ordinary men for exercising their creative faculties and for acting in conformity to their sense of justice and fair play. The socialists of Western Europe and the United States retain a

---

[24] *Zur Psychologie des Sozialismus,* p. 382.
[25] *Ibid.,* p. 384.

limited place for the class struggle, by admitting the necessity for organized activity of working-men's groups in self-defense against employers who seek to impose oppressive conditions of labor upon them.
They make their political appeal, however, to all sections of the people.
The leaders speak not of class war and revolution but of liberty and fraternity. Socialism, they maintain, must be "rooted in political democracy"
and kept dependent upon majority consent. Socialism is to be achieved not
through struggle "for power between vested and unvested interests,"
but through the "efforts of the whole life of society for freedom."
Socialists will gain power "by constitutional means," "without bloodshed"; and they will govern in strict accord with public opinion. Their
rule "will be entirely beneficent"; their dealings "with high and low,
rich and poor, will be marked with broad-minded toleration and equity."
The task of socialism is to make the democratic philosophy of "the
worth and dignity of man" a working fact.[26]

Thus most of the socialist leaders outside of Russia now discard or
greatly discount the basic dogmas of Marx. Following the more academic
theorists, they generally reject his economic interpretation of history
and his vision of the socialist revolution. The theoretical critics of Marx
easily find defects in all parts of his doctrinal system.[27] But to refute
the strict rational validity of a theory does not prove that it has not
left permanent and significant influences upon subsequent thought and
practice. We no longer accept the abstract principles of democracy laid
down in Rousseau's *Social Contract* and the American and French
Declarations of the eighteenth century; we consider their postulates of
human equality and of government by consent to be entirely inadequate
as representations of actual human traits or of the actual ways in which
men set up and operate their political institutions. At the same time, we
recognize the profound influence which these dogmas have exerted upon
later forms of political discussion and constitutional change. Economists
have thrown overboard the labor theory of value, but they acknowledge
that there are valid elements in Marx's discussions of surplus value and

[26] Sidney Webb, "The Labour Party on the Threshold," Fabian Tract no. 207,
the Chairman's address at the annual conference of the Labour Party, 1923; J
Ramsay MacDonald, *A Policy for the Labour Party* (1920); J. H. Thomas, *When
Labour Rules* (1921); Norman Thomas, *America's Way Out* (1931).
[27] The following works contain good examples of adverse, but fair, conservative criticism of Marxian doctrines: O. D. Skelton, *Socialism: a Critical Analysis*
(1911); F. R. Salter, *Karl Marx and Modern Socialism* (1921); Rudolf Eucken,
Socialism: An Analysis, translated by Joseph McCabe (1921).

that he helped to show the defects in the classical doctrine of an economic order operating on assumptions of subsistence wages and unregulated competitive profits. Philosophers of history hold that Marx attributed too much weight to economic factors, but admit that his writings helped to create an understanding of the influences which the modern development of industry has exerted upon the forms and policies of social organization and upon prevailing criteria of social justice. The sociologists reject Marx's too precise identification of economic status and social class, but agree that economic conditions play a leading part in determining the issues and alignments of social conflicts and political rivalries. The political scientist believes that the Marxian conception of the socialist state—established by a proletarian revolution, controlled by manual workers, and operating all the essential industries—sets a goal that stands no chance of realization in any period that we can now foresee; but they hold also that the Marxian forecast has been realized in some of the actual trends in economic life—through our elaborate fabric of industrial legislation; our effective organization of skilled labor for collective bargaining; and our direct governmental provision of vast social services in the fields of education, highways, intercommunication, sanitation, and the supply of local utilities. If we do not have collective and public enterprise in the form and extent that Marx advocated and prophesied, we do have more of it than the creed of *laisser-faire* can account for; and our private or individual enterprise is of a variously limited and diluted sort. Marx's writings and the organized workingman's movement he led have been important factors in the spread of ideas that have been extensively applied during the last seventy-five years. "If one were to pick out the half-dozen men who most profoundly moved the world from the middle of the nineteenth century," said a leading British journal recently, "Marx would have to be one of them." [28]

POST-WAR SOCIALISTS OF THE LEFT

The influence of Marx's writings and activities, though it extends widely, is still most obvious within the socialist movement. Even in regions where the theoretical spokesmen and parliamentary leaders of the larger socialist groups attempt to discard or ignore his major doctrinal tenets, the actual movement of socialism is somewhat closely

[28] *Manchester Guardian Weekly*, April 8, 1926.

bound to his creed. The Marxian slogans continue to arouse the emotions and aspirations of millions of workers organized in the socialist parties of the Western countries; his doctrines seem to them to explain the hardships they suffer unjustly and unnecessarily and to embody the most hopeful remedies. Even the reformist leaders and theorists accept, more or less vaguely, the essential Marxian propositions: that the system of private capitalism creates economic differences which lead inevitably to class antagonisms; that the ownership of capital tends, in so far as it is not restricted by law, to become more concentrated and more exploitative of the workers; and that the only secure remedy is a general socialization of capital, to be achieved through the acquisition of political supremacy by the workers organized into national political parties.

Although most of the Western socialist leaders propose slow and pacific means for this political transition from capitalism to socialism and regard the latter stage as an inevitable fulfilment of democracy, there are still the more "orthodox" socialists who insist upon the necessity of holding on to the revolutionary aspects of Marxism. They repudiate the policy of interclass collaboration and would separate themselves from those who are interested in democracy as sufficient in itself. Thus certain socialists in Germany criticized the revolution of 1918 as a mere "popular" movement, aiming at a more comfortable life within the framework of the capitalist system; it was, they said, a political revolution, broadening slightly the basis of popular control, but not a social revolution designed to supplant a capitalists' by a working-men's organization of economic relations.[29] The Independent Labour party of Great Britain, at its Easter conference of 1933 (shortly after the Nazi accession to power and the complete suppression of the German socialist party—oldest and, outside Russia, largest of all the socialist parties of the world), renounced its faith that socialism could be achieved through democracy, proposed coöperation (though not affiliation) with the British Communist party and the Third International, and committed itself (somewhat vaguely) to the policy of revolutionary socialism. Certain socialist writers have pointed to the post-war reactionary dictatorships in Europe as evidences of the breakdown, for socialist purposes, of traditional parliamentary methods and as warnings that violence and illegality may be the inevitable weapons of socialists, if existing rulers prevent all radical economic change and practice or tolerate

[29] See Rosa Luxemburg, *Die Krise der Sozialdemokratie* (1919).

violent and illegal measures to check the advent of socialism.[30] Socialists of this sort are anxious to rid themselves of the taint of "liberalism" and to defend themselves from the taunt that they are weary of heroic efforts. The differentiation between these left-wing socialists and the still further left-ward Russian Communists consists chiefly in the less exclusive emphasis the former place upon the idea of an immediate and bloody seizure of autocratic governmental power by the workers. They express a more definite preference for the road of reason and discussion and retain some hope that the present wielders of political and economic power will allow the inevitable march to socialism to proceed on that road. Their position is that, although abrupt and fundamental social changes are necessary and are to be achieved by the efforts of workers ready to act without the active coöperation of other groups, violence and dictatorship are methods only of last resort, to be employed occasionally and temporarily and only when capitalists resort first to those weapons.

The Socialists of the Third International make no such reservations. Socialism, they say, must be definitely and constantly identified with a revolutionary struggle of a working-class for a society of free workers. The socialist's outlook must be one of persistent hostility to the capitalists and their economic system; his whole life should be colored by this outlook. Socialism cannot be advanced except upon the assumption that it is irreconcilable with all other social creeds. The workers, therefore, must rely principally upon force for installing themselves in power and upon governmental censorship, propaganda, and coercion for exercising thenceforth their authority autocratically until they have destroyed the last remnants of capitalism.

SELECT BIBLIOGRAPHY

GENERAL REVIEWS OF SOCIALIST THOUGHT AND PRACTICE SINCE 1914

Balch, Emily, *Approaches to the Great Settlement* (New York, 1918).
Boudin, Louis B., *Socialism and War* (New York, 1916).
Dutt, R. Palme, *The Two Internationals* (London, 1920).
"Excerpts from Socialist War Manifestoes," *Intercollegiate Socialist,* III (1914), 12–15.
Frankel, Emil, "Present-day Tendencies in the German Socialist Movement," *Journal of Political Economy,* XXXIII (1925), 60–80.

---

[30] See Harold J. Laski, *Democracy in Crisis* (1933), especially Ch. IV.

Humphrey, A. W., *International Socialism and the War* (London, 1915).

James, E., "Un nouveau théoricien du socialisme: Henri de Man," *Revue de métaphysique et de morale*, XXXVI (1929), 113–144.

Laidler, H. W., "The European War and Socialism," *Intercollegiate Socialist*, III (1914), 3–11.

——————, *History of Socialist Thought* (New York, 1927), Ch. XXIX.

Lorwin, Lewis L., *Labor and Internationalism* (New York, 1929).

Maxe, Jean, *De Zimmerwald au bolchévisme* (Paris, 1920).

Reports and Proceedings . . . of the . . . Congress of the Labour and Socialist International (Zurich, 1923, 1925, 1928, 1932).

Rockow, Lewis, *Contemporary Political Thought in England* (New York, 1925), Ch. V.

Stroebel, Heinrich, *The German Revolution and After,* translated by H. J. Stenning (London, n.d.)

Trachtenberg, Alexander, *The American Socialists and the War: a Documentary History of the Attitude of the Socialist Party toward War and Militarism since the Outbreak of the Great War* (New York, 1917).

Usher, H. B., "Socialism: Dogmatic and Empirical," *Contemporary Review*, CXXX (1926), 161–167.

Vandervelde, Émile, "Ten Years of Socialism in Europe," *Foreign Affairs*, III (1925), 556–566.

Walling, W. E., *The Socialists and the War: a Documentary Statement of the Position of the Socialists of All Countries, with Special Reference to Their Peace Policy, Including a Summary of the Revolutionary State Socialist Measures Adopted by the Governments at War* (New York, 1915), Pt. II.

Walling, W. E. and Others, *The Socialism of To-day* (New York, 1916).

WORKS IN CONTEMPORARY SOCIALIST THEORY (OUTSIDE RUSSIA)

Bauer, Otto, *Der Weg zum Sozialismus* (Vienna, 1919, twelfth ed., 1921).

Benedict, Bertram, *The Larger Socialism* (New York, 1921).

Bernstein, Eduard, *Die deutsche Revolution: ihre Ursprung, ihr Verlauf, und ihr Werk* (Berlin, 1921).

Brailsford, H. N., *Socialism for Today* (London, 1925).

Cole, G. D. H., *A Guide Through World Chaos* (New York, 1932).

Dalton, Hugh, *The Capital Levy Explained* (London, 1923).

De Man, Hendrik, *Zur Psychologie des Sozialismus* (Jena, 1926).

——————, *The Psychology of Socialism,* translated from second German edition by Eden and Cedar Paul (New York, 1927).

Glasier, J. B., *The Meaning of Socialism* (Manchester, 1919; New York, 1920).

Greiling, W., *Marxismus und Sozialisierungs-theorie* (Berlin, 1923).

Grottkopp, Wilhelm, "Sozialismus und Wirklichkeit," *Archiv für Sozialwissenschaft und sozial Politik*, LVI (1926), 789–798.

Hillquit, Morris, "Marxism Essentially Evolutionary," *Current History*, XXIX (1928), 29–35.

Kautsky, Karl, *The Labour Revolution*, translated by H. J. Stenning (London, 1925).

Korsch, Karl, *Marxismus und Philosophie* (Leipsic, 1923).

Laidler, H. W., *Socialism in Thought and Action* (New York, 1920).

Laski, Harold J., *Democracy in Crisis* (Chapel Hill, N. C., 1933).

Leichter, Otto, *Die Wirtschaftsrechnung in der sozialistischen Gesellschaft* (Vienna, 1923).

Luxemburg, Rosa, *Die Krise der Sozial-demokratie* (Berlin, 1919).

MacDonald, J. Ramsay, *Socialism: Critical and Constructive* (London, 1921).

——————, *A Policy for the Labour Party* (London, 1920).

Neurath, Otto, *Wesen und Weg zur Sozialisierung* (Munich, 1919).

Snowden, Philip, *Labour and National Finance* (London, 1920).

Sombart, Werner, *Der proletarische Sozialismus* (Jena, 1924).

Stroebel, Heinrich, *Sozialisierung: ihre Wege und Voraussetzungen* (Berlin, 1921).

——————, *Socialism in Theory and Practice*, translated by H. J. Stenning (London, 1922).

Thomas, J. H., *When Labour Rules* (London, 1921).

Thomas, Norman, *America's Way Out: a Program for Democracy* (New York, 1931).

——————, *The Socialist Cure for a Sick Society* (New York, 1932).

Webb, Sidney and Beatrice, *A Constitution for the Socialist Commonwealth of Great Britain* (London, 1920; New York, 1921).

——————, *The Decay of Capitalist Civilization* (New York, 1923).

CONTEMPORARY CRITICISM OF SOCIALIST THEORY

Boucke, O. F., *The Limits of Socialism* (New York, 1920).

Carver, Thomas N., "The Fundamental Error of Marxism," *Current History*, XXIX (1928), 18–23.

Corbett, J., "Labour and the Gradualists," *Fortnightly Review*, CXXII (1924), 797–807.

Eucken, Rudolf, *Der Sozialismus und seine Lebensgestaltung* (Berlin, 1920).

——————, *Socialism: an Analysis*, translated by Joseph McCabe (London, 1921).

Gough, George W., *The Economic Consequences of Socialism* (London, 1926).

Hearnshaw, F. J. C., *A Survey of Socialism* (London, 1928), Chs. IX–X.

Joseph, H. W. B., *The Labour Theory of Value and Karl Marx* (London, 1923).

Laski, H. J., "The Value and Defects of Marxist Philosophy," *Current History*, XXIX (1928), 23–29.

Mises, Ludwig, "Neue Beiträge zum Problem der sozialistischen Wirtchaftsrechnung," *Archiv für Sozialwissenschaft und Sozialpolitik*, Vol. LI (1924).

Muhs, Karl, *Anti-Marx: Betrachtungen über der inneren Aufbau der Marxschen Oekonomik: Bd. I. Der Produktionsprozess des Kapitals* (Jena, 1927).

Nicholson, J. Shield, *The Revival of Marxism* (New York, 1920).

Salter, F. R., *Karl Marx and Modern Socialism* (London, 1921).

Skelton, O. D., *Socialism: a Critical Analysis* (Boston and New York, 1911).

Scott, John W., *Karl Marx and Value* (London, 1920).

Wells, H. G., *The World of William Clissold*, 3 vols. (London, 1926), I, pp. 163 ff.

CHAPTER VI

THE SOCIALISTS OF SOVIET RUSSIA

ORIGINS AND POLICY

SOME writers have suggested that the present order in Russia is to be explained mainly as the product of the whole of Russian history and only incidentally as an attempt to apply the revolutionary doctrines of Marx. The Communist rulers, they say, carry on an old tradition of governmental absolutism, reproducing in somewhat different forms a policy of espionage and coercion begun by the Tartar rulers of the fourteenth century, revived by Ivan the Terrible in the sixteenth century, and maintained generally by the Romanov tsars from the early seventeenth century on. These writers recognize that the existing despotism is applied for basically different ends; but Russian history, they say, supplies an explanation for this also; for the extreme restraint that the present working-men's régime imposes upon the liberties of all who seek private wealth is but the natural reaction against the policy of the old despotism, which served only the interests of property-owners and held down to the lowest possible level of human existence the masses whose arduous labors made possible the private wealth. Again—the established church of Russia generally supported the callous and unenlightened régime of the tsardom and at times even encouraged the harsh suppression of protests against it; so, it is said, the Russian Communists of to-day derive their hostility to religion from the persistent indifference of the church to the temporal hardships of the common men, for whose welfare the present rulers maintain their socialist autocracy. These are legitimate and plausible hypotheses, as general explanations of the present order; but they have not been and probably cannot be specifically verified by any searching of records far back into Russian history. The immediate origins of the Soviet régime have been authentically set forth, however, by a number of competent writers; and their accounts can be summarized briefly in the following pages.[1]

[1] For historical and descriptive accounts of Russia from the early nineteenth century to the revolution of February–March, 1917, see the list on pp. 184–185.

There is no doubt that the men who have ruled Russia since November, 1917, are professed disciples of Marx. A Marxian socialist party had been organized in Russia two decades earlier. Like the socialist parties of other countries, it addressed itself principally to the problems of an urban proletariat. Its most influential leaders, however, understood that no socialists could govern Russia unless they made the agricultural workers (constituting four fifths of the population of Russia) their allies, or at least their acquiescent followers. Even Trotsky—bitterly opposed, in recent years, to any substantial concessions to the peasants—appears to acknowledge that the radical Marxian group would not have come into power in 1917 if either the tsardom or the provisional government that superseded it had been able to solve the peasant problem.[2]

Most of the peasants were, until the reforms of the seventh decade of the nineteenth century, serfs—bound to the soil, subject to the disciplinary powers of the landowners, and, though possessing small holdings in their own right, legally unable to sell or otherwise transfer their holdings; pursuing crude methods of cultivation, they obtained with difficulty the bare means of subsistence. There were other features of centralization and oppression in the traditional order. The legal powers of the tsar were absolute; actual government was in the hands of small groups of the nobility and upper bureaucracy supporting the tsar; and there were the familiar methods and institutions of autocratic government: centrally appointed and controlled administrative officers throughout the country; a summary and corrupt administration of justice; and a secret police, clothed with arbitrary and inquisitorial powers and assisted by *agents provocateurs,* for the detection of political offenders. There was, finally, no representative government, no public education, and relatively little freedom of inquiry in political matters.

Occasionally, for several centuries past, the peasants, provoked by some immediate or unusual grievance, engaged in a local uprising; but they were too ignorant and inexperienced and too widely dispersed for any effective revolt. From the later years of the eighteenth century on there was a continuous current of intellectual protest, coming generally from persons outside the peasant class—from priests and university teachers and occasionally merchants and even army officers. Expressions of sympathy for the peasants appear in the contemporary Rus-

[2] See his *History of the Russian Revolution,* I (1932), Chs. I, III, IX, and XX.

sian literature, as in the poems of Alexander Pushkin in the early nineteenth century and in the novels of Turgenev and others later in the
century.[3] Now and then there were abortive attempts at insurrection by
the middle-class reformers, as in the famous mutinies of December,
1825. Sometimes the tsars themselves, as Catherine II (1762–1796) and
Alexander I (1801–1825),[4] put forth schemes for political or cultural reforms, to be achieved by governmental *fiat;* but the projects that were
put into effect were narrowly limited in scope, or they were soon revoked
if they seriously threatened any vested interests.

In the middle of the nineteenth century there were, for a while, pros-
pects that Russia might fall in with the liberal movements of the Western world. Notable reforms were put into operation by Alexander II
(1855–1881), with the support of influential members of the nobility.
These men had come to recognize some of the inhumanity of the Russian social order. They were becoming aware also that the system of
serfdom was, under existing commercial and industrial conditions, economically unprofitable and that other antiquated institutions in Russia
were holding her back in her competition, in war and peace, with the
more progressive nations of the West. In the first decade of Alexander's
reign, the serfs were freed from the arbitrary powers of the landlords,
made owners of the communal lands, and given small individual allotments; representative assemblies—the *zemstvos*—were set up in the
provinces and empowered to provide roads, schools, and experimental
farms, and to serve other local industrial and cultural needs; there was
an extensive reorganization of the courts—abolishing the secret inquisitorial system in criminal trials and removing corruption from the
courts; and greater freedom was accorded to the press. These measures,
however, produced in fact little or no substantial change in the autocratic structure of the government or in the aristocratic character of the
whole economic and social order. The zemstvos were undemocratic in
composition and were permitted to exercise no really deliberative powers;
although the administration of justice remained on a definitely higher
plane, summary methods still prevailed for the trial of political offenses;
and political censorship and espionage reappeared in full vigor.

Particularly significant was the disillusionment over the consequences
of the "emancipation" of the serfs. The new land regulations gave the

[3] See Peter Kropotkin, *Russian Literature: Ideals and Realities* (second ed., 1916).

[4] See, e.g., Georges Vernadsky, *La chute constitutionelle de l'empire russe de l'an 1820* (1925), traduit du russe par Serge Oldenbourg (1933).

peasant little opportunity to earn a comfortable living and left him bereft of any stimulus to enterprise. His possession could be transferred to others against his will and without compensation for the money or labor he had put into improvements; he was subject, not only to heavy redemption payments for his allotment, but also to high land, capitation, and other taxes; in most cases the area assigned to his use was so inadequate that he rented additional land at a price which he could pay only by working on the lands of his former landlord; his earnings from both allotted and rented lands were frequently so small that he had to hire himself, and perhaps his wife and children, in the home or fields of the landlord; and he was generally without any real instruction in improved methods of cultivation. Thus the peasants, although freed from legal serfdom, remained in a condition of economic and social bondage, unable to realize their yearnings for comfort and independence.

In the last quarter of the century the movements for reform or revolt were extensive and varied. Some of the efforts were of a very visionary sort, projecting schemes out of actual relation to the needs of the Russian masses. Young intellectual noblemen, having traveled and studied in Western Europe, returned to Russia full of remorse for oppressive conditions for which they considered their own families to be responsible and offered vague suggestions for putting into application at home the new ideas of freedom and progress they had learned in the West. There were also more practical movements, and these, before the end of the century, fell into three main currents: a middle-class movement for liberal constitutional reform; a revolutionary agrarian movement for a socialism built on Russian lines but to be achieved by acts of terrorism against landowners and governmental agents; and a Marxian, industrial-socialist, movement, which early in the twentieth century split into right and left wings.

The first of the practical movements was led chiefly by intellectuals of the liberal professions and provincial gentry and drew support from educated men generally. This group sought orderly steps towards constitutional monarchy and parliamentary government on the Western model; and they endeavored meanwhile to persuade the existing authorities to bring about a juster and more practical settlement of the land question and a larger measure of local self-government. The leaders of this group carried on their discussion and action chiefly in the zemstvos. Early in the twentieth century they formed themselves into a Constitutional Democratic party, which took the leading part in the deliberations of the national parliaments set up by the reforms of 1905, and again in the provisional government following the overthrow of the tsardom in the revolution of March, 1917.

The second group, known as the "populists" (*narodniki*), appealed directly to the peasants, who were to be made economically and socially dominant in Russia through a development of traditional Russian institutions; they proposed to extend the territorial scope and enlarge the authority of the rural village (*mir*) in a common ownership of the land and to restore the old handicraft association (*artel*) as the form of organization for industrial administration; the emancipation of the masses, they believed, would come about through a distinctively agrarian and coöperative socialism and would not have to wait until Russia became industrialized on the large scale assumed in the system of Western socialism. The dominant group among the populists saw no hope, however, for any legal and peaceful or even for any nationally organized revolutionary transition from landlordism to peasant socialism; the rulers of the old order must be got rid of and assassinations and other sporadic acts of violence were the only practical means. The Social Revolutionary party, organized in 1901, was made up principally from a fusion of remnants of the populist group.

The third group appealed not to the peasants but to a new class of discontented workers. In the last quarter of the century there was a rapid expansion of industrial production in Russia, chiefly in textiles, machine-making and other manufactures, and in the mining of coal and iron. This development brought on other economic changes: a growth of the ancillary enterprises of trade, transportation and communication, and a rapid increase in urban population, including a wage-earning group becoming increasingly conscious of its capacity for concerted action. Actual living conditions among this new proletariat were generally bad: low wages, long hours of labor, small and unsanitary dwellings, and a harsh factory discipline. The urban workers, like the peasants, had no legal means of agitation for change: trade-unions and collective bargaining were forbidden, participation in strikes was punishable by imprisonment or exile, and governmental espionage restrained the dissemination of ideas of moderate reform. Occasionally the government would enact temporizing measures of relief, as by slightly shortening the work day or feebly limiting the disciplinary powers of the employers. These measures could not satisfy the workers. An increasing destitution facilitated the spread of revolutionary ideas among them and afforded the occasion for the rise of parties that gave first place to the interests of an industrial working class.

Marx's *Kapital* had been translated into Russian in 1872, and the socialist intellectuals began at that time to turn their attention to the urban workers. During the next two decades small Marxist groups were formed; and from these groups there was organized, in 1898, the Russian Social Democratic party, led by G. Plekhanov (leading Russian exponent of Marxism), J. O. Martov, P. B. Axelrod (a former follower of the anarchist Bakunin), Vera Zasulich, and V. I. Lenin. The party appeared to be united in doctrine. It adopted the familiar formulae of class struggle, conquest of power by the organized proletariat, and socialization through nation-wide political action. At the second congress of the party (in Brussels and London, 1903), disputes arose over questions of party composition and organization; one group, led by Martov and Axelrod, contending for a broad basis of socialist membership and a loose party organization; the other group, led by Lenin, insisting upon an exclusively revolutionary membership and a highly centralized and militarized direction of party policy. The latter faction, soon capturing a majority of the Russian Marxians, were known as the Bolsheviks, and the moderate minority group were called Mensheviks.[5] The disputes between the two factions developed almost immediately into differences over matters of tactics and general program. According to the Mensheviks, the socialist movement in Russia should proceed according to the course outlined by Marx, so that the final revolutionary stroke would have to wait upon the steady building-up of an organized proletarian majority, accompanying a long process of capitalist development and degeneration. They were willing meanwhile to enter into alliances with liberal groups among the bourgeoisie. According to the Bolsheviks, it was the general stage in the development of world capitalism, not the particular stage within a given country, that, in the Marxian prognosis, determined the proper time for the socialist cataclysm; the typical course would not have to be repeated in each separate country. The Bolsheviks, appealing mainly to the industrial proletariat but seeking support also from the poorer peasantry, advocated immediate preparation for an early revolution.

Meanwhile the Russian autocracy was blindly preparing the way for the success of a revolutionary policy. Reactionary groups were almost

[5] From the Russian *bolshinstvo,* meaning "majority," and *menshinstvo,* meaning "minority."

continuously in control during the reigns of the brutally despotic Alexander III (1881–1894) and the weak and superstitious Nicholas II (1894–1917). Their policy appeared to be determined by a fanatical belief that the principles of autocracy, nationalism, and orthodoxy could be ruthlessly maintained against all resistance or criticism. They showed themselves to be no less opposed to open, deliberate, and peaceful agitation than to secret, illegal, and violent action. When the *zemstvos*, controlled by the Constitutional Democrats, sent up moderate complaints and petitions, the central government responded by curtailing their powers, disbanding some of them, and exiling their leaders. The tsar and his advisers also dealt relentlessly with the efforts of religious and racial minorities to secure some measure of autonomy in caring for their special cultural interests, and they condoned the pogroms against the Jews. The exasperation and despair which this policy induced brought on a widespread feeling that a just and humane order could be achieved in Russia only by intimidation, through assassination or insurrection. Governmental terrorism was met by revolutionary terrorism. There were riotous mutinies by peasants seeking to get possession of surplus lands on the landlords' estates. Secret societies were formed, to convert the educated youth to insurrectionary methods, or maintain a revolutionary zeal among the peasants, or prepare acts of violence against agents of the government.[6]

The Russo-Japanese War of 1904–1905, growing out of Japanese opposition to the imperialist designs of Russia in Northern China and ending in a humiliating defeat for Russia, revealed the weaknesses of the autocracy. The conduct of the war disclosed glaring stupidity and crookedness among members of the court clique and the higher bureaucracy, brought new miseries to the workers, and spread dissatisfaction among all sections of the people. Progressive as well as revolutionary parties came into open and aggressive opposition to the tsardom. The suddenly intensified discontent was manifested in deputations to the tsar, strikes among railway and factory workers, mass processions in the cities, uprisings by peasants, mutinies on warships, disaffection in the army, and a further series of political assassinations. The government attempted to quell the disturbances by drastic measures of force.

---

[6] In the seventies, several provincial governors were assassinated. Tsar Alexander II was slain in 1881, after surviving three previous attempts on his life; thirty-three years later came the assassination of the notorious Plehe, who, as Minister of the Interior, had been responsible for the prosecution of thousands of political agitators.

Not succeeding in this, it turned to a temporary policy of concession and reform. In the autumn of 1905, the tsar, under the advice of Count Witte, issued a manifesto promising that in the succeeding year he would summon a Duma, or national parliament, to be elected by all groups of the population; that henceforth no law would come into force without the approval of this representative assembly; and that the people would now be permitted to enjoy fundamental rights of civic liberty, including freedom of speech, conscience, and association.

These concessions appeared to establish constitutional government for Russia, but in actual practice no such result was realized. The ruling groups were unwilling to permit the application of constitutional ideas; their desires were rather to get promptly back to the old order. Another period of governmental repression set in. The first and second Dumas were dissolved by the tsar, who then claimed and exercised the right of legislation by decree. He also changed the system of election and representation in such ways as to reduce substantially the representation of the peasants and wage-earners and enlarge that of the higher nobility. The Duma became impotent as a body sharing governmental powers with the tsar, although its sessions served, to a very limited degree, as a medium for the propagation of liberal political ideas.

Thus Russia, in the twentieth century, despite its industrial progress, its literary and artistic eminence, its increasing cultural and economic contacts with Western peoples, remained relatively unenlightened and inhumane in its political and social policy. Although the press remained somewhat freer than it had been before 1905, the aristocracy and bureaucracy, in order to maintain themselves in power, were still relying extensively upon artificial means—a centrally controlled secret police and a pervasive system of espionage. Progressive and radical elements in the population were, however, gaining in experience and cohesion by formulating and discussing their complaints and proposals, occasionally in sessions of the zemstvos and the Duma and more generally in their political parties and secret societies. At the same time, the landowners were declining in wealth and social prestige, and the cleavage between them and the people was becoming greater. The desire for change was spreading and becoming more explicit. The masses were becoming vaguely aware that not primarily the evil intention of landlords and officials but the social and political system itself was responsible for the ills they suffered.

Thus when the World War began the groups in control had taken no effective steps toward the solution of any of the pressing social and political problems of Russia; and there was a growing belief in the improbability of any settlement by peaceful, evolutionary, and constitutional means. The conduct of the government during the war strengthened the factors of revolution. The early exhaustion of ammunition, the successive defeats of the Russian armies, the rapidly spreading privation due to the blockade, the general disorganization of trade and transport, and through it all the unmistakable evidences of governmental inefficiency and obstinacy and the rumors of intrigue and immorality in the imperial court, brought on increasing disillusionment and discontent among the people and disaffection and desertion in the army. The government persisted in punishing criticism and rejecting all proposals for change, however moderate. Practically all accounts agree that the final collapse of the tsarist régime came about chiefly through its own rottenness.

The revolution of March, 1917, was the work of no single class or political party and had no outstanding leaders and no definite program or objective. [7] Mensheviks, Bolsheviks, Social Revolutionaries, and Constitutional Democrats played their several parts in the protests, demands, and threats during the few weeks preceding the abdication of the tsar on March 15. Members of the first three groups took part in fomenting the strikes, processions, riots, and other mass demonstrations of that period; their leaders joined in bringing together, three days before the abdication, the Petrograd council (Soviet) of Workers' and Soldiers' Deputies, and in formulating the demands put forth by that body for a Constituent Assembly—to be elected by universal suffrage and to be pledged to a radical political and social change. The Mensheviks and Social Revolutionaries, although continuing to participate in the activities of the Petrograd and provincial soviets, looked upon the March revolution as a definitive event—the inevitable first stage in a long movement towards socialism; they appeared to agree that a distinctively socialist revolution would have to wait until the end of the process of capitalist development under a bourgeois-democratic régime, which meanwhile they—as moderate or radical critics —would support. Lenin (returning from exile in April) maintained, on the other hand, that Russia, although not economically ready for complete socialism, was politically ready for the transfer of power to

[7] For accounts of Russia in 1917, see the list on pp. 185–186, *infra.*

the workers and that the soviets were the appropriate agencies for bringing about such a revolution.

The progress of events in the half-year following the revolution was
favorable to the triumph of Lenin's views. The provisional government
rapidly lost popular support outside of bourgeois groups, chiefly because
it continued to carry on the war without any radical redefinition of
war aims and persisted in the notion that after a few years a constitutional monarchy, or even a republic, could be set up in Russia without
any immediate and extensive plans for economic reform. Its educated
and public-spirited, but inexperienced and hesitant, leaders could satisfy
neither those who were attached to the old régime nor the workers and
peasants who hoped for a prompt realization of their aspirations for
a new economic and political standing in the nation. During the summer
a reconstituted cabinet brought about some improvements in administration and succeeded for awhile in stirring the armies to increased efforts;
but it was unable to overcome the indifference or hostility of the masses
to a continuation of the war or to cope adequately with the tremendous
economic difficulties.

Meanwhile the restless workers were pushing the soviets into a left-
ward policy and Bolsheviks were rapidly displacing Mensheviks and
Social Revolutionaries in the leadership of the soviets. In September
they gained a slight majority in the Moscow soviet and a commanding
majority in the Petrograd soviet, whose "Military Revolutionary Committee" now became their main organ of action. This body demanded
the creation of a soviet government for Russia and put forth promises
of immediate peace and of land, homes, food, and power for the masses.
On November seventh, the army soviets, aided by deserting garrisons
of the provisional government, forcibly took possession of the agencies
of government. A second All-Russian Congress of Soviets, convening
on the following day, formally ratified the Bolshevist program and
vested governmental authority in a "Council of People's Commissars,"
composed wholly of Bolsheviks, with Lenin as President and Trotsky
as commissar of foreign affairs.[8] These new rulers concluded peace
with Germany in the following March; and in the course of the next
three years they consolidated their power, suppressing peasant revolts

---

[8] Other important members of the Council were Rykov, commissar of internal
affairs; Stalin, commissar of nationalities; and Lunacharsky, commissar of education.

and defeating the white Russian armies (of Koltchak, Yudenitch, Denikin, and Wrangel), which, aided by the European Allies and the United States, sought either to restore Russia to her former rulers or to set up constitutional government on the Western model. The Bolsheviks became the successful group in seizing and holding the reins of government in the Russian chaos because they had the most popular appeals for the peasants, workers, and soldiers; the most consistent social theory; the greatest skill in adapting their theory to pressing practical needs; the best working organization; and the boldest and ablest leadership.

The outstanding leaders have been Lenin (from the origin of the Bolshevist group until his death in 1924), Trotsky (from 1917 to 1924), and Stalin (since 1924).

Lenin's father was a government inspector of schools who, in Lenin's youth, received a patent of nobility from the government in recognition of faithful services. Lenin himself was graduated from a classical preparatory school; entered the University of Kazan, from which he was expelled because of his radical political activities; and later took work, as a non-resident, in the University of St. Petersburg, where he passed the final examinations in 1891. A period of banishment in Siberia gave him opportunity to clarify and systematize his socialist ideas, acquire a mastery of several foreign languages, and prepare his first important books. In the two decades following the founding of the Social Democratic party of Russia he was—although living most of the time as an exile in various European countries—the dominant personality among the Bolsheviks, formulating their doctrines, directing their tactics as a more or less underground group, and leading them to power in 1917; and, until his death, he was constantly the directing genius in the Soviet government. In his brief theoretical writings he set forth a systematic political doctrine with considerable dialectical skill and a fair historical perspective; he was highly effective as a speaker before popular audiences; and as head of the government of Russia he displayed rare qualities of practical statesmanship in exceedingly difficult domestic and international situations. A disinterested and qualified writer has described Lenin as probably having done "more to deflect the course of world history than any political figure since Napoleon." [9]

Trotsky, son of a successful Jewish farmer, was generally in active

[9] William H. Chamberlin, *Soviet Russia: a Living Record and a History* (1930), p. 83.

association with the Marxian socialists of Russia. He took a prominent part in the revolution of 1905, and, like most of the other revolutionary leaders, spent most of his adult life under the tsardom in exile. He was not, however, definitely aligned with the Bolsheviks before 1917. At the time of the March revolution he was in New York City, where he had just begun the editorship of a revolutionary Russian newspaper. He returned as directly as possible to Russia, joined the Bolsheviks in July, was made chairman of the Petrograd soviet in September, and thenceforth played a part, second only to that of Lenin, in organizing the revolution and carrying on the Bolshevist government, until the party dissensions after Lenin's death. As commissar of foreign affairs (1917–1918) and commissar of the army and navy (1918–1925) he conducted the negotiations leading to the Brest-Litovsk peace treaty with Germany, created the new Soviet army, reorganized the railway system, and directed the militant communism of the period from 1918 to 1921. He has been generally described as the most effective of the Bolshevik orators, and his brilliant writings have made significant contributions to the exposition of Communist doctrines. Stalin, son of a Georgian village shoemaker, was a revolutionary socialist since youth and a leader among the Bolsheviks for several years before 1917. He has been in the ruling clique from the beginning of the Communist régime and the predominant figure in party and governmental affairs since 1925.[10]

The Communist rulers appear, in many of their characteristic acts and utterances, to be zealous doctrinaires. There is probably no country in the world that is governed with more thorough devotion to an ideal or more unwavering ideas as to the general course to be pursued in realizing that ideal. Nevertheless, they change their tactics, for they are realists as well as idealists.[11] The tactical changes have been

[10] Rykov, premier since Lenin's death, and Kalinin, chairman of the All-Russian Executive Committee, are, like Stalin, the sons of peasants. Many of the other leaders have come from "higher" social strata. Chicherin, commissar of foreign affairs from 1918 to 1930, is of an old and distinguished family of the nobility and held office in the Russian diplomatic service under the tsardom. Lunacharsky, commissar of education, 1917 to 1929, had been a brilliant playwright and literary critic; Krassin, late Soviet ambassador to France and to England, had been a successful engineer and business man; Krylenko, state attorney-general for several years, a lawyer and army officer; Rakovsky, formerly Soviet ambassador to England and to France, a doctor of medicine. Nearly all of the leaders had been active in revolutionary movements from early youth and served terms in prison or in Siberian exile.

[11] For a brief selection from the vast number of books and articles describing and commenting on the Bolshevist régime, see the list on pp. 186–188, *infra*.

principally in the economic field. At all times they have deliberately maintained a "mixed" economic system, with private enterprise, public enterprise, and combinations of the two—the proportions fluctuating as conditions change. The constant feature is the centralized direction of the whole system by a single compact group driving towards an unchanging goal. Bourgeois resistance, civil war, and foreign invasion forced upon them in the beginning a more rapid, extensive, and centralized socialization of industry than they had planned for. This policy, followed for about three years, was successful politically in the sense that it contributed to the success of the government in repelling invasions and suppressing the counter-revolution. In its economic results, it failed. The attempt had been undertaken under exceptionally difficult conditions—in a country of primitive methods of cultivation, limited technical knowledge, and inadequate methods of transportation—and at a time of unusual depletion of productive energies, due to the enormous loss of man power and the bungling administration of supplies during the World War. In 1921 the government—faced by a woefully inadequate production of the necessaries of life, a rapidly depreciating currency, a loss of public credit, an increasing number of persons dependent upon public support, and serious threats of revolt—took stock of the situation, acknowledged its temporary economic setback, and announced a new policy, involving various concessions to peasants and foreign capitalists and widely restoring private trade, though with severe restrictions on profits.

The "new economic policy" of 1921, like the "war communism" it succeeded, was adopted to meet an emergency. The tactics have continued to change, as in the measures initiated in 1928 for collectivizing the farms and in the "five-year plan" for speeding up the pace of industrial and agricultural production. These later changes have involved new combinations of public and private business. At some points the socialist aims are obvious, as in advantages given to the collective over the individual farmers, by way of lower taxation, easier credit, *etc*. At other points there are new "surrenders to capitalism," as in the favors granted to the technical intelligentsia, the partial substitution of piece-work ("payment by results") for equal pay in coal-mining and other industries, the use of bonuses, promotions and salary increases to stimulate productivity, and the allowance of increased inequalities in the incomes of private traders. Certain insignia of social approval—the "Order of Lenin" and the "Red Banner of Toil"—are awarded for exceptional achievements in production. The rulers of Russia recognize that a general improvement in the standard of living is a prerequisite for the success of the Communist policy.

Throughout all these changes in economic tactics the underlying social policy remains the same. The constant aims have been to make Russia more nearly self-sufficient, to secure more comfortable living conditions and wider cultural opportunities for the masses, and above all, to keep the reins of economic and political control in the hands of that minority most devoted and tenacious in driving towards the ultimate socialist victory. Since the beginning of the Bolshevik régime, the government has administered directly the basic functions of banking, transport, electric power, and foreign trade. Where in other businesses it makes concessions to private enterprise, it exacts a socialist *quid pro quo*, by imposing higher taxes, denying voting rights, and enforcing rigid labor standards. The Russian Soviet system is a thoroughgoing experiment in proletarian political socialism.

The rulers of the system believe that they can keep the experiment going and maintain themselves in the control of it only by persistent propaganda and inexorable censorship and coercion. The governmental apparatus of Soviet Russia has been largely an annex to a single party. In 1918 the Bolsheviks adopted the name "Russian Communist Party," which, with the formation of the "Union of Socialist Soviet Republics," in 1923, became the "All-Union Communist Party" of Russia. This party selects its members with great care and it has a thoroughly centralized management. Elections to the principal governing organs—the local soviets, the provincial congresses, the national legislative and executive body (the "Union Central Executive Committee"), and the nominally supreme "All-Union Congress of Soviets"—are controlled by the small "political bureau," which dominates the deliberations of both party and governmental assemblies and determines, as far as party exigencies require it, the appointments to public administrative offices. By virtue of closely interlocking directorates, the controlling personnel of the Russian government, the Communist party of Russia, and the Third International are largely identical. The party has applied its discipline to some of its most distinguished members. In 1924 the controlling group removed Trotsky from the command of the army and from the inner circles of the party because of his vigorous criticisms of the government's concessions to peasants and industrial capitalists and his persistent agitation for an intensive revolutionary propaganda in foreign countries. It expelled him from Russia in 1928 when he defied the party again by urging a more ruthless policy in forcing the well-to-do peasants into the collective farms. This rigorous discipline has brought most other revolters to terms—notably, Kamenev and Zinoviev, who followed Trotsky for awhile, and Bukharin, who sought to moderate the party policy.

The Communist governors of Russia rule with an iron hand. They inflict severe penalties not only for acts of sedition or insurrection but also for any conduct that tends to impede them in the execution of their plans. They strive to control popular opinion by systematically disseminating their own doctrines and rigorously restricting the circulation of opposing ideas. They teach communism in the schools, in order to impose a "proletarian morality" upon the youth of the land, as, they believe, the ruling groups in other countries impose a "bourgeois morality" upon their children. Through such measures they endeavor to prevent their massive experiment from going to pieces and to indoctrinate the present and coming generations in Russia with the whole ideology of a communist social order.[12]

THE COMMUNIST DOCTRINES

Lenin is the immediate doctrinal authority for the Russian Communists.[13] Trotsky's writings are illuminating in their brilliant polemical passages, as where he defends his party against its Western socialist critics, or, in his later works, denounces the "disloyal" Communists who triumphed over him in the intra-party conflicts after Lenin's death; several of his books give impressive expositions of the cultural and spiritual aims of the Russian system. The works by other Communists— notably, N. Bukharin, editor, from 1918 to 1929, of *Pravda* (leading newspaper of the party), and Stalin—are useful mainly as résumés of Lenin's ideas.

Lenin as a young man professed his adherence to Marx and never subsequently wavered in this faith. The other theorists also proclaim Marx as their master and the *Communist Manifesto* as their gospel;

---

[12] See further, *infra*, pp. 182–183.

[13] The authoritative doctrines of the Communists are to be found in the works of the men who have been the controlling personalities in the actual government of Soviet Russia—notably, Lenin, Trotsky, Bukharin, and Stalin—and in the theses and resolutions of the Third International. See the list on pp. 188–189, *infra*. For critical expositions of the Communist doctrines, by non-Communists, see the list on pp. 190–191.

they describe their revolution as an attempt to realize that gospel. A primary object of Lenin's *State and Revolution,* written in the middle of 1917, was to show, by extensive quotations from the works of Marx and Engels, that the projected revolution and the Communist rule to follow it would be, although different from what the Western socialists would approve, yet absolutely true to Marx. In the prolonged controversy, during the first few years of the new régime, between Trotsky and Lenin, on the one side, and Kautsky—leading theorist for the orthodox socialists after Marx's death—on the other, the principal point in issue was not the justice or expediency of the Communist program but its validity as an attempt to carry out Marx's ideas.[14]

The Communist theorists hold strictly to Marx's economic interpretation of history and to his conception of class war as the basic fact in all social evolution. There are, however, differences in emphasis in the attack on modern society, and there are important features in the Communist program that distinguish it from the program ordinarily envisaged by Marx.

The Communists, following Marx, insist on the differentiation of their program from all programs that seek to unite or reconcile opposing economic classes by mitigating the differences between them or by peacefully and gradually modifying the social institutions which have developed under the influence of those differences. As long as there are some who live mainly by labor and others who live mainly by investment and by directing the labor of others, hostility between the two groups is inevitable. Those who own no means of production are forced to sell their labor to the small groups who do. Moreover, the capitalist system is not only essentially exploitative; it is also inefficient. The owners of capital cease to produce goods when they cannot sell them at a profit, and frequently they cannot sell goods at a profit because under the unequal distribution of wealth the people who need the goods are unable to buy them. Thus all members of society suffer from the anarchy of capitalism; the competition between producers

[14] See especially the following: Lenin, *The State and Revolution* (1917), *The Proletarian Revolution and Kautsky the Renegade* (1920); Karl Kautsky, *The Dictatorship of the Proletariat* (1920), *Terrorism and Communism* (1920); Trotsky, *The Defence of Terrorism* (1921). Cf. also *Theses and Statutes of the Third (Communist) International Adopted by the Second Congress . . . 1920* (Publishing Office of the Communist International, Moscow, 1920), pp. 13 ff; *Theses and Resolutions Adopted at the Third World Congress of the Communist International . . . 1921* (Contemporary Publishing Association, New York, 1921), pp. 49 ff.

causes waste of energy, periodically recurring crises of overproduction and unemployment, and a general disintegration of productive forces.

Although the Communists repeat the familiar Marxian indictment of modern society, they give greater emphasis to another criticism. The essential fault in capitalism, they say, is neither the inequality in distribution nor the inadequacy of production of the necessities of life. The fatal evil is the inequality of power, and the goal to be striven for is an equality not of wealth but of social status and cultural opportunity. The achievement of that goal involves the destruction of a political as well as of an economic system. For the state, in any of its typical contemporary forms, is inextricably associated with the capitalist order. Its historic rôle has been to serve the interests of those who own property, to support them in their domination over the property-less, and to suppress all attempts to shake off that domination. Laws in the modern state are generally only the formulations of the desires of capitalists; even when they are not, judges interpret and apply them as if they were. Thus the modern state is an agency for the maintenance of the *status quo*. It treats those who oppose the social supremacy of property-owners as enemies of the state and, therefore, of society itself. This is true of all existing forms of the state. However democratic the structure of government, the real repositories of political authority are the owners of wealth, who, by their possession of the main organs of propaganda and education—the schools and colleges, the churches, and the press—control the political and social opinions of the workers.[15] Accordingly, democracy, as it actually operates, is not popular rule, but bourgeois rule; congresses and parliaments, presidents and cabinets, are merely agencies of bourgeois class domination. The only private rights that are recognized are those of bourgeois groups; for others—censorship and denial of free assembly, martial law, and pogroms.

How, according to the Communists, is the modern political and economic system to be ended? Its dissolution, they say, in the orthodox fashion, will come about partly through its own development and degeneration. Marx explained this to mean that capitalism must prepare the way for socialism, both destructively, by creating those conditions of concentration, overproduction, unemployment, and poverty that make the workers in every way ready for a socialist revolution; and constructively, by developing the instrumentalities of large-scale

---

[15] N. Bukharin and E. Preobraschensky, *The A B C of Communism* (1922), p. 44.

production to a point where the proletarians can use them for socialist purposes. In the course of these changes all the workers would acquire experience in coöperative action and develop an *esprit de corps* that would make them competent for political rule.

The régime of the Russian Communists was set up in a country least prepared, according to this Marxian hypothesis, for a socialist revolution.[16] Large-scale industry had barely got under way; industrial laborers numbered less than one tenth of the total population, and they had had only very limited experience in any sort of deliberate, open, concerted activity. Marx, it is true, at one time expressed the hope that when socialist revolutions occurred in the industrialized countries of Europe, Russia might, in a revolution at the same time, be able to pass directly from its system of village communal land-ownership into a system of state socialism and thus escape suffering the "fatal conditions of a capitalist system" through which the other countries had had to pass.[17] The revolution of November, 1917, however, met neither the general conditions described by Marx nor the specific conditions which he indicated as possible for a Russian revolution. It did not come as the climax of a long course of economic and political development in Russia; it had no connection with the communal system of the old villages; and it was not supported by socialist revolutions in other countries.

Lenin maintains, nevertheless, that the Russian revolution took place in essential accord with Marx's theory. For economic and political developments in the industrial world at large had by 1917, he explains, prepared the way for a successful socialist revolution in any particular country where an existing capitalist régime was in a situation of unusual instability. The great industrial nations had been greatly weakened by their competitions for the control of foreign markets and unexploited regions and by the excessive economic wastes and disorders of the World War that grew inevitably out of this destructive rivalry. The conditions prerequisite for the success of a revolution in a particular country are, according to Lenin, as follows: first, there must be an organized group of aggressive and resolute revolutionists, clearly

[16] For discussions of the relations of Russian Communism to Marxism, see the following: Boris Brutzkus, *Die Lehren des Marxismus im Lichte der russischen Revolution* (1928); Morris Hillquit, *From Marx to Lenin* (1921); H. W. Laidler, *History of Socialist Thought* (1927), Ch. XXVII; A. Landau-Aldanov, *Lénine* (fifth ed., 1920), Pt. II, Ch. I.

[17] See D. Ryazanoff, *The Communist Manifesto of Karl Marx and Friedrich Engels*, pp. 262–265.

conscious of their objective; secondly, although this group will inevitably be small in numbers, it must be supported by an active discontent among the people generally; finally, the revolution must be undertaken when the defenders of the old order are weak and divided. Russia, he believed, completely satisfied these conditions in 1917.[18]

Thus Lenin's doctrine is consistent with the evolutionary phase of Marx's socialism in this general sense—it holds that a socialist revolution can occur only when economic and political developments have prepared the way for it. Although the November revolution of 1917 took place under circumstances different from the specific expectations of either Marx or the Bolsheviks themselves, the latter promptly proclaimed the revolution to be fundamentally a vindication of the former's prophecy. The "Manifesto" put forth by the constituent congress of the Third International, in March, 1919, begins with the following declaration:

Seventy-two years have gone by since the Communist party announced their program to the world in the form of a Manifesto drawn up by the two greatest teachers of the proletarian revolution, Karl Marx and Friedrich Engels. . . . Development has continued on the lines indicated in the party's Manifesto. The period of the last decisive struggle has begun later than was desired or expected by the apostles of social revolution. But it is here; it has come. We Communists, representatives of the revolutionary proletariat in different countries in Europe, America and Asia, now assembled in the powerful Soviet city of Moscow, both feel and consider ourselves to be the followers of, and participants in, a cause for which the program was drawn up seventy-two years ago.[19]

Lenin agreed with Marx in the contention that, although the natural development of capitalism creates the conditions for its own destruction, its actual overthrow must be by deliberate action of the workers themselves; and their action must be through political means. The methods of trade-unionism or even syndicalism will not do. Wage-earners cannot squeeze out property-owners either by making bargains with them or by striking or committing acts of violence against them. They must put themselves in possession of the organized coercive power of the whole community and use this power to expropriate the capitalists and then set about the long task of building up a completely commu-

[18] *The Revolution of 1917*, Vol. I (Vol. XX of his *Collected Works*, 1927–), pp. 116–129, and *passim*.
[19] Resolutions of the Congress of the Third International, March, 1919.

nistic society. In other words, they must get control of the state. They can do this, Lenin maintains, only by force. The capitalists' control of the vehicles of information and discussion makes it impossible for the workers to elect majorities to the parliaments of existing democracies. "The substitution of a proletarian for the capitalist state is impossible without a violent revolution." [20] The leaders of the revolution of November, 1917, had had the proper sort of experiences to indoctrinate them with this idea. Trotsky relates that in a meeting of Bolsheviks in July of that year, with 175 delegates present (representing 112 local groups), a questionnaire filled out by 171 of the delegates revealed that 150 of them had been arrested a total of 549 times, 110 had suffered a total of 245 years in prison, 24 had spent a total of 73 years in penal settlements, and 55 had been in exile for a total of 127 years.[21]

The Russian Communists attach great historical significance, for the cause of socialism, to the Paris Commune of 1871, which they regard as a genuine expression of Marx's doctrine of political revolution. In their theoretical discussions and in their propaganda they use the Commune—and Marx's commentary on it (in *The Civil War in France*)—as a proof of the socialist orthodoxy of their own revolution. Marx, they show, hailed the brief revolutionary régime of 1871 as the "storming of heaven" and "a glorious harbinger of a new society," and he contrasted it with the visionary and inadequate movements of 1789, 1830, and 1848. The Western socialists, Lenin says, have forgotten all this and have gone back to the bourgeois methods of peaceful, democratic, piecemeal change. The Paris Commune failed, Lenin contends, only because it was too moderate and lenient in its immediate program of constructive action. He interprets the Commune as a spontaneous and violent uprising of socialist working-men, followed by a thoroughly undemocratic, antiparliamentary, governmental régime.[22]

Marx's other writings show that he gave less emphasis than the Russians do to the inevitability and importance of violence in a socialist revolution. He admitted, as we have seen, that an armed uprising might

[20] Lenin, *The State and Revolution* (1917), p. 23.
[21] *History of the Russian Revolution*, II (1932), 308.
[22] Cf. particularly, in this connection, Edward S. Mason, *The Paris Commune: an Episode in the History of the Socialist Movement* (1930). Mr. Mason, in this original and exhaustive study, shows that the Commune, though violent, was not essentially either proletarian or socialist; such elements were involved in it, but there were others also. He indicates that Marx himself, as well as other socialists of the time, exaggerated the socialist and proletarian factors in the insurrection; and he makes clear the way in which the Russian Communists have restored and assiduously exploited this earlier "legend" of the Paris Commune.

in many instances be an inevitable factor in the final seizure of political power by the proletariat.[23] Particularly in a country like Russia, where the people had long been accustomed to violent rule by a military despotism, the transition to socialist rule might naturally take an insurrectionary form; and even in other countries the capitalist groups might refuse to yield the reins of control unless overcome by force. Marx's general program, however, gave chief place to propaganda and organization—information and explanation, peaceful and legal agitation—as the means of developing a class feeling among the workers, cultivating their political intelligence, and uniting them into a political body. By these means they would become, by the strength of their numbers, organization, and understanding, efficient both for a revolution—if that should prove to be necessary—and for maintaining an orderly socialist government of the community. The Communist program attaches more importance to conspiracy, intrigue, and incitation to disorder, as means both for disseminating socialist ideas and sentiments and for sapping the moral and practical foundations of the existing order.

The Communists contend also that, since the conditions that determine the success of any socialist revolution are world-wide, the revolution should be conducted, as far as possible, on a world-wide scale. Their aim is to set up an international community of proletarian states and, eventually, a single state controlled by the united workers of the world, with all racial and national boundaries forever destroyed. The method of working for this revolution to establish the "International Soviet Republic" must be principally through "propaganda and agitation," which means not academic discussions and "casual" speeches but energetic dissemination of Communist ideas and watchwords and persistent training in the tactics of revolution. More specifically, the means of preparation for world revolution are, according to resolutions of the Third International, as follows: electioneering activity by Communist parties (the parties to be formed "underground" in countries where they are proscribed by law); maintenance of a Communist press and distribution of books, leaflets, and posters; arrangement of Communist "reading circles, festivals, Sunday rambles, etc."; organization of Communist labor unions and an aggressive participation in strikes; and exploitation, for Communist purposes, of regular military operations in the several countries. In carrying out the last-mentioned form of revolutionary preparation, "the anti-military

[23] See *supra,* Ch. II, pp. 54, 56–59.

agitation of a pacifist nature" must be avoided, for Communists are not non-resistants. They should utilize the existing "army, rifle clubs, citizen guard organizations, etc., for the purpose of giving the workers military training for the revolutionary battles to come." In general, the organizers in each country "must look upon every member of the party and every revolutionary worker as a prospective soldier in the future revolutionary army." [24]

The Communist program embodies mainly, however, a policy not of destruction but of constructive achievement through positive governmental action. In its economic phases the policy is essentially similar to that of Marx; in its political phases there are distinctive features of some importance.

The Communists agree with Marx in holding that the immediate task before socialists, after they have put themselves in active control of the government of a state, is to establish a rational and just organization of economic relations. By substituting collective for individual ownership of the means of production and distribution they will release productive energies of the people—now absorbed in wasteful efforts of competition among owners and in conflicts between owners and workers —for more effective struggles against the forces of nature. The process of socialization cannot, however, be carried through all at once. The new régime will not, in the beginning, have at its disposal the organization and experience sufficient for administering directly the whole economic life of the community. Trial alone will show how rapidly the socialization can proceed. The Communists have always recognized that the destruction of capitalism could not, particularly in a country of retarded economic development, be achieved by "sudden frontal attacks." Lenin pointed this out, three years before the "retreat" of 1921. All agree that the road to communism is "long and complex." The essential thing is that none but Communists mark out the course. When they "contract the area" of their progress, they do not change its direction; and they surrender no socialist principles. But to retain the control they frequently change their tactics. "A Marxist," said Lenin in 1917, "must take cognisance of living life, of the true facts of reality . . . he must not continue clinging to the theory of yesterday, which, like every theory, at best only outlines the main and the general, only approximately embracing the complexity of life." [25]

[24] *Theses and Resolutions Adopted at the Third World Congress of the Communist International . . . 1921* (see note 14, p. 161, *supra*), pp. 84–92, 114.
[25] In his "Letters on Tactics," in *The Revolution of 1917*, I, 121.

"The peculiarities of the present situation," he said in 1919, make it necessary "to be cautious, to retreat, to wait, to go slowly," "to compromise with the bourgeoisie" at some points in order "to be meticulously rigorous" in more important places.[26]

In other words, they "make economic concessions," says Bukharin, "in order not to be forced to make political concessions." Although, as we have seen, a Communist revolution destroys the "existing political system," it holds on to some traditional political weapons. The instrumentalities of coercive government must continue in use until the long task of building the new order is completed. Communist policy, after the dispossession of existing wielders of political and economic power, is determined by two aims: to prevent the capitalists from recapturing power and to maintain social stability and efficiency. It takes time to consolidate the work of a proletarian revolution, for the revolution is to bring about not social disorder or impotence but the preservation and advancement of civilization. Just as a state controlled by capitalists has been the indispensable organ for the maintenance of capitalism, so now the working-men's state is to be the chief agency for a proletarian reconstruction of society. As the capitalists needed the state in order to exploit the proletariat, so now the latter need the state to repress their former exploiters. Accordingly, "the road to socialism lies through the highest possible intensification of the principle of the state." [27]

Moreover, the state will continue to be, as it has been in all past ages, a class organization and an institution of armed force. [28] It can never be what democrats and moderate socialists have attempted to make it—a corporate community in which different economic classes coöperate by way of bargain and compromise. The communist state, like every other state, will be an organization for the domination of one class over the rest of society. It will be avowedly, what other states are in fact, undemocratic. It will represent the proletariat without any pretense of representing an entire nation. It is a dictatorship of the proletariat; and this implies that only proletarians rule, that they rule through proletarian, as distinguished from capitalist, institutions, and that they rule coercively.

Who are the proletariat? The constitution of Soviet Russia explicitly

[26] Lenin, *The Soviets at Work* (fifth ed., 1919), p. 43.
[27] Trotsky, *The Defence of Terrorism* (1921), p. 157.
[28] Lenin, *State and Revolution*, pp. 7, 12–16, 26, and *passim*.

denies rights of voting and eligibility to monks, clergymen, private merchants, and traders; to members of the former reigning dynasty and former members of the police, gendarmerie, and secret service of the tsardom; and to all who employ the labor of others in order to obtain profits. It accords these political rights to all citizens, of either sex, eighteen years of age, who acquire "the means of living through labor that is productive and useful to society," or are "soldiers of the army and navy of the soviets," or are "citizens of the two preceding categories who have lost their capacity to work." Thus work, or willingness to work, in the common interest is the supreme and sufficient qualification for a voting citizenship in the proletarian dictatorship.[29]

Here, then, is the formal basis for a political democracy; for the group defined by the constitutional qualifications for the suffrage contains an "immense majority" of the entire nation; the constitution declares, moreover, that political rights are in the "plenipotentiary representatives" of "the toiling masses." However, the Communists, as we have seen, profess no faith in the familiar institutions and methods of democracy. The devices of modern republican government, they maintain, are suited to the economic system in which they were evolved and to no other. Communism, in destroying the capitalist order, cannot take over the political agencies of capitalism and adapt them to its own ends. It must create new institutions; a commonwealth of workingmen has place only for working-men's constituencies for political representation and only for working-men's associations for the extra-governmental discussion of political policy. It must, therefore, have: first, formal governing councils, representing all the workers, grouped according to their interests as laborers; and, secondly, a compact political body, composed of those who, by virtue of their superior competence and devotion, can be wisely and safely entrusted with the task of framing and discussing proposals for submission to the official bodies chosen by the rank-and-file workers. Accordingly, the essential institutions of the Communist dictatorship in Russia are the soviets and the Communist party.

The soviets came into the Communist system somewhat by accident, with no structure or theory for them in the beginning. "The Russian Communist party . . . strove to realize Soviets before the exact and scientific system for the Soviet authority had been worked out," de-

[29] Constitution of the Russian Socialist Federated Soviet Republic (as revised in May, 1925), Arts. 1–8, 68–9.

clared Zinoviev in 1920.[30] Councils composed of delegates chosen by working-men grouped in their factories or workshops were active in the general-strike movement in the revolution of 1905. Similar councils played an important part in the February-March revolution of 1917, and from this time on they continued in existence and spread to the provincial towns and the villages and to the army. In the succeeding months the Bolsheviks, finding it easier to obtain majorities in these councils than in the provisional parliament, ignored the latter and used the former as the forums for their revolutionary discussion and propaganda. Then, after a successful experience with the soviets in the November revolution and in the early months of the new government, the leaders devised for them a standard structure, which was incorporated in the constitution of 1918.

Lenin, in August, 1917, had written of "the destruction of parliamentarism"; he said, expounding Marx's comments on the Paris Commune of 1871: ". . . the way out of parliamentarism is to be found, of course, not in the abolition of the representative institutions and the elective principle, but in the conversion of the representative institutions from mere 'talking shops' into working bodies." [31] He did not at that time indicate a name or form for the latter. Most subsequent statements of the Communist doctrine represent the soviet system as indispensable in any truly socialist state and as essentially in contrast with the representative system of a democracy. A soviet represents working-men only and represents them in natural working-men's constituencies—grouped in factories, workshops, or unions—rather than in residence districts, which correspond to no real unities in the economic and social interests of working-men. Parliamentarism, it was formally set forth by the Second Congress of the Third International, is a "democratic" form of rule only for a bourgeois class society. It cannot be the form of the organization for the future Communist society, which recognizes no classes; and it cannot be the form for the transitional society of the proletarian dictatorship, for it undertakes to represent a "national will," which is purely "fictitious," made up of the imaginary wills of the several territorial groups. "The immediate historical task of the working class" is to destroy "the whole machinery of the bourgeoisie . . . and all the parliamentary institutions with it, whether

[30] *The Second Congress of the Communist International as Reported and Interpreted by Official Newspapers of Soviet Russia* (Washington, D.C., 1920, Government Printing Office), p. 66.

[31] *State and Revolution* (Vanguard Press ed.), p. 153.

they be republican or constitutional-monarchial," and to "create in its place a new proletarian apparatus. . . . The only form of proletarian dictatorship is a republic of Soviets." [32] "Above all," declared Bukharin, "the Russian Revolution solved the question of the forms of the dictatorship. It solved the question as to what should constitute the power of the proletarian state. The Soviets, the Soviet power—that is the form which was born of our Revolution. In the beginning, one could still think perhaps that the Soviets were a specifically Russian product. But the further experiences of Western Europe showed that this was the general form rooted in the fundamental conditions of the war of the working class against the bourgeoisie. And it is for just that reason that all who advocate the dictatorship of the proletariat must support the Soviet power." [33]

The Communist writers, however, are not specific in indicating the distinctive significance of their soviet system. Some of them maintain that the scheme establishes a thoroughly democratic system of representation for the proletariat. The common pursuit that brings workers together into a factory or union creates among them a consolidated interest and opinion in matters of social policy. A local soviet, composed of representatives from these single-minded groups, will, therefore, in choosing delegates to the next higher soviet body, reflect accurately the various shades of interest and opinion of the several original constituencies. Moreover, in all stages in the choice of representatives —from local soviet to the All-Russian Congress of Soviets—the representatives are delegates, not deputies; they serve for short terms, possess only the authority of express mandates from the body that chooses them, and are subject to an unlimited right of recall. Finally, no soviet body is limited by any other governing organ; there are no upper legislative houses representing other groups of the people and no independent executive and judicial departments. The Council of People's Commissars (the "Cabinet" of the Russian state) is chosen by the Central Executive Committee (depository of supreme governing power between sessions of the Congress), which in turn is chosen by the All-Russian Congress of Soviets. So authority goes, in a single channel, from bottom to top. There are nowhere any "checks and balances" to thwart the "popular" proletarian will, expressed in choosing the man-

[32] *Theses and Statutes of the Third (Communist) International Adopted by the Second Congress* (see note 14, p. 161, *supra*), pp. 44–46.
[33] In *Soviet Russia*, IV (1921), 162. Cf. also his article "A Program of Marxism," *Labour Monthly*, IV (1923), 75–92.

dated delegates. Thus according to this formal analysis of the soviet constitution, rank-and-file working-men are the ultimate sovereign.

Lenin has somewhat vaguely summarized "the character of the soviet organization" as follows: "The Socialist character of the Soviet democracy—that is, of proletarian democracy in its concrete particular application—consists first in this: that the electorate comprises the toiling and exploited masses—that the bourgeoisie is excluded. Secondly in this: that all bureaucratic formalities and limitations of elections are done away with—that the masses themselves determine the order and the time of elections and with complete freedom of recall of elected officials. Thirdly, that the best possible mass organization of the vanguard of the toilers—of the industrial proletariat—is formed, enabling them to direct the exploited masses, to attract them to active participation in political life, to train them politically through their own experience, that in this way a beginning has been made for the first time actually to get the whole population to learn how to manage and to begin managing." [34]

Some outside commentators have described the soviet system as a form of occupational or functional representation; the voters, it is said, are grouped into economic instead of territorial constituencies, so that the representative councils may take account chiefly of the interests that differ according to type of work rather than place of residence. But an occupational or industrial system of representation appears to have only a very limited application in the Russian system. The local city soviets, it is true, are made up for the most part of delegates chosen by workers grouped by factories and labor unions, with "district" representation retained only for housewives and other workers not organized into unions or assembled in workshops. Each rural soviet, however, is made up mainly of representatives of the peasants of the locality; and the scheme of representation in the county, provincial, and national congresses is mainly geographical. There are, for example, no mining, textile, or railway working-men's representatives in the All-Russian Congress of Soviets; there are only representatives of the various city soviets and provincial congresses. [35]

In any event, the system of soviets supplies in fact only the form of a working-men's democracy. The party officials who control the

[34] *The Soviets at Work* (fifth ed., 1919), p. 39.
[35] See Paul H. Douglas, "Occupational Representation," *American Journal of Sociology*, XXIX (1923), 128–157.

policy of the Communist party are, as we have seen, largely identical with the governmental officers who control the armed forces of the nation; and these same men supervise the elections and dominate the deliberations of the soviet bodies to whatever extent they deem necessary in order to secure the ultimate decision they desire.

Generally the Communist writers do not deny this; for it is their explicit doctrine that until the masses have been made ready—by practical experience, technical knowledge, social outlook, and moral conviction—to participate in the activities of a completely communistic society, the actual direction of social policy must be in the hands of that minority whose interest and point of view most faithfully represent the long-run interest and point of view of the entire working population. "The revolutionary supremacy of the proletariat presupposes within the proletariat itself the political supremacy of a party, with a clear program of action and a faultless internal discipline. . . . The Party includes in its ranks only the most class-conscious and devoted; and only in careful selection does it widen its ranks." [36] Thus the "general will" of the proletariat is to be represented and given effect only in the Hegelian way—by vesting decision and power in the hands of those best qualified, intellectually and morally, to discover and execute the "real will" of the whole proletariat; in the hands, that is, of men who are most expert in diagnosing the causes of the disorders from which the masses actually desire deliverance and in discovering and applying the proper remedies.

Finally, a dictatorship of the proletariat, according to the Russian doctrine, means not only a denial of political and economic privileges to all non-workers and a rule by the élite among the workers but also a very autocratic and coercive exercise of governmental authority. "The party of the proletariat," says Bukharin, "must be inexorably set on the attainment of its object. Its task is not to bargain with the bourgeoisie but to overthrow them and break their resistance." [37] Force, the Communists point out, is always the major weapon with which a ruling class confronts those who challenge its political and economic supremacy: thousands were slain by the tsar in suppressing the revolution of 1905; Koltchak, in 1920, shot even the moderate adversaries to his Siberian dictatorship; the white terrorists in Hungary, in 1921, pursued the same methods, in a more extreme degree. Force, moreover,

[36] Trotsky, *The Defence of Terrorism*, pp. 100, 102.
[37] Bukharin and Preobraschensky, *The A B C of Communism*, p. 75.

always plays its most prominent part in political action when a new social group has come into power and has to fight to retain its advantage. The groups that are being dislodged do not peacefully yield their ground. It is "foolishness," says Kamenev, to recognize violence as the proper offensive means for seizing power and not admit it also as the means of defense against the groups who seek to recapture their former positions.[38]

How far does this political doctrine—of rule by a proletarian minority, directing the deliberations of working-men's councils and applying summary governmental repression in enforcing political conformity—accord with an orthodox Marxian conception of the socialist state?

The general idea of a temporary period of rigorous domination by a working-class government over the rest of the nation can be found in Marx's writings. On several occasions, we have seen, he spoke of a transitional socialist state, which he described as "nothing else but the revolutionary dictatorship of the proletariat." [39] The socialist critics of Lenin maintain that Marx meant socialist government by a proletarian majority and not despotic rule by a socialist minority within the proletariat. They point out that in works written in reference to revolts of the mid-nineteenth century Marx condemned the "class parliaments" projected in the schemes of the bourgeois revolutionists; and in the *Communist Manifesto* he proclaimed the democratic aims of a proletarian revolution. "The first step in the working-class revolution," says the *Manifesto*, "is the raising of the proletariat to the position of the ruling class, the victory of democracy. . . . The proletarian movement is the conscious movement of the immense majority in the interests of the immense majority." Moreover, the Paris Commune, which he approved, was based, in principle, upon universal suffrage.[40] Proletarian rule thus understood, it is said, has both the rational or idealistic justification of bringing the largest possible number of normal human beings into the enjoyment of political privileges and the practical justification of a government by those whose preponderance in physical power can be maintained without any resort to extreme methods of political repression.[41]

Marx's program, it is said again, contained no suggestion for

[38] Kamenev, *The Dictatorship of the Proletariat* (1920), p. 12.
[39] See *supra*, Ch. II, pp. 59–60.
[40] Kautsky, *The Dictatorship of the Proletariat*, p. 44.
[41] Hillquit, *From Marx to Lenin*, pp. 61–62.

abandoning the traditional method of grouping voters so that their representatives were chosen by place of residence. Differences at this point between the Communists and the Western Marxians are, however, not important. As we have seen, there is only a very limited application of a specifically occupational or industrial representation in the Soviet system. Moreover, socialist parties and writers in the West have now incorporated occupational groupings into their systems of political organization. Most of the contemporary schemes give place to both residential and industrial representation in order that the political assemblies may reflect both consumers' interests, which differ in the different localities, and producers' interests, which vary by vocation or industry.[42]

What Marx ordinarily had in mind, when he sketched the governmental structure of a socialist state, was a rule by the general body of manual laborers, who, in any Western industrial state, would constitute in fact a majority of the total population. The dictatorship would consist in the fact that this political majority would govern by rules of its own, designed solely for its own requirements, and in defiance or disregard of the interests, desires, and laws of any minority aggressively hostile to it.[43] Thus the proletarian dictatorship, in Marx's system, would be only a special application of the traditional creed of the unlimited prerogatives of popular sovereignty. The doctrine of the Russian Communists does not recognize any such prerogatives.

More important still is the divergence between Marxism and Communism on the question of rule by the sword as a means of holding political supremacy and of conducting the affairs of government. The older Marxians have always recognized that any working-class government must be fully prepared to suppress, by military means if necessary, the counter-revolutionary movements almost certain to appear after any socialist revolution; but they have not looked upon martial law, espionage, and the summary administration of justice as methods of a normal régime under socialist auspices. Accordingly the Western socialists criticize not only the undemocratic structure of the Communist government but also its arbitrary and oppressive rule: its suppression of speech, its severe punishment of anti-Communists, and its generally officious and onerous regimentation of economic and social life. A centralized despotism, the critics admit, was doubtless temporarily

[42] See *supra,* Ch. V, pp. 132–133.
[43] Hillquit, *From Marx to Lenin,* pp. 55–57,

unavoidable in saving Russia from subjugation by foreign powers and from demoralization and dismemberment within. But to continue a "government by bayonets, without popular support," after the period of invasion and civil war has passed, will inevitably reintroduce exploitation of the masses by the ruling minority and will develop among the latter a class feeling clearly differentiated from a truly proletarian class consciousness. Kautsky, in a work written expressly to show the un-Marxian character of Russian communism, holds that the forms of democracy are adequate for emancipating the Russian workers—peasants as well as urban wage-earners—from subjection to the old aristocracy and that socialism can be attained in Russia, as everywhere else, by parliamentary methods. Even such a radical revolutionary socialist as Rosa Luxemburg criticized (in an essay written in 1918) the Communists' narrow interpretation of dictatorship. She held that the dictatorship should be that of the proletarian class—not of a party or faction within it—and that it should be conducted in the open daylight, with every opportunity and invitation for criticism and for active participation by the rank and file.[44]

Lenin himself, speaking on various occasions in April, 1917, stated a not substantially different conception of the impending Communist society. He described the Paris Commune of 1871, his pattern for the soviet state, as having been based on "direct, immediate, and absolute rule of the majority"; insisted that the Bolsheviks, although as yet in a minority, realized the need of "winning a majority," and that they desired "all public offices to be elective, all officials to be subject to recall at any time" and "the building up of the entire state administration from the bottom by the masses themselves, their actual participation in every step of practical life, their active rôle in the administration." In May, however, he declared that if the soviets should succeed in seizing the government, they would set up "a state not in the ordinary sense of that word," but a "dictatorship," resting "not on the law, not on the formal will of the majority, but on direct and open force." [45] It would be a state governed in the interest, but controlled only ultimately by the will, of the workers and peasants—the great majority in the Russian nation. He later explained that practical conditions forced upon the communist rulers a system of government by a party

[44] Kautsky, *Dictatorship of the Proletariat;* Luxemburg, *Die russische Revolution,* a pamphlet published posthumously (Frankfort, 1922).

[45] *The Revolution of 1917* (see note 18, *supra,* p. 164), at pp. 124, 203, 225, 230, 281.

oligarchy, ruling in behalf of the proletarian masses, yet relying not at all on their initiative or voluntary coöperation but on an energetic direction by the oligarchy itself. Other Communists have likewise related the rule by violence to the actual difficulties confronting them after they had seized the reins of government: counter-revolutionary movements, with financial and military aid from hostile foreign nations; attempts to assassinate the Communist leaders; returning soldiers made desperate by their recent hardships; the former land-owners and bourgeoisie determined to resume their former manner of life; the formerly exploited workers and peasants, unintelligent and inexperienced, expecting privileges of wealth and leisure to come to them immediately, but unwilling to work on the intensive scale imperative if complete industrial and financial disintegration was to be escaped. Nothing but resolute and coercive regimentation could overcome the resistance, or the inertia, of such groups.

More frequently, however, the Communists set forth a broader conception of force as an instrumentality of government. Their doctrine is that force is the characteristic attribute of all political rule and that under no conditions is there any place for individual liberty under the state. "When it becomes possible to speak of freedom," they quote from Engels, "the state as such ceases to exist." "No organization except the army," says Trotsky, "has ever controlled man with such severe compulsion as does the state organization of the working-class in the difficult period of transition. . . . The state, before disappearing, assumes . . . the most ruthless form," and "embraces authoritatively the life of the citizens in every direction." [46]

The Communist aims, as set forth in the books of Lenin, Trotsky, Bukharin, and Stalin, are faithfully reflected in the resolutions, "theses," and "statutes" adopted by the congresses of the Third International. The following passages appear to give a fair summary of the general program:

The victory of Socialism over Capitalism—as the first step to Communism —demands the accomplishment of the three following tasks by the proletariat, as the only really revolutionary class:

The first task is to lay low the exploiters, and above all the bourgeoisie as their chief economic and political representatives; to defeat them completely; to crush their resistance; to render impossible any attempts on their part to re-impose the yoke of capitalism and wage-salary.

[46] Trotsky, *Defence of Terrorism*, p. 157.

The second is to inspire and lead in the footsteps of the revolutionary advance guard of the proletariat, its Communist party—not only the whole proletariat or the great majority, but the entire mass of workers and those exploited by capital; to enlighten, organize, instruct, and discipline them during the course of the bold and mercilessly firm struggle against the exploiters; to wrench this enormous majority of the population in all the capitalist countries out of their state of dependence on the bourgeoisie; to instill in them, through practical experience, confidence in the leading role of the proletariat and its revolutionary advance guard.

The third is to neutralize or render harmless the inevitable fluctuations between the bourgeoisie and the proletariat, between bourgeois democracy and Soviet Power, on the part of that rather numerous class in all advanced countries—although constituting a minority of the population—the small owners and proprietors in agriculture, industry, commerce, and the corresponding layers of intellectuals, employees, and so on.[47]

The working class and the Communist Parties of all countries prepare themselves not for a period of quiet agitation and organization, but for prolonged struggle which capital will now force upon the proletariat, in order to beat it into submitting to all the burdens of capitalist policy. In this fight the Communist Parties must develop the highest militant discipline. Its Party leaders must coolly and deliberately consider all the lessons of the fight, they must prudently review the battlefield, uniting enthusiasm with the greatest deliberation. They must forge their militant plans and their tactical course in the spirit of collective thinking of the entire Party, giving due consideration to all criticism by comrades of the Party. But all the Party organizations must unhesitatingly carry out the course adopted by the Party. Every word and every step of every Party organization must be subordinated to this purpose. The Parliamentary factions, the press of the party, the party organizations must unwaveringly obey the order given by the party leadership.[48]

The Communists may seem to be interested mainly in economic affairs, but to that end, as well as for other equally important ends, they are concerned with the whole intellectual and cultural life of the citizen. They are concerned with religion because they consider it to be inconsistent with Communism and indeed a definite obstacle to the realization of their program. They renounce all religion for themselves and seek to destroy the religious faith of others. Members of

[47] *Theses and Statutes of the Third (Communist) International Adopted by the Second Congress . . . 1920* (see n. 14, p. 161, *supra.*), pp. 10–11.
[48] *Theses and Resolutions Adopted at the Third World Congress of the Communist International . . . 1921*, p. 198.

the Communist party are pledged to atheism, and the Constitution disfranchises priests and ministers of all sects. The law, it is true, does not prescribe atheism as a qualification for voting rights or prohibit the profession or practice of any religion. When priests have been prosecuted, the charge has been, not heresy, but use of an ecclesiastical office in abetting sedition or organized disobedience to law. The central government has even authorized the local soviets to allow voluntary religious associations the use of seized church properties. The Communist authorities, however, are aggressively hostile to religion. They seek to exterminate it altogether, both by narrowly limiting the activities of religious associations, so as to deprive them of opportunities for gaining any sort of social or moral hold on the masses, and by positive measures aimed at educating the minds of the youth away from attitudes of faith in a divine intervention in the affairs of man. The government, though permitting these associations to exist and to carry on their ceremonial worship and moral exhortation, denies them the right to engage in civic or philanthropic activities, prohibits religious instruction in the schools, limits the circulation of religious publications, and promotes an antireligious propaganda in newspapers, magazines, public lectures, and moving pictures.

In the minds of some commentators, Russian Communism has, despite these antireligious professions and practices, become religious in its prevailing mood.[49] There is, it is said, an official and popular "apotheosis" of Lenin: hundreds visit his shrine every day; his statues are set up in public places; pictures of him are put in positions of special honor in factories, schools, and private homes; streets, railroad stations, and societies of all sorts are named for him; he is cited as authority on every sort of subject; school children are taught to glorify him. Moreover, the religious mood of Communism appears not only in this "Lenin myth," but also in the fervor with which men, women, and children devote themselves to the pursuit of far-away goals, entirely separate from any prospect of selfish advantage to themselves.

---

[49] On the "religious" or "mythical" aspects of Russian Communism, cf. the following: Herbert Bury, *Russia from Within* (1927), Chs. III and XI; M. d'Herbigny, *L'aspect religieux de Moscou* (1926); A. A. Bogolepoff and others, *Der Staat, das Recht und die Wirtschaft des Bolschewismus*, pp. 39-69; J. M. Keynes, *Short View of Russia*, Ch. XIII; H. J. Laski, *Communism*, pp. 51-52, 159-161; Lancelot Lawton, *The Russian Revolution* (1927), Chs. XXIX, XXXIV, XL-XLIII; Anne O'Hare McCormick, *The Hammer and the Scythe* (1928), Ch. X; Matthew Spinka, *The Church and the Russian Revolution* (1927); Dorothy Thompson, *The New Russia* (1928), Ch. IV.

Thus the more ardent Communists, it is said, act generally in the mood and discipline of a holy order. They are, says Professor Laski, "as a party, comparable to nothing so much as the Society of Jesus. There is, in both, the same rigorous and unyielding set of dogmas, the same iron loyalty capable of unlimited self-confidence. The Jesuit who set out to preach his faith in China or the unknown Arctic North-West is not dissimilar to the Communist who volunteers to bury the infected corpses in the cholera epidemic. Like the Jesuit, the Communist has no personal end to secure; he feels himself essentially the servant of a great idea. Like the Jesuit also, the Russian Communist has the assurance that he works for a cause that is bound in the end to triumph. . . . It is this assurance that they have the truth (and, with it, the future) on their side which makes the Bolsheviks so impatient of, and so intolerant to, criticism and dissent. Like all the great spiritual fanatics of history, they cannot help but equate disagreement with sin." [50]

These moods and activities of the Communists are, however, not inconsistent with their atheism, unless every fanatical and self-sacrificing pursuit of a distant goal is to be considered an adventure in religion. The Communists are always working for glories to be realized in this world, and in nothing that they do in pursuing these glories is there any indication that they rely on any sort of other-worldly aid or fear any sort of other-worldly judgment on their efforts. It is in this thoroughgoing repudiation of the supernatural that the Communists may properly be regarded as consistently antireligious. If the wrongs of man are to be righted, only human ingenuity, they believe, can find the way; and it must set about the task at once and be heroically persevering in the task.

This Communist hostility to religion, we have seen, has been explained as a special product of Russian history. To all outward signs, it is true, there is a fundamental incongruity between the program of Communism and the social attitude of the dominant Russian church under the tsardom of the nineteenth century. That church, in both its creed and practice, appeared to be an integral part of the social autocracy which the Communists have sought to destroy. The Holy Synod, ruling body of the church, was presided over by a Chief Procurator appointed and controlled by the tsar; and although some local priests were definitely liberal in their political opinions, others served as recruiting agents for the army of the tsar, and some of them

[50] H. J. Laski, *Communism*, pp. 51–52.

assisted his secret police in apprehending persons charged with political offenses. The church and the tsardom appeared to work hand in hand in the suppression of religious and political heresy. Pobiedonostsev, Chief Procurator during the stirring period of the last quarter of the nineteenth century, was a leading prophet of social reactionism and advocated a stern repression of all religious dissent and of every liberal movement in education and politics.[51] When the tsar, in 1905, under threat of revolution, proclaimed freedom of conscience and opinion, a synod of orthodox bishops denounced the concession. The Russian church taught generally that political authority, like ecclesiastical authority, is derived from God, so that disobedience to government is disobedience to God. Thus the Communists had practical reasons, out of their immediate experience and observation, for associating religion with an opposition to all aggressive efforts of the common man to improve his earthly status.

However, the Communists hardly need that specific record of the Russian church to establish or confirm their belief in the irreconcilability between religion and Communism. Their own explanation of the incompatibility rests on a broader theoretical basis and draws its evidence from a wider historical field. Most existing churches, they believe, approve or tolerate the social system that the Communists wish to destroy. Either the churches do not like the condition of human brotherhood which the Communist seeks to establish in this world or they distrust or fear or regard as superfluous the measures which Communists regard as indispensable in bringing that condition to pass. Whether selfishly or from a vague conception of some generally beneficent purpose to be served by their approval, the church leaders are friendly, or at least deferential or timid, in their attitude to the owners of great wealth. And religion generally, the Communists maintain, preaches contentment with one's earthly lot and submission to the powers that be, or advocates only a passive resistance to these worldly conditions. Thus it is, as Marx said, "opium for the people," quieting their restiveness under existing injustices, either by its appeals for divine intervention to right the wrongs or by its mystic intimations of a contentment to be attained independently of the experiences of which the sufferers are most immediately conscious. Communists regard it as their task to protect oppressed peoples from these delusions. Therefore, they endeavor to rid the ignorant masses of all hope that the hard-

[51] Bernard Pares, *A History of Russia* (second ed., 1930), pp. 391–394, 404.

ships they suffer here can be set right save by human effort or made good by compensatory privileges to be enjoyed in another world.

The earthly glories which the Communists seek to bring to the common man are not, however, merely material glories. The rulers of Russia are diligent in extending and improving popular education and in promoting science, literature, and the drama, and, to a lesser degree, music and art.[52] Their activity in these fields, it is true, has been subordinated, particularly since 1928, to their economic and political policy. They insist, for example, that the teaching and writing of science and philosophy should not be in conflict with the Marxian ideology; they often make books and plays serve the socialist cause by visualizing the government's experiments in communism or by glorifying generally the ideals and emotions of a communistic society; and, in vaguer ways, they attempt to have music and the play of children prepare the proper emotional and ideological milieu for the Communist order. In a broader sense, on the other hand, their political and economic measures are means for their moral and cultural ends. For they recognize, Trotsky has explained, that man does not live by physical activity alone. They seek, therefore, not only a fairer division of material goods and greater leisure for ordinary men but also a finer all-round development of human personality. The moral purpose of their educational policy is, on the one hand, to train man to discipline his animal impulses, and, on the other hand, to give him a sense of his "social relationship" by making him aware of his dependence upon others for the social privileges he enjoys, so that he acts responsibly, recognizing a duty to work with others in serving a common interest. The Soviet authorities strongly support Maxim Gorky's efforts to preserve old and cultivate new literary and artistic treasures in Russia.[53] Their general cultural objectives are to enlarge the information and understanding of the common man, cultivate his critical mind, make him refined in manners and speech, develop his artistic appreciation, and supply him with the physical means for a high order of intellectual and artistic activities.

---

[52] See the following works of Trotsky: *Problems of Life,* translated by Z. Vengerova (1924), *Literature and Revolution,* translated by Rose Strunsky (1925); and cf. the following comments: John Dewey, *Impressions of Soviet Russia* (1929), Ch. III; C. H. Herford, "The Culture of Bolshevist Russia," *Contemporary Review,* CXXXI (1927), 591–599; H. J. Laski, *Communism,* pp. 157–158; Avrahm Yarmolinsky, "New Ideas and Ideals in Soviet Russia," *Current History,* XXII (1925), 402–407; Alexander Bakshy, "Maxim Gorky: Russia's Literary Idol," *ibid.,* XXXVIII (1933), 571–576.

[53] Alexander S. Kaun, *Maxim Gorky and His Russia* (1931), pp. 482 ff.

They have a "humanistic" creed and are inspired by a faith that they can create a society in which all normal men will be able to realize native potentialities of intellectual and æsthetic enjoyment now enchained only by an unfavorable social environment.

CONCLUSION

Economic and political measures predominate in the Communist program as long as the unfavorable environment persists. If the privileges of social life are to be made available equally to all who share the burdens of that life, society must be made the owner of the instrumentalities of labor. This socialist system of distribution and ownership is so completely in opposition to the capitalist system of allotting privileges unequally, without any relation to differences in effort, that the transfer of control from capitalists to socialists has to be by a process that is abrupt and violent; there can be no gradual and voluntary combination of the opposing groups nor any merging of their policies by a process of concession and compromise. A catastrophic social revolution is the first step in the achievement of communism. The next, and longer, step is the concentrated and coercive rule made necessary, on the one hand, by the counter-efforts of a minority bent on regaining their privileges of the old order, and, on the other hand, by the inertia of a majority inexperienced and undisciplined in the ways of the new order.

It is chiefly in this emphasis upon the impossibility of a free and democratic socialistic government—resting on consent of the governed and recognizing no private rights against itself—that the Russian Communists may be said to differ from the orthodox Marxians in the Western states. In this aspect of their doctrine, their affiliations are rather with such groups as the Fascists of Italy or the European and American writers who sneer at the "delusions" of democracy and liberalism. The Communists share a widely prevalent belief that popular government and individual freedom are nothing but obstacles to the efficient execution of any consistent social policy. Many writers, of widely varying social doctrines, hold that rule by a minority, forcibly guiding an incompetent and inert majority and denying any claims of particular interests against the collective interest, is the mark of every community that attempts to act in any organic way.[54] The Communists qualify this general doctrine of aristocratic and authoritarian collectivism by the

[54] See *infra*, pp. 328–331, 477–478.

specification that every coercive political rule over a community is inevitably by and for the immediate benefit of some class within the community. Political authority is never an expression of social solidarity; where there is solidarity, the authority is not needed. The state is always the organization of a class, controlled by the most intelligent, energetic, and class-conscious minority within the class. The Communist state, its spokesmen contend, is, however, unique in that it represents the largest class within the community and is a definite preparation for a future class-less and state-less society. Meanwhile, it governs frankly in the interest of one class and against that of another. In this policy it is always raising up a hitherto submerged group and bringing down a privileged group. The Communist policy, therefore, in contradistinction to the policy of capitalism, progressively diminishes rather than accentuates the differences between the two classes and thereby gradually merges them into a single community. Indeed, the Communist program is intended to destroy eventually every group that insists on remaining a class. Thus proletarian class rule is an intermediate, transitional, stage of society between capitalist class rule and the class-less commonwealth of the future. And when classes disappear, coercive social rule disappears. The Communists, following Marx again, hold that under socialism the state "withers away." For them, as for most other schools of political doctrine, freedom is the ultimate goal. "State power, which is the embodiment of class rule, vanishes in proportion to the vanishing of classes." "The proletariat only needs the state *temporarily*." [55]

Generally, however, the Communists acknowledge that the temporary period of proletarian state omnipotence, intervening between capitalist dictatorship and the free communism of the future, may be a "long historic epoch." Anarchism, in their doctrine, is something to be achieved—and with great difficulty. It is in no sense a way of achieving the ideal organization of society.

SELECT BIBLIOGRAPHY

HISTORICAL ORIGINS OF THE RUSSIAN COMMUNIST RÉGIME: MODERN
RUSSIA, BEFORE MARCH, 1917

Alexinsky, G., *Modern Russia*, translated by Bernard Miall (London, 1913).
Hindus, Maurice G., *The Russian Peasant and the Revolution* (New York, 1920), Chs. I–XIII.

[55] Nikolai Bukharin, "A Programme of Marxism," *Labour Monthly*, IV, 83; Lenin, *The State and Revolution*, pp. 17, 63.

Karpovich, Michael, *Imperial Russia, 1801–1917* (Boston, 1932).

Korff, Baron Sergius, *Autocracy and Revolution in Russia* (New York, 1923). ·

Kovalevski, M. M., *Russian Political Institutions* (Chicago, 1902).

Makeev, Nicholas, and O'Hara, Valentine, *Russia* (London, 1925), Chs. I–V.

Mavor, James, *An Economic History of Russia,* 2 vols. (New York, 1914), Vol. II.

————————, *The Russian Revolution* (London, 1928), Bk. I.

Miller, Margaret S., *The Economic Development of Russia, 1905–1914* (London, 1926).

Nol'de, B., *L'ancien régime et la révolution russe* (Paris, 1928).

Nötzel, Karl, *Die soziale Bewegung in Russland* (Stuttgart, Berlin, and Leipsic, 1923).

Olgin, Moissaye, *The Soul of the Russian Revolution* (New York, 1917).

Pares, Bernard, *A History of Russia* (London, 1926; second ed., New York, 1930), Chs. XVI–XXIV.

————————, *Russia and Reform* (New York and London, 1907).

Robinson, Geroid Tanquary, *Rural Russia under the Old Régime* (London and New York, 1932).

Vernadsky, George, *A History of Russia* (rev. ed., New Haven and London, 1930), Chs. VI–XIII.

Wallace, Donald M., *Russia* (rev. and enl. ed., London and New York, 1912).

Williams, Harold W., *Russia of the Russians* (New York, 1914).

THE REVOLUTIONS OF 1917

Bukharin, N., *Vom Sturze des Zarismus bis zum Sturze der Bourgeoisie* (Zurich, 1918).

La chute du régime tsariste (Documents transcrits; Paris, 1927).

Florinsky, Michael T., *The End of the Russian Empire* (New Haven, 1931).

Golder, F. A., *Documents of Russian History, 1914–1917,* translated by Emanuel Aronsberg (New York, 1927).

Kerensky, Alexander F., *The Catastrophe* (New York and London, 1927).

————————, *The Prelude to Bolshevism: the Kornilov Rebellion* (London, 1919).

Kramar, Karel, *Die russische Krisis,* translated from the Russian by A. Schebek (Munich and Leipsic, 1925).

Lenin, V. I., *The Revolution of 1917,* translated by Joshua Kunitz and M. J. Olgin, Vol. XX of *Collected Works* (New York, 1927–   ).

Lenz, J., *The Second and Third Internationals* (New York, 1931).

Lockhart, R. H. Bruce, *British Agent* (New York, 1932).

Mavor, James, *The Russian Revolution* (London, 1928), Bks. I–III.

Oldenbourg, Serge, ed., *Le coup d'état bolchéviste, 20 octobre–3 décembre*

1917. Recueil des documents relatifs à la prise du pouvoir par les bolchévistes (Paris, 1929).

Pares, Bernard, *History of Russia* (London, 1926), Ch. XXIV.

Petrunkevitch, Alexander; Harper, Samuel N.; and Golder, F. A., *The Russian Revolution* (Cambridge, Mass., 1918).

Trotsky, Leon, *History of the Russian Revolution,* translated by Max Eastman, 3 vols. (New York, 1932).

Vernadsky, George, *History of Russia* (New Haven and London, 1930), Chs. XIII–XIV.

———————, *The Russian Revolution, 1917–1931* (New York, 1932).

•

THE COMMUNIST LEADERS

Chamberlin, William H., *Soviet Russia: a Living Record and a History* (Boston, 1930), Ch. IV.

Eastman, Max, *Leon Trotsky: the Portrait of a Youth* (New York, 1925).

Essad-bey, *Stalin: the Career of a Fanatic* (New York, 1932).

Fülöp-Miller, René, *Lenin and Ghandi,* translated from the German by F. S. Flint and D. F. Tait (London and New York, 1927).

Levine, Isaac Don, *The Man Lenin* (New York, 1924).

———————, *Stalin* (New York, 1931).

Mirsky, D. S., *Lenin* (Boston, 1931).

Trotsky, Leon, *Lenin* (New York, 1925).

———————, *My Life* (New York, 1930).

Vernadsky, George, *Lenin, Red Dictator* (New Haven, 1931).

THE GOVERNMENTAL POLICY OF SOVIET RUSSIA

Arnot, R. Page, *The Russian Revolution: a Narrative and a Guide for Reading* (London, 1923).

Baldwin, Roger, *Liberty under the Soviets* (New York, 1928).

Batsell, W. R., *Soviet Rule in Russia* (New York, 1929).

Brailsford, H. N., *The Russian Workers' Republic* (New York and London, 1921).

———————, *How the Soviets Work* (New York, 1927).

Bron, Saul G., *Soviet Economic Development and American Business: Results of the First Year Under the Five-Year Plan and Further Perspectives* (New York, 1930).

Burns, Emile, *Russia's Productive System* (New York, 1930).

Chamberlin, William H., *Soviet Russia: a Living Record and a History* (Boston, 1930).

———————, *The Soviet Planned Economic Order* (Boston, 1931),

———————, "The Brain Worker in the U.S.S.R.," *New Republic*, LXIX (1931), 34–36.

Chase, Stuart, Dunn, Robert, and Tugwell, R. G., eds., *Soviet Russia in the Second Decade: a Joint Survey by the Technical Staff of the First American Trade Union Delegation* (New York, 1928).

Counts, George S., *The Soviet Challenge to America* (New York, 1931).

Dobb, Maurice, *Russian Economic Development since the Revolution* (London, 1928; second ed., 1929).

Dobbert, Gerhard, ed., *Red Economics,* by Walter Duranty, W. H. Chamberlin, H. R. Knickerbocker and others (Boston and New York, 1932).

Eastman, Max, *Since Lenin Died* (London, 1925).

Economic Review of the Soviet Union (New York, 1927–1933, fortnightly).

Eckardt, Hans von, *Russia* (New York, 1932).

Farbman, Michael, *Piatiletka: Russia's Five-year Plan* (New York, 1931).

Feiler, Arthur, *The Russian Experiment,* translated from the German (New York, 1930).

Fischer, Louis, *Machines and Men in Russia* (New York, 1932).

———————, *The Soviets in World Affairs* (New York, 1930).

Florinsky, Michael T., *World Revolution and the U.S.S.R.* (New York, 1933).

Foreign Policy Reports, Vol. III, No. 15, *Evolution of the Soviet Government, 1917–1927* (New York, 1927).

———————, Vol. VIII, Nos. 1 and 2, *The Political Structure of the Soviet State* (New York, 1932).

Ginsburg, Benjamin, "Science under Communism," *New Republic*, LXIX (1932), 207–9.

Harper, Samuel N., *Civic Training in Soviet Russia* (Chicago, 1929).

———————, *Making Bolsheviks* (Chicago, 1931).

Hecker, Julius, *Religion under the Soviets* (New York, 1927).

Hindus, Maurice, *Broken Earth* (London, 1926).

———————, *Red Bread* (New York, 1931).

———————, *The Great Offensive* (New York, 1933).

Hoover, Calvin B., *Economic Life of Soviet Russia* (New York, 1931).

Information Service, Federal Council of the Churches of Christ in America, Vol. IX, No. 28 (1930), "The Third Act of the Russian Revolution."

Kaganovitch, L. M., *La structure du parti communiste de l'U.R.S.S. (Bolchévik)*, translated from the Russian (Paris, 1926).

Kramar, Karel, *Die russische Krisis* (Munich and Leipsic, 1925), pp. 336–689.

Lawton, Lancelot, *An Economic History of Soviet Russia,* 2 vols. (London, 1932).

Scheffer, Paul, *Seven Years in Soviet Russia* (New York, 1932).

Smith, Jessica, *Woman in Soviet Russia* (New York, 1928).

Soviet Union Review, published monthly by the Soviet Union Information Bureau (Washington, D. C.).

Soviet Union Year-book, compiled and edited by A. A. Santalov and Louis Segal (London, 1925–   ).

Stekoll, Harry, *Through the Communist Looking Glass* (New York, 1932).

"Ten Years of Bolshevism: a Symposium," *Current History,* XXVII (1927), 153–237.

Thompson, Dorothy, *The New Russia* (New York, 1928).

Timoshenko, Vladimir, *Agricultural Russia and the Wheat Problem* (Stanford University, 1932).

Tobenkin, Elias, *Stalin's Ladder* (New York, 1933).

Vernadsky, George, *History of Russia* (New Haven and London, 1930), Chs. XVI–XX.

Ward, Harry F., *In Place of Profit* (New York, 1933).

White, William C., *These Russians* (New York, 1931).

Woody, Thomas, *New Minds: New Men?* (New York, 1932).

Yakovlev, Y. A., *Red Villages* (New York, 1931).

Zelitch, Judah, *Soviet Administration of Criminal Law* (Philadelphia and London, 1931).

THE COMMUNIST DOCTRINES: WORKS OF THE RUSSIAN COMMUNISTS

Bukharin, Nikolai, *The Economic Theory of the Leisure Class* (New York, 1927).

——————, *Historical Materialism: a System of Sociology,* translated from the third Russian edition. (New York, 1925).

——————, *Imperialism and World Economy* (New York, 1929).

——————, *Karl Kautsky und Sowjetrussland* (Vienna, 1925).

——————, "A Programme of Marxism," *Labour Monthly,* IV (1923), 75–92.

——————, *Programme of the World Revolution* (Glasgow, 1920).

——————, "What is New in the Russian Revolution," *Soviet Russia,* IV (1921), 162–163.

Bukharin, Nikolai, and Preobraschensky, E., *The ABC of Communism,* translated from the Russian by Eden and Cedar Paul (London, 1922).

Ilin, M., *New Russia's Primer* (Boston, 1931).

Kamenev, L. B., *The Dictatorship of the Proletariat* (Detroit, 1920).

Lenin, V. I., *Collected Works,* completely revised, edited and annotated (New York, 1927– in process).

——————, *The Revolution of 1917,* translated by Joshua Kunitz and M. J. Olgin, *Collected Works,* Vol. XX (in 2 vols.).

——————, *Toward the Seizure of Power,* translated by M. J. Olgin and Alexander Trachtenberg, *Ibid.,* Vol. XXI (in 2 vols.).

——————, *"Left-wing" Communism, an Infantile Disorder* (London, 1920).

——————, *The Proletarian Revolution and Kautsky the Renegade* (London, 1920).

——————, *Selections from Lenin*, translated by J. Fineberg, 2 vols. (London, 1929).

——————, *The Soviets at Work*, an address delivered in 1928 (fifth ed., New York, 1919).

——————, *The State and Revolution: Marxist Teaching on the State and the Task of the Proletariat in the Revolution* (Detroit, 1917).

Stalin, Joseph, *Leninism*, translated from the Russian by Eden and Cedar Paul (New York, 1928).

——————, *The New Russian Policy* (New York, 1931).

Trotsky, L., *The Defence of Terrorism: a Reply to Karl Kautsky* (London, 1921).

——————, *Literature and Revolution*, translated by Rose Strunsky (New York, 1925).

——————, *Our Revolution: Essays on Working-class and International Revolution, 1904–1917*, collected and translated by M. J. Olgin (New York, 1918).

——————, *Problems of Life*, translated by Z. Vengerova (New York and London, 1924).

——————, *Whither Russia? Towards Capitalism or Socialism* (New York, 1926).

——————, *History of the Russian Revolution*, 3 vols. (New York, 1932).

Third (Communist) International, *Theses and Statutes . . . Adopted by the Second Congress . . . 1920* (Publishing Office of the Communist International, Moscow, 1920).

——————, *Theses and Resolutions Adopted at the Third World Congress . . . 1921* (Contemporary Publishing Association, New York, 1921).

——————, *V^e congrès . . . 1924: Compte rendu analytique* (Librairie de l'Humanité: Paris, 1924).

"Constitution of the Russian Communist Party," Text in *Current History*, XXV (1926–1927), 713–721.

COMMUNIST DOCTRINE IN OTHER COUNTRIES

Foster, William Z., *Toward Soviet America* (New York, 1932).

Lenz, Joseph, *Was Wollen die Kommunisten* (Berlin, 1927).

Oneal, James, *American Communism: a Critical Analysis of Its Origin, Development and Programs* (New York, 1927).

Paul, William, *The State: Its Origin and Function* (London, 1917).

Rappoport, Charles, *La révolution mondiale* (Paris, 1921).

Strachey, John, *The Coming Struggle for Power* (New York, 1933).

CRITICAL EXPOSITION BY NON-COMMUNISTS

Brailsford, H. N., *The Russian Workers' Republic* (New York and London, 1921).

Brameld, Theodore B., *A Philosophical Approach to Communism* (Chicago, 1933).

Brutzkus, Boris, *Die Lehren des Marxismus im Lichte der russischen Revolution* (Berlin, 1928).

Bury, Herbert, *Russia from Within* (London, 1927).

Colton, Ethan T., *The XYZ of Communism* (New York, 1931).

Dewey, John, *Impressions of Soviet Russia and the Revolutionary World* (New York, 1929).

Douglas, Paul H., "Bolshevism," in Charles E. Merriam and Harry E. Barnes, eds., *Political Theories, Recent Times* (New York, 1924), pp. 254–266.

Eastman, Max, *Marx, Lenin and the Science of Revolution* (London, 1926).

Gurian, Waldemar, *Bolshevism: Theory and Practice,* translated by E. I. Watkin (New York, 1932).

d'Herbigny, M., *L'aspect religieux de Moscou en Octobre, 1925, Orientalia Christiana,* Vol. V, No. 3 (Rome, January, 1926).

Herford, C. H., "The Culture of Bolshevist Russia," *Contemporary Review,* CXXXI (1927), 591–599.

Hillquit, Morris, *From Marx to Lenin* (New York, 1921).

Hindus, Maurice, *Humanity Uprooted* (New York, 1929).

Hopper, Bruce, *Pan-Sovietism* (Boston, 1931).

Internationale Vereinigung für Rechts-und Wirtschafts-philosophie, *Der Staat, das Recht und die Wirtschaft des Bolschewismus* (a symposium, Berlin, 1925).

Kautsky, Karl, *The Dictatorship of the Proletariat,* translated by H. J. Stenning (Manchester, London, etc., 1919).

——————, *Terrorism and Communism,* translated by W. H. Kerridge (London, 1920).

Keynes, John M., *Laisser-faire and Communism* (New York, 1926).

——————, *A Short View of Russia* (London, 1925).

Laidler, Harry W., *History of Socialist Thought* (New York, 1927), Chs. XXV and XXVII.

Landau, Mark A., *Lenin,* authorized translation from the French (New York, 1922).

Laski, H. J., *Communism* (New York and London, 1927).

Luxemburg, Rosa, *Die russische Revolution* (Frankfort, 1922).

McCormick, Anne O'Hare, *The Hammer and the Scythe: Communist Russia Enters the Second Decade* (New York, 1928).

MacDonald, J. Ramsay, *Dictatorship and Revolution* (London, 1920).

Mason, Edward S., *The Paris Commune: an Episode in the History of the Socialist Movement* (New York, 1930).

Mautner, Wilhelm, *Der Bolschewismus* (Berlin, 1920), Pt. III.

Nitti, Francesco, *Bolshevism, Fascism and Democracy*, translated by Margaret M. Green (London and New York, 1927).

Pasvolsky, Leo, *The Economics of Communism, with Special Reference to Russia's Experiment* (New York, 1921).

Postgate, R. W., *The Bolshevik Theory* (New York, 1920).

Russell, Bertrand, *Bolshevism: Practice and Theory* (New York, 1920).

Shaw, Bernard, "The Dictatorship of the Proletariat," *Labour Monthly*, I (1921), 297–317.

Spargo, John, *Bolshevism: the Enemy of Political and Industrial Democracy* (New York, 1919).

——————, *The Psychology of Bolshevism* (New York, 1917).

Spinka, Matthew, *The Church and the Russian Revolution* (New York, 1927).

"La Technique Révolutionnaire du Bolchévisme," *Revue des deux mondes*, XL (1927), 271–299.

Walling, W. E., *Sovietism: the ABC of Russian Bolshevism—according to the Bolshevists* (New York, 1920).

Yarmolinsky, Avrahm, "New Ideas and Ideals in Soviet Russia," *Current History*, XXII (1925), 402–407.

CHAPTER VII

THE ANARCHISTS

HISTORICAL SKETCH

ANARCHISM is the doctrine that political authority, in any of its forms, is unnecessary and undesirable. In recent anarchism, theoretical opposition to the state has usually been associated with opposition to the institution of private property and also with hostility to organized religious authority.

Doubts as to the moral and social legitimacy of state authority have been expressed since the earliest periods of political speculation. Some of the Stoics of ancient Greece belittled the importance of political institutions and taught that the way to the good life was to be found not in the rightly organized state (where Plato and Aristotle sought it) but in a social condition in which men are able to act freely in response to natural instincts of sociability and justice; these philosophers held that it was unreasonable to subject benevolent and reasonable men to the control of political magistracies, composed often of inferior members of the community. Various sects of the Middle Ages held that religion was an adequate guarantee for a just and orderly civil life and that men united in their Christian faith should be permitted to live under the control of that faith alone, free from any restraint by the state.[1] Several poets and philosophers in modern times have disparaged political coercion as generally a violation of the rights of human personality and have vaguely argued that man's natural reasonableness and sociability constitute the best possible foundation for a just and happy social life.[2]

Instances such as the foregoing show simply that serious disparagement of political authority is no new thing. More immediate sources of the main ideas of recent anarchism are to be found in other places:

[1] Such were the doctrines of the Arminians in the ninth century and the Anabaptists in the fifteenth century.

[2] These views appear at places in the writings of the Benedictine monk, Rabelais (1495–1553), and of the French prelate, François Fénelon (1651–1715).

in the familiar seventeenth century and eighteenth century doctrines of freedom and equality as natural human rights; in the economic dogmas (set forth by the eighteenth century physiocrats and the later classical economists) of a natural order of society, distinguished from a society restrained and directed by political authority; in the psychological dogmas that lie at the basis of these and other doctrines of economic individualism—the assumptions that each individual seeks only his own interest and is intelligent enough to pursue his interest successfully with little help from organized society; finally, in the socialist doctrine that existing political arrangements sanction economic institutions which take from laborers the values they create. The more narrowly individualistic implications of any of these doctrines are not generally accepted by anarchists. Most anarchist doctrines rest upon assumptions of the predominance of the social and coöperative, not the self-seeking and competitive, instincts of man.[3]

William Godwin (1756–1836)—son of a Calvinist minister, a minister himself for a brief period, and an author of novels, plays, children's stories, and miscellaneous works in social theory—has often been called the first modern anarchist; he was the first clearly to associate opposition to political authority with an attack on private property.[4] He maintained that ordinary men act reasonably and justly when their normal desires for self-expression and fair dealing have not been perverted by unfair economic conditions, maintained by the coercive intervention of the state. He admitted, however, that even if the most natural and equitable social relations were now restored, there would for a long period be some men whose conduct would require restraint. Vestiges of the authoritative state will, therefore, have to remain until, through the steady work of enlightened and just government, the perverted instincts of this unfortunate minority are brought back into their normal modes of expression. Thus Godwin's doctrine was not fully anarchistic, nor did he designate it by any such name. Nevertheless, the greater part of his theoretical work was devoted to an exposition of the social and moral ills created by public government and private property, which, he believed, sanction and sustain one another.

[3] For general accounts of modern anarchism, see the titles on pp. 226–228, infra.

[4] Godwin was the husband of the celebrated feminist, Mary Woolstonecraft, and the father-in-law of Shelley. His most important political work, *An Enquiry concerning Political Justice,* was first published in 1793. See C. H. Driver, "William Godwin," in *The Social and Political Ideas of Some Representative Thinkers of the Revolutionary Era,* F. J. C. Hearnshaw, ed. (1931), pp. 141–180.

A somewhat similar sort of utopian anarchism appears in the works of Thomas Hodgskin (1787–1869), in post-Waterloo England. He became a convinced and extreme individualist as a result of reading Adam Smith. The theory of an ultimate and underlying harmony—which the classical economists tended to assume—Hodgskin made the central point of his teaching. He believed that the whole universe "is regulated by permanent and invariable laws." Man is part of this vast system, so that "his conduct is influenced, regulated, and controlled or punished in every minute particular by permanent and invariable laws, in the same manner as the growth of plants and the motion of the heavenly bodies." Consequently there is no need whatever for legislation or for planning. The preëstablished harmony of self-interest achieves itself when man is left unhindered. Therefore, "all law making, except gradually and quietly to repeal all existing laws, is arrant humbug."

Along with this teaching Hodgskin combined the individualistic doctrine of the right to the whole produce of labor. That principle, he believed, was guaranteed and underwritten by Nature herself. It is the natural property right in contradistinction to the existing artificial right. When all present laws are repealed, Hodgskin believed and taught, this natural property right would be automatically achieved, and all men would secure their deserts in proportion to the efforts of their labor.

Hodgskin did not delineate the form of a community without government; and in most of his utterances he appeared willing to retain political authority, provided that it should withdraw its sanctions from the unjust system of private industrial property and confine its tasks to maintaining peace and order. In promulgating the labor theory of value as a doctrine of revolt he appears to have had a considerable influence on that generation of London working-men which later supported the Chartist movement (1838–1848). It is also possible that he had some influence on another extreme individualist, Herbert Spencer. Both men were, for a few years in the forties, on the staff of the London *Economist*, and Spencer's *Social Statics* (published in 1851) shows close affinities with the general trend of ideas in Hodgskin's various works.[5]

---

[5] For the paragraphs on Hodgskin the writer is indebted almost exclusively to Professor C. H. Driver of King's College, London; see his "Thomas Hodgskin and the Individualists," Ch. IX, in *Social and Political Ideas of Some Representative Thinkers of the Age of Reaction and Reconstruction*, F. J. C. Hearnshaw, ed., (1932); also Élie Halévy, *Thomas Hodgskin* (1903) and the forthcoming biography of Hodgskin by Driver. Hodgskin's chief works, from which the above quotations come, are: *Labour Defended aaginst the Claims of Capital* (1825);

Pierre Joseph Proudhon (1809–1865) was probably the first to call himself an anarchist. Son of a cooper, reared in poverty, but obtaining a college education through heroic effort, he moved to Paris as a young man, under a pension from the *académie* of his home town. In Paris he at once came into close associations with radical socialists congregated there and served a brief prison term for writing seditious articles following the revolution of 1848.[6] Basing his doctrine on the Golden Rule and the natural law of justice, he derived therefrom the right of every one to the full product of his own labors. His first published work was entitled *What Is Property?* His answer was that it was "theft." In the same work he declared: "I am, in the full sense of the word, an anarchist."[7] His most specific complaint against the state was that it had evolved out of the system of private property and had sustained the inequitable incidents of that institution. He condemned political authority also on the broader ground that it implied the dominance of passion over reason, justice, and understanding. In some of his writings he explained that in condemning property he had in mind chiefly that form of it made up of accumulations from profits, interest, and rent; and his specific economic proposals seemed intended only to eliminate the monopolistic and exploitative features from private property, rather than to destroy the institution altogether. He drew up a plan for a "Bank of the People," to issue "labor notes" which would represent units of labor, measured solely by duration, and would be loaned, without interest, to any one offering his capacity and promise to work as security. Proudhon's more elaborate fiscal proposals constitute a system of "mutualism," under which individuals and voluntary associations would be enabled to engage in productive enterprise through gratuitous credit supplied by coöperative banking associations. He described his mutualism as "positive anarchy." He believed that his banking plan would eventually eliminate all private capital by rendering it incapable of earning interest and that the plan would so encourage and facilitate voluntary coöperation generally that any sort of coercive social organization would become unnecessary.

Popular Political Economy (1827); *The Natural and Artificial Right of Property Contrasted* (1832).

[6] Proudhon's works are published in 26 volumes (*Œuvres complètes*, 1868–1876). There is a new edition in process (1923–   ). See especially his *Qu'est-ce que la propriété* (1840) in Vol. V of the 1923 ed., and *Système des contradictions économiques ou philosophie de la misère* (1846), *ibid.*, Vols. II–III. For a recent evaluation of his ideas, see L. Maury, "Sur Proudhon," *Revue bleue*, LXVI (1928), 278–280.

[7] *What Is Property?* translated by Benj. R. Tucker (1876), p. 272.

It is the fiscal part of Proudhon's doctrine that became most widely known and most influential. Proudhon mutualists were predominant in the French labor movement in the sixties and seventies. Continental immigration into the United States brought his ideas into this country, where practical experiments were undertaken by his disciples. Most of the disciples voiced his opposition to state socialism and to governmental aid or interference, but their positive anarchism, like Proudhon's, went little further than an occasional suggestion that, if mutualism were established, justice and good would prevail to such a degree that all occasions for authoritative intervention in the intercourse of men would disappear.[8]

Most of the American anarchists of the mid-nineteenth century derived their ideas directly from older intellectual traditions: the eighteenth century romanticist beliefs in man's innate goodness and free will, the orthodox labor theory of value, and the utilitarian doctrine of intelligent self-interest. And they developed their ideas in direct reference to American social questions—e.g., slavery, and, later, the labor problems arising from the rapidly increasing industrialism of the sixties and seventies.[9] Radical abolitionists broadened a denunciation of the United States government—on the ground of its violation, through slavery, of man's natural right "to his own body" and the fruits "of his own labor"—into a condemnation of all government as based essentially on violence. Many of them preached "non-resistance"—a refusal to take any part in government or to countenance the use of force either in support of or against government. Henry David Thoreau (1817–1862), following the transcendentalists in their beliefs in man's natural impulses to goodness and in his perfectibility under the guidance of his free and reasonable will, argued for the supremacy, under all conditions, of conscience over the law. He urged both passive and active resistance

---

[8] See *Proudhon's Solution of the Social Problem* edited by Henry Cohen (1927), from a revised form (first in 1849) of articles written in 1848 by Charles A. Dana in Paris, printed in the New York *Tribune,* and published in *The Spirit of the Age*—a weekly, edited by William H. Channing.

William B. Greene (1819–1878) was the most thoroughgoing American follower of Proudhon. Born at Haverhill, Mass., he was a student for a short while at West Point Military Academy and later at the Harvard Divinity School. He was a Unitarian minister for a brief period, was a member of the Massachusetts constitutional convention of 1853, and served as a Colonel in the Civil War. See his *Mutual Banking* (1850), *Sovereignty of the People* (1868), and *Socialistic, Communistic, Mutualistic and Financial Fragments* (1875).

[9] For an extensive account of anarchism in the United States, see Eunice M. Schuster, *Native American Anarchism* (1932), which contains a useful bibliography on pp. 188–197.

to the American government in the struggle against slavery, ardently defended John Brown's raid and other acts of violence in that struggle, disparaged all claims for the good achievements by governments in the past, and held up the ideal of a future society without any government.[10] More systematic doctrines of anarchism were set forth by Josiah Warren (1799–1874) and his disciple Stephen Pearl Andrews (1812–1886), and later by Benjamin R. Tucker (1854–   ) and his disciples —particularly Lysander Spooner (1808–1887). These men, like Greene and most of the leaders of the antislavery non-resistants, were well-born, somewhat conventionally educated, New Englanders, interested generally in radical economic and social reforms.

Warren published the first anarchist journal in the United States— the *Peaceful Revolutionist* (a weekly, lasting only a few months). He resided for a brief while in the Owenite settlement at New Harmony; operated a bank of the same general sort as Proudhon's later "Bank of the People," but with "repugnance" as well as time of labor considered in the evaluations of the labor notes; conducted a "time store" for two years, with its merchandise valued in terms of the time and repugnance of labor; and established several brief-lived colonies, in which the inhabitants carried on small farms and trades and exchanged their products through the medium of the labor notes.[11] Basing his social doctrine on the universal natural law of self-preservation, he argued that man's need for governmental protection to-day arises from evils originating not in his own nature but in the unfortunate "errors" committed by his forefathers in setting up the institutions of private property and coercive government. For the direction of general community affairs, Warren proposed a council of experts whose decisions would have only the weight that reasoning and persuasion in support of them could give. He advised working-men to renounce all interest in political affairs and confine their activities to voluntary coöperative

---

[10] See particularly his *Civil Disobedience* (1864), in *The Writings of Henry David Thoreau*, IV (1906), 356–387.

[11] Warren, often called the first American anarchist, was born in Boston, son of a distinguished general of the Revolutionary War. Andrews was born at Templeton, Mass., studied at Amherst College, and later qualified for the practice of the law; his popular fame rests chiefly upon his vigorous abolitionist activities and his researches and propaganda in the fields of phonography and spelling reform. See Josiah Warren, *Equitable Commerce* (1852) and *True Civilization* (1863); William Bailie, *Josiah Warren, the First American Anarchist* (1906); Stephen P. Andrews, *The True Constitution of Society in the Sovereignty of the Individual* (1852), *The Labor Dollar* (1877)—reprinted from Tucker's short-lived *Radical Review*.

efforts; if that were done, profits and poverty would be gradually eliminated from society and the need for government would eventually disappear.

Benjamin Tucker accepted for the most part the economic proposals
of Proudhon and Greene and acknowledged Warren's influence in forming his general social doctrines.[12] In 1881, he established a magazine,
Liberty, which, issuing semiweekly until 1907, acquired a considerable
reputation as an exponent of philosophical anarchism. In 1893 he published a volume of his articles selected from this magazine, with the
title—*Instead of a Book, by a Man Too Busy to Write One: a Fragmentary Exposition of Philosophical Anarchism.*

Tucker made intelligent self-interest the basis of his doctrine. "Anarchists," he said, "are egoists in the farthest and fullest sense." They
totally discard "the idea of moral obligation." All men have "the right,
if they have the power, to kill or coerce other men and make the entire
world subservient to their ends." With Tucker, man's natural self-
interest leads logically to a society in which all men are prevailingly
free, for liberty is the most effective agency of order, as well as the chief
ingredient of happiness. Liberty means the enjoyment of "rights," which
are simply the practical limits which self-interest places upon might;
men form associations in order to secure a better definition and recognition of these limits. Stable society is essential to the enjoyment of
liberty; but any social infringement of liberty, beyond the point where
a limitation is necessary to prevent interference by one individual with
the liberty of another, is an "invasion." "The nature of the invasion is
not changed, whether it is made by one man upon another man, after
the manner of the ordinary criminal, or by one man upon all other men,
after the manner of an absolute monarch, or by all men upon one man,
after the manner of a modern democracy." Political authority, therefore, should be eliminated from society; for at all periods of history,
and whatever the form of government, the state has violated the principle of liberty. It has always put restraint upon non-invasive as well as
invasive acts. "This is the anarchistic definition of government: the subjection of the non-invasive individual to an external will." [13]

[12] Born at South Dartmouth, Mass., Tucker was a student at a Friends'
Academy and later at the Massachusetts Institute of Technology. While in Boston
he met Warren. From early youth he was actively interested in movements to
improve the conditions of labor. Starting adult life as a printer, he was for several
years on the editorial staff of the Boston *Globe,* but abandoned that position in
order to devote his efforts to the elaboration and dissemination of his own ideas.

[13] Tucker, *Instead of a Book,* p. 23.

The most prevalent and characteristic forms of the invasive action of the state, according to Tucker, are taxation, military protection, and the administration of justice. Taxation is the compulsive exaction of a man's earnings for services which, in many cases, he does not want. Military defense and judicial protection are services which should be supplied in the same way that all other social needs are supplied, in a country whose government acts according to the traditional principles of *laisser-faire;* they should be sought and paid for by those who demand them. The state has no more right to monopolize and compel acceptance of such services than it has the right to monopolize and impose educational and benevolent services or a regulation of private property. The state is also invasive because it coercively protects the ownership of industrial property by those who perform no labors on the property. It compels acceptance of an economic system under which the surplus values produced by laborers are allotted, in the form of rent, interest, and profits, to those who do not labor.

In place of the state, Tucker would have associations formed by individuals freely contracting. Every such association should have the right to enforce upon its members whatever regulations the members agree upon, including an obligation to pay taxes—if that is part of the agreed conditions of membership. But entrance into any association should be without compulsion and members should retain the right of secession. Among the most important of these associations would be the societies for defense—for protection of members of the community against those who violate essential social laws by invasive acts. Tucker recognizes the right of the defensive associations to employ, against invasive individuals, all the repressive and punitive measures now employed by the state.

The essential distinctions between Tucker's doctrine and non-anarchist doctrines are that the former makes membership in, and positive support of, any political, i.e., force-employing, association, a matter of free choice on the part of each individual, and allows no association to claim a monopoly of this or any other sort of social service. Thus there may be competing associations for defense. A political citizenship by birth, or involuntary citizenship of any sort, is excluded by Tucker's system. No one is to be compelled to join a defensive or other association, and none but members will be compelled to pay taxes to any association. A defensive association will employ coercion against non-members not to exact allegiance, fiscal support, or acceptance of beneficent services but only to prevent and punish invasive acts. This, according to Tucker, is still anarchism. "The subjection of the *invasive* individual is not government, but resistance to and protection from government." [14] Moreover, the necessity for such repression will soon cease. The disposition to invasive action is produced solely by the oppressive action of an authority which demands the loyalty and coöperation of unwilling individuals and enforces upon all an inequitable economic system. When coercive government disappears, crimes will disappear.

There have been respectable and thoughtful followers of Tucker, some of whom are still living.[15] The most significant anarchism of the later nineteenth and earlier twentieth centuries, however, in the United States as elsewhere, is the revolutionary doctrine set forth by followers of the Russians, Bakunin and Kropotkin.

None of the anarchists whom we have considered expected that political authority could be got rid of suddenly or that it should be attacked in a violent revolt. Godwin, Proudhon, and the New England anarchists, we have seen, recommended only a gradual elimination of political government, and that only by peaceful methods: opening the eyes of the people to injustices under the existing order, education in the principles of anarchy, the practice of passive resistance, and a renunciation of all part in political activity. Moreover, none of them, except Tucker, and, more briefly, Warren, proposed any system for a comprehensive organization of a community from which the state had been removed; and Tucker retained agencies of organized coercion in the social order he proposed.

Anarchist ideas of a more menacing sort had appeared in the writings of several Germans—notably Johann Kasper Schmidt (1806–1856), an obscure school teacher, who wrote under the pseudonym of "Max

14 *Instead of a Book*, p. 39.

15 Lysander Spooner (1808–1887), becoming in late life a convert to the views of the much younger Tucker, was the most violent of any of the New England anarchists in verbal assaults on the Constitution and government of the United States. He had been a radical abolitionist and a vigorous critic of the social evils arising from monopoly and large-scale industry. He was born in Athol, Mass., and prepared himself for the law. In 1884 he operated a private mail route between Boston and New York, in a successful effort to compel the government to reduce its postage rates. See his *Natural Law or the Science of Justice* (1882); *A Letter to Thomas F. Bayard Challenging His Right and that of All the Other So-called Senators and Representatives in Congress—To Exercise Any Legislative Power Whatever over the People of the United States* (1882); *A Letter to Grover Cleveland on His False Inaugural Address, the Usurpations and Crimes of Lawmakers and the Consequent Poverty, Ignorance, and Servitude of the People* (1886).

Stirner." Stirner's doctrine is exclusively individualistic.[16] To him the individual is the only reality, and the supreme law for every individual is his own interest and pleasure. The only right is might. "Whatever I do, I do for my own sake," though I make pretensions to humaneness and liberality. "We have only one relation to one another, that of utility, of usableness, of use."[17] Thus the state is unnatural because it represses the individual in the supposed interest of the community. "The state has never any object but to limit the individual, to tame him, to subordinate him, to subject him to something general." "I am the mortal enemy of the state."[18] To get rid of the unnatural, individual-repressing, political institutions, any means are to be used that give promise of success. Experience shows that insurrection and violence are necessary in order to bring about any substantial transformation of an existing order of society.

Stirner's work hardly falls into the regular course of recent anarchist doctrine. It is not a reasoned argument for a society organized on the lines of purely voluntary coöperation. Its main theme appears rather to be an appeal for the rights of civil disobedience; a protest—chiefly in terms of scorn and ridicule—against any sort of subordination to constitutional restraints—whether set up voluntarily or coercively—on intelligent self-interest. His attitude is in part like that of the Russian nihilists; and it is similar to Nietzsche's exaltation of the rights of the strong to rule over and exploit the weak.[19] His doctrine involves an attack on the state in so far as political authority stands in the way of a vindication of the strong man's inevitable will to power. Although his *Ego and His Own* enjoyed considerable popularity for a brief period, he left no important body of disciples. Interest in his ideas revived at the time that Nietzsche's ideas were spread abroad, in the last decade of the nineteenth century.

[16] He taught in a government school, 1833–1835, and in a private school for girls, 1839–1855. He was translator of several standard works in classical political economy, and he wrote a brief account of the French Revolution; see John H. Mackay, *Max Stirner* (Leipsic, 1898, etc.), and J. G. Huneker, *Egoists* (1909), Ch. X. His reputation as a theorist rests on his *Der Einzige und sein Eigenthum* (1845), translated, by S. T. Byington, as *The Ego and His Own* (1913). Several contemporaries of Stirner, less extreme in their anarchism, exercised probably greater influence upon the workingmen of their time, notably, Moses Hess (1812–72), Karl Grün (1817–87), and Wilhelm Marr (1819–72); none of these made significant contributions to the evolution of ideas.

[17] Stirner, *The Ego and His Own*, pp. 426, 385.

[18] *Ibid.*, pp. 298, 339.

[19] For the Nihilists, see *infra* in this chapter, pp. 219–220; for Nietzsche, *infra.* pp. 312–313, 342–343.

The most systematic and thoroughgoing anarchist doctrines in modern times appear in the writings of Michael Bakunin (1814–1876) and Prince Peter Kropotkin (1842–1921). These high-born, cultivated writers sought to show the orderly, evolutionary, scientific aspects of their anarchist creeds; they recommended violence, but only in a carefully organized revolution, not in isolated and irresponsible acts of assassination and destruction; and they outlined comprehensive schemes of organization for a society without political control. Their arguments are thoroughly permeated by the familiar socialist criticisms of private property, but they add other criticisms, and in their programs of social reconstruction they are radically different from the socialists. They condemn the centralized control in the Marxian system, and would eliminate collective as well as private ownership of industrial property. Although there is much in common between these two brilliant Russians, there are also significant points of difference in their criticisms, in their programs, and in the general spirit of their social philosophy.

Both Bakunin and Kropotkin were born of old families of distinction among the Russian nobility. Both were trained for military life and as young men served as officers in the army. Their experiences gave them first-hand observation of the despotic and terroristic policies of the Russian civil and military administration in their day. Their reactions turned them to socialist and revolutionary, and soon to anarchist, views.[20] Their writings and their direct participation in insurrectionary movements in various European states brought them into conflict with the political authorities on several occasions; both served several terms in prison and spent most of their later years in exile—Bakunin in Switzerland; Kropotkin in France for several years and then, for the last years of his life, in England.

BAKUNIN

Bakunin, the son of a diplomat and a student at the universities of St. Petersburg and Moscow, spent twelve years in prison and was twice sentenced to death. He is regarded as the founder of an extensive movement of anarchism among proletarian groups of Europe in the later nineteenth century. His activities were predominantly in the field of

---

[20] A useful account of the life and activities of Bakunin is M. Nettlau, *Michael Bakunin: eine Biographie*, 3 vols. (1896–1900). The best account of Kropotkin's life is his own *Memoirs of a Revolutionist* (1899).

practical agitation and organization. His writings—although in a style
that is vivid, eloquent, and incisive—are lacking in orderliness of arrangement; most of them he left uncompleted at his death. His influence was due chiefly to his industry, courage, devotion to his cause,
and skill in organizing and directing the intrigues of secret societies.

Bakunin founded his doctrine of anarchism upon what he described
as a scientific basis.[21] The whole evolution of man, he argued, is from
a condition in which animal impulses and physical restraints control his
conduct toward a condition in which ideal ends and sanctions predominate. Human history "consists in the progressive negation of man's
original bestiality, the evolution of his humanity." [22] Political authority,
private property, and religion are natural institutions for the lower
stages of man's development, for they are associated, in one way or
another, with physical desires and fears: private property cultivates
man's interest in material goods; the state supports private property
through its physical compulsions; religion sustains both state and
property, and it also appeals to man's desire for physical comfort and to
his fear of physical suffering after death. These institutions, characteristic
expressions of man's primitive nature, are, under the natural laws of
human evolution, destined to disappear.

Bakunin is explicit and uncompromising in rejecting all institutions
of political control, even those resting on universal suffrage. Despotism,
he holds, lies not in the form of the state but in its essence; and the
most democratic devices are of no avail whatever in modifying this
essential character of the state.[23] The ignorance and inexperience of the
masses make them helpless against the intrigues of the economically
powerful classes, who can mold any form of political machinery to their
own advantage. In this sense Bakunin's repudiation of the state has an

---

[21] The following is a collection of Bakunin's works: Michael Bakunin, Œuvres,
edited by J. Guillaume, 6 vols. (Paris, 1907–1913).

The analysis here given of Bakunin's ideas is based chiefly on the following
of his works: Fédéralisme, socialisme, antithéologisme (1867–1868), Œuvres, I,
1–205; Articles écrits pour le journal l'égalité (1868–1869), ibid., V, 11–218;
L'Empire Knouto-Germanique et le révolution sociale (1870), ibid., II, 287–455;
III, 7–177; Dieu et l'état, ibid., I, 261–326.

For analysis of Bakunin's doctrines, cf. the excellent article by Samuel Rezneck,
"The Political and Social Theory of Michael Bakunin," American Political Sci-
ence Review, XXI (1927), 270–296; and also the following: Eduard Bernstein,
"Karl Marx und Bakunin," Archiv für Sozialwissenschaft und Sozialpolitik, XXX
(1910), 1–29; F. Brupbacher, Marx und Bakunin (1913); Paul Eltzbacher,
Anarchism, Ch. VI.

[22] Œuvres, III, 37. Cf. also, I, 275,

[23] Ibid., II, 326 ff.

economic basis. The system of private property in the means of production keeps the masses of men in subjection to the owners of capital; the state rests upon and perpetuates this system. The object of every political system is to confirm and organize the exploitation of workers by property-owners.[24]

However, although the *raison d'être* of political authority is the perpetuation of an oppressive economic condition, its essential vice, according to Bakunin, lies even more in its moral and intellectual features. The state is morally debasing to all members of a civilized community— to those who govern as well as to those who are governed, for it acts by compulsion rather than by enlightenment and persuasion. In every act of the state, the judgment and will of the private citizen is displaced by a command of some public agency. Morality and intelligence in human conduct consist solely in performing good and reasonable acts that are approved as good or recognized as reasonable by the doer. An act done under dictation is wholly lacking in moral or rational quality. Thus the inevitable tendency of state action is to degrade the moral and intellectual levels of those subject to its authority. Political authority also demoralizes those who participate in its exercise. To occupy a position of political power engenders attitudes of superiority quite out of relation to any actual distinction in merit. Among those who exercise the power, natural sentiments of coöperation and fraternity are supplanted by traditions of prerogative, class differentiation, and sacrifice of individual welfare to the interests of public office. Thus the state makes tyrants or egoists out of the few and servants or dependents out of the many.

Private property, which is both the ground of existence and the consequence of the state, creates physical and moral evils of all kinds. To the millions of workers, it brings economic dependence, laborious toil, ignorance, and social and spiritual immobility; for the few wealthy, it provides superfluous luxury and special opportunities for physical pleasure and artistic and intellectual enjoyment. Religion is an evil, both because it sanctions evil institutions and because it is incompatible with man's better nature. It is consciously used by the possessors of economic and political privilege to sanctify their unnatural superiority.[25] It diverts man's interest and effort from important affairs in the actual world of humanity; develops his fancy, superstition, and credu-

[24] *Œuvres*, II, 311, 326.
[25] *Ibid.*, III, 127 ff.

lity; and aborts his reason and insight. Religious faith should be displaced by science and knowledge; the fiction of future divine justice, by the actuality of present human justice.

The goal of anarchism is, according to Bakunin, to be attained both through evolution and revolution. Anarchism has both a scientific and an insurrectionary technique. The "current of events and facts" flows automatically towards the anarchist goal. The task of anarchists is to eliminate the impediments to that current, both by removing ignorance of the natural laws of social evolution and by demolishing the institutions which interfere with the evolution. An anarchist revolution means the destruction of all that is commonly understood in the expression "public order." The destruction will require some measures of violence. It cannot be effected through the ballot; and inevitably there will be some bloodshed, as a result both of the stupidity of those who will stubbornly attempt to resist and of the natural feelings of revenge which many, in the first moments of their uprising, will feel towards their former oppressors.[26] Although Bakunin deprecated such acts of personal vengeance, he did not minimize the severity and thoroughness of the anarchist revolution: it will involve the forcible dissolution of churches, the army, courts, police, legislative assemblies and administrative offices, and the invalidation of all titles to property.

How is an anarchist revolution to be organized? There will be, in a capital or other key city, voluntary associations of faithful anarchists, organized by "barricades" (grouped, that is, by streets or quarters of the city). The barricades will send representatives, instructed and recallable, to a council for the whole city, which, in turn, will create out of its membership committees for the various functions of revolutionary administration. The task of this revolutionary organization will be, on the one hand, to execute thoroughly the program of destruction: the prompt suppression of all political institutions; the immediate distribution, among workers' societies, of all productive property; and the initiation of measures to guarantee that no new authoritative organization of any sort—not even a proletarian or socialist dictatorship—will be set up. On the other hand, in order to consolidate the revolution on a national scale, the council will send agents, as propagandists and agitators, to the provincial and rural communities, in order to secure their participation by informing them as to the actual ends and achievements of the revolution.

[26] *Œuvres,* V, 45 ff.

When the state and private property disappear, what shall take their places? Bakunin did not maintain that the whole problem of human welfare would be solved by eliminating political authority and private property. It is true that he put emphasis upon the destructive phases of anarchism and disparaged any detailed discussion of the future organization of society. But he had full appreciation of the social aspects of man's life and recognized the need for a regular organization of human relations.[27] Every advance in human evolution, he said, every release of man from subjection to the forces of his physical environment or from enslavement to his own animal instincts, has come about through the sympathetic collaboration of man with his fellows. Human freedom has no meaning apart from society. For freedom is not a merely negative concept; it denotes more than the mere absence of external restriction of one's faculties; it means the ability to act in response to the characteristic impulses of a rational being. The true liberty of a human individual postulates, on the one hand, a recognition of his freedom by others, and, on the other hand, an equal respect on his part for the freedom of others. A hermit, a cannibal, or a slave-master cannot be regarded as morally free. "Liberty is not a matter of isolation, but of mutuality; not of separation, but of combination; for every man, it is only the mirroring of his humanity (that is, of his human rights) in the consciousness of his brothers." [28] Bakunin calls this the principle of "solidarity," by virtue of which a man feels himself as fully free only when he sees about him others enjoying the same freedom.

In place of the state, therefore, Bakunin would establish a free society, from which all classes and all relations of authority have disappeared and in which every one, without distinction of race, color, nationality, or belief, is permitted to labor and enjoy the fruits of his labor, on equal terms.[29] The basis of this free society will be contract and voluntary association, instead of law and compulsive allegiance. As the coöperation will rest upon the natural needs and inclinations of men, whatever organization is necessary will develop from the bottom upwards. The new society will operate on these basic economic principles: society itself will own the land and all materials and instruments of production; it will permit them to be taken into possession by those persons, acting individually or in freely formed associations, who are

---

[27] *Œuvres,* I, 141, 286.
[28] *Ibid.,* I, 278.
[29] On the character of the new society, cf. *Ibid.,* I, 112; II, 347, 392; V, 75.

willing to use them productively; every individual will then be permitted to share freely in the enjoyment of the products to the extent of his needs, subject only to the condition that he has, to the best of his ability, contributed his labors to the productive efforts. Local associations may combine into larger territorial combinations, provided that at every stage there is no compulsion about it. And the coöperation need not stop at existing "national" lines. The abolition of the state will mean the end of political boundaries. "There will be a free union of individuals into communes, of communes into provinces, of provinces into nations, and finally of nations into the United States of Europe, and later of the whole world." [30] The associations will have a system of law that needs no penal sanctions, for it is made up of rules which the members perceive to be necessary in keeping society going.

Bakunin conceived this order of society not as an inspiring ideal for the remote future but as a goal to be soon achieved, probably before the close of the nineteenth century. The immediate task of those who foresee the course of evolution is, he said, to organize and expedite the revolution. This is to be done by both education and intrigue. The policy of repression pursued by existing governments makes it necessary for the anarchist campaign to be carried out through secret societies of the faithful. The chief work of these societies will be, not to commit acts of terrorism, but to free the masses of men from their economic ard political superstitions and bring back into operation their more natural ideas and emotions. This will lead naturally to an heroic and effective coöperation in overthrowing the institutions which only unreasoning fears and abnormal feelings have sustained and in setting up a society founded on voluntary association and mutual good will.

KROPOTKIN

Kropotkin's writings are vivid and interesting and display a scientific temper as well as a breadth of sympathy.[31] He sought to give evolutionary and historical bases to his doctrines. He maintained that the method of the natural sciences was the only way to reach conclusions as to the

[30] *Œuvres*, I, 16–17.
[31] The account here of Kropotkin's doctrines is based chiefly on his following works: *Paroles d'un révolté* (1885); *La conquête du pain* (1888; sixteenth ed., 1921), in translation *The Conquest of Bread* (1907); *Anarchist Communism: Its Basis and Principles* (1905), republished from articles in *The Nineteenth Century and After*, February and August, 1887; *L'anarchie dans l'évolution socialiste*, (1885), in translation *The Place of Anarchy in Socialist Evolution* (1886).

nature of man and society. He was a student of biology and human geography, and some of his anarchist propositions are stated in terms of generalizations in these fields, buttressed by an array of concrete data. He represented his doctrine as based not on metaphysical conceptions of natural rights but on ideas of the actual course of human evolution. The laws of natural evolution, he held, apply alike to animals and their groupings and to men and human society. They define the processes of an increasing adaptation to surrounding conditions of life —the development of organs, faculties, and habits that render more complete the accommodations of individuals and groups to their environment.

Kropotkin placed distinctive emphasis upon two phases of this evolution. He contended, in the first place, that in both individual and social life natural evolution takes place not solely through a process of steady development but also, at times, through accelerated, abrupt, apparently disruptive transformations. In the normal course of the life of an individual, vital forces operate in an orderly manner; but when these are interfered with, by misdirected applications of human volition, the effects of the interference may accumulate until they cultivate forces of resistance of such strength that they later break forth in what appears to be an organic disease, but which is in reality only a necessary means of bringing natural processes back into their normal course. Likewise in social life, there is the slow and steady progress from lower to higher forms of organization, but there are also the quick and revolutionary movements forward. The normal efforts of human society towards the goals of social evolution may be obstructed by misinformed or interested opposition. New ideas, that appear naturally and that are necessary for the continued progress of mankind, attempt to come forth into the actual life of society, but their action is sometimes blocked by the inertia of the ignorant and indifferent or by the perverted aims of those who have selfish interests in retaining old traditions and conditions. On such occasions there is the need for great events that break the immediate course of history and draw mankind out of old ruts into new roads, but still on the main highway.[32]

The second, and more important, principle in Kropotkin's evolutionary theory is found in his conception of the predominant part played in evolution by the coöperative, as distinguished from the competitive, attributes of animals and men. The law of organic evolution is, he main-

[32] *Paroles d'un révolté,* pp. 17–24; "La necessité de la révolution."

tains, primarily a law of mutual aid, not of conflict. Individuals and species that survive are those endowed with the most effective faculties for coöperation in the struggles to adapt themselves to their environment; those in which the competitive qualities predominate over the coöperative tend eventually to disappear. The higher the species the more perfectly developed are the dispositions and capacities for coöperation. Kropotkin devoted an entire book to the demonstration of this principle.[33] The book is full of concrete evidences, drawn widely from observation and study of the organs and habits of animals—especially of the wild life on the Russian steppes, where the struggle is with an exceptionally adverse environment. He argued that the law of mutual aid manifests itself, in social life, in a principle of equality, justice, and social solidarity, which is nothing but the golden rule; the one fundamental requisite for the attainment of the goal of social evolution is—"Do to others as you would have it done to you in like case."

What then are the hindrances to the progress of human society towards its natural goal? They are, primarily, the state and private property, but also religious authority, which is the servant and sanctifier of political oppression and economic privilege.

The state, Kropotkin held, is without any natural or any historical justification. It is opposed to man's naturally coöperative instincts. Its structure and its manner of action are determined by the fallacious assumption that men's characteristic and prevailing impulses are competitive and unsocial, so that restraint and compulsion are necessary in order to maintain society. Political authority, moreover, contravenes that basic psychological principle according to which the development of human faculties comes about principally through the performance of spontaneous, self-imposed acts. Here we find again the ancient Stoic faith that justice is immanent in human nature and that conformity to its dictates can be secured best by cultivating man's natural reasonableness and goodness rather than by subjecting him to the coercive commands of organized authority. Men lived together for ages without any politically enforced rules. The state is of relatively late historical origin, having displaced the freer, more natural associations of earlier civilization, when the relations of men were regulated by habits and usages learned, like hunting and agriculture, from the years of childhood. Laws, in their earliest forms, were simply the customs that served to maintain society. State-enacted law appeared only when society be-

[33] *Mutual Aid a Factor of Evolution* (1902).

came divided by economic conditions into mutually hostile classes, one of them seeking to exploit the others. As political authority developed, laws came more and more to be merely rules confirming the customs that proved advantageous to the ruling groups and gave permanence to their economic supremacy. Thus laws to-day are either superfluous or harmful; they consist in part of customs which, because beneficial to society, would be observed without the state's sanction, and in part of rules which, because beneficial to property-owners, are sustained only by fear of the power exercised by that ruling minority.[34]

Kropotkin argued that history reveals both the state's incompetence for the achievement of any high purpose and its positive contribution to human suffering and injustice. The state has not protected the factory laborer and the peasant from exploitation by capitalists and landowners or secured food for the needy or work for the unemployed. It has not been the guardian of inherent rights of the individual; "freedom of the press and association, the inviolability of the home, and all the rest, are respected only so long as the people make no use of them against the privileged classes." [35] Neither the protective nor the beneficent services of the state are either necessary or effective. The people, acting spontaneously, can defend themselves against domestic brigands and foreign aggressors; history shows that standing armies have always been defeated by citizen armies and that invasion is most effectively thwarted by popular uprisings. Nor is government successful in protecting us against ill-disposed persons at home; prisons are more effective in spreading vice than in checking it. Finally, the cultural and benevolent activities of government are superfluous; when men are released from their economic and political dependence, voluntary activity will supply all that is needed for both education and charity.

Kropotkin believed these facts to be true of all forms of state. The transformations of absolute monarchies into parliamentary governments have effected no change in the essential character of the state. A representative system based on universal suffrage is now unworkable.[36] Men cannot be taken out of the mass and entrusted with the management of public affairs; they are unfitted for such a task, unacquainted with the problems with which governments are supposed to deal. "Representative government has accomplished its mission; it has given a mortal blow to

---

[34] *Paroles d'un révolté,* pp. 226–227.
[35] *Ibid.,* pp. 28–29.
[36] Cf. *Ibid.,* pp. 169–212.

court-rule; and by its debates it has awakened public interest in public questions. But to see in it the government of the future socialist society is to commit a gross error. Each economic phase of life implies its own political phase; and it is impossible to touch the very basis of the present economic life—private property—without a corresponding change in the very basis of the political organization." [37]

The evil quality of private property is inherent in its essential character and manifest in its actual effects. By its nature it is an offense against justice, for under it a minority retains the major benefits created by the combined efforts of multitudes of men of both present and past generations. Kropotkin's doctrine of the broadly social basis of value is like that of the Fabians.[38] The existing values of any industry represent, on the one hand, the discoveries, inventions, and labors of many past centuries and, on the other hand, the present-day activities of varied and widely scattered groups of men—those who serve the industry directly as well as those who construct the machines for it, plow and dig for its raw materials, transport its products, and carry on its technical research.[39] "Science and industry, knowledge and application, discovery and practical realization leading to new discoveries, cunning of brain and of hand, toil of mind and muscle—all work together. Each discovery, each advance, each increase in the sum of human riches, owes its being to the physical and mental travail of the past and present. By what right, then, can any one whatever appropriate the least morsel of this immense whole and say—This is mine, not yours?" [40]

Actual social conditions reveal the consequences of private property: among the masses—want and misery, millions unemployed, children of retarded growth, constant debts for the farmers; among the wealthy few—prodigality, ostentation, idleness, leading to the pursuit of the coarser pleasures, debasing the press, and inciting war.[41] And this whole economic condition is inextricably bound up with the political system. Historically, the parasitic institutions of state and property entered together into the midst of the free institutions of our ancestors; and the whole reason for the existence of political authority to-day lies in its function of protecting property.

What will follow the disappearance of the state and private property?

---

[37] *Anarchist Communism,* p. 28.
[38] Cf. *supra,* p. 104.
[39] *Anarchist Communism,* pp. 14–16.
[40] *The Conquest of Bread,* p. 9.
[41] *Paroles d'un révolté,* pp. 5–6.

Kropotkin's picture of future society is, in many details, like the one drawn by Bakunin. Men will continue to live together, but they will no longer be held together by governmental authority.[42] Free association will prevail throughout society. Individuals prosecuting the same ends will combine into groups and these groups into larger associations, the course of organization proceeding from the simple to the complex according to actual needs and desires. As the demands appear groups will be formed to build houses, construct roads, make tools, conduct schools, etc. These groups will join into leagues and unions with various blendings and interlacings as economic and social interests dictate.[43] All associations will be formed through voluntary contracts, whose observance will in general be assured by the necessity felt by every one for friendly coöperation with his neighbors. Within each group those exceptional individuals who fail to live up to their obligations will be expelled from membership. Disputes will be settled by voluntarily established courts of arbitration. Since this social order will be based upon principles of freedom and justice, the incitement to antisocial acts will largely disappear. Where such acts do occur, moral influence and sympathetic intervention will normally suffice to suppress them; in the rare cases where this is ineffective, fear of expulsion from the various fellowships, or of forcible intervention, either by individuals or by unorganized mass action, will supply the necessary corrective.

Economically, the new order will be that of complete communism. So far as ownership is concerned there will be no discrimination between goods for production and goods for consumption. Kropotkin regarded as fallacious and impracticable the doctrine that productive goods— machines, factories, raw materials, land, means of transportation— should be the property of the community, while finished products— dwellings, clothing, provisions—should remain under private ownership. The house that shelters us, the clothing that covers us, the coal and gas we burn, the food we eat, the books from which we draw instruction, are just as necessary for useful production as are machines, factories, and raw materials.[44]

Every normal individual will be driven into some association, both by his natural impulse to labor when his work can be done under conditions which he regards as just and by the natural unwillingness of a

42 *L'anarchie dans l'évolution socialiste,* p. 24.
43 *Paroles d'un révolté,* pp. 115–116.
44 *Ibid.,* p. 136.

society of workers to share the products of its labors with those who refuse to work. The associations will be formed on the following sort of contract: "We are ready to guarantee to you the use of our houses, stores, streets, means of transportation, schools, museums, etc., on condition that from your twentieth to your forty-fifth or fiftieth year, you apply four or five hours a day to some work recognized as necessary for life. Choose yourself, when it pleases you, the group you wish to join, or organize a new group, provided that it undertakes to do some necessary service. For the rest of your time associate yourself with whom you like, for recreation, art, or science, according to your taste. Twelve or fifteen hundred hours of work annually, in some group producing food, clothing, or shelter, or engaging in activities of public health or transportation—that is all we ask of you. In return we guarantee to you all that our groups produce." [45] Although the products will be shared only by those who work, or are willing to work, the distribution will be on the basis, not of service, but of need. "Put needs above works and recognize the right to live first of all: then recognize the right to the comforts of life for all who take part in production." [46] Every laborer will be permitted to satisfy freely his needs from all that is abundant; less plentiful objects will then be allotted according to needs, with preference for children, the aged, and the weak.[47]

Under such an organization of production and distribution, the quantity of goods, Kropotkin believed, will be sufficient for all to live in comfort; and the goods will be of better quality than under the present system. Even under the existing system—with its loss of productive capacity, due both to the frequent endeavors of capitalists to limit production and to the waste of work in making worthless objects of luxury—production is increasing more rapidly than population. In a system where men choose their labors in response to natural, creative impulses rather than under the goad of wage-slavery, men will work both more skilfully and more diligently.[48] In his *Fields, Factories, and Workshops,* Kropotkin undertook to show that, if production were organized and carried on in accordance with the teachings of science and experience, a relatively small amount of non-irksome labor would be sufficient to maintain every one in health and comfort.

[45] *Conquête du pain,* pp. 203–204.
[46] *Ibid.,* p. 229.
[47] *L'anarchie dans l'évolution socialiste,* p. 13, and *Anarchist Communism,* pp. 20–21.
[48] *The Conquest of Bread.* p. 182.

Kropotkin believed that the natural course of events was moving towards the goal he pictured. The anarchist, he said, "merely points out in which direction evolution goes", describing "what he considers to be the next phase of evolution. It is no longer a matter of faith; it is a matter for scientific discussion." [49] Already, he argued, the part played by government is becoming less important, as compared with the coöperative activities in which citizens voluntarily engage. Millions of transactions are now entered into and executed daily without any governmental intervention; agreements are faithfully kept not under the incentive of fear of punishment, but because of a desire to retain the confidence and respect of one's neighbors or a natural habit of keeping one's word; large railway systems and manufacturers' associations are organized by voluntary agreement; private organizations for the nobler pursuits of benevolence and culture are formed—life-boat and hospital associations, the Red Cross, societies for scientific study. Even where the sphere of governmental activity expands, the communist principle is continually asserting itself: the public bridge and free road supplant the toll bridge and turnpike; government-owned museums, libraries, schools, parks, paved and lighted streets are made free to all; public water and tramway charges are fixed at figures to make these services available equally to poor and rich.[50]

Although Kropotkin believed that the inevitable trend of social evolution was towards the anarchist goal, he did not believe that the goal could be reached through a wholly gradual and peaceful process. The evolution must culminate in a revolution. An uprising in one country will spread into a general European revolution, probably lasting from three to five years.[51] The revolution will be, in its first phase, destructive and violent; existing governors must be deposed, prisons and forts demolished, the spirit of mutual aid revived. "A frightful storm is needed to sweep away all this rottenness, to vivify torpid souls with its breath, and to restore to humanity the devotion, self-denial, and heroism, without which a society becomes senile and decrepit, and crumbles away." [52]

After the basic instruments of coercive authority are forcibly removed, the people will proceed to expropriate private property, peasants expelling landowners, workers driving out factory owners, those

[49] *Anarchist Communism*, p. 4.
[50] *Ibid.*, pp. 21–28.
[51] *Paroles d'un révolté*, p. 90.
[52] *Ibid.*, pp. 246. 280, 342.

having inadequate homes moving into dwellings that contain surplus space. Then there must follow the work of a constructive reshaping of society. This will be through a purely voluntary procedure. No government, no transitional dictatorship, will be required; that would mean death to the revolution. "If the dissolution of the state is once started, if once the machinery of oppression begins to weaken, free associations will be formed automatically. When coöperation is not forced by government, natural wants will bring about a voluntary coöperation. Overthrow the state and a free society will rise up at once on its ruins." [53]

Kropotkin considered some of the common criticisms of anarchism and offered answers to them.[54] He insisted generally that anarchism does not mean chaos or confusion. It means hostility to the state and to the peculiar social relations which the state sustains, but it is not true that where there is no government there is disorder. Moreover, order that is merely the consequence of the strong arm of government is of doubtful benefit. He considered more specifically the objections that, in the absence of political authority, men would fail to keep agreements, refuse to work, and commit antisocial acts.

In the first place, agreements, Kropotkin said, are essentially of two kinds—forced and voluntary. In the former case, the agreement is accepted by one of the parties out of sheer necessity, as when a workman sells his labor to an employer because otherwise his family would starve; the fear of political authority is necessary to guarantee the observance of such an agreement, but the agreement itself is unjust, so that it is no valid criticism to say that it will not be observed under an anarchist system. In the case of agreements entered into not under duress of unjust economic necessity but voluntarily and in response to the reasonable requirements of coöperation and exchange, no force is necessary to secure observance; they would be carried out as faithfully in an anarchist society as in a political society.

Secondly, Kropotkin argued that distaste for work is not the natural disposition of man. Men normally prefer work to idleness. Any existing unwillingness to work is due mainly to conditions which anarchism will eliminate: underpayment for long and laborious hours; work of such character and duration as to destroy all opportunities

---

[53] *Ibid.*, pp. 116–117, 243–245. Kropotkin set forth the procedure in considerable detail; cf. *The Conquest of Bread*, pp. 75–95, 100–104, 110–113.
[54] Cf. *Conquest of Bread*, Ch. XII; *Anarchist Communism*, pp. 22–35; *Paroles d'un révolté*, pp. 97–104.

for higher enjoyment; ill health caused by unsanitary conditions of employment. Only overwork, unhealthy work, unfairly remunerated work, is repulsive to man. Where these conditions are eliminated, there is no problem of the non-worker.

Thirdly, Kropotkin maintained, there is no natural disposition in men to violate the useful customs of society. The antisocial deeds that are perpetrated now are the consequences of perverted social rules. Most crimes are due directly or indirectly to the injustices of the existing system of production and distribution, not to the perversity of human nature. When a man—himself and his family in need of the bare necessities of life, others about him living in superfluous ease and luxury—commits a crime, he does so under the impulsion of conditions that will disappear when anarchism prevails. For the future society will not only remove existing incentive to crime; through its care to see that each is in youth trained for some handicraft, through its provision of education and decent homes for all and its promotion generally of the institutions of voluntary coöperation and mutual aid, it will so develop social health and competence and a general regard for one another's interests that positive incentives to good conduct will be firmly established and there will be no need for organized repression.

Kropotkin rejected conventional religion on both scientific and spiritual grounds. Religion, he believed, is either "a primitive cosmogony," "a rude attempt at explaining nature," or it is an ethical system which, through its appeals to the ignorance and superstition of the masses, cultivates among them a tolerance of the injustices they suffer under the existing political and economic arrangements.[55] He was willing, however, to apply the term "religion" to his conception of a social morality that develops spontaneously among the masses of the people. Such a natural religion he believed to be essential to any society, in the sense that no society can exist without certain moral habits and rules that evolve unconsciously and as a consequence of which men respect one another's interests and rely upon one another's words. A morality of this sort is anterior to and independent of formal religious creeds. It grows out of the social conventions that begin as soon as men begin to live together. Habits of mutual support and of self-sacrifice for the common well-being are necessary conditions for the welfare of the group in its struggle for life. The individuals who survive and thrive are those who best accustom themselves to a life in society. "A morality which

[55] *Anarchist Communism*, pp. 32–35.

has become instinctive is the true morality, the only morality which endures while religions and systems of philosophy pass away."

In all that Kropotkin wrote he placed emphasis upon man's sense of social responsibility, his feelings of human brotherhood, and his disposition to engage in labors that satisfy both an impulse to create and a desire to see commodities produced in amounts sufficient to meet the needs of his fellowmen. He regarded these natural human attributes as adequate guarantees of peace, order, and fair dealing in a society that has got rid of the unnatural institutions of private property and political coercion.

The numerous and devoted followers of Bakunin and Kropotkin added no essentially new ideas. Prominent among these disciples have been Élisée Reclus, Jean Grave, and Émile Gautier in France; Enrico Malatesta in Italy; and Emma Goldman, a Russian-American. Reclus who was a distinguished geographer, is the most important of this group. Although he drew from Kropotkin the principal counts in his indictment of the modern political and economic order, he showed some originality in presenting the evidences. He proposed chiefly nega- tive and pacific measures for getting rid of political authority. Abstain from voting, he urged, and do not petition your government for redress of your grievances or resort to the courts for redress of your injustices.[56] Malatesta, trained for the medical profession which he gave up for the sake of anarchism, wrote a brief work in support of Kropotkin's idea of "mutual aid" in biological evolution as the scientific justification of anarchism. Grave, Gautier, and Goldman restated other parts of the theoretical systems of Kropotkin.[57]

ANARCHIST PROPAGANDA BY DEED

The doctrines of Bakunin and Kropotkin were spread among the working-men of Europe through numerous journals, some of them ably edited, most of them very short-lived, each—after an unsettled

---

[56] Reclus (1830–1905) was banished from France following his participation in the commune of 1871. He was granted an amnesty in 1879 as the result of numerous petitions from scientists of distinction. In 1892 he was appointed pro- fessor of comparative geography at the University of Brussels, where he remained until his death.

[57] For titles of the works of the writers named in this paragraph, see the biblio- graphical list on pp. 225–226, *infra,* and for the numerous other anarchist writers of the nineteenth century, see Max Nettlau, *Bibliographie de l'anarchie* (1897).

existence of a year or two—succumbing to the pressure of governmental espionage or its own financial stringency. Scores of anarchist clubs were formed, often with names such as "The Indomitable," "The Oaken-hearted," "The Panther of Battingnolles," or "The Bomb Throwers," that indicated the zeal and bravado of the members. Bakunin and his associates made vigorous efforts to win over to anarchism the International Workingmen's Association; they succeeded in obtaining control of most of the branches in Italy, Spain, Southern France, and Belgium, and of many branches in Switzerland and a few other regions; but they were finally, after a bitter contest, expelled from the International in 1872.[58]

Johann Most attempted to incite and organize practical activities in behalf of anarchism in Germany and the United States.[59] Banished from Prussia and then from England, he came to the United States in the early eighties. Here his skill and vigor, as a speaker, writer, and organizer, brought a small and subterranean anarchist movement somewhat into the open. Anarchist journals and associations sprang up in various parts of the country. The International Working People's Association, organized at Pittsburgh in 1883, adopted a manifesto, prepared by Most, advocating "relentless, revolutionary, and international action" to achieve the anarchist goal. In the columns of his *Freiheit* (a weekly published in New York City), Most urged his followers to practise guerilla warfare against the dominant classes, and gave explicit directions for the use of nitro-glycerin, bombs, and poison.[60] Following the execution of the anarchist leaders charged with responsibility for the May-day disorders in Chicago, in 1886, the movement in the United States disintegrated; the associations were dissolved and the periodicals went out of existence or were taken over by German-American socialists; and Most (having served a year in prison for advocacy of the use of dynamite) abandoned his anarchist teachings. In the nineties the anarchist propaganda was revived, under the leadership of Emma Goldman, joined later by her husband, Alexander Berkman, and other young radicals from Europe. These anarchists were outspoken in their denunciation of contemporary economic and political

[58] Cf. *supra*, p. 67.
[59] Most (1846–1906), in his youth, was active in the socialist movement in Germany. He served a term in prison in the early seventies and was a socialist member of the *Reichstag* from 1874 to 1878.
[60] See Rudolf Rocker, *Johann Most, das Leben eines Rebellen* (1924); Emma Goldman, "Johann Most," *American Mercury*, VIII (1926), 158–166.

institutions. They were not very explicit, however, in urging immediate measures of revolutionary action, and they were generally unmolested, until the time of the World War, when imprisonments and
deportations put an end to even an academic advocacy of revolutionary
anarchism. Small anarchist group associations and journals survive to-
day in the United States, but their views are of a very placid and
visionary sort.

Impetus to the practical program of European anarchism, in its more
immediately destructive phases, came perhaps less from Bakunin and
Kropotkin than from certain of the Russian nihilists.[61] Nihilism is a
broader term than anarchism, indicating more sweeping negations—a
repudiation generally of established ideas, institutions, and standards.
It appears in several variously crossing currents in the cultural life of
nineteenth century Russia. The term was first applied in the fields of
literary and artistic criticism, where, in the early nineteenth century,
those who strongly opposed a prevailing conventionalism attempted to
throw overboard all traditional standards and held up spontaneity and
naturalism as the qualities most worth while in all forms of artistic
expression. Closely related were the "realistic" philosophers, who exalted natural science and empiricism as opposed to the abstract and
speculative methods of prevailing philosophy. In religion and morals,
the nihilist attitude was manifested in a disparagement of authoritarianism, orthodoxy, transcendentalism, and formalism, and in a cultivation
of atheism or deism in religion, and of hedonism, experimentalism, and
humanism in ethical doctrine. The whole nihilistic trend appeared to
be a natural reaction against the inertia, unenlightenment, and inhumanity then prevailing in the high places of church, state, and
society in Russia.[62]

The political phases of nihilism are illustrated typically in the teachings of Sergei Netschaiev (1848–1882), son of a court official, and, in
early life, a teacher in a parochial school. He eagerly adopted Bakunin's
revolutionary views and joined with him in organizing secret clubs of
students in St. Petersburg, Moscow, and other Russian cities. His ideas,
expounded in several pamphlets and in a journal which he established,

[61] On the basic ideas of Russian nihilism, cf. Karl Nötzel, *Die soziale Bewegung
in Russland* (1923), Bk. II, Chs. I–II; Thomas G. Masaryk, *The Spirit of Russia*,
II, Ch. XIV, especially p. 69 ff.
[62] The philosophical, religious, and moral standards of nihilism are revealed in
various Russian writings—particularly in works of philosophical criticism by
Chernichevsky (1828–1889), Drobrolubov (1836–1861), Pisarev (1840–1868), and
in famous novels, most notably Ivan Turgeniev's *Fathers and Sons*.

are distinguished by the emphasis they place upon the violent, immediately destructive phases of the anarchist program. He collaborated with Bakunin in the composition of a "Revolutionary Catechism," which set forth in detail the tasks of the revolutionist. The fulfilment of these tasks, the Catechism taught, demands a complete dedication to the inexorable revolution, and a breaking away from all sentimental ties and from all moral or conventional restraints. Every means for the attainment of the anarchist goal is advised—poison, the dagger, the torch, the halter. Assassination is to be employed both to get rid of the chief opponents of the revolution and as a means of propaganda—for its psychological effect. Netschaiev's characteristic creed was that the word has no value unless it results in a deed and that it is no concern of anarchists to devise the future organization of society; if we get rid of the unnatural institutions that exist to-day the proper forms of organization will evolve out of the experiences of the future.

The doctrine of an anarchist "propaganda by deed"—the idea that social regeneration can be achieved only through acts that inspire dread and horror in those now in control of the institutions of social order —was taken up by anarchist groups throughout Europe and became a characteristic phase of anarchist tactics.[63] Effects of the nihilistic and anarchistic propaganda are seen in overt acts in various parts of the world: insurrectionary May-day demonstrations; antimilitarist and antipatriotic propaganda in the armies; assaults upon the lives of persons in high public office.[64]

This terrorism of assassination, however, is not the sort of anarchist activity that Bakunin and Kropotkin advocated. Bakunin, though offering extenuations for such inevitable deeds, generally deplored them

[63] For description of the practical activities of nihilists and anarchists, cf. the following: Jacques Prolo, *Les anarchistes* (1912), Vol. X in *Histoire des partis socialistes en France*, Alexandre Zévaès, ed., 11 vols. in 3, (1911–1912); Stepniak (S. M. Kravchinski), *Nihilism as It Is* (1894), and *Underground Russia*, translated from the Italian (1883; fourth ed., London, 1896); Alphons Thun, *Geschichte der revolutionären Bewegungen in Russland* (1883); E. A. Vizetelly, *The Anarchists* (1911).

[64] Conspicuous instances are the attempts, in 1878 and 1879, to assassinate Emperor William I of Germany, King Humbert of Italy, and King Alphonso XII of Spain; and the assassinations of the Russian General Trepoff (prefect of police) in 1871, Tsar Alexander II in 1881, President Carnot of France in 1895, the premier of Spain in 1898, and King Humbert in 1900; also the Chicago Haymarket riot in 1886, and Alexander Berkman's attempt to kill banker Henry C. Frick in 1895. Connections with anarchist teachings were also seen in later acts of violence—the assassination of President McKinley in 1901; the attempts on the life of King Alphonso XIII in 1906, of the Mikado in 1910; and the assassination of King George of Greece in 1913.

none the less, regarding them as unwise and futile. They tend, he said, to a perversion of the pure and exalted aims of the sincere anarchist. Moreover, they are impotent; for privilege and authority inhere, not primarily in men, but in institutions. It is private property, the state, the church, that must be got rid of, not property-owners, politicians, and priests. Kropotkin also argued that, although in an anarchist revolution there will be inevitably some taking of life and annihilation of property, provoked by feelings of revenge on the part of those who have experienced the extremes of suffering and oppression, yet these acts form no part of anarchist policy. The anarchist revolution will not be a reign of terror; for it is a movement inspired by noble motives. The rank-and-file revolutionists will be restrained by sympathy for their victims; and the leaders know the teaching of history—that a reign of revolutionary terror is only a preparation for a more rigorous governmental autocracy. The appropriate policy for anarchists is an organized, and if necessary, violent overthrow of governments, but it is not assassination and terrorism.

Anarchists and socialists have the same goal—a classless and stateless society—but their roads diverge sharply. The revolutionary socialists of Soviet Russia, we have seen, maintain that socialists cannot avoid the long route through the coercive dictatorship of the proletariat; whereas the anarchists deny that coercion and censorship can lead to a society organized on principles of freedom and voluntary coöperation. "We do not at all disagree with the anarchists," said Lenin, "on the question of the abolition of the state as a final aim"; but "Marxism differs from anarchism in that it admits the necessity of the state and state power in a revolutionary period in general, and in the epoch of transition from capitalism to Socialism in particular." [65] The anarchists exalt individual freedom and rely upon its universal and constant effectiveness. A socialist society, they believe, is no step forward unless liberty replaces force as the basis of its constitution. They acknowledge the inevitable interdependence of men in society and recognize the necessity of organized social coöperation in serving the physical, intellectual, and spiritual needs of man. They deny that the long coercive régime of capitalism can be destroyed by a long, equally coercive, proletarian rule. Accordingly the contemporary an-

[65] *The State and Revolution* (1917), p. 63; *The Revolution of 1917 (Collected Works)*, I, 140.

archist, Emma Goldman, finds only disillusionment in Soviet Russia; for she sees centralization, censorship, and governmental terrorism in operation. She does not believe that a free and classless society can be achieved in any such fashion. A transitional social order, she contends, must bear an essential likeness to the permanent order that is to replace it. "The means to further the revolution must harmonize with its purposes." "No revolution can ever succeed as a factor of liberation unless the MEANS used to further it be identical in spirit and tendency with the PURPOSES to be achieved." [66]

The socialists, notably the Russian Communists, stand for a change of class dictatorships—a reversal of the relations of hostile classes, so that the serving class of yesterday becomes the ruling class of to-day—with a faith that thereby a classless society will be reached to-morrow, far ahead. The anarchist, on the other hand, stands for a reversal of the principles of social order—immediately—so that voluntary coöperation displaces its opposite, coercion, as the rule of society. Violence, he contends, is proper only as a weapon of defense—of organized resistance to authority. It is not a means of coöperation, and is not, therefore, a means of action in a "socialist" order truly conceived. When violence is "institutionalized" it is no longer an instrument for achieving freedom for any one.

TOLSTOI

Some anarchists, we have seen, contend that violence is inadmissible even as a means of resistance or revolution. Anarchism is not necessarily a doctrine that countenances force in an organized revolution. Before Bakunin, the idea of any sort of aggressive action as a method for destroying political authority had rarely been suggested. Earlier anarchist writers, with few exceptions, had either omitted any discussion of the means of getting rid of the state or proposed only the methods of education, persuasion, and example.

The most celebrated among recent advocates of this pacific sort of anarchism was Count Leo Tolstoi, probably the most widely known Russian of the later nineteenth century and one of the greatest literary figures of recent times. He was the son of a wealthy landowner of noble

[66] *My Further Disillusionment in Russia* (1924), pp. 175, 178. Cf. also by the same author, *My Disillusionment in Russia* (1923), and *Living My Life* (1931), Vol. II, Chs. LII and LIII.

rank. After graduating from a university, he spent five years in the army and served as an officer in the Crimean War. His experiences and impressions in that war were set forth in several brief books, which won for him immediately a reputation for powers of vivid realism and incisive psychological analysis. He spent most of the remainder of his life on his ancestral estate in Yasnaya Polyana, engaged in practical efforts to relieve poverty and ignorance among the masses and in writing books that portrayed the lives of peasants and landlords, and that set forth particularly the artificiality and emptiness of life among the latter. In his later life, his writing came to be generally of a definitely socio-philosophical nature. His social doctrines appear in his third great novel, *Resurrection,* and in several dramas and short stories, but most completely in brief brochures, appearing between 1880 and 1893.[67] Throughout all his writings there appear his hatred of a life of luxury, sophistication, and oppression, and his exaltation of honest labor and simple living.

Tolstoi's doctrine has been called Christian anarchism. He rejected many of the traditional dogmas of Christianity—particularly, the trinity, the divinity of Christ, and personal immortality—but he was thoroughly Christian in his ethics. He scorned the Russian Church because he believed that it had, by supporting the tyranny of the Russian state and condoning the idle and selfish lives of the Russian upper classes, foresaken entirely the teachings of Christ. He based his social and political philosophy not upon the creed of any Christian sect but directly upon the Gospels. He regarded the various Christian creeds as in some cases incomprehensible and in other cases sharply opposed to the principles of Christianity—preaching rigidity where Christ taught progress, and cultivating arrogance and selfishness where He exalted humility and charity. Tolstoi described Christianity as a simple code of moral rules, offering the one adequate solution for the problems of human conduct. Christ's teachings, he held, show that the only rational activity of man is love—renunciation of personal comfort for a neighbor's sake, suppression of purely animal impulses, withdrawal from all striving for happiness and prestige.

Both the state and private property are, in Tolstoi's theory, incompatible with true Christianity. The state is based on force and

[67] His earlier novels, *War and Peace* and *Anna Karenina* (1875–1876), also have great social and ethical themes. Most important among the briefer works are *The Gospel in Brief, What I Believe, What Shall We Do Now?* and *The Kingdom of God within You.*

executes its will through armed men—policemen and soldiers, trained to kill; thus it transgresses Christ's command not to resist evil by force.[68] Under private property a few are enabled to enjoy superfluous comforts and luxuries made possible by the labors of the many who live in want; [69] this is an offense against Christ's exhortations to charity and human brotherhood.

Tolstoi said little as to the future organization of society. He did not consider that it was possible or necessary to set forth the details of a new social order. "The future . . . will only be what men and circumstances make it." [70] In general he laid stress upon individual regeneration and regarded most institutional schemes for reforming society as futile. He was emphatic in condemning force as a means of social reconstruction: force in all its forms is forbidden by the Christian doctrine, and insurrections and conspiracies lead always to new governmental tyrannies. The only effective methods are those of enlightenment and example. Awaken the consciences of the people; live according to the principles of love and equality; practise passive resistance; refuse obedience to the clearly un-Christian commands of a government; and, where practicable, refuse to pay taxes or to serve on juries.

Tolstoi has had devoted, but relatively few, followers. In indirect and supplementary ways, however, his pacific teachings probably aided the aggressive movements that led finally to the destruction of the old social and political autocracy of Russia.[71] His insistence that the real strength of Russia was the strength of her toiling masses possibly offered some encouragement to the assertive demands of the peasants. His attacks upon the sanctity of the governing aristocracy may have added some adherents to insurrectionary movements among the urban workers. Kropotkin believed that Tolstoi's vivid pictures of Russia's whole social system and his fervent appeals for more benevolent ways of living greatly stirred the consciences of many landowners who had hitherto been complacent in the face of the inequities of the order of which they were a part. Tolstoi himself was apparently not interested either in liberal-democratic movements or in the revolutionary plans of the socialists, anarchists, and nihilists. Despite his vigorous protests against autocratic rule and his bitter denunciation of the callousness of those who supported that rule, the tsar's government made no seri-

[68] Cf. particularly *The Kingdom of God within You*, p. 219 and *passim*.
[69] See the vivid details in *What Shall We Do Now?*
[70] *The Kingdom of God within You*, p. 326.
[71] Cf. *supra*. Ch. VI. *

ous effort to restrain him. Those who wielded an authority resting on force saw no reason for interfering with a man who condemned any sort of forcible resistance to authority.

SELECT BIBLIOGRAPHY

ANARCHIST WRITERS

Andrews, Stephen Pearl, *The Science of Society: No. 1: The True Constitution of Government in the Sovereignty of the Individual as the Final Development of Protestantism, Democracy, and Socialism* (New York, 1851).

——————, *The Labor Dollar* (Boston, 1877).

Bakunin, Michael, *Œuvres*, James Guillaume, ed., 6 vols. (Paris, 1907–1913).

——————, *Gesammelte Werke*, 3 vols. (Berlin, 1921).

——————, *God and the State*, translated by Benj. R. Tucker (fifth ed., Boston, 1885).

Gautier, Émile, *Le Darwinisme social* (Paris, 1880).

Goldman, Emma, *Anarchism and Other Essays* (New York, 1910).

——————, *Living My Life*, 2 vols. (New York, 1931), *passim*.

Grave, Jean, *La société mourante et l'anarchie* (Paris, 1893).

Greene, William, *Mutual Banking* (West Brookfield, Mass., 1850).

——————, *Sovereignty of the People* (Boston, 1868).

——————, *Socialistic, Communistic, Mutualistic and Financial Fragments* (Boston, 1875).

Kropotkin, Peter Alexander, *Memoirs of a Revolutionist* (Boston and New York, 1899).

——————, *Paroles d'un révolté* (Paris, 1885).

——————, *L'anarchie dans l'évolution socialiste* (Paris, 1885).

——————, *The Place of Anarchy in Socialist Evolution,* (London, 1886).

——————, *La conquête du pain* (Paris, 1888; sixteenth ed., 1921).

——————, *The Conquest of Bread* (New York and London, 1907, and other editions).

——————, *Anarchist Communism: Its Basis and Principles* (London, 1905).

——————, *Fields, Factories, and Workshops* (Boston, 1899, and numerous other editions).

——————, *Mutual Aid a Factor of Evolution* (London, 1902, etc.).

——————, *Ethics, Origin, and Development* translated from the Russian by Louis S. Friedland and Joseph R. Piroshnikoff (New York, 1924).

Malatesta, Enrico, *Anarchy* (San Francisco, 1900).

Most, Johann, *Die freie Gesellschaft* (New York, 1884).

Proudhon, Pierre Joseph, *Œuvres complètes*, 26 vols. (Brussels, 1868–1876; new ed. in process (Paris, 1923–   ).

——————, *Qu'est-ce que la propriété* (1840), in Vol. V of *Œuvres* (ed. of 1923–   ).

——————, *What is Property?* translated by Benj. R. Tucker, 2 vols. in one (Princeton, Mass., 1876).

——————, *Système des contradictions économiques ou philosophie de la misère* (1846), Vols. II and III of *Œuvres* (ed. of 1923–   ).

Reclus, Élisée, *Évolution et révolution* (Geneva, 1880; sixth ed., Paris, 1891).

——————, *Evolution and Revolution*, translated (third ed., London, 1886).

——————, "Anarchy: by an anarchist," *Contemporary Review*, XLV (1884), 627–641.

——————, *L'Évolution, la révolution, et l'idéal anarchique* (Paris, 1898).

Spooner, Lysander, *Poverty: Its Illegal Causes and Legal Cure* (Boston, 1846).

——————, *Natural Law or the Science of Justice. A Treatise on Natural Law, Natural Justice, Natural Rights, Natural Liberty, and Natural Society—Showing That All Legislation Whatever is an Absurdity, a Usurpation, and a Crime* (Boston, 1882).

Thoreau, Henry David, *Civil Disobedience* (1864), Vol. IV in *The Writings of Henry David Thoreau*, 20 vols. (Boston and New York, 1906).

Tolstoi, Count Leo, *The Gospel in Brief* (1880), in *Complete Works* (New York, 1899), Vol. IX.

——————, *What I Believe* (1884), *ibid.*

——————, *What Shall We Do Now?* (1885), *ibid.*, Vol. XIV.

——————, *On Life* (1887), *ibid.*

——————, *The Kingdom of God within You* (1893), *ibid.*, Vol. VIII.

Tucker, Benjamin R., *Instead of a Book, by a Man Too Busy to Write One: a Fragmentary Exposition of Philosophical Anarchism* (New York, 1893; second ed., 1897).

Warren, Josiah, *Practical Details in Equitable Commerce* (New York, 1852).

——————, *True Civilization: An Immediate Necessity and the Last Ground of Hope for Mankind* (Boston, 1863).

HISTORICAL AND CRITICAL ACCOUNTS

Adler, Georg, "Anarchismus," in *Handwörterbuch der Staatswissenschaften* (second ed., Jena, 1898–1901), I, 296–327.

Bernstein, Eduard, "Karl Marx und Bakunin," *Archiv für Sozialwissenschaft und Sozialpolitik*, XXX (1910), 1–29.

Bailie, William, *Josiah Warren, the First American Anarchist* (Boston, 1906).

Brupbacher, F., *Marx und Bakunin: Ein Beitrag zur Geschichte der internationale arbeiter Assoziation* (Munich, 1913).

Eastman, Max, *Marx, Lenin and the Science of Revolution* (London, 1926), Pt. II, Ch. II.

Eltzbacher, Paul, *Der Anarchismus* (Berlin, 1900).

——————, *Anarchism*, translated by S. T. Byington (New York and London, 1908).

Douglas, Paul H., "Anarchism," pp. 203–210 in *Political Theories, Recent Times*, Charles E. Merriam and H. E. Barnes, eds. (New York, 1924).

Kirkup, Thomas, *History of Socialism* (fifth ed., London, 1913), Ch. X.

Mackay, John Henry, *The Anarchists: a Picture of Civilization at the Close of the Nineteenth Century*, translated by George Schumm (Boston, 1891).

Masaryk, Thomas G., *The Spirit of Russia: Studies in History, Literature, and Philosophy*, translated from the German by Eden and Cedar Paul, 2 vols. (London and New York, 1919), Chs. XIV and XIX.

Nettlau, Max, *Bibliographie de l'anarchie* (Brussels, 1897).

——————, *Biographie de Bakounine*, 3 vols. (London, 1896–1900).

——————, *Der Vorfrühling der Anarchie: ihre historische Entwicklung von den Anfängen bis zum Jahre 1864* (Berlin, 1925).

——————, *Der Anarchismus von Proudhon zu Kropotkin: seine historische Entwicklung in den Jahren 1859–1880* (Berlin, 1927).

——————, *Anarchisten und Sozialrevolutionäre: die historische Entwicklung des Anarchismus in den Jahren 1880–1886* (Berlin, 1931).

Osgood, Herbert L., "Scientific Anarchism," *Political Science Quarterly*, IV (1889), 1–36.

Prolo, Jacques, *Les anarchistes* (1912), Vol. X of *Histoire des partis socialistes en France*, Alexandre Zévaès, ed., 11 vols. in 3 (Paris, 1911–12).

Rezneck, Samuel, "The Political and Social Theory of Michael Bakunin," *American Political Science Review*, XXI (1927), 270–296.

Rolland, Romain, *Vie de Tolstoi* (Paris, 1911).

——————, *Life of Tolstoi*, translated by Bernard Miall (London, 1911).

Schuster, Eunice M., *Native American Anarchism: a Study of Left-Wing American Individualism* (Northampton, Mass., 1932), in Smith College Studies in History, Vol. XVII.

Stammler, Rudolf, *Die Theorie des Anarchismus* (Berlin, 1894).

Stanoyevich, M. S., "Tolstoi's Theory of Social Reform," *American Journal of Sociology*, XXXI (1926), 577–600, 744–761.

Stepniak (S. M. Kravchinski), *Nihilism as It is* (London, 1894).

——————, *Underground Russia*, translated from the Italian (New York, 1883).

Thun, Alphons, *Geschichte der revolutionären Bewegungen in Russland* (Leipsic, 1883).

Vizetelly, E. A., *The Anarchists* (New York, 1911).

Zenker, E. V., *Anarchism: a Criticism and History of the Anarchist Theory* (New York and London, 1897).

CHAPTER VIII

THE SYNDICALISTS

A NOVEL social doctrine for working-men emerged from the French labor movement of the late nineteenth century. The doctrine came in part from the anarchists and in part from Marx; but there are some peculiar features, and the whole combination is distinctive. The doctrine is called "syndicalism," a word derived from *syndicat*—the ordinary French term for labor union. When, in the last decade of the century, there appeared, within the chief national organization of labor unions in France, a division between moderate and radical wings, the opposing policies were designated as "reformist syndicalism" and "revolutionary syndicalism" respectively; when the revolutionary wing gained control of the organization, its general policy came to be known simply as *"syndicalisme."* [1] The corresponding word was soon regularly applied to similar doctrines of smaller labor groups in other countries. The chief tenets of the doctrine appeared more or less independently in the several countries, but it was in France that it received its most elaborate formulation and its most persistent and vigorous assertion. Syndicalism, loosely defined, holds that the workers alone must control the conditions under which they work and live; the social changes they need can be achieved only by their own efforts, by direct action in their own associations, and through means suited to their peculiar needs.

HISTORICAL BACKGROUND OF FRENCH SYNDICALISM

As to why this doctrine became predominant in the French labor movement during the two decades preceding the World War, several explanations have been offered. Some commentators have attempted to show a relation of syndicalism—with its faith in a spontaneous and direct working-man's uprising against oppression, its emotional appeal to the sentiments of class solidarity, its trust in the "myth" value of the

[1] See Félicien Challaye, *Syndicalisme révolutionnaire et syndicalisme réformiste*, (1909).

general strike—to characteristic psychological traits of the French race. More often, however, and more convincingly, explanation is sought in recent French history. The actual facts and conditions of the industrial and political evolution of France, from the time of the Revolution to the last decades of the nineteenth century, show why the usual devices of an economic or political contest were unavailable to French working-men, who, therefore, were compelled to find new weapons. They could not use ordinary trade-union methods. The relatively late persistence of small-scale industry in France made it difficult for wage-earners to combine into large national units in the manner essential for any persistent and successful pursuit of a purely industrial conflict. Moreover, French law, during most of this period, variously hampered the efforts of workers to form unions and conduct strikes. Then, too, the working-men of France felt that they could not successfully pursue the program advocated by Marx. The frequent and abrupt breaks in French constitutional development in the nineteenth century tended to cultivate a skepticism towards politics as a method of reform. When finally, therefore, in the active industrial era of the late nineteenth century, French working-men became strongly organized, they were prepared to reject both trade-unionism and political socialism as their means of salvation and to yield ready assent to those who proposed more radical and direct methods of social strife.

The details of this historical background, from the late eighteenth century to the advent of syndicalism a hundred years later, can be sketched only briefly here.[2] At the very beginning of the period we find, among the dominant groups of the Revolutionary era, an extreme hostility to associations of every sort. This attitude was an inheritance from pre-Revolutionary days. The guilds and corporations of the *ancien régime* had, in many instances, become a narrow and selfish oligarchy. The exclusive privileges and arbitrary powers they possessed—in fixing the quantity, quality, and price of commodities and in determining the conditions for entering the various crafts and trades which they controlled—had been widely regarded, by moderate as well as radical reformers, as one of the chief social oppressions of that age.

[2] Cf. especially Louis Levine, *Syndicalism in France* (second rev. ed., 1914); Hubert Lagardelle, *L'évolution des syndicats ouvriers en France de l'interdiction à l'obligation* (1901); G. D. H. Cole, *Self-Government in Industry* (1917), pp. 303–321; and for the later period: Sylvain Humbert, *Le mouvement syndical* (1912); Paul Louis, *Le syndicalisme français d'Amiens à Saint Étienne, 1906–1922* (1924); Fernand Pelloutier, *Histoire des bourses du travail* (1902). See also the list on pp. 257–258, *infra*.

Moreover, an antagonism to special group activities fitted in well with the political ideas of the leaders of the Revolution, who were, generally speaking, *doctrinaire* individualists and *doctrinaire* democrats. Their "natural-rights" theory recognized individual interests, on the one hand, and the general interest, on the other hand, but no intermediate interests. The theory, standing for the private rights of the individual and for the sovereignty of the "general" will, had no place for any associations less than the community. Accordingly, legislative enactments of the Revolutionary era dissolved the old guilds, prohibited the formation of "particular" associations for defense of "alleged common interests," and forbade any gatherings that were designed to limit the free economic activities of individuals.

For various reasons, the conservative and semiliberal régimes of the first half of the nineteenth century retained and extended these prohibitions and applied them particularly to workers, imposing severe penalties for strikes and other forms of concerted activity by wage-earners. Despite the restrictions, the workers organized, in several ways. They set up travelers'-aid and mutual-benefit societies, which, although falling technically within the law's proscriptions, were generally unmolested because of their normally innocent purposes. They organized secret societies, propagating the radical proletarian ideas then current in Europe. Finally, they formed associations to pursue the methods of the labor union; these bodies also, because of the law's undiscriminating injunctions, were generally secret. The government of the Second Empire, in its first years, attempted to suppress associations of all sorts, because of the organized participation of working-men in the revolution of 1848. Later, however, Louis Napoleon came to look upon wage-earners as a potential source of popular support for his régime, and he sought to cultivate their good will by relaxing the restrictions on their organized action. A law of 1864 established a right to strike, and a ministerial proclamation four years later announced that there would be no governmental interference with associations having peaceful aims.

The active trade-union movement that got under way, following this change of governmental policy, was checked again in the general conservative reaction after the revolutionary commune of 1871; the unions were suppressed and many of their leaders were executed or banished. In the gradual liberalization of the social policy of the Third Republic, the governmental attitude changed again to toleration and then to active encouragement—but for ends other than those in which the workers were chiefly interested. Waldeck-Rousseau, minister of interior (1883–1885) in the cabinet of Jules Ferry, devised a plan to utilize the unions for public purposes: they would be encouraged to serve as agencies of conciliation between employers and workers; as forces of defense against assaults upon the Republic by monarchists, clericals, and other antidemocratic groups; and as organs to aid the government in the elaboration of labor legislation.[3] Conformably to these ideas, a law of 1884 authorized the formation of unions and again established the right to strike. The movement for organization developed rapidly, and in 1886 a national federation of the unions was created, chiefly for the purpose of consolidating the activities of local groups in times of industrial dispute.

There remained, however, several obstacles to the successful functioning of labor unions through the normal methods of strikes and collective bargaining. As already indicated, the relatively decentralized type of French industry made it difficult to form strong national organizations of wage-earners, which are essential for consolidating the efforts of the workers in their industrial conflicts. Moreover, the national federation of unions had acquired affiliations with the parliamentary socialists who, under Guesde's leadership, were interested in the unions only as agencies of propaganda and electioneering. The law of 1884, though legalizing combinations and strikes, withheld the right to use one of the indispensable instrumentalities of the strike—namely, picketing, even in its orderly forms. The workers, moreover, objected to the requirement of official registration for their union officials; and they were generally distrustful of the aims of the government. Finally, uncompromising antagonism on the part of many employers tended to weaken the influence of the more conservative labor leaders. The combined effect of all such factors was to impel the workers generally towards other forms of association than the trade union and towards the more unconciliatory methods of conflict.

The organs through which the distinctive notions of revolutionary syndicalism were first put forth were not the *syndicats* but the *bourses du travail* or "labor exchanges." The first of these was established in Paris in 1887; others were soon formed in various provincial towns.

---

[3] For the ideas of Waldeck-Rousseau and the "Radical" party group, see J. Paul Boncour, *Le fédéralisme économique* (second ed., 1901), especially the preface by Waldeck-Rousseau.

They were created, in the first instance, mainly to serve as employment agencies; but they also had social and educational functions: maintaining libraries, journals, and lecture courses; supplying help for sick, unemployed, and traveling workers; and serving as working-men's social clubs. Soon they became centers of vigorous activity not only in these services of mutual aid and education but also in organizing the workers for their economic conflicts and supplying moral and practical support in time of strikes.[4] A national federation of the bourses (*Fédération des Bourses du Travail de France*) was formed in 1893, and became at once the chief center of the labor movement, in both its practical and theoretical phases. In 1895, largely under its initiative, a new and comprehensive national organization of wage-earners was formed —the General Federation of Labor (*Confédération Générale du Travail*). This organization—the "C.G.T."—was thereafter the chief national labor organization in France.

At the very beginning there was a division in the Confederation between a moderate trade-union, but also political-socialist, group and a radical, antipolitical group. The latter soon acquired the ascendancy. Its general policy was to repudiate all pacific measures. It would oppose all bargaining with employers, who were to be treated as perpetual enemies, and all appeals to the state, which was to be regarded as chief support of the social system in which employers occupied the key positions. It would approve all measures whereby the workers, by their own "direct" efforts—including violence, if necessary—might push out the capitalists and take over the management of industry and the control of social life generally.[5]

The triumph of "revolutionary syndicalism" in the policy of the Confederation appears to have been due, in considerable measure, to the efforts of theorists, both within and without the active labor movement —notably, Fernand Pelloutier and other French disciples of Bakunin and Kropotkin; and Georges Sorel (1847–1922), a civil engineer, of a philosophical turn of mind, who in middle age had become interested in practical social problems.

Pelloutier (1867–1901) was perhaps the first to adopt fully the idea

---

[4] The municipalities at first, looking upon the bourses as agencies of pacification, gave them substantial encouragement, granting subsidies and providing halls for them. As their activities became more aggressive, this support was withdrawn.

[5] See Félicien Challaye, *op. cit.* (note 1, p. 229, *supra*), and Alexandre Zévaès, *Le syndicalisme contemporain* (1911), Ch. VII.

that French working-men must pursue their aims in complete dissociation from the rest of the nation. He was of bourgeois origin, a Radical Republican in his first political years, and then a socialist of the Guesdist faction. He parted from the Guesdists on the issue of the general strike, which he unsuccessfully defended before a socialist congress in 1892. Soon after that he revealed his leanings towards the ideas of Bakunin. As part of a plan to keep the bourses out of the control of political socialists, Pelloutier was made secretary of the national federation of bourses in 1894, and he held this post until his early death seven years later. The rapid growth of these groups was due in large measure to his energy and organizing ability. Under his leadership, anarchist communists came into the bourses in considerable numbers; and their influence upon the policy of the Confederation was strengthened both by the dissensions among the socialists and by the government's partiality—as it seemed to the workers—for employers, in times of critical industrial disputes.

While Pelloutier was impressing upon the French labor movement his idea that the workers must attain their salvation by their own coöperative efforts, acting through their local labor exchanges, Sorel made his first appearance as a theorist for wage-earners by claiming for the unions this same exalted function. He set forth this idea in a magazine article, entitled "The Socialist Future of Trade Unions," which concluded with the assertion that "the whole future of socialism resides in the autonomous development of workingmen's syndicats." [6]

In all subsequent expressions of syndicalist theory and policy there is this basic idea of Pelloutier and Sorel—that the social transformation to be sought by the proletariat must be a self-transformation and that the institutions through which existing society is to be displaced by a new society are institutions that grow out of and are built up by the working class through its unaided efforts and in defiance of political authority. The elaboration of this idea is to be found in pamphlets and brief books by active leaders of the Confederation—notably, Pelloutier, Victor Griffuelhes, Émile Pouget, Émile Patuad, and Léon Jouhaux (secretary of the Confederation since 1909); also in the somewhat more elaborate works of theorists outside the practical movement—notably, Sorel, Hubert Lagardelle, and Edouard Berth; and in the records of the debates and resolutions of the Confederation.

[6] The article, appearing in 1897, was published in pamphlet form in the following year: *L'avenir socialiste des syndicats.*

THE DOCTRINES OF REVOLUTIONARY SYNDICALISM [7]

The syndicalists called themselves a "new school" of socialism. They threw overboard both the reformist plans for conciliation and the orthodox schemes for a proletarian conquest of power through political methods. Social classes, they argued, differ from one another not only in their economic interests but also in the ideas and institutions that grow out of the diverging interests. Each class evolves its own standards of right and wrong and its own special organs of defense and control. The substance of history lies in the successive efforts of each class to impose upon society its peculiar juridical opinions and institutions. The territorial, military state reflects the ideals of property-owners and can serve their interests well enough; when rival groups of property-owners seek to control the state, political parties are the appropriate forms of association in such a competition. Wage-earners, however, in pursuing their immediate interests and following their social impulses, fall naturally into other sorts of groupings; and it is in these groupings that they can act most effectively in their efforts to reconstruct society in such a way as to make it fit their permanent interests as a community of workers.

Thus the working-men's association, in the syndicalist system, is not, like the British or American trade-union, merely a group formed to protect and aggrandize the material interests of its members; it has higher and more comprehensive aims than short hours and high wages. Its primary purpose is to raise the worker to that position of dignity and independence for which his function as a producer fits him. Productive work, the syndicalist argued, is the highest manifestation of human personality, the affirmation of man's creative power; at least the work is of such character when it is really his own work, performed voluntarily and with objectives and under conditions which he, alone or in collaboration with fellow workers, determines.[8] Where

---

[7] The works of leading syndicalist theorists are listed on p. 258, *infra.* The most useful are the following: Victor Griffuelhes, *L'action syndicaliste* (1908); Hubert Lagardelle, *Le socialisme ouvrier* (1911), especially Pt. II, Ch. II; Georges Sorel, *L'avenir socialiste des syndicats* (1898), *La décomposition du Marxisme* (1908), *Réflexions sur la violence* (1906; translated as *Reflections on Violence,* 1915); Émile Pouget, *La Confédération Générale du Travail* (1908; second ed., 1910).

For expositions of syndicalist doctrine see Louis Levine, *Syndicalism in France* (1913), Chs. V, VI, VIII; Georges Guy-Grand, *La philosophie syndicaliste* (1911); Roger Soltau, *French Political Thought in the Nineteenth Century* (1931), Ch. XIV; and the other titles listed on pp. 258–259, *infra.*

[8] Hubert Lagardelle, *Le socialisme ouvrier,* p. 340.

employers, as owners of the materials and instruments which the laborer manipulates, fix the conditions of labor, then there is no really creative work by the laborer. The whole social and political hierarchy of to-day is a large-scale reproduction of the bonds of dependence that hold the workers in each factory subject to the factory-owner. Present-day society is "made in the image of the present-day workshop." When the workshop is free, society will be free and the workers' sense of dignity and spirit of independence will be revived.

The syndicalists believed that their ideal of "free work in a free society" could be nourished most naturally in those groups that reflect directly the primordial, creative impulses of men. More concretely, they believed that ordinary labor unions, organized by craft or industry, and local labor councils or bourses, together with the national federations and confederations of these bodies, are the proper agencies both for conducting a working-men's revolution and for managing the affairs of society after the revolution. Workers, moreover, should confine themselves to the methods appropriate to their peculiar experiences and aims. They cannot, to any good purpose, borrow bourgeois devices of bargaining and electioneering, which serve only the interests of property-owners. Their tactics must be those of working-men's "direct action," in the appropriate forms of the strike, sabotage and (less important) the boycott and the label.[9]

The syndicalists admitted some utility in the strike as ordinary trade-unionists use it—to force an employer to improve or maintain existing conditions of employment. But the syndicalist strike is essentially a more formidable and exalted undertaking than the ordinary strike. It is primarily a demonstration of the latent social power of wage-earners: by simultaneously quitting work in essential industries, they can paralyze the whole economic and social life of the community and thus force privileged groups to yield to their demands. Particular strikes, however extensive, should, therefore, be regarded chiefly as means of preparation and training for a final and mighty general strike by which the workers are to make themselves the masters of society.

The idea of the general strike was not original with the syndicalists.[10]

[9] For syndicalists' accounts of their tactics, see especially, Émile Pouget, *La Confédération Générale du Travail*, pp. 40–50, and Victor Griffuelhes, *L'action syndicaliste*.

[10] For historical sketches of the general strike, see the following: Meredith Atkinson, "The General Strike in History," *Nineteenth Century*, XCIX (1926), 795–804; Wilfrid H. Crook, *The General Strike* (1931); Arnold Roller, *The Social*

In the early nineteenth century, labor leaders in England and France had proposed a concerted and organized stoppage of work in essential industries as the only sure means for compelling the dominant social groups to take action for redress of the economic and political grievances of wage-earners. Thereafter the plan occupied almost continuously a prominent place in radical labor agitation. On various occasions national and international socialist bodies debated it as a possible way to overthrow a reactionary government, to stop a war, or even to bring on the socialist conquest of political power. Both the orthodox Kautsky and the revisionist Jaurès admitted that socialists might properly use strikes to achieve particular political changes that furthered their cause. Aristide Briand, the ablest "independent socialist" in France in the late nineteenth century, vigorously championed the general strike as the means for a working-men's revolution, and he persuaded the National Federation of Syndicalists to endorse the plan. Most socialists opposed it, Jules Guesde characterizing it as a method certain to fail until the workers were completely organized and not needed when they were. In the nineties, however, under pressure of the propaganda conducted by Pouget and Pelloutier, the C.G.T. accepted the general strike, with greatly amplified notions as to its function and significance. It then became a cardinal feature in the syndicalist program.

The syndicalist general strike is not the familiar "sympathetic strike," in which various groups of workers that have no particular quarrel with their employers quit their jobs in order to force attention to the demands of some other group engaged in an unsuccessful strike. It is different also from the ordinary "political strike"—used as a means of upsetting an oppressive political régime or of intimidating a government into granting particular concessions. This latter conception of the strike, as a means of popular political pressure, gained prestige in France in the middle of the century, when it was defended by two well-known literary men of the time—a journalist, Émile de Girardin, and the famous novelist and poet, Victor Hugo; these men suggested, and described in vivid detail, a general *croissant des bras* as the best method whereby the people of France could circumvent the despotic plans of Louis Napoleon. In later years the political strike was put to practical test, in other countries, with successful results on several important occasions. Thus, in 1893, it was a general strike, accompanying other

General Strike (1905); Émile Vandervelde, *La grève générale en Belgique* (1914); Alexandre Zévaès, *Le syndicalisme contemporain*, pp. 343–350.

mass demonstrations, that, when other means had failed, finally fright-
ened the government of Belgium into enacting a democratic suffrage;
and strikes in a similar manner helped to obtain suffrage extensions in
Sweden, in 1902, and in Austria five years later. In Russia, in 1905,
the tsar's promise to set up certain institutions of constitutional government was induced chiefly by a general strike in St. Petersburg and a
stoppage of the railways throughout the country. A political strike,
finally, played an essential part in defeating the "Kapp Putsch" of
March, 1920, in Germany. When monarchist and military groups (led
nominally by Dr. von Kapp, but actually by Generals von Ludendorff
and von Lüttwitz) had seized the capital and expelled the chief officials
of the Republican government, the organized workers of Germany,
responding to an appeal from President Ebert, laid down their tools and
thus enabled the Republican forces to expel the counter-revolutionaries.
Occasionally the C.G.T. admitted that strikes might be properly used to
exact from a government some particular action of benefit to the organized workers. Generally, however, the syndicalists looked upon political
reforms as futile and delusive; and they intended the strike to be used
mainly for antipolitical purposes.

The distinctive features of the syndicalists' strike are to be found
in the general mood in which it is to be conducted and in its sweeping
revolutionary aims.[11] Every strike, they contended, is to be regarded as
a method of training and discipline and as a means of arousing sentiments of class solidarity. A special interpretation of the inspirational
aspect of the syndicalist strike was given by Sorel, who, in his *Réflexions sur la violence,* laid great emphasis upon the myth value of
the general strike.[12] Every effective social movement, he maintained, has
its myth. The masses of men are stirred into persevering and heroic
action not by practical or scientific demonstrations of some rationally
desirable goal but only by appeals to the imagination. Sorel cited examples from history to show how social myths, picturing ideal conditions that could never be attained, had none the less, through their
effects on human emotions, produced profound social consequences,
giving new directions to the thought and conduct of men throughout
long periods of time. Thus the early Christians, inspired by their

---

[11] For the syndicalist conception of the general strike, see especially Hubert
Lagardelle, *La grève générale et le socialisme* (1905) ; Georges Sorel, *Matériaux
d'une théorie du prolétariat* (1919), pp. 61 ff.; Victor Griffuelhes, *L'action syndicaliste,* pp. 27–37.
[12] See especially pp. 177 ff.; and cf. *Matériaux,* pp. 89 ff.

vague anticipations of the early reappearance of Christ and the total destruction of the pagan world, developed a doctrine and discipline that radically transformed their own and later generations, although the apocalyptic myth itself was never to be realized. Sixteenth century reformers dreamed of a religiously regenerated Europe; their dreams never came true, but their activities, which would not have been carried on except for these dreams, brought about vast and permanent changes in church and state. The eighteenth century political dogmas of freedom and equality were irrational and impossible, yet they radically modified the whole course of constitutional development in the Western world in the succeeding century. Sorel, therefore, disparaged any attempt to judge the general strike by considerations as to "how far it can be taken literally as future history." "Everything which its opponents endeavor to establish," he said, "may be conceded without reducing in any way the value of the theory which they think they have refuted." [13]

Most of the syndicalists, it appears, found little value in Sorel's idea of the strike as an effective "social myth." They did, however, agree that the effectiveness of a strike could not be measured by its immediate practical results. They too attached importance to strikes as means of evoking and strengthening the appropriate sentiments for a wage-earners' war against capitalists and the state. A general strike, they said, brings all groups of workers into a coördinated and coöperating class, intensifies their class consciousness, and cultivates a militant feeling among them. As economic strife becomes more intense, every strike becomes less the separate act of a special group of workers and more the act of a class fighting for the ultimate triumph of its formidable revolutionary aims. The magnitude of the aims constitutes the characteristic feature of the syndicalist strike. It is a means of direct action for a general economic and social revolution; a weapon for forcing a general capitulation of employers and governors to workers.[14] Its special utility lies not in its superiority to particular strikes as means for securing concessions from property-owners or parliaments but in its superiority to political, trade-union, or anarchist methods for bringing about the fundamental social transformation which syndicalists seek to achieve.

Sabotage, the boycott, and violence were, therefore, according to the

[13] *Reflections on Violence*, pp. 135–136.
[14] Victor Griffuelhes, *L'action syndicaliste*, p. 33.

active syndicalists, proper incidents of an industrial conflict. The term "sabotage" indicates a policy of injuring an employer's property or business through sluggish, bungling, wasteful, or positively damaging acts—done either while the worker remains on the job or in connection with strikes.[15] It may take the non-violent forms of slow work for long hours, poor work for low pay, meticulous observance of instructions so as to increase costs of production, or telling the truth to customers so as to injure the sale of articles; or it may take the violent form of destroying materials and mutilating machines and tools. The C.G.T., in 1897, adopted unanimously a resolution approving the use of sabotage and the boycott, especially when these means appeared to be necessary in order to make a strike succeed; and later resolutions confirmed this position. Some of the theorists condemned sabotage. Syndicalism, they argued, is a philosophy of workers' control of society. Working-men must, therefore, constantly prove themselves fit for that task. In all that they do they should show their respect for the dignity of productive work and refrain from conduct that commits them to any sort of imperfect or uncraftsmanlike performance. Sorel, however, as well as the practical leaders, generally defended proletarian violence, both in destructive sabotage and in the use of whatever forms of force proved necessary in overcoming a capitalist or governmental resistance to a revolutionary general strike. Since workers and employers are at war, the moral standards of war must prevail. Sorel, moreover, saw something ennobling in physical violence and regarded it as an essential factor in developing courage, vigor, and self-respect among the workers.[16]

The syndicalist program of direct action involves a negation of political action. We have seen that experience and theory worked together

[15] The word is derived from the French *sabot* ("wooden-shoe"); so that sabotage perhaps originally indicated the throwing of a wooden clog into machinery, or working like one who wears wooden shoes ("travailler à coup de sabots"). Cf. John Spargo, *Syndicalism, Industrial Unionism and Socialism* (1913), pp. 140 ff. The French syndicalists are said to have borrowed the idea originally from a *ca-'canny* ("go-slow") policy practised and preached by an English industrial union in the nineties. For a syndicalist explanation of the whole theory and practice, see Émile Pouget, *Sabotage* (1911; translation, 1913).

[16] See his "Apology for Violence," an appendix to *Reflections on Violence*, p. 297.

The boycott—the refusal to take employment with or purchase articles made by a firm regarded as unfair in its dealings with workers—and the label—to indicate work done under union conditions, are incidental forms of direct action, which, as employed by syndicalists, reveal no novel aspects, except in so far as they are occasionally glorified by syndicalists as indications of the resources which the workers, as monopolists of labor and near monopolists of consumption, have at hand for use in their warfare with the rest of the community.

in creating among French working-men a distrust of politics. They could not forget the state's tardy and reluctant recognition of the 'wage-earners' rights to organize and act concertedly for the protection of the valid interests of working-men. They were antagonized also by more positive manifestations of unfriendliness on the part of the French state —in the partiality displayed by the national government in favor of employers in times of serious industrial conflict. In the years imme-diately preceding the definitive triumph of the revolutionary over the moderate group in the Confederation, the army and police had been used vigorously against strikers. The syndicalists contended that the army's essential task appeared to be that of defending not the nation but the capitalist groups within the nation: in war the army served the imperialistic designs of international financiers; in peace it sup-pressed strikes; it was never used in the cause of the workers. The syndicalists pointed out that in strikes near the Franco-German border, in 1905, German and French troops were used indiscriminately on both sides of the border, proving thus that governments give little heed to a national boundary in times of conflict between employers and wage-earners. Thus the syndicalists were persuaded to accept Marx's maxim that "the proletariat has no country." Their antipolitical attitude was confirmed, moreover, by evidences of injustice and incompetence in the policy of the national government of France. The Boulanger episode and the Dreyfus, Panama, Carnot, and other scandals occurred in the years when the syndicalist policy was being developed; and famous authors, entirely outside the labor movement (Taine, Zola, Anatole France), supplied eloquent pictures of parliamentary inefficiency and intrigue in that period.

The state, the syndicalists argued, is theoretically wrong because it embodies an impossible ideal of social unity. Society is essentially pluralistic, and no political constitution can make it otherwise. Through all of Sorel's writing there runs this idea of the futility of political action and of the fallacy of the democratic belief in some fundamental identity of human interests that can harmonize the diverging and opposing in-terests of the several economic groups in a capitalist society.[17] Thus the syndicalists often condemned the political activity not only of reformist socialists, with their compromises and alliances with liberal groups, but also of orthodox socialists, who sought to acquire control

[17] *Illusions du progrès*, pp. 9–10; *Décomposition du Marxisme*, pp. 53 ff.; *Matériaux d'une théorie du prolétariat*, pp. 56, 263, 286.

of a government and use its machinery to reconstruct the whole economic order for the benefit of the workers.[18] The syndicalists' goal was the same as that of both reformist and orthodox socialists—a common, working-men's, ownership of the means of production and exchange; but syndicalists did not believe that the way to that goal lay through political action of either the reformist or orthodox sort.

Although the syndicalists believed that the workers could not rely on political action and did not need that as their means of salvation, yet, as long as the state remained in existence, there could be no objection, they said, to using its services in incidental ways. The official position of the syndicalist associations was one of political neutrality. The C.G.T. consistently refused all coöperation with socialist or other political parties and opposed participation by syndical organizations in political campaigns and elections. It conceded full discretion to the individual syndicalist to vote and act otherwise politically as he pleased. It also admitted that workers might properly, under certain conditions, join in efforts to obtain legislation favorable to their associations. Thus they might work to secure the enactment of measures giving legal recognition to the unions or assigning to the latter such functions as the operation of public employment bureaus or the inspectional tasks necessary for the enforcement of factory legislation.[19] Moreover, the syndicalists agreed that, where an act of the government beneficial to the workers could be secured by aggressive acts which intimidate the government into the action desired, then the government's concession could be accepted, since it had been obtained by direct action of the workers. They pointed with pride to the several occasions on which the French Parliament had enacted labor legislation obviously under pressure from the united efforts of working-men, acting under syndicalist auspices, in public meetings, street demonstrations, and strikes.[20]

Syndicalism, it is thus seen, was mainly a creed of opposition—of aggressive action against the institutions of capitalist economy and political government. Both in its negations—its general repudiation of private ownership and of political action—and in its affirmations—its positive technique of direct action—it was concerned with methods for getting rid of existing instruments of oppression, not with the ways of administering social affairs after the success of their destructive

[18] On the relations of the syndicalists to the Socialist party of France, cf. Sylvain Humbert, *Le mouvement syndical*, pp. 74–88.

[19] Cf. Sorel, *L'avenir socialiste des syndicats,* pp. 17 ff.

[20] Cf. Pouget, *Confédération générale du travail,* p. 46.

efforts. It offered, therefore, a policy primarily of revolution, not of administration. Most syndicalists held that it was not necessary or reasonably possible to plan constructively for the future organization of society. The sufficient task for the present is that of inspiring and directing wage-earners in the activities of defense and attack. The more metaphysical theorists—Sorel and Berth—argued, moreover, that any attempt to depict the details of the future order would dispel those visionary intuitions in which lay the chief power of syndicalism.

The only attempt to set forth fully the forms of a future syndicalist society is to be found in a book, *How We Shall Bring About the Revolution,* by the ex-anarchists Patuad and Pouget.[21] According to this somewhat romantic prophecy, the syndicalist revolution (which the authors describe in vivid detail) will be followed by the permanent, constructive tasks of syndicalism. For these tasks the existing syndical associations will, for the most part, be sufficient. Ordinary functions of management will be in the hands of industrial unions, which will have possession of buildings, machinery, and equipment in the several industries and will exercise immediate direction of production and execute general rules for special cases. The authors appear to have generally in mind the local unions; but they assign certain nation-wide services, such as the post office and the railroads, to national federations of workers; the latter, however, are to leave as much autonomy as practicable to the local unions. There will be other national federations to supply technical information and expert advice to the local bodies. Finally, a comprehensive national body, like the existing C.G.T., will have the function of deciding matters that demand uniform treatment in all industries, such as the care of children, the aged and the sick, the determination of minimum and maximum ages for work and the length of the normal work-day, and the definition of standards of remuneration.

The authors recognize that in the new society there will be need for certain disciplinary sanctions, but these will be distinctive in kind. There will be boycotts for profiteers, and banishment for idlers and for those who otherwise show their unwillingness to adjust themselves to the new order. Each union will pass judgment upon any of its members in case of "anti-human acts"; it may decree "a moral punishment," in the form of a boycott or, in extreme cases, may remand the culprit

---

[21] Émile Patuad and Émile Pouget, *Comment nous ferons la révolution* (1909); translation by Charlotte and Frederic Charles—*Syndicalism and the Coöperative Commonwealth: How We Shall Bring About the Revolution* (1913).

to a general meeting of the unions, where a sentence of banishment can be imposed, reserving to the accused a right of appeal to the national federation and finally to the central committee of the general trade-union congress. Certain of the more heinous offenses will be spontaneously dealt with through acts of summary justice inflicted by eye-witnesses. Prisons and court-houses will, however, be abolished, for crimes will decrease in number because there will no longer be any occasions for the antisocial acts "caused by misery, inequality, or the evil deeds of capitalism"; and the better social environment will tend to eliminate the offenses that result from physiological defects and mental disease.[22]

The authors admit also the need for a defensive militia: syndicalist policy, they explain, is not "the resignation and non-resistance preached by Tolstoi." But the military arrangements will differ radically from those of the present. There will be no professional army, no military schools, no barracks or other offensive armaments. In each union there will be an armed troop, for protection against counter-revolutionary disturbances. Purely defensive arms will be assigned by the central labor exchanges to the battalions in the several unions. These military bodies will be so directly identified with the ordinary groupings of the working masses that they cannot conceivably act against working-men's interests. The people, having made their work free, will simply have "the common sense to arm themselves in order to protect their conquered liberty." [23]

As already indicated, most syndicalist writers regarded as untimely and futile any attempt to present a comprehensive picture of the future organization of society. Some of the writers discussed the proper allocation of functions to local unions, federations of unions, bourses, and the general confederation of labor, respectively; the allotment generally accorded with that indicated by Patuad and Pouget, except that in most instances there was a more explicit assignment to the bourses of the function of supplying community needs in the way of public health and other utilities. Generally nothing was said as to the methods of dealing with foreign aggression, crime, or rebellion.

Syndicalists explained the similiarity as well as the originality of their doctrine in relation both to Marxism and to communist anarchism.

---

[22] *How We Shall Bring About the Revolution,* pp. 125–127, 152–153.
[23] *Ibid.,* pp. 156–158.

Generally they described their system as a logical development of Marx's basic doctrines, retaining his hypotheses and carrying his main arguments to their logical conclusions but at the same time removing fallacies in current interpretations of Marxism and correcting mistakes made by Marx himself, due to the fact that his prophecies and proposals were made in the very early stage of the organized labor movement. Syndicalists emphasized Marx's conception of the class war, accepted the idea of a social evolution tending towards the complete demolition of the traditional state, and at the same time insisted (perhaps more than Marx) upon the volitional element in that natural movement.[24] Lagardelle showed that Marx, on several occasions, indicated working-men's associations as the proper agencies both for maintaining working-class solidarity and for suppressing the wage system. Marx's general position, according to Lagardelle, was that the institutions through which the workers' emancipation is to be progressively achieved will be those that evolve naturally out of the struggle between proletariat and bourgeoisie.[25]

Sorel maintained that the general strike is essentially Marxian. Although it does not appear in Marx's sketch of the tactics of socialism, it expresses better than anything else the spirit of class war. It forces all citizens into two clearly defined, mutually hostile, groups, as ordinary economic operations do not. It preserves a constant and ardent spirit of revolt, while political methods of any sort bring on concessions and collaborations which tend inevitably to a reconciliation on terms that leave the workers in a subordinate position. Sorel admitted an apparent incompatibility between his own and the Marxian conception of the development of the class conflict. Marx emphasized the part which increasing poverty and exploitation would play in developing a revolutionary disposition among the proletariat, while Sorel maintained that strikes succeed best in periods of increasing prosperity, because only in such times can peasants and artisans be united with proletarians by visions of the "rosy-colored" future: "If you once identify revolution and general strike it then becomes impossible to conceive of an essential transformation of the world taking place in a time of economic decadence." [26] The opposing opinions can be reconciled, according to Sorel, for Marx meant simply that the preparation of the

---

[24] Cf. Sorel, *L'avenir socialiste des syndicats,* and *Réflexions sur la violence,* pp. 257–267; translation, pp. 195–204.

[25] Cf. Lagardelle, *Le socialisme ouvrier,* pp. 349–357.

[26] *Reflections on Violence,* pp. 148–149.

proletariat for the revolution depends upon conditions which create a "stubborn, increasing, and passionate resistance to the present order of things." Since such resistance, in its most effective form—the strike— is induced rather by the well-being than by the abasement of the prole- tariat, the error of Marx's specific prophecy in no way invalidates his essential argument. "The new school," Sorel concluded, "does not wish to restrict itself to the formulas of Marx; . . . it does not in the least feel itself bound to admire the illusions, the faults and the errors of the man who did so much to work out revolutionary ideas; it endeavors to separate what disfigures the work of Marx from what will immortal- ize his name." [27]

Syndicalists, Lagardelle explained, rejected both the economic and the political fatalism of the followers of Marx. They discountenanced the belief that concentration of industry, centralization of capital, de- crease of the middle class, and increase of the proletariat would of themselves destroy capitalism and elevate the proletariat to the pre- dominant position in society; and they repudiated the socialists' faith that the workers "have only to possess themselves of the state in order to change the face of the world." [28] Lagardelle argued that Marx's prophecy represented the concentration of industry, the increasing misery, and the other attendant changes in capitalist development not as in themselves all-sufficient in the evolution of socialism but rather as factors creating the conditions which workers can utilize for their own ends. Moreover, in indicating the seizure of political power as the indispensable means whereby the working class could, at the proper time, complete the socialist transformation of society, Marx did not mean that the workers should take over to their own uses the tradi- tional machinery of the state but rather that they must assume com- plete control over the whole of social life.

The revolutionary socialists of Soviet Russia agree with the revolu- tionary syndicalists in insisting upon the right of and the necessity for the superior minority to exercise control over the apathetic and unin- telligent majority and in making an effort to give an important place to functional associations in the administration of the affairs of society. The earlier "Social Revolutionaries" of Russia had propagated both doctrines. Apart from certain general features of a socialist program, however, the marks of a common parentage do not appear, and the

[27] *Reflections on Violence,* p. 97.
[28] Lagardelle, *Le socialisme ouvrier,* pp. 329–330.

admixture of other blood and the operation of dissimilar environments show their effects. The Russian Communists place little reliance upon the syndicalist devices of direct action. They have no taste for the general strike as an "energizing myth"; and they argue that experiences, notably the outcome of the Russian insurrection of 1905, have proved the utter inadequacy of strikes and sabotage as principal weapons for a social reconstruction. They hold that workers' associations, acting alone, are ineffective for either revolt or government.

Here then is the chief point at issue between socialism—revolutionary or reformist—and syndicalism, and it indicates a theoretical affiliation—but not an identity—between syndicalism and anarchism. As socialists have ridiculed the syndicalists' idealization of the general strike, so the revolutionary syndicalists repudiated the socialists' blind faith in the magic virtue of control through legal coercion. Syndicalists and anarchists looked upon voluntary "interest" associations as adequate both for the achievement of the revolution and for the administration of social affairs after the revolution. They discredited political action not only because they regarded the state as reflecting, in its whole structure and activity, the characteristic ideals of a capitalist-controlled society but also because reliance upon state intervention seemed to them to be inconsistent with their faith in the self-sufficiency of the organized, class-conscious workers.

We have seen the part that anarchists played in founding the associations within which the syndicalist policy was developed. The men who immediately followed Pelloutier in directing syndicalist propaganda—notably, Griffuelhes, Pouget, and Yvetot—preached generally the doctrine that the state should either be removed here and now or that it should be utilized only in so far as absolute necessity dictates; and such, apparently, was the position of Sorel. The prevailing syndicalist attitude, however, was represented perhaps more faithfully by the more moderate spokesmen, Lagardelle and Berth. Although they denied any "theoretical obligation" to the state and any admission of its "permanent character," they yet maintained that bourgeois institutions could be "eliminated only as they are replaced by working-class institutions"; so that "working-class democracy has need a while yet for political democracy." This position is clearly distinct from that of the orthodox anarchists. The latter demanded absolute abstention from political activity on the part of individuals as well as associations: the state being essentially an unjust and irrational institution, any recognition of it is inconsistent with true anarchist faith. Anarchism addressed itself to the individual and ordered him not to vote or interest himself in any way in the activity of the state; whereas syndicalism, although recognizing that political methods are not normally the proper methods for the accomplishment of its tasks and insisting upon the political neutrality of all syndical bodies, yet gave to the individual workers the freedom to utilize political parties and other agencies of democracy.[29] Thus Lagardelle contrasted the realism and pragmatism of syndicalism with the intellectualism and dogmatism of anarchism.

Some syndicalist theorists, moreover, not only admitted a limited use of political methods but recognized also that the several syndical associations in the future society would themselves exercise a coercive authority. Although political authority and force would be discarded, sovereignty would remain. Sovereignty in a syndicalist system, it was explained, would reside not in a king, or lords, or the people but in national associations of workers. The superiority of syndicalist to political authority would consist in the fact that it would be organic, not mechanical, like that of the state, which rests solely on the state's power to instil fear of punishment. Syndicalist authority, although in exceptional cases applying coercion to abnormal members of society, would rest generally upon a natural accord of homogeneous interests and opinions among the members of the association in which the sovereignty inheres.[30] The different sovereigns would be separated not by fictitious territorial or national boundaries but by the real lines of division created by the varying services which social life requires; these lines would divide society not into antagonistic or competing factions but into coöperating associations of a consolidated working-men's community.

Thus in two senses the revolutionary syndicalist was less definitely anti-authoritarian than the anarchists. He permitted some supplementary use of ordinary political agencies for the immediate ends of syndicalism; and his system left room for some organized coercion in managing society after the syndicalist revolution. The coercion would be "direct"—applied not by a comprehensive territorial state but by the several co-equal and autonomous associations of workers.[31]

---

[29] See *supra,* pp. 203–204, 209–211, 223–224.

[30] See Sergio Panunzio, "Syndicalisme et Souveraineté," *Le mouvement socialiste,* XXXIV (1913), 59–73.

[31] This may be the sort of society the political "pluralists" (to be considered *infra,* Ch. XVIII) have in mind.

Minority labor groups in other countries have employed certain of the tactics of revolutionary syndicalism. In some countries, as in Italy under the leadership of Arturo Labriola and Enrico Leone, the policies and the ideas behind them have been largely reproductions of French syndicalism. In the case of other groups—notably, the American "I.W.W."—the policies, evolving in distinctive environments, have been largely independent of French influences.[32]

The I.W.W. (Industrial Workers of the World) was founded at Chicago, in 1905, through a merger of several associations, brought together by a common distrust of the too conservative American Federation of Labor and the too doctrinaire Socialist party, a special concern for the interests of unskilled laborers (generally overlooked by the A.F.L.), and a vague hope of uniting on a plan of action more aggressive than collective bargaining—to which the A.F.L. mainly confined itself—and more direct than political socialism.[33] Prominent leaders in the original meeting were William Haywood (secretary of the Western Federation of Miners), Eugene Debs and A. M. Simons (leaders of the orthodox Socialist party), Daniel De Leon (an official of the more revolutionary Socialist Labor party), and W. E. Trautman (an industrial unionist, opposed, or indifferent, to political action). Dissension between direct-actionists and political-socialists led soon to the withdrawal of the latter; this left the original association a smaller but more homogeneous body.[34]

Certain leaders of the I.W.W. were doubtless influenced, in some measure, by the works of Sorel, Pouget, and other syndicalist writers, as well as by personal contacts established by visits of Haywood and W. Z. Foster to France. The influences were probably reciprocal, but the most authoritative students hold that the two movements developed, for the most part, independently of one another.

Cardinal features of the I.W.W. policy—industrial unionism, regional alliances of workers from various industries, the disparagement of political action, and the practice or threat of violence—had been

---

[32] See André Tridon, *The New Unionism* (1913; second ed., 1917), Chs. VI–XIII.

[33] See Paul Brissenden, *The I.W.W. A Study of American Syndicalism* (1919; second ed., 1920); J. S. Gambs, *The Decline of the I.W.W.* (1932), and other titles on p. 259, *infra*.

[34] Its membership has consisted principally of unskilled workers in railway construction and the textile mills, migratory laborers in lumbering and grain harvesting in the West, and workers in steel mills and coal mines.

The faction that split off formed an independent association, known for awhile as the "Detroit I.W.W." and later as "The Workers' Industrial Union." It has been less widely active than the "Chicago I.W.W."

familiar in the policies of earlier labor associations in the United States: notably, the Knights of Labor, founded in 1869 and dominating the labor movement in the late seventies and early eighties; the Western Federation of Miners, organized in 1892; the American Railway Union, formed under the leadership of Eugene Debs, in 1893; the Western Labor Union, founded in 1898, largely on the initiative of the W.F.M.; and the American Labor Union, formed in 1902 from a union of the W.F.M. and the W.L.U. Conditions in many of the industries affected by these unions were such that the ordinary processes of the strike and collective bargaining, even when conducted throughout a whole industry, were ineffective against the resources and strategies of the owners, who were frequently aided by sympathetic state and local governmental authorities—through injunctions, the national guard, and the police. Often a contest between owners and workers took the form of violent direct action on both sides.

It is difficult, however, to construct any clear and coherent system of doctrine from the various pronouncements of the association. One of its spokesmen has declared that its policy includes "all tactics that will get the results sought with the least expenditure of time and energy." [35] The "Preamble" of the 1905 platform proclaims a general policy of implacable class war and militant direct action. "The working-class and the employing class have nothing in common. . . . Between these two classes a struggle must go on until the workers of the world are organized as a class, take possession of the earth and the machinery of production, and abolish the wage-system." It is a fallacy of trade-unionism that it misleads the workers into the belief that they have interests in common with their employers and that it divides the workers into competing groups. The new policy is "to unite all the industrial workers of the world into one body" and to discountenance political action of every kind, whether in the peaceful form of balloting and lobbying or in the revolutionary political form of using labor organs as clubs "with which to beat their way into possession and control of government." The I.W.W. is not to engage in "the useless task of attacking governments that oppress us. . . . The government is the stick or club in the hands of the economic masters of every country. Leave the stick alone and turn upon the masters. . . . The socialist stick is as bad as the capitalist stick." [36]

[35] Vincent St. John, *The I.W.W.* (1913), p. 17.
[36] *Preamble and Constitution of the Industrial Workers of the World* (1914 ed.),

The membership of the I.W.W. has always been small—reliably esti-
mated, at its highest point in the textile strikes of 1912, as around
100,000. Recently the number has declined rapidly. Many of the most
active members were imprisoned during the World War for interfering
with enlistments or retarding the production of munitions. Others have
met a similar fate under the post-war State statutes against "criminal
syndicalism." Some of the leaders, including Haywood and Foster,
have deserted to the Communists, and others have withdrawn in disputes over tactics. The I.W.W. activity, however, has helped spread
the idea of industrial unionism, which forms the principle of organization for some of the strongest of the newer unions in the United States
and is a main tenet of the American Communists.[37]

For a brief period some of the leading ideas of revolutionary
syndicalism flourished in important sections of the British labor movement.[38] The mass strikes of 1911–1913 were planned and directed by
men who had had direct and extended contacts with the French syndicalists and the American I.W.W. Tom Mann, Guy Bowman, James Con-
nolly, Ben Tillett, and Will Thorne organized a brief-lived "Industrial
Syndicalist League" and urged on the movement for industrial unionism, which John Burns, Mann, Thorne, and Tillett had initiated in the
eighties. Through numerous speeches and pamphlets they spread abroad
the doctrine that neither bargaining with employers nor political regulation of employment conditions but only the destruction of capitalism
could deliver the workers from their social bondage; and that only the
working-men themselves, by concertedly laying down their tools and in
other ways displaying their massed strength, could accomplish the
destruction. The strikes alarmed the nation, forced concessions from
employers in some instances, and hastened the enactment of legislation
strengthening the labor organizations. The movement itself collapsed,
through the effective measures of repression taken by the government
and the failure to win over the main labor bodies, which remained

pp. 4, 15, 19–20. Generally, as a matter of policy, the organization has allowed
its members liberty to vote as they choose; and its spokesmen have generally
described the official attitude as non-political, rather than antipolitical.

[37] Professor Brissenden estimates the membership, in 1930, as less than 10,000.
See his article, "Industrial Workers of the World," in the *Encyclopaedia of the
Social Sciences*, Vol. VIII. He there points to the influence of the I.W.W. in forcing
the A.F.L. to pay some attention to unskilled workers and also in promoting the
organization of Negro laborers.

[38] W. M. Citrine, *The Trade Union Movement of Great Britain* (1926);
Max Beer, *History of British Socialism*, Vol. II, Ch. XVIII; Tom Mann, *From
Single Tax to Syndicalism* (1913).

committed to collective bargaining and to gradual nationalization or reform through orthodox political methods. Nevertheless, the agitation of Mann and his associates left permanent marks on the British labor movement; on the one hand, in furthering the organization of large and aggressive unions, formed on industrial lines; on the other hand, in preparing the way for a favorable reception to guild socialism and other, more limited, schemes for a direct working-men's control of the conditions of their work.

THE "NEW SYNDICALISM" IN FRANCE

The World War and post-war conditions produced radical changes in the character and policy of organized syndicalism in France.[39] Soon after the war began the General Confederation of Labor abandoned its antimilitarism and antistatism, joined the socialists in entering into a truce with the government, and coöperated actively in the various economic arrangements for furthering a successful conduct of the war. The syndicalist daily, *La Bataille Syndicaliste,* belied its title by editorial utterances almost chauvinistic in temper. There was an aggressive and growing antiwar minority, but the Confederation remained, for the duration of the war, formally a united body.

The critical economic and social troubles of the early post-war period created new dissensions between the moderate, nationalistic majority and the militant minority in the Confederation. The disputes related to both international and domestic policies. The two factions agreed in demanding amnesty for political prisoners, in criticizing generally the conservative reaction in Europe, and in condemning the French intervention in aid of the Russian counter-revolutionaries; but they divided sharply over the question of affiliation with the Russian Communists. In domestic matters the issues arose over methods for bringing pressure upon the government in order to force it to take action for the restoration of constitutional liberties and for the improvement of living conditions. In 1920, the officials of the Confederation, under clamorous pressure from the left wing, declared a May-day general strike in support of a national strike by the railway workers. The complete fail-

[39] On the policy of the C.G.T. during and after the War, see the following: Marjorie R. Clark, *History of the French Labor Movement, 1910–1928* (1930); Léon Jouhaux, *Le syndicalisme et la C.G.T.* (1920); Lewis L. Lorwin, *Labor and Internationalism* (1929), Ch. XXII and pp. 644–645; Roger Picard, *Le mouvement syndical durant la guerre* (1928); Paul Louis, *Le syndicalisme français, d'Amiens à Saint-Étienne* (1924), Ch. II; David J. Saposs, *The Labor Movement in Post-War France* (1931).

ure of this attempt and the ensuing quarrel as to the causes of the failure intensified the discord. A definite split between the two wings occurred in January, 1922. The minority group formed a new national organization—the "General Confederation of United Labor" (the "C.G.T.U."—*Confédération Générale du Travail Unitaire*), which soon acquired a membership of about half the number of the older organization. This new confederation adopted the revolutionary doctrines of the Communist International, with which it is now formally affiliated. The older organization has forsworn revolutionary tactics of all sorts.

The new policies of the old C.G.T. have been described in addresses and journalistic articles by Jouhaux, Perrot (former secretary of the Union of the Syndicats of the Seine), and others; [40] and a comprehensive exposition of the philosophy of the new movement has been given by Maxime Leroy in his *Techniques nouvelles du syndicalisme*. Leroy, Jouhaux, and Perrot characterize the post-war doctrine as broader and more constructive, differing from, yet logically developing out of, the earlier syndicalist notions. The change, they maintain, is an entirely natural evolution from youth to age. [41] As a young nation, struggling to maintain its security and independence, fortifies itself, as far as it can, with impassable military and economic frontiers, so a rising working class has to establish its own integrity by isolating itself from the rest of the nation. But as with nations, so with economic classes—when their special interests and their right to exist have been generally and explicitly acknowledged, then they can with safety recognize the rights of other nations or classes and coöperate with them in the pursuit of interests that are essentially common. The time has come, therefore, for the workers to abandon their narrow conception of class war. They should now seek to perpetuate those processes of inter-group collaboration that proved effective in war time. Workers can now safely admit that production is not simply a matter of hand labor, that the whole process involves administration, invention, research, artistic craftsmanship, distribution, and even use and consumption. The production of any basic commodity or service demands a proper coördination among manual laborers, technicians, managers, artists, scientists, carriers, purveyors, users—all vitally concerned in the quality, quantity, and price of that utility. [42]

[40] These have appeared in the daily *Bataille*, weekly *Atelier*, and monthly *Voix du Peuple*.
[41] Leroy, *Techniques nouvelles du syndicalisme* (1921), Ch. II.
[42] *Ibid.*, Ch. XIII.

The new syndicalists wish, therefore, to supplant the negative, destructive tactics of the older syndicalism by a positive and comprehensive policy. As the revolutionary syndicalists contrasted proletarian direct action to the political indirect action of the socialists, so now Leroy contrasts the newer syndicalist technique of "institutions" with the older technique of "conspiracy." Likewise Perrot argues that, since capitalism persists less by virtue of its financial resources than by its peculiar services—its organization of production, exchange, and credit—it can be displaced not by a stoppage of production or by negligent or destructive action but only by a "revolution of institutions." The workers must prove that they are capable of participating in the management of production and that they know how to serve the collective interest.[43]

Accordingly the newer syndicalists condemn violence and dictatorship. There is, they say, nothing proletarian about violence; it has been the weapon of malcontents of all ages and was inherited by proletarians from the bourgeois insurrectionary parties of the eighteenth and nineteenth centuries. The World War and its treaties have demonstrated the futility of victories by armed force. The post-war Bolshevist régime in Russia has refuted Sorel's contention that proletarian violence, being in the nature of a war, would be conducted according to rules of war which protect non-combatants and defeated antagonists. It is impossible to assign to violence a rationally limited place, for violence is essentially the negation of moderation and reason and the domination of instinct. A dictatorship, like war, requires a highly centralized organization, and an arbitrary authority and iron discipline, whereas syndicalism is democratic, federalistic, pacific. The "revolution of institutions," it is admitted, implies a radical transformation of the existing political and economic structure of society and may involve abrupt breaks with the past; but these sudden ruptures must be regarded only as incidents, lacking any decisive influence upon the fundamental changes which syndicalists seek to achieve.[44]

The new syndicalists have made concrete proposals for a coöperative control of industry. Committees of the Confederation, collaborating with representatives of consumers' associations and the organized civil servants, have drawn up plans for the management of public and private enterprises. For each publicly owned industry, the plans provide a tri-

[43] *Techniques nouvelles du syndicalisme*, Ch. V.
[44] *Ibid.*, Ch. V: "Qu'est ce que la Révolution?"

partite scheme of management, in which equal representation is given to (1) producers—i.e., all manual and technical workers, (2) users, and (3) the public; and for private industry they set up a system of joint management by owners and workers. The plans preserve the right to strike for the wage-workers in both public and private industries. Leroy admits that the strike has no theoretically justifiable place in the proposed system; for it amounts to a putting in question by a single group of decisions reached not arbitrarily by a self-centered faction but deliberately by representatives of all the groups. The strike, he explains, is retained "less out of respect for the exercise of a legitimate faculty than to satisfy one of the fundamental beliefs of the working class, which does not consider itself to be actually free except to the extent that it is free to use this particular means." [45]

The new syndicalism is in some respects a return to the ideas of Waldeck-Rousseau and his associates four decades ago. As the latter planned to bring labor unions into collaboration with the state, so Jouhaux and Leroy plan to have the state supervise and coöperate with the unions. The proposals apparently contemplate a division between the governmental organization for preserving order and administering justice, on the one hand, and the state's agencies for carrying out its supervisory economic and cultural functions, on the other hand; although the method of division is not clearly indicated in the detailed schemes that have been published. Leroy contends generally, however, that by separating public political from public economic agencies and by vesting ordinary industrial management in the hands of bodies broadly representative of all grades of workers, there can be established a national ownership, distinct from other familiar types of ownership: from private ownership, with its familiar capitalist abuses of waste, oppression, and exploitation; from state or municipal ownership of the traditional sort, administered by a bureaucracy out of contact with the various interests concerned; from associated consumers' ownership, with its tendencies towards a slightly modified capitalistic system; and from coöperative producers' ownership, which neglects the legitimate interests of consumers and the public.

Thus the post-war syndicalists accord an important place to general social interests and to political authority as the spokesman and defender of these interests. They would, in the first place, set up above all industry a national, broadly representative, economic council—to prepare

[45] *Techniques nouvelles du syndicalisme*, pp. 159–160.

general plans for the organization of production and distribution and to approve or disapprove general policies of administration proposed by the bodies that operate the several industries. They would, in the second place, reorganize the state, modify its functions, and, by transforming economic relations, reduce to a minimum the occasions for the exercise of its coercive power. They recognize that there will be conflicts of interest among citizens and that consequently there must be tribunals to adjudicate, and other agencies to execute judgments, with power to apply coercion when necessary. The state will be needed also to maintain military defense and conduct foreign intercourse. But the most important tasks of the future syndicalist state will be, on the one hand, to collaborate in the management of production by selecting representatives of the collective interest and, on the other hand, to provide the means of education and artistic expression and enjoyment for the masses and to encourage intellectual inquiry and technical invention. The state will become, "through all its laws and in all its services, an impulse to initiative, invention and economic heresy, with the same zeal with which the traditional state restrains spontaneity and innovation. It will endeavor to guide rather than restrain; its legislation will become more and more a means of enlightenment rather than dictation." [46]

Thus the larger bodies of organized labor in France have abandoned the revolutionary syndicalism of the pre-war period. The present exponents of that earlier doctrine are to be found in a new international organization, founded in Berlin, in 1923, under the name of the old "First International" (of the years 1862–1876)—the "International Workingmen's Association." The spokesmen for this revolutionary-syndical International direct attention to the opposition of their policy both to the pacifism of the International Federation of Trade Unions (with which the C.G.T. and most of the larger national organizations of labor unions in other countries are affiliated) and to the extreme politicalism of the Russian Communists, with their reliance upon armies, police, partisan courts, and the other traditional agencies of governmental oppression. The resolutions and debates of the new "I.W.M.A." restate most of the ideas of the pre-war syndicalists: they repudiate collective bargaining and political action and insist upon independent action by working-men's associations in strikes, sabotage, boycotts, and

[46] *Techniques nouvelles du syndicalisme,* p. 125.

other mass demonstrations—in preparing for general national strikes and the final revolutionary world strike. The organization has a small membership, chiefly in Germany, the Scandinavian countries, Mexico, and Argentina.

The most important influences of the earlier French syndicalism are, to be found to-day in other places: on the one hand, in the revival, chiefly in Fascist Italy and Communist Russia, of the Sorelian philosophy of violence as an indispensable means of bringing about any fundamental social regeneration; on the other hand, in the national guilds and industrial parliaments of Guild Socialists, the "Corporations" of the Fascists, and the schemes for "industrial nationalization" and "joint-control" put forth by various groups of socialists and liberal collectivists to-day.[47]

SELECT BIBLIOGRAPHY

BIBLIOGRAPHIES OF SYNDICALISM

Levine, Louis, *Syndicalism in France* (second rev. ed., New York, 1914), pp. 427–435.
Zimand, Savel, *Modern Social Movements* (New York, 1921), pp. 213–226.

HISTORICAL BACKGROUND OF FRENCH SYNDICALISM

Challaye, Félicien, *Syndicalisme révolutionnaire et syndicalisme réformiste* (Paris, 1909).
Cole, G. D. H., *Self-Government in Industry* (London, 1917), pp. 303–321.
Humbert, Sylvain, *Le mouvement syndical* (Paris, 1912), Vol. IX of *Histoire des partis socialistes en France,* ed. by Alexandre Zévaès, 11 vols. in 3 (Paris, 1911–1912).
Lagardelle, Hubert, *L'évolution des syndicats ouvriers en France de l'inter-diction à l'obligation* (Paris, 1901).
Levine, Louis, *Syndicalism in France* (second rev. ed., New York, 1914), Chs. I–IV–VII.
Louis, Paul, *Le syndicalisme français d'Amiens à Saint-Étienne, 1906–1922* (Paris, 1924).
Pawlowski, Auguste, *La Confédération Générale du Travail* (Paris, 1910).
Pelloutier, Fernand, *Histoire des bourses du travail* (Paris, 1902).

[47] See *supra,* 132–133, 173–177, *infra,* 268–270, 478–481, 549.

Weill, Georges J., *Histoire du mouvement social en France, 1852–1924* (third ed., Paris, 1924), Chs. IX, XII, XV, XVI.

Zévaès, Alexandre, *Le syndicalisme contemporain* (Paris, 1911).

WORKS OF LEADING SYNDICALIST THEORISTS

Berth, Édouard, *Les nouveaux aspects du socialisme* (Paris, 1908).

Griffuelhes, Victor, *L'action syndicaliste* (Paris, 1908).

Lagardelle, Hubert, *La grève générale et le socialisme* (Paris, 1905).

——————,*Le socialisme ouvrier* (Paris, 1911).

Patuad, Émile, and Pouget, Émile, *Comment nous ferons la révolution* (Paris, 1909). *Syndicalism and the Coöperative Commonwealth.* (*How We Shall Bring About the Revolution*) translated by Charlotte and Frederic Charles (Oxford, 1913).

Pouget, Émile, *La Confédération Générale du Travail* (Paris, 1908; second ed., 1910).

——————, *Le sabotage* (Paris, 1910).

——————, *Sabotage*, translated by A. M. Giovanitti (Chicago, 1913).

Sorel, Georges, *L'avenir socialiste des syndicats* (Paris, 1898).

——————, *La décomposition du Marxisme* (Paris, 1908; second ed., 1910).

——————, *Les illusions du progrès* (second ed., Paris, 1911).

——————, *Réflexions sur la violence* (Paris, 1905).

——————, *Reflections on Violence*, translated by T. E. Hulme (New York, 1914).

——————, *Matériaux d'une théorie du prolétariat* (Paris, 1921).

CRITICAL EXPOSITION OF SYNDICALISM

Acht, Anton, *Der moderne französische Syndikalismus* (Jena, 1911).

Brentano, Lujo, *Ueber Syndikalismus und Lohnminimum* (Munich, 1913).

Cole, G. D. H., *World of Labour* (London, 1913), Chs. III and IV.

Douglas, Paul, "Syndicalism," pp. 216–227 in *Political Theories, Recent Times,* Charles E. Merriam and H. E. Barnes, eds. (New York, 1924).

Dimnet, Ernest, "Syndicalism and Its Philosophy," *Atlantic Monthly,* CXI (1913), 17–30.

Guy-Grand, Georges, *La philosophie syndicaliste* (Paris, 1911).

Harley, J. H., *Syndicalism* (London, Edinburgh, and New York, n.d.).

Hunter, Robert, *Violence and the Labor Movement* (New York, 1914).

Laidler, Harry W., *History of Socialist Thought* (New York, 1927), Ch. XXII.

Lasserre, Pierre, "Georges Sorel: Théoricien de l'Imperialisme," *Revue des deux mondes,* XLI (1927), 144–166.

Levine, Louis, *Syndicalism in France* (New York, 1914), Chs. V, VI, VIII.

MacDonald, J. Ramsay, *Syndicalism: a Critical Examination* (London, 1912).

Russell, Bertrand, *Proposed Roads to Freedom* (New York, 1919), Ch. III.

Spargo, John, *Syndicalism, Industrial Unionism and Socialism* (New York, 1913).

Soltau, Roger, *French Political Thought in the Nineteenth Century* (New Haven, 1931), Ch. XIV.

THE I.W.W. AND SYNDICALISM IN VARIOUS COUNTRIES

Brissenden, Paul, *The I.W.W.: A Study of American Syndicalism* (New York, 1919; second ed., 1920).

Brooks, John Graham, *American Syndicalism: the I.W.W.* (New York, 1913).

Citrine, W. M., *The Trade Union Movement of Great Britain* (Amsterdam, 1926).

Gambs, J. S., *The Decline of the I.W.W.* (New York, 1932).

Groat, George G., *Organized Labor in America* (New York, 1916), Chs. XXVII and XXVIII.

Haywood, William D., *Bill Haywood's Book* (New York, 1929).

Hoxie, R. F., *Trade Unionism in the United States* (New York and London, 1917), Ch. VI.

Industrial Workers of the World, *Preamble and Constitution*, 1905; amended 1906–1914 (Chicago, 1914).

The I.W.W.: What It Is and What It Is Not (Chicago, n.d.).

Levine, Louis, "Development of Syndicalism in the United States," *Political Science Quarterly*, XXVIII (1913), 451–479.

Mann, Tom, *From Single Tax to Syndicalism* (London, 1913).

Parker, Carleton H., "The I.W.W.," *Atlantic Monthly*, CXX (1917), 651–662.

St. John, Vincent, *The I.W.W., Its History, Structure and Methods* (Cleveland, 1913).

Saposs, David J., *Left Wing Unionism* (New York, 1926).

Tridon, André, *The New Unionism* (New York, 1913; second ed., 1917).

THE "NEW SYNDICALISM" IN FRANCE

Jouhaux, Léon, *Le syndicalisme et la C.G.T.* (Paris, 1920).

Leroy, Maxime, *Les techniques nouvelles du syndicalisme* (Paris, 1921).

Lorwin, Lewis L., *Labor and Internationalism* (New York, 1929), Ch. XXII and pp. 644–645.

Louis, Paul, *Le syndicalisme français* (Paris, 1924), Chs. II and III.

Maxe, Jean, *De Zimmerwald au bolchévisme* (Paris, 1920).

Picard, Roger, *Le mouvement syndical durant la guerre* (Paris, 1928).

Clark, Marjorie R., *A History of the French Labor Movement* (Berkeley, Calif., 1930).

Saposs, David J., *The Labor Movement in Post-War France* (New York, 1931).

CHAPTER IX

THE GUILD SOCIALISTS

MARXIAN socialism and revolutionary anarchism are proletarian doctrines, each standing for an absolute power over economic and social life, to be exercised either through a territorially organized, worker-controlled state or through the severally organized occupational groups of workers. Guild socialism is like these doctrines in that it would withdraw from owners of capital both the power to determine the conditions under which laborers work and the right to derive profits out of what laborers produce. But it recognizes other bonds and interests than those of workers or producers, and it places less emphasis upon the purely economic phases of producers' interests. The guild-socialist doctrine was set forth by English intellectuals in the first and second decades of the twentieth century. Its basic ideas first appeared in writings by A. J. Penty, an architect; A. R. Orage, a schoolmaster, journalist, and philosophical essayist; and S. G. Hobson, a journalist and public lecturer. The three were members of the Fabian Society and the Independent Labour party, until they became dissatisfied with the persistence of these organizations in holding on to the ideas of centralized political socialism. Penty entered and left the regular socialist movement under the influence of considerations similar to those which had moved William Morris a half-century earlier. Like Morris, he believed that the modern industrial system made any sort of artistic or creative work impossible, and he joined the socialists because they were attacking modern industrialism. Also like Morris, he soon came to the conclusion that the socialists had no solution of the problem, for they were preoccupied with economic returns for the worker and proposed no plans for restoring that spontaneous and creative activity which the modern system of minute divisions of labor had destroyed. In other words, large-scale industry, whether in public or private hands, is concerned with producing and distributing salable goods and ignores all considerations of beauty and craftsmanship. Penty, therefore, advocated a return to medieval conditions of production, under which artisans,

261

in small local groups, controlled the work of their crafts. Orage and Hobson were less interested in the purely æsthetic aspects of the revolt against modern industrialism but were equally desirous of securing for workers larger opportunities for creative and self-directed activity. These two, in the columns of the *New Age* (founded in 1907 by members of the Fabian Society and edited by Orage), made vigorous attacks (borrowed from both Marx and Morris) upon modern capitalism, criticized also the centralized collectivism of contemporary socialism, and gradually reshaped the original Orage-Penty proposals, for a restoration of medieval guilds, into an elaborate scheme for national guilds, properly adjusted to modern political and economic conditions.[1]

The movement soon gained other able adherents. The most active among them was G. D. H. Cole, a recent graduate of Oxford and fellow of Magdalen College, Oxford. He had joined the Fabian Society as an undergraduate and had participated in the organization of the Society's Research Department, but he parted company with them when he failed to persuade them to abandon their affiliations with political Labourites and Liberals. He had been made ready for the guild-socialist ideas by his sympathetic study both of the writings of French syndicalists and of Professor F. W. Maitland's reasonings on the origins and inherent legal rights of the medieval and early modern corporation. Cole, in a dozen books and pamphlets, amplified the critical and constructive ideas of guild socialism in elaborate detail, and he became the best-known and most influential figure in the movement. Professor R. H. Tawney, Bertrand Russell, and R. de Maeztu (a journalist), contributed the theory of the functional basis of property rights: they maintained that property has its moral justification and its valid claim for social protection only in so far as it is associated with some social service. This theory became a cardinal doctrine in the later works of Hobson and Cole.[2]

---

[1] Penty's ideas were set forth in a book published in 1906, *The Restoration of the Guild System.* Orage's views were first presented the following year in an article in the *Contemporary Review,* under the title "Politics for Craftsmen."

The *New Age,* a small weekly of moderate socialist leanings, was a medium of expression for some of the most brilliant publicists and literary critics of the day. The Orage-Hobson articles were reprinted in a book, edited by Orage and published in 1914 under the title, *National Guilds—an Inquiry into the Wage System and the Way Out.*

[2] For titles of the guild-socialist books of Cole, Tawney, Russell, and de Maeztu, see the list on p. 286, *infra.* Others who contributed substantially to the development and clarification of the doctrine are Major C. H. Douglas, an engineer; Mr. and Mrs. Hammond, well-known industrial historians; Norman Angell;

In 1915, W. Mellor (an official of a building-employers' association), M. B. Reckitt, and others organized the National Guilds League, which became the chief center of guild-socialist propaganda.[3] The League published a monthly magazine (*The Guildsman,* later *The Guild Socialist*), issued pamphlets and leaflets, and sold books written by its leading members. The League, though small in membership, was active and influential during the six years of its existence. It found receptive audiences in several sections of the British labor movement, where similar trends of opinion had been developing independently. In several instances, during the decade preceding the World War, strikes had been terminated by arrangements that recognized some rights of industrial self-government for the workers. The successful "shop-stewards" movement during the war further confirmed the confidence of many labor-unionists in their powers of independent action. Meanwhile, American ideas of industrial unionism and French syndicalist doctrines were being preached extensively among British working-men. The acute industrial depression after the war inclined the workers generally to consider new proposals for attacking the wage system. Thus the guild socialists brought to British working-men ideas for which they were somewhat prepared by experience, and there were close affiliations between the guild socialists and important groups of trade-unionists.[4]

Industrial conditions, in 1919, suggested to some of the guild socialists that the time was propitious for putting their theory into practice in one important industry. There was an acute need for a large number of new dwelling houses in the industrial centers, and private enterprise had proved unable to supply the need. Measures taken by the national

H. N. Brailsford; George Lansbury, labor journalist and member of Parliament; and C. E. Bechhofer.

[3] See the following: G. D. H. Cole, "The National Guilds Movement," in *Monthly Labor Review* (U.S. Bureau of Labor Statistics), IX (1919), 24–32; S. G. Hobson, *Guild Principles in War and Peace* (1917), Ch. I; M. B. Reckitt and C. E. Bechhofer, *The Meaning of National Guilds* (second ed., 1920), Ch. I; Niles Carpenter, *Guild Socialism: an Historical and Critical Analysis* (1922), Chs. I–III.

[4] J. M. Paton, who had been a leader of the aggressive shop-stewards in Glasgow, was made organization secretary of the National Guilds League. He first suggested the guild-socialist tactics of "encroaching control," a process of gradual displacement of capitalist-owners through orderly action by workers' associations. Frank H. Hodges, secretary of the Miners' Federation, was for awhile a member of the Executive Council of the League; and the mines-nationalization bill drafted by the Federation was deliberately formed upon guild-socialist principles. The National Union of Railwaymen, the Railway Clerks Association, the National Union of Teachers, and the Union of Postal Workers borrowed guild-socialist proposals in their projects for the reorganization of their respective industries.

government—in subsidizing building employers, granting financial support to local governing authorities, and restricting rent charges—proved inadequate. Private builders found that they could pay wages satisfactory to the workers and still make profits only when they built expensive homes and factories. The building workers maintained that they could produce all the cheap dwellings needed, provided they could be assured of conditions guaranteeing continuity of employment and pay. Early in 1920 representatives of the several building trade-unions in the Manchester district formed a builders' guild, with S. G. Hobson as secretary, and proposed to the Manchester city council the construction at cost of as many dwellings as the council deemed necessary. Similar guilds were formed in other cities in England and Wales; and they organized a National Buildings Guild, closely affiliated with the National Federation of Building Trade Operatives.[5]

After several months of negotiation the national government finally agreed to give its financial support to a limited number of contracts between the guilds and the local authorities, as a basis for experiment. The contracts were made in some twenty-odd cities, and a thousand or more dwellings were built; the buildings were reported to be satisfactory both as to price, which was lower than that at which private contractors could build, and as to quality, which was universally admitted to be good. In the summer of 1921, however, the government withdrew its support, refusing to allow its financial grants to local authorities to be used any longer for such purposes. With the general lowering of wage levels and an increase in unemployment, the workers' control over the labor supply had become less effective; and the building guilds went out of existence a half-year later. Other producers' guilds had been formed in a few smaller industries. Meanwhile the whole organized movement of the guild socialists was declining, and the National Guilds League was finally dissolved in 1925. Cole has repudiated most of his guild socialism and the others have turned their attention to other matters.

THE GUILD-SOCIALIST CRITICISMS

The guild-socialist indictment of present society was in part similar to the traditional socialist attack. It made the familiar argument that

---

[5] See Amy Hewes, "Guild Socialism: a Two Years' Test," *American Economic Review*, XII (1922), 209–237; G. D. H. Cole, "A Building Guild for Great Britain," *New Republic*, XXII (1920), 25–27; Niles Carpenter, *Guild Socialism*, pp. 329–335.

the exchange values of commodities are chiefly dependent upon labor, while the laborer's wage is dependent upon the cost of his subsistence, and the surplus of the values he produces goes to landowners, investors, and entrepreneurs. Either, therefore, the present wage system should be abolished, or wages, profits, rents, and interest should be apportioned upon a fundamentally different principle. The guild socialist made also a broader economic argument. It is no longer possible, he maintained, to hope for a steady increase of production under the traditional organization of economic life. Education and experience have revealed to wage-earners that their subsistence is not necessarily or permanently dependent upon their producing indefinite profits for the capitalist. They have indeed learned to expect that, in many cases, limitation rather than enlargement of production is the most effective guarantee of an increased return for laborers. In other words, that relation between work and reward which was immediate and obvious in the pre-capitalist system becomes, to say the least, indirect and uncertain in the capitalist system and almost non-existent in large-scale industry. Consequently, the incentives to productive effort become weaker, strikes and curtailment of exertion become the rule, and production becomes constantly a more speculative adventure.

The characteristic attack of the guild socialists lies, however, in their moral and psychological arguments, rather than in their strictly economic criticisms. They assail the doctrine that a right of property exists for its owner's sake, without any predominant relation to a social purpose, and that the organized community is under obligation to guarantee this right even for owners who render no useful social service. They consider the unsoundness of present society to lie chiefly in the fact that the whole organization of its economic life is based upon the principle not of performance but of acquisition.[6] They protest against the "dehumanizing" consequences of the machine system, under which the processes of production are so minutely distributed that the working life of each laborer consists wholly of routine repetitions of automatic responses and no worker is able to discern his own work in the finished product. His labors suppress rather than stimulate his craftsmanship impulses. For guild socialists, therefore, the main economic problem is to find a way of restoring the spirit of craft, to devise a system that develops in workers not merely skill but also pride in their work and an

---

[6] See especially G. D. H. Cole, *Chaos and Order in Industry* (1920), and R. H. Tawney, *The Sickness of an Acquisitive Society* (1920).

interest not primarily in the amount they earn but in the form and quality of what they make.

The guild socialists attacked also the present political structure of society. Political democracy, they said, at its best guarantees to ordinary men the opportunity not to govern themselves but only to choose their governors and that only in the field of "political" activity. Even within this limited sphere, the method of choosing representatives is essentially undemocratic; for we choose, for a large number of disparate purposes, men who are qualified to represent us in reference only to a limited number of those purposes. Under a perfect operation of the system we may secure representatives who reflect generally our opinions on questions of regional needs. Yet we entrust these same men with the decision of other critical questions that have no relation to territorial lines. They determine issues between producers and consumers, landlords and tenants, employers and employees; and in no case are these groups segregated into corresponding localities. In so far, then, as political governors adjust interests that are not regional, our political constitution is undemocratic, however democratic the forms of suffrage and nomination may be. Still other matters of vital concern to the ordinary citizen fall outside the jurisdiction of our political agencies as defined by our traditional political doctrine. A political democracy makes no pretense of guaranteeing to workers any substantial participation in determining the conditions under which they work. It does just the opposite. By guaranteeing traditional property rights, it lends its protection to the arbitrary control that owners of machines exercise over the conditions under which wage-earners may operate those machines or that landowners exercise over the conditions under which land-workers may cultivate the soil. Thus our society is fundamentally undemocratic because the democratic principle does not extend beyond the state and because it operates only partially within the state.

A SOCIETY OF GUILDS

Society, the guild socialist holds, will not be completely democratic until it is organized on a functional basis. There should be "as many separately elected groups of representatives as there are distinct and essential groups of functions to be performed. . . . Man should have as many distinctly and separately exercised votes as he has distinct social purposes or interests." [7] Each industry and each technical and

[7] G. D. H. Cole, *Self-Government in Industry* (1917), pp. 33-34.

cultural service should be administered by a coöperative organization
of all who work within the industry or service. A guild is defined as "a
self-governing association of mutually dependent people organized for
the responsible discharge of a particular function of society." [8] Each
guild must include all workers who take any part in the particular service for which the guild exists, whether their work is skilled or unskilled,
manual, technical, clerical, administrative, or managerial. The guild
must, moreover, be self-governing to the fullest extent compatible with
the fulfilment of its obligation to the community whose needs it exists
to supply. It is thus an autonomous but not absolutely free group.

There was no unanimity among the guild socialists as to how far it
would be actually possible to carry this process of dividing social life
into functions and of establishing an occupational group for the autonomous administration of each function. All went beyond the industrial sphere and extended the system to the several professions—education, law, the drama, medicine, and public health.[9] They also proposed
guilds, with membership based on place of residence, to supply the
collective economic needs of the community in such matters as water,
light, and sewage and garbage disposal. For the needs of personal and
domestic consumption, where consumers are not contiguously placed
territorially, they suggested that there might be guilds formed on the
general plan of the existing consumers' coöperative societies.

There were some differences of opinion among the guild socialists
as to whether the main guild units would be local or national organizations. A minority, typified in Penty and Stirling Taylor, maintained
that, if guild socialism perpetuated large-scale organization, it defeated
its own primary object, which was to protect the freedom of each
worker and secure to him opportunities for the full manifestation of
his instinct of craftsmanship. If the main decisions affecting the work
of the laborer were to be made by large national organizations, bureaucracy would become inevitable and the individual worker would be

[8] On the whole structure of the proposed guild system see the following:
S. G. Hobson, *National Guilds and the State* (1914, 1919), Pt. II, Chs. III–VII,
XIII and *Guild Principles in War and Peace* (1917), Ch. III; G. D. H. Cole,
Self-Government in Industry, Chs. IV–VIII and *Guild Socialism Restated* (1920,
1921), Chs. III–VI; M. B. Reckitt and C. E. Bechhofer, *The Meaning of National
Guilds,* Ch. VIII; Niles Carpenter, *Guild Socialism,* pp. 158–176.

[9] Hobson suggests, however, that ministers, artists, authors, journalists, inventors, and pure scientists might be left out of the guild organization altogether,
dealing with the guilds through voluntary contracts or receiving subsidies from
them. See *National Guilds and the State,* Pt. II, Ch. VI; and cf. Cole, *Guild Socialism
Restated,* pp. 103, 107 ff.

about as much submerged as under the capitalist system. According to this group, the moral salvation of the worker could be achieved only by reëstablishing the local craft or industrial group as the main source of control.[10]

A majority of the guild socialists regarded a restoration of anything like the structure of the medieval guild system as undesirable and impracticable. They acknowledged that, in order to recapture as much as possible of the spirit of that system, a considerable degree of local autonomy would be necessary. But there must also be strong national organizations: only in that way could advantage be taken of the existing trade-union movement and guild structure adapted to the inevitable conditions of large-scale production. The degree of centralization would have to vary according to the nature of the industry. In a typical industry like that of coal-mining, the national organs—representing all who are engaged, by hand or brain, in the work of the industry—would determine the adjustment of supply and demand, provide raw materials, sell the products not sold by the particular mine, decide general principles of organization and production, establish general standards of safety and workmanship, organize research, and represent the mining industry in its relations with other guilds and with consumers' organizations. The local guild would still be left with wide discretion in the application of the general principles and standards established by the national organization and also in experimenting with new methods and products.[11]

Cole and Hobson set forth in minute detail the internal structure of the guilds in order to show how, with due regard to the practical needs of the community, each guild organization would be autonomous in its external relations and democratic internally—in fixing conditions of

---

[10] A. J. Penty, *The Restoration of the Guild System* (1906), *Old Worlds for New* (1917), *Post-Industrialism* (1922); G. R. Stirling Taylor, *The Guild State* (1919).

[11] The number of guilds and the lines of demarcation between them were matters which the guild socialists were willing to leave to be determined by considerations of practical convenience at the time the system was put into operation. Thus there might be one guild for the entire service of transit, with highways, railroads, and navigation as dependent branches; or each of the latter might constitute a separate guild. Similarly, the building industry might be an independent guild or it might be combined with furniture-making, ship-building, and machine-making into a large construction guild. Hobson suggested the following main guilds for Great Britain: (1) transit; (2) agriculture; (3) mines and quarries; (4) metals, machines, implements, and engineering; (5) building construction, furniture, and decoration; (6) paper, printing, books, stationery; (7) textiles; (8) clothing; (9) food, tobacco, drink, and lodging.—*National Guilds and the State*, p. 227.

membership, selecting officials, and allocating powers among the different offices. Each guild association would be so organized as to secure, on the one hand, the necessary unification and coördination of production on a national sale and, on the other hand, the protection of valid differences among localities and crafts and the encouragement of individual initiative and self-expression. Most of the writers would make each guild substantially autonomous in prescribing qualifications for membership and terms of apprenticeship and in admitting and excluding members, although generally they proposed safeguards in the matter of expulsion by providing that no one should be expelled save for cause (to be determined by an "overwhelming majority") and that appeals should be allowed from local to national guild bodies. In selecting officials, for those whose work is leadership and direction, there would be direct election by guild members with a limited right of recall; for those whose work is predominantly technical, there would be appointment by committees chosen by the members. "At every stage," said Cole, ". . . wherever a body of men has to work under the supervision of a leader or officer, it must have the choice of that officer; every committee must be appointed directly by those over whose work it is to preside." [12]

[12] *Self-Government in Industry*, p. 255. For each "shop" (e.g., the drawing office or foundry of an engineering works) there would be a shop committee elected by ballot of all the workers of the shop, "to look after the interests and efficiency of the shop, both in making rules and in generally supervising their execution"; for each "works" (e.g., a whole engineering works of a given locality) there would be a works committee composed of representatives elected by the workers of each shop—to coördinate the interests and activities of the several 'shops. For each district there would be a committee composed partly of representatives of each works, elected by the respective works committees, and partly of representatives of each craft, chosen by all members of the respective crafts working in the district; its function would be to coördinate production in that particular industry throughout the district and to conclude necessary arrangements with other guilds of the district as well as with the local "public" authorities. There would be two national guild bodies in each industry: a national assembly or "delegate meeting," composed of representatives chosen by each craft in the industry, to serve "both as a final appeal court and as the initiator of the general lines of Guild policy"; and a national executive committee, composed partly of representatives from each district, chosen by all the workers in the industry in that district, and partly of representatives of each craft, chosen by national balloting of the several crafts. Workers of each shop would elect a shop foreman; the members of a clerical department, a clerical head; the manual laborers of a works, a works manager. All the clerical workers would elect a general clerical manager, and the works committee would elect a general works manager. The district committee would choose a district secretary, mainly for statistical work in coördinating supply and demand. The Executive Committee of the national guild would nominate, and the Delegate Meeting elect, a general secretary of the guild. Finally, there would be works experts chosen by the works

Every vital service in society would be organized into a national guild, and its constitution would reflect the essential interests of the workers actually engaged in supplying that service. This plan for the several national guilds, however, makes no provision for meeting needs that arise out of the close interdependence of the different economic groups. Railroads and machine industries are directly dependent upon iron, steel, and coal; manufacturing industries are dependent upon the agencies of distribution; textile and clothing industries are closely inter-related; most industries are dependent upon the mines. This inter-dependence can be met in part by agreements among the several guilds providing for "exchange of representation," "the equivalent of some inter-locking directorates of to-day," the interchange of "guild ambassadors" or "special joint committees," and finally a national "Industrial Guild Congress," representing all national guilds. This body, according to Cole, "would be the final representative of the Guild System on its industrial side and would have the vital functions of laying down and interpreting the essential principles of guild organization and prac-tice. It would be, in fact, on questions requiring central coördination, the Guild legislature, and, either itself or through a subordinate organ, the ultimate court of appeal in purely Guild questions. . . . It would act as the representative of the Guilds as a whole in their common external relations, both with other parts of the body social and with other organizations abroad. One of its functions, and by no means the most important, would be to adjudicate on inter-Guild difficulties and disputes, the local Guild councils acting as normal courts of first in-stance on such questions. But its most important internal Guild func-tion would be that of laying down the general principles of Guild con-duct, in the form of general regulations within which each Guild would have to work." It would levy taxes upon the various guilds to obtain the sums needed to defray expenditures for these common guild objects. It would serve as representative "of the 'producers' outlook' in negotia-tion with representatives of the 'consumers' outlook' in matters of im-portance to the community as a whole." [13]

The writers offered these sketches of a guild constitution as illustra-tions, not as rigid models. The particular machinery would have to be adapted to the requirements of the several industries and to limitations

committee, district experts chosen by the district committee, and "traveling" and "national" experts chosen by the National Executive Committee.

[13] Cole, *Guild Socialism Restated*, pp. 68–71; Hobson, *National Guilds and the State*, pp. 230–231; and see Carpenter, *Guild Socialism*, p. 176.

arising out of the habits and experiences of the workers. "The new system," said Cole, "will have to make its way gradually and it will not be perfectly and securely established until it too has become an instinct and a tradition. . . . We must not . . . concentrate our attention too much on the difficulties which would attend its instantaneous introduction; we must try to imagine it as it would be after a period of experience, when the workers were getting used to it, and the purely internal difficulties had been overcome." [14]

The guild socialists took generally the position that the transition from capitalist society to the guild-socialist commonwealth must be principally through evolution—a natural and gradual, though consciously guided and expedited, development of the existing industrial situation.[15] This did not mean that they would rely chiefly upon political methods. In their view the most that working-class political action could do was to support those governmental measures that facilitated the economic transitions necessary for guild socialism. But they believed it impossible, in a capitalist society, to consolidate the workers politically in such way as to enable them to obtain control of a political government; or even if the control were obtained, the changes necessary for the realization of guild socialism could not be effected through legislation. The state, in its organization and technique, was not, according to guild socialists, a fit instrument for making the changes they desired.

Fundamental economic transformations, it was argued, can be secured only through economic means. What are these means? In general, the workers must exercise to the fullest the latent potentialities of their labor power. Accordingly, they must evolve a working-class organization and policy capable of realizing that power in full effect. This can be best achieved by enlarging and developing the existing trade-union movement. This demands an expansion of trade-union membership, including the organization of workers now largely unorganized—the unskilled laborers and the "black-coated" clerical, technical, and managerial workers. It involves also a modification of the present trade-

[14] G. D. H. Cole, *Guild Socialism Restated*, pp. 55–56.
[15] On the tactics of guild socialism, see especially the following: S. G. Hobson, *National Guilds and the State*, Pt. I, Ch. X and Pt. II, Ch. XIV; G. D. H. Cole, *Self-Government in Industry*, Ch. V, *Guild Socialism Restated*, Chs. X–XI; M. B. Reckitt and C. E. Bechhofer, *The Meaning of National Guilds*, Chs. V, VII; Niles Carpenter, *Guild Socialism*, Ch. VII.

union structure: first by establishing an industrial, in place of a craft, basis of membership, both because the industrial union provides a stronger force to use against the capitalist and because it is the only form consistent with the broader purposes of guild-socialism—namely, to control industry, not merely to better conditions of employment; and, secondly, by democratizing the internal structure of the trade-union, making the workshop or its equivalent the basis of organization, since a place of work represents a far greater unity of interest than a place of residence.[16]

While perfecting their organization the workers should pursue a policy of "encroaching control"—"wresting bit by bit from the hands of the possessing classes the economic power which they now exercise, by a steady transference of functions and rights from their nominees to representatives of the working-class." This is not the familiar system of "joint-control," under which employers and employees serve together upon the same committees and councils; "encroaching control" means the gradual transfer of functions from employers' hands to employees' hands. Nor does it involve anything like profit-sharing, which has inevitably the tendency of further entrapping the workers in the capitalist system. "Encroaching control" means, specifically, that the workers should secure the right to choose the workshop foreman, to regulate discipline in the shop, and to hire and discharge workers. They should also work for the institution of the "collective contract," under which the employer agrees to a lump-sum compensation for a given output of a shop, the workers' association then apportioning the work and distributing the sum according to its own regulations.[17]

This gradual guildizing process should be carried on not only in private industries but also in publicly owned enterprises—for example, the post office and the municipally owned utilities. The detailed steps here may not be in all instances the same as in private industry. In particular, the entering into arrangements for joint control between the government and civil servants' organizations may be temporarily permissible here. The guild socialists, however, did not look upon the further extension of nationalization or municipalization as necessarily leading towards their goal or as a means upon which principal reliance could be placed even where nationalization was accompanied by guildi-

[16] G. D. H. Cole, *Self-Government in Industry,* pp. 132 ff., 141; *Guild Socialism Restated,* p. 194.
[17] *Ibid.,* pp. 196–201.

zation. They accepted existing movements for nationalization as inevitable parts of a general liberalizing evolution of society but approved the specific proposals only if they included provisions for workers' participation in control. The guild socialists also proposed, as another means in their plan for a piecemeal supersession of capitalism, that independent guilds be immediately set up in selected industries, where the conditions were such that successful experimentation could be carried out.

The method of gradual and peaceful displacement and dispossession of capitalists had the practical advantage, the guild socialists maintained, of saving the workers, the public, and innocent capitalists from unnecessary suffering; it had also moral and psychological value in progressively demonstrating the uselessness of any capitalistic participation in control.[18] However, a definitive replacement of capitalism by guild socialism might require some measures more obviously compulsive in character; forcible expropriation might be necessary in order to overcome resistance by capitalists to the policies of gradual supersession. In such cases the state could be used as the agency for carrying out expropriation; the typical policy should fall between absolute confiscation, on the one hand, and compensation based upon current standards of commercial value, on the other. The state should offer "consideration," or "compassionate allowances," instead of compensation, to existing owners. The writers made varying suggestions as to the forms which this lenient treatment should take. Generally they "suggested a system of terminable annuities extending over two generations"; but they did not agree as to the extent to which the annuities should approximate the actual incomes being received at the time the properties were taken over. "No cut-and-dried scheme can actually prescribe in advance for society all the circumstances of a situation which can not possibly be foreseen with any exactness. . . . Common sense will surely suggest that it is far better to conciliate the newly dispossessed than to excite them by harsh treatment to revolt against the new order."[19]

Guild socialists recognized the possibility of occasional action of a more violent character—compelled by the obstinate resistance of the possessing classes or by a mob psychology on the part of either

[18] Cole, *Guild Socialism Restated*, p. 206.
[19] Reckitt and Bechhofer, *The Meaning of National Guilds*, pp. 379–382; S. G. Hobson, "Claim and Counter-claim," *New Age*, vol. XXI, new series (1917), pp. 382–384.

property-owners or workers. They generally regarded an organized insurrection as futile, since it presupposed the arming of workers to an extent impossible until the dissolution of the capitalist system had proceeded to a point at which its overthrow could be obtained without violence. They also repudiated "direct action," for its success would depend upon such a superiority in the workers' economic strength as could be achieved only after the evolutionary process had gone much further than at present.

The thing to be aimed at, said Cole, "is not early revolution, but the consolidation of all forces on the lines of evolutionary development with a view to making the 'revolution,' which in one sense must come, as little as possible a civil war and as much as possible a registration of accomplished facts and a culmination of tendencies already in operation." [20]

THE POLITICAL THEORY OF THE GUILD SOCIALISTS

Guild socialism is like the earlier French syndicalism in its aversion to all doctrines that make productive activity dependent upon political authority. It would protect the worker not only against exploitation by capitalists but also against any bureaucratic suppression of his craftsmanship. Its object is to make work more interesting and the whole economic structure of society more democratic. Unlike syndicalism, however, it would not eliminate the state from society. Guild socialism is an attempt to reconcile the syndicalist idea of special producers' interests with the political idea of general or public interests. It regards neither the territorial nor the professional grouping in society as by itself complete. "Certain common requirements are best fulfilled by the former and certain others by the latter." Thus the state remains an indispensable institution of society, although there are many forms of common action in which the state has no proper part.[21]

There were differences of opinion among guild socialists on the position and sphere of the state in a guild-socialist society. In some of the earlier discussions of the apportionment of functions among political and guild bodies, there were suggestions that the national guilds congress

---

[20] *Guild Socialism Restated*, pp. 183–185, 187, 206.

[21] On the political aspects of guild socialism, see the following: Hobson, *National Guilds and the State*, Pt. II, Ch. XVI; Cole, *Self-Government in Industry*, Chs. III, VII; *Guild Socialism Restated*, Chs. VII–VIII; Reckitt and Bechhofer, *The Meaning of National Guilds*, 349–383; Carpenter, *Guild Socialism*, 176–190.

would be made the final authority in all purely industrial matters, while the state would remain supreme in all purely political affairs; or, in reference to economic functions, the former would represent the citizens as producers, while the latter would represent them as consumers.

Hobson and Cole recognized, however, that such generalizations were inadequate and that the problem of the place and function of the state required a fuller and more exact analysis. There are certain "political" functions to be performed. Agencies, democratically constituted and at the same time efficiently organized, must exist to perform them. Should these agencies simply make up another guild—the political guild—on a parity with any one of the industrial and civic guilds? Or should there be superimposed upon the multiple functional classification of society a twofold general division, whereby the political organization of society is differentiated from the whole system of industrial and civic guilds? If the latter arrangement is adopted, what will be the relations between the two systems? Will they be co-equal systems or will one be supreme over the other? In other words, will they be mutually independent, or will they be interrelated either through the ultimate supremacy of one over the other or through the subordination of each to a common superior?

These were perplexing questions for the guild socialist. For he did not, like the anarchist, deny the need of organized physical force—of military defense and coercive authority for protection from crime and tort; nor, like the syndicalist and pluralist, did he generally evade such questions. He recognized that there are certain essential social needs that cannot be met save through the activities of an institution organized upon some such basis as that of the existing state; he acknowledged also that this institution (whether or not it is to be called "the state") must continue to be endowed with some of the powers and privileges by virtue of which the state to-day is enabled to claim for itself a unique social position in society—a position traditionally designated as "sovereign." On the question as to what is to remain of the traditional sovereignty of the state, guild socialists were not in agreement. Contrast at this point is usually made between the views of Hobson and those of Cole.

Hobson's view was that a guild-socialist society must be one in which the state continues to be the representative of the community at large, as distinguished from all other associations, each of which represents some part of the community. The state remains supreme, even though it delegates many of its functions to other associations. It will perform fewer functions but possess no less authority. It will continue to be the original source of power, the final arbiter, the peculiar representative of the individual in his capacity as citizen as distinguished from his capacity as producer or consumer. In this sense, Hobson declared, "we remain socialists." [22]

What does this mean concretely? Each industrial guild will remain normally autonomous in the administration of its economic affairs: it will decide what goods to produce and what prices to charge for them; it will fix wages, have its own banks, issue its own credit; and it will hold the necessary plants and tools, as trustee of the state. The state will be owner of the plants and tools, leasing them to the various guilds; it will decide questions of fair play in general economic policy—in relation, for example, to complaints against the importation of cheap foreign labor or against wage-exploitation by a guild; it will decide other matters of public policy on appeal from the guild congress; it will be a court of final appeal in case of disputes between guilds, when the guild congress proves unable to settle them. The state will levy taxes on the guilds, with the primary object of obtaining the revenues for financing both its own activities and those gratuitous services provided, under state auspices, by the civic guilds; it will be empowered also to apply taxation in such way as to modify the fiscal policies of the guilds. Generally speaking, the tax levies will tend to be the equivalent of economic rent—that is, the earnings of a guild not needed for depreciation, capital provision, or insurance.[23] The state will finance the various civic guilds which supply gratuitously the amenities in the way of education, health, etc.; and it will determine the broad policies of these guilds.

Beyond these functions in relation to the industrial and civic guilds, the state, according to Hobson's description, will have other duties to perform more directly. Peculiarly important among these original and independent functions of the state is that of formulating and enforcing civil and criminal law. Much of the existing legal work of government may lapse. Laws concerning rent, interest and profits, master and servant, and landlord and tenant, will become less important in an economic system which is not organized primarily in the interest of landlords,

[22] See A. R. Orage, ed., *National Guilds: an Inquiry into the Wage System and the Way Out* (1914), p. 133. The book is a reprint of articles appearing in the *New Age* in 1912 and 1913.

[23] *Guild Principles in War and Peace*, p. 60. Cf. Cole, *Self-government in Industry*, third ed., pp. 283–286.

capitalists, and entrepreneurs. Crimes that spring from poverty will largely disappear. Hobson was not so visionary as to hope that all criminality would vanish or that no legal sanctions would be required for vindicating the rights of individual guild members. Civil and criminal law will remain, and in its making and administration the state will be immediately concerned. The state will have also the obligation of supplying military protection. Though a country organized on guild-socialist principles will not make aggressive war, wars against it may occur; so it will need an army and navy for defense. Finally, the state must control international economic relations, which, with the growing supremacy of the pacific principles of guild socialism, may be expected to become more intimate and complex than under the present conditions of selfish economic nationalism.

Cole's doctrine was more pluralistic, in expressed intention at least. He made an explicit effort to place the state upon the level of the guilds and thus to be entirely rid of the sovereign, omni-competent state. In his scheme, the state, though indispensable, will be regarded not as the source of authority of other indispensable groups of society but as simply one in a system of coördinate, co-equal groups. Like every other régime, it must have as much power, and only as much, as is necessary for the performance of its peculiar function in society.

Cole's doctrine, in its economic aspects, represented an effort to harmonize the right of the consumer to control use and consumption with the right of the producer to control production. The guild organization of society, in order to satisfy the producer's just demand for responsibility and self-government, must control conditions of production; the state, to satisfy the consumer's just claim for an equitable division of the nation's produce and for full provision of the goods and services which he properly requires, should own the means of production and regulate prices and the distribution of income. An association organized on the basis of territorial representation is fit to represent the citizens as consumers.

The state also, as the association in which men meet on the ground of identity, would, in Cole's earlier conception, have "political" duties—defense of the community, control of marriage and divorce, the protection and education of children, care of defective and dependent persons, prevention and punishment of crime. But not even in these activities would it act as sovereign. The difficulty of exact definition of the respective functions of the state and the guilds creates opportunities for rivalry and conflicts of interest and competence. A superior coördinating authority above both the guilds and the state will be necessary to adjudicate such conflicts, and it must be a joint body representing all the associations. It will act normally not as a legislative or administrative authority but as a court of appeal—a deciding, not an initiating, body. This "Democratic Supreme Court of Functional Equity" will deal with matters common to all associations; and it will possess supreme powers of coercion, maintaining ultimate control over "the whole paraphernalia of law and police." Such a scheme of social organization eliminates the sovereign state, but it retains both the state and sovereignty, ascribing the latter to a body higher than the state.[24]

In his latest important work on guild-socialist theory, Cole not only rejected Hobson's claim that the state has "the supreme task of expressing the spirit of the community and the positive power of coordinating and directing the activities of all the various parts of the social structure," but represented himself also as now "destroying" the idea that the state represents the consumer and as definitely excluding the state "from a place in the control of economic and civic services alike." In this later view the state is left with very little to do; for Cole here reached the conclusion that substantially all the essential economic and civic needs of society permitted the institution of corresponding associations so organized as to operate on functional rather than territorial lines. The only important exception, and this Cole represented as only a possible or tentative exception, was the function of dealing "with the whole sphere of personal relationships—questions of personal conduct and of personal property relations." Cole thus expected that the state would " 'wither away' to a very considerable extent"; it would "ultimately disappear altogether, either after a frontal attack, or by atrophy following upon dispossession of its vital powers." [25]

Despite this accentuated disparagement of the state, Cole's later attitude is no more pluralistic than his earlier attitude. It is indeed quite the contrary. For it is in his later guild-socialist books that his more elaborate discussion of "the *communal*, as distinct from the functional, organization and working of Guild Society," appears. Here he maintained that it is not sufficient to provide a system of economic guilds for production and commerce; of civic guilds for civic services; of con-

[24] *Social Theory*, Ch. VIII.
[25] *Guild Socialism Restated*, pp. 119–120, 123.

sumers' societies, collective utilities, cultural and health councils for users' needs. These must all be organized into a single system whereby "the communal spirit of the whole society can find expression." [26] This essential coördinating body must be entirely dissociated from the present political machinery of society and not be regarded in any sense as the successor of the state. The state of the past and present is an organ of class domination, whereas the communal organization of guild society is to be an organization of social coöperation. The political machinery of to-day is essentially one of coercion, of order and authority externally imposed, whereas the principles of guild socialism require that the communal, as well as the specific functional, institutions of society shall be expressive of spontaneity and self-government. Finally, the state, in its present politically democratic form, is organized upon a fallacious principle of representation—an assumption that persons chosen upon the single basis of place of residence are qualified to reflect all the varied interests and ideas of the people miscellaneously assembled in such districts.

The commune—the coördinating organization in guild society—must have a structure essentially different from that of the state. It must be predominantly representative of all the several councils, which are themselves representatives of the various functional organizations of producers and consumers; although a certain degree of representation on a territorial basis may be combined with this functional representation. In short, there must be local and regional federations of the various guilds and a national communal body representing both the national guilds and the regional communes.

What are to be the powers and functions of the commune in its local, regional, and national organizations? [27]

In the first place, the commune will have extensive and important duties in relation to financial matters. This includes an ultimate control of prices. Cole gave an illustration of the manner of the exercise of this control in the case of milk somewhat as follows: the proper distributive guild will propose to the appropriate consumers' coöperative society a price based upon what the former pays to the agricultural guild, plus the cost of distribution; if these two bodies agree, the figure agreed upon becomes, normally, the price; if they disagree, the matter goes to the commune for final decision. The commune, moreover, will

---

[26] *Guild Socialism Restated,* p. 119.
[27] See the summary in *Guild Socialism Restated,* pp. 139–140.

have, "for social reasons," independent power to fix prices above or below the agreed prices and to allocate the surplus or loss realized from such a price. The financial powers of the commune will include also the allocation of financial resources among the various industries and services. It will exercise this function chiefly through its power to revise and ratify the budgets of the various guilds, with full opportunity accorded to the several guilds or other interests concerned to present their points of view and participate in the discussion of the proposed budget. All this involves two other financial powers for the commune: (a) taxation, which will take the form of assessing certain sums upon the guilds, leaving to each guild the function of taxing its individual members or otherwise raising the allotted sum; (b) the ultimate control of the issue of credit, whether banks are to be directly maintained and administered by the several guilds or by the Guild Congress.

Secondly, the commune will settle issues between the functional bodies arising from differences on matters of policy, in cases where such differences prove unsolvable by action of guild councils or the Guild Congress. Thirdly, the commune will be the authority for the partition of powers among the various functional bodies; both by enacting the "constitutional laws" that define the respective spheres of these bodies, and, through its judicial system, by adjudicating disputes as to the interpretation and application of such laws.

Cole designated his fourth group of communal functions as "questions not falling within the sphere of any functional authority." These include such matters as the following: (a) declaring war and peace and controlling the armed forces (although the army and navy are to be organized internally on guild lines); (b) controlling foreign relations, particularly determining international political relationships and international economic and civic questions that become involved with political questions or that may be referred by the economic and civic guilds; (c) fixing the boundaries of towns, townships, and regions; (d) controlling personal and private property relationships. It has already been indicated that this last-mentioned group of functions might be delegated to the surviving state, whose coercive laws, however, would require ratification by the commune.

Finally, the commune will exercise powers of compelling individuals and functional bodies to conform to its laws and decisions. Coercion of individuals will be exercised through the familiar methods of criminal prosecution. Coercion of groups will, presumably, be applied in the form of the economic boycott. Cole argued that coercion in any form would be invoked only as a last resort; and he expected that occasions for it would be extremely rare in a guild-socialist society, where reliance is placed chiefly upon argument and communal opinion and where every group is entrusted, as far as possible, with the administration of its own affairs and is given every reasonable opportunity to present its claims in matters decided by the commune.

Both Hobson and Cole proposed to establish "public" (that is, state or communal) ownership of the principal resources and instrumentalities of production and distribution but to entrust operation in these fields, as in private enterprise, to the working personnel associated in the several guilds.[28] In other fields they would admit private ownership of capital and allow the owner to hire out his capital at rates which the several guilds agreed to pay. This system permits the owner to receive interest but denies him profits (which should go to the general community) and withholds from him the right to dominate the industry in which his capital is invested. The state, or commune, must also control "private" economic enterprise through taxation and a varied regulation of prices, wages, and working conditions.

In taxation, the state (with Hobson) or the commune (with Cole) would make lump-sum assessments upon the several guilds, leaving to the latter the task of raising the sums assessed by levying taxes upon their members. The amount to be assessed upon any guild would in general be equivalent to its surplus earnings—the balance of revenues over current expenditures and the necessary charges for depreciation and insurance.

Prices would generally be fixed in first instance by the guilds, acting severally or by inter-guild agreements. However, in Cole's system, definite provision was made for a price regulation by the commune, when social interests required a revision of prices. Hobson apparently contemplated that the state's power over prices would be only indirect—a consequence of its policy of taking surplus earnings through taxation. Hobson also set up a principle of valuation of commodities or services according to time of labor, as an ideal standard for the measurement of price; but he indicated that such a method of price determination

---

[28] On the economic policies of guild socialism, see especially Hobson, *National Guilds and the State*, Pt. II, Ch. VIII, and *Guild Principles in War and Peace*, pp. 120–124; Cole, *Guild Socialism Restated*, pp. 72–74.

would probably not be practicable in the early stages of a guild-socialist system.

In the matter of payment for work, both Cole and Hobson provided for an initial determination by the guilds, with a revisory power in the commune or state; and both proposed that the individual worker should continue to receive payment during periods of unemployment caused by sickness, accident, old age, shortage of demand, or other industrial conditions: these are circumstances for which the worker is not responsible and for which, therefore, he should not be permitted to suffer. Unemployment payments should be regarded as essential "industrial maintenance"—a natural charge upon the several industries; every industry should be compelled to maintain its own unemployed, who are in reality "its own labor reserves."

The guild socialists frequently indicated uniformity of pay as an ideal, not realizable during the early stages of guild socialism. "I assume," said Cole, "that equality of income cannot, and must not, be made a condition of the establishment of the Guild system; for I am convinced that the moral and psychological conditions which would make such equality possible could develop only in the atmosphere of a free Society, and even there only by a gradual process. It is essentially true that equality, if it proves, as I think it must, the only solution of the problem of income, can only develop out of the actual experience of free and democratic industrial and social conditions, and I am sure that when it does come, it will come, not in the absurd guise of 'equality of remuneration,' but in the destruction of the whole idea of remuneration for work done, and the apprehension of the economic problem as that of dividing the national income, without regard to any particular work or service, among the members of the community." [29]

An explicit aim of the guild socialists was to secure a more extensive diffusion of social control than we have in present society—to allow the individual to distribute "his loyalties and obligations among a number of functional bodies." [30] Their system provides for diversification in forms of representation and methods of social control. Nevertheless, it also recognizes fully the need for a comprehensively representative agency of unification and coördination among the manifold functional groups and the necessity of endowing that communal organization with

[29] *Guild Socialism Restated*, pp. 72–73.
[30] Cole, *Social Theory* (1920), p. 140.

ultimate powers of control over the most vital concerns of social life. Although the commune or state will have a system of representation different from that of the present state and although it will delegate administrative tasks, as far as practicable, to smaller bodies, still it will have an authority which, in range and in types of sanction, is not essentially different from that of the traditional state. It will make war and decide upon peace; it will determine international political relations; it will allocate capital- and labor-power among the different economic guilds, ratify their budgets (including salary items), assess taxes upon them, control their credit issues, and, on appeal, fix prices; it will define the spheres of competence of the various guilds and settle disputes of policy between them; finally, it will define and punish crimes and exercise a general "police power."

Cole's commune and Hobson's state appear then to be no less "sovereign" than the traditional state. Both writers expected, however, that tendencies to an arbitrary, oppressive, all-absorbing use of communal or political authority would be weaker in a guild-socialist society. In the first place, their system, they anticipated, would insure such a logical and just distribution of rights and obligations and would so broaden the opportunities for self-expression that occasions for the exercise of the disagreeable phases of social authority would diminish; there would be less litigation and fewer wars and crimes. In the second place, as many communal or political functions as possible would be assigned to regional and local bodies; this would mitigate the tendency to arbitrariness inherent in any highly centralized system.

CONCLUSION

Like the earlier socialist doctrines, guild socialism would put an end to, or greatly modify, the employer-employee, master-servant relation in economic life. Like both Marxian and Fabian socialism and unlike anarchism and syndicalism, it retains the state and invests it, as representative of the community, with important attributes of power. But, in theory at least, it strictly circumscribes the functions of the state: it is unlike the more familiar socialist schemes and like anarchism and syndicalism in its idea that control over the conditions of work should rest neither in owners of capital nor in the organized community but in the laborers themselves, of all grades, grouped not on territorial but on professional or occupational lines.

Despite the brief life of the guild-socialist movement, it left behind many important influences. Trade-unionists, socialists, the post-war syndicalists, and empirical collectivists of various sorts now widely accept guild-socialist doctrines in their schemes for the administration of nationalized industries and the control of private enterprise.[31] Some of the changes demanded by guild socialists and moderate post-war syndicalists are being carried out in the United States through the extensive reorganization of industrial control put into operation in 1933. Under the National Recovery Act of this year, the national government has assumed unprecedented authority over hours, wages, prices, the rate of production, and the conditions of competition; but it attempts to exercise its authority with the active participation of groups of the people most directly affected. It has wages and hours in a given industry settled, in first instance, by agreement between the employers and laborers in the industry, through negotiation between representatives of their own associations; it makes its price regulations after consulting the opinions of consumers chiefly concerned; and it surrounds its central administrative board with advisory committees representing laborers, employers, and consumers. Here then is an attempt to set up new organs that are to act according to a policy of neither private nor public enterprise but of a joint enterprise in which employers, wage-workers, consumers, and the government (speaking, if necessary, for any private group that appears to come out badly in the voluntary agreements) are joint partners. The government is decidedly the dominant partner and exercises its power freely to force the agreements it considers best.

These features of the "new deal" in the United States were devised less to carry out a theory than to remedy the immediately pressing troubles of unemployment, overproduction, and the like or, in the words of the National Recovery Act, to meet the "national emergency . . . hereby declared to exist." Theory, however—in the sense of a general predilection for certain methods of action or a general criterion for assessing the success of the methods—is present, implicitly or explicitly, in even the most practical consideration of political questions. Moreover, an actual trial of new expedients, set up under whatever "merely practical" incentives, leads often to new theories or to an acceptance of theories that have hitherto been rejected or ignored.

The guild-socialist writers have directly influenced certain theorists—

[31] Cf. *supra*, pp. 132–133, 255–256, and *infra*, Ch. XX.

particularly by suggesting or endorsing the "pluralist's" doctrine that freedom and equality, under the conditions of modern industry, can be secured not by substituting a collectivist democratic régime for an aristocracy or plutocracy, as the autocrat of society, but only by extensively partitioning power among a variety of generally autonomous working groups, each associated on the basis of some specific economic or cultural function in the service of the community.[32]

The guild socialist would have each industry administered by the organized coöperation of all workers—manual, technical, managerial—in the industry not in order that these workers may conserve for themselves all the values they create but in order that they may best develop their creative impulses and best execute their social functions. In this conception, the function of each producer is, on the one hand, a personal one: in producing he realizes his instinct for creation to the extent that the craftsmanship aspect of his function is not completely obliterated by a system in which control of his activity rests wholly in the hands of property-owners. The producer's function is, on the other hand, a social function, in two senses: in the first place, his opportunity for productive activity is dependent largely upon the past and present activities of the members of the community generally; in the second place, his work is truly creative only to the extent that he produces services or commodities which satisfy human needs. Because of these social aspects of all productive activity, there must be some organization whereby the community can express its wishes and its criticisms as to the way in which its needs are met and its credits acknowledged by the producers. The guild socialist, therefore, retains the sovereign state, although he may call it a "commune." But he would redefine the functions of the state and modify its constitution. He would have most of the ordinary industrial and civic services administered by democratically organized, internally self-governing associations of actual workers; and he would have these associations also recognized as the regular agencies for expressing popular opinion on public questions. His contention is that the principle of democracy should not be confined to that limited sphere of social life which we ordinarily designate as "political"; it should be applied to the whole of economic and cultural life. The fundamental demand of guild socialism, in other words, is that the whole structure of society should be made democratic.

[32] Cf. *infra*, Ch. XVIII.

SELECT BIBLIOGRAPHY

THE THEORISTS OF GUILD SOCIALISM

Cole, G. D. H., *Self-Government in Industry* (London, 1917).
——————, *Labour in the Commonwealth* (New York, 1918).
——————, *Chaos and Order in Industry* (London, 1920).
——————, *Social Theory* (New York, 1920).
——————, *Guild Socialism Restated* (London, 1920; New York, 1921).
Hobson, S. G., *Guild Principles in War and Peace* (London, 1917).
——————, *National Guilds and the State* (London, 1914, 1919).
——————, "Claim and Counter Claim," *New Age*, Vol. XXI, new series (1917), pp. 382–384.
Maeztu, R. de, *Authority, Liberty and Function* (London, 1916).
Orage, A. R., "Politics for Craftsmen," *Contemporary Review*, XCI (1907), 782–794.
——————, *An Alphabet of Economics* (London, 1917).
——————, *National Guilds: an Inquiry into the Wage System and the Way Out* (London, 1914).
Penty, A. J., *The Restoration of the Guilds System* (London, 1906).
——————, *Old Worlds for New: a Study of the Post-Industrial State* (London and New York, 1917).
——————, *A Guildsman's Interpretation of History* (London, 1920).
——————, *Post-Industrialism* (London, 1922).
Reckitt, M. B., and Bechhofer, C. E., *The Meaning of National Guilds* (New York, 1918; 1920).
Russell, Bertrand, *Proposed Roads to Freedom* (New York, 1919), Chs. III–VI.
Tawney, R. H., *The Sickness of an Acquisitive Society* (London, 1920).
Taylor, G. R. Stirling, *The Guild State* (London, 1919).

DESCRIPTIVE AND CRITICAL ACCOUNTS

Carpenter, Niles, *Guild Socialism: an Historical and Critical Analysis* (New York and London, 1922).
Cole, G. D. H., "The National Guilds Movement," *Monthly Labor Review* (U. S. Bureau of Labor Statistics), IX (1919), 24–32.
——————, "A Building Guild for Great Britain," *New Republic*, XXII (1920), 25–27.
Douglas, Paul H., "Guild Socialism," in *Political Theories, Recent Times*, C. E. Merriam and H. E. Barnes, eds. (New York, 1924), pp. 227–234.

Field, G. C., *Guild Socialism* (London, 1920).

Hewes, Amy, "Guild Socialism: a Two Years' Test," *American Economic Review*, XII (1922), 209–237.

Laidler, Harry W., *History of Socialist Thought* (New York, 1927) Ch. XXIII.

Wallas, Graham, *Our Social Heritage* (New Haven, 1921), pp. 104–121.

PART II

THE CONTROVERSY OVER DEMOCRACY

CHAPTER X

THE DEMOCRATIC TRADITION

THE CASE FOR DEMOCRACY

THE explanation and appraisal of democracy has been a favorite theme of discussion since the earliest times of political speculation. We derive the word from the ancient Greeks, and there has been little change in its formal meaning. Herodotus, in the fifth century B. C., understood democracy to mean the "multitude's rule," or a society in which there is "equality of right" (ἰσονομία) and the holders of political office "are accountable for what they do therein." [1] So the late James Bryce, endeavoring only to make the conception more concrete, defined the term as "a government in which the will of the majority of qualified citizens rules, taking the qualified citizens to constitute the great bulk of the inhabitants, say, roughly, at least three fourths, so that the physical force of the citizens coincides (broadly speaking) with their voting power." [2]

The arguments for democracy have been set forth in three principal, variously interrelated forms: namely, the doctrine of natural rights, first appearing, as a defense of democracy, in the later Middle Ages; the theory that the standard of utility, or of the happiness of the many, makes democracy the preferable form of government; and the idealist doctrine, set forth most explicitly during the last half-century, that only democracy makes possible the full realization of the most characteristic potentialities of human personality.

The theory that man has a natural right to participate in government received its first full expression, in the terms that became the prevailing formulas of later democratic doctrine, during the seventeenth century— notably in England, where "Independents," "Levellers," and protagonists of the "Commoners'" representatives in Parliament set forth the grounds of their resistance to the autocratic claims of the Crown, the Established Church, and the hereditary nobility. A Levellers' pamphlet

[1] *History*, Bk. III, Ch. LXXX; Bk. VI, Ch. XLIII. See the translation by A. D. Godley, 4 vols. (1921).
[2] Bryce, *Modern Democracies*, I (1921), 22.

during the Puritan Revolution of the mid-century asserted that "We the people" derive "from Adam and right reason" certain "naturall rights" of liberty, property, freedom of conscience, and equality in political privilege.[3] And the "Agreement of the People," a formal draft of a republican constitution, in 1647, declared that it is "equal, necessary and of natural right that the people, by their own representatives, should choose their own laws." [4] In the same period, John Milton, setting up a more carefully reasoned argument in defense of republican ideas against the claims of royal and ecclesiastical absolutism, based his whole argument on the principle that "all men naturally were born free"; and from this principle he derived "the liberty and right of free-born men to be governed as seems to them best." [5] Likewise, when John Locke sought to establish a scientific justification for the parliamentary revolution of 1688 and to construct a theoretical foundation for the whole structure of a just and rational political authority, he took as his major premise the principle that "to understand political power right" we must begin with a recognition of the natural and original freedom of all men "to order their actions and dispose of their possessions and persons as they think fit, within the bounds of the laws of nature, without asking leave or depending upon the will of any other man." He then argued that the only sort of political society justifiable, on the basis of this "perfect" freedom of man in the natural state, was one in which the people incorporate themselves into "one body politic, wherein the majority have a right to act and conclude the rest." [6] This is the central idea of the later classics of democracy, such as Rousseau's *Social Contract*, Paine's *Rights of Man*, and the great "Declarations" of the American and French Revolutions. Many of the most significant events of modern political history—the growing supremacy and gradual democratization of the British House of Commons, the achievement of American independence from Great Britain, the overthrow of the old autocracy in France, the later movements for written constitutions and representative parliaments—have been widely interpreted as efforts to vindicate this claim that ordinary men have an inherent right to determine the form and personnel of their governments.

[3] Quoted in C. H. Firth, *The Clarke Papers* (1891), preface, p. lx.
[4] See Samuel R. Gardiner, *Constitutional Documents of the Puritan Revolution* (second ed., 1899), p. 333.
[5] *On the Tenure of Kings and Magistrates,* 1649, in *English Prose Writings of John Milton,* Henry Morley, ed. (1889), p. 362.
[6] *Two Treatises of Government* (1690), Bk. II, Secs. IV and XCV.

The notion survives—if not in the explicit argument, at least in the tacit assumptions, of contemporary demands for popular self-government—that although men are not naturally the same in intelligence, energy, thrift, inventiveness, and perseverance, yet all normal men—just as they have equal rights to life, freedom, and access to the courts of law—have equal rights to a voice in government because they have equal stakes in the justice and efficiency of governmental action.

The utilitarian argument, as we have seen, is that, since political government has no other end than the well-being of the individual men and women that make up society and since each individual's well-being ought to count for as much as that of any other individual, a society is properly organized politically to the extent that its constitution and policy tend to promote the interests, conserve the rights, and extend the capacities and opportunities for happiness of the greatest number of individuals in the community.[7] Democratic government satisfies these requirements, since it is least likely to subordinate the welfare of the majority of the community to that of any part. Democracy means government by those who have the greatest concern for and the greatest awareness of the interests and rights of the people generally. The natural self-interest of human beings is the best security against political action that is oppressive or tolerant of oppression.

It is also contended, in the utilitarian argument for democracy, that in so far as governments promote human welfare through the efficient and equitable discharge of the primary political functions—furnishing protection from internal and external enemies, settling disputes, providing the means of education, and supplying certain other essential and common needs—democratic governments have actually produced results at least as satisfactory as those achieved under monarchies and aristocracies. It is also contended that in certain functions, as in alleviating poverty and removing traditional economic and social injustices, they have been more prompt and thoroughgoing than other forms of government.

The late James Bryce, in his *Modern Democracies,* gave perhaps the best descriptive appraisal of the actual workings of recent democracy. Equipped in an unusual degree with the resources of both an active statesman and a scholarly observer, he analyzed the structure and activities of the formal institutions of government in the leading democracies (except England) of the nineteenth and early twentieth centuries, de-

[7] *Supra*, p. 11.

scribed the operation of political parties, the press and public opinion in these countries, and showed how they had dealt with industry, science, art, morality, and religion. He stated his general conclusion that the modern experiment in popular government had justified itself. Although no form of government could revolutionize or perfect human nature and all forms had their characteristic defects, the defects of democracy had been, in recent times, less ruinous than those of other forms. Both as a political expedient for the elimination of sources of suffering, fear, and injustice and as an agency for the positive stimulation and cultivation of the cultural life of individuals, modern popular government, he maintained, had proved to be less ineffective than modern aristocracies and monarchies. If democracy "has not brought all the blessings that were expected, it has in some countries destroyed, in others materially diminished, many of the cruelties and terrors, injustices and oppressions" of former times. "However grave the indictment that may be brought against democracy, its friends can answer, 'What better alternative do you offer?' " [8]

The idealist conception of democracy, in the forefront of the argument for at least a half century, is concerned primarily with less tangible values: not with democracy's demonstrable benefits in preserving order and security, extending physical comforts, and providing means of education and culture, but with its effects in developing the latent intellectual and spiritual qualities of individuals. Democracy's superior virtue, it is argued (following John Stuart Mill), lies in the fact that it calls into activity the intelligence and character of ordinary men and women. Government by a superior individual or group—however wise, vigorous, and benevolent—fails, Mill contended, in the most essential requirement of good government: it encourages the citizen to devote his intelligence and energy to material and selfish pursuits and pleasures and limits to a significant degree the opportunity and occasion for him to exercise his really human capacities.[9] Participation in the control of public affairs removes the individual from narrow egotism and enlarges the range of his interest and imagination. In harmony with this approach to the question it has been argued more recently that, in deciding whether to extend the suffrage to some hitherto unenfranchised group, the main consideration should be, not the degree or quality of

[8] *Modern Democracies*, II, 585, 668–669.
[9] *Considerations on Representative Government* (1861), Chs. II and III; and compare with this L. T. Hobhouse, *Liberalism* (1911), pp. 228 ff.

political intelligence the members of this group have shown, but the sort
of intelligence they are likely to display if they are afforded the stimulus
and opportunity which enfranchisement will supply. Thus a determined
demand for the suffrage should be taken as a reliable indication of the
possession of just the right sort of social sensitiveness and political
aptitude that should be accepted as the criteria of fitness for the
suffrage.[10]

THE PROBLEM OF REPRESENTATION

Recent commentaries on the machinery of democracy have been concerned generally with the devices for discovering and applying whatever
community opinions there are or that can be evoked on matters of general and public import. Here we have discussions of the interrelations
between executive and legislative departments and between upper and
lower legislative houses, and the familiar debates on the initiative and
referendum, the popular nomination and recall of elective officers, the
"short ballot," the legislative regulation of political parties, the simpli-
fied and more consolidated forms of local government, the "merit" system of appointment, and the methods for strengthening executive leadership in legislation.[11] These devices are advocated as means, on the one
hand, for making governmental officers more promptly and faithfully
responsive to popular opinion and freeing them from domination by
party machines and vested economic interests and, on the other hand,
for arousing and informing a popular interest in political questions and
concentrating that interest upon the policy-forming officials. Where the
justification or criticism of the devices has gone to their fundamental
merits, the discussions have generally centered upon such questions as
the following: What is the proper scope of popular participation in
government? Is the power of voters strengthened or weakened by de-
creasing the number of elected officers? Should the function of the
voter be confined to choice of principal officers and the determination of
questions of fundamental constitutional organization and function or
should it be extended to cover questions of ordinary legislative policy?
What is the proper distribution of control between legislative and executive branches of the government in the decision of questions of public

[10] L. T. Hobhouse, *op. cit.*, pp. 232–236.
[11] For the United States, cf. R. G. Gettell, *History of American Political
Thought* (1928), Ch. XVI; and C. E. Merriam, *American Political Ideas, 1865–
1917* (1920), Ch. IV.

policy? How far is it practically essential and democratically safe to apply standards of expertness for the selection of public officers? To what extent is conspicuous responsibility an essential feature of democratic government? How far is popular control extended or limited by consolidation or diffusion of responsibility among the different agencies of government? The voluminous discussion of these questions, which still goes on, has been mainly in terms of practical efficiency. They are, in many cases, valuable examinations on the technique of popular government, but they bring forth no new ideas on the values of democracy.

The development of the democratic conception is revealed not only in the liberalization of its conception of the politically qualified members of the community but also in the transformations of its notions as to the appropriate methods for ascertaining and giving expression to the desires of such persons. Universal adult citizenship suffrage is now generally understood as essential but yet not sufficient for making government a faithful reflection of the political genius of a people. How can the desires of the voters be discovered? And what sort of technique of representation and administration secures most precisely and readily the translation of their opinions into actual achievement? In all modern states whose governments are based on the democratic principle there has been constant discussion of problems relating to the scope of popular participation in government; the methods of representation; and the structure, procedure, and interrelations of governmental agencies.

The most fundamental problem is the question of representation. "Pure democracy"—in which the politically qualified members of the community meet together for the discussion and decision of public questions—is universally regarded as suitable only for small communities with simple collective needs; it has never widely existed and has now generally disappeared. The recent forms of direct voting on political issues can, even under the most favorable conditions, be employed for relatively few questions. The democracy of the modern world is a representative democracy; and the problem is to secure a system of voting that insures the election of representatives who reflect as completely as possible the varieties of opinion of the electorate.

The traditional, and still prevailing, system of voting for representatives is by territorial groups. Although in the early parliaments of modern European states, the several "estates"—nobility, clergy, commoners—were represented in separate houses, the commoners' representatives were always chosen from territorial districts. There was no explicit theory behind the first appearance of this system of representation. It was simply the most natural and convenient system for grouping the large body of common people. The later theoretical justification rests upon the assumption that the interests within any region are fundamentally unified and that they vary from region to region.

These assumptions have been widely challenged in recent years. It is argued that in two ways the traditional system of representation falls needlessly short of the democratic ideal of government by universal or unanimous consent of the people: the system represents the voters in groups that are rarely homogeneous in political needs and opinions; and it represents only majority or plurality fractions of the several groups, leaving substantial minorities without any voice in government.

To remedy the first and more fundamental defect, many recent publicists have advocated a radically different grouping of voters for purposes of representation. They contend that the territorial system, even where it provides for representation of minorities within the several districts, still fails to make the elected body a true mirror of the balance of opinion in the electorate because a particular region is rarely identified with any particular interest or opinion. Each district is the habitation of such various, often conflicting, economic and social needs and views that no clear mandate to the chosen delegate can be fused out of them; consequently what he represents is only one or several among minority groups; or no group is represented, the persons chosen to office being those who are facile in the elaboration of principles so vague as to avoid offense to any of the groups.

Some of the critics of the territorial system have proposed an economic or occupational grouping—the explicit representation of manufacturers, agriculturalists, bankers, laborers, merchants, the liberal professions, governmental employees, etc. People engaged in the same kind of work or owning the same kind of property, have, it is said, more in common than people living in the same district. The chief political issues are economic issues, and each economic group has certain specific rights or interests upon which its members are peculiarly informed.[12]

The specific proposals for professional or industrial groups are gen-

[12] For discussions of professional representation, see the following: Charles Benoist, *La crise de l'état moderne* (1902), *Pour la réforme électorale* (1908); Léon Duguit, *Manuel de droit constitutionnel* (1911, 1918), pp. 176–179; H. L. McBain and Lindsay Rogers, *The New Constitutions of Europe* (1921), Ch. XIII; H. A. Overstreet, "The Government of Tomorrow," *Forum*, LIV (1915), 6–17.

erally somewhat vague in defining the composition of the groups, fixing the distribution of representation among them, and arranging the inter-relations of the occupational bodies among themselves and with the territorially representative bodies, if these latter are to be retained.[13] Many commentators express doubts as to whether a democratic repre-sentation can be actually achieved through any practicable plan for ex-plicitly grouping people on the basis of their economic or occupational position. Such groups, it is said, are indefinite and impermanent in their composition; they are interdependent; and the vocational interest is not the only, and not always the chief, determinant of social align-ment.[14] Many essential occupations form no distinct interests in rela-tion to fundamental political questions. It is difficult both to define the groups and to distribute individuals among them properly. Even where groupings fairly definite and stable in composition can be identified, their interdependence is such that it is fallacious to regard their real political interests as either conflicting or separable. Basic interests in the way of safety, order, and health are common to all groups; where these interests vary in the specific requirements for their protection, the variations generally follow territorial rather than vocational lines. And the features that unite or differentiate citizens, emotionally and practically, are racial, religious, and sectional, as well as occupational.

Contemporary opinion generally looks with more favor upon the proposals for minority and proportional representation; for the latter systems retain the territorial constituencies—which do correspond to actual unities of interest in important political issues—and at the same time remedy in some measure the inadequacies of territorial representa-tion. They make it possible for political groupings to be formed on occu-pational or other lines, but they do not require any legal definition of the groups. By distributing votes rather than voters, they secure an alignment of voters on the basis of any interest that is actually domi-nant in the minds of the voters when they mark their ballots. The schemes, in varying forms, are in operation for the election of national parliaments in a dozen or more European states; and they exist more widely for the election of the councils of a number of cities of the

---

[13] The general idea is a basic principle in such widely varied constitutional sys-tems as those of the Guild Socialists, on the one hand, and the Fascists, on the other hand; and it is applied, to a limited extent, in the soviet system of the Rus-sian Communists. Cf. the immediately preceding chapter, at p. 279, and also Ch. VI, *supra,* at pp. 169–173 and Ch. XVII, *infra,* at p. 469.

[14] Cf. Paul H. Douglas, "Occupational Representation *versus* Proportional Rep-resentation," *American Journal of Sociology,* XXIX (1923), 128–157.

United States, Canada, South Africa, and several European countries.[15]

The obstacles to the further extension of the systems of proportional and minority representation have been chiefly of a practical sort. Thus the Hare system of the single transferable vote—which, by its method for counting ballots, makes possible a very exact apportionment of representatives among various interest groups in proportion to the size of the groups—is met with the objection that it appears to the ordinary citizen to be mysteriously complicated, its results depending upon luck or pure chance. The simpler plans of minority voting—such as the "limited voting" in Spain and Portugal, the "cumulative voting" for the lower house of the Illinois legislature, and the "list" system in Belgium and other countries—are criticized because they require, for their effective operation, a highly centralized party discipline in order to make the electors in the several groups vote solidly. With respect to all such systems it is said that, where a large number of small groups are represented, the result is that decisions in an elective assembly can be reached only through bargains and compromises among blocs and factions. These difficulties—together with the superficial simplicity of the territorial system, the force of inertia behind the latter, and the consideration that the under-representation of certain minorities in some districts is generally offset by an over-representation of certain opposing minorities in other districts—appear to be the chief factors that have caused the older system to be retained in most of the states of the world to-day, despite the demonstrable evidence that many of the objections to the newer systems have not been supported by actual experience under them.

A more significant trend in the contemporary discussion of the technique of democracy is to be seen in the writings of those who recommend other methods for recognizing the political importance of occupational and cultural groups. It is proposed not to make these groups the constituencies to be represented in political assemblies but to devolve important social functions upon them and allow them wide autonomy in the discharge of such functions. It is here contended that the essential principle of democracy involves more than a popularization of the formal structure of political government. Inevitably only a very small

[15] For recent descriptions of the systems of proportional and minority representation, see John R. Commons, *Proportional Representation* (1907); C. G. Hoag and G. H. Hallett, *Proportional Representation* (1926); J. H. Humphreys, *Proportional Representation* (1911); H. L. McBain and Lindsay Rogers, *New Constitutions of Europe*, Ch. V.

fraction of the citizens can specialize in the work of politics. No improvements in the representative machinery can make it possible to evoke expressions of popular will or opinion on more than a very limited number of issues. Democracy means participation by the people generally in the control of the conditions under which they live. In many instances this can be best achieved not through strengthening popular control over the ordinary political assemblies or through enlarging the functions of the latter but only through extending self-government into spheres other than those directly administered by political agencies.[16] It is said that self-government and equality of opportunity are as essential in economic as in political affairs and that industry as well as government should be made a social institution. An industrial democracy should, therefore, be set up within, or parallel to, political democracy. Workers should be enabled to acquire not merely a more adequate share in the products of the joint labors of their employers and themselves but also a more effective voice in managing the combined efforts. The familiar trade-union tactics of strikes and collective bargaining accomplishes this end in some measure, but the workers should be brought into a more regular and positive participation in the control of industry. Accordingly, there are numerous plans for having the employees of an industry choose their representatives to meet with representatives of the employers for the purpose of settling grievances and discussing working conditions.[17] Various forms of these joint councils are in operation and there are varying opinions as to their effectiveness. Generally, in all the schemes in operation, the ultimate decision remains with the owners, whatever the formal arrangements; and the prevailing opinion among serious students of the systems is that the councils are useful as means for maintaining industrial peace or promoting industrial efficiency, rather than for enabling the general body of workers to supplant or join the owners as the real masters of modern economic life.

Some students of the contemporary political scene believe that none of the familiar schemes of group representation and inter-group co-

---

[16] Cf. Joseph Berthélemy, *La problème de la compétence dans la démocratie* (1918); A. G. Gardiner, "The Twilight of Parliament," *Atlantic Monthly*, CXXVIII (1921), 248–255; H. J. Laski, "Democracy at the Crossroads," *Yale Review*, new series, IX (1919–1920), 788–803; G. W. Thompson, "The State and Modern Democracy," *Quarterly Review*, CCXLVIII (1927), 18–25.

[17] Cf. W. Jett Lauck, *Political and Industrial Democracy* (1927); Report on "Industry's Manifest Duty," by the Executive Council of the American Federation of Labor, 1923.

operation go far enough, and that in order to achieve any real democratization of our social life we need a more fundamental reorganization of our traditional social structure. The problem, they say, is not merely to free workers from subservience to employers but to release all functional groups from the compulsions of the organized community as a whole. Thus political "pluralists," we shall see, join guild socialists and syndicalists in opposition to the constantly widening sway of political government and in the demand for a general devolution of social control. A political theory that is realistic, they maintain, must recognize that the modern community is made up essentially of groups rather than of individuals, and that the ordinary citizen can be organically linked with the community only through the various intermediate associations into which his more intimate interests naturally draw him. He can impress the stamp of his will and opinion only on those decisions that relate to matters he can understand and in the formulation of which he can collaborate with others with whom he feels some special bonds of vocational or cultural interest. The associations formed on these bonds, therefore, should become substantially autonomous in both policy and administration. The regular political agencies should confine their activity chiefly to matters of defense and education.[18]

Even the pluralists ordinarily admit, however, that there are general as well as special group interests within the community and that special interests have to be forced or directed into many carefully contrived coördinations and compromises among themselves. They generally agree also that the state is the proper organ to make these adjustments and that it can successfully discharge its functions of social integration only if it is democratically constituted. On those broad issues whose proper determination concerns not any group particularly but the community as a whole the will of the greater number of citizens should prevail over the will of any minority among them. Thus pluralism, as we shall see more fully, retains a good deal of monism and readmits the democratic principle of majority rule into the government of both the particular association and the general community.

THE TREND TOWARDS DEMOCRACY

From the late eighteenth century until very recently there was a widespread opinion that a movement towards democracy was part of

---

[18] See *infra,* Ch. XVIII.

the great process of man's development from savagery to civilization and from lower to higher stages of civilization. Popular writers and orators saw something inexorable and universal in the movement and serious students of social history gave considerable support to the opinion. They drew their proofs both from the ethnologist's descriptions of the succession of political forms among primitive and semicivilized peoples and from the historian's chronicles of the development of political institutions among civilized nations. These accounts show, it is maintained, that political government takes origin in a community's more or less unconscious acceptance of the patronage and domination of some single family, caste, or class; that with the growth of political experience, this aristocratic rule becomes an hereditary right (recognized as such by the community), but it becomes also (from the fact of this social recognition), a responsible, increasingly limited authority; that in the normal course of later development among civilized peoples (illustrated from the familiar political annals of the nations of Western Europe), there are added elective bodies which, with the broadening distribution of wealth and the progress of popular enlightenment, become gradually more democratic in their constitution and steadily acquire greater powers in government, until they finally supplant altogether the traditional agencies of autocracy.[19]

Although democratic opinion has become less optimistic and aggressive since the middle of the nineteenth century, a belief still prevails widely among both popular and learned writers that the main trend is from autocracy to democracy. In 1906 an able political writer in Canada declared: "It is hardly to be denied that the principle of democratic rule has now become a permanent and essential factor in political institutions and that it alone can form the basis of the state of the future."[20] Three years later a leading American sociologist maintained that in the working out of a law of the survival of the fittest among political forms, democracy outlasts all others. "The world is clearly democratizing," he declared; "it is only a question of how fast the movement can take place, and what, under varying conditions, it really involves."[21]

---

[19] See R. M. MacIver, *The Modern State* (1926), pp. 133–145; and for general accounts of the progress of democracy in the modern world, see H. A. L. Fisher, *The Republican Tradition in Europe* (1911); A. E. Duchesne, *Democracy and Empire* (1916); Alan F. Hattersley, *A Short History of Democracy* (1930).

[20] Stephen Leacock, *Elements of Political Science* (1906), p. 51.

[21] Charles H. Cooley, *Social Organization* (1909), p. 120.

The main political movements of the nineteenth and early twentieth centuries supplied illustrations of an apparently democratic trend. At the close of the Napoleonic wars there ,was one limited monarchy (England), one small and moderate democracy (Switzerland) in Europe, and one democracy (the United States) in the Western hemisphere. Governments in the rest of the world were generally in the hands of hereditary kings and nobles, who ruled alone or with slight restraint by assemblies that represented only limited groups of the people. During the succeeding century, ending with the outbreak of the World War, popular government was widely extended: democratic constitutions were set up throughout the Western hemisphere; France and three minor countries were added to the republics of Europe; and in the remaining monarchies of Europe (save in Russia) representative parliaments were established and ministries made politically subordinate to the parliaments—except in Germany; so that the number of limited monarchies in Europe increased from one to twelve or more, and three Asiatic countries adopted that form. Meanwhile successive suffrage changes in the several countries had steadily enlarged the proportions of citizens entitled to participate in the choice of parliamentary representatives.

Many of the transformations that arose from the upheavals of the World War seemed to strengthen the traditional faith in some sort of historic law of democracy. Popular revolutions, peaceful or bloody, swept away—by assassination, deposition, or forced abdication—a tsar, a sultan, three emperors, and nearly a score of minor kings, grand dukes, dukes, and princes. Elective parliaments were set up in most of the regions where hereditary autocracies had ruled before the war.

Accordingly, among many students of social history the idea persists that the dominant political movement is towards democracy; and this trend, they hold, has proceeded so rapidly and extensively in modern times that democracy must be regarded as the only normal form of government for enlightened nations of the present-day world. Professor R. M. MacIver, reviewing (in 1926) the general evolution of political forms from the primitive institutions of semicivilized races to the higher complex systems of the advanced states of to-day, concludes that "in spite of reverses, the main trend of the state . . . is towards democracy." [22] Professor Edward P. Cheyney—maintaining (in 1927) that "the great course of human affairs" is controlled by laws, verifiable from a consideration and comparison of the phenomena of history—

[22] *The Modern State*, p. 340.

describes, as one of the great laws of history "a law of democracy, a tendency for all governments to come under the people." This law, he believes, will work with compelling force against any present-day attempt to thwart it.[23]

On the other hand, even friends of democracy now doubt the validity of some of the assumptions of the traditional democratic doctrine and are skeptical as to its workability in traditional forms within the present-day social environment. They point to the difficulties—material and psyschological or spiritual—that democracy has to confront. They feel that the justification for democracy, as traditionally understood, may have rested upon certain sociological and philosophical assumptions no longer accepted; and its success may have been dependent upon practical economic and social conditions that no longer prevail. They recognize that democracy—either because of the unsuitability of the environment or the intrinsic defects of the theory itself—does not accomplish actually what the theory expects of it. Democracy, it is feared, suits only the conditions of small-scale industry.

Large-scale industry creates industrial despots within the societies organized politically as democracies; and the former rather than the latter make the decisions that affect most seriously the welfare of the masses of workers and consumers. They do this directly through their power to fix the income and living conditions of the workers and the cost of the necessities of life for the inhabitants generally. They determine indirectly the decisions of the agencies of democracy through their control of the means whereby the social opinion upon which democracies depend is formed. Democratic institutions, accordingly, do not solve the pressing problems for the masses in present-day industrial society. They do not remove poverty, the uncertainties of unemployment, or the wide inequalities in the distribution of wealth. Workers look increasingly to other devices than democracy when they have issues of vital importance to settle. They use the organized strength of their unions to force employers into collective bargains or they resort to some of the shorter cuts of "direct action." Moreover, when a political democracy plays a part in settling these and other social problems, it has now to act on a territorial scope that fits the extensive units of contemporary industry. Consequently its most important agencies are so remote from the masses of people that they lose all touch with popular opinions and desires. Finally, philosophers and psychologists are no

[23] *Law in History and Other Essays*, pp. 7–10 and 18–20.

longer confident that men normally act under the influence of their reasoning faculties. They are skeptical concerning the power of the masses of men—however well they may be equipped with democratic political agencies—to reach decisions based on rational analysis of alternative programs of action intended to bring about conclusions that protect their interests and satisfy their real desires.

There are a considerable number of writers who hold that the trend of events now runs against democracy. They point out that the transformations of the World War created new autocracies as well as new democracies; although hereditary rule of the old sort has disappeared—save in unimportant or remote countries such as Lichtenstein, Afghanistan, or Abyssinia—virile autocracies of another sort have sprung up in Italy, Hungary, Poland, Russia, and other states of Europe, and also, somewhat later, in Asiatic and Latin-American countries. The dictatorships, it is contended, show their powers of survival; for they are meeting unusual difficulties with a vigor, initiative, concentration of effort, and persistence of policy that were displayed by none of the constitutional monarchies or democracies they supplanted and that few of the existing democracies are able to maintain. The impressions of these observers are exemplified in the recent statement of an American publicist who asserts his belief that the "movement which had dominated the world since the American and French revolutions" is now apparently to be reversed, and the present era may "ultimately be known as the era which overthrew democracy." [24]

Some contemporary observers hold, moreover, with many earlier writers, that popular government has not actually existed even in countries whose constitutions have been nominally democratic; that democracy has accordingly never been a valid theory, either as a political ideal or as a description of political facts. They write of the "false assumptions," the "receding tide," the "impossibility," of democracy, and of the "historic necessity of oligarchy." The challenges of the right and the ability of democracy to survive come now from both conservative and radical quarters; and they appear in the varied forms of emotional appeal, rational criticism, and revolutionary action.

What are the specific complaints against democracy? And what types of state do the critics regard as more normal and genuine than democracy, or as at least more competent in actual performance?

[24] John Corbin, in the New York *Times,* January 6, 1924, *Book Review,* p. 11.

SELECT BIBLIOGRAPHY

THE MEANING, DEVELOPMENT, AND VALUES OF DEMOCRACY

Barnes, Harry E., "Democracy, History of," in *Encyclopædia Americana.*

Brown, Ivor, *The Meaning of Democracy* (London, 1920; 1926).

Bryce, James, *Modern Democracies,* 2 vols. (New York, 1921).

Carpenter, William S., *Democracy and Representation* (Princeton, 1925).

Cheyney, Edward P., *Law in History and Other Essays* (New York, 1927), Ch. I.

Duchesne, A. E., *Democracy and Empire* (London and New York, 1916).

Fisher, H. A. L., *The Republican Tradition in Europe* (London and New York, 1911).

Hadley, Arthur T., *Undercurrents in American Politics* (New Haven, 1915), Ch. I.

Hattersley, Alan F., *A Short History of Democracy* (Cambridge, Eng., 1930).

Heinberg, J. G., "History of the Majority Principle," *American Political Science Review,* XX (1926), 52–68.

Hobhouse, Leonard T., *Liberalism* (New York and London, 1911), Ch. IX.

Mill, John Stuart, *Considerations on Representative Government* (London, 1861), Chs. I–IV.

Porter, Kirk H., *History of Suffrage in the United States* (Chicago, 1918).

Shepard, Walter J., "Theory of the Nature of the Suffrage," *Proceedings of American Political Science Association,* 1912, pp. 106–136.

THE STRUCTURE AND TECHNIQUE OF DEMOCRACY

Barthélemy, Joseph, *La problème de la compétence dans la démocratie* (Paris, 1918).

Benoist, Charles, *La crise de l'état moderne. De l'organisation du suffrage universel* (Paris, 1902).

——————, *Pour la réforme électorale* (Paris, 1908).

Bondy, William, *The Separation of Governmental Powers* (New York, 1893).

Bryce, James, *Modern Democracies,* 2 vols. (New York, 1921).

Commons, John R., *Proportional Representation* (New York and Boston, second ed., 1907).

Delbrück, Hans, *Government and the Will of the People,* translated by Roy S. MacElwee (New York, 1923).

Douglas, Paul H., "Occupational Representation *versus* Proportional Representation," *American Journal of Sociology,* XXIX (1923), 128–157.

Gardiner, A. G., "The Twilight of Parliament," *Atlantic Monthly,* CXXVIII (1921), 248–255.

Gettell, Raymond G., *History of American Political Thought* (New York, 1928), Ch. XVI.

Goodnow, Frank J., *Politics and Administration* (New York and London, 1900).

Hoag, C. G., and Hallett, G. H., *Proportional Representation* (New York, 1926).

Laski, Harold J., "Democracy at the Crossroads," *Yale Review,* new series, IX (1919–1920), 788–803.

Lauck, W. Jett, *Political and Industrial Democracy, 1776–1926* (New York, 1926).

Leibholz, G., *Das Wesen der Repräsentation unter besonderer Berücksichtigung des Repräsentativ-systems* (Berlin and Leipsic, 1929).

Lowell, A. Lawrence, *Public Opinion and Popular Government* (New York, 1913).

McBain, Howard L., and Rogers, Lindsay, *New Constitutions of Europe* (Garden City, 1922), Chs. XII–XIII.

McCulloch, Albert J., *Suffrage and Its Problems* (Baltimore, 1929).

McDonald, William, *A New Constitution for a New America* (New York, 1921).

McIver, R. M., *The Modern State* (Oxford, 1926), Chs. V, XI, XII.

Merriam, Charles E., *American Political Ideas, 1865–1917* (New York, 1920), Ch. IV.

Mill, John Stuart, *Considerations on Representative Government,* Chs. V–XVIII.

Ostrogorski, M., *Democracy and the Organization of Political Parties,* translated from the French by Frederick Clarke (New York and London, 1902; 1922).

Thompson, G. W., "The State and Modern Democracy," *Quarterly Review,* CCXLVIII (1927), 18–25.

Weyl, Walter E., *The New Democracy* (New York, 1912).

CHAPTER XI

THE ATTACK ON DEMOCRACY

THE numerous complaints against democracy vary greatly and are not always consistent one with another. It is difficult to recapitulate them in any orderly manner. The difficulty arises in part from some confusion as to the essential features of the political structure or creed that is being attacked. Neither the advocacy nor the disparagement of democracy is ordinarily set forth in precise and systematic form. Both advocates and opponents generally agree that "the essence of democracy is equality," but on both sides there are wavering ideas as to the exact implications of that essential principle.

Human equality is sometimes discussed as if it meant sameness, or an equivalence in general competence. Thus common criticisms challenge what is imputed to democracy as its basic hypothesis—namely, its assumption that men are equal because they are closely alike in mental, moral, and spiritual qualities. Manifestly they are not; at any stage of their development, they show wide differences in physical vigor, moral stamina, and capacity to learn by training and experience. So the critics take pains to show that democracy is an irrational or impossible ideal because nature decrees inequality among men, and conquest, patronage, and control of the weak by the strong, the stupid by the wise, the timid by the courageous, the poor by the rich. This sort of criticism is common and easy but not very important, for few serious protagonists of democracy have ever held that all men are equally or similarly intelligent, virtuous, energetic, clever, or thrifty. The protagonists generally admit that men differ in these and other respects, but deny that the differences are inconsistent with a theory of democracy.

The democratic doctrine does, however, rest upon some sort of belief in human equality. It holds that men are equal one to another, not in the sense of having the same or equally worthy qualities in general, but in the sense of possessing beneath the observed differences some more basic and universal attribute or manhood by virtue of which each should by right—and can with safety—be treated as the equal of every

308

other in reference to certain functions and privileges in society. It holds also that the general level of political wisdom and virtue is as high among the whole body of people as among any identifiable minority. Thus the most important issue between advocates and antagonists of democracy arises out of their opposing answers to two questions: Are differences in social status or economic success, in intellectual or professional achievement, reliable indications of differences in real political intelligence? And are such differences safe grounds for any discrimination in the allotment of fundamental political rights? In other words, is there any way of discovering and segregating special groups, distinguished by their superior fitness in political affairs? The democrat answers these questions negatively. He has confidence in the political competence of ordinary men, trusting, in the long run, their honesty and common sense, their feeling for order and sense of justice, their desire and capacity to choose relatively fit men for public office. He holds generally that, as a matter of both natural justice and proved success, political power should be shared by all normal adult citizens. Any relevant criticism must argue that democracy's method of allotting political power is apt, in the nature of the case, to work more inequitably and inefficiently than other available methods, or that experience shows that it does so work in actual practice.[1]

RULE BY AVERAGE MEN

Some of the criticism of democracy consists chiefly in descriptions of the characteristic imperfections of ordinary men, without reference particularly to the manifestations of their mediocrity in the actual workings of political institutions. Government by popular majorities, it is said, means rule by the average man, who is generally unintelligent, controlled in his opinions and conduct more by emotion than by reason, of limited knowledge, lacking the means of leisure necessary for the acquisition of information and understanding, and suspicious of any superior ability in others. What political virtue, it is asked therefore, is there in mere superiority in numbers? What standard of judgment can make us believe the opinion of any 55 per cent of the people to be wiser or fairer than that of the other 45 per cent?[2] What quality has

[1] For titles of the works of recent critics of democracy, cf. the lists on pp. 332–334 and p. 352, *infra*.

[2] Cf. Walter Lippmann, "Why Should the Majority Rule," *Harper's Magazine*, CLII (1926), pp. 399–405.

the majority in greater amount or higher value, except the one quality of superior force? Is not majority rule merely rule by greater physical power? What better reason is there that every one should have equal power in politics than that every one should have equal power in law or medicine, or in business, farming, bricklaying, or forging?

The critics also contend that democracy shows its actual inexpertness and unfairness in the policies it puts into operation. Its program of action is characterized by a superficial sentimentalism, a disparagement of excellence, an unfriendliness to true scientific and artistic progress, and an intolerance of freedom in thought and conduct. Democracies either are undiscriminating or they select for their sympathy the defective and dependent, the incompetent and improvident—those who fall behind in the inevitable competitions of social life. Popular opinion will not support the courts in repressing crime because the democratic disposition both belittles individual moral responsibility and exalts sympathy for the underdog as the sublimest of all virtues. A short-sighted humanitarianism leads a democracy, in its policies of economic and social reform, into all sorts of artificial and meddlesome schemes for suppressing competition and equalizing wealth and social position. A democracy is interested not in promoting the worth of exceptional individuals but in increasing the comforts of ordinary individuals. The mediocre majority endeavors constantly to bring individuals of distinctive capacity and achievement down to its own level. Equality is not only democracy's initial hypothesis but also its constant objective.

Democracies, the indictment proceeds, though often favorable to superficial innovation, are unfriendly to freedom of inquiry and to fundamental changes in the domains of knowledge, art, and social organization. The ordinary man is a tradition-loving, custom-respecting, habit-following being. His inertia shows itself both in small matters—the tenacity with which he clings to familiar ways of cooking, eating, and dressing—and in larger matters—his fear of novel social customs and legal institutions. Only the individual of exceptional intellectual and spiritual quality is able to release himself from the deadening restriction of habit and convention. Discoveries and inventions, new ways of living or thinking, make slow progress among the masses. Democracies are, therefore, the most conservative of all forms of state. "There is," said Henry Sumner Maine, "no belief less warranted by actual experience, than that a democratic republic is, after the first and in the long run, given to reforming legislation." The great eras of legal reform were those in which political power rested in the hands of autocrats—Roman emperors of the early Christian period, Charles the Great in the ninth century, the monarchic French governments of the seventeenth and eighteenth centuries. "It seems to me quite certain that, if for four centuries there had been a very widely extended franchise and a very wide electoral body in this country, there would have been no reformation of religion, no change of dynasty, no toleration of dissent, not even an accurate calendar. The threshing-machines, the power-loom, the spinning-jenny, and possibly the steam-engine, would have been prohibited." [3] Gustave Le Bon has expressed the same idea. "Had democracies," he said, "possessed the power they wield today at the time of the invention of mechanical looms or of the introduction of steam-power and of railways, the realization of these inventions would have been impossible or would have been achieved at the cost of revolutions and repeated massacres. It is fortunate for the progress of civilization that the power of crowds only began to exist when the great discoveries of science and industry had already been effected." [4] Contemporary American critics cite, as characteristics of democratic policy, the recent acts of political authorities in the American commonwealths in prohibiting the teaching of evolution and in restraining the scientific and impartial presentation of the facts of American history.

Thus the critics contend generally that democracy is, of all forms of state, the most unfriendly to liberty and individuality. The man of a characteristically democratic temperament neither desires freedom for himself nor tolerates it in others. American democracy punishes those who protest publicly against its abridgement of its own constitutional guarantees of free speech and assembly. Genuine liberty is quite outside the comprehension and imagination of the ordinary man and beyond his capacity to defend; to maintain it demands more self-reliance, courage, and resoluteness than he possesses. Having no sense of the dignity and social worth of his own personality, he has no appreciation of these values in others. He lends ready support to any sort of political or social pressure that tends to standardize human behavior—particularly, where the standardization is a leveling down to his own mental and spiritual plane. A democracy, therefore, is the most meddlesome, morally and intellectually, of all policies. It seeks to protect the community from superior or unusual individuals by regulating their deeds and utterances

[3] Maine, *Popular Government* (1886), pp. 65–66, 67, 98.
[4] *The Crowd: a Study of the Popular Mind* (second ed., 1897), p. 83.

so as to bring them into accord with ordinary ways of acting and thinking.

In much of this criticism there appears the direct or indirect influence of the German philosopher, Friedrich W. Nietzsche, whose writings, in the eighteen seventies and eighties, contain perhaps the most excoriating invective ever uttered against democracy.[5] He bitterly challenged the political and ethical doctrines that all men are in any sense equal, and also the habits of mind that go with such doctrines. Out of the various moral systems, of this past, two primary and contrasting types, he declared, still prevail—the morality of power and the morality of servility and fear.[6] The latter is the creed of Christianity, which opposes the triumph of the strong and assertive over the weak and servile. Christianity is a religion for the masses. It preserves the inefficient, cowardly, and degenerate and wages war upon the higher types of men. Thus it thwarts the processes of evolution through selection, for it fights vice, illness, poverty, and other conditions of decadence, which, if left undisturbed, would remove the unfit. It "appeals to the disinherited everywhere; it consists of a foundation of resentment against all that is successful and dominant; . . . it takes up the cudgels for idiots, and utters a curse upon all intellect. Resentment against those who are gifted, learned, intellectually independent: in all these it suspects the element of success and domination." "I regard Christianity as the most fatal and seductive lie that has ever yet existed"; its *"morality of paltry people* . . . is the most repugnant kind of degeneracy that civilization has ever yet brought into existence." [7] Christianity is responsible for democracy and socialism, with their "petty virtues," their "sensuous comfortableness," their happiness of the greatest number, their idealization of weakness, their depreciation of genuine excellence and sentimental concern for the underdog.

Nietzsche's denunciation of Christianity and democracy contains, in a colorful and extreme style, what is expressed or implied in many fa-

[5] Cf. Nietzsche's *Werke* 19 vols. (Leipsic, 1895–1913); *The Complete Works of Friedrich Nietzsche,* a translation edited by Oscar Levy, 17 vols. (Edinburgh and London, 1910–1913).

Nietzsche's moral, social and political ideas are scattered through a number of his works. They perhaps appear in their simplest form in his *Beyond Good and Evil (Complete Works,* Vol. XII); they are also in his *Thus Spake Zarathustra (ibid.,* Vol. XI), and *Will to Power (ibid.,* Vols. XIV–XV).

For brief expositions of Nietzsche's ideas, cf. Georg Brandes, *Friedrich Nietzsche,* translated from the Danish by A. G. Chater (1914).

[6] See *Beyond Good and Evil,* XII (*Complete Works*), 227–256.

[7] *Will to Power,* XIV (*Complete Works*), 130, 163–164.

miliar attacks on democratic policies to-day. These policies, it is said, reflect the emotions of unsuccessful men: fear on the part of the masses living near the margin of subsistence, that unless they obtain a redistribution of wealth they will fall below that margin; desire of the incompetent and unimaginative to prevent any one else from engaging in intellectual and artistic activities which they themselves cannot comprehend and enjoy. Because the multitude is intolerant of superiority and individuality, democracies either tyrannize on their own part over minorities or else yield themselves to the leadership or domination of men who best exemplify the popular jealousy of success and independence. From all of this it follows that, of all forms of government, democracy is the most inefficient and extravagant, the most factional and intolerant, the most hostile or indifferent to true progress.

AN UNSCIENTIFIC DOGMA

Criticisms such as the foregoing have been familiar since the earliest recorded discussions of forms of government.[8] What is most distinctive in the contemporary criticism is to be found in the attempts to build an indictment of democracy upon newer scientific foundations, borrowed chiefly from psychology and biology. Various writers now attempt to prove their criticisms by explaining the psychology of "mobs" or "crowds," the laws of heredity, and the showings of recent measurements of the levels of human intelligence.

It is a familiar idea among sociologists that groups of men often act in ways strikingly different from the normal ways of the individuals who compose the group; just as certain chemical elements constitute, when combined, a new sort of substance possessing properties distinct from the properties of any of the elements forming the compound. In any sort of assemblage of men, the group mind tends to submerge the individual mind, and emotion tends to overbalance reason as the motive force determining action. Certain sociologists have described in detail the peculiar psychological and moral traits of crowds and have

---

[8] As in the writings of Herodotus, Xenophon, Aristophanes, and Plato in the fifth and fourth centuries B. C.; Jean Bodin in the sixteenth century; Algernon Sidney in the seventeenth century; Alexander Hamilton, John Adams and Edmund Burke in the eighteenth century; Thomas Carlyle, James Fitzjames Stephen, and Ernest Renan in the nineteenth century. Particularly in American books and journals of to-day we find democracy belabored and ridiculed in terms closely similar to those in which "American" political and social customs were sneered at in British journals of the eighteen seventies and eighties.

pointed to the relations of these traits to the characteristic weaknesses of democracy.[9] The characteristics of a group, they explain, are determined by qualities which the members have in common; and individuals resemble one another chiefly in their subconscious, instinctive qualities; they differ in their conscious, more rational and spiritual, attributes. Accordingly, in crowds, the responses of men are largely reflex manifestations of primitive impulses and their higher and more individualized thoughts and aspirations tend to disappear. Each member of the crowd loses his sense of individual personality and responsibility, his consciousness of self-action; he acts impulsively and yields readily to the influence of suggestion and to the contagion of the feelings of others in the crowd. Groups of any sort, therefore, are apt to act under momentary stimuli, without premeditation; they are moved by simple and undiscriminating generalities or by purely emotional appeals. Persons who, acting separately, are reasonable, peaceful, and law-abiding, may compose a group that is impetuous, belligerent, and disorderly.

There is also, it is said, a more practical aspect to the distinctive characteristics of crowd action. Each member of a group is protected by his anonymity and acquires a sense of power from the combined forces of others in the group. He feels competent and secure in yielding to impulses which, acting alone, he might, from a sense of fear or impotence or shame, be inclined to restrain. An isolated man knows that he cannot safely or successfully set fire to a palace, or loot a store, or hang a suspect, or ostracize a political or religious heretic. As member of a mob, lynching party, klan, or league for the preservation of religious or political orthodoxy, he becomes conscious of a might bestowed upon him by the numerical strength of his associates.

Whatever the cause, then, we find frequent instances where individuals in groups participate in the expression of sentiments or in the commission of acts that are contradictory to their normal character and habits. Even among the best of men, group action reflects the common, primitive sides of their natures and reduces the opportunity and stimulus for individualized thought and conduct on a higher plane. The conclusion is that political democracy is bad because in all of its most

9 Gustave Le Bon, *Psychologie des foules* (1895; thirteenth ed. 1908), translated as *The Crowd: a Study of the Popular Mind* (1917); Scipio Sighele, *La foule criminelle: essai de psychologie collective* (1901); William Trotter, *Instincts of the Herd in Peace and War* (1916, 1919). Cf. also Martin Conway, *The Crowd in Peace and War* (1915).

characteristic institutions and policies it depends upon mass expressions—balloting at the polls and voting in juries, legislative assembles, and party meetings. Le Bon pointed out that juries render verdicts which every individual juror may condemn; legislatures enact laws which each legislator may recognize as improper. And it seems easily evident to any observer that men who—in their individual dealings with their fellow-men—are fair, generous, and reasonable, become fanatical, intolerant, and selfish when they go to the polls or to conventions and mass meetings as members of their political parties.

Obviously, it is conceded, there must be group action in any political society, whatever the form of government. What the critics contend is that democracies exhibit in an exaggerated degree the traits of crowd psychology. The electorates and assemblies of a democracy are made up, for the most part, of ordinary men, who are inclined—even as individuals—to act more under the control of emotion than of reason. In the councils of aristocracies, on the other hand, the effects of crowd psychology are somewhat restrained; the stronger minds and more balanced temperaments of the individual members of these bodies afford some protection from the degenerating influences of crowd emotionalism.

Thus a theory of the relations of crowd psychology to the defects of democracy has to be supplemented by a theory as to the dissimilarities in native capacity among human beings. If the intellectual and moral differences of men are inborn and important and not substantially modifiable by training and environment, then the theory of democracy is wrong. Many of the contemporary critics make this their main line of attack.[10] They attempt to solve problems of political control and governmental policy by the principles of genetics, and, more directly, by the biometrists' records of kinship among distinguished men and the psychologists' measurements of human intelligence.

Most of these critics, it must be said, have had no direct experience

[10] See the titles on pp. 333–334, *infra*. The writers listed stress the relative importance of heredity, as compared with environment and training, in determining the success and achievements of men, and on that ground they offer objections to certain "democratizing" policies of contemporary governments. Not all of them argue that aristocracy is thereby proved to be preferable to democracy as a form of political organization. The more sweeping repudiation of democracy, in terms of laws of heredity, is found in the listed writings of Prescott Hall, Alleyne Ireland, N. J. Lennes, and H. L. Mencken and is implied in parts of the listed works of Wm. McDougall, Karl Pearson, Lothrop Stoddard, Lewis M. Terman, and A. E. Wiggam.

with biological experiments and observations. Accordingly, they base their specific political conclusions upon very general statements of the laws of heredity. These laws state that only the germinal structure, not "acquired characteristics," form the source of heredity. New characters, not derived from the parents, sometimes appear in the germ plasm of an organism, and these characters, being congenital, are inherited by the progeny; but changes produced by environment and training are not transmitted from parent to offspring. Moreover, the human germ plasm is not a vague mass of plastic potentialities but a highly differentiated substance, possessing specific mental and moral tendencies. In applying these laws to man and political society, the critics maintain that the most significant differences among men are the hereditary differences, and that the variations in the achievements of men are definitely related to fixed characters in the native germ plasm. Thus the democratic doctrine is held to be wrong, either because it underrates the importance of the native differences among individuals or because it assumes that such differences can be substantially qualified in their effects by favorable or unfavorable conditions of environment and training.

The validity of this biological criticism of democracy depends upon the fullness and exactness of our knowledge as to the ways in which the characteristics of organisms in general—and of man in particular—are related to unit characters in the germinal structure. In other words, it must be shown, not merely that men differ in native capacities and that environmental effects on the forms of expression of native capacities are not perpetuated by heredity, but also that the most important varieties of behavior we observe among normal men are due mainly to specific differences in the native germ plasm and not to environment and training. Geneticists have demonstrated, by experimental breeding, the germinal bases for a wide variety of characteristics of plants and the lower animals; they have shown, for example, that certain features—colors in flowers, shapes of leaves, sizes of beans, susceptibilities to diseases—depend upon the presence of specific determining factors in the germ plasm. These scientists, however, recognize the relatively limited scope of their knowledge of the relation of human traits to elementary germinal characters. They have no doubt that the principles of heredity which they find operating among plants and lower animals apply also to man; but they acknowledge that their understanding of human heredity is relatively inexact or incomplete because of the difficulty of tracing the hereditary transmission of human features: human beings have no pure lines, and they are such slow-breeding animals that the geneticist cannot control his observations in experimental breeding.[11]

Biometrists, it is true, by statistical studies of certain identifiable physical characters, have reached conclusions as to the effect of inheritance in influencing height, color of eyes, shape of head, length of arm, reproductive fertility, and various other anatomical and physiological features of man. Generally, however, they acknowledge their uncertainty as to the full effects of heredity in determining man's mental and moral traits.[12] Their doubt is due in large measure to difficulty in defining and appraising these traits and in isolating them from environmental influences. We identify and characterize innate mental capacities only by inference from observations or records of the conduct or achievements of the individuals whom we study; and ordinarily we make our scrutiny only after the individuals have reached a stage where environment has had some opportunity to affect the forms of expression of the innate capacities.

The critics of democracy often make use of the canvasses that show the prevalence in certain families—as the "Jukes," "Kallikak," and "Nam" families in the United States and the "Markus" family in Germany—of various mental and moral defects, such as feeble-mindedness, tendency to insanity, habitual criminality, vagabondage, chronic alcoholism, sexual irregularity.[13] It need be noted here only that there is no unanimity among contemporary geneticists, of scientific training, as to the full weight of heredity in determining any of these imperfections, although there appears to be a decidedly prevailing opinion that there is an inheritance of feeble-mindedness. The biological issue between aristocracy and democracy relates, however, to the ques-

[11] E. G. Conklin, *Heredity and Environment* (1927), p. 116. Cf. W. E. Castle, *Genetics and Eugenics* (1924), p. 337.
[12] For typical examples of scientific works that maintain the predominance of heredity in determining the quality of human achievement, see the following: Ellsworth Huntington and L. F. Whitney, *The Builders of America* (1927); P. Popenoe and R. H. Johnson, *Applied Eugenics* (1918); H. E. Walter, *Genetics* (1913).
[13] Richard L. Dugdale, *The Jukes* (1877); A. H. Estabrook, *The Jukes in 1915* (1916); H. H. Goddard, *The Kallikak Family* (1919); J. Jörger, "Die Familie Markus," *Zeitschrift für der gesammte Neurologie und Psychiatrie*, XLIII (1918), 76–116.
On the general subject of the inheritance of human defects, cf. the following: Karl Pearson, *The Scope and Importance to the State of the Science of National Eugenics* (1911); H. H. Goddard, *Heredity of Feeble-mindedness* (1911); Michael F. Guyer, *Being Well-Born* (1927).

tion of differences not between normal and abnormally inferior persons but between normal and superior persons or between the various levels of mental capacity within the wide range of normal persons. Here the biologists have very little to offer. As already indicated, they acknowledge that they know little as to the descent of normal mental traits among men. The critics of democracy rely extensively, therefore, on the one hand, upon various canvasses of the ancestry of men of exceptional ability; and, on the other hand, upon recent tabulations of the correlations between children and parents with respect to the levels of general intelligence.

The statistical study of the inheritance of superior human capacity was begun by Sir Francis Galton over sixty years ago, in his investigation into the "heredity of genius." [14] He made elaborate biographical summaries to show that eminent judges, statesmen, military commanders, literary men, scientists, artists, divines, and sportsmen had had a relatively large number of eminent relatives in the same fields; he believed, therefore, that his summaries established a "decided law of distribution of genius in families." In some of the summaries he attempted to demonstrate that there was a specific inheritance of superiority—that illustrious men in a given field had a disproportionate number of descendants or other kinsmen in the same field. But the prevailing use of such canvasses has been to show not that specific intellectual or artistic talents are inherited but that intellectual and artistic superiority in general is inherited; the superiority may manifest itself in varying forms among the kinsmen. Galton, and others following him (notably Alphonse de Condolle in France and Karl Pearson in England), presented statistical tables to show that men of distinction in science, literature, political position, and other fields are generally descended from parents whose superior ability is demonstrated by their economic or social position in the community or by the vocational class to which they belong. Thus Galton indicated the somewhat excessively large number of English scientists that were descended from the "nobility and gentlemen," and Condolle's tables showed the relatively high percentage of European scientists who were descended from the "noble, wealthy gentlemanly classes." [15]

The contemporary critics of democracy make use of later canvasses

---

[14] Galton *Hereditary Genius* (1870).

[15] Francis Galton, *English Men of Science* (1874), p. 22; Alphonse de Condolle, *Histoire des sciences et des savants* (1873); Karl Pearson "On the Inheritance of Mental and Moral Characters in Man," *Biometrika*, III (1904), 131–190.

that deal chiefly with a distribution by large occupational groups. Professor J. McKeen Cattell, recording the ancestry of 885 leading American men of science, found that the professional classes—constituting 3 per cent of the total population—contributed over two fifths of the scientists; manufacturing and trade—containing about a third of the population—contributed about a third of the scientists; while agriculture—containing two fifths of the population—contributed only one fifth of the scientists. Havelock Ellis' canvass of over a thousand "British men of genius" showed that over a third came from the professional classes and only a fifth from the far more numerous groups of clerks, mechanics, farmers, and laborers. Galton's and Condolle's tables, as well as Edwin L. Clarke's recent canvass of American men of letters, also show a similarly disproportionate distribution among the different vocational groups. The canvasses appear to show generally that a high percentage of distinguished men in recent times have come from professional groups; a proper percentage from manufacturing, financial, and trading groups; and a relatively small percentage from the large agricultural and wage-laboring groups.[16]

Another method used to demonstrate the inheritance of intellectual superiority is to take some particular group of relatives and show the large number of proficient individuals among them. This method is exemplified in the popular American canvasses of the distinguished posterity of a seventeenth century Connecticut couple—Richard Edwards and his talented wife, Elizabeth Tuttle. It is shown that the descendants of this famous pair include two presidents of the United States and an impressive number of senators, congressmen, judges, college presidents, professors, clergymen, authors, lawyers, and physicians.[17]

Recently the newer devices of psychologists in measuring "general intelligence" have been exploited extensively in attempts to show that mental differences within the general range of normal individuals are widely inherited and that this fact proves invalid the theory and policy

[16] J. M. Cattell, *American Men of Science* (third ed., 1921), pp. 783–790. Havelock Ellis, *A Study of British Genius* (1904, 1927), pp. 373–380. Edwin L. Clarke, *American Men of Letters, their Nature and Nurture* (1916), *passim*. The several tabulations are reproduced in Lewis M. Terman, *Mental and Physical Traits of a Thousand Gifted Children, Genetic Studies of Genius*, I (1925), 64–65. Cf. also, Catharine M. Cox, *Early Mental Traits of Three Hundred Geniuses*, II (*ibid.*, 1926); William T. J. Gun, *Studies in Hereditary Ability* (1928); Edgar Schuster and Ethel M. Elderton, *The Inheritance of Ability* (1907).

[17] See C. B. Davenport, *Heredity in Relation to Eugenics* (1911), pp. 225–228. Cf. *infra*, Ch. XIV, p. 361.

of a democracy. The psychologists' earlier tests were usually limited to measuring specific qualities of perception, such as accuracy of vision and discrimination in taste and smell, or strength of memory, quickness of response, and capacity of attention. Within the last two decades rapid developments have been made in attempts to measure intelligence in a more general sense. The newer tests have been widely regarded as showing that individuals can be differentiated not only as to their specific mental traits but also as to their mental levels, so that they may be classified as of superior, average, or inferior general intelligence. The aim of these psychologists and of many of the popular writers has been to show that these differences in the mental levels of normal human beings are congenital.[18] They reach these conclusions, not by comparing the children's levels, as established by the tests, with similarly established levels of the parents, but by showing correlations between the test-ratings of the children with the occupational positions of the parents. Thus Professor Terman shows that of 1,000 children whom his tests classify as "gifted," 31.4 per cent were descended from parents of the professional class, 50 per cent from parents of the semi-professional and business groups, 11.8 per cent from skilled laborers, 6.6 per cent from semi-skilled and slightly skilled laborers, and 0.13 per cent from common laborers.[19]

Somewhat closely related to this idea of a biological differentiation among the several social and vocational classes within a given community is the idea that there are congenital differences, of great social and political significance, between the various races of the world; the two ideas are frequently intermingled in contemporary attacks upon democracy. Many critics contend generally that the future advance of civilization depends upon the maintenance of the purity of some race which they regard as biologically superior to the other races of the world.[20] This is not a new attitude. At all periods of history there has been a tendency for each tribal, racial, or national group to regard

[18] See C. C. Brigham, *A Study of American Intelligence* (1923); N. J. Lennes, *Whither Democracy* (1927); C. S. Yoakum and R. M. Yerkes, *Army Mental Tests* (1920). Cf. *infra*, Ch. XIII, pp. 359–361.

[19] Terman, *Mental and Physical Traits of a Thousand Gifted Children* (*supra*, p. 319, n. 16), p. 64.

[20] For a general exposition and criticism of the literature on this subject, see F. H. Hankins, "Race as a Factor in Political Theory," *Political Theories, Recent Times*, C. E. Merriam and H. E. Barnes, eds. (1924), Ch. XIII; and for a bibliographical list, see S. J. Holmes, *A Bibliography of Eugenics* (1924), pp. 277–287.

itself as physically, culturally, and morally superior to any other such group. The Hebrews regarded themselves as the "chosen people"; Greeks looked upon non-Greeks as "barbarians," unintellectual and uncivilized; Romans regarded non-Romans as undisciplined and inefficient; Japanese and Chinese looked down upon one another, both looked down upon both darker and lighter races; to the Chinese all Westerners were barbarians. In recent times the idea of race superiority has been vaguely and varyingly applied to larger and smaller racial or linguistic groupings. The early nineteenth century German philosopher, J. G. Fichte, not only recognized this universal tendency of racial egoism but himself maintained that the German people were the superior people whose duty it was to spread German culture over all of Europe.[21] Later in the century we find ideas of Russian, Slavic, Aryan, Teutonic, Baltic, Nordic, or French supremacy.

Perhaps the most influential of the later nineteenth century exponents of the idea of racial superiority was the French diplomat and writer, Count Arthur Joseph de Gobineau. He held that neither physical environment nor social conditions could explain the advances of civilization; the ethnic was the most important factor in history. He considered the only thoroughly civilized race to be the Aryans—represented chiefly by the Persians in Asia and the Teutonic peoples of Europe.[22] After Gobineau, Houston Stewart Chamberlain was the most extreme of the advocates of the idea of German-Teutonic race superiority.[23] He maintained that all the great achievements in the modern world—in science, invention, art, religion, philosophy, economic theory, and political doctrine and practice—came from Teutons of the modern German race.

The typical contemporary form of the theory of race superiority is the Nordic doctrine.[24] The eager advocates of this doctrine hold that virtue, vigor, and intelligence belong peculiarly to Nordics and that the bad

[21] *Reden an der deutsche Nation,* 1808 and 1824, in *Sämmtliche Werke,* VII (Berlin, 1846), 257–499.

[22] *Essai sur l'inégalité des races humaines* (first French ed., 1853–1855), translated as *The Inequality of Human Races,* by Adrian Collins (1915).

[23] Among the other disciples of Gobineau were Georges Vacher de Lapouge, in France; and Ludwig Woltmann and L. Schemann, in Germany. For titles of the works of these men, see the list on pp. 334–335, *infra.* For a critical exposition of their views, see F. H. Hankins, *The Racial Basis of Civilization: a Critique of the Nordic Doctrine* (1926).

[24] Leading exponents of this idea are Madison Grant, Lothrop Stoddard, A. E. Wiggam, Clinton S. Burr, Carl C. Brigham, and Professor Henry Fairfield Osborn, in the United States; William McDougall, in England; and Hans F. K. Günther, Eugen Fischer, and Fritz Lentz, in Germany.

features of modern civilization come chiefly from Asiatic, Mediterranean, Alpine, and East Baltic races. Some of the Nordicists draw their evidences from the achievements, not only of Germans, Scandinavians, and Anglo-Saxons, but also of Latins and South Europeans. Thus Professor Henry Fairfield Osborn, in his enumeration of great men of Nordic ancestry, includes the following Italians and Frenchmen, in each of whom he finds traces of Nordic blood: Galileo, Titian, Leonardo da Vinci, Coligny, Racine, Colbert, Richelieu, Lafayette, Rochambeau, Lamartine, Napoleon, Joffre, Foch, Rodin, and Anatole France. He names also, as "presumably" or "probably" of Nordic origin, Kossuth, Kosciusko, and Pulaski; and he asserts that "Columbus, from his portraits, authentic or not, was clearly of Nordic ancestry." [25] He draws the practical conclusion that in the United States dependence must be placed chiefly upon the "Anglo Saxon branch of the Nordic race," "for leadership, for courage, for loyalty, for unity and harmony of action, for self-sacrifice and devotion to an ideal." [26] A. E. Wiggam maintains that the Nordic race "has contributed a vast share of all political wisdom and scientific discovery to the modern world." [27] Lothrop Stoddard summarizes the matter as follows: "The white race divides itself into three main species—the Nordics, the Alpines, and the Mediterraneans. All three are good stocks, ranking in genetic worth well above the various colored races. However, there seems to be no question that the Nordic is far and away the most valuable type, standing, indeed, at the head of the whole human genus." [28]

Extreme assertions of Nordic superiority have been made by Madison Grant in the United States and Hans Günther in Germany. Grant draws his evidences from all periods of the history of civilization and from all parts of Europe. "Greek states," he says, "in which the Nordic element was most predominant outlived the other states"; "the old aristocratic and military classes" of Southern Europe to-day are derived chiefly from Nordic families of "the Teutonic type"; thus "the amount of Nordic blood in each nation is a very fair measure of its strength in war and standing in civilization." [29] Again: "The backbone of western civilization is racially Nordic, the Alpines and Medi-

[25] Letter to the New York *Times*, April 8, 1924, p. 18.
[26] Preface to fourth edition of Madison Grant's *Passing of the Great Race*, (1921), p. xi.
[27] *New Decalogue of Science* (1922), p. 35.
[28] *The Rising Tide of Color against White World Supremacy* (1920), p. 162.
[29] *The Passing of the Great Race* (1916), pp. 147, 170, 175.

terraneans being effective precisely to the extent in which they have been nordicized and vitalized. . . . If this great race, with capacity for leadership and fighting, should ultimately pass, with it would pass that which we call civilization. It would be succeeded by an unstable and bastardized population, where worth and merit would have no inherent right to leadership and among which a new and darker age would blot out our racial inheritance. . . . Such a catastrophe cannot threaten if the Nordic race will gather itself together in time, shake off the shackles of an inveterate altruism, discard the vain phantom of internationalism and reassert the pride of race and the right of merit to rule." [30]

Günther distinguishes five racial types in Europe—the Nordic, the Mediterranean, the Dinaric, the Alpine, and the East Baltic—and makes extensive comparisons of their physical and mental character- istics. He contrasts "the radiant . . . kindly . . . decided . . . ex- pression" of the Nordic eye to the "dull, incommunicative, or even sullen" expression of the Alpine eye, or to the "sullen . . . gloomy . . . harder" expression of the East Baltic eye. He describes the "truth- fulness," "energy," "prudence," "steadfastness," "fairness," and "sense of reality" of the Nordic race and its "fitness . . . for statesmanlike achievements"; the "reflective, hard-working and narrow-minded" quality of the Alpine without "any real boldness in thought or deed"; and the visionariness, irresoluteness, mental confusion, brutality, and nihilism of the East Baltic and its "lack of any really creative power." Historically, he finds that Nordic elements were the dominant factors in the rise to prestige of such ancient countries as Assyria, Greece, and Persia. The chief peril of civilization to-day is in the threatened "de- nordicization" of Germany, England, and the United States: a result of the fact that in these countries "the higher classes, who on the average have more Nordic blood than the lower," have a lower birth-rate and also suffer greater losses in war—due to their superior fighting vigor and their greater "war-like disposition," which makes them "the first to rush into the fight." This tendency is further strengthened through the "mistaken 'love of mankind,'" manifested by Western peoples in re- cent times when "'philanthropy' and 'social measures' have devoted themselves most to those with inferior hereditary qualities: the weak, the unstable, the work-shy, the harlot, the tramp, the drunkard, the weak-minded, even the criminal." The great sums required for mis-

[30] Introduction to Stoddard's *Rising Tide of Color*, p. xxix.

guided public and private charity come mainly from gifts and taxes that force the "very classes richest in Nordic blood to a further restriction on the number of children," while the inferior classes, among whom the non-Nordic elements are relatively strong, are thereby enabled to maintain a higher birth-rate.[31]

The "Third Reich," set up by Adolf Hitler and the "Nazis" in March, 1933, has made this "race science" a cardinal feature of its policy. It purges the schools of "non-Germans," destroys "un-German" books, and excludes books by "non-Aryans" from the public libraries. Although this appears in fact to be mainly an item in a program of expelling Jews and Jewish influences from important places in the educational, professional, and industrial life of Germany, it has been officially proclaimed as a part of a comprehensive plan to maintain the racial purity of the German nation. The Minister of Education announced that the significance of the Nordic races in the development of civilization was to be taught in the schools. The future citizens of Germany would thereby, he declared, come to understand that the "world-dominant peoples" of the present age—the Germans, the English, and the North Americans—attained their intellectual and political superiority by virtue of their Nordic blood, and that the future prosperity and prestige of Germany would depend upon the maintenance of an unchallenged supremacy of the Nordics (often officially designated also as "Germans" or "Aryans") in the whole political, business, and cultural life of the nation.[32]

Most of the exponents of this idea of race superiority maintain that a crossing between two races ordinarily produces not a new intermediate type, halfway between the two parent stocks, but a mongrel type substantially like the inferior of the two races crossed; the lower race being of a more "primitive" type, its characteristics are more "ancient" and "deep-seated," and are, therefore, dominant. "It must be borne in mind that the specializations which characterize the higher races are of relatively recent development, are highly unstable and when mixed with generalized or primitive characters, tend to disappear. Whether we like to admit it or not, the result of the mixture of two races, in the long run, gives us a race reverting to the more ancient,

---

[31] Hans F. K. Günther, *The Racial Elements of European History*, translated from the second German edition of his *Rassenkunde Europas* (1926), by G. C. Wheeler (1927), pp. 23, 42, 50, 240, 243, 248, 249, and Chs. III and VIII, *passim*.

[32] Cf. *infra*, pp. 486–488.

THE ATTACK ON DEMOCRACY 325

generalized and lower type." [33] Accordingly the popular American application of the Nordic doctrine is the contention that the descendants of the original English, German, and Scandinavian settlers and of the earlier immigrants from Northern Europe—in other words, the racial elements now generally in the upper economic and social groups of Americans—should be maintained in their positions by restrictions on the immigration of non-Nordics. "Heredity and eugenics," says Wiggam, "are asking America just two great questions. The first is: Are we replacing the noble strains, the great family lines of our forebears, with weaker, slower, and lower streams of immigrant blood? The second is: Are the great native stocks—the living foundations of empire—that created our rich and multitudinous environment and made America the most luxurious abode in the whole earthly life of man— are they reproducing their own kind?" [34]

What specifically do these arguments concerning the hereditary transmission of differences in intelligence among individuals and the congenital differences between racial groups have to do with the theory of democracy?

In so far as scientists have attempted to make political applications of genetic principles, they have generally confined themselves to suggestions that governments should take steps to facilitate a natural biological selection. In most instances, their proposals have been concerned chiefly with the elimination of the abnormally unfit by sterilization of the feeble-minded and other devices to prevent breeding by the clearly inferior. Some eugenicists, including Galton and Pearson, have advocated a more positive policy, proposing measures not only to get rid of our worst but also to increase our best inheritance. Raise the level of the human race, they have urged, by encouraging those of higher ability to mate with one another and to have more than the average number of children; discourage those of mediocre ability from having numerous children; prohibit those who have abnormal hereditary defects from having any children.

The scientists, however, have not usually sought to use their methods or data in establishing conclusions as to the proper location of political authority or the proper scope of governmental policy.[35] Occa-

[33] *Passing of the Great Race,* pp. 15–16. See also the works of Wiggam and Stoddard.
[34] A. E. Wiggam, *Fruit of the Family Tree* (1924), p. 188.
[35] For excellent studies of the whole subject of human heredity, see the follow-

sionally a scientist makes a broad generalization that appears to give support to the arguments of the popular writers. Thus Professor Osborn said recently that the modern study of biology "has compelled us to realize the superior force and stability of heredity as being more enduring and potent than environment"; and Professor Edward M. East has declared that "no matter what value one may assign to precept and example in moulding the mind of man, his mentality is due fundamentally to his hereditary endowment, to his inborn traits." [36] Accordingly, various writers whose chief work has been outside the fields of scientific biology bring up the immutable germ plasm in their effort to destroy the democratic dream. Lothrop Stoddard says sweepingly that "man is moulded more by heredity and less by environment than any other creature" and that human intelligence is "an inborn quality whose capacity is predetermined by heredity." [37] "Biology warns us," says A. E. Wiggam, "that nearly all the happiness and nearly all the misery of the world are due, not to environment, but to heredity; that the differences among men are, in the main, due to differences in the germ cells from which they are born. . . . The social classes which you seek to abolish by law, are ordained by nature." [38]

It is in just this identification of hereditary superiority with varyingly defined "social classes" that the most characteristic tendency in the contemporary criticism of democracy is to be found. The writers contend generally that in the intense competitions of modern society, with its highly specialized division of functions, those individuals best fitted by native endowment to meet these competitions not only survive but tend to rise to the more comfortable and secure positions in the community. Men of higher native capacities, it is maintained, are found chiefly in the socially, professionally, and economically "upper classes." Thus Professor Terman draws the following conclusions from his vocational classification of the parents of a thousand gifted California children. "In spite of all our efforts to equalize educational opportunity, the ten-year-old child of the California laborer competes for

ing: S. J. Holmes, *The Trend of the Race* (1921); Franz Boas, *Materials for the Study of Inheritance in Man* (1928); Herbert S. Jennings, *The Biological Basis of Human Nature* (1930). Cf. also note 12, p. 317, *supra,* and the list on p. 377, *infra.*

[36] Osborn's *Introduction* to Madison Grant's *Passing of the Great Race* (1916), p. viii. E. M. East, *Heredity and Human Affairs* (1927), p. 67.

[37] *Revolt against Civilization* (1922), pp. 48, 74.

[38] *The New Decalogue of Science* (1922), p. 243.

high I.Q. rank no more successfully than the laborer's son competed for the genius rank in Europe a hundred years ago. This statement is based on a comparison of the relative number in our group and in the Galton-de Condolle-Ellis genius groups of individuals whose parents belonged to the unskilled or semi-skilled labor classes. Previous studies had only demonstrated the superiority of the higher occupational and social classes with respect to the number of finished geniuses produced, and it was only natural that many should prefer to explain this superiority on the ground of educational opportunity. We have demonstrated that the superiority of the same occupational and social classes is no less decisive when the compared offspring are at an age at which educational opportunity is about as nearly equalized as an enlightened democracy can make it." [39]

The general idea here is that average intelligence ascends as we ascend the economic and social scale. Wage-earners, small business men, farm tenants, small farmers have a generally lower mental capacity and moral stamina than professional men, big business men and others of the upper social strata. The social and economic inequalities existing at any given time are held to reflect fairly accurately the natural and ineradicable differentiations in native endowment. The leaders of to-day are the only ones that can be depended upon to produce the leaders of the future. "We have pretty good evidence," says Professor William McDougall, "that capacity for intellectual growth is inborn, that it is hereditary, and also that it is closely correlated with social status." [40] "A given population," says Lothrop Stoddard, "tends to become more and more differentiated biologically, the upper social classes containing an ever larger proportion of persons of superior native endowments while the lower social classes contain a growing proportion of inferiors." [41] Not all the popular critics take an equally extreme position. The general trend of their "scientific" argument, however, is to show that a democratic constitutional system is unscientific as well as impractical because it ignores the true laws of heredity and fails to make its political classification correspond to a natural biological stratification, revealed generally in an existing economic and social stratification.

[39] Terman, *op. cit.*, pp. 634–635.
[40] McDougall, *Is America Safe for Democracy?* (1921), p. 67.
[41] *The Revolt against Civilization* (1922), p. 74.

THE IMPOSSIBILITY OF DEMOCRACY

In the criticisms of democracy there is often involved, explicitly or implicitly, the idea not only that democracy is ethically unjustifiable and practically inefficient in so far as it operates at all but also that it is nowhere actually in operation. The essential features of this argument do not vary greatly in the different discussions; and we shall cite here only a few striking statements by distinguished writers, who take as their main theme in their discussion of democracy the idea that democracy is impossible, rather than peculiarly undesirable, as a way of allotting political power.

The late Vilfredo Pareto—although recognizing that the democratic dogma, like other political myths, has important practical consequences in impelling men to act in certain ways—maintained that all the terms we use to distinguish forms of political rule are worthless "from the logico-experimental point of view." In other words, actual power is never where we imply that it is when we describe a given state as a monarchy, aristocracy, or democracy. Almost everywhere "there is a not very numerous governing class, which keeps itself in power partly by force and partly by consent of the much more numerous class of the governed." The proportions of force and consent and the ways in which they are applied vary in different communities, but the variations do not follow the differences in the legal or theoretical forms of state. Behind the parliaments of so-called democracies, as well as behind all public despots, there is a minority that plays the major part in the real decisions of government. At times, it is true, the actual rulers have to do obeisance to the whims of princes and parliaments, but not for long; soon they resume their power and exercise it with a greater effectiveness than that of the occasional power wielded by the formal government. In democracies the people are permitted to believe that the official government is actually controlled by their will. The ruling minority concedes to the populace a formal right to decide "general" questions, to which the proper officials may only give "concrete" application; but in the exercise of this latter function, the officers have all the freedom they need to make any sort of application which they, or the minority whom they serve, desire. "A governmental system in which the 'people' expresses its 'will' (if we could suppose that the people has a will), without factions, intrigues and cliques, exists only in the state of the pious desires of theorists." "Our democracies in France,

Italy, England and the United. States tend more and more to be demagogic plutocracies." [42]

Professor Robert Michels (like Pareto, a Swiss Italian) has described the organization and operation of political parties as an exemplification of the oligarchic character of the so-called democracies of the modern world. He undertakes to show that the citizens generally, however fully endowed with political rights, take no effective part in governing. The political interest of the populace manifests itself not in making decisions on issues but in eagerly following and venerating a trusted leader. "The masses experience a profound need to prostrate themselves, not simply before great ideals, but also before the great individuals who in their eyes incorporate such ideals." Only a small number of men have the disposition—the self-esteem, the desire for popular adulation, the willingness to endure the sacrifices and labors which leadership requires—to put themselves in ruling positions. The capacities and means of leadership are various: oratorical skill and political trickery, or real intellectual superiority and special technical competence in affairs of government. Michels is not fully clear in elaborating his main theme. In some places he appears to be describing oligarchic rule as only a condition of temporary crisis into which democracies inevitably fall; in others he appears to regard oligarchy as inherent and constant in all social organization. The latter seems to be his prevailing view. Every society, he believes, has a leadership that not only proposes but also commands. Democracies cannot escape "the law of the historic necessity of oligarchy." However broad the suffrage and however direct the forms of nomination and election, the elected generally rule the electors, and without much limitation. If democracy is "the least of evils" among forms of political organization, it is only because its ideals and institutions hold those in authority to the least oppressive and callous type of leadership. "The majority of human beings, in a condition of eternal tutelage, are predestined by tragic necessity to submit to the domination of a small minority and must be content to constitute the pedestal of an oligarchy." [43]

Oswald Spengler, in his sweeping views of the movement of Western

---

[42] Vilfredo Pareto, *Traité de sociologie générale*, 2 vols. (1917), Vol. II, Secs. 2,239 ff., especially Secs. 2,244, 2,253, 2,257, 2,259, 2,681. The French edition is a translation, by Pierre Boven (under the author's supervision), of Pareto's *Trattato di sociologia* (1916).

[43] Robert Michels, *Political Parties: a Sociological Study of the Oligarchical Tendencies of Modern Democracy*, translated from the Italian by Eden and Cedar Paul (1915). The quoted passages are from pp. 73, 417, 424–425, and 407.

civilization, maintains that whatever elements of real democracy the modern world has known are doomed to extinction. The World War simply brought to near completion a development that had been going on for a century. The eighteenth century gospel of "freedom, justice, humanity, progress" rests upon a faith in the social omnipotence of free human reason; but average men are endowed with little reason and have little freedom to use what reason they possess. All the institutional and ideological paraphernalia of modern democracy facilitate rather than obstruct the operation of despotic rule. The forms of election and the slogans of electoral campaigns, the free school and the popular press, delude the masses into the belief that their formal rights are actual power. To extend the suffrage makes more difficult its free and effective exercise. Popular education only increases the number of those subject to the power exercised by newspaper-owners. "The rights of the people and the influence of the people are two different things. . . . One can make use of constitutional rights only when one has money. . . . That a franchise should work even approximately as the idealist supposes it to work presumes the absence of any organized leadership operating on the electors (in *its* interest) to the extent that its available money permits. . . . The Press to-day is an army with carefully organized arms and branches, with journalists as officers, and readers as soldiers. . . . Here, as in every army, the soldier obeys blindly, and war-aims and operation-plans change without his knowledge. The reader neither knows nor is allowed to know the purposes for which he is used. . . . It is permitted to everyone to say what he pleases, but the Press is free to take notice of what he says or not. It can condemn any 'truth' to death simply by not undertaking its communication to the world—a terrible censorship of silence, which is all the more potent in that the masses of newspaper readers are absolutely unaware that it exists. . . . As the English kingship became in the nineteenth century, so parliaments will become in the twentieth, a solemn and empty pageantry. As then sceptre and crown, so now peoples' rights are paraded for the multitude, and all the more punctiliously the less they really signify." [44]

These are illustrations of a widely held opinion that the people in a democracy rule only nominally; that the inert, unorganized masses are

[44] Oswald Spengler, *The Decline of the West*, translated by Charles Francis Atkinson, 2 vols. (1919), especially Vol. II, Chs. XI–XII. The quotations are from Vol. II, pp. 455, 456, 462–463, 464.

always controlled by some alert, resolute, organized minority—military despots, big business men, party managers, or social reformers—who are skilful in adjusting popular ideas and emotions to the limited interests or beliefs of some small group. And this minority leadership is rarely a leadership by the capable or high-minded. Democracies operate oligarchically but not aristocratically. The men who most readily win a popular following are not prophets or statesmen but politicians or tyrants; not the men of excellence in wisdom and courage but those who know how to appeal to passion and fear, rather than to reason and conscience. Some of the critics describe the typical democratic leader as the rhetorician, the sycophant, the electioneer—the glib and shallow person who gains a popular hearing and maintains his prestige by his skill in flattering the plain people and a readiness to adapt his own professed convictions to their superstitions and prejudices; he feeds the masses on fictions of liberty, equality, and self-government and plays upon their religious and racial partisanship.[45] According to others, the typical democratic leader is the domineering, swashbuckling, discipline-imposing, militant despot. The popular idols of their times, declares H. L. Mencken, have been Nero, Torquemada, Danton, Mussolini; not Socrates, Christ, Galileo, Savonarola; each of the latter was put to death with encouragement or applause, or at least with complacent acquiescence, from the mob of plain people.[46] "The multitude," said Le Bon, "erect their loftiest statues, not to benevolent statesmen but to tyrants who have vigorously oppressed them. . . . The type of hero dear to crowds will always have the semblance of a Cæsar. His insignia attracts them, his authority overawes them, and his sword instills them with fear. . . . It was the most enthusiastic of the Jacobins who acclaimed Bonaparte with greatest energy when he suppressed all liberty and made his hand of iron severely felt." [47]

Thus the critics contend generally that there is no such thing as an actual political democracy in the sense of a community in which political decisions are constantly made from a consensus of opinions of a

---

[45] The critics draw their examples not only from among recent American mayors, governors, senators, and presidents but also from conspicuous leaders in other spheres of American life. Professor Babbitt cites with approval the challenge by a foreign critic who asked: "What must one think of a country . . . whose most popular orator is W. J. Bryan, whose favorite actor is Charlie Chaplin, whose best known evangelist is Billy Sunday, and whose representative journalist is William Randolph Hearst?" *Democracy and Leadership* (1924), p. 255.

[46] Mencken, *Notes on Democracy* (1926), pp. 64–68.

[47] Le Bon, *The Crowd*, p. 61.

majority of the people. Most men, it is said, are incapable of forming or formulating their own will or opinion. The average man has no will or opinion on most questions of social significance. What appears as his decision is in reality only a manifestation of submission or acquiescence or applause evoked by more efficient men, moved by good or evil intent. The multitude is always subject to a few dominating spirits, acting in promotion of their own individual glory or in safeguarding the interests or promoting the ideals of the group to which they belong.

SELECT BIBLIOGRAPHY

GENERAL CRITICISMS OF DEMOCRACY

Babbitt, Irving, *Democracy and Leadership* (Boston and New York, 1924).

Belloc, Hilaire, *The House of Commons and Monarchy* (London, 1920).

Benoist, Charles, "Les maladies de la démocratie," *Revue des deux mondes,* XXVI (1925), 761–774; XXVII (1925), 540–560; XXX (1925), 801–818; XXXVII (1927), 572–587.

Cecil, Lord Hugh, *Conservatism* (London, 1912).

Conway, Martin, *The Crowd in Peace and War* (New York, London, etc., 1915).

Cram, Ralph Adams, *The Nemesis of Mediocrity* (Boston, 1917).

Crisp, Dorothy, *The Rebirth of Conservatism* (London, 1931), especially Ch. III.

Faguet, Émile, *The Cult of Incompetence,* translated by Beatrice Barstow (London, 1911).

Hasbach, Wilhelm, *Die moderne Demokratie: eine politische Beschreibung* (Jena, 1912).

Hollis, Christopher, *The American Heresy* (London, 1927).

Inge, William R., *Labels and Libels* (New York, 1929).

Ireland, Alleyne, *Democracy and the Human Equation* (New York, 1921).

Kales, Albert M., *Unpopular Government in the United States* (Chicago, 1914).

Kent, Frank R., *Political Behavior* (New York, 1928).

Lanessan, J. M. A. de, *La crise de la république* (Paris, 1914).

Le Bon, Gustave, *La psychologie politique et la défense sociale* (Paris, 1910).

————, *Psychologie des foules* (Paris, first ed., 1895; thirteenth ed., 1908). Translation: *The Crowd: a Study of the Popular Mind* (London, 1896, etc.).

Lewis, Wyndham, *The Art of Being Ruled* (London, 1926).

Lecky, W. E. H., *Democracy and Liberty,* 2 vols. (New York, 1896).

Lilly, William S., *First Principles in Politics* (London, 1899).

Ludovici, A. M., *The False Assumptions of Democracy* (London, 1921).

Maine, Henry Sumner, *Popular Government* (New York, 1886).

Mallock, William H., *Aristocracy and Evolution: a Study of the Rights, the Origin, and the Social Functions of the Wealthier Classes* (London, 1898).

——————, *The Limits of Pure Democracy* (second ed., London, 1918).

Mencken, H. L., *Notes on Democracy* (New York, 1926).

Michels, Robert, *Political Parties: a Sociological Study of the Oligarchical Tendencies of Modern Democracy,* translated from the Italian by Eden and Cedar Paul (New York, 1915.)

Nietzsche, Friedrich W., *Beyond Good and Evil,* in *The Complete Works of F. N. Nietzsche,* edited by Oscar Levy (Edinburgh and London, 1910–1913), Vol. XII.

——————, *The Will to Power,* in *Complete Works,* Vols. XIV–XV.

Ortega y Gasset, José, *The Revolt of the Masses;* authorized translation from the Spanish (London, 1932).

Ostrogorski, M., *Democracy and the Party System in the United States* (New York, 1910).

Pareto, Vilfredo, *Traité de sociologie générale,* 2 vols. (1917–1919), Vol. II, Ch. XII, Secs. 2,239–2,267.

Spengler, Oswald, *The Decline of the West,* translated by C. F. Atkinson, 2 vols. (New York, 1926–8), Vol. II, Chs. XI–XII.

Stoddard, T. Lothrop, *The Revolt against Civilization: the Menace of the Under Man* (New York, 1922).

Treitschke, Heinrich von, *Politik,* 2 vols. (Berlin, 1897–1898); translated as *Politics,* by Blanche Dugdale and Torben de Bille, 2 vols. (New York, 1916).

Wells, H. G., *Anticipations of the Reaction of Mechanical and Scientific Progress upon Human Life and Thought* (New York and London, 1902).

Wiggam, Albert E., *The Fruit of the Family Tree* (Indianapolis, 1924).

——————, *The New Decalogue of Science* (Indianapolis, 1922).

CRITICISM OF DEMOCRACY IN TERMS OF BIOLOGY

Brigham, C. C., *A Study of American Intelligence* (Princeton, 1923).

Cox, Catharine M., *The Early Mental Traits of Three Hundred Geniuses. Genetic Studies of Genius,* Vol. II (Stanford University, 1926).

Ellis, Havelock, *A Study of British Genius* (London, 1904; rev. ed., 1927).

Galton, Francis, *Hereditary Genius* (New York, 1870; 1914).

——————, *English Men of Science: Their Nature and Nurture* (New York, 1890).

——————, *Noteworthy Families: an Index to Kinships in Near Degrees between Persons whose Achievements are Honourable, and Have Been Publicly Recorded* (London, 1906).

Guyer, Michael F., *Being Well-Born* (Indianapolis, 1927).

Hall, Prescott F., "Aristocracy and Politics," *Journal of Heredity,* X (1919), 166–168.

Huntington, Ellsworth, and Whitney, L. F., *The Builders of America* (New York, 1927).

Ireland, Alleyne, "Democracy and the Accepted Facts of Heredity," *Journal of Heredity,* IX (1918), 339–342, and X (1919), 360–367.

Lennes, N. J., *Whither Democracy? Does Equalizing Opportunity Create Hereditary Social Classes?* (New York and London, 1927).

McDougall, William, *Is America Safe for Democracy?* (New York, 1921).

Pearson, Karl, "On the Inheritance of the Mental and Moral Characters in Man, and Its Comparison with the Inheritance of the Physical Characters," *Biometrika,* III (1904), 131–190.

——————, *The Scope and Importance to the State of the Science of National Eugenics* (Cambridge, Eng., 1911).

Popenoe, Paul, and Johnson, Roswell, *Applied Eugenics* (New York, 1918).

Schuster, Edgar, and Elderton, Ethel M., *The Inheritance of Ability* (London, 1907).

Stoddard, Lothrop, *The Revolt Against Civilization: the Menace of the Under Man* (New York, 1922).

Terman, Lewis M. *The Mental and Physical Traits of a Thousand Gifted Children. Genetic Studies of Genius,* Vol. I (Stanford University, 1925).

Walter, Herbert E., *Genetics* (New York, 1913).

Wiggam, Albert E., *The Fruit of the Family Tree* (Indianapolis, 1924).

——————, *The New Decalogue of Science* (Indianapolis, 1922).

Yoakum C. S, and Yerkes, R. M., *Army Mental Tests* (New York, 1920).

THEORIES OF RACE SUPERIORITY

Brigham, C. C., *A Study of American Intelligence* (Princeton, 1923).

Burr, Clinton Stoddard, *America's Race Heritage* (New York, 1922).

Chamberlain, Houston Stewart, *Die Grundlagen des neunzehnten Jahrhunderts* (second ed., Munich, 1900), translated as *The Foundations of the Nineteenth Century,* by John Lees, 2 vols. (New York and London, 1910).

Condolle, Alphonse de, *Histoire des sciences et des savants* (Geneva, Basle, Lyons, 1873).

Cram, Ralph Adams, *The Nemesis of Mediocrity* (Boston, 1917).

Fischer, Eugen, *Rasse und Rassenentstehung beim Menschen* (Berlin, 1927).

Fischer, Eugen, and Lenz, Fritz, *Grundriss der menschlichen Erblichkeitslehre und Rassenhygiene* (Munich, 1921).

Gobineau, Joseph A. de, *Essai sur l'inégalité des races humaines*, 4 vols. (Paris, 1853–1855), translated as *The Inequality of Human Races*, by Adrian Collins (London, 1915).

Gould, Charles W., *America, a Family Matter* (New York, 1922).

Grant, Madison, *The Passing of the Great Race* (New York, 1916).

Günther, Hans F. K., *Rassenkunde Europas* (second ed., Munich, 1926), translated as *The Racial Elements of European History* (New York, 1928).

Osborn, Henry Fairfield, Introduction to Madison Grant, *The Passing of the Great Race* (New York, 1916 and 1921).

Sadler, William S., *Long Heads and Round Heads, or What's the Matter with Germany?* (Chicago, 1918).

Schemann, Ludwig, *Die Rasse in den Geistes-wissenschaften: Studien zur Geschichte des Rassengedankens* (Munich, 1928).

Stoddard, Lothrop, *The Rising Tide of Color against White World Supremacy* (New York, 1920).

Vacher de Lapouge, Georges, *Les Sélections sociales* (Paris, 1896).

Wiggam, Albert E., *The Fruit of the Family Tree* (Indianapolis, 1924).

—————————, *The New Decalogue of Science* (Indianapolis, 1922).

Woltmann, Ludwig, *Politische Anthropologie* (Eisenach and Leipsic, 1903).

CHAPTER XII

SUBSTITUTES OR CORRECTIVES FOR DEMOCRACY

IF democracy is undesirable, or unworkable and unrealizable, what can be had in its place? Is a society in which political control is expressly vested in a single ruler or in some minority group preferable, in contemporary life, to one that permits all normal citizens to share voting rights equally?

KINGS OR DICTATORS

Faith in monarchy has not entirely disappeared. There still survives the idea that important governmental decisions demand a unity and vigor of which all groups, democratic or aristocratic, are incapable and which only a powerful king or dictator can supply.

In France there is a militant, well-organized movement, having as its definite objective the early reëstablishment of a powerful, hereditary kingship in that country.[1] The movement has aggressive and accomplished spokesmen—notably, Léon Daudet, Charles Maurras, and Jacques Bainville.[2] These writers vehemently denounce the weaknesses

[1] There are active royalist groups in Austria and Hungary to restore the Hapsburgs; in Bavaria, for the Wittelsbachs; and in Prussia, for the Hohenzollerns. Friends of the exiled King Alfonso and Grand Duke Cyril are vaguely looking forward to counter-revolutionary royalist *coups* in Spain and Russia, respectively. These movements have evolved no significant literature on the theory of monarchy.

[2] For titles of their works, see p. 352, *infra*. For an account of the activities of the royalists, see Jean Carrère and Georges Bourgin, *Manuel des partis politiques en France* (1924); and for an exposition of their theories, see Roger Soltau, *French Political Thought in the Nineteenth Century* (1931), Ch. XII.

The activities of the royalists center chiefly around the *Ligue d'Action Française*, founded in 1898 as a nationalist and antisemitic organization and later adopting royalism as its principal idea. The League publishes a daily newspaper, *l'Action Française*, and has various agencies of study and propaganda, such as a library, a monthly magazine, and an institute for lectures and discussions. The participants in the movement appear to come partly from formerly noble families, who aspire to rise out of their present obscurity and penury into the power and prestige they enjoyed under the old régime, and partly from the families of prosperous tradesmen, who vaguely aspire to a social prominence more in proportion to their economic position than they have been able to achieve under the French Republic.

and iniquities of French politics since republican ideas first invaded France in the eighteenth century and brought about her degradation —from her position, under Louis XIV, as the most distinguished and powerful of all the nations, to her present "second-rate" place in world affairs. They state their positive program with eloquence and lucidity, though without much logical coherence. Their royalism is in part a derivation from their extreme nationalism. The supremacy of national above all group and individual interests can be maintained, they argue, only by a government that is unified and constant in its policy, certain and strong in the execution of its will, and competent to protect the nation from all wavering and weakness in its intercourse with other nations and from any sort of internal disunity and disorder. A republic has no such government: its parliaments continually shift their policies, rarely devote them to public ends, and are never strong in enforcement. Power, stability, and the supremacy of national interests can be maintained only by monarchs; and the whole inheritance and training of a king creates in him a devotion to affairs of state and a disposition to perpetuate his country's traditions.

The program of the French royalists includes a unique admixture of centralization of political authority, devolution of administrative functions, and ecclesiastical autonomy for the Roman Church. The destruction of the privileges of the corporations of the old régime was, they hold, one of the greatest crimes of the Revolution. For the roots of nationalist devotion grow deepest in the natural attachments of individuals to church, neighborhood, craft, and kin. When monarchy is restored, then the ancient liberties of local, vocational, family, and ecclesiastical associations can be safely revived.

The royalist program calls for the reëstablishment of the crown, by restoring the Duke of Guise, heir of the Bourbon and Orleans families, to the throne; the abolition of parliament as a legislative body; and the institution in its place of an annual assembly, representing provincial assemblies and having the sole function of controlling national finances. It makes the ministers responsible solely to the king and places all major national decisions exclusively within his power. These changes, the royalists contend, would restore French politics to that lofty plane where public power and influence is the rightful heritage of those who, through blood, tradition, and training, are the chief possessors of political wisdom.

The royalists make no pretense of allegiance to the theological and moral doctrines of the Roman Catholic Church. Maurras calls himself a "Catholic atheist," ridicules the Christian creed of human equality and universal brotherhood, and repudiates the Church's standards for sex morality and other matters of personal conduct. When the royalists have defended the Church against outside political attacks upon its ecclesiastical independence and against inside attempts to modernize or liberalize its doctrine and policy, it is because they have recognized the close affiliation between monarchical and ecclesiastical traditions in France. They look upon the Church as the supreme embodiment of the principles of legitimacy and autocracy in the modern world. The Church preserves its traditional organization, rigidly enforces its discipline, and countenances no changing or challenging of its creed. This attitude won for the royalists the fervent devotion of thousands of lay Catholics, and friendliness, or tolerance, from high ecclesiastical officials. These ties have recently been broken. The increasing bitterness and recklessness of the royalists in their political activities brought the Church to realize that it could not hope to retard or modify republican anticlericalism if it condoned violent assaults upon the government of the Republic. It may also be said, more generally, that there can hardly be a permanent accord between Catholicism and any creed that preaches the unqualified supremacy of political authority over every other allegiance. Active ecclesiastical support of the royalists ceased in 1923; and three years later the Pope issued a decree forbidding Catholics to associate themselves with the movement.

In the first years after the World War, the adroit and violent invectives of Daudet and Maurras made a wide popular appeal among students in the lycées and universities. These youths, having observed the governmental blunders and injustices during the periods of war and reconstruction, had come to doubt the reasonableness, efficiency, and justice of contemporary republican institutions. In recent years the royalist activity has taken more of a fascist direction—characterized by a fanatical chauvinism and by vague notions that, by vehement upbraiding and a conspicuous parading and disturbing the peace, they can wreck parliamentary government and put control of affairs in the hands of a small clique of militant patriots, who will reinvigorate France's national life, humiliate her enemies and rivals, extend her domains, and restore her cultural and political prestige.[3]

[3] The French royalists have assiduously exploited to their own aims almost every crisis through which the Third Republic has passed: the Boulangist movement of 1889, the Dreyfus affair of 1894, the Agadir incident of 1911, and the

The royalists' objections to democracy are in many respects like those of the other critics. It does not seem likely, however, that any trend towards democracy in the contemporary world will be seriously checked or modified by any of the projects for restoring hereditary monarchs to positions of power. Most of those who bemoan the unintelligence of democracies would generally endorse the warning by an ardent French critic, that "an intelligent king is a rare, even an abnormal thing." [4]

In another form, however, the principle of a one-man political rule now finds practical expression in Italy and in several countries of Central and Eastern Europe, where dictatorships have been set up during the last decade and a half.[5] Each of the dictators put himself in power chiefly by means of armed force; destroyed all effective opposition, in the early stages of his régime, by a policy of governmental terrorism; and retains the use of censorship and a summary judicial procedure as normal means for dealing with political minorities. Yet each is approved, it appears, by substantial numbers of the more intelligent citizens and is widely acclaimed by the populace. It is not difficult to find explanations for the origins of the dictatorships and for the practical successes which, in some measure at least, they achieve. On the one hand, the World War, or the conditions of the terms of peace, left each of the countries in a condition of exceptional economic and social disorder; on the other hand, the normal operation of parliamentary institutions was made impossible or difficult by a general popular lassitude, in reaction from an extraordinary war discipline, and by the failure of rival democratic groups to agree on any common program to meet the emergency. Where the choice appeared to lie only between a perpetuation of such conditions and a submission to the iron hand of a rule which, although destroying self-government and individual liberty, seemed able to meet immediate needs—in the way of balancing budgets, stabilizing currencies, and maintaining order—the people chose, or accepted, the latter alternative.

Algeciras affair of 1906. In recent years they have, on occasions, exercised an influence on political decisions quite out of proportion to their numbers, particularly in determining specific lines of attack adopted by the conservative factions in Parliament; as in the assault upon Caillaux and Malvy in 1917, leading to the accession of Clemenceau to the premiership and the prosecution of the two former ministers; and again in their support of French occupation of the Ruhr.

[4] Émile Faguet, *The Cult of Incompetence*, translated by Beatrice Barstow (1911), pp. 62–63.

[5] See F. Cambo, *Les dictatures* (1930); Henry R. Spencer, "Dictatorship," in *Encyclopaedia of the Social Sciences*, Vol. V (1931).

Some critics of democracy claim that, when unusually difficult problems have to be faced, even the older democracies confess their impotence and surrender to emergency dictatorships. Premier Poincaré, it is pointed out, "saved the franc" in 1926 by persuading the French parliament to give him a "doctor's mandate" in reorganizing the finances of the nation. The British, in the autumn of 1931, escaped financial and social disaster only by yielding to Prime-minister MacDonald's emotional plea that the voters give him and his associates *carte blanche* in devising the fiscal and economic measures to deliver the country from its crisis, with only vague intimations as to what his measures would be. The Congress of the United States, in 1933, blindly conferred on President Roosevelt the vast discretionary powers he demanded—to inflate the currency, institute governmental economies, and regulate production, prices, and working conditions in private industry and trade—as the only way to restore prosperity. If these steps were necessary, then, the critics contend, democracy is discredited; for the test of a good form of government is to be found in the measure of its success in meeting the difficulties of a crisis; any form of government may work tolerably in times of prosperity and peace.

The theoretical justification of dictatorship has been set forth most extensively by Mussolini and the other spokesmen for Italian Fascism —to be reviewed later.[6] The Fascist theorists, we shall see, characterize their doctrine as a "new conception of civil life"; the novelty consisting essentially in an emphatic repudiation of the assumptions, ideals, and methods of modern democracy. It is the object of the Fascists to displace the visionary, disintegrating, enfeebling creeds of equality and freedom by a realistic doctrine of an organic, hierarchically constituted nation, whose few most virile citizens assist a dictator in holding the multitude to the task of realizing destinies more exalted than the petty aims of commonplace men.

RULE BY THE ÉLITE

Neither a revolutionary dictatorship nor a monarchy of the older type is the form of polity proposed by most of the contemporary critics of democracy. They seek rather an aristocratic government. Every community, they hold, should adopt—or have imposed upon it—some system for putting its best members into governmental office and for in-

[6] In Ch. XVIII, *infra*.

vesting them with the function not of discovering and effectuating popular opinion but of fashioning out of their own minds the major political decisions and seeing that the decisions are properly executed.

But how shall the "few wise," who are to take command of the "innumerable foolish," be discovered and endowed with political authority? [7] Most critics of democracy are certain that the multitude lack not only wisdom to rule but also capacity to choose wise rulers, so that an aristocracy cannot be set up by popular vote. Few of the writers are specifically clear in any positive proposals. Most of them either do not make such an attempt or else they describe their aristocrats in only vague terms. It is difficult, where there is no hereditary nobility, to find some concrete mark for identifying the politically superior members of a community.

Wealth is a mark of definite differentiation, but few regard it as a reliable sign of political wisdom. William H. Lecky, it is true, pointed to the advantages in a combination of wealth with an hereditary social and political status—a condition realized in the traditional British constitution, which "assigns to a wealthy class a large circle of necessary duties and makes the gratuitous discharge of public functions the appanage and sign of dignity." [8] More recently, the late William H. Mallock set forth, in more specific form, the case for an economic aristocracy. His *Aristocracy and Evolution* was a plea for the social and political supremacy of able men generally, but the argument was elaborated chiefly in economic terms. Mallock believed that the modern advances of civilization had been made chiefly in the economic field and that economic progress had been brought about principally through the agency of the aristocrats of industry. He maintained that the whole increase in the *per capita* wealth during the last hundred years had been due exclusively to the intelligence and energy of a few inventors, capitalists, employers, managers, and financiers.[9] The laborer's capacity had remained just what it was. Without the new machines and processes with which the genius of the inventors had provided the wage-earner or without the superior organization of personnel and distribution supplied by great business managers, the laborer could create no more

[7] See Thomas Carlyle, *Shooting Niagara* (1867) in *Critical and Miscellaneous Essays,* V (New York, 1909), 186.

[8] W. H. Lecky, *Democracy and Liberty,* I (1896), 384.

[9] William H. Mallock, *Aristocracy and Evolution: a Study of the Rights, the Origin, and the Social Functions of the Wealthier Classes* (1898), especially pp. 204 ff.

wealth for himself or others than a century ago. Mallock's chief aim was to prove that the future advance of social welfare depended upon the continuance of the wage system of production and the competitive system of distribution, and that owners of capital, by controlling jobs, wages, and prices, must continue to direct the economic life of the community. He had also in mind, however, a vague idea of a more general supremacy of industrial leaders in the affairs of the community. He did not, however, define any way for setting up this plutocratic society.

The idea of an economic aristocracy does not appeal to most of the critics of democracy and is particularly uncongenial to those who write under the influence of Nietzsche. Although Nietzsche seemed occasionally to accept economic success as a significant indication of superior worth and to regard economic self-interest as an important factor in accomplishing the elimination of the weak by the strong, yet his aristocrat was not the successful business man or the wealthy man of any sort. On the contrary, much of his political discussion was in the nature of an attack upon financially entrenched mediocrity in the modern state. His hostility to democracy rested to a considerable degree upon his belief that such a system of government was favorable to the rise to influence of wealthier groups and unfavorable to the supremacy of the intellectually and culturally superior.

Contemporary writers share this idea that a characteristic fault of democracy is its exaggeration of the significance of wealth. A. M. Ludovici, a disciple of Nietzsche, says: "The greatest indictment of modern society is perhaps the frequency with which vulgarity and the meanest attainments in will and intellect achieve phenomenal material success." Wealth, he continues, endows with power "people who are neither wise, virtuous, characterful nor resolute," and "condemns to impotence, obscurity and ignominy, people who would be eminently fitted to wield power." [10] "The most cursory survey of our world," declares Lothrop Stoddard, "is enough to show that in politics, finance, business, and most other fields of human activity, a large proportion of the most influential figures are persons of decidedly mediocre intelligence and character." [11]

Nietzsche's political ideal appeared to be that of a rule by the strong, hardy, aggressive members of the community. He looked forward to a

[10] A. M. Ludovici, *The False Assumptions of Democracy* (1921), pp. 40, 42, 124.
[11] Lothrop Stoddard, *The Revolt against Civilization,* p. 226.

world governed by men so highly differentiated from ordinary men—in courage, patience, self-discipline, austerity, and aggressiveness—as to constitute in reality a higher species of the human being. This new world, he maintained, could be reached if we would simply let the evolution, which has already moved from ape to man, proceed on to the *Ueber-mensch*.[12] Put no restraint upon the superior man's desire for power, and this impulse will, in its expression, lead gradually through successively superior types of men to an aristocracy that will rule the masses. Out of such an aristocracy there will arise, still further in the future, a new race; and the slow transformations will continue until ultimately the species, man, is superseded by a higher species, "superman." Existing governments should support this evolution by wise systems of eugenics and education. The eugenic policy should be both restrictive—the prohibition or limitation of the offspring of inferior people in order to secure the elimination of the unfit—and positive—the selective improvement of superior stocks by a regulation of marriages. Education should be confined chiefly to selected individuals. Although Nietzsche attached great importance to the significance of congenitally superior traits, his faith in education as a means of improving the race was strengthened by his belief in the inheritance of acquired characteristics.

Through much of the popular writing against democracy to-day there runs this conception of an aristocracy conceived in naturalistic terms. If we would only let nature take its course, it is said, or assist nature in taking its course, the stronger and more capable men would come to the top, socially and politically. The state should, therefore, do little to preserve or train the weak and unsuccessful members of society and much to encourage the strong and successful. Still the writers are not clear in identifying the biologically superior groups. Some seem to regard as naturally best those who are prominent or successful economically and socially (and "social" success seems here to be often understood in the popular or fashionable sense of the word). Others hold variously that the best stocks are to be found in the middle classes, or among those who show unusual capacity in scientific or professional achievement, or who have a high rating in the recently devised formal measurements of "general intelligence." The general argument is that, whether or not any scheme can be devised for directly investing the biologically select with political power, the state should have

[12] Nietzsche, *Thus Spake Zarathustra* (*Complete Works*, Vol. XI), Ch. LXXIII.

some method for discovering its persons of superior natural endowment and should devise measures for promoting their training and reproduction. Few go beyond that to the point of proposing that we adopt some particular scheme for vesting political power directly in some socially superior group. Most admit that we cannot specifically identify and segregate our proper rulers; for not only high intelligence but also proper character and emotional temperament are essential to a proper exercise of political power.[13]

Perhaps the most impressive advocacy of aristocracy to-day is, therefore, to be found in the works of those who describe aristocratic leadership in broadly ethical, humanistic, cultural terms and make no attempt to phrase their arguments in the terminology of biology or other natural sciences. They revive old beliefs that perpetual values can be recognized and preserved, fruitful changes devised and executed, only where the rulers and guides of the people are the few who stand above and apart from the multitude in character, manners, and wisdom— made fit to govern both by their native capacities and by their manner of living. It is the idea of Carlyle and Ruskin, who looked regretfully back to the Middle Ages when feudal lords ruled and protected the humble classes. So also William H. Lecky lauded the hereditary aristocracy of his day, in whom, he said, you find the nobleman's freedom from sordid motives, an indifference to the emoluments of public office, and a superior public spirit and devotion.[14] Heinrich von Treitschke (in the eighteen seventies) had most forcefully proclaimed this ideal of a cultural aristocracy. Civil society, he maintained, is essentially aristocratic in structure; its coherence and growth depend upon recognized and accepted differentiations among its members—in economic condition, social prestige, and political influence. There can be no sure advances in learning and art, save where ordinary people apply their energies to the production of the necessities and conveniences of life. The masses must forever remain the masses. The multitude must "plow and forge and dig in order that a few may write and paint and study." [15]

This idea of a cultural aristocracy, supported by the rough work of the masses, appears to-day—variously elaborated and illustrated, and,

---

[13] "A teamster may possess great emotional interest and sound character, and thus, with but moderate intelligence of the abstract type, may make a splendid voting citizen. The college professor or doctor may have great intelligence, but lack sadly the temperamental elements of character required for sound citizenship."—A. E. Wiggam, *The New Decalogue of Science*, p. 148.

[14] *Democracy and Liberty*, I (1896), 379 ff.

[15] Heinrich von Treitschke, *Politics*, translated, 2 vols., I (1916), 41.

in some instances, intermixed with ethical considerations—in the writings of such men as Dean Inge, T. S. Eliot, Count Keyserling, Hilaire Belloc, and Irving Babbitt.[16] Dean Inge has argued, in general terms, that social inequality, associated in some degree with differentiation in political power, is essential to the production of human individuals of the highest type. Eliot writes of the advantages of a government by men characterized by their "spiritual and intellectual conduct on a high plane"; he seems to see such men best typified to-day in the elegant, literary, orthodox Anglican churchmen of his adopted country. Count Keyserling has in mind some sort of social-intellectual aristocracy, exemplified in the social leaders of contemporary Hungary and Spain. With Professor Babbitt, the natural aristocrats are those possessed of a superior ethical and æsthetic sensitiveness, a higher power of subordinating their naturalistic and expansive impulses to their spiritual and rational faculties, and a clearer appreciation of constant moral and cultural values. Almost the whole of Babbitt's political and social philosophy has to do with the importance of respecting and obeying traditional standards of worthy conduct. This, in matters of private conduct, means the subordination of man's baser, appetitive instincts to a self-discipline developed through habits of living under the direction of one's higher faculties. A political aristocracy is simply a society that evolves and follows the type of public leadership which respect for such standards implies.

No systematic résumé of the political doctrines of this group of critics can be given. The writers do not attempt to set forth their ideas in any logically articulated form. Their political comments are significant as eloquent and forceful expressions of the general political preferences of certain men who have read widely and who believe that they find their preferences confirmed by the revelations of history. They make their disparagement of democracy empirical only by citing examples of the evil deeds of democracies of the past and present. They do not define the forms for an aristocratic organization of modern society or consider whether any actual aristocracies have been relatively free from the vices they find in democracies.

MIXED GOVERNMENT

Other writers seek relief from the defects of democracy in more specific ways, combining aristocratic with democratic devices rather

[16] See the titles on p. 352, *infra*.

than rejecting the latter altogether. The proper form of government for a community fit for universal suffrage, they say, is a constitution based on a general but not a uniform distribution of political rights. Each individual should count—not equally but according to his worth. This is an old idea. Justice, the ancients said, implies a proportionate rather than an identic allotment of privileges and duties. Aristotle argued that political justice is a relative—not an absolute—principle, which finds its expression only in a constitutional assignment of political functions in accordance with men's varying merits. In both ancient and modern times there have been various devices for giving wealth (as in Solon's laws of the seventh century, B. C., and in the "three-class" system of voting established by Prussia in the nineteenth century) or education (as in the recent Belgian system of plural voting) its proper extra weight in a system of general voting.[17] We need say here only that, according to most observers, experience has not revealed much of really aristocratic value in any of the schemes of group or plural voting. There is a more persistent faith in the possibility of balancing the influence of popular assemblies by the powers of other bodies farther removed from control by mass opinion: second legislative houses representing sections of the population not adequately represented in an election by universal suffrage, and courts (with judges appointed for life or for long terms) vested with the power to review and nullify legislative enactments.

Most states to-day have bicameral legislatures; and in some of them the composition of the smaller or upper chamber is such that extra representation is afforded to select cultural, professional, or economic groups.[18] There is, however, no agreement as to the proper way for constituting an upper house so as to make it really a reflection of the more competent political opinion of a nation. The writers generally acknowledge that accession by birth no longer supplies, if it ever did supply, a valid test. They have more confidence in the pos-

[17] Said John Stuart Mill: "Until there shall have been devised, and until opinion is willing to accept, some mode of plural voting which may assign to education, as such, the degree of superior influence due to it, and sufficient as a counterpoise to the numerical weight of the least educated class; for so long the benefits of completely universal suffrage cannot be obtained without bringing with them, as it appears to me, more than equivalent evils."—*Considerations on Representative Government*, p. 171.

[18] Cf. H. B. Lees-Smith, *Second Chambers in Theory and Practice* (1923); James Bryce, *Modern Democracies* (1921), Vol. II, Ch. LIV; H. L. McBain and Lindsay Rogers, *The New Constitutions of Europe* (1922), Ch. III; Pierse Loftus, *The Creed of a Tory* (1926), Pt. II, Ch. II.

sibilities of either an executive appointment from special categories—men of experience in high offices of state or church or of distinguished achievement in science, literature, art, invention, or business—or an indirect election of members having special qualifications and serving for long terms of office. The theory is that a chamber composed on some principle other than that óf direct representation of a numerical majority of the electorate will, whether its power be equal and concurrent with that of the more popular chamber or merely a right to secure delay and reconsideration, supply some antidote for the mischiefs of complete democracy.

The power of courts to pass upon the validity of legislative enactments is distinctively an American contrivance. The "imitations" in a few other constitutional democracies [19] make, in either theory or practice, only very limited approaches to the system of judicial review as it is maintained in the United States; although several European publicists—particularly in France and, since the adoption of the Weimar Constitution, in Germany—have advocated a full incorporation of the principle in the constitutions of their respective countries. The typical American defense of the principle appears to be determined chiefly by a fear of democracy's reckless dealings with traditional privileges of private property-owners, although the advocates ordinarily state the case in more general terms.[20] Free government, they hold, implies not only that the people are represented in their legislative assemblies but also that certain stable legal principles are maintained as checks upon the popular will and certain fundamental rights of persons and property are recognized as outside the competence of any government, however constituted. The advocates of a "judicial veto" rarely define specifically the basic principles and rights that are to operate as checks upon legislative power. The checks are vaguely named, by such general phrases as "natural and inherent rights of persons or property," "tradi-

[19] Canada, Australia, Mexico, Argentina, Brazil, Venezuela.

[20] There is a voluminous literature on the subject in the United States and a recently increasing discussion by European publicists. See Charles G. Haines, *The American Doctrine of Judicial Supremacy* (1914), and "Some Phases of the Theory and Practice of Judicial Review of Legislation in Foreign Countries," *American Political Science Review*, XXIV (1930), 583–605; R. L. Hale, "Judicial Review *versus* Doctrinaire Democracy," *American Bar Association Journal*, X (1924), 882–886; A. Blondel, *Le contrôle juridictionnel de la constitutionnalité des lois* (1927); Léon Duguit, *Traité de droit constitutionnel* (second ed., 1921–1925), Vol. III, Ch. III, Secs. 45–46; and the article "Judicial Review," by Edward S. Corwin, in the *Encyclopaedia of the Social Sciences* (Vol. VIII) with the bibliographical list following the article (pp. 463–464). See also Ch. XIII, *infra*, pp. 365–369.

tional or fundamental principles of law," or "due process of law." The writers contend that courts, rather than popularly elected legislatures, are the most competent interpreters of traditional political principles and the surest guardians of admitted civic rights.

Some contemporary writers, mainly in England, would assign this moderating function to a "monarch." The ills to which the democratic body politic is peculiarly subject, they say, cannot be cured or prevented by a mere injection of aristocratic antidotes. The stronger dose of a power concentrated in one man is needed. Lord Hugh Cecil has, accordingly, argued for a restoration of active governmental initiative to the British crown, so that there may be one official, trained in "the arts and manners of the past," who is enabled, by his exalted position, to view public issues in complete detachment from factional, local, and transitory considerations.[21]

Hilaire Belloc has contended at greater length for a restoration of some form of monarchy.[22] The House of Commons, he argues, ruled effectively and equitably only when it was an aristocracy—that is, a house of the gentry. A truly aristocratic government exists only when the proper qualities and moods for it are present among both the governing and the governed. In other words, there must be, on the one hand, a minority that is worthy of popular respect or that at least knows how to elicit it and, on the other hand, a populace that desires to be ruled by its betters. Neither of these conditions exists in contemporary England. The temper for an aristocracy has disappeared from both the House of Commons and the people. The former—with its conspicuous demagoguery, corruption, party intriguing, subservience to millionaire newspaper-owners, general ineptitude, and lack of any *flair* for the national traditions—has lost its aristocratic character and disposition. The people, on their part, have no ability to distinguish whatever aristocrats there are. The new urban populace—in contradistinction to the old rural yeomanry—no longer recognizes "the gesture of a gentleman." It is immersed in practical problems of subsistence and security (which the paternal rich formerly solved for it); and it is intellectually perverted by the heritage of the egalitarian philosophy of the French Revolution.

The only moderator for the governments of the great states of to-day, Belloc continues, is a monarch: not necessarily an hereditary ruler or a

[21] Lord Hugh Cecil, *Conservatism* (1912), pp. 223–229.
[22] Hilaire Belloc, *The House of Commons and Monarchy* (1920).

self-constituted dictator or even an indeterminately serving elected head. What is required is a single person ("normally an adult man") exercising positive powers in government "for some considerable period" ("perhaps better for life"). A monarchy may come about "through a return to power" of hereditary rulers; through "an elective machinery"; or (is this, written in 1920, prophetic?) "through the accidental popularity of one man in some important crisis of the commonwealth." It may come "in any one of a thousand ways. . . . But come Monarchy must, if the greatness and the homogeneity of the nation are to be maintained." For even the industrial masses of to-day have not lost their hero worship, their desire to place responsibility on a single powerful official, their fear of such an official in conspicuous control of the coercive forces of the nation, or their trust in his power to protect the weak against oppression.[23]

In a different vein, and with somewhat vaguer detail, R. H. Gretton has maintained that every community needs a "kingship," or its proper equivalent for that office.[24] In the contemporary constitutional monarchies, the royal heads survive, he believes, not by having lost their powers, nor by mere inertia and the force of tradition, but by virtue of the permanent values of their office. And the functions of that office are not merely ceremonial and ornamental; they are effective and fulfil demands of government that can be satisfied in no other way. For a representative assembly, in either a monarchy or a republic, does not and cannot govern; it only, as John Stuart Mill explained, discusses, advises, amends, and accepts or rejects. Political leaders, within or outside the government, initiate and direct the policies of government. If these officials are politically responsible for their measures, the responsibility is actually only to party factions that control the assembly. Every state needs, therefore, one single official who is above all factionalism. Standing before the nation as a symbol of its unity and continuity, he should have power not only to warn and to mediate but also to act more positively whenever his forceful intervention is required in order to uphold the integral life and progress of the people. The need is satisfied most fully and naturally by an hereditary kingship, by reason of its permanence, its association with long national tradition, and its independent tenure. Republics, however, can have also their formal

---

[23] The quotations are from Belloc, *op. cit.*, pp. 110, 173, and 188.
. [24] R. H. Gretton, *The King's Majesty: a Study in the Historical Philosophy of Modern Kingship* (1930).

heads, who can be made to stand above the party-controlled cabinets and parliaments. "The Supreme Magistracy of Republics tends in fact to become more and more analogous to royalty. . . . Republics may not know the name of king, but they all present an institution which only a study of kingship can satisfactorily explain." [25]

In the varied plans for weighted voting, select upper chambers, courts of constitutional review, royal or presidential moderators, and other aristocratic or monarchic checks and balances for a democracy, there is generally no attempt to allot positive powers of ruling to some one or more of the intellectually, morally, culturally, or biologically superior members of society. The theory is rather that relief from the faults of democracy can come only through superseding the idea of any sort of personal rule—whether by the one, few, or many—by the idea of an institutional or legal supremacy. In other words, in place of government by will of the people, we must have government by fundamental and unchanging—or by slowly and imperceptibly changing—law. Under this theory, popular government can be made tolerable only by setting up above the ordinary governing bodies a constitution (written or unwritten) embodying definitions of governmental powers and individual rights, so that basic principles and traditional policies can be changed only with unusual caution and deliberation; a constitution, moreover, which so spreads the process of decision among various political bodies that the will of the people, or of any group among them, can prevail only after whatever is merely transient, impulsive, or factional has been filtered out of it. Every democracy needs to have certain independent and expert officials whose function it is not to issue decrees reflecting their own desires or beliefs but to discover the more basic needs or the more permanent aims of the nation and to devise the measures that fulfil these needs and aims. Courts and upper legislative chambers can check an impetuous popular decision when it violates a more permanent national will embodied in classic legal documents or in traditionally established legal practices.

[25] Mr. Gretton cites, with fair plausibility, the presidency of the French Republic. But he is also of the opinion (surprising even in 1930) that the "most successful" and "wisest" presidents of the United States "have tried to produce, in face of the extreme difficulties which the American Constitution opposes to such an effort, something like the relations of a Constitutional sovereign with Congress."—*Op. cit.*, pp. 14–15.

CONCLUSION

We have then, in varying expressions, a repudiation of the doctrine that places individuals and minorities in political subservience to majorities. Most of the critics rest their case mainly with a demonstration of the fallacies of that doctrine. They do not go far in attempts to describe the formal substitutes for democracy or to define specifically the personnel of an aristocracy. In so far as they have a constructive theory, it appears, most significantly, first, in their advocacy of an institutional control of the sort indicated above; and, secondly, in exhortations to the common man to submit himself voluntarily to a personal guidance by his betters. Through much of the writing against democracy there runs the idea that aristocracy can be brought about by persistently cultivating a conviction or feeling among ordinary people that they are not competent, through direct vote or unrestricted choice of representatives, to decide political questions or to be the main influence in the decision. They should admit their incompetence and look respectfully and trustfully to those who excel them in political wisdom. "The whole meaning of aristocracy," says Belloc, "is the provision of a sort of worship addressed to the few that govern. . . . 'The Aristocracy' in an aristocratic state is . . . not a caste (though it may be a caste), least of all a plutocracy, but essentially *an oligarchy enjoying a peculiar respect from its fellow-citizens.*" [26] Thus in all spheres of social life, the writers contend generally, a community should offer its superior men inducements attracting them to positions of influence and it should give these men full opportunity to exercise their influence and suppress that of others. Economic and cultural progress comes about not through developing the productive capacities or increasing the privileges of the masses but only through cultivating the talents of the "exceptionally gifted minority." "The many," declared Mallock, "can prosper only through their participation in benefits which, in the way alike of material comfort, opportunity, cultural and social freedom, would be possible for no one unless the many submitted themselves to the influence or authority of the super-capable few." [27] Or as Faguet put it: "A democracy can live only on condition of producing an aristocracy or permitting an aristocracy to produce itself!" [28]

[26] *The House of Commons and Monarchy,* p. 13.
[27] William H. Mallock, *The Limits of Pure Democracy* (second ed., 1918), p. 392.
[28] *The Cult of Incompetence,* p. 95.

SELECT BIBLIOGRAPHY

Babbitt, Irving, *Democracy and Leadership* (Boston and New York, 1924).

Bainville, Jacques, *Histoire de France* (Paris, 1924). *History of France,* translated by A. and C. Gauss (New York, 1926).

Belloc, Hilaire, *The House of Commons and Monarchy* (London, 1920).

Blondel, A., *Le contrôle juridictionnel de la constitutionnalité des lois* (Paris, 1927).

Cambo, F., *Les dictatures* (Paris, 1930).

Cecil, Lord Hugh, *Conservatism* (London, 1912).

Daudet, Léon, *L'avant-guerre* (Paris, 1913).

——————, *Le stupide dix-neuvième siècle* (Paris, 1922).

Eliot, T. S., *For Lancelot Andrewes: Essays on Style and Order* (New York, 1928).

Gretton, R. H., *The King's Majesty: a Study in the Historical Philosophy of Modern Kingship* (London, 1930).

Hearnshaw, F. J. C., *Conservatism in England* (London, 1933), pp. 22 ff., 298 ff.

Inge, William R., *Outspoken Essays: Second Series* (London, New York, etc., 1922).

Keyserling, Count Herman, *Europe,* translated by Maurice Samuel (New York, 1928).

Lecky, W. E. H., *Democracy and Liberty,* 2 vols. (New York, 1896).

Loftus, Pierse, *The Creed of a Tory* (London, 1926).

Ludovici, A. M., *The Defense of Aristocracy: a Text-book for Tories* (London, 1915).

Mallock, William H., *Aristocracy and Evolution: a Study of the Rights, the Origin, and the Social Functions of the Wealthier Classes* (London, 1898).

——————, *The Limits of Pure Democracy* (second ed., London, 1918).

Maurras, Charles, *Enquête sur la monarchie* (Paris, 1900–1909).

——————, *Trois idées politiques* (Paris, 1898).

Nietzsche, Friedrich W., *Thus Spake Zarathustra,* in *Complete Works* (Edinburgh and London, 1910–1916), Vol. II.

Spencer, Henry R., "Dictatorship," in *Encyclopædia of the Social Sciences,* Vol. V (1931).

Treitschke, Heinrich von, *Politics,* translated by Blanche Dugdale and Torben de Bille, 2 vols. (New York, 1916).

Wells, H. G., *Democracy under Revision* (London and New York, 1927).

——————, *The World of William Clissold,* 3 vols. (London, 1926), Vol. II, pp. 322–368.

CHAPTER XIII

THE DEFENSE OF DEMOCRACY

THE traditional doctrine of democracy has been in part, as we have seen, a theory of original rights of man—a view that government is made in virtue of those rights and must conform to them. Under that theory, men have a natural right to participate equally in political power, just as they have a natural right to be free from enslavement or to appeal on equal terms to judicial tribunals for protection of their lives and possessions against assault or trespass. Democratic doctrine is still set forth in these terms. The contemporary doctrine tends to lay greater stress, however, upon a more nearly empirical phase of human equality. It looks upon government as a contrivance of human wisdom to serve certain fundamental human needs which normal men understand and in which they are equally concerned. Thus democracy is now primarily a theory that, however men may differ in certain qualities, they do not differ significantly in their fitness to participate in political power; and the theory holds that governments constituted on a broadly popular basis do actually, in the long run, serve more efficiently and justly than governments representing select social groups.

The contemporary critic of democracy summarily rejects the traditional theory of natural rights as a mere metaphysical hypothesis, unsustained by any possible evidence and without practical value in solving any of the actual problems of political life. His more detailed attack, as we have seen, is directed against the democratic assumptions as to the equality of men in political capacity. He maintains that the assumptions are disproved both by science and by experience. Science, he says, shows that genetic differences among men mark off sharply an exceptional minority clearly superior to the general run of average men; that we can identify the men who are endowed with the best germinal gifts, for they generally find their way into "upper" social groups of one sort or another; and that the democratic method of allotting political power is, therefore, a "biological injustice." [1] He main-

---

[1] A. E. Wiggam, *The New Decalogue of Science* (1923), p. 40. Cf. Lothrop Stoddard, *The Revolt Against Civilization* (1923), p. 266.

tains also that the records of history and the observation of contemporary experience prove democracies to be actually more inefficient, unstable, and oppressive than other forms of government.

The democrat meets his critics on their own ground. He believes that if biology and history do not positively prove the validity of the democratic doctrine, at least they do not disprove it; and he can balance his critic's biological and historical arguments with opposing and equally authentic reasoning from the same fields.

DEMOCRACY AND BIOLOGY

The democrat has no difficulty in showing that prevailing attempts to use biological arguments in disparaging democracy reveal badly muddled ideas as to precisely what the state of genetic knowledge is to-day; or that most of those who make the biological attack are attempting to cultivate a field with which they are not sufficiently familiar. The scientists' knowledge of what human characters breed true and what do not is relatively slight.[2] They know little as to the presence or absence of definite human characters whose modes of hereditary transmission follow precise Mendelian lines, or as to what characters in any given human individual are dominant and what recessive. Good and bad characteristics are apparently not, for the most part, unit characteristics; and we do not know what are the elementary characters in the native germ plasm that in combination make one man better than another; nor do we know what specific features or combinations of features lie at the basis of such qualities as imagination, good judgment, foresight, or sense of justice. Moreover, we have no precise knowledge as to the extent to which tendencies or potentialities sheathed in the native germ plasm are modifiable by environment, experience, and training. It appears to be certain that economic conditions of the parents and other childhood surroundings do variously check or promote the development of the native capacities of any individual.

Peculiarly untenable, it appears, are the arguments of those who mingle the question of racial inequality with the issue of democracy *versus* aristocracy and seek to find a biologic or blood basis not only for varieties in intellectual capacity among individuals but also for differences in the levels of culture among the various peoples of the world.[3] Anthropologists differentiate races according to superficial

---

[2] See pp. 358–364.
[3] *Supra,* pp. 320–325.

features, such as color of skin and shape of head, and believe that these have definite biological bases not modifiable by changes in environment. They make little claim to knowledge of any differences in sensory and native mental traits. They are only beginning to conduct scientifically safeguarded tests to discover what racial dissimilarities of the latter sort exist and have applied these tests only to races widely differentiated in physical appearance.[4]

When the newly devised "mental tests" have been employed in comparing whites and Negroes in the United States, the results have usually given a higher rating for the whites.[5] These tests, however, have not been made under conditions which could insure that the possibilities of environmental influences were completely eliminated. In a recent examination of Negroes and whites in Jamaica, where the two groups had received generally similar education and lived under generally similar environmental conditions, the results appeared to show some superiority of the Negroes over the whites in sense of rhythm and in the discrimination of time intervals in music; some superiority of the whites over the Negroes in copying geometric figures, drawing models, and fitting blocks into holes; and an equality between the two groups in the accurate repetition of numerical figures.[6] When the ordinary tests have been used to compare American whites with Chinese, Japanese, and Hindus, no differences in favor of the whites have generally been revealed.[7] Certain neurological comparisons of whites, Negroes and Indians have shown a somewhat larger and more complex brain structure

[4] For criticisms of the popular doctrines of racial superiority, see the list on pp. 377–378, *infra.*

[5] See the following: S. L. Pressey and G. F. Teter, "A Comparison of Colored and White Children," *Journal of Applied Psychology,* III (1919), 277–282; Robert M. Yerkes, "Psychological Examining in the United States Army," *Memoirs of the National Academy,* Vol. XV (1921); Edward L. Thorndike, "Intelligence Scores of Colored Pupils," *School and Society,* XVIII (1923), 569–570. See also the summaries in Pitirim Sorokin, *Contemporary Sociological Theories* (1928), pp. 294–297.

[6] Charles B. Davenport, "Do Races Differ in Mental Capacity?" *Human Biology,* I (1929), 70–89.

[7] See Marvin L. Darsie, *The Mental Capacity of American-born Japanese Children,* Comparative Psychology Monographs, Vol. III (1925); Percival M. Symonds, "The Intelligence of the Chinese in Hawaii," *School and Society,* XIX (1924), 442; Gregory D. Walcott, "The Intelligence of Chinese Students," *ibid.,* XI (1920), 474–480; Lewis M. Terman, *Mental and Physical Traits of a Thousand Gifted Children,* Genetic Studies of Genius, I (1925), 55–57; Karl T. Waugh, "A Comparison of Oriental and American Student Intelligence," *Psychological Bulletin,* XVIII (1921), 106; Kwok T. Yeung, "The Intelligence of Chinese Children," *Journal of Applied Psychology,* V (1921), 267–274.

in the whites than in the other two races.[8] Since within many ethnological groups there have been centuries of inbreeding, there may be *a priori* reasons for expecting that there are differences among them in the structures of sense organs and nervous systems; but actual measurements are yet too limited in range and application to afford evidences for any extensive generalizations.

The prevailing opinion among anthropologists is that between heredity and environment as factors determining the differences among "racial" or cultural groups no precise comparison can be made; neither factor has been carefully measured.[9] Physical environment alone does not appear to be the determining influence; for we find varying cultures appearing in similar environments, similar cultures appearing in different environments, cultural characteristics of a given people persisting through changes in environment, whole civilizations disintegrating without change of environment, "high" civilizations developing in unfavorable environments, "low" civilizations in favorable environments. On the other hand, it equally appears that blood is not the overwhelming factor; for we find similar cultural traits appearing among peoples of distinct racial heredity, and vast cultural changes occurring among a people whose racial composition has not changed.

The difficulty in the discrimination is increased by the fact that many of the so-called races of to-day are in reality of mixed racial composition. Slavs, Anglo-Saxons, or Celts are primarily political or ethnological, not strictly anthropological or zoölogical, groups. The Nordic, Alpine, and Mediterranean races of Europe are each "so thoroughly mixed," says Professor Tozzer, "that it is difficult, outside of the Scandinavian countries and the southern tip of Italy, to find any countries or communities where one of these races is in anything like a pure state."[10] And we can say little as to whether racial crossings create hereditary results that are prevailingly bad or prevailingly good; we have no exact evidences that either crossing *per se* or inbreeding *per se* is harmful. We do know that there has been a constant mingling of racial

[8] See Robert B. Bean, "Some Racial Peculiarities of the Negro Brain," *American Journal of Anatomy,* V (1906), 353 ff.

[9] See A. A. Goldenweiser, *Early Civilization* (1926), p. 295; Robert H. Lowie, *Culture and Ethnology* (1917), p. 62; A. M. Tozzer, *Social Origins and Social Continuities* (1925), p. 51; Clark Wissler, *Man and Culture* (1923), pp. 296-297.

[10] Tozzer, *Social Origins and Social Continuities,* p. 42. Cf. also A. C. Haddon, *The Races of Man and Their Distribution* (1924), pp. 189 ff., and F. H. Hankins, *The Racial Basis of Civilization,* Pt. II, Chs. III and VII.

types in all periods of the history of civilized mankind and that the civilizations we call "great" have generally appeared in areas inhabited by populations of heterogeneous racial composition.[11]

It is not denied that, in any given era, there are differences in the cultural attainments of different ethnological or national groups, nor that the differences may be due in part to biologic heredity and natural selection. But it is contended that no scientific case has been established in support of the claims of a biologic supremacy of some particular racial group, such as the Aryans, Teutons, Nordics, Anglo-Saxons, Celts, or Jews. Extensive claims, we have seen, have been made in behalf of the Teutons or Nordics, and both anthropometric and historical arguments have been offered to support them. There is, for example, the familiar contention that the Teuton or Nordic group is characterized by dolichocephaly or "long-headedness"; that the aristocratic or dominant social groups in Western Europe, in ancient, medieval, and modern times, have been predominantly dolichocephalic; that "within any specific race, its more dolichocephalic elements are dominant" and "occupy the higher social strata"; and that "all dominant races are dolichocephalic." [12] The claims appear to be refuted by a variety of anthropometric evidences: many of the most primitive peoples, showing no signs of mental superiority, are definitely dolichocephalic; recent statistical measurements of the cranial indices of gifted children and of adults in the higher social groups show no predominance of dolichocephaly; and other comparisons indicate that murderers are no more brachycephalic than the people generally, and the latter no more so than high professional men.[13] Nor have the advocates of Nordic superiority made any better case in their use of historical evidences. It has been shown that most of the cultural features of modern civilization —in the way of scientific invention and discovery, social institutions, industrial and agricultural methods, moral and religious creeds, and æsthetic forms—appeared first among non-Nordics; and they have

[11] See Roland B. Dixon, *The Racial History of Man* (1923), *passim;* Vernon Kellogg, "The 'Nordics' and the Rest," *New Republic,* XXXV (1923), 278–280.

[12] Georges Vacher de Lapouge, *L'aryen, son rôle social* (1899), p. 395. Cf. also *ibid.,* pp. 40 ff., 410 ff.; B. S. Bramwell, "Observations on Racial Characteristics in England," *Eugenics Review,* XV (1923), 480–491, 556–570, especially 448 ff. and 570.

[13] Paul Topinard, *Anthropology* (translation, 1878), pp. 236–242; Lewis M. Terman, *Mental and Physical Traits of a Thousand Gifted Children,* pp. 166–167, 170; F. G. Parsons, "The Cephalic Index of the British Isles," *Man,* XXII (1922), pp. 19–23; Arthur MacDonald, *Man and Abnormal Man* (1905), p. 19; and the discussion and references in Pitirim Sorokin, *Social Mobility* (1927), Ch. X.

been subsequently developed, refined, and added to by brachycephalic as well as by dolichocephalic types, and by Mediterranean, Alpine, and Caspian groups as well as by Nordic or Teuton "Aryans." [14] Indeed the evidences of history are said to show that the most important features in the culture of any modern racial group are not original but are borrowed from other racial groups and that Nordics have borrowed as extensively as any of the others.[15] In short, the prevailing conclusion among scientific students of modern racial groups appears to be this: differences in manners, institutions, customs, and achievements are probably due in some measure to differences in blood and in some measure to conditions of climate, topography, and other features of the physical environment; but they are mainly the consequences of varying elements in the cultural heritage, historical experiences, and inter-racial contacts of the several groups.

With respect to all the attempts to build doctrines of political and racial aristocracy upon biological principles, the democrat asks his opponent to be at least as cautious as the biologists themselves—from Darwin over a half-century ago to the leading geneticists of to-day. "With civilized nations," Darwin said in 1871, "continued progress depends in a subordinate degree on natural selection." [16] In "man's intellectual and moral nature," said Alfred Russel Wallace two decades later, there are certain admirable and socially beneficial qualities which are of no utility in the struggle for life and which, therefore, cannot "have developed by variation and natural selection alone." [17] "An ever-increasing number of well-meaning persons," Professor Edward M. East warns us, "read a page or two from a biological encyclopædia, and are so surprised by the changed outlook it gives them they forthwith see the answer to every problem immediately." There are, he says further, "few undisputed facts thus far born in the genetic laboratories having an immediate practical application to the course of human

---

[14] Cf. E. Houzé, *L'Aryen et l'anthroposociologie* (1906), pp. 31–33; Roland B. Dixon, *The Racial History of Man*, pp. 514–516.

[15] Robert H. Lowie, *Culture and Ethnology*, p. 34; Tozzer, *Social Origins and Social Continuities*, p. 42; Clark Wissler, *Man and Culture*, p. 295. See also Thomas R. Garth, *Race Psychology: a Study of Racial Mental Differences* (1931); the author, in this survey of the scientific studies, made during the past half-century, to determine the mental capacities of races, reaches the conclusion that "we have never, with all our researching, found indisputable evidence for belief in mental differences which are inherently racial."

[16] Darwin, *Descent of Man* (1871), p. 143.

[17] Wallace, *Darwinism* (1889), p. 463.

progress in the social sense." [18] Professor Raymond Pearl offers a more
emphatic rebuke. "The literature of eugenics," he says, "has largely
become a mingled mess of ill-grounded and uncritical sociology, economics, anthropology, and politics, full of emotional appeals to class
and race prejudices, solemnly put forth as science, and unfortunately
accepted as such by the general public." [19] "Until we know how much
the environment is responsible for," says Thomas Hunt Morgan, "I
am inclined to think that the student of human heredity will do well to
recommend more enlightenment on the social causes of deficiencies rather
than more elimination in the present deplorable state of our ignorance
as to the causes of mental differences." And again: "If within each
human social group the geneticist finds it impossible to discover, with
any reasonable certainty, the genetic basis of behavior, the problems
must seem extraordinarily difficult when groups are contrasted with
each other, where the differences are obviously connected not only with
material advantages and disadvantages resulting from location, climate,
soil, and mineral wealth, but with traditions, customs, religions, taboos,
conventions, and prejudices." [20] Eugenics, says Professor Lancelot Hogben more recently, "has become identified with ancestor worship, anti-
semitism, colour prejudice, anti-feminism, snobbery, and obstruction to
educational progress." [21]

But what can the democrat say as to the showing of the intelligence
tests, elaborately developed in recent years by psychologists and educational experts and adduced by many contemporary critics of democracy as offering a guidance which the biologists cannot supply?
These tests, it seems to be generally agreed, show different levels in certain
forms of intelligence and generally measure the levels consistently—
that is, if a group of adults take the tests on different occasions the
resulting scores of the several individuals of the group remain approximately the same; or if the tests are applied to a given group of
children at different ages, the children maintain generally the same
relative ranking at a later age as that which the tests showed at any
earlier age. [22] Moreover, the tests appear to demonstrate that the capacity
which they measure generally reaches its maximal development at the

[18] East, *Mankind at the Crossroads* (1923), p. 341.
[19] Pearl, "The Biology of Superiority," *American Mercury*, XII (1927), 260.
[20] Morgan, *Evolution and Genetics* (1925), pp. 205, 207.
[21] Hogben, *Genetic Principles in Medicine and Social Science* (1932), p. 209
[22] Edwin G. Boring, "Intelligence as the Tests Test It," *New Republic*, XXXV
(1923), 35–37.

age of from fourteen to sixteen, so that it is not susceptible of elevation by later training and experience. There are differences, however, among the experts themselves as to the effects of environmental conditions in influencing the test-ratings of the children. In a recent symposium among experienced testers, reports were made of conclusions from experiments designed specifically to reveal the relative importance of "nature and nurture" in their effects on intelligence. Some reported that a change from a poor to a good environment produced no appreciable effect on the intelligence rating of the children under examination. Others described the results of their experiments as indicating "that an improvement in environment produces a gain in intelligence" and "that the character of the home is an important factor in the development of the child's intelligence." [23]

What is it that, at best, the mental tests do measure? Not all of a man's qualities and not even the whole of his mental capacity. They may measure certain special abilities whose potentialities for development stop somewhere in the 'teens. They do not measure certain other special abilities which are of great importance as factors of success or usefulness and which are subject to further development throughout normal adult life. There is now no confident agreement as to just what the tests do reveal. Certainly they do not measure courage, steadiness, initiative, inventiveness, capacity for leadership, or a sense of social responsibility. It is even doubted that they measure intelligence in any "general" sense. "There is," declares a psychologist, "no such thing as a test of pure intelligence. . . . Measurable intelligence is simply what the tests of intelligence test." [24] "The intelligence tests we are using are undoubtedly lopsided," says a professor of education; "they test particularly, and almost exclusively, an abstract intelligence which is able to react to spoken and written words"; it is therefore most unscientific to suppose that they yield "a complete and scientific diagnosis of the whole of a pupil's mental capacity and ability." [25] Most psychologists and educators appear now to agree that there are numerous traits which, although not revealed by any formal tests yet devised, are of fundamental importance in determining the quality of human conduct or the

[23] *Nature and Nurture: Their Influence upon Intelligence. Twenty-Seventh Yearbook of the National Society for the Study of Education* (1928), pp. 260, 211 and 330.

[24] Boring, *loc. cit.* (*supra*, p. 359, n. 22), p. 37.

[25] J. Ralph McGaughy, "Tendencies in Supervision," *Teachers College Record,* XXIX (1928), 583.

ability of individuals to make social adjustments satisfying to themselves and others; they further agree that many such traits are to a
significant degree subject to development under the influence of training
and environment.

The democrat denies also that the biographical studies of kinships
among eminent men disprove his doctrine. As to the popular American
canvasses of the numerous notables descended from the brilliant Elizabeth Tuttle, the democratic rejoinder is that the family to which she
belonged did not display qualities which would give any assurance of
such a worthy heritage. Elizabeth herself was divorced by Richard Edwards, "on the ground of her adultery and other immoralities"; one of
Elizabeth's sisters murdered her own son; and one of her brothers
murdered a sister.[26] What eugenist could foresee that a family which,
in one group of brothers and sisters, contained an adulteress, an in-
fanticide, and a sororicide would produce the many able clergymen, university presidents, scientists, jurists, and statesmen of the future?
Sir Francis Galton's study of English judges showed that, of the one
hundred able judges whom he listed as ancestors of able judges, ninety
were apparently the sons of fathers of average standing, and only ten
had eminent fathers.[27] Scientific geneticists of to-day express doubts as
to the practical implications of the tables set up to demonstrate the
inheritance of exceptional ability. Professor Raymond Pearl shows that,
of the eighty-five poets given most extensive mention in the *Encyclopædia Britannica,* only three were descended from parents of sufficient
distinction to be mentioned separately in the *Encyclopædia;* that of
the sixty-three prominently mentioned philosophers, most were the
sons of obscure clergymen, shopkeepers, peasants, watch-makers, clerks,
or petty office-holders; and that only five of the eminent philosophers
produced any descendants of distinction.[28] Other canvasses have been
made of the lowly parentage of great men of the past. We are reminded
that Jesus was the son of a carpenter and Leonardo da Vinci the illegiti-
mate son of a domestic servant; that Shakespeare's father was a butcher
and glover; Beethoven's, a "confirmed drunkard"; Schubert's, a peasant; Farraday's, "a poor blacksmith"; Carlyle's, a stone-mason; Lin-
coln's, a "roving carpenter"—"poor white trash"; Pasteur's, a tanner;
Browning's, a clerk; and that Socrates' mother was a mid-wife; Beetho-

[26] Clarence Darrow, "The Edwardses and the Jukeses," *American Mercury,* VI
(1925), 147–157.
[27] Cf. *supra,* Ch. XI, p. 318, n. 15.
[28] See *supra,* p. 359, n. 19.

ven's, the "daughter of a cook"; and Schubert's, "an ignorant drudge." [29] The author of one of the canvasses, a distinguished geneticist, concludes that "most of the great leaders of mankind come from humble parents." [30] Certainly, numerous examples can be adduced to show that intellectual and artistic excellence often appear in unsuccessful and apparently incompetent families, whom no scientific observer could identify as the bearers of the genius-producing genes.

Professors E. L. Clarke and J. M. Cattell—from whose canvasses of the occupational distribution of the fathers of American men of literature and science Professor L. M. Terman and others have drawn data for their conclusions as to the correlations between innate ability and occupational status—drew no such conclusions themselves.[31] Both challenged the extreme claims of Galton and Pearson as to the great predominance of heredity over opportunity in determining the achievements of men. "There have been," said Clarke, "three especially important factors in the development of American men of letters: a good heredity furnishing stock capable of being developed, an education adequate to develop latent ability, and a social environment furnishing incentive to the naturally endowed and amply educated to turn their attention to literature." [32] The differences in ability, Professor Cattell believed, "may be properly attributed in part to natural capacity and in part to opportunity"; in the present state of our knowledge we cannot heavily weight one factor over the other. "On the one hand, the specific character of performance and degree of success are determined by family position and privilege as well as by physical heredity; on the other hand, marriage, chiefly determined by environment, is an important factor in maintaining family lines." It is peculiarly difficult to find reliable evidences of any hereditary lines of separation between "upper" (professional and business) and "lower" (agricultural and artisan) classes in the United States. "Five or ten generations back," Cattell continued, "most of us have ancestors of nearly the same average physical, intellectual, and social conditions; and selection for ability within this short period must be slight and transient." [33]

[29] Edward G. Conklin, "Biology and Democracy," *Scribner's Magazine*, LXV (1919), 403–412; Fred Eastman, "The Parents of the Great," New York *Herald Tribune*, Nov. 6, 1932, Magazine Section, p. 15. Cf. also Conklin's "Heredity and Democracy," *Journal of Heredity*, X (1919), pp. 161–164.

[30] Conklin, "Biology and Democracy," *Scribner's Magazine*, LXV (1919), p. 411.

[31] See *supra*, Ch. XI, p. 319, n. 16.

[32] Clarke, *American Men of Letters: Their Nature and Nurture* (1916), p. 99.

[33] Cattell, *American Men of Science: a Biographical Dictionary* (third ed., 1921), pp. 786, 788, 785.

Thus the prevailing opinion among scientists appears to be that our knowledge of human heredity is so limited that we can give only very dubious answers to the most significant questions about it.[34] "The single human individual," says Professor Herbert S. Jennings, "has not a single definite prearranged fate or tendency, but a vast number of capabilities, a vast number of keys, as it were, through which the environment may play upon him; a multitude of impulses, tendencies toward action in diverse directions." [35] We cannot measure innate capacity by achievements, for we cannot differentiate the effects which opportunity has had upon the achievements. The mental traits we observe in adults are often the product of an environment that obscures the nature of the inheritance. Environment influences the development of the individual from the beginning of the life of the fertilized egg. Heredity, it is true, supplies a pattern that sets certain limits to the range of variety in the future development of the individual, so that it is not possible, by controlling his training and environment, to make any sort of individual we like out of him. The limits of this hereditary pattern are wide, however, so that we cannot, by selective mating, determine the fate of the individual offspring and make anything we like out of him. In any event, we can identify the biologically superior only incompletely and inconclusively. Biologists generally believe that extremely low grades of intelligence—feeble-mindedness, for example, breed true; [36] but they generally deny that either high or mediocre intelligence breeds true. Moreover, although the biologists agree that human traits produced by environment and training are not inheritable, they do not contend that worthy and useful traits are not created or developed by environment and training; and they do not contend that the varieties of behavior and achievement we observe among normal men are due mainly to specific differences in native endowment. Certainly no way has yet been discovered for selecting out of the total

[34] For general discussions of the biological bases of human traits, by scientific students of heredity, see the bibliographical list on p. 377, *infra*.

[35] Jennings, *The Biological Basis of Human Nature* (1930), p. 170.

[36] Scientists now often express doubts as to the state of our knowledge concerning the heredity of feeble-mindedness. "The often-quoted cases of the Juke and Edwards families," declares Professor J. M. Cattell, "are more largely due to environment and intermarriage within that environment than to the persistence of the traits of one individual through several generations."—(*American Men of Science*, p. 788.) Professor Lancelot Hogben points out also that "feeble-mindedness" is not a mental condition that has been scientifically defined, and that we have no definite knowledge of the hereditary bases of the various conditions we vaguely describe by that general term. (*Genetic Principles in Medicine and Social Science*, 109 ff.)

population those individuals with genes for high mental capacity; and
we have little or no scientific knowledge as to the descent of the normal
mental attributes of men.

If the conclusions of the scientists do not show any incompatibility
between biology and democratic doctrine, what do the lessons of experience prove? What, in the first place, has the democrat to say as to
the charge that popular governments have acutally been, in spheres of
morals and opinion, the most intolerant and tyrannical of all forms of
government and have lent themselves most readily to the inclinations
of average men to impose their beliefs and standards of conduct upon
superior and unusual individuals? His reply is that the charge rests
both upon a misinterpretation of the democratic ideal and upon a mis-
representation of the actual records of democratic governments.

The creed of democracy, it is contended, does not imply faith in the
infallibility of majority opinion. Democracy means government by the
many rather than by the one or the few; but it means more than that.
Theorists in explaining democracy, statesmen in advocating or defending it, constitution-makers in constructing it, have had in mind not only
the conception of a government representing the general body of citizens
but also the conception of government limited in its powers over individual citizens. The association of popular government with limited
government is a characteristic feature of most of the classic defenses of
democracy. Pericles (in the fifth century B. C.), extolling the Athenian
democracy, explained not only that its government was "in the hands,
not of the few, but of the many," but also that its laws gave equal
justice to all and allowed every one to enjoy himself in his own way.
The "dead heroes" of the Peloponnesian War had preferred death rather
than life in subjection to a state (Sparta) that exalted strong authority
and methodical order above individual liberty and free debate. Modern
democratic theorists have generally championed popular rights against
government as well as over government. Milton, in the seventeenth
century, wrote eloquent appeals for both popular sovereignty and toleration: he argued that, although ultimate political authority rested, by
natural right, in the people, yet such an authority included no right to
dictate opinions and private morals; human intelligence and character,
he pointed out, had no chance to grow if law sought to fix the forms

of their expression. The eighteenth century revolutionary "Declarations" in America and France had no more to say of government by consent of the governed than of the obligation upon all governments to refrain from arbitrary interferences with individual liberty.

When a national constitutional system was being set up in the United States, it was the radical democrats who were the most solicitous as to how private rights would fare under a strong centralized government. In the constitution as drafted by the Convention of 1787, there was no detailed formulation of private rights of speech, religion, press, assembly, and petition, or of the traditional guarantees of fair trial before the courts. The more aristocratic and conservative leaders, such as Hamilton and Madison, argued that a government founded upon popular representation needed no limitation by a definition of rights reserved to the individual; in other words, popular choice, direct or indirect, of the principal political officers was a sufficient guarantee of the protection of those rights. The more thoroughgoing democrats were not reassured by the argument; and it was their agitation that insured the addition of a "bill of rights" to the Constitution. When Jefferson, leader of democratic opinion, became President, he set forth, in his inaugural address, his conception of the essential requirements of a true democracy; these included not only rule by the majority but also equal and exact justice and freedom of religion and the press.[37] John Taylor of Caroline—philosophical exponent of Jeffersonian democracy and leading critic of the aristocratic ideas of Hamilton and Adams— described, as fundamental in the democratic features of the American Constitution, both equality of civic and political privileges and limitation upon governmental powers—the latter to be secured partly through a distribution of the functions of government among three departments and partly through a constitutional reservation to the individual of the rights of a free conscience, religion, and press.[38]

The doctrine that a popular majority is morally justified in doing anything it wants to do is a doctrine that has rarely been put forth by important democratic theorists in any age. It is generally only in reference to privileges of private property that the aristocrat is more critical of governmental intervention than the democrat. "Conservatives" and "progressives" in the United States, we have seen, have frequently joined

---

[37] *The Writings of Thomas Jefferson*, ed. by Paul Leicester Ford, VIII, pp. 1–6.
[38] Taylor, *Inquiry into the Principles and Policy of the Government of the United States* (1814), Section VI.

issue over the proper position of the courts as guardians of these privileges against arbitrary regulations by popular legislative bodies. Conservative opinion maintains that private property cannot be made duly
secure unless judges are accorded unlimited and final discretion in nulli-
fying enactments which they regard as violative of property rights.[39]
Progressives oppose that extreme position. They do not ordinarily contend that the courts should lack the power to nullify legislative infrac-
tions of clear and specific provisions of a formal constitution; their
objection is rather to the judicial power to invalidate legislation on the
grounds of its violation of vague requirements of "freedom of contract," "fundamental ideas of property," "vital principles of government," and "the essential nature of all free governments." [40] These
requirements, though the courts generally find them to be embodied
in the constitutional command of "due process of law," are statements
of general political—not technical legal—principles; and judges know
no more about them than any one else. The position of the critic of
judicial review is that, although every government should be so constructed as to safeguard individual freedom, there is no reason why
judges should have the exclusive function of defining the ingredients of
that freedom. It is proper that legislatures should be bound to accept
an expert legal opinion of a court as to the meaning of such technical
expressions as *ex post facto*, "bill of attainder," or "jury trial"; it is
not proper, however, to hold the people bound to accept an obscure
political theory of a court as to whether certain restrictions of the activities of some individuals are reasonably necessary in order to safeguard freedom of activity for others. In deciding such questions, the
argument proceeds, a judge is as subject as any one else to the influence
of his social environment and his training; there can, therefore, be
no assurance that courts will be more effectively solicitous than rep-

[39] Cf. *supra*, Ch. XII, pp. 347–348.
[40] These expressions are from majority opinions in Calder *v.* Bull, 3 Dallas,
386 (1798), and Loan Association *v.* Topeka, 20 Wallace, 655 (1874).
For criticisms of the American doctrine of judicial supremacy, see the following: Gilbert Roe, *Our Judicial Oligarchy* (1912) ; A. M. Kales, *Unpopular Government in the United States* (1914), Ch. XVII; Roscoe Pound, "Liberty of
Contract," *Yale Law Journal*, XVIII (1909), 454–487, and "Courts and Legislation," *American Political Science Review*, VII (1913), 361–383; Thomas Reed
Powell, "The Logic and Rhetoric of Constitutional Law," *Journal of Philosophy,
Psychology and Scientific Methods*, XV (1918), 645–658; Theodore Roosevelt,
"The Judges, the Lawyers and the People," *The Outlook* (New York), CX (1912),
1003–1007. For surveys of the literature on the question, cf. R. G. Gettell, *History
of American Political Thought* (1928), pp. 555–565, and C. E. Merriam, *American
Political Ideas, 1865–1917* (1920), Chs. V and VI.

resentative assemblies in safeguarding substantial interests of all groups in the community. Indeed judges may, from the nature of their technical training and their circumscribed social contact, find it peculiarly difficult to consider such questions in the light of general interests.

The issue over judicial review in the United States arises sharply in reference to decisions of the Supreme Court on the validity of statutes that limit freedom of contract in order to protect substantial interests of working-men or the public. It is admitted on both sides that, under the due-process-of-law clauses of the fifth and fourteenth amendments of the federal Constitution, statutes may abridge liberty of contract only where there are reasonable grounds for the abridgement, and that there may be such grounds if there is a reasonable connection between the limitation and some admittedly lawful object of governmental control. The question as to whether there are valid grounds for the limitation depends, therefore, upon an interpretation not of legal principles but of social, economic, or even physical, facts; and upon such facts the judge is not ordinarily better informed than the legislator. Thus the issue in *Lochner v. New York* [41] (in which the United States Supreme Court held invalid a statute limiting the hours of labor in bakeshops to not more than sixty hours a week or ten hours a day) was the question as to whether or not there was "some fair ground" for thinking that work in a bakeshop was sufficiently unhealthful to justify the New York legislature in limiting the right of contract as to hours of labor in that trade. This was clearly a question of fact, not of law; a physiological question, upon which the legislature had been extensively supplied with supporting expert opinion before it enacted the statute. *Adkins v. Children's Hospital* [42] involved the constitutionality of a statute of Congress setting up a board empowered "to ascertain and declare standards of minimum wages adequate to supply the necessary cost of living to women workers and to maintain them in health and to protect their morals." The Supreme Court, in holding the statute unconstitutional, stated its disagreement with Congress as to a "prevalent connection" between immorality and very low wages; it also declared that it was not convinced by the arguments as to actual benefits resulting from the operation of similar statutes in several of the States; or it found the arguments "only mildly persuasive." Here again the differences between the Court and Congress rested on opinions concerning social facts upon which the judges were

[41] 198 U. S. 45, 1905.
[42] 261 U. S. 525, 1923.

probably not so well informed as many of the people who had advocated the legislation before Congress.

Judges, in their ordinary training and experience, it is said, have no opportunity or occasion to study political and legal questions in their general social bearings. When they consider the economic effects of a statute, they naturally and honestly consider the consequences with which they are most familiar or which they can best understand; and these are the probable effects of the statute upon the interests of economic and professional groups with whom the judges have lived in closest contact. Accordingly, the courts sometimes appear to invalidate an act simply because of its intention to accomplish economic results which the judges do not approve, or (in the words of Chief Justice Taft) "to carry out economic views which the court believes to be unwise and unsound." [43] Even where this unconscious prejudice is not the dominant factor in the decision, the legal training of the judge, it is said, creates in him such an extreme devotion to the sanctity of formal precedent that he feels bound, in many significant instances, to obstruct the valid aims of a democracy. A vague economic doctrine of *laisser-faire* comes to be conceived as a clear legal principle, made obligatory by constitutional provisions on liberty, property, and due process. If judges, under the color of maintaining a vague constitutional requirement of due process of law, have the power to nullify social legislation which they consider novel, not reasonably necessary, or essentially unwise, then the people, said Theodore Roosevelt, become the victims of "perfunctory legalism" and the constitution is perverted "into an instrument for the perpetuation of social and industrial wrong." [44]

Ordinarily the critics of judicial review demand not an abolition of the power but rather a limitation of it or a modification of the manner of its exercise. Some propose formal limits—such as requiring an extraordinary majority among the judges in decisions invalidating statutes, providing for a direct or indirect popular referendum on the court's action, or allowing a legislative body or the voters to over-ride an adverse decision in such cases. Others propose that the formal power of the court be left as it is, and that efforts be made to "educate" the judges and thereby persuade them to interpret laws and constitutions on the basis of a legal logic or philosophy different from that of the

---

[43] In his dissenting opinion in Adkins v. Children's Hospital.
[44] *Proceedings of Ohio Constitutional Convention* (1912), p. 378.

traditional case-law system of the United States.[45] Judges, they argue, should understand that formal analysis of written laws and traditional legal usages is but one of the functions of a judge; for all law is a means to an end, and the end is to obtain not only stability and certainty in legal relations but also progress and justice. Judges must, therefore, give consideration to the broad social effects of legal institutions and doctrines. They should be educated to understand that legal flexibility is one of the essential conditions of both order and progress and that legal theory must be built upon practical considerations which recognize the priority of common interests to individual interests, and of the ends of the law to the legal machinery itself. All the critics agree that some way should be found to prevent or dissuade judges from setting aside— as clearly unreasonable and therefore violative of "due process"—legislation which many admittedly reasonable men have deliberately and persistently advocated on the basis of an extensive and expert study of relevant facts.

The contemporary democrat is usually willing to accept the familiar admonitions of De Tocqueville and Mill, that, even in democracies, means must be found for protecting individuals against those who seek, through governmental prohibitions and compulsions, to impose on others their own habits, creeds, and affiliations. He maintains, however, that this problem is equally before all forms of state; intolerance and the disposition to standardize human conduct are no greater in democracies than in other polities. Indeed, the inclination to establish conformity to type, to shape all individuals into approved molds of opinion and conduct, is not a peculiarity of government in any of its forms. Contemporary experience abundantly shows that the source of that sort of tyranny may just as likely be some organized private group—a trade-union, chamber of commerce or professional association; a church, luncheon club, "constitutional" league, or "reform" society. Where these groups seek political means for the application of their tyranny, monarchies and aristocracies lend themselves to the attempts as readily as democracies. At a time when we witness in Fascism and Sovietism such outstanding assertions of a minority's right to impose its will on all, it can hardly be seriously contended that the disposition to tyrannize over dissentients

---

[45] Cf. Roscoe Pound, "The Need of a Sociological Jurisprudence," *Green Bag*, XIX (1907), 607–615; Oliver Wendell Holmes, Jr., "The Path of the Law," *Harvard Law Review*, X (1897), 457–478.

is a weakness peculiar to majorities. The Fascist minority proclaims its right to relentless supervision over the daily lives of all citizens in order to safeguard the supreme interests of the corporate state. The Communist minority in Russia declares the necessity of its iron-handed rule over the masses, until the latter are persuaded, by centuries of education and experience, of the inevitability of communism.[46] Certainly it would be difficult to show generally, from the records of history, that democracies have been peculiarly unfavorable to intellectual independence and individual self-discipline or that freedom of speech and the press has fared exceptionally well under monarchic and aristocratic governments.

But if democracies are not more intolerant, are they not more inefficient than other forms of state? The democrat claims that his critics do not survey the evidences impartially. They offer examples of the foolish and unjust deeds of democratic assemblies but do not compare these with the recorded mistakes of the agencies of aristocracies. The critics point back to periods of enlightened administration and cultural progress under the governments they approve but ignore other periods that show the same advantages experienced under democratic auspices. The source of the political troubles of modern communities is to be found, the democrat maintains, not in the institutions of popular government but in universal human weaknesses and in the maladjustments of all established institutions to the complex conditions of modern society. History, he believes, supplies no grounds for the hope that a transfer of political power from the general body of citizens to any special class would bring on a more just and efficient social order.

Occasionally the democratic advocate to-day goes further and seeks to make a positive historical case for democracy. He contends that it was under the régime of republican institutions that Athens and Rome made their greatest contributions to civilization and that in both countries degeneration came about under oligarchic and monarchic rule. A competent historian in the United States has sought to make a case for democracy from the modern history of England.[47] He argues that her monarchy of the early seventeenth century and her aristocracy of the early nineteenth century taxed more oppressively and inequitably, spent public funds more recklessly and unscrupulously, managed colonial de-

---

[46] See *supra,* Ch. VI, pp. 172–173, 176–177, and *infra,* Ch. XVII, pp. 477–478.
[47] Edward P. Cheyney, "Historical Tests of Democracy," in *Law in History and Other Essays* (1927), Ch. IV.

pendencies more blunderingly and inhumanely, and gave less encouragement to science and literature, than her democracy of the early twentieth century. Others have shown that in mid-nineteenth century England it was the democratic reformers who led the successful movement to bring honesty and efficiency into the civil service by substituting standards of merit for appointment and promotion in place of the patronage and nepotism that had developed under an aristocratic rule.

The protagonist of democracy finds his faith strengthened by the movement of political events since the World War. The success with which the older democracies (England and her self-governing dominions, the United States, France, Switzerland, and the Scandinavian countries) and most of the new democracies (Czechoslovakia, Finland, and Estonia) have weathered the storms of postwar adjustment and the later economic disorders of the period of the "depression," supply him with new evidences of the efficiency and durability of democracy. He avers that none of these countries has abandoned democracy for dictatorship, even in emergencies. The extraordinary powers, recently vested in the executive heads of some democracies, were not exacted through any threat of armed force but were granted—and are still revocable—through regular constitutional channels; there are no new armed forces to support the powers; no representative assemblies have been abolished or their composition altered, no opposition political parties dissolved, no novel limitations imposed on assembly and discussion or summary methods established for the trial of political offenses. He contends, therefore, that a popular impression that there has been less democracy in the world since the War, or that there has been a recent "breakdown of democracy," is not borne out by the facts. The dictatorships, on the one hand, flourish only in countries that were undemocratically governed before the war; they represent, therefore, no real loss to democracy. On the other hand, the new constitutions of Czechoslovakia, the Baltic states, and Spain, represent net gains to the cause of democracy; for they are operating with fair success, under difficult conditions, in countries that were formerly autocratically governed.[48]

[48] Cf. John Dickinson, "Democracy Has Not Broken Down," *The World*, Sunday, May 20, 1928, editorial section, p. 1; J. M. Kenworthy, "Can Democracy Survive," *The Outlook* (London), LIX (1927), pp. 423–424; Walter Lippmann, "The Strength of Democracy," in the *Herald Tribune* (N. Y.), March 30, 1933; Simeon Strunsky, "Democracy Still Stands Firm," in the New York *Times*, Sunday, May 21, 1933, magazine section. Cf. *supra*, p. 303.

CONCLUSION

Evidences such as the foregoing indicate the sort of empirical argument that can be made in defense of democracy. Nothing has yet been written, however, that will definitively settle the question in this manner. Indeed it appears that no thoroughly scientific or empirical case can be established in support of democracy, aristocracy, or any other form of state. The criteria for distinguishing the forms are not very precise, and on all sides there is apt to be some assembling of *ex parte* testimony. Frequently the advocate of any one of the forms begins with some sort of emotional bias and then, deliberately or unconsciously, selects the particular scientific doctrines or historical evidences that seem to confirm his prejudices, or that at least enable him to refute the exaggerated claims of his opponents. There appears to be nothing in science or history to indicate that the predilections of the democratic theorist are unsound.

The prevailing democratic theory to-day is, however, relatively moderate in its pretensions—disillusioned as to some of the claims made by its earlier dogmatists. The theory admits, first, that democracy will not succeed under all sorts of conditions; secondly, that, even where conditions are favorable for its success, it must recognize the limits of its fruitful competence; and, thirdly, it must submit itself to the test of full and critical examination of its performance.

Democracy then, its advocates agree, in the first place, is unrealizable in an unsuitable social milieu. Its success is dependent upon the existence of a "civic" sense among the people generally: a rational like-mindedness and an imaginative sympathy that in some degree transcend economic and cultural differences, and a general disposition among the people to put into high governmental office the sort of persons who act largely under the influence of such attitudes. It presupposes also that the citizens have enough intellectual and moral vigor (whether derived from heredity or experience) to withstand persistent deception by demagogues and to apply some discriminating judgments to the policies of their chosen leaders. It is a typical democratic belief that the peoples of Western Europe and of all English-speaking countries have these essential political virtues in a measure sufficient for the general success of democracy and that democracy can also be set up, in gradual instalments, among other more or less civilized peoples, if popular education and equalization of economic opportunity are extended among them at the same time.

In the second place, the serious advocate of democracy agrees that, if it is to be effective, it must keep its action within proper limits. General popular voting should be confined to the decision of basic issues —the popular election of only a few, most important, policy-determining officials, or the acceptance or rejection by popular vote of only the most fundamental measures; the general governmental policy must allow as much territorial and functional devolution as practicable; the individual cannot participate effectively in deciding general issues until he has had some experience in deciding local or vocational issues with which he is in more intimate association.

Thirdly, democracy needs free and informed discussion of governmental affairs. The people do not govern merely by having a right to choose their governors. They must have also the opportunity to understand and criticize what these officers are doing. A democracy, therefore, requires a system of general education, an intelligent and independent press, and freedom of association and discussion. Education must be general not merely in the sense that it is available to all but also that it is not overspecialized or mainly factual; and it must be of a sort to supply the incentives and develop the potentialities for free and effective thinking on political questions. Public authority must, if the private press does not, provide means for supplying the citizens with correct and intelligible description and interpretation of the aims and methods of those who hold public office.[49] And all citizens must have full opportunity for association, discussion, and peaceful protest; democracy is not so much the right of each to have his ideas adopted as it is the right and opportunity of each to have his ideas heard and to hear the ideas of all others.

Thus moderate democratic and moderate aristocratic doctrines are not far apart to-day. Just as the latter does not challenge the former's ideal of equality of opportunity and of assignment of political function according to merit rather than social position, so the former does not challenge the latter's ideal of government by those fitted to govern. The troublesome problems are how to define the qualities that make men fit to govern and how to discover the men who are endowed with these

[49] Cf., *passim*, the following: Walter Lippmann, *The Phantom Public* (1925); H. J. Laski, *The Dangers of Obedience and Other Essays* (1930), and *Liberty in the Modern State* (1930).

qualities. The democrat has no major premise as to the sameness of ability among members of the community; he simply denies that we can discover any close correlation between natural or biological superiority and economic or professional position, or that we have any evidence that the general political capacity of average men is lower than that of any determinable minority group. Accordingly, he is skeptical of all schemes for improving government on conventionally aristocratic lines—by assigning special political powers to members of the learned professions, superior technicians, persons of high social station, or successful business men. Neither distinction in scientific or artistic achievement nor success in business gives any assurance of an unusual endowment in the qualities of a wise governor: good judgment, intellectual courage, a high sense of honor, and a breadth of interest and information in reference to public affairs. Several writers have recently recorded deeds and utterances, just before and during the "depression," of practical American aristocrats—captains of industry and conservative statesmen —revealing defects of public wisdom and foresight in the very types of "superior men" exalted by the contemporary censors of democracy.[50] It can also easily be shown that the censors, in writings berating the common man's romanticism and shallow reasoning on public questions, display these weaknesses themselves; for they glibly set up great social laws on the basis of slight and selected evidences drawn from a very inexpert reading of history and the biological sciences. What men then, the democrat asks, possess unusual wisdom outside their special fields? "It does not follow," even Le Bon admitted, "that because an individual knows Greek or mathematics, is an architect, a veterinary surgeon, a doctor, a barrister, he is endowed with a special intelligence on social questions." [51] "It is doubtful," a distinguished classical scholar said recently, "whether actual history shows the political judgment of the so-called upper educated classes to have been sounder than that of the masses." [52]

Particularly in groups do bankers, lawyers, engineers, professors, or artists appear to act as emotionally, as fully under the reflex influence of subconscious impulses, as do "common" men. Le Bon, whose description of "crowd psychology" has supplied arguments for many at-

[50] See, for example: Edward Angly, *Oh Yeah?* (1931); Arthur Pound and Samuel T. Moore, eds., *They Told Barron* (1930), and *More They Told Barron* (1931); Gilbert Seldes, *The Years of the Locust* (1933).

[51] Le Bon, *The Crowd: a Study of the Popular Mind* (translation, 1922), p. 212. Cf. *supra*, Ch. XI, p. 314.

[52] Paul Shorey, in an address before the Convocation of the University of the State of New York, October 21, 1927.

tacks on democracy, insisted that crowd characteristics were not peculiar to assemblages of the rank and file. "As soon as a few individuals are gathered together they constitute a crowd, and, though they should be distinguished men of learning, they assume the characteristics of crowds with regard to matters outside their specialty." "In a crowd men always tend to the same level; and, on general questions, a vote recorded by forty academicians is no better than that of forty water-carriers." [53] In other words, when it is a matter of forming a common decision on matters of general interest, specialists in their several fields are apt to bring to the common task only the intelligence and sentiments of average men.

The problem of leadership under any form of constitution is perhaps, as Plato understood it to be: how to find, not the captain of industry, military hero, social patrician, scholar, or technician; but the philosopher —the man of well-balanced mind and temperament, possessing the capacity and disposition to look upon public questions in their general, intrinsic, and permanent, rather than their factional, or superficial, and ephemeral aspects. What sort of organization is likely to bring forth and maintain a following for such a leader? Have not, one advocate asks, monarchies and aristocracies often exalted their selfish and incompetent men and trampled upon their great men? [54] And to Mencken's assertion that it was the mob of plain people that repudiated Socrates, Christ, Savonarola, and Galileo, the democrat can reply that it was Aristophanes, prominent aristocrat, who led the assault upon Socrates; that Savonarola had a strong popular following and was defeated only when he incurred the disfavor of the social and ecclesiastical patricians of his day; and that monarchic and aristocratic groups played the chief parts in the prosecutions of Christ and Galileo.

Thus the democrat believes that no other method is better than the democratic method for identifying and bringing to the top the men of high political character, and that democracy, more nearly than other forms, confines these men to their function of leadership and prevents them from becoming dictators. Finally, it is said, democracy brings peculiar benefits, of a moral or spiritual sort, to the rank and file. To treat men as equals makes them more coöperative in spirit and more active in efforts to mitigate inequality.

[53] Le Bon, *op cit.*, pp. 48–49, 211–212.
[54] Ivor Brown, *The Meaning of Democracy* (revised ed., 1926), Ch. XII.

The democrat then, on the one hand, does not concede that the records show aristocracies and monarchies to be actually more competent than democracies in providing a community with efficient administration and stable public order; and he maintains, on the other hand, that such advantages are less secure and less broadly beneficial where they are conferred or imposed by a ruling minority than where they are obtained in a manner involving some conscious response and collaboration on the part of the persons affected. He holds that no minorities are ever so superior in wisdom and self-control that they do not constantly require both the enlightenment and the restraint which come from the necessity of persuading the minds and wills and maintaining the confidence and respect of the people whom they seek to lead. In short, the rank and file are generally able to make a relatively intelligent discrimination between a group that intends to further the public interest and some other group, animated by narrower motives; and their participation in political power is indispensable for developing in them the interest in government, respect for law, and coöperative feeling which are in some measure essential to stable government in any community too enlightened and virile to be controlled mainly by fear of coercion.

SELECT BIBLIOGRAPHY

THE GENERAL DEFENSE OF DEMOCRACY

Bascom, John, "The Alleged Failure of Democracy," *Yale Review*, IX (1900), 253–264.

Brown, Ivor, *The Meaning of Democracy* (London, 1920; 1926).

Bryce, James, *Modern Democracies* (New York, 1921), Vol. II, Chs. LVIII–LXVIII, LXXIV, LXXX.

Burns, Cecil D., *Democracy: Its Defects and Advantages* (New York, 1929).

Cheyney, Edward P., *Law in History and Other Essays* (New York, 1927), Ch. IV: "Historical Tests of Democracy."

Corwin, Edward S., *The Democratic Dogma and the Future of Political Science, and Other Essays* (Shanghai, 1930): title essay.

Ellwood, Charles A., "Democracy and Social Conditions in the United States," *International Journal of Ethics*, XXVIII (1917–1918), 499–514.

Kenworthy, J. M., "Can Democracy Survive?" *The Outlook* (London), LIX (1927), 423–424.

Lindsay, A. D., *The Essentials of Democracy* (Philadelphia, 1929).

Masaryk, Thomas G., *Les problèmes de la démocratie* (Paris, 1924).

Michel, Henry, *La doctrine politique de la démocratie* (Paris, 1901).

Montgomery, Richard, "The Essence of Democracy," *New Age*, XXXVIII (1925–1926), 175–177, 187–189, 201–202.

Morley, John, *Critical Miscellanies*, 4 vols. (New York, 1886–1908), IV, 265–326: "Democracy and Reaction."

Sait, Edward M., *Democracy* (New York and London, 1929).

Smith, T. V., *The American Philosophy of Equality* (Chicago, 1927).

——————, *The Democratic Way of Life* (Chicago, 1926).

Soltau, Roger, *French Political Thought in the Nineteenth Century* (New Haven, 1931), Ch. XIII.

Woolf, Leonard, *After the Deluge: a Study of Communal Psychology* (New York, 1931), especially Pt. II, Ch. III.

Wright, Henry Wilkes, *The Moral Standards of Democracy* (New York, 1925).

THE BIOLOGISTS' DISCUSSION OF HUMAN TRAITS

Carr-Saunders, Alexander M., *Eugenics* (New York, 1926).

Castle, William E., *Genetics and Eugenics* (Cambridge, Mass., 1924).

Conklin, E. G., "Biology and Democracy," *Scribner's Magazine*, LXV (1919), 403–412.

——————, "Heredity and Democracy," *Journal of Heredity*, X. (1919), 161–164.

——————, *Heredity and Environment* (Princeton, 1922), pp. 249–256, 287–315.

Cook, O. F., and Cook, R. C., "Biology and Government," *Journal of Heredity*, X (1919), 250–253.

East, Edward M., and Jones, D. F., *Inbreeding and Outbreeding* (Philadelphia, 1919).

Hogben, Lancelot, *Genetic Principles in Medicine and Social Science* (New York, 1932).

Jennings, Herbert S., *The Biological Basis of Human Nature* (New York, 1930).

Kellogg, Vernon, *Mind and Heredity* (Princeton, 1923).

Morgan, Thomas Hunt, *Evolution and Genetics* (Princeton, 1925).

Parker, George H., *What Evolution Is* (Cambridge, Mass., 1926), Ch. V.

Pearl, Raymond, "The Biology of Superiority," *American Mercury*, XII (1927), 257–266.

SCIENTIFIC CRITICISM OF THE DOCTRINES OF RACE SUPERIORITY

Boas, Franz, *The Mind of Primitive Man* (New York, 1911).

Davenport, C. B., "Do Races Differ in Mental Capacity?" *Human Biology*, I (1929), 70–80.

Dixon, Roland B., *The Racial History of Man* (New York, 1923).

Dorsey, George A., "Race and Civilization," Ch. X of Charles A. Beard, ed., *Whither Mankind* (New York and London, 1928).

Garth, Thomas R., *Race Psychology: a Study of Racial Mental Differences* (New York, 1931).

Goldenweiser, A. A., *Early Civilization* (New York, 1922).

Haddon, A. C., *The Races of Man and Their Distribution* (Cambridge, Eng., 1924).

Hankins, F. H., *The Racial Basis of Civilization: a Critique of the Nordic Doctrine* (New York and London, 1926).

Kellogg, Vernon, "The 'Nordics' and the Rest," *New Republic,* Vol. XXXV (1923), 278–280.

Kroeber, A. L., *Anthropology* (New York, 1923), Chs. IV and VII.

Lowie, Robert H., *Culture and Ethnology* (New York, 1917).

Ogburn, William F., *Social Change, with Respect to Culture and Original Nature* (New York, 1922).

Tozzer, A. M., *Social Origins and Social Continuities* (New York, 1925).

Wissler, Clark, *Man and Culture* (New York, 1923), especially Chs. VI, XIII, XV.

Zollschan, Ignaz, *Das Rassenproblem unter besonderer Lagen der judischer Rassenfrage* (Vienna, 1910).

PART III

POLITICAL AUTHORITY AND INDIVIDUAL LIBERTY

CHAPTER XIV

THE OPPOSITION TO STATE INTERFERENCE

THE PROBLEM OF A CRITERION

THE most persistent of all political questions is this: To what extent or in what spheres may government properly control individual conduct? The problem is considered important by all except the political absolutists, who hold that the authority of the supreme government of a state—although it may be restrained by the commands of God, the laws of physical nature, or rules of expediency—is morally omnicompetent and irresponsible in its dealings with private citizens and subjects. All others set limits to state authority in the rights and interests of individuals.

It is generally agreed that the problem of defining the proper limits to political authority is not solved by perfecting the form of government according to either aristocratic or democratic standards of perfection. On the one hand, men of high intelligence and lofty ideals are often, as political rulers, intolerant and meddlesome, or unwisely benevolent and paternalistic. On the other hand, majority rule is no guarantee against oppressive governmental interference with individuals and with minority groups; the "self-government" of a democracy, as Mill pointed out, is not the government of each man by himself but the government of each by the rest of the community. There are always some groups that try to use government to exploit other groups or to protect or reform them by means that destroy incentives or opportunities for self-development.

Inevitably, if there is to be a comprehensive organization of society, there must be some governmental restraints upon individual choice. The problem is to discover what sort of activities of the individual must be controlled by government and in what acts he should be left free from governmental guidance or restraint and permitted to do as he pleases. This is the most difficult of all the problems of political theory. No clear and practical solution has ever been found. When we oppose some particular governmental intervention, we are apt—ignoring the numerous governmental interferences upon which we constantly rely and the varied governmental assistance which we constantly accept without question— to express an unbounded faith in the ability of every normal individual to take care of himself and an unqualified distrust of governmental action. Or if we attempt to define the criterion for discriminating between the kind of intervention which safeguards and that which destroys the values of individual freedom, the criterion is usually a very general one, and there is never certainty as to how it is to be applied.

If the criterion is "natural rights"—so that government may interfere to safeguard those rights but may not infringe them and may not intervene where they are not threatened—we still have the questions as to what, in concrete cases, the natural rights are and what sort of governmental action violates them or what sort of private conduct destroys them so that governmental intervention is necessary for their protection. We may agree that man has inherent and inalienable rights to life, liberty, property, and the pursuit of happiness, but disagree, for example, as to whether these fundamental rights give to every man a right to jury trial in all ordinary criminal cases, to compensation in all instances where private property is taken for public use, and a right not to be taxed except for a public purpose. Some undertake to define these and other familiar claims as natural rights which no state can justly infringe and which a court must sustain whether or not they are incorporated in the formal law of a state; others define them as legal rights—that is, rights in so far as they are embodied in constitutions or other forms of established law.[1] In other words, we differ as to whether these are rights in themselves or only means to some more universal and fundamental rights which, under various conditions, can be protected as well by other means. We thus disagree as to what natural rights are, how they should be maintained, and what their relative values are when they come into conflict with one another.

There are similar difficulties when attempts are made to supplant or supplement the criterion of natural rights by some more practical test. Commonly an effort is made to draw a distinction between conduct that affects others and conduct that affects only the doer. Here the argument of John Stuart Mill is the fullest and most familiar. "The only purpose," he said, "for which power can be rightfully exer-

---

[1] Cf. Loan Association v. Topeka, 20 Wall. 655 (1875), Monongahela Navigation Co. v. U. S., 148 U. S. 312 (1893); and see Charles G. Haines, *The Revival of Natural Law Concepts* (1930).

cised over any member of a civilized community, against his will, is to prevent harm to others." [2] In so far as the consequences of an act affect only the doer, government has no excuse for intervening. The warrant for the restraints imposed by society must never be sought in the good, physical or moral, of the individual restrained. It is not the task of laws and conventions to compel a man to be prudent, temperate, or self-respecting. Let him acquire these virtues by experiencing the penalties that fall naturally upon any one who neglects them. Where a government interferes in matters of opinion and moral conduct, it is apt to interfere in the wrong place, restraining innocent forms of enjoyment and enforcing prevalent modes of conduct upon those who dissent in no harmful ways. This checks wholesome variety in discussion and behavior and supports an unimaginative popular opinion in efforts to reduce all individuals to common types.

This is probably the most widely accepted principle for the determination of the proper scope of political interference, but there are uncertainties in applying it. All may agree, for example, that, on the one hand, government should not punish a man for drinking intoxicating beverages, even when he drinks to the extent of injuring his moral character or his physical and mental health; but that, on the other hand, government may properly punish him for offensive manifestations of intoxication in public, or for driving on the public highways while intoxicated. Beyond this point there is sharp disagreement, although all accept the principle that a government should interfere only with conduct that affects the welfare of others substantially, directly, and adversely. One side contends that government has no warrant to prohibit the general traffic in intoxicating beverages because it thereby restrains sales to the vast number of buyers who affect only themselves by their consumption of the beverages. The other side argues that, since consumption of the beverages often leads directly to neglect of lawful dependents and to violent and reckless behavior in public, a general prohibition upon the manufacture and sale is in reality a restraint upon a business that facilitates an indulgence likely to cause injury to others. Similar difficulties appear in applying the principle to questions as to the propriety of legislation limiting freedom of contract in fixing hours and wages of labor. One side maintains that where laborers enter a contract under the pressure of no physical threat or otherwise traditionally

[2] Mill, *On Liberty* (1859), p. 23, and see Chs. I and IV. Page references are to the second edition (Boston, 1863).

unlawful act by the employer, the injuries they suffer from long hours or low wages are self-inflicted and are not properly a concern of government. The other side maintains that the community generally suffers from any physical weakening or social degradation of workers by long hours and low wages; or that differences in the economic situations of employers and wage-workers, respectively, enable the former actually to dictate terms of a contract, so that the latter do not voluntarily assent to the contracts from which they receive injury; in either case a government, in setting limits to terms of the contract, is preventing employers and wage-earners from entering into agreements that harm the community; or it is restraining one party to the contract from forcing injurious terms upon the other.

Obviously we can make no rigid discrimination between acts that concern the doer and those that concern others. The criterion serves only as a rough and general guide for those who maintain that the qualities we value most are cultivated not by obedience but by free volition, and that human progress is impossible where legislation or social opinion narrowly confines the fields within which every normal individual may give expression, in thought, speech, and action, to his peculiar attributes. "Society," it is said, "gains in sanity, health, and security by suffering each man to speak his mind freely, to follow his own feeling, tastes, sentiments, to plan his life as best he can according to his own notion, rather than by coercing him into a life approved by his fellows." [3]

There are other criteria, and the form of the argument varies according to the particular sort of freedom that is advocated. One man exalts individual freedom in morals and opinions and yet supports extensive governmental regulation of private industrial activity; another supports restraints upon moral conduct and upon political and economic discussion and yet calls himself an individualist because he opposes political interference in the distribution of wealth.

The word "individualism" appears to have been first used in the early nineteenth century as a term of general ethical significance, indicating the characteristic disposition of the type of person who refrains from interfering with others and demands that they refrain from interfering with him. Soon the term was employed in its political sense, as the name for a doctrine that governmental institutions and policies should be appraised solely according to their effects on the welfare of

[3] Silas Bent, "Freedom of Speech, Conscience and the Press," in *Freedom in the Modern World*, H. M. Kallen, ed. (1928), p. 142.

individuals. The doctrine also implies that, in ordinary matters of moral and economic conduct, governments, either by their restraints or their services, can contribute little to individual welfare and indeed tend to destroy it if they go any further than to suppress crimes and torts, maintain public order, and provide a secure monetary system and a few other of the basic and universal economic needs of a trading community. Political individualism in this general sense, we have seen, was part of the heritage of ideas in the middle of the nineteenth century, closely related to the dominant ethical and economic doctrines of that period. There were the Protestant-Christian doctrine of the supremacy of individual conscience over ecclesiastical authority, the natural-rights doctrine of human equality and freedom, and the classical-economic assumption that the normal individual is the best judge of his own interests and in pursuing them best serves the interests of the rest of society.

NON-INTERFERENCE IN MORALS AND OPINIONS

The contemporary arguments for moral and intellectual freedom contain little that is new. When a government makes what appear to be unusual or exaggerated efforts to standardize belief and conduct, then we find, for the most part, restatements of the classic arguments of Luther, Milton, Locke, Spinoza, Fénelon, Montesquieu, Voltaire, and Mill: [4] matters of belief, these men maintained, can be determined only by the powers of rational persuasion or by divine revelation and inspiration; coercive efforts to establish uniformity in morals and opinions are sure to fail; man has a natural right to be free in matters of opinion and private morals; and peace and happiness flow from a policy of toleration.

All these ideas survive in the contemporary case for freedom of speech; but the main contentions are three, and they are closely related: a policy of restraint hampers the intellectual and moral development of the individual restrained; it deprives society of an indispensable means for discovering truth and securing its widest and most effective acceptance; and it makes popular government impossible. [5] Milton

[4] See particularly, John Milton, *Areopagitica*, 1644; John Locke, *Letters on Toleration*, 1690–1706; and Mill, *Liberty*.

[5] In the later nineteenth century, the works of Charles Renouvier (1815–1903) contain perhaps the most effective defense of moral and intellectual liberty; see his *Science de la morale* (1869).

In the early twentieth century, Émile Faguet's *Le libéralisme* (1912) is important. Among the most recent works, the following state the case incisively:

stressed the first idea and Mill the second. "Reason is but choosing," said Milton, and liberty is the nurse of character and wit; there is no exercise of intelligence or virtue where there is no opportunity to make up one's mind as to what is right and true; the minds and souls of men stop growing if they feed only upon what is fed out to them by authoritative custodians of truth and goodness.[6]

Mill made the now familiar argument that an opinion which political authority or social convention seeks to discredit often turns out to be true and that, even though events might prove it to be partially or wholly false, society would suffer from the suppression of it.[7] In the first place, governments, majorities, and social aristocrats are not infallible. Majorities and authorities of the past have held opinions which we now consider erroneous; Socrates and Christ were condemned by both government and public opinion for holding doctrines contrary to those approved as right by the prevailing moral and patriotic judgments of their times; and it is likely that some of the cranks of to-day hold views which future generations will find to be right. Secondly, the opinions which government or social convention seeks to suppress may contain portions both of truth and error; the discrimination between the two and the replacement of the erroneous element by the truth are made possible only by discussion and trial. Finally, even though the opinion which some group seeks to suppress proves to be wholly wrong, present and future generations suffer by the silencing of it; for an imposed belief is a belief held without understanding of its ground and meaning and therefore without conviction. Such a belief fails to exert its natural effect upon disposition and conduct. It is collision with error and adverse opinion that creates the clearest impression of the meaning of one's opinion and the greatest confidence in its validity and in the practicability of living according to it. It is liberty in contradicting and disproving a prevailing opinion that is most likely to win over the adherence of dissenters. "The beliefs which we have most warrant for have no safeguard to rest on but a standing invitation to the whole world to prove them unfounded."[8] It is a poor service to any creed—Christianity,

Harold J. Laski, *Liberty in the Modern State* (1930); Everett Dean Martin, *Liberty* (1930); and the titles by H. M. Kallen (*supra*, p. 384, n. 3), and Zechariah Chafee, Jr., *infra*.

For bibliographies on freedom of speech, see Zechariah Chafee, Jr., *Freedom of Speech* (1920), pp. 377–386; Theodore Schroeder, *Free Speech Bibliography* (1922).

[6] Milton, *Areopagitica* (Morley ed., 1884), p. 329.
[7] Mill, *Liberty*, Ch. II.
[8] *Ibid.*, pp. 40–41.

democracy, capitalism, or communism—to prevent the free criticism of it.

In the United States, these ideas of Mill have been stated incisively by Justices Holmes and Brandeis of the Supreme Court, in various opinions setting forth their interpretations of the meaning and scope of the guarantees of free speech and due process in the American constitution: "The best test of truth is the power of the thought to get itself accepted in the competition of the market"; in frank expression of conflicting opinion "lies the greatest promise of wisdom in governmental action"; and the founders of the American republic "believed that freedom to think as you will and to speak as you think are means indispensable to the discovery and spread of political truth." [9]

Contemporary discussion places particular emphasis upon the third contention mentioned above—the importance of free discussion as an essential requirement of popular government. Democracy, it is said, is unrealizable without freedom of political discussion. A right to vote gives a man no real part in controlling government unless he is free to form his own opinions about his vote, to hear what others have to say about the issues, and to persuade others to adopt his opinions. Here, moreover, it is not merely a question of the absence of restraint; presence of opportunity is equally essential.[10] Forming opinions freely requires more than being permitted by law to express and publish opinions freely; it requires also an actual access to relevant information and interpretation. True opinion can prevail in a contest with false opinion only where the facts to which the opinions relate are equally available to both sides. The impediments to popular freedom of opinion now arise no more from direct repression by governments and dominant social groups than from the unreliability and inadequacy of the existing means of supplying the people with the facts and points of view out of which may be formed opinions that can in any rational sense be considered free. The citizens generally are victimized by official propaganda during wars and by unofficial propaganda in times of peace. Political parties, partisan newspapers, associations of working-men, business men, and farmers, leagues for the advocacy of "reforms" or for the defense of "security"—all these agencies constantly put forth distorted or one-sided

[9] Dissenting opinion of Justice Holmes in Abrams v. U. S., 250 U. S. 616 (1919), at p. 630; dissenting opinion of Justice Brandeis in Gilbert v. State of Minnesota, 254 U. S. 325 (1920), at p. 338; and Brandeis' concurring opinion in Whitney v. California, 274 U. S. 357 (1927), at p. 375.

[10] See Laski, *Liberty in the Modern State, passim.*

argument and information.[11] The ordinary individual cannot by himself, however, obtain the knowledge that will enable him to think freely about the problems of government, even on the limited number of issues that should be properly submitted to popular decision. How can it be supplied to him? The intelligent advocate of democracy and individualism now recognizes that these creeds need not so much a defense of their virtues as a demonstration of ways for insuring that those who report and interpret political facts and proposals do so honestly, impartially, and intelligibly.

However, the individualist argument proceeds, democracies, as well as other forms of government, do often fail not only in providing the means of free discussion but also in adequately recognizing the right itself.[12] Freedom of speech is unnecessarily restrained when governments, in war times, punish honest criticism of war aims and methods; when, in peace times, legislative assemblies expel members for their unorthodox political or economic doctrines; when public school boards dismiss or discriminate against teachers on similar grounds; or when city police dissolve public meetings assembled to advocate opinions discredited by those in control of government. Even judges, it is complained, on some occasions lend their support to the policy of repression; for they permit prosecutors to browbeat unpopular witnesses and to bring in testimony, as to a defendant's political views, that has no relation to the crime with which he is charged; or they refuse to set aside the conviction of a "radical" even when it has been shown that the conviction has been obtained through the use of perjured testimony;[13] and in labor disputes, they issue injunctions that prohibit not only criminal acts but also peaceful picketing, orderly parades, and the public utterance of honest arguments in support of a strike.[14]

[11] On recent propaganda, see the folowing: Edward L. Bernays, *Propaganda* (1928); Harold D. Lasswell, *Propaganda Technique in the World War* (1927); Arthur Ponsonby, *Falsehood in War-time* (1928); Peter Odegard, *Pressure Politics* (1928).

On the control of public opinion by newspapers, cf. the titles by Angell, Belloc, Lippmann, Sinclair, and Villard on p. 405, *infra;* and on the general subject of public opinion in a democracy, the titles by Graves, Lippmann, Lowell, and Sait, *loc. cit.*

[12] See E. S. Bates, *This Land of Liberty* (1930); Everett Dean Martin, *Liberty;* Leon Whipple, *The Story of Civil Liberty in the United States* (1927).

[13] See Felix Frankfurter, *The Case of Sacco and Vanzetti* (1927); Ernest J. Hopkins, *What Happened in the Mooney Case* (1932); Arthur Garfield Hayes, *Trial by Prejudice* (1933), and the titles in the immediately preceding note.

[14] See *Limiting Scope of Injunctions in Labor Disputes: Hearings before a Subcommittee of the Committee of the Judiciary, United States Senate, 70th Congress, 1st session, on S. 1482* (Government Printing Office, Washington, 1928).

All advocates of "free speech" admit the necessity of some governmental limits upon it; for speech, the individualist has to acknowledge, is in some cases—as in libel and slander, indecent or blasphemous utterances in public, or words clearly and directly instigating insurrection or disorder—an injury to others of the sort that governments, under any positive political creed, are meant to deal with. The practical difficulty is in finding reasonable and workable tests of what are proper uses and what are abuses of freedom of speech. In relation to obscenity and blasphemy, the theory attempts to find some midway position: accepting, on the one hand, a suppression where there are clear reasons for believing that the public utterance will degrade public morals or incite crime; opposing, on the other hand, any censorship for the purpose of protecting society against religious or ethical heresy.[15] As to political discussion and criticism, the contention is that governmental restraint should be imposed only when the utterances create an obvious danger that they will bring about directly some forcible resistance to government or some breach of the peace. The consistent and courageous individualist is willing to permit the public expression of any sort of criticism of government or the advocacy of any sort of political doctrine—even that which condemns all government and condones violent means to secure its overthrow—provided only that the utterances, considered in the circumstances in which they are delivered, create no reasonable grounds for believing that they will provoke promptly some act of violence.[16] Speech, it is said, should be judged by its probable and immediate effects, not by its possible and remote tendency to provoke insurrection or other crime. There is no justification, for example, in punishing utterances on the grounds that they might "induce an uprising against government . . . at some indefinite time in the future." [17]

The records of history, the individualist contends, prove the futility of repression as a means of maintaining political security. "If there were virtue in repression, the Bourbons would still be on the throne of France, the Romanoffs would still be on the throne of Russia, Spain would still be a great empire, the Hapsburgs would still rule a Holy

See also Felix Frankfurter and Nathan Greene, *The Labor Injunction* (New York, 1930).

[15] Chafee, *Freedom of Speech*, pp. 170–172.

[16] *Ibid.*, pp. 213–228. See also Justice Holmes' majority opinion in Schenck *v.* U. S., 249 U. S. 47 (1919) and the minority opinions of Justices Holmes and Brandeis in Abrams *v.* U. S., 250 U. S. 616 (1919) and Schaefer *v.* U. S., 251 U. S. 466 (1920).

[17] From Justice Holmes' dissenting opinion in Gitlow *v.* People of New York, 268 U. S. 652 (1925), p. 673.

Roman Empire, and the Federalist party might still be in power in Washington." [18] Tolerance of protest would doubtless not have perpetuated, but it might have prolonged, these régimes; a policy of tolerance, moreover, would have insured a less abrupt and destructive transference of power into new hands and would have made more likely the transmission of the virtues of these régimes to those succeeding. Governments should, therefore, in the interests of their own security, welcome outspoken criticism and vigorous protest. Thus it may be, and indeed frequently is, a profoundly patriotic and orderly spirit that inspires defense of the right to criticize government. "No government," said Thomas Jefferson, "ought to be without censors. . . . If virtuous, it need not fear the fair operation of attack and defense." [19]

However, the advocate of freedom of opinion and conduct is not preeminently interested in the security of governments. National solidarity and political stability are not, he maintains, ends in themselves. The paramount aim of all social institutions is the free development of human personality. Political authority is, therefore, good only in so far as it helps to make possible that development. The supreme test of human progress is the measure of intellectual and moral freedom that individual men and women enjoy.

ECONOMIC LAISSER-FAIRE

The designation "individualist" is now claimed generally by those who are less interested in moral and intellectual than in economic freedom. Their concern is to show the values of a governmental policy that puts the fewest possible limitations upon the acquisition and use of private property. This economic individualism appears now to be a creed of conservatism. It is set forth as the doctrinal basis for arguments against socialism or against some proposed new regulation of prices, profits, wages, or working conditions.

Economic individualism has not always been a defense of established economic interests. The British "Radicals" of a century ago appealed to the orthodox dogma of *laisser-faire* when they sought legislative intervention in behalf of wage-earners, tenants, and poorer people generally.[20] These reformers were individualists, in the sense that they be-

---

[18] Frank I. Cobb, "Free Speech, Its Value and Perils" (an address delivered in 1920), in John L Heaton, ed., *Cobb of "The World"* (1924), pp. 355–356.

[19] In a letter to President Washington, September, 1792: *The Writings of Jefferson,* Paul Leicester Ford, ed., Vol. VI, p. 108.

[20] Cf. *supra,* Ch. I, pp. 15–16.

lieved that the normal individual knew best his own interest and how to pursue it and that in pursuing his own interest he also, without intending it, served the common interest as well. Their general policy was one of non-interference in economic affairs. Government, they argued, should intervene in order to reëstablish "free trade" in foreign commerce, remove traditional restrictions on workers' combinations, and put the poor in an equal position with the rich in contests before the courts; it should then let competition operate without legal restraint. Although there are inevitable rivalries of interest, as a consequence of which the successful achievements of some may bring temporary losses and discomforts to others, yet the rivalries must not be regulated by authority; for experience shows that those who benefit from a competitive pursuit of economic gain are more numerous than those who suffer from it.

The general doctrine of *laisser-faire* appeared, in many respects, to work well in practice in the eighteenth century, when the removal of traditional economic restraints, surviving from feudalism, facilitated the development of commerce and industry. In the early nineteenth century also the doctrine appeared in some degree to fit an actual economic system, characterized by free exchange; practical conditions at that time appeared to make it economically and socially desirable to rely generally on the sort of adjustments the doctrine assumed to be automatic. Soon the practical conditions changed; an increasing concentration in the management of industry and trade and a waxing collective strength of labor power, leading consumers to believe that non-interference does not always guarantee the fulfilment of their needs, and even inducing property-owners to believe, in many instances, that a complete absence of governmental aid or restraint does not always best serve their interests. The changing conditions and notions have brought on an increasing limitation, by both private and public action, of the field of free competition; so that trusts, trade agreements, labor unions, and collective bargains, on the one hand, and tariffs, bounties, and labor laws, on the other hand, have become familiar features of an industrial community.

The arguments for *laisser-faire* to-day are generally pleas for the preservation of a legal *status quo* against novel limits upon freedom of contract and against further transfers of economic enterprises from private to public hands. Throughout the constant shiftings of the lines between non-interference and regulation, the case for the former policy is usually set forth in terms either of abstract dogmas or of empirical generalizations held to fit all conditions. Owners of property, it is said, should be free (within certain admitted limits assumed to be axiomatic) to accumulate as much property as they can by what means they choose (within the traditional laws of crime, tort, and contract) because private property is a natural right of man; or because free competition in the pursuit of wealth is the only way of maintaining natural relations of supply to demand; or because it is the only way of conserving the effects of a natural selection and reproduction of the fittest individuals in a competitive struggle for existence; or because experience, illuminated by our common sense, shows us the harmful moral and practical consequences of governmental attempts to minimize the effects of an unequal distribution of wealth.

This eclectic approach to economic individualism appears effectively in the writings of two of the most widely influential sociologists of the later nineteenth century—Herbert Spencer and William Graham Sumner.

Spencer's intellectual heritage predisposed him in various ways to a creed of individualism. He began his sociological studies with *a priori* assumptions of natural rights, with the familiar belief in natural economic laws, and with the Non-conformist's antipathy to authority. He shared also the prevalent conception of human history as orderly and beneficent change—a continuous, naturally operating progress towards more enlightened ways of living and towards a more perfect equilibration of social forces. His main arguments against governmental interference, however, were set forth, not with these traditional conceptions, although they constantly reappear, but with doctrines drawn from the natural sciences. An individualistic policy for modern governments could be proved to be right by the laws of both universal and organic evolution.

The universal process of evolution, according to Spencer, is a movement from uniformity and incoördination to diversity and coördination; in all phenomena, inanimate and animate, there is a development from "an indefinite, incoherent homogeneity to a definite, coherent heterogeneity": the earth and other planets evolved out of indefinite liquid masses into their present complex structures; the evolution of organic life has proceeded from the simple forms of lower organisms to the specialized structures and functionings of the higher animals.[21] So also

---

[21] In Spencer's *First Principles* (first published in 1862) and his *Principles of Sociology* (first published 1878–1880), Pt. II.

in social evolution, Spencer argued, as civilization advances, human groups become more heterogeneous in composition and more diversified in internal organization and activity, and the parts of any group become more interdependent. In a tribe of savages, all engage in similar activities; destroy part of the tribe, and those surviving live pretty much as before; but cut off the coal-mining or wheat-growing groups from the rest of a modern community and fatal suffering ensues. Political policy must be accommodated to this universal progress from the like to the different.[22] The autocratic government of a primitive society may properly impose a rigid discipline that restrains a too free differentiation of individuals. In civilized society, governments must accept the inevitable individuation and automatic equilibration of parts; any extension of state activity beyond what is necessary to protect individual freedom of action tends to impede the increasing specialization and the spontaneous interaction of interdependent individuals that are essential factors of social evolution.

Spencer's chief influence upon the later attempts to establish a scientific basis for economic individualism comes from the arguments he made in applying to human progress the law of organic evolution through natural selection. As a consequence of the continuous struggle for existence between individual organisms striving to adapt themselves to their environment, those best fitted—by attributes with which they are born or which they acquire in the course of the struggle—to cope with their surroundings generally survive and leave offspring. As the offspring generally inherit these adaptive qualities of their progenitors and as inferior types of individuals are persistently eliminated in the struggle, this process of survival and reproduction of the best and destruction of the inferior accomplishes a gradual improvement of the stock. Any attempt by government to interfere with the eternal struggle for existence is an attempt to modify nature. The essential end of government is to support nature—to maintain as far as possible a condition under which each adult receives the good results and suffers the evil results of his own nature and conduct.[23] The state has, therefore, two, and only two, sorts of duties. Its primary function—the function which formed the original motive of political organization—is defense

[22] Spencer, *Principles of Sociology,* Pt. V, Chs. XVIII–XIX.
[23] This argument is made chiefly in *The Man versus the State* (1884), published also in *Social Statics and the Man versus the State* (1892), Chs. III and IV, and *Justice* (1879), Pt. IV of the *Principles of Ethics,* Ch. XXVI.

against external attack; its secondary function is to prevent encroachments reciprocally among the individuals within the political
community; for the success of either sort of aggression destroys the
natural relation between conduct and consequence. The state's sole
domestic duty, in other words, is to preserve justice. Spencer's formula
for justice is this: "every man is free to do that which he wills, provided
he infringe not upon the equal freedom of any other man"; and a man
infringes on the equal freedom of another only when he breaks contracts or commits crimes or torts. The state, therefore, must confine
its functions to supplying military protection, repressing crime, and
preventing or redressing torts and breaches of contract.[24]

On the basis of this biological argument, reinforced by a detailed
recital of the actual blunders of government regulation, Spencer went as
far as a man bound by tradition could go in a specification of the things
modern governments should not do.[25] He opposed all organized charity,
public or private, all state aid to education or industry, and all governmental operation or regulation of industry. Compulsory and public
education, poor relief, and social legislation are futile attempts to change
natural conditions; they attempt to perpetuate the weak and put them
on the same plane as the strong, to preserve the unfit at the expense of
the fit. Government should let poverty and unsanitary housing alone,
so that weaker types may sooner die out; it should let industrial competition alone, however intense, for by such competition the best individuals come to the top. It should not operate the mint or the post office
or erect lighthouses and life-saving stations because none of these activities fall within the sole justification of state activity—namely, the
restraint of one man from interfering with the equal freedom of another.
But what, in Spencer's conception, is this "equal freedom," with which
the state may not properly interfere but which it is the state's duty to
protect? It is freedom to enjoy "natural rights"—the familiar rights to
life, liberty, and property. Spencer does not explain why the state can,
without interfering with the natural elimination of the unfit and survival of the fit, protect the weak against the strong in safe-guarding life,
liberty, and property.

Sumner's eloquent and forceful advocacy of individualism was in-

---

[24] *Justice*, Ch. VI.
[25] For Spencer's specification of his narrowly individualistic views of state
functions, cf. his *Essays: Moral, Political and Æsthetic* (new and enlarged edition, 1866), Chs. II and IX; *The Man versus the State; Justice*, Chs. VI–VIII,
XXV–XXIX.

fluenced by the biological writings of Darwin and Huxley and by Spencer's application of biological principles to social phenomena.[26] He was an ardent and persistent opponent of the American policy of tariff protection and a vigorous critic of governmental intervention in the industrial and moral life of the community. "Let it be understood," he said, "that we cannot go outside of this alternative: liberty, inequality, survival of the fittest; non-liberty, equality, survival of the unfittest. The former carries society forward and favors all its best members; the latter carries society downwards and favors all its worst members."[27] Sumner followed Spencer also in a theory that social phenomena are subject to laws which man's efforts cannot modify. "The truth is that the social order is fixed by laws of nature precisely analogous to those of the physical order. The most that man can do is by ignorance and self-conceit to mar the operation of social laws."[28] Laws of society determine, in various ways, a natural relation of immorality and indolence to poverty and disease, of virtue and industry to health and prosperity. Although the laws do not appear, in their immediate results, to work with invariable perfection, they operate best when no efforts are made to interfere with them. Let nature alone, and eventually she will cure vice and sloth. Competition "is a law of nature. . . . Nature submits to him who most energetically and resolutely assails her. She grants her rewards to the fittest, therefore, without regard to other considerations of any kind."[29] Another law determines, in civilized society, normal relations between supply and demand and regulates naturally and justly the competing economic interests of the members of society. The wage-system and private ownership of capital are accordingly essential parts of modern industrial organization. To attack capital is to attack "the foundations of civilization."[30]

Throughout Sumner's attack on socialism, paternalism, and other schemes for political control of industry, he combined with his appeal to natural social and economic laws an appeal to the teachings of ob-

[26] Sumner's individualistic ideas appear in several of his books and in numerous essays and addresses. For an exhaustive bibliography of his writings, some of the most important of which were first published posthumously, cf. William Graham Sumner, *The Forgotten Man and Other Essays*, edited by Albert Galloway Keller (1918), pp. 499–518.

[27] Sumner, "The Challenge of Facts" (composed, according to Professor Keller, in the eighties), in *The Challenge of Facts and Other Essays*, edited by Albert Galloway Keller (1914), p. 25.

[28] *Ibid.*, p. 37.

[29] *Ibid.*, p. 25.

[30] *Ibid.*, pp. 27–28, 39.

servation and experience. "All experience is against state regulation." [31] Experience shows the supreme value which the struggle to win a fortune has in developing practical efficiency, sound judgment, and strength of character. It shows also that most governmental action for improving the condition of the less successful members of society accomplishes, in equal degree, an impairment of the condition of others. Charitable and regulatory laws, although they may be enacted in behalf of the "poor," "weak," and "unfortunate," actually protect the idle, negligent, inefficient, and intemperate at the expense of the industrious and prudent. These latter are the self-reliant, and, therefore, generally forgotten, men who pay the taxes and bear the other economic burdens caused by the foolish sentimentality of the "reformer, social speculator, and philanthropist." The "forgotten man" is "the simple, honest laborer, ready to earn his living by productive work. We pass him by because he is independent, self-supporting, and asks no favors. He does not appeal to the emotions or excite the sentiments. He only wants to make a contract and fulfill it, with respect on both sides and favor on neither side. He must get his living out of the capital of the country. The larger the capital is, the better living he can get. Every particle of capital which is wasted on the vicious, the idle, and the shiftless is so much taken from the capital available to reward the independent and productive laborer." [32]

Contemporary biological criticisms of the collectivist tendencies of

[31] "The Forgotten Man" (composed in 1883), in *The Forgotten Man and Other Essays* (*loc. cit.*, n. 26, *supra* p. 395), p. 480.

[32] *Ibid.*, p. 476. See also the following familiar passage: "Such is the Forgotten Man. He works, he votes, generally he prays—but he always pays—yes, above all, he pays. He does not want an office; his name never gets into the newspaper except when he gets married or dies. He keeps production going on. He contributes to the strength of parties. He is flattered before election. He is strongly patriotic. He is wanted, whenever, in his little circle, there is work to be done or counsel to be given. He may grumble some occasionally to his wife and family, but he does not frequent the grocery or talk politics at the tavern. Consequently, he is forgotten. He is a commonplace man. He gives no trouble. He excites no admiration. He is not in any way a hero (like a popular orator); or a problem (like tramps and outcasts); nor notorious (like criminals); nor an object of sentiment (like the poor and weak); nor a burden (like paupers and loafers); nor an object out of which social capital may be made (like the beneficiaries of church and state charities); nor an object for charitable aid and protection (like animals treated with cruelty); nor the object of a job (like the ignorant and illiterate); nor one over whom sentimental economists and statesmen can parade their fine sentiments (like inefficient workmen and shiftless artisans). Therefore, he is forgotten. All the burdens fall on him, or on her, for it is time to remember that the Forgotten Man is not seldom a woman." *Ibid.*, pp. 491–2.

Cf. also "The Challenge of Facts" (*loc. cit.*, n. 27, *supra*), p. 43, and *What Social Classes Owe to Each Other* (1883), p. 21.

modern democracy add nothing to the arguments of Spencer and Sumner, although they bring the scientific terminology somewhat up to date and introduce new illustrations of the biologically degenerating effects of contemporary programs of economic and social legislation.[33] These programs are unscientific and impractical, it is said, because they derive their impulse from an unscientific optimism which assumes that each generation can biologically uplift the race through its measure of poor relief, sanitation, education, and trade regulation. All that is a gross biological error. We cannot improve the human stock by saving and strengthening its weaker units. As long as an organism continues to propagate, the cells of the germ plasm from which it took its start are immortal and are not permanently affected by anything happening to the organism after birth. We can change inheritance patterns, one half of which each parent contributes, only in two ways; we can improve prevalent patterns by breeding from best parents, and we can deteriorate them by breeding from the worst.

In primitive life, it is argued, as well as in the earlier stages of modern civilization, natural and sexual selection worked more actively: defective children were allowed, deliberately or unwittingly, to perish; wars tended to preserve and multiply the stronger stocks; the struggle for existence tended to eliminate the disgenic classes of society. To-day we set aside or retard natural and sexual selection; we cherish defectives and permit them to breed; we allow wars to destroy more of the better than of the inferior stocks; and we encourage the best stocks to remain relatively sterile. The evil is not so much that a collectivist policy preserves the unfit but that it permits them to produce other human beings as unfit as they are, physically, mentally, and morally. Statistics of feeble-mindedness and insanity, for example, show the increasing proportions of these abnormal stocks in the populations of Great Britain and the United States.[34] An equally significant disproportion appears when we compare average and superior stocks: unskilled workers have more children than skilled workers; laborers, skilled and unskilled, have more children than scientists and professional and business men; artisans have more children than artists. Stocks whose members have attained the highest eminence are the ones that are dying

---

[33] Cf. Alleyne Ireland, *Democracy and the Human Equation* (1921); F. C. S. Schiller, *Eugenics and Politics* (1926); A. E. Wiggam, *The New Decalogue of Science* (1923); Lothrop Stoddard, *The Revolt Against Civilization* (1922), Ch. III.

[34] Cf. Elliott R. Downing, "Human Inheritance," Ch. XIV in *The Nature of the World and of Man,* edited by Horatio Hackett Newman (1926).

out, their places being taken by mediocre families. The social legislation of democracies not only thwarts the elimination of the unfit but
burdens the fit; the funds for social reform are derived almost wholly
from taxes imposed upon the economically successful, who are thus led
to postpone marriage and limit their offspring.

According to this argument, the logical conclusion from Darwinism
is a policy of economic non-interference by the state—the tolerance, or
even encouragement, of a competition that ensures the triumph of the
capable over the incapable members of society. You cannot improve the
human stock by improving the social environment or mitigating inequality in the distribution of wealth; the effects of such changes are
not transmitted to future generations. The fundamental error of a collectivist policy is that it seeks to have the incompetent flourish on equal
terms with the competent and thus ignores or seeks to remove the competition that eliminates the unfit. The biologic individualists do not ordinarily define what they mean by "fittest" individuals; they do not indicate whether they mean physical, intellectual, artistic, or moral fitness.
Often they appear to identify fitness with success in the accumulation
of wealth. They are generally advocating, in terms of a newly developed
social biology, what the earlier *laisser-faire* economists and utilitarians
had preached in terms of the nature of man, the natural laws of production and exchange, or the proved requirements of human happiness.

Economic individualists also generally oppose the intrusion of any
doctrine of labor-created or community-created values into a discussion of the distribution of wealth. Some absolutely reject, or wholly
ignore, the claims for such values. Others acknowledge that in diverse
and indirect ways all values are in part the product of the abilities and
activities of innumerable individuals and of the securities and conveniences supplied by organized communities; and yet they maintain
that this principle applies so universally and indiscriminately that it
cannot serve as a practical or just guide for determining the scope and
direction of governmental policy. In other words, although the community and the state, as well as various individuals other than the
owners, play a part in the creation of all values, that part in any given
instance is so indeterminate and subordinate that it should not be cited
to justify any governmental impairment of an owner's property claims.
All attempts to discriminate between earned and unearned increments
of value must, therefore, be rejected.[35]

[35] See Lord Hugh Cecil. *Conservatism* (1912), Ch. V.

Some writers go further and for the fiction of labor-created values oppose their fiction of owner-created values. An owner is entitled to freedom in the use of his property because he has rightfully acquired it. He has "earned" his wealth by the industry and intelligence which he has applied in accumulating it or by the self-denial and self-control which he has exercised in using it. "Capital" is the creation only of the thrift and foresight of its owners. The major premise in this argument seems to be that all wealth—everything which is produced beyond what laborers need for the bare maintenance of themselves and their families —is the product of the intelligence, skill and energy of those who own the materials and instruments of production. Production is regarded as essentially an individual, not a collective, function; skill is regarded as an individual inheritance or gift, not in any sense a social product or asset. The owner has, therefore, a general right "to run his business as he pleases"; and the state has no right to interfere in order to transfer any of the benefits of his business to others.

These individualists do not ordinarily demand that society should be inhumane in the face of actual distress or utterly indifferent to de-graded living conditions among workers. But they would have the conditions relieved not by regulation but by voluntary charity and by lessons in prudence. Persuade landowners and employers to deal benev-olently with tenants and laborers; encourage the latter to live indus-triously, temperately, and thriftily. Where public aid proves to be necessary to supplement private effort, let the intervention by the state be understood as an act not of justice but of mercy. No one—either the poor, the unemployed, or the low-waged—has any "right" to be supported or assisted by the state.[36]

In many instances, a creed of individualism is made up of little more than assertions that certain disliked regulations are "of a socialistic sort," or violate "sound principles of government," or go against tradi-tion.[37] If there are more positive elements in this unspecified doctrine of individualism, they are generally only the vaguely surviving postulates of classical political economy—that "economic forces" fix "natural" re-lations between supply and demand and operate for the best possible

[36] Cecil, op. cit., pp. 181–182; and cf. Frédéric Le Play, La réforme sociale en France (1864), and L'organisation du travail (1870).

[37] See, for example, the articles by Elihu Root, Henry Cabot Lodge, E. H. Gary, and Augustus P. Gardner, in Truxton Beale, ed., The Man versus the State: a Collection of Essays by Herbert Spencer . . . with Critical Comments, by Elihu Root, H. C. Lodge and others (1916).

good of all who, by their efforts and sacrifices, deserve that good. The creed assumes that without regulation there is, among buyers and sellers, a perfect competition which determines normal and proper prices, and such a complete mobility of labor that an unrestrained competition among employers and wage-earners secures the best attainable arrangements of wages and working conditions. Any governmental interference with this free and open competition is nothing more than a futile effort to substitute "artificial" for "natural" relations in the modern economic order. The "proper" functions of government are ordinarily only defense against outside foes, "maintenance of justice and security," and "provision of a monetary system." [38]

The common contention in all these doctrines of narrower individualism is that existing economic differences arise from differences in natural endowment or in the chances of fortune; the state is not morally or practically competent to adjust such differences. Where the state does not interfere, the share of wealth that each individual receives is generally a faithful measure of what he has contributed to the total wealth. The chief economic concern of government, therefore, should be to sustain private property and whatever inequalities appear with it. The state offends against justice and discourages effort and thrift when it seeks to modify an existing distribution of wealth by laws regulating wages or profits, or takes out of private hands the ownership and operation of industrial and commercial services, or sets up schemes of social insurance or of governmental supervision of maternity and infancy.[39]

The individualism of those who have made any analytical or historical study of modern economic life is generally of a more moderate and flexible sort. It is an empirical individualism, permitting government to intervene where experience and common sense show that the intervention is likely to promote human welfare. It makes no claim of an absolute natural or moral right in private ownership or of something permanently fixed in the traditional boundaries of state activity. There is explicit acknowledgment that private efforts do not supply adequately all the common economic needs of a civilized community, so that there can be no sweeping condemnation of all governmental enterprise; and

[38] Fred R. Fairchild, "Government Saves Us from Depression," *Yale Review,* XXI, new series (1931–1932), 661–683.

[39] For these extremely individualistic ideas, see the titles by Harry F. Atwood, Ernest J. P. Benn, John W. Burgess, Thomas Mackay, William H. Mallock and David A. Wells, *infra,* pp. 405–407; and cf. also the works listed by Irving Babbitt, Wilbur C. Abbott, and Otto H. Kahn.

that normal individuals, pursuing severally their valid aims, often come into conflicts that harm themselves and others, so that government in many instances may properly restrain acts which are not wrong under the traditional forms of the law. The specific programs of this moderate individualism vary widely; but they generally leave ample room for many of the familiar economic activities of contemporary governments in fixing uniform weights and measures, imposing requirements upon industrial establishments in order to safeguard the health and safety of employees and the public, taxing imports to protect domestic prices, limiting immigration to uphold domestic living standards, regulating the prices and services of private monopolies, restraining the unfair practices of competitive enterprises, preventing waste of natural resources, and conducting certain of the simpler forms of non-competitive business enterprise—such as postal communication and water supply. The programs exclude governmental ownership of enterprises that are now commonly in private hands, such as railroads, factories, mines, banks, and public utilities; and they generally resist any governmental limitation upon the prices and profits of private enterprises, except for carefully safeguarded limitations in the case of public utilities. The essential aim is to preserve private property as a socially safe institution: private ownership should be regulated to the extent, and only to the extent, that experience shows to be clearly necessary in order to keep the institution operating smoothly in the actual conditions of modern industrial communities.[40]

This economic individualism to-day hardly undertakes to stand on any strict theoretical definition of the province of the state in relation to private property. It is rather a general defense of the latter institution and of the modern "capitalistic" system. The theoretical defense is still variously set forth: private property, it is said, is some sort of a natural right; or a requirement of natural justice, or an indispensable means of adapting the economic life of the community to natural relations between supply and demand; or a normal method of expressing and cultivating characteristic and worthy impulses of normal human beings; or an essential product—and instrumentality—of a natural struggle for existence in the course of which fit individuals drive unfit individuals out of existence and thereby gradually improve the human

[40] For this moderate, empirical individualism, see the following: Thomas N. Carver, *Essays in Social Justice* (1915), *Principles of Political Economy* (1919); Harold G. Cox, *Economic Liberty* (1920); J. A. R. Marriott, *Economics and Ethics;* Hartley Withers, *The Case for Capitalism* (1920).

stock. These theoretical ideas survive in the contemporary individualism; but other arguments, of a more empirical and scientific tenor, now have greater sway.

Thus it is maintained that the long history and wide prevalence of private ownership, and the beneficial effects of its uses, prove its survival value.[41] Individual ownership prevails among the most primitive peoples, and private ownership of industrial capital is the essential feature in the capitalistic structure of modern civilized nations. "If historic records show anything it is that private property was present as far back as they exist and that the feeling for it has always been intense." It is so fixed "in the mores" that "to complain of it is like finding fault with the way a chemical element behaves."[42] Even in Russia, private capitalism shows its survival value, for the powerful socialist group that attempts to destroy it there has found it necessary to reëstablish much of it and to utilize extensively the services and wealth of capitalists of other countries. Moreover, wherever the system has been in operation, it has brought shorter hours, higher wages, better dwellings, clothing, and food, greater security against preventable ills, and wider opportunities for culture and pleasure than workers ever enjoyed under any pre-capitalist system; it has supplied consumers with an increased supply of the necessities and conveniences of life; and it is the only system which can secure a satisfactory adjustment of supply to demand. Finally, essential public enterprises depend for their financial support upon revenues derived from the wealth that private enterprise produces. The writers contrast the waste, extravagance, inefficiency, and corruption in governmental services with the thrift, industry, and honesty of private enterprise. Public officials, it is said, have no direct economic self-interest in the efficiency and economy with which governmental action is conducted, for their income is not dependent upon keeping expenditures below actual costs. So with the rapidly expanding governmental activity in recent years we have increasing governmental deficits and debts and the mounting tax burdens on private industry. Moreover, governmental regulation and ownership

---

[41] For an able anthropological defense of private property, see A. G. Keller, *Man's Rough Road* (1932), Ch. VIII. For typical defenses of modern capitalism, see the following: Ernest J. P. Benn, *Confessions of a Capitalist* (1925); Dorothy Crisp, *The Rebirth of Conservatism* (1931), Ch. II; J. Lawrence Laughlin, "The Logic of Capitalism," *Yale Review*, XIII, new series (1924), 289–301; L. Pohle, *Kapitalismus und Sozialismus* (fourth ed., 1931); Hartley Withers, *The Case for Capitalism*.

[42] A. G. Keller, *Man's Rough Road*, pp. 140, 127.

are not only inefficient and costly in themselves, but also, by making the results of individual efforts insecure, they impair the efficiency of private enterprise.[43]

Underlying this historical and empirical defense of private ownership, there is frequently the idea that the validity of the institution is proved by human psychology, so that to attack the institution is to go against some fundamental law of human nature. This idea has been expressed in a somewhat philosophic form by A. M. Ludovici, a leading contemporary disciple of Nietzsche. Human development is primarily a matter of increasing the conscious and voluntary activities of man, and this expansion of his activity both results in and is dependent upon an extension of the things which he can manipulate under his own control. Man's cultural improvement comes about through an expression of his instinct to extend his attributes into the world of phenomena outside himself. To hamper this instinct in any way is to obstruct a natural development of the most characteristic capacity of the human species. Only in very rare instances can the expression of this instinct be found except in material objects. A man grows by bringing these objects under his possession and control. Private property, therefore, is an essential condition of human progress—"a principle of life." It "constitutes the gratification, nay the very necessity, of one of the deepest instincts of man." An attack upon it is an "attack on Life itself." [44]

Others state the psychological case more generally. It is said that the desire to possess and to excel in the possession of material goods is a basic and morally beneficent human characteristic and an indispensable stimulus to the proficient production of commodities essential to the life and progress of a civilized society. There is no way of effectively destroying the desire or replacing the stimulus, and there is no way of conserving the benefits of private property without tolerating also the wide inequalities in wealth and in the social power that depends upon wealth. All the material amenities of modern civilization are the products of a competitive pursuit of wealth; and men compete not for equality but for superiority; the dominant motive of human endeavor is to surpass, not merely to equal, one's neighbor. Thus inequality in the distribution of wealth is an inevitable consequence of the operation of those motives which alone impel men to the pain and labor

---

[43] Fairchild, "Government Saves Us from Depression" (*loc. cit.* n. 38, p. 400, *supra*).

[44] Ludovici, *False Assumptions of Democracy* (1921), pp. 33, 35, 32.

that produce the wealth. A governmental policy that attempts to distribute wealth equally among unequally competent and industrious individuals undermines individual character, drys up the springs of productive activity, and deprives the community of its natural leaders in economic and cultural progress. Diligent, thrifty, resourceful, inventive individuals come forth in a society where government intervenes only to relieve actual distress, prevent clear violation of clearly established rights and interests, and supply community needs that private effort cannot adequately supply. We derive both individual and social benefits, both moral and economic values, from a policy that allows the widest practicable range of individual choice in the acquisition and use of property. Under such a policy, it is maintained, the members of the community are most likely to develop habits of prudence in preparing for the uncertainties of business and the infirmities of old age and to apply energy and ingenuity in mastering the forces of nature and devising and perfecting the arts of industry.

SELECT BIBLIOGRAPHY

DEFENSE OF FREEDOM OF OPINION AND MORAL CONDUCT

Bates, Ernest Sutherland, *This Land of Liberty* (New York and London, 1930).

Chafee, Zechariah, Jr., *Freedom of Speech* (New York, 1920).

Desjardins, Arthur, *De la liberté politique dans l'état moderne* (Paris, 1894).

Faguet, Émile, *Le libéralisme* (Paris, 1903).

Faulkner, Harold W., "Perverted American History," *Harper's Magazine,* CLII (1926), 337–343.

Harvey, George B. M., *The Power of Tolerance and Other Speeches* (New York and London, 1911).

Heaton, John L., ed., *Cobb of "The World", a Leader in Liberalism: Compiled from his Editorials* (New York, 1924).

Kallen, Horace M., *Individualism; an American Way of Life* (New York, 1933).

——————, ed., *Freedom in the Modern World* (New York, 1928).

Laski, Harold J., *The Dangers of Obedience, and Other Essays* (London and New York, 1930).

——————, *Liberty in the Modern State* (New York and London, 1930).

Martin, Everett Dean, *Liberty* (New York, 1930).

Mill, John Stuart, *On Liberty* (London, 1859; Boston, 1863).

Prins, Adolphe, *De l'esprit du gouvernement démocratique; essai de science politique* (Brussels, 1905), Ch. I.

Renouvier, Charles, *Science de la morale* (Paris, 1869).

Russell, Bertrand, "Freedom in Society," *Harper's Magazine,* CLII (1926), 438–444.

Ryan, John A., *Declining Liberty and Other Papers* (New York, 1927).

Schroeder, Theodore, *Free Speech Bibliography* (New York, 1922).

Seagle, William, *Cato; or the Future of Censorship* (London, 1930).

Whipple, Leon, *Story of Civil Liberty in the United States* (New York, 1927).

—————————, *Our Ancient Liberties* (New York, 1927).

PROPAGANDA, THE PRESS, AND PUBLIC OPINION

Angell, Norman, *The Press and the Organisation of Society* (London, 1922).

Belloc, Hilaire, *The Free Press,* (London, 1918).

Bernays, Edward L., *Propaganda* (New York, 1928).

Graves, W. Brooke, ed., *Readings in Public Opinion, Its Formation and Control* (New York and London, 1928).

Lasswell, Harold D., *Propaganda Technique in the World War* (New York and London, 1927).

Lippmann, Walter, *Liberty and the News* (New York, 1920).

—————————, *Public Opinion* (New York, 1922).

Lowell, A. L., *Public Opinion and Popular Government* (New York, 1913).

Odegard, Peter, *The American Public Mind* (New York, 1930).

—————————, *Pressure Politics* (New York, 1928).

Ponsonby, Arthur, *Falsehood in War-time* (New York, 1928).

Sait, Edward M., *American Parties and Elections* (New York, 1927), Chs. IV, V.

Salmon, Lucy M., *The Newspaper and Authority* (New York, 1923).

Sinclair, Upton, *The Brass Check* (Pasadena, 1919).

Villard, Osward Garrison, *Some Newspapers and Newspapermen* (New York, 1923).

Young, Kimball, and Lawrence, R. D., *Bibliography on Censorship and Propaganda* (Eugene, Oreg., 1928).

ECONOMIC INDIVIDUALISM

Abbott, Wilbur C., *The New Barbarians* (Boston, 1925).

Atwood, Harry F., *Back to the Republic, the Golden Mean: the Standard Form of Government* (Chicago, 1924).

Babbitt, Irving, *Democracy and Leadership* (Boston and New York, 1924), Ch. VI.

Beale, Truxton, ed., *The Man versus the State* (New York, 1916).

Benn, Ernest J. P., *Confessions of a Capitalist* (London, 1925).

——————, *The Return to Laisser Faire: the Case for Individualism* (London and New York, 1928).

Burgess, John W., *The Reconciliation of Government with Liberty* (New York, 1915).

Carver, Thomas N., *Essays in Social Justice* (Cambridge, Mass., 1915).

——————, *Principles of Political Economy* (Boston, etc., 1921).

Cecil, Lord Hugh, *Conservatism* (London, 1912).

Cox, Harold G., *Economic Liberty* (London, 1920).

Crisp, Dorothy, *The Rebirth of Conservatism* (London, 1931), Ch. II.

Fairchild, Fred R., "Government Saves Us from Depression," *Yale Review,* New Series, XXI (1931–1932), 661–683.

Fay, Charles N., *Too Much Government, Too Much Taxation* (Garden City, N. Y., 1923).

Guyot, Yves, *Where and Why Public Ownership Has Failed,* translated from the French by H. F. Baker (New York, 1914).

Hearnshaw, F. J. C., *The Social and Political Ideas of Some Representative Thinkers of the Victorian Age* (London, etc., 1933), Ch. III, "Herbert Spencer and the Individualists."

Hoover, Herbert, *American Individualism* (New York, 1922).

Inge, William R., *Outspoken Essays: Second Series* (London and New York, 1922).

Ireland, Alleyne, *Democracy and the Human Equation* (New York, 1921).

Kahn, Otto H., *Our Economic and Other Problems: a Financier's Point of View* (New York, 1920).

Keller, A. G., *Man's Rough Road* (New York and New Haven, 1932). Ch. VIII, and *passim.*

Laughlin, J. Lawrence, "The Logic of Capitalism," *Yale Review,* XIII, new series (1924), 289–301.

Mackay, Thomas, ed., *A Plea for Liberty; an Argument against Socialism and Socialistic Legislation* (New York, 1891).

Mallock, William H., *Aristocracy and Evolution: a Study of the Rights, the Origin and the Social Functions of the Wealthier Classes* (London, 1898), especially Bk. IV, Ch. IV.

——————, *Social Equality* (New York, 1882).

Marriott, J. A. R., *Economics and Ethics: a Treatise on Wealth and Life* (New York and London, 1923).

Pohle, L., *Kapitalismus und Sozialismus* (fourth ed., Berlin, 1931).

Requa, Mark L., *The Relation of Government to Industry* (New York, 1925).

Schiller, F. C. S., *Eugenics and Politics* (London, 1926), especially Chs. I–III.

Spencer, Herbert, *Essays: Moral, Political and Aesthetic* (new and enl. ed., New York, 1866), Chs. II and IX.

——————, *Justice* (1879), Pt. IV of *Principles of Ethics* (New York, 1891–1893), Chs. VI–VIII, XXV–XXIX.

——————, *The Man versus the State* (New York, 1884).

——————, *Principles of Sociology* (New York, 1878–1880, 1897–1898), Pt. I, Ch. I; Pt. II, Ch. III.

Stoddard, Lothrop, *The Revolt against Civilization* (New York, 1922).

Sumner, William Graham, *The Challenge of Facts and Other Essays* (New Haven, 1914).

——————, *The Forgotten Man and Other Essays* (New Haven, 1918).

——————, *What Social Classes Owe to Each Other* (New York, 1883; reprint, New Haven, 1925).

Wells, David Ames, *Recent Economic Changes and Their Effect on the Production and Distribution of Wealth* (New York, 1889).

Wiggam, A. E., *The New Decalogue of Science* (Indianapolis, 1923).

Withers, Hartley, *The Case for Capitalism* (London, 1920).

CHAPTER XV

PHILOSOPHICAL GROUNDS FOR STATE INTERVENTION

THE traditional doctrine of economic individualism regards political action, particularly in the economic field (except action in protecting private property and enforcing contracts), as artificial, going counter to moral, economic, or biologic laws, and thereby interfering with the normal physical development and spiritual improvement of the human race. No political society has ever been operated in accordance with that doctrine. No government has ever confined its activities within the sphere which the dogmas of individualism mark out. Organized communities have, in all periods of history, restrained as well as protected the property-owner. The scope and forms of the restraints and the degree of their directness have greatly varied from time to time. If we consider the evolution of human society as a whole, we can hardly find any persistently predominant trend towards either more or less governmental intervention. In the early modern age, it is true, certain restraints that are frequently characterized in contemporary political writing as of a peculiarly "collectivist" sort were not generally in force; there was, for example, relatively little governmental control of working conditions or direct regulation of prices or wages; and no substantial body of public opinion then believed that practical needs demanded any such intervention. The prevailing forms of industrial enterprise have changed since that time—machine processes displacing handicraft production and dislodging workers from the control of their working materials and instruments, and large corporate enterprises destroying the equal bargaining power of consumers, as well as of workers.

The changes in industrial methods have, in the minds of many observers, produced some evil consequences: new forms of ill health and economic insecurity for workers; and such an increasing concentration in the management of industrial capital that the ordinary individual's chance of enjoying the advantages of modern civilization has seemed to rest increasingly in the hands of small numbers of capital-owners who, accepting the teachings of economic individualism, act upon the assumption that in "running their own business" they have no general social obligations beyond those embodied in the traditional laws of crime, contract, and tort, and that they serve the general interest best by pursuing their own economic gain. Since the early nineteenth century, there has been a growing body of opinion, among both law-makers and theorists, that the practical conditions which justified the former policy of non-intervention no longer exist; that the unregulated market devices for determining wages and working conditions, fixing amounts to be produced, and setting prices no longer supply adequately our common needs or bring about a distribution which agrees with our normal standards of fair play; and that in many ways governmental intervention can improve conditions by action clearly outside the traditional fields of punishing crimes, redressing torts, and enforcing contracts. Throughout this period the scope of economic legislation has constantly expanded; government has increasingly intervened to fix maximum hours of labor; prescribe sanitary precautions in industrial establishments; supply public aid to the aged and disabled; require the insurance of workers against the risks of their employment; and fix, by one means or another, the prices and services in private enterprises engaged in supplying certain common necessities and conveniences.

The most influential proponents of this legislation have often been in the same camp with socialists in practical movements for the special taxation of great wealth and the public ownership of basic utilities, and they have accepted the general socialist doctrine that a fairer distribution of wealth and a more adequate supply of the necessities of life are proper objects of governmental activity. Generally, however, they have not set as their goal, near or remote, the destruction of the system of private property. The theorists have sought to find a social philosophy to fit a collectivist but, as they interpret it, non-socialist trend in governmental activity. Rejecting the economic determinism of both socialism and individualism, they have set forth a theory that recognizes the moral and social as well as the material and directly self-seeking aspects of human behavior and that regards political agencies, not as mere devices either for suppressing disorder, settling disputes, protecting property, or guaranteeing an adequate supply and equitable distribution of economic goods, but as natural expressions of the varied aims of normal men, or at least as peculiarly useful instrumentalities in a coöperative pursuit of these aims. Somewhat typical forms of a theoretical justification for a political program of moderate collectivism have appeared in the French doctrine of "solidarity" and in the political "idealism" of an important group of British philosophers.

THE DOCTRINE OF SOLIDARITÉ

French social doctrine in the middle of the nineteenth century appeared to be generally dominated by the deductive methods and *laisser-faire* conclusions of the English classical economists. About this time, however, there set in a new tendency. The influences came in part from German economists of the historical school, who effectively exposed the highly abstract nature of the assumptions of economic individualism, expressed their distrust of general "economic laws," and pointed to the actual variability in the scope of political action—the functions of governments differing according to differences in physical environment and changing according to changes in the general institutional structure of the community. More directly, the particular developments in French collectivist doctrine were influenced by the theories of French sociologists and moral philosophers, who, in opposition to the assumptions of the classical economists, brought forward general hypotheses of their own as to the nature of man and society and set forth their belief in the "reality" of the social bond. They sought to overthrow the hypothesis that human society is less natural than its members or that political activity is somehow outside the normal, instinctive, spontaneous phases of the life of man.

Auguste Comte, "founder" of sociology, in the fifth decade of the century, described human society as the highest stage in organic evolution, embodying the completest development of that natural harmony of organization and action—all parts of a complex and self-existent system working together spontaneously in sustaining the life of a whole—which we find, in less perfect operation, in plants and animals; and he ascribed to the state the essential function of maintaining in full vigor the organic "solidarity" of society.[1] A half century later, René Worms developed in elaborate detail this organismic conception of society. Worms pointed to the specific analogies between societies and ordinary organisms, in their structure and functioning. Society, he maintained, is *"un être véritable"*—"a living whole composed of parts themselves living."[2] Human individuals, variously grouped by natural bonds into the

[1] Auguste Comte, *Cours de philosophie positive*, 6 vols. (1830–1842; fifth ed. 1892–1894), especially IV, 235 ff., 308–309, 417; VI, 712 ff.
[2] René Worms, *Organisme et société* (1896), p. 38.

historic institutions of human society, are its organs. Worms' elaboration of these analogies—in his descriptions of the "anatomy," "physiology," and "pathology" of societies—has no light to shed on any particular problem of governmental function. We are concerned here only with his general contention that a national political society differs from ordinary organisms only in its greater complexity and plasticity of structure and the predominantly psychic nature of the bonds that hold its elements together. These differences make the society a "super-organism"—"*un organisme avec quelque chose de plus.*" [3] The state is a society that has become conscious of its unity and has incarnated the ideas and sentiments of its unity in institutions and laws. It is the super-organism become a super-personality, having its own life so distinct from and superior to the lives of its members that to save its own it does not hesitate at times to require the destruction of the lives of these lesser beings. "Does not he who sacrifices himself for his country believe in the reality of the being for whom he abandons his life? And if his act, in the eyes of all, passes for heroism and not for folly, is it not because all, unconsciously or not, share his belief?" [4] The acceptance of this conception of the state, Worms declared in another place, "condemns that radical individualism which would elevate each human being into a being all-sufficient in himself, since the theory establishes, against that policy, the reality of the collective being, and the necessity of an indissoluble connection among all its elements." [5]

The attempts to draw literal analogies between human societies and living organisms were, in France as elsewhere, soon abandoned; and the organismic conception of the state has survived (with insignificant exceptions) only in the older Hegelian form: the state an end in itself; its evolution controlled by its own laws; its functionally differentiated parts, interdependent and inseparable, all existing for and dependent upon a vigorous life of the corporate national society. [6] The biologic analogy, it is true, was retained in another form in the attempt to apply to political society the doctrine of survival and selection through mutual aid. [7] The advocates of coöperation through state-sanctioned voluntary associations or through the state itself have, however, relied chiefly upon ethical and juristic notions.

[3] *Organisme et société*, p. 394.
[4] *Ibid.*, p. 46.
[5] *Annales de l'Institut International de Sociologie*, IV (1898), 301.
[6] Cf. *supra*, pp. 25–26, and F. W. Coker, *Organismic Theories of the State* (1910).
[7] Compare Kropotkin's argument from mutual aid to anarchism, *supra*, pp. 208–209.

Certain moral philosophers in France—notably, Alfred Fouillée and Charles Renouvier—sought to reconcile ethical with practical and scientific (i.e., biologic) approaches to the problem of governmental policy. Society, Fouillée maintained, is both organic and contractual in its origin and nature—a "contractual organism." [8] It is, as an organism, composed of individual units and functional groups whose concurring activities maintain the organic unity, consciously accepting the reciprocal obligations which life in society requires of them; a society does not, like an animal or plant, live by virtue of the reflex functioning of its parts; the strength of its vitality depends upon the extent to which its members understand their common aims. There is no consciousness and volition in society itself and no social mind or will as a distinct entity; consciousness and will are in the individual members; but the social instincts of these members and their rational comprehension of their dependence upon others lead them deliberately to maintain the organic union and to set up "organs of direction"—the agencies of political government. Renouvier also sought, in more general and familiar terms, to combine practical with idealistic justifications of a creed of coöperation. [9] His position was, in brief, this: The task of the social philosopher is to show not only that the ideals of human brotherhood and charity are worthy inspirations for fair and generous dealings with one's fellows but also that the ideals have "realistic" foundations, in the sense that each individual, however superior his natural endowments or inherited privileges, is actually dependent upon the coöperation of his fellows for the attainment of his own success and happiness. We also find in Renouvier's writings the notion of the "quasi-social-contract," which became a cardinal feature in the later doctrine of French "solidarism."

The term "solidarity" was apparently first used by one of the minor utopian socialists of the early nineteenth century—Pierre Leroux, who is also credited with having invented the word "socialism." Comte adopted the term as an appropriate designation for his own conception of the organic interdependence of men in society. Some of the French orthodox economists—notably Bastiat—adopted the word and the conception but deduced individualist conclusions, arguing that, since one man's conduct affects so directly and extensively, for good or ill, the

---

[8] *La science sociale contemporaine* (1880; second ed., 1885), bks. ii–iii; *Le socialisme et la sociologie réformiste* (1909), pp. 357–416.

[9] *La science de la morale* (1869), Vol. II, Chs. XXXVI–XXXVII.

welfare of all his fellows, the state must do nothing to weaken the individual's sense of responsibility for the social consequences of his acts; or that, since the solidarity of a society is perfected through an increasing differentiation among its members, a hands-off governmental policy is essential in order to maintain and intensify the differences. In 1889, Charles Gide, distinguished French economist and historian of economic doctrines, proposed "solidarity" as the name for a "new school" of social economy.[10] Theorists and practical politicians—notably the leaders of the new "Radical" (later "Radical-Socialist") party in French politics—were, he explained, seeking a creed "of the nature of a *via media* between economic Liberalism [i.e., "Individualism"] on the one hand and socialism on the other. It must repudiate *laissez-faire* equally with the socialization of individual property; it must hold fast to the doctrine of the rights of man and the claims of the individual while recognizing the wisdom of imposing restrictions upon the exercise of those rights in the interests of the whole community." The Social-Catholic creed of authoritarianism and the socialist creed of universal equality were, he believed, just as unrealistic and unworkable as the "Liberal" creed of individual isolation and freedom; and he set up "solidarity" not mainly as a theory or ideal but as "just a fact, one of the best-established facts of history and experience and the most important discovery of our time." [11]

Gide credited Léon Bourgeois with the chief influence in making the doctrine of solidarity popular both in academic circles and among various groups of practical reformers. Bourgeois, an active political leader as well as social theorist, published, in 1896, a series of magazine articles setting forth the "scientific," "practical," and "juristic" aspects of the doctrine.[12] His scientific argument employed the familiar doctrine of evolution through mutual aid: coöperation and collective control are primary factors in organic and social evolution; only those animal species survive that possess the instincts and organs disposing and qualifying them for a life of mutual aid; a nation that shows itself unable or unwilling to act in coöperation with other nations and in an organized and disciplined manner internally will be eliminated in the

---

[10] On the evolution of the solidarist conception, see Charles Bouglé, "L'évolution du solidarisme," *Revue politique et parlementaire*, XXXV (1903), 480–505; Charles Gide and Charles Rist, *History of Economic Doctrines* (translation, 1915), pp. 344–345, 439, and Bk. V, Ch. III.

[11] Gide and Rist, *History of Economic Doctrines*, pp. 592–593, n. 2.

[12] Léon Bourgeois, *Solidarité* (1896; seventh ed. 1912).

intensive competitions between nations. Bourgeois gave greater emphasis, however, to the conception of quasi-contract—the idea of liabilities created by benefits received instead of by promises made. Arguing from the quasi-contracts of ordinary law—as in the case of obligations incurred, under certain conditions, by the acceptance of payment not due or of services not explicitly contracted for—he set forth the general idea that society is based upon a contract; a contract not in Rousseau's sense of individuals surrendering generally their rights to the community in return for equal shares of voting power over the community, but in the sense of obligations incurred by virtue of the acceptance of the benefits of social life. The individual's tacit acknowledgment of his social obligations is attested by his residence in the community, acceptance of its protection and aid, and constant utilization of the common social heritage.

The solidarist doctrine of quasi-contract had a strong hold among French jurists. Thus Joseph Charmont, professor of law in the University of Montpelier, argued that ownership of property creates for the owner as many obligations as rights; by the mere fact of his ownership, and not by any undertaking or any fault on his part, he incurs liabilities: to his employees—for accident or disease incurred in the course of employment, and to the public—to keep his property free from peril to the general health and safety. Laws that define these liabilities are not the formulations of limitations upon rights; they are directions for the execution of implied contractual obligations.[13]

Gide doubted the utility of the doctrine of the quasi-contract and, as already indicated, preferred to put his emphasis upon the "fact" of solidarity—that each is harmed by the failures of others and helped by their successes, or that each, from motives both of self-interest and a natural sympathy for human suffering, is naturally concerned in the well-being of others, so that a policy of coöperation rather than competition fits the facts of human experience. Thus solidarity for Gide is primarily a scientific or practical, rather than an idealistic or juristic, conception. When society, through its political agencies, grants public aid to the poor and disabled or intervenes to promote the coöperative activities of private associations, it does so as an act not of charity but of self-preservation—in the broadest sense of this term. He seemed willing to accept Charmont's general conception of law as the means

---

[13] Joseph Charmont, *La renaissance du droit naturel* (1919; second ed., 1927), Ch. VII: translation in *Modern French Legal Philosophy*, Ch. VII.

whereby a community protects itself from the dissolution that comes from an excess of the competitive activities of men. He was inclined, however, to lay stress upon the voluntaristic aspects of the doctrine. "Solidarism," he said, "is State Socialism in a French garb, but possessed of somewhat better grace in that it does not necessarily imply the coercive intervention of the State, but shows considerable respect for individual liberties." [14] He did not object to governmental coercion when private interests proceeded on the assumption that merciless and purely self-regarding competition, rather than mutual aid, was the normal rule for life in society; but he believed that a general reliance on state intervention (as by the German academic socialists) left too little opportunity for a normal development of the naturally coöperative dispositions of men; and he directed attention to the popularity of the solidarist doctrine among the voluntary-associative movements in France—the syndicalists, mutualists, and various coöperative producers' and consumers' societies.

POLITICAL IDEALISM IN RECENT BRITISH PHILOSOPHY

The British idealists made little effort to point to the limits of the state's competence in advancing voluntary coöperation. They did not set state action in opposition to individual action as normal means for developing human personality and cultivating the social instincts of men. They believed that individual self-development was in no way circumscribed by assigning to the state a comprehensive and exalted sphere of action.[15]

The idealist political doctrine is founded in ethics and is a reaction against the naturalistic, utilitarian realism of the individualists—against the sort of theoretical analysis that estimates human welfare in terms of material, tangible comforts and satisfactions and maintains that the

[14] Gide and Rist, *History of Economic Doctrines,* p. 592.

[15] The leading idealists were Oxford men—graduates of Oxford and later fellows and lecturers there. The following are the most important and influential of the Oxford idealists: Edward Caird (1835–1908); Francis Herbert Bradley (1846–1924); Thomas Hill Green (1836–1882); Bernard Bosanquet (1848–1923), lecturer at University College, Oxford, later professor of moral philosophy at St. Andrews. Caird's interest was mainly in metaphysical and religious questions. Others who accepted in somewhat varying forms the ethical and political ideas of Bradley, Green, and Bosanquet, are the following: William S. Lilly (1840–1919), William Wallace (1844–1897), David C. Ritchie (1853–1903), W. H. Fairbrother (1859–1903). For titles of the works of these authors, cf. the list on pp. 431–432, *infra* and for later writers who follow generally the political doctrine of Green, see pp. 429–430, *infra*.

nature of the state or of a man can be fully apprehended through a study exclusively of outward, concrete facts. Many individualists, of course, would not have accepted this description of their creed. It is, rather a statement of what the idealist thought that the individualist ought, if he were to be consistent, to mean. The general philosophy of the Oxford group is called "idealist" because it attempts to define and judge man and his institutions according to their ideal natures and aims, rather than their actual appearances. Man is more than a series of sensations and experiences; social institutions are more than their particular manifestations in forms and policies. Idealism in this sense is not synonymous with visionariness or subjectivism—the fashioning of conjectures or goals that are out of all touch with human experience. But it does maintain that a world of ideas exists as truly as the world of facts through which ideas make themselves apparent to the perceptions of man and that the former world is the more permanent and substantial world.

Like any other ethical doctrine, this idealism starts with a certain conception of the nature of man and a resulting interpretation of his social life. It distinguishes between the specific, voluntary acts of an individual, on the one hand, and his real will, on the other hand. The latter indicates the sort of life he wants to lead, the type of man he aims to be. His particular acts may, as a consequence of his ignorance or under the pressure of immediate physical needs, seem to point in another direction. But his will must be considered in terms of his more constant motives, or, in other words, of his ideals. Our reason enables us to distinguish reality from appearance, "a function from its derangements," [16] the purposes and destinies of institutions from their historic origins and changes. Thus to understand an institution is to discover the ideas and spiritual forces that bring it into existence and keep it going; and we can achieve such an understanding even though no single actual institution, in its observable form and activity, reveals fully those ideas and forces. The essential importance of a social institution consists in the fact, not that it supplies certain means of maintaining physical life or of satisfying physical needs and desires, but that it embodies certain standards of conduct accepted by its members as right in controlling their relations.[17]

[16] Bernard Bosanquet, *Social and International Ideals*, p. 310.
[17] Cf. George H. Sabine, "Bosanquet's Theory of the Real Will," *Philosophical Review*, XXXII (1923), 641.

The idealist approaches political questions from this general philosophical viewpoint. He observes actual men and actual institutions, good and bad. But his generalizations or conclusions are not determined wholly or predominantly by such observations, as if he had no independent capacity for discriminating between the failures and vices of men and their more perfect conduct. He perceives the part that selfishness and narrow ambitions play in the lives of statesmen and in the evolution of political institutions; but he recognizes behind these weaknesses something which he holds to be more constant and universal, more rational and spiritual. Studying political activity in all its phases, he recognizes a prevailing trend or purpose towards the realization of an end which his reason and moral judgment approve. So he appraises the state by ideal standards, though the standards are, of course, definite standards which actual men set up and seek to achieve. Political society, under this conception, is what men intend it to be. The state is what actual states "claim to be, and pretend to be even when they are not." [18]

This idealist doctrine restores to political thought the most characteristic idea of ancient Greek political philosophy, as expressed in the great works of Plato and Aristotle. In the Greek theory of the classical age, the state is the supreme means to the good life, and its ethical importance surpasses its economic, legal, and political phases. The British doctrine is also in part a revival of early nineteenth century German philosophy; and the Oxford philosophers show clearly the influence of Kant and Hegel, in terminology, method, and metaphysical conceptions. The German idealist philosophy appeared as a general refutation of eighteenth century naturalistic rationalism. The latter, we have seen, regarded the state as the product of deliberate negotiation among men, who set up political society to serve their conscious needs; and it represented the individual as the source of rights, the state as an artificial creation by man to protect his original rights, and the political will of the community as simply a summation of the wills of the individual citizens. [19] The German idealist philosophy described the state as original and organic in nature, the source of individual rights, and the embodiment of a general community will which might be very different from, and even substantially independent of, the wills of a majority of

[18] Bosanquet, *Social and International Ideals,* p. 310.

[19] This last clause states not the actual eighteenth century doctrine but rather a somewhat inexact or exaggerated description of Rousseau's conception of the general will as it appeared in the idealist criticism.

the citizens.[20] British idealism likewise appeared as a reaction against the empirical utilitarianism and economic individualism dominant in British writing throughout the earlier part of the nineteenth century. It represents the state as an institution whose true nature we may best discover not by observation of actual political institutions but by abstract analysis of political conceptions.

From the standpoint of general philosophy, probably F. H. Bradley is the most important among the British Idealists. His essay on "My Station and Its Duties" (in his *Ethical Studies,* published in 1876) contains the basic psychological and ethical phases of the general creed. A man, Bradley held, has, as a moral being, no reality apart from the family and community to which he belongs. An individual is what he is by virtue, on the one hand, of certain original mental and physical attributes, and, on the other hand, of the language he speaks, the ideas and sentiments that language carries into his mind, the examples and social customs he follows, the institutions that protect and enlighten him. The former, he inherits from his ancestors; the latter he derives from the society within which he lives. Native capacities remain unrealized, undeveloped, save in so far as they utilize the social heritage; so there is very little room left for "individuality." An individual apart from the community is an abstraction. He can realize his possibilities as a perfect man only to the extent that he is a perfect member of his community, fulfilling faithfully the duties of the particular place which he occupies in the nation. He may, within limits, choose his position in society, but he does not determine the duties and privileges that belong to the position.[21] Apart from the community to which he belongs, he cannot find the sort of activity which makes him really himself. Each owes his moral quality and his opportunity to realize whatever spiritual and intellectual attributes he possesses to the organized society in which he lives.

The most extended and concrete suggestions for a practical application of the idealist doctrine were made by Thomas Hill Green.[22] He was

---

[20] Cf. *supra,* pp. 8–9, 25–26.

[21] Bradley, *Ethical Studies,* pp. 156, 159, 182.

[22] For a sketch of Green's life, see *Works of Thomas Hill Green,* R. L. Nettleship, ed., III (London, 1885–1888), cvii ff. Green was the son of a rector; was educated at Rugby and Balliol College; was lecturer in history and Greek philosophy; fellow, and later tutor at Balliol; and in the last few years of his life professor of moral philosophy in the University. He engaged in practical movements of political and social reform. He made public speeches in support of suffrage extension; took part in the campaign for educational liberalization, by such means as public maintenance of education, compulsory attendance, and the elimination of

a teacher of philosophy, but a philosopher who in all of his teaching and writing manifested profound interest in the immediate ethical and political problems of the community in which he lived. And in many ways he displayed, as far as his poor health and limited talents as a public speaker made possible, his devotion to the aim which determined his whole ethical and political creed: "the removal of all restrictions which law can remove in the free development of English citizens."

The key to Green's political doctrine is supplied by his general ethical doctrines, revealed both in his criticism of conventional deterministic and utilitarian ideas and in his exposition of his own views on the nature of the moral man and of moral conduct.[23] You cannot, Green maintained, explain man in purely naturalistic terms, as the helpless product of physical forces within and without his body. He possesses a free intelligence—a self-distinguishing consciousness not explainable as a part of the processes of nature. He possesses a free will—free in the sense that it is determined by his own ideas and motives, as well as by outside stimuli and by his physical wants and impulses. The expressions "good" and "bad" have ethical significance only in so far as applied to acts "in which a self-conscious individual directs himself to the realization of some idea"—to the attainment of some consciously entertained purpose in which for the time he seeks satisfaction.[24] The moral quality of any act depends upon the nature of the object in which the doer seeks satisfaction; the moral character of a man depends upon

sectarian religious instruction; was active in temperance organizations, advocating public restrictions upon the number and hours of public houses; was for a short period a member of the Oxford school board and of the Oxford town council; and contributed generously both of time and money to the promotion of high school education in that town.

[23] Green's philosophy appears chiefly in his interpretation of other philosophers, particularly the Greeks and Hume, Kant, Mill, and Spencer. Most of his works were published posthumously. The collected edition is the *Works of Thomas Hill Green*. His general ethical doctrines are set forth in his *Prolegomena to Ethics*, not contained in the collected edition of his works, but published separately in 1883. His political doctrines are set forth extensively in the following works: *Lectures on the Principles of Political Obligation*, delivered before his Oxford class in 1879–1880 (*Works*, II, 334–553) ; his lecture on *Liberal Legislation and Freedom of Contract*, delivered during the election campaign of 1881 (*Ibid.*, III, 365–386) ; and his *Four Lectures on the English Commonwealth*, delivered before a philosophical society in 1867 (*Ibid.*, III, 277–364).

In the analysis of Green's ethical and political ideas, I have been particularly aided by the following: W. H. Fairbrother, *The Philosophy of Thomas Hill Green* (1896), Ch. VI; John Maccunn, *Six Radical Thinkers* (1907), Ch. VI; R. L. Nettleship, "Memoirs," in the *Works of Thomas Hill Green*, III (1885–1886), xi–clxi; David G. Ritchie, *The Principles of State Interference* (1891; second ed., 1896), Essay 4.

[24] *Prolegomena to Ethics* (third ed., 1890), p. 160.

the nature of the objects in which he generally seeks satisfaction.

The utilitarian standard for the moral value of an act is the tendency of the act to produce a maximum of pleasure for the largest possible number of men; for Green, the standard is a tendency to contribute to the perfection of mankind. Green acknowledged that in modern Europe the doctrine of utilitarianism had been of great social value. It had supplied a practical point of view from which to criticize certain traditional precepts and institutions that produced effects contrary to true morality. Whatever its theoretical invalidity, it had improved social conduct by impelling those who were disposed to act morally to consider a wider range of persons, when they weighed the consequences of their acts. In other words, though utilitarians were mistaken in identifying the highest good with the greatest net amount of pleasure enjoyed by the greatest number of persons, they had improved the standard of social action by "insisting that it is the greatest number whose highest good is to be taken into account." [25] Nevertheless, the utilitarian creed, Green maintained, was theoretically invalid and, if logically carried out, would lose its practical value. A general habit of deciding action by a calculation of consequences in the way of pleasures and pains places impediments in the way of social progress. When a man feels himself under a general obligation to produce as much pleasure and prevent as much pain as possible, he will find it necessary to avoid causing discomfort or disappointment to himself or to friends and neighbors, and he will be predisposed to swim with the stream of social opinion. On the other hand, a man really governed by a sense of moral obligation often finds it imperative to ignore questions of pleasure, for himself or others, and to disregard apparent claims of society, in order to seek satisfactions—possibly in art or science—that cannot be reduced to terms of the pleasures and pains of any number of persons.

The standard of morality which Green set up is that of development from a less perfect to a more perfect human life. This he considered the most dependable, least obscure, guide and inspiration to right conduct. "The true good of man is the perfection of human life." This does not mean a mere attainment of individual excellence. The complete man is a thoroughly social man; the good man cannot seek an interest private to himself or a good in which others cannot share. The person whose excellence the moral man seeks is not an abstract, isolated self; it is a self affected by and affecting the manifold interests of

25 *Prolegomena to Ethics*, p. 384.

other persons. The social interest of man is as primary a fact, and as relevant to the consideration of his moral character, as his individual interest. His moral ideal is an ideal of a good common to himself and others. On the other hand, the recognition of the social aspect of human excellence does not involve the sacrifice of the individual to the excellence of a community abstractly conceived. Human progress can take place only through the progress of human personalities. The life of society is a life lived by individuals. But personal life is common life. In the history of civilization, the gradual elevation of man's moral conceptions has shown itself not only in an elevation and clarification of the quality of his ideals but also in a social broadening of his moral vision—an extension of the range of persons whose welfare is seen as part of the common good.[26]

Green rejected not only utilitarianism but also the doctrine of natural rights—the idea that a human being is born with certain liberties of action and certain vested interests in material things of use to him; or that he possessed such liberties and claims in some pre-social condition and retains them as legal and moral rights after entering organized society; and that man's rights in society are valid only in so far as they can be proved to be compatible with his pre-social, or "natural," rights. Green denied that there are any such things as rights independent of and prior to society. A natural right is only a right that is necessary to the fulfilment of a purpose regarded as natural to man because conformable to the qualities that distinguish him from other beings. Because he is naturally a moral, rational, and social being, those freedoms of action are natural to him that are means to the fulfilment of his vocation as such a creature. Thus natural rights are rights which *should* be enjoyed by a normally rational and moral man living in a rationally constituted society. They belong only to men capable of being influenced by the idea of a common good and are effective only in a society whose members recognize a common good as contributing to their own ideal good.[27] They are the conditions under which the realization of the moral capacity of a man is made possible. Natural rights have political significance in so far as they admit of enforcement through political agencies. A man has natural rights of property, for example—rights, under certain conditions, to bring under his control material

[26] *Prolegomena to Ethics*, pp. 217–218.
[27] Cf. W. H. Fairbrother, *The Philosophy of Thomas Hill Green*, pp. 110–111; George H. Sabine, "Bosanquet's Theory of the Real Will," (see n. 17, *supra*, p. 416), pp. 638–639.

objects instrumental to the satisfaction of his valid needs or to the expression of his valid emotions; the vindication of such rights is a proper function of the state as an agency for the promotion of the moral development of its citizens; but it is equally the state's obligation to prevent the use of the proprietary claims for ends opposed to the common good.

All the Oxford idealists have emphasized the influence of a man's social contacts. Each individual is the sort of man he is not primarily because of his native endowment or the physical environment in which he lives but because of the sort of conventional and institutional relationships in which he finds himself. The standards of conduct and opinion which these conventions and institutions express and to which he habitually conforms go far towards determining his character and success. If he is removed from the pressure of law, custom, and social opinion, then his character becomes that of a hermit—on a low plane, culturally, intellectually, and spiritually, and lacking the essential attributes of what we understand as human personality.

THE POLITICAL DOCTRINE OF THOMAS HILL GREEN

The object of Green's most important political work, the *Principles of Political Obligation*,[28] was to demonstrate, on the basis of his general moral philosophy, the ethical position of the state—the extent to which political authority is justifiable and obedience to law morally obligatory. Political institutions, he held, are to be judged according to their contributions to the development of the character of the citizens. For a man to live a life which he can call his own life, morally speaking, he must be able to count on certain freedom of action in the attainment of his aims. This is possible only where there is a common recognition, by members of the society in which he lives, that such freedom is for their common good. This recognition is expressed in laws. So when an individual submits to the authority of the institutions through which laws are formulated and executed, he is simply allowing his life to be regulated by conditions without which he would be unable to live a life really his own. Thus the function of law and the state is to assist man "to realize his reason, i.e., his idea of self-perfection, by acting as a member of a social organization in which each contributes to the better being of all the rest." The ethical value "of the institutions of

28 See n. 23, *supra*, p. 419.

civil life lies in their operation as giving reality to the capacities of will and reason and enabling them to be really exercised." [29]

All this implies that to have a community which can be called a politically organized community, there must be present an element of conscious political volition among its members—a feeling that the coercive authority holding them together and controlling their common action exists for their good and reflects in part their ideas as to what is essential for their good. It is, of course, true that the supremacy of laws involves restraints upon individual inclinations. The idealist philosophy justifies political compulsion and punishment. But an essential element of legal supremacy, as distinguished from mere superior physical force, is a consciousness, on the part of most of the individuals restrained, that submission to the restraints is for a common good. This does not mean that each particular act of conformity to law is secured through such an understanding, without the operation of other motives or impulses: certain laws may be obeyed by those who regard them as unjust and who submit only because of fear of the penalties of non-obedience; others are observed through force of habit, without any thought of the common good the laws are intended to serve. What Green means is this: that in a truly political society submission to law in general must be a habit of conformity founded upon a consciousness of a common good to be secured, rather than either a habit of submission based upon fear of punishment or a blind and inert following of custom. Disobedience and disloyalty are likely to appear where the average citizen feels that the laws are enacted for the benefit of special rather than common interests or that the state is protecting private advantages instead of maintaining common rights.

Thus Green recognized that a supreme coercive power is an essential attribute of the state; the protection of common rights requires forcible intervention by the state. But coercion, according to his doctrine, is not the creative or primary sustaining factor in the state; force vindicates rights but does not originate them. Superior coercive authority is an indispensable attribute of the state, essential to the maintenance of its existence and to the effective execution of its duties; but it does not make the state. Organized force is political in its nature only if exercised for the maintenance of rights, in accordance with law, and in conjunction with a popular conviction of the appropriateness of the exercise. A state is an aggregation of persons among whom common rights and

[29] *Principles of Political Obligation*, Par. 7.

interests are in general mutually acknowledged. A society cannot exist as a political community unless these rights and interests are habitually recognized and acknowledged without any forcible intervention by the state. In a state fear is needed as a motive only to restrain that minority of citizens "in whom civic sense is lacking, and for the occasional reinforcement of the law-abiding principle in others." [30]

Thus, according to Green, you must find the justification for government in the motives that prompt general obedience to it. The function of the state is essentially and exclusively a moral function. The constant object of its laws and institutions is to assist the individual in realizing his ideal of self-perfection as a member of a social group in which each member contributes to the better existence of all the others. State action is legitimate to the extent that it promotes individual freedom—in the sense of self-determined conduct directed towards reasonable ends. This does not imply that individual morality can be achieved by action of the state, or enforced by laws. The morality of an act depends upon the will of the doer—his disposition and motive in acting as he does; and the latter are inside the individual, wholly beyond the reach of laws and officers. Acts done under external compulsion of any sort lack the quality of moral acts. The state can promote morality only indirectly and through its dealings with external matters. It can do much to aid the individual of spontaneously good will. It can, on the one hand, render services which aid his naturally developing consciousness of the common good and which encourage him to impose moral duties upon himself; and it can, on the other hand, by forcible interferences in the conduct of others, remove obstacles to his self-realization.

The state's characteristic work, according to Green, is that of removing external hindrances to the voluntary performance of good acts. In executing this task it has much more to do than defend the community from foreign attack and check traditional crimes and torts. It must help to create social conditions in which there will be the fewest possible impediments in the way of each individual making the best of himself. This means, in many cases, that the state has to interfere in social life—positively, creatively—in order to see that the well-disposed individual has not only formally but actually the opportunity of doing or enjoying things "worth doing or enjoying." Thus a so-called "freedom of contract" can be properly limited in many ways, for it is "valuable only

[30] *Principles of Political Obligation*, p. 432.

as a means to an end." That end, continues Green, "is what I call freedom in the positive sense: in other words, the liberation of the powers
of all men equally for contributions to a common good. No one has a
right to do what he will with his own in such a way as to contravene
this end." [31] There is accordingly no obligation upon the state to protect contracts which defeat the end for which alone it enforces contracts.

Green held strictly to the principle that the state's task is to make
possible the achievement of the good life by the individual for himself
and that government cannot compel the individual to choose good
rather than evil ways of living. But this principle does not create, for
Green, any presumption in favor of *laisser-faire*. There are circumstances in which many individuals cannot choose reasonable ends without active intervention by the state, to provide the kind of environment
in which they have the chance to make the best of themselves morally
and intellectually. An individual, with high native capacity, may be confronted by impediments to full self-realization, arising from his ignorance and his lack of means for removing ignorance, or from fraud
or carelessness on the part of others with whom he has to deal. The
state, in providing public education, regulating the structure and management of factories, defining conditions of land tenure, preventing the
adulteration of foods, is not trying to impose civic goodness upon parents, factory-owners, landlords, food-purveyors; it is trying to set free
whatever potentialities for civic goodness are possessed by children,
factory-workers, tenants, and consumers.

Thus Green ardently defended the labor, health, and educational
legislation of his day—legislation, which, because it in one way or another limited the power of individuals to do as they pleased with what
they called their own, was widely and vigorously opposed in the name
of "individual liberty" and "freedom of contract." Just as earlier in the
century the liberal reformer saw that governmental action could promote individual liberty by removing restrictions on freedom of contract,[32] so Green believed that government, through the collectivist
legislation of his day, was enhancing individual liberty by adding restrictions upon freedom of contract. Accordingly, the state is justified in
prohibiting parents from doing as they will with their children, if parents choose to put their children to work in industries harmful to them

---

[31] *Liberal Legislation and Freedom of Contract*, III (*Works*), 371–372.
[32] Cf., *supra*, pp. 15–16.

or to let them go without elementary education. It is justified in prohibiting persons from erecting houses according to their choice, if it regards such houses as dangerously unsanitary either for the community or for those compelled, by economic conditions, to rent them.[33]

Green found the chief source of the abuses of private property in the origin of land-ownership and in the liberties that had been allowed to the owners. "The appropriation of land by individuals," he said, "has in most cases been originally effected, not by the expenditure of labour or the results of labour on the land, but by force. The original landowners have been conquerors." Early land-ownership created the institution of serfdom. When later developments in industry created new demands for laborers, the latter were drawn from among the descendants of men trained in the habits of serfdom or from others not in a situation to contract freely for the sale of their labor. Green nowhere indicated a complete and detailed program of land reform. He did not advocate confiscation of the unearned increment of land; he regarded the whole matter as too intricate to be dealt with in that sweeping way. He proposed legislation of the following sorts: prohibiting agreements between landlord and tenant that reserve the game to the landlord; withholding legal sanction from settlements that interfere with the future distribution or improvement of the land or that prevent the holder from converting his land into money or dividing it among his children; guaranteeing to outgoing tenants the value of unexhausted improvements made by them.

Although Green justified a manifold political regulation of the economic activities of individuals, his doctrine was not socialistic. He respected private ownership of property in general, regarding it as a natural instrumentality for the realization of human capacity, an essentian means of the "free life"; and he accepted economic inequality as an inevitable concomitant of inequality in native capacity. By appropriating commodities and shaping them to fit human needs, man satisfies natural wants and expresses worthy, socially valuable emotions. The political recognition of such a right is one of the conditions to the fulfilment of our ideals. Ownership of property enhances the power of the

---

[33] In the same spirit, Green advocated limitation upon freedom of contract in the matter of intoxicating beverages. Drunkenness, he held, is not a vice which is the concern merely of the drunkard: "however decently carried on, the excessive drinking of one man means an injury to others in health, purse, and capability" —as, for example, through the impoverishment of members of his family.—*Liberal Legislation and Freedom of Contract*, pp. 383–384.

moral individual to live for the common good, to fulfil his social functions. The abuses of private ownership or of any other privilege recognized by society do not establish a reason for abolishing the privilege.
The state does, however, have a definite obligation to do its utmost to
prevent or abolish the abuses. Where some owners constantly use their
property in ways that interfere substantially with ownership by others,
there may be an occasion for governmental limitation upon freedom in
the acquisition and disposition of property. If ownership is "needed to
moralize a man," how can it be said that the state must tolerate uses
of property which create a large property-less proletariat? The socialists
hold the multiplication and degradation of this class to be due to private ownership of productive property; Green finds the cause in the
abuses of ownership, which political regulation can correct without destroying the system of private property.

In his lecture on "Liberal Legislation and Freedom of Contract,"
Green analyzed the various legal restraints on industry and showed
their relation to his principles of state interference. As already indicated, he maintained that it is the function of the state to limit all contracts which create conditions producing physical degeneration or a
deterioration of the moral forces of the community. No limitations of
this nature can weaken the spirit of self-reliance and independence of
any one; they are only restraints which, by removing some of the
weight of ignorance and unhealthful environment with which many
persons would otherwise have to struggle, make these persons freer to
improve their talents and exert themselves in pursuing the higher ends
of human existence.

Thus Green ascribed to the state definite duties in defining the economic rights and controlling the social relations of men. However, although in this way he gave concrete application to his general philosophical conception of the high importance of the state for the moral
welfare of man, he was not a state-absolutist; he did not conceive
political organization as an end in itself. Although the rights of the
individual derive only from his position as member of the state, yet in
states as actually organized, the persons who hold the reins of power
often foster institutions and practices which the rationally moral individual regards as wrong, opposed to the common good. If a state fails
persistently in serving the high moral purpose for which it exists—
namely, making possible the self-realization of its citizens—it loses its
claims upon the allegiance of the latter, who then have rights against

the state or at least against the government in which the state is then imperfectly actualized; and they may be justified in repudiating or resisting its commands.

Green warned, however, that claims of rights against the state must be made with great circumspection. The citizen cannot claim to have such rights as might exist in an assumed stateless "state of nature" or some other hypothetical condition in which all individuals are assumed to be able to act irrespectively of one another. Nor can he regard every customary privilege or power as a right—a freedom which, because he has been enjoying it, he may continue to enjoy. Where new conditions create new needs for regulation of his activities, he may not plead a traditional right against the regulation; nor may he pay supreme regard to his individual opinion in determining whether in a given case an obligation to obey or a right to disobey exists. No one has a right to resist a law merely because the law requires him to do something which his inclination or judgment does not approve.

The conditions under which protest or opposition on the part of the citizen are morally justified are, Green explains, as follows: he must regard a definite social good as obtainable through successful opposition; and he must be convinced that a substantial part of the community shares his opinion. In other words, resistance to governmental authority is a right where there is *general* recognition that such resistance will promote a *public* good.[34] Then practical consideration must be given to the probable consequence of successful resistance. If the indications are that disregard of a law or a revolt against the government will result in general disorder, the resistance may not be justifiable; a substitution of general anarchy for the rule of law would bring on oppressions greatly outweighing those created by a submission to unjust laws.

The citizen moved to protest a law on moral grounds has, therefore, several questions to consider. Is his objection to the law founded on concern for the well-being of the community or only for his own comfort and pleasure? Can modification of the law be obtained constitutionally and peaceably? If not, what chances are there that forcible resistance will lead to wise modification of the law? Is the social conscience of the community capable of seeing the situation as he sees it? If the matter is important enough to suggest the overthrow of the existing government, what chance is there that the capacity and temper of

---

[34] *Liberal Legislation and Freedom of Contract*, p. 453.

the people are such as to insure that anarchy will not result? Or is the evil of the law so great that the risk of anarchy should be taken? "There can be no right to disobey the law of the state except in the interest of the state, that is, for the purpose of making the state in respect of its actual laws more completely correspond to what it is in tendency or idea, viz., the reconciler and sustainer of rights that arise out of the social relations of men." [35]

Some political idealists (e.g., Bosanquet, and, as a spokesman for Fascism, Giovanni Gentile), we shall see, have exalted political authority much higher than this and have allowed little or no room for claims by the individual, in any circumstances, against the moral supremacy of the state.[36]

The more moderate views of Green have been followed in the works of several recent writers of distinction—notably, Benedetto Croce, in Italy; Sir Henry Jones, John Watson, J. S. Mackenzie, Ernest Barker, H. J. W. Hetherington, R. F. A. Hoernlé, and H. A. L. Fisher, in England; and Professors William E. Hocking and Norman Wilde, in the United States.[37] These men hold generally with Green that only as a member of a political community is a man really a man in the truest sense of the word—that is, a being whose conduct is determined by rational and moral aims as distinguished from the merely physical desires and impulses which determine the behavior of lower animals. They generally agree also that, although the state has only ethical aims and depends for its vigor upon some sort of community of moral ideals among its members, yet it now has numerous, perhaps principally, economic tasks to perform—making a free moral life possible by preventing the glaring economic inequality that unrestrained competition creates. They hold that the end of the state is to maintain social conditions in which there are the fewest possible impediments in the way of each well-disposed individual making the best of himself, morally and intellectually. Private property exists only because society has recognized it as an aid to the moral and intellectual development of man. Governments accordingly both protect and limit private property, in so far as its uses create aids or obstacles to the moral and intellectual development of the citizens. There is in no sense a "right" of private property except as it is founded upon social

---

[35] *Liberal Legislation and Freedom of Contract*, p. 453.
[36] *Infra*, Chs. XVI, XVII.
[37] For titles of their works, see *infra*, pp. 431–432. On the ideas of Jones and Watson, see Lewis Rockow, *Contemporary Political Thought in England*, Ch. III.

recognition. However superior the economic talents of an individual may be, he is dependent upon his state both for practical success in the exercise of those talents and for the moral satisfaction that comes from a sense of having exercised them for some purpose which his moral judgment recognizes as worthy and useful. The fulfilment of a valid claim to property is in every way dependent upon the rendering by the state of those services which experience shows to be necessary both for protecting the property and for preventing its use in a way harmful to the interests or contrary to the ethical standards of the community. When a government, therefore, enforces certain standards of safety and health in industry or itself provides certain economic services, as by supplying gas or cleaning streets, it is no more "interfering" in "private economic rights" than when it enforces contracts or gives military and police protection to private property. In all such instances it is simply aiding in the maintenance of conditions which a rational and moral individual recognizes as essential to the intellectual and moral freedom and welfare of himself and others.

SELECT BIBLIOGRAPHY

THE DOCTRINE OF SOLIDARITÉ

Bouglé, C., "L'évolution du solidarisme," *Revue politique et parlementaire,* XXXV (1903), 480–505.

Bourgeois, Léon, *Solidarité* (Paris, 1896; third ed., 1902).

Charmont, Joseph, *La renaissance du droit naturel* (Paris, 1910; second ed., 1927).

Durkheim, Émile, *De la division du travail social* (second ed., Paris, 1902).

Fouillée, Alfred, *La propriété sociale et la démocratie* (Paris, 1884).

—————, *La science sociale contemporaine* (Paris, 1880; second ed., 1885).

—————, *Le socialisme et la sociologie réformiste* (Paris, 1909).

Gide, Charles, and Rist, Charles, *History of Economic Doctrines,* translated by R. Richards (Boston, etc., 1915), Bk. V. Ch. III.

Michel, Henri, *L'idée de l'état: essai critique sur l'histoire des théories sociales et politiques en France depuis la Révolution* (second ed., Paris, 1896), Bk. V, Ch. III and pp. 625–653.

—————, *La doctrine politique de la démocratie* (Paris, 1901).

Renouvier, Charles B., *La science de la morale,* 2 vols. (Paris, 1869).

THE IDEALIST DOCTRINE

Barker, Ernest, *National Character and the Factors in its Formation* (New York and London, 1927), Chs. V, VI.

Bosanquet, Bernard, "The Duties of Citizenship," pp. 1–27, in *Aspects of the Social Problem,* by various writers, edited by Bernard Bosanquet (London and New York, 1895).

——————, *The Philosophical Theory of the State* (London, 1899).

——————, *Social and International Ideals: Being Studies in Patriotism* (London, 1917).

Bradley, F. H., *Ethical Studies* (London, 1876).

Fisher, Herbert A. L., *The Common Weal* (London, 1924).

Green, Thomas Hill, *Prolegomena to Ethics,* A. C. Bradley, ed. (first ed., Oxford, 1883; third ed., 1890).

——————, *Lectures on the Principles of Political Obligation,* II (*Works of Thomas Hill Green,* R. L. Nettleship, ed., 3 vols., London, 1885–8), 334–553.

——————, *Four Lectures on the English Commonwealth,* III (*Ibid.*), 277–364.

——————, *Lecture on Liberal Legislation and Freedom of Contract* (*Ibid.*), pp. 365–386.

Hetherington, H. J. W., *Social Purpose: a Contribution to a Philosophy of Civic Society* (London and New York, 1918).

Hocking, William E., *Man and the State* (New Haven, 1926).

Hoernlé, R. F. A., *Idealism as a Philosophy* (New York, 1927).

Jones, Henry, *The Working Faith of the Social Reformer* (London, 1910).

——————, *Principles of Citizenship* (London, 1919).

Lilly, William S., *First Principles in Politics* (London, 1899).

Mackenzie, J. S., *Fundamental Problems of Life* (London and New York, 1928).

Muirhead, J. H., *The Service of the State: Four Lectures on the Political Teaching of T. H. Green* (London, 1907).

——————, "Recent Criticisms of the Idealist Theory of the General Will," in *Mind,* XXXIII, new series (1924), 166–175, 233–241, 361–368.

Ritchie, David G., *The Principles of State Interference: Four Essays on the Political Philosophy of Mr. Herbert Spencer, J. S. Mill, and T. H. Green* (first ed., London, 1891; second ed., 1896).

Wallace, William, *Lectures and Essays* (Oxford, 1898).

Watson, John, *The State in Peace and War* (Glasgow, 1919).

Wilde, Norman, *The Ethical Basis of the State* (Princeton, 1924).

Wilson, Roland K., *The Province of the State* (London, 1911).

CRITICAL EXPOSITION OF POLITICAL IDEALISM

Chin, Y. L., *The Political Theory of Thomas Hill Green* (New York, 1920).

Fairbrother, W. H., *The Philosophy of Thomas Hill Green* (London, 1896).

Haldar, Hiralal, *Neo-Hegelianism* (London, 1927).

Hobhouse, Leonard T., *The Metaphysical Theory of the State: a Criticism* (London and New York, 1918).

Hoernlé, R. F. A., "Bernard Bosanquet's Philosophy of the State," *Political Science Quarterly*, XXXIV (1919), 609–631.

Joad, G. E. M., *Essays in Commonsense Philosophy* (Swarthmore, Pa., 1919).

Lindsay, A. D., "T. H. Green and the Idealists," Ch. VII, *The Social and Political Ideas of Some Representative Thinkers of the Victorian Age*, F. J. C. Hearnshaw, ed. (London, etc., 1933).

Maccunn, John, *Six Radical Thinkers* (London, 1907), Ch. VI.

Rockow, Lewis, *Contemporary Political Thought in England* (New York, 1925), Ch. III.

Sabine, George H., "Bosanquet's Theory of the Real Will," *Philosophical Review*, XXXII (1923), 633–651.

Waddington, M. M., *The Development of British Thought from 1820 to 1890* (Toronto, 1919), pp. 165–182.

CHAPTER XVI

"REASON OF STATE" AND THE DOCTRINE OF POLITICAL AUTHORITY BY FORCE

THE AUTHORITARIAN TRADITION

THERE are creeds that exalt the corporate political community above the individual, or any number of individuals, and that recognize no valid claims on the part of the citizen either to share in governing his community or to have some sphere of personal freedom and self-determination honored by the community as outside the limits of its authority. Advocates of such creeds hold not simply, with the recent collectivist, that the state has positive services to render and that it must play, directly or indirectly, an ever-increasing part in economic and cultural life. They go further and hold that the state is, for all citizens and in all matters, the highest arbiter of conduct and opinion and is entitled to choose its own means of vindicating its supremacy.

This is sometimes called the Hegelian philosophy of the state. Hegel greatly glorified the state and regarded its authority as inevitably embodied in an autocratic and powerful government.[1] He recognized a sovereignty of the general will, it is true, but believed that only wise rulers know what that will is. He acknowledged also that the individual has rights and interests but held these to be derived from and dependent upon man's political affiliations; they are not retained from some hypothetical condition of life existing prior to or independent of political life. According to Hegel, what is best in human personality comes from the individual's organic membership in the community. He believed also that a moral and rational exaltation of the state elevates the citizen spiritually, evoking in him a devotion that tends to enlarge his personality and purify his aims of selfishness and narrow-mindedness. The Hegelian doctrine was given concrete form in autocratic constitutions set up in the German states during the first half of the century. Particularly in the Prussian constitution of 1851 and in academic

[1] See *supra,* pp. 8–9.

treatises upon that document, we find full assertions of the principle of irresponsible political authority.[2] Later in the century, we have seen, certain British philosophers took over in part the Hegelian doctrine; and some of them, notably Bernard Bosanquet, went as far as Hegel in exalting state authority.[3]

Bosanquet's argument proceeds somewhat as follows. Man's true individuality is realized only through an expression of his real will; and the latter is essentially identical with the general will, which is realized only through the state. In other words, a man, as man, is a moral being; as a moral being, he must will whatever conditions make moral life possible; but there is no such thing as moral conduct for an individual living in isolation from his fellows. The state, therefore, in maintaining the social conditions necessary for "the good life," is realizing the will of every truly moral individual. Under Bosanquet's view, accordingly, the supreme duty of man is the development of his social capacities. The life of any individual or the work of any association smaller than the state has value only "as embodying some element of the common good." [4] The rule of political justice is with Bosanquet as it was with Plato: Each is to be and do that which his special place in society requires of him. "There are higher claims than that of justice to individuals as such." [5] Within the large political communities of today, there is such a multitude of corporate interests, competing one with another as well as with the interests of the whole community, that it is difficult for the ordinary individual to see, through the maze of his more immediate and obvious relationships—to his church, family, and neighborhood, and to his workshop, trade-union, or professional association—his relationships to the general community. He is not apt

[2] Cf. L. von Rönne, *Das Staatsrecht der preussischen Monarchie*, (1856–1863; fourth ed., 1881–1884) ; and for a slightly less extreme view, Herman Schulze, *Preussisches Staatsrecht* (1872–1877; second ed., 1888). For summaries of Prussian constitutional theory, cf. J. H. Robinson, "A Brief Sketch of the Origin and Nature of the Prussian Constitution," *Annals of American Academy of Political and Social Science,* supplement to Vol. V (1894), 203–221; and W. W. Willoughby, *Prussian Political Philosophy* (1918), Ch. V.

[3] Cf. *supra*, Ch. XVI. For Bosanquet's political ideas see his works as follows: *The Philosophical Theory of the State* (1899) ; "The Duties of Citizenship," pp. 1–27 in *Aspects of the Social Problem,* edited by Bosanquet (1895) ; "Three Lectures on Social Ideals," pp. 189–249 in his *Social and International Ideals* (1917). For critical analysis of his ideas, see R. F. A. Hoernlé, "Bernard Bosanquet's Philosophy of the State," in *Political Science Quarterly,* XXXIV (1919), 609–631; George H. Sabine, "Bernard Bosanquet's Theory of the Real Will," in *Philosophical Review,* XXXII (1923), 633–651.

[4] "Duties of Citizenship," p. 10.

[5] *Social and International Ideals,* pp. 209, 211.

to realize the extent to which the life and character of each of these smaller groups is bound up with the life of the nation. The tendency is to over-rate the relative importance of the smaller groups: each individual comes to judge everything in the light of the interests not of the community but of his vocation or class. The purpose of political organization is to counteract this tendency.

Bosanquet thus felt the need of emphasizing the importance of that association which "includes all the other interests and associations, and makes them possible." The lesser associations are partial, leaving out "whole provinces of our lives and whole masses of our fellow citizens." [6] The state, because it is more comprehensive in its membership and competence than the other associations, is ethically superior to the latter; it is "the supreme community." It stands at the head of a hierarchy of social institutions, not only controlling in physical power but morally preëminent also. In differences of opinion between the state and the citizen the state is necessarily right. A man's true morality, as well as his real happiness, consists primarily in filling satisfactorily his appointed place in the organized community. Human excellence consists in the doing by each individual of that which it pertains to him to do by virtue of his citizenship; his success is bound up with his discharge of civic duties; his most important duty is that of conformity to the politically sanctioned modes of conduct. The state may, therefore, legitimately do whatever is required for the preservation and improvement of the organized life of the community and is the sole judge of what is so required. It can and will, when need arises (of which it is the sole judge), "prohibit and prevent the expression in external acts of any loyalty but that to the community which it represents." [7]

Until Italian Fascism appeared, this profound and somewhat mystic reverence for political authority found, in recent times, its fullest and most consistent expression in tsarist Russia. Philosophers and journalists of the nineteenth century elaborated, in varying forms, the idea of the superiority of Slavic to Western European civilization, and they generally described the orthodox Greek Catholic Church and the political system of the tsardom as the supreme embodiments of Slavic superiority. [8] In the latter half of the century this Slavo-philism became

---

[6] "Duties of Citizenship," p. 8.

[7] *Social and International Ideals*, pp. 283–284.

[8] For expositions of absolutist doctrines in Russia in the nineteenth century, cf. Thomas G. Masaryk, *The Spirit of Russia: Studies in History, Literature and*

a narrowed and intensified Russophilism, whose leading exponents were generally united in their abhorrence of the democratic, liberalizing forces invading Russia from the West. They regarded religious ortho-doxy, social aristocracy, monarchical government, and centralized ad-ministration—sustained by subservience and inertia among the masses —as indispensable conditions for a safe and orderly national progress. They believed that the misfortunes of modern Russia came not from an excess but from an insufficiency of absolutism. Any governmental or social institution that diminishes the scope of independent activity of the central monarchy tends, they held, to weaken the vitality and security of national life. They disparaged, therefore, not only con-stitutions and parliaments but also independent courts and jury trials and all the ordinary agencies of popular political opinion, such as pub-lic schools, autonomous universities, and independent newspapers.

The governmental system of tsarist Russia was organized and operated on these authoritarian principles.[9] The supreme task of the bureaucracy, it appears, was to suppress rebellion or outspoken com-plaint, and the test of an efficient administrator was the ability with which he curbed insubordination of any sort. The provincial governors, according to a very circumstantial account given by one of them, were mainly occupied in searching out malcontents, revolutionary or peace-ful.[10] A citizen had to show a passport in moving from one locality to another; and he had to secure, from the provincial governor, a "certifi-cate of political responsibility" in order to enter college or to enter journalism or one of the professions—such as medicine, law, or teaching. It appears from the detailed description written by the last chief of the tsar's *ochrana* (or secret police) and completed just before his death in exile from Communist Russia, that this organization had similar duties.[11] The description shows the police employing the familiar de-vices of despotism: searching residences, making arrests, and opening

Philosophy, translated from the German by Eden and Cedar Paul, 2 vols. (1919), especially Vol. II, Chs. XV–XVI; Paul N. Miliukov, *Russia and Its Crisis* (1905), especially Chs. II–IV; Julius F. Hecker, *Russian Sociology* (1915), Pt. I, Ch. II; Alfred N. Rambaud, ed., *The Case of Russia: a Composite View* by A. N. R., Vladimir G. Simkovitch, J. Novicow, Peter Roberts, and Isaac A. Hourwich (1905).

[9] For description of the administrative system of Russia under the tsars, see Sir Donald M. Wallace, *Russia* (second ed., 1905), Chs. VIII, XXIV, and *passim;* Moissaye J. Olgin, *Soul of the Russian Revolution* (1917), Ch. VII; *The Memoirs of Count Witte,* translated by Abraham Yarmolinsky (1920), *passim.*

[10] S. D. Urosov, *Memoirs of a Russian Governor,* translated from the Russian by Herman Rosenthal (1908).

[11] A. T. Vassilyev, *The Ochrana: the Russian Secret Police* (1930).

private correspondence without warrants; assuming various disguises in order to act as *agents provacateurs* and gain admission to membership in socialist and revolutionary societies; banishing political suspects without trial. Other accounts show the strict press censorship and the suppression of assembly and petition. The censors rejected not only all direct criticism of government but also all fiction that exalted liberty or disparaged oppression; and a petition for redress of grievances or a meeting for discussion of social or political conditions was ordinarily considered to be "disorder" and, therefore, a thing to be suppressed by force.

The assumptions upon which the tsar and his ministers ruled the Russian nation were eloquently stated by Pobiedonostsev, Chief Procurator of the Holy Synod from 1880 to 1905.[12] The tsar, he maintained, should be regarded as unlimited by law, custom, public opinion, or moral judgment, and as designated by God to be guardian and custodian of the nation and the orthodox church. A "constitution" for Russia should have but one formula—an oath of allegiance obligating Russian subjects to care for the welfare of the tsar. Those who neglect this obligation in any detail are criminals and traitors. All laws are an abomination because they limit the free will of the supreme ruler and his agents. "If a person whose duty it is *to act*, meets restricting instructions on every step in the law itself and in its artificial formulations, if he is always exposed to the danger of overstepping a certain line of demarcation, then the administrator loses himself in doubts and is weakened by the very thing that was intended to furnish him with power."[13] The tsar alone, with what counsel from others he chooses to obtain, should formulate and proclaim public policy. Any spontaneous political action or expression emerging from the people is irrelevant; parliaments and elections are instruments serving only selfish group interests. No agency of public administration or education should be outside the hands of the state; the administration of justice, education, the press are exclusively governmental functions.

---

[12] See K. P. Pobiedonostsev, *Reflections of a Russian Statesman* (1898). President Masaryk has described Pobiedonostsev, as "the man whose opinions were long dominant among the ruling class of Russia, . . . the man whose desperate attempt to suppress the progressive movement of the Russian youth and the Russian intelligentsia was largely responsible for the deplorable situation of the country. . . . Whoever wishes to know what had been going on in Russia under Alexander III and Nicholas II must study the mental, scientific, and journalistic characteristics of Pobiedonostsev."—*Spirit of Russia*, II, 197–198.

[13] *Reflections of a Russian Statesman*, p. 48.

Trial by jury is an "absurd and dangerous" institution—an obstruction both to effective enforcement of order and to equitable adjustment of disputes, even in countries where, as in England, it is deeply rooted in historical tradition and experience. A jury is necessarily a motley group, selected in so haphazard or artificial a way as to render it utterly incompetent for any rational and discriminating appraisal of facts. The press and popular education are other "great falsehoods" of modern civilization. The former, pretending to express popular opinion and professing informed judgments on art, literature, and the conduct of government, is really the mouthpiece of ignorant and unscrupulous money-makers or notoriety seekers, spreading gossip and prejudice in place of fact. By its selection and classification of news and rumor and the special illumination which it casts upon them and by its power to elicit popular attention and approval by satisfying the common man's fondness for sensation and scandal, it can reward and punish whom it chooses; so that if the press is uncontrolled, no government can withstand its destructive activity. As to popular education, anything beyond reading, writing, arithmetic, fear of God, and devotion to the tsar is superfluous and dangerous. The people have no uses for science and literature. On the other hand, they do need superstition, which education destroys; for superstition is "the natural, elementary power of inertia"—the ballast that keeps the ship of state in equilibrium through the long course of history; to eradicate it is to destroy social stability. Teachers and journalists who fight blind faith with knowledge are nourishing an evil spirit, luring simple and humble people from the safe fold of order and security, leading them astray into barren fields of skepticism, challenge, and doubt.[14]

Pobiedonostsev was sincerely and profoundly disturbed by the growing influence of liberal Western ideas in literature and political discussion. Russia, he complained, "has become hideous, insane and false beyond belief, because all order and consistency have vanished from our development, because all discipline of thought, feeling and morals has been relaxed among us. In public and family life all *simple, organic relations* have been shattered and destroyed, and their place has been taken by intruding *institutions and abstract principles,* mostly false or falsely applied to life and practice." "The task of authority is great and holy. Authority worthy of its name inspires people and adds wings to their actions. To see authority of this kind, to feel its inspiring in-

[14] *Reflections of a Russian Statesman,* Chs. IV–VI.

fluence is a great joy for every one who loves the truth, who seeks for light and virtue." [15]

Frequently those who exalt political authority regard physical coercion as the proper instrumentality of authority.[16] Force is said to be the normal means whereby a governmental régime maintains a nation's prestige, cultural influence, and commercial supremacy in the world at large and holds the allegiance of citizens at home. Thus a general doctrine of political authoritarianism becomes a creed of dominance by intimidation—militancy in international relations and forcible suppression of political dissent in domestic government. To-day this creed is preached and practised most thoroughly in Russia and Italy.[17] The Communist and Fascist doctrines of coercivism, however, embody ideas that were widely current in the political philosophy of the late nineteenth and early twentieth centuries; and their vogue was widely extended by the World War.

There are differences of opinion as to the propriety of tracing back to Hegel's influence the recent doctrines of political ruthlessness. Hegel repudiated the doctrines of force advocated by some of his contemporaries. In his system, "will," not "force," was to be the consolidating factor of national allegiance. He was seeking to cultivate proper intellectual and moral attitudes towards the state. The reason of man must be persuaded to understand the position and function of political authority in the life of the nation. The citizen should look up to his state—embodied in the person of the Prince as unlimited sovereign—in order that political authority may be unhindered in its sublime work of nourishing a nation's distinctive culture, manifested in its religion, moral code, science, and art. Hegel did not lay stress upon the importance of a policy of military aggression and expansion or upon the physically coercive aspects of a nation's political preëminence.

The combination of a general sanctification of political authority with a specific indication of physical power as the most natural expression and instrumentality of the authority, appears most completely in the historical and political writings of Heinrich von Treitschke, in the eighth decade of the nineteenth century. The dominant idea in Treitschke's *Politik* is that power is the most distinctive attribute of

---

[15] *Reflections of a Russian Statesman,* pp. 72, 258.
[16] See more fully, pp. 450 ff., *infra.*
[17] Cf. *supra,* pp. 168, 173–4, 177, and *infra,* pp. 479–481.

the state and that the state is morally justified in applying its power without concern for individual aims and interests.[18] Treitschke, a Saxon, worshiped the old "state-builders" of Brandenburg and Prussia. Inclined in his youth to a military career, he was turned by deafness to the vocation of a scholar and teacher. He was a pupil of several of the famous nationalist historians of Germany. He held, with these, that the ultimate moral warrant for a coercive state absolutism is to be found in the fact that the strong state is the natural and indispensable conserver of national culture; and he accepted their teaching that only Prussian arms could unite the German people. His ideas were confirmed and clarified by the successful wars of Prussia against Austria and France. Henceforth he was in no doubt that German independence and unity were made possible only by the *Machtpolitik* of the Prussian military monarchy. From this he argued generally that the most significant and indispensable service which political organization renders to a society is that of compulsive unification and stabilization. It takes a strong, centralized, militaristic state to give strength and orderliness to a people. The state, through its power, establishes order, peace, law, among the eternally clashing interests that make up a national society. Accordingly, the state's first duty is to maintain itself constantly in a position to render this peculiar service. This implies that it must be nationalistically constituted, aristocratically organized, and equipped with a strong army and an efficient police. It should normally seek no other means of making its will prevail than the means of force; it should not endeavor, in any particular exercise of authority, to appeal to the conscience and reason of its subjects; always it should demand obedience, not ask for approval.[19]

Treitschke was a professor of history successively at Leipsic, Freiburg, Kiel, Heidelberg, and Berlin. All his lectures and writings were

---

[18] Treitschke's political doctrines appear in their most complete and systematic form in his *Politics;* translated by Blanche Dugdale and Torben de Bille, 2 vols. (1916). The original, *Politik* (1897–1898), was published posthumously from his lectures delivered at the University of Berlin in 1874 and succeeding years; and the lectures were, to a considerable extent, an elaboration and systematization of his earlier controversial essays on current German politics. Other important works of Treitschke are the following: *Deutsche Geschichte im neunzehnten Jahrhundert,* 5 vols. (1879–1894); *Historische und politische Aufsätze,* 4 vols. (1886–1897).

For critical expositions of Treitschke's ideas, see the following: H. W. C. Davis, *The Political Thought of Heinrich von Treitschke* (1914); Adolf Hausrath, *Treitschke: His Doctrines of German Destiny and of International Relations* (1914); J. W. Headlam, "Heinrich von Treitschke," *English Historical Review,* XII (1897), 727–747.

[19] *Politics,* especially Vol. I, chs. I–III. See further at pp. 451–2, 454, *infra.*

constantly pervaded by this conception of the historic greatness of Germany and the exalted destiny that stood before it, under a vigorous and aggressive Prussian and Hohenzollern leadership. He was immensely and almost universally popular, his lectures attracting large and varied audiences; and he left a considerable number of disciples in Germany, particularly among the university professors; and many of his ideas have been followed by statesmen and publicists in other countries.[20]

NATIONALISM, IMPERIALISM, AND MILITARISM

The doctrine of state absolutism is now commonly associated with creeds of "nationalism"; for it is a "nation," rather than a ruler or government, to whom the citizen is called upon to surrender his individuality. It is true that the idea of nationality has also been associated with ideals of political freedom; nationalist and democratic doctrines have operated together in movements for political independence and popular government. The doctrine of government by consent, in other words, has been held to imply not only the right of the general body of citizens in a given political community to select their own form of government and choose their own governors but also the right of any given "national" group to become or remain a separate state, independent of any other nation. This liberal ideal of nationalism was realized in familiar realignments of political affiliations during the nineteenth century: the successful revolt of the Greeks against Turkey and the separation of the Belgians from Holland, in the first half of the century; the mid-century efforts of Hungarian and Italian minorities to gain their freedom from Austria; the creation of the German empire and the kingdom of Italy; the achievement of Roumanian and Serbian independence from Turkey; and the Irish "home-rule" movement. The ideal has persisted. It became a slogan of propaganda among the Allies in the World War and a cardinal point in President Wilson's statement of war aims, when he demanded a "readjustment of frontiers

[20] Treitschke was editor of the *Preussische Jahrbücher* from 1866 to 1889; and he was for several years, in the seventies, a member of the imperial Reichstag.

For statements of views by his academic disciples, cf. *Modern Germany in Relation to the Great War*, by various German writers (1916): a translation, by W. W. Whitelock, of *Deutschland und der Weltkrieg* (1915). It is a collection of essays by German and Austrian university professors, presenting recent German conceptions of German cultural ideals and political doctrines. Cf. also W. W. Willoughby, *Prussian Political Philosophy*, Chs. II–V.

. . . along lines of nationality." Thus it was in execution of a principle of national self-determination that the Peace of Versailles took away minorities from the German, Austro-Hungarian, and Ottoman empires and either restored them to older politico-racial affiliations—Alsace-Lorraine to France, part of Schleswig to Denmark, the southern Tyrol to Italy—or set them up as independent states—Poland, Czecho-slovakia, Yugoslavia.

What is it that makes a nation and endows it with this right of political self-determination? [21] Early nineteenth century philosophers and historians sought some simple and specific basis of nationality. They found the essential national bond to inhere variously in a unity of blood, speech, or geographical situation. These and other factors of a sentiment of nationality are, however, variously interdependent; and any attempt to find some single source of nationality is now generally regarded as futile. Anthropologists and historians now generally consider that a sense of nationality is primarily the product of historical experiences and cultural traditions. They attempt to say nothing more precise than that when a number of persons have, through a long period of time, lived in close contact with one another and in some way separated from other groups, there develop among them similar habits of behavior and similar notions as to what is desirable and admirable in human conduct, and these common habits and beliefs become embodied in social customs and rules which the group as a whole desires to preserve.[22] In other words, a nation is a group of people who consider themselves to be a nation; regarding themselves as essentially alike in their standards of conduct and belief (i.e., as "culturally homogeneous"), they desire to control their own social life—in religion, law, and politics.

[21] Cf. Harry E. Barnes, article on "Nationalism" in *Encyclopedia Americana,* Vol. XIX; Max S. Handman, "The Sentiment of Nationalism," *Political Science Quarterly,* XXXVI (1921), 104–121; Carleton J. Hayes, *Essays on Nationalism* (1926), and the titles by Delaisi, Le Fur, Mitscherlich, and Rose, listed on p. 459, *infra.*

[22] See Ernest Renan, "Qu'est-se q'une Nation?" an address at the Sorbonne in 1882; published in his *Discours et conferences* (1887).

The cultural-traditional conception of nationality was first fully set forth by the Swiss theorist, J. K. Bluntschli; see his *Gesammelte kleine Schriften* 2 vols. (1879–1881), Vol. II; and his *Theory of the State,* a translation of Vol. I, sixth edition (1875–1876), of his *Lehre vom modernen Stat.*

A nation, says Prof. Carleton Hayes, "is any group of persons who speak a common language, who cherish common historical traditions, and who constitute, or think they constitute, a distinct cultural society in which, among other factors, religion and politics may have played important though not necessarily continuous rôles."—*Essays on Nationalism,* p. 21. Cf. also pp. 354 ff., *supra.*

Various writers have set forth the cultural values of this distribution of mankind into culturally distinct and politically autonomous groups. Civilization, it is said, advances by diversification as well as by assimilation; and this holds for racial and national as well as for individual types. No one nation exhibits within itself the whole range of human culture. Any nation achieves significance for humanity only in respect to certain unique national attributes. Thus the division of the peoples of the earth into differing, continually competing, political groups contributes to the richness of civilization. Each nation has special virtues from the preservation of which all humanity benefits. It is, said Treitschke, in the "abundance of these limited qualities that the genius of humanity is exhibited." [23] Here again a creed of "nationalism" might be logically associated with a creed of political freedom and equality, for the most beneficial cultivation of the characteristic qualities of a nation is possible only when that nation is allowed opportunity to develop freely its peculiar customs and institutions. One people cannot enrich and invigorate itself from the spiritual resources of another unless relations of comity and coöperation are maintained between them. Each nation, having the right and obligation to defend its independent existence, is equally obligated to acknowledge the same right in other nations and to recognize that its own aims must be limited by the rights and interests of the others.

Some writers have maintained, however, that this right of independent existence belongs only to the better peoples of the world—those who have spiritual and cultural values peculiarly worth preserving and disseminating.[24] They argue, moreover, that a highly civilized nation has the right and obligation not only to protect its independence and administer its internal affairs without interference from others but also to expand its sway, by force if necessary, over more backward peoples. A superior nation, it is said, has a world vocation; it has no right to bury its talents or to exploit them selfishly. This was the common theoretical argument supporting the movement of colonial expansion of the later nineteenth century, whereby "low-cultured" races of Africa and the Pacific islands were brought under the sway of the states of Europe and America. The latter were simply assuming the "white man's burden." Imperialism was as much a duty as a right, decreed by

[23] *Politics,* I, 19, and cf. Count Hermann Keyserling, *Europe* (1928), pp. 329 ff.
[24] Cf. J. R. Seeley, *The Expansion of England* (1883); Benjamin Kidd, *Control of the Tropics* (1898); Paul Rohrbach, *Der deutsche Gedanke in der Welt* (1913), translated by E. von Mach, with the title, *German World Policies* (1915).

some law of the development of civilization. The advent of the United States as a great colonial power, in the last decade of the century, was declared by a leading American sociologist to be "a matter of destiny" —"as certain as the advent of spring or summer"; the "exceptional" and "stupendous" reserves of energy, initiative, and inventiveness of the American people were, he said, gaining a natural outlet, to the advantage both of themselves and the peoples held in dependence; to oppose this expansion of the American political domain was to engage in "idle contention against cosmic law." [25]

Such a defense of an expansive nationalism rests obviously upon the hypothesis that the physically powerful peoples are the best peoples; that in general civilization progresses towards higher stages as nations strong in material wealth and military organization extend their sway over nations less advanced in these respects. Some of the advocates offer verification of the hypothesis by showing specifically the benefits brought to communities subjugated through the colonial expansion of a powerful state. They point to barbaric institutions—like slavery—eradicated; pestilences exterminated; governmental efficiency increased and official corruption reduced; better methods of production introduced; standards of living elevated; and opportunities afforded, under proper restraint and direction, for training in the art of self-government.

Other advocates of a physically aggressive nationalism rest their case primarily upon the interests of the powerful nation. They may set forth vague ideals of an ultimate world mission to be served, but their main argument asserts the right of a strong nation to extend its sway with little or no specific regard to rights and interests of the weak peoples submerged in the process of expansion. A "great nation," it is said, has the right not only to defend itself against direct attack but also to resist whatever threatens interests of essential importance to its independence and prosperity. Moreover, for any nation to survive, it has more to do than preserve its territorial integrity, protect its material resources, and vindicate its honor. It must also grow—expand its domain, increase its military strength, exalt its national prestige; otherwise it will fall into decay and succumb in the inevitable competition between nations. The nations that succeed best in protecting their interests and enlarging their spheres of political and economic influence prove thereby their prior right to survive. War, moreover, is the natural

[25] F. H. Giddings, *Democracy and Empire* (1900), p. 270.

instrumentality of national expansion and its outcome is the test of the right to expand. "It is war that makes nations." [26]

Militant nationalists to-day often use old metaphysical arguments for war and revive the martial allegories of religions of antiquity. Conflict between states, it has been said in both ancient and contemporary writings, is a manifestation of a universal principle of existence. Everywhere change and progress proceed only from the struggle for survival between irreconcilable forces—Good against Evil, Light against Darkness, the Strong (and thereby worthy) against the unworthy Weak. The eternal conflict is between forms and forces that are sanctioned and those that are not sanctioned by God or Nature; and the naturally or divinely Right force can maintain its inherent superiority only by constant assault upon the Wrong and ultimately weaker force that opposes it. Those who seek a more direct or explicit divine approbation of war find it in the familiar pictures, in sacred books, of the Divine Being as a God of Battle, instigating and presiding over wars and revealing His will in the outcome. In Christian countries, the apologists for war specifically deny that the Christian Gospel—with all its praise of brotherly love, peace, and good will—contains any condemnation of war. The sayings of Christ, it is maintained, do not always mean what they seem to mean. In the simple metaphors of His sermons and parables, He sought to soften the inevitable animosities of mankind; but He was not laying down definite standards of conduct which He expected or desired to have set up as obstacles to a vindication of the power and prestige of "great nations." [27] To interpret the Christian Gospel as a condemnation of war would be to represent the Messiah as repudiating Jehovah, who was the Lord of Battles; and it would put Christianity in opposition to some cosmic principle of conflict. For whether or not there is a Divine will behind it all, "the law of struggle is a fundamental law of nature," and war is "a permanent and inextricable part of the universal web of human things." [28]

Although the recent theoretical advocates of war restate these metaphysical and theological arguments, they bring in also supporting historical, biological, and ethical reasons for war. They maintain that, from the beginnings of recorded history, the fundamental interests

[26] Walter Bagehot, *Physics and Politics* (1873), p. 77.

[27] See the rectorial address on "Idealism in International Politics," delivered by Lord Birkenhead before the students of Glasgow University; reported by the *Manchester Guardian*, November 8, 1923.

[28] Henry Arthur Jones, *Patriotism and Popular Education* (1919), p. 98.

of different political communities have been continually in opposition, and with the advance of civilization, wars have tended to increase rather than diminish in scope and intensity; moreover, war generally facilitates the survival and development of the more virile races of mankind; and it has permanent cultural and moral value in maintaining and diffusing civilization and cultivating worthy human traits.

It is a familiar theory that states originated as incidents or consequences of war; government, it has often been said, began as military government—in the form of the coördinated action and centralized direction necessary for repelling or attacking a neighboring tribe or for holding in subjection a captured people. According to this theory, states begin as organizations for war, and war remains the chief factor in political evolution. "Since the long-headed men first drove the short-headed men out of the best land of Europe, all European history has been the history of the superposition of the more military nations over the less military." [29] Efficiency, inventiveness, and orderliness are indispensable factors of military strength; so that the most military nations have been essentially the most progressive nations—industrially, culturally, and politically. Thus war has been the principal means by which humanity has risen to its present level of civilization.

Some of the writers who have insisted upon this sort of historical validity in the wars of the past have yet contended that there has been a prevailing trend towards the disappearance of war—a trend revealed in the results of the wars themselves. The nations, they say, that have been the most efficient in war have been basically the most highly cultured and most peace-loving nations. Civilization depends in an increasing measure upon the arts of peace; and the more civilized nations have had to fight to preserve the peace of the world. In England's suppression of the Scottish highlanders, in Russia's subjugation of the Caucasus, and in the nineteenth century conquests in Africa and Asia by Western countries, orderly communities were suppressing turbulent communities. War was being used as an agency of peace. Furthermore, in order for the more enlightened, and thereby the more pacific, communities, to be able to go on doing their civilizing work, they must keep strong and warlike enough to suppress the nations that will not keep the peace. Permanent peace will be achieved when the process is completed—through the concentration of an overwhelming preponder-

---

[29] Walter Bagehot, *Physics and Politics*, p. 49. See also generally, Franz Oppenheimer, *The State* (1914).

ance of military strength in the hands of the most pacific communities. Thus the history of civilization has revealed a long war to end war.[30] Certain writers, on the other hand, have found in history a demonstration of the permanence and increasing significance of war and its arts as factors in the progress of civilization. As civilization advances, wars, they maintain, become more frequent, more protracted, and more destructive. Thus the task of war is eternal. There is always contention for survival and dominance between the more and the less civilized nations, and the struggle will continue to take the form of armed strife, defensive and aggressive. "The appeal to arms," said Treitschke, "will be valid until the end of history." [31]

The biological-historical case for war has drawn support from a few distinguished scientists. Ernst Haeckel—first and most influential apostle of Darwinism in Germany—who was diligent in making broad philosophical and sociological applications of his biological ideas, contended that egoism, which he characterized as a universal biological law, manifested itself in human society in a sort of racial cannibalism.[32] The earth, he said, has insufficient resources for all the racial groups that appear upon its surface. The weaker groups perish not only through their incapacity to compete effectively in the common struggle for the limited supply of the means of life but also through their inability to defend themselves against conquest and ultimate annihilation by the stronger groups. Karl Pearson likewise characterized international strife as part of "the natural history of mankind." A "scientific view of life," he maintained, must recognize that human progress comes about through an eternal contest not only between individuals but also of race against race. As a superior nation increases its internal efficiency by taking steps to insure that its weaker stocks die off, so it achieves

[30] See Walter Bagehot, *op. cit.;* John Fiske, "Manifest Destiny" (1880), in his *American Political Ideas Viewed from the Standpoint of Universal History* (1911), pp. 93–144; W. G. Sumner, "War" (1903), in his *War and Other Essays* (1911), pp. 3–40; A. G. Keller, *Man's Rough Road* (1932), Ch. IX; M. A. Vaccaro, *Les bases sociologiques du droit et de l'état* (1898), Chs. IV, V.

[31] *Politics*, I, 29.

See also the following: Freiherr Colmar von der Goltz, *Das Volk in Waffen* (1883, and later editions), translated as *The Nation in Arms* (1887, etc.); S. R. Steinmetz, *Die Philosophie des Krieges* (1907); Homer Lea, *The Valor of Ignorance* (1909); Karl Lamprecht, *Krieg und Kultur* (1914); Friedrich von Bernhardi, *Deutschland und der nächste Krieg* (1912), translated as *Germany and the Next War* (1914); Max Scheler, *Der Genius des Krieges* (third ed., 1917); and the writers listed in notes 33–35, *infra*. For an analysis of such doctrines, cf. P. Sorokin, *Contemporary Sociological Theories* (1928), Ch. VI.

[32] Haeckel, *Die Welträtsel* (1899), translated as *The Riddle of the Universe* (1901); *Der Kampf um den Entwickelungsgedanken* (1905).

external efficiency—and thus advances the evolution of the whole human race—by continually contending with other strong nations and crushing out the weaker nations. It can prove its equality with other superior nations only by constantly "struggling" with them for trade routes, sources of raw materials, and food supplies. When it comes into contact with inferior groups, it either surrenders any claim to superiority by mixing with them or adapting its ways to their ways or vindicates its superiority by ejecting the inferior groups or exploiting them to its own uses. We cannot, Pearson declared, escape "the victory of the physically and mentally better organized. . . . The path of progress is strewn with the wreck of nations; traces are everywhere to be seen of the hecatombs of inferior races, and of victims who found not the narrow way to greater perfection. Yet these dead peoples are, in very truth, the stepping stones on which mankind has arisen to the higher intellectual and deeper emotional life of to-day." [33]

Popular writers adopt these general biological arguments and place exclusive emphasis upon war as the form of the selective struggle between nations. They extend the argument by showing how war operates also as an agency of internal selection. Thus they maintain that, although deaths in battle destroy a disproportionate number of the better type of individuals (since armies are composed of selected youth), yet this disgenic effect of war is more than offset by the good effects from the larger number of the weak and indigent taken off by the famine and disease that come in the wake of war.[34] One writer argues that "during the economic distress of war, ordinarily prohibiting the increase of families, it is the most robust of constitution who are likely to yield to the sexual impulse"; thus better offspring are insured. Another argues that the virile men of a victoriously invading army improve the stock of the peoples of a conquered territory by the "large progeny" the invading soldiers leave behind in the regions they temporarily occupy.[35]

Such writers also exalt war for its direct cultural, moral, and spiritual benefits. War, they say, is an essential factor of national cohesion, a means of spreading civilization from one nation to another, and a

[33] Pearson, *National Life from the Standpoint of Science* (1900), p. 64.

[34] See, for example, S. B. Luce, "The Benefits of War," *North American Review*, CLIII (1891), 672–683; Hudson Maxim, *Defenseless America* (1915); Henry Arthur Jones, *op. cit.*, n. 28, p. 445, *supra*.

[35] Corrado Gini, "The War from the Eugenic Point of View," in *Eugenics in Race and State* II (1923), pp. 430–431; Hudson Maxim, *op. cit.*, p. 274.

general physical and psychical tonic for citizens of the fighting nations. War, said Treitschke, consolidates a people, reveals to each individual his relative unimportance, sweeps away factional hostilities and group selfishness, and intensifies patriotism and national idealism. When two nations are at war, each comes more fully to know and respect the other, and the exchange of good qualities is made easier. Finally, it is said, war begets various individual virtues—valour, industriousness, inventiveness, orderliness, "habit of obedience," "cleanliness," "temperance," "moral stamina," "spiritual enlargement." The excesses of idleness, luxury, extravagance, and sentimental sympathy for the weak and indigent come in times of peace; and the periods of prolonged peace in the history of a nation are the sluggish, spiritless, degenerate stages in its cultural development. The achievements of peace do not "stir our souls to their finest responses." "The grandeur of history lies in the perpetual conflict of nations." [36]

These arguments for war have not been developed with any sort of logical precision or completeness. They have been generally submitted as axioms. They could hardly be offered in any other form. We have no historical or other empirical data for a closely reasoned argument either for or against war as a "natural" instrumentality of international policy. Generally the historians and ethnologists have not attempted to establish conclusions as to the extent to which wars in the past have elevated rather than degenerated the general scale of civilization, whether successes in wars have been due to the superior virtues of the conquering group or to the accidents of good fortune, or how far the spread of civilization has been brought about by military conquest and how far through a displacement of backward by advanced peoples as a result of the higher efficiency and fecundity of the latter. Moreover, no scientific student of human behavior could seriously undertake to observe systematically the qualities that appear to become most active in times of war and find out in that way whether wars contribute more to the good than to the evil sides of human nature. Finally, the biological theory of natural selection through survival of the fittest hardly supplies any argument for war as a normal and essential phase of the relations between states. Biologists now generally discredit that sort of interpretation of the theory, for the doctrine of natural selection serves only to show how those forms survive that succeed in adapting them-

---

[36] Henry Arthur Jones, *op. cit.*, p. 105; Treitschke, *Politics*, p. 21. See also S. R. Steinmetz, *op. cit.*, *passim;* and the titles listed in n. 35, *supra*.

selves to the conditions of survival. It contains no hypothesis as to what methods of adaptation generally succeed. Accordingly, it gives no preference whatever to conflict over coöperation in the relations between the forms that struggle to survive.

THE STATE AS PHYSICAL POWER

The idea that war generally brings positive human benefits, apart from its specific utility as a weapon of national defense, is essentially associated with a broader doctrine of "power" as something of supreme value in itself, both in man and in human society.[37] The individual to be most admired, according to this doctrine, is the strong man who compels other men to act in fulfilment of his will. At times the power-worshipers admit that spiritual and intellectual capacities may be as effective as physical capacities as factors of the compelling strength, but generally they appear to have physical power principally in mind. The whole conception is related to Nietzsche's glorification of the "masterly" virtues of man. Nietzsche, we have seen, denounced the Jewish-Christian-bourgeois moral creeds as doctrines of decadence; for, he said, they protect and foster the weak; and weakness is the greatest of all human vices. The essential attribute of a being that is really a man is a "will to power." The "good" man is the man who understands, acknowledges, and cultivates this impulse in himself and glorifies and courageously practises the aggressive, combative virtues that harmonize with the impulse. The truly moral person has no place for the vulgar and slavish virtues of humility, self-sacrifice, pity, gentleness.[38]

The theory of political absolutism applies to states this moral philosophy of power. The great state is the one that dominates over other states and governs its own citizens by the compulsions of force rather than reason. According to this conception, the motive that supplies the impulse to the forming of a political society and thereafter determines its structure and controls its policy is not, as Marxians and certain individualists have maintained, economic—the craving for material possessions and pleasures; nor is it, as the ancient Greeks and

---

[37] This appears in the works of Nietzsche, Treitschke, and Haeckel; see the references *supra*, p. 312, n. 5; p. 440, n. 18; p. 447, n. 32.

For critical analysis of the general idea of the state as force, see William E. Hocking, *Man and the State* (1926) Ch. V; John Watson, *The State in Peace and War* (1919), pp. 167 ff. Compare also the ideas of the Russian Communists and the Fascists, Ch. VI, *supra*, and Ch. XVII, *infra*.

[38] See *supra*, pp. 312–313.

the nineteenth century idealists held, the aspiration of man to develop his higher spiritual and rational faculties; and it is not, as the liberal democrat considers it to be, the desire to protect the unfortunate and maintain just and generous relations among all members of the community. Everywhere the dominant political motive has been love of power, passion for self-assertion. The economic motive operates, in political action, chiefly as servant of the power motive. Moreover, a state, in order to be powerful and eminent, must be guided by hard and ambitious men. Every statesman who has served his country well has been strong-willed; strongly nerved; personally enjoying power in itself; finding, in the cultivation of the strength and prestige of his state, an enhancement of his own personality. Political history, said Treitschke, is largely the record of the combat between such men. "The features of history are virile, unsuited to sentimental or feminine natures. . . . The ruling nations are not so much the races rich in mental endowment, but rather those whose peculiar gift is force of character." Culture is born and matures more naturally and happily in periods when statesmen and the state are strong: Chaucer, in the time of the British conquerors of France; Shakespeare under Elizabeth; Milton under Cromwell; Scott and Byron in the time of British victories over France again.[39]

Advocates of the strong state sometimes discuss the relation of political authority to the ethical nature of man and acknowledge that the state does have ultimate moral and cultural ends to which its power should be subservient. The state, it is said, is under obligation to vindicate individual rights, protect the interests of lesser associations, and conserve and improve the cultural values of the nation; and as the grandest institution for the moral elevation of humanity, it is necessarily subject to moral law. Thus Treitschke, commending Machiavelli for having introduced into political thinking the fruitful idea that the state is power, criticized him for having omitted any consideration of the necessity that political power, having been achieved, should justify itself by its exertion for the highest moral welfare of man.[40] In other words, the evil of Machiavellianism is not in the immorality of its means but in its neglect of any great moral purpose. Machiavelli was right in maintaining that, when the salvation of the state is at stake, there is no place for considerations as to the purity of the means it

[39] *Politics*, I, 21, 24.
[40] *Ibid.*, I, 83–88.

employs to preserve itself; but he was wrong in implying that the state exists in order to exist. So also Napoleon's policy was wrong not because it sought great power for France but because it was a mere land-grabbing scheme and was not conceived as a necessary part of a comprehensive plan for the permanent consolidation and development of French national culture.[41]

The power of the state, Treitschke continued, should be regarded as something to be used in the service of high national ends. The culture of a nation clusters about its political system. The state cannot, therefore, leave it to the pleasure of parents as to whether their children should be nurtured and educated; or to the chances of private initiative as to whether art should be cherished and supported. "Art is as indispensable to men as their daily bread." [42] Moreover, governments must constantly intervene in the relations between private citizens and associations in order to restrain their selfishness and conciliate their rivalries in the thousands of collisions that are inevitable in the complex civilization of modern times. However, as state activity widens, it should become more indirect and moderate in its methods—less in the manner of direct compulsion, restraint, or service; more in the manner of clearing away impediments, spurring on, enlightening. The ultimate object of political authority is individual freedom. The state, therefore, has to set limits to its activities. It must allow free development of religious faith and the fearless seeking after knowledge. "In all questions of conscience every man must decide for himself alone." Both "the state and public opinion must allow the individual to develop his individual character both in thought and in act." "The most precious and especial possession of our nation, . . . which will yet constitute the German state a new phenomenon in political history, is the German's invincible love of personal freedom." [43]

Thus in Treitschke's elaboration and illustration of his general doctrine, we find specific ideas that can be mutually reconciled only with great difficulty: on the one hand, views narrowly autocratic, aristocratic, nationalistic, militaristic; on the other hand, explanations and qualifications that make him appear to be a supporter of moderate and liberal government, in a state more concerned in improving the moral and physical welfare of its subjects than in advancing its own power

[41] *Politics*, II, 587 ff.
[42] *Ibid.*, I, 76.
[43] *Freiheit und Königthum* (fourth ed., 1871), in Treitschke, *Historische und politische Aufsätze*, 4 vols., III (1896), 17.

and prestige—a paternalistic state, it is true, but one safeguarding individual initiative, fair in its international policy, and resorting reluctantly to war.

Professor Friedrich Meinecke (distinguished editor of the *Historische Zeitschrift*) has recently attempted, in a book setting forth historically and critically the principle of "reason of state," to explain this interweaving of militarist and idealist conceptions in absolutist theories of the nature and aims of the state.[44] States, says Meinecke, like individuals and lesser associations, have a two-sided character—"biologic," elemental, egoistic, on the one hand; ethical and social, on the other hand. So reason of state is constantly in danger of degenerating into advantage of state—into a nationalist egoism, that is, which blends easily with advantage of the statesman and becomes a mere Machiavellian technique for tyrants, without ethical implications. But the long trend is in the other direction. History reveals a general, though intermittent, ascent towards a political world in which the more elementary forces fall slowly into the background and power is striven for less as an end in itself and more as an indispensable means to the spiritual well-being of the community. The zest for power tends to become sublimated into nobler forms. There is a pragmatic basis for this tendency. The successful statesman—although working zealously for the maintenance and enlargement of state power and inevitably stimulated in those efforts by a conscious, personal ambition as well as by a subconscious instinct for power—recognizes also that the strength of his community is produced through the cultivation of ethical and legal values and that power itself is made insecure through any persistent or radical distortion of these values. The security of the whole structure of political authority depends first, upon the existence of a satisfied community, capable of rendering and willing to render political service or obedience, and second, upon an international good faith and good will. Blindly growing power destroys itself.

What Meinecke seeks to demonstrate is that this dualistic conception

[44] *Die Idee der Staatsräson in der neueren Geschichte* (1924). During the World War many British, French, and American commentators on Treitschke ignored his statement of liberal political aims and methods; the writers were then seeking to show, in the most emphatic way, his influence on the German military and imperial policies that brought on the war. See the following: Ernest Barker, "Nietzsche and Treitschke: the Worship of Power in Modern Germany," *Oxford Pamphlets*, Vol. IV, No. 20 (1914); John Adam Cramb, "Treitschke and Young Germany," in his *Germany and England* (1914); Émile Durkheim, "*Germany Above All*": *German Mentality and War*, translated by "J. S." (1915); A. T. Hadley, "The Political Teachings of Treitschke," *Yale Review*, IV (1914), 235–247.

of the state is essential for all political thought and action. The statesman must find some intermediate position between a blind apotheosis of
Machtpolitik, on the one hand, and, on the other hand, an idealism
that admits no compromise between moral right and political necessity
and attempts to place the state absolutely under the domains of law
and morality. Meinecke acknowledges that this intermediate position
can never be exactly found nor even indicated with any close approach
to precision. Neither the statesman nor the populace can be entirely
freed from primitive emotional impulses. Zest for largeness of power is
ever in their blood. In the matter, for example, of extending the territorial domain of a state, it is often beyond the capacity of either
government or people to discriminate between what is imperatively
needed for legitimate reasons of state and what is desired out of a
sheer joy of expansion. Neither the historian nor the political philosopher can define the limits between *Kratos* and *Ethos;* neither can
determine how far, at any given moment in the life of a state, free play
must still be given to the love of power and desire to dominate that
have gradually elevated primitive man into the sort of being whom history calls civilized, and how far, also in the interest of civilization, such
a motive must be restrained by considerations of right and law.

Although the authoritarians thus justify the coercive and aggressive
state by the cultural and moral ends it serves, generally they do not set
up these ends as juristic or ethical limits to political power. The state,
they believe, is essentially an organization of irresponsible power. "If,"
said Treitschke, "the state neglects its strength in order to promote the
idealistic aspirations of man, it repudiates its own nature and per-
ishes." [45] The state's duty to preserve and strengthen itself takes precedence over all other obligations. Its essential task internally is to uphold and impose its will upon all within its bounds; externally, its
primary duty is to look out for its own welfare. In its execution of these
inevitable obligations, the state should not be judged by the ethical
canons that are applied to individual behavior. The moral standards for
state action are set by its own peculiar nature and ultimate objects. The
state at times must disregard familiar norms of law and morality. From
the very nature of its function, it comes up against forces that drive it
into violations of right.

This conception of the strong state as the servant of world civilization passes easily into a general exaltation of greatness of political

[45] *Politics,* I, 91.

power and vastness of domain, unassociated with any sense of moral responsibility. The doctrine tends to become a provincial, often insolent and mercenary, and generally amoral, conception of national rights and destiny. A state, it is contended, has under all conditions a right to protect its interests, including purely economic interests, without reference to any essential contribution it can make to the civilization of the world. It has also the right to defend its "national honor," for insults or slights unavenged invite disregard of substantial national interests. A "great" state should disregard rights and interests of backward, impotent peoples. Even in disputes between powerful states, it is impossible to place much reliance upon either traditional law or abstract right. Their intercourse must be controlled by calculations of self-interest, on both sides. The principles of law for the relations between states are not clearly defined, and there can be no impartial tribunals for adjudication. International controversies should be frankly recognized as disputes in the adjustment of which there is no standard of right and justice to which a common appeal can be made. The most important disputes between states are conflicts of interest, which cannot be settled by law. "Law," said Lord Hugh Cecil, in 1912, "supposes common ground between contending parties; but in a conflict of interests there is no common ground." [46] Thus the approved policy appears to be that of "Sacro Egoismo!"—"My Country, right or wrong!"—"Deutschland über Alles!"

This policy of intransigence in international affairs becomes naturally associated with a policy of governmental irresponsibility in internal affairs. The general doctrine is that a state exists to uphold the interests of a sovereign political community against all other interests—whether of other communities or of its own citizens—by whatever means are expedient. The corporate nation, moreover, can deal with other nations and with its own citizens only through an established governmental régime, which therefore becomes the depositary of the irresponsible political authority; and irresponsible authority has, in secular affairs at least, to depend chiefly upon physical coercion as the means of maintaining its supremacy. Thus a theory of political absolutism adopts generally the creed that might makes right; and in Treitschke's words, "weakness must always be condemned as the most disastrous and despicable of crimes, the unforgiveable sin of politics." [47]

[46] *Conservatism* (1912), p. 206, also pp. 202, 208.
[47] *Politics*, I, 95.

This political philosophy of violence serves both "radical" and "conservative" social groups equally and in both cases may be used in support of attitudes of either loyalty or disloyalty to an established government. Economic, social, or religious groups whose interests and ideals are effectively sanctioned by existing law most readily appreciate the advantages of respect for legal authority; they are foremost in invoking the full force of government to suppress private violence and restrain outspoken criticism of the law. When, however, existing law appears to be in conflict with established social interests, then the authority of the interest may be rated higher than that of the law; the advocate of "law and order" becomes contemptuous of law and may advocate disorder or even armed rebellion.

There are many familiar examples of the illegal violence of conservatives. In the eighteen eighties, the Conservative party of Great Britain successfully sponsored summary measures by the British government in dealing with disorders among the South-Irish agitators for "land-reform" and "home-rule." Three decades later the same party was directly and openly implicated in a North-Irish armed insurrection against the government, which was preparing to put into effect a home-rule enactment of Parliament. Sir Edward Carson (formerly crown prosecutor of the rebellious South Irish and later attorney-general) led a large armed assemblage in Belfest in a solemn pledge to resist home-rule by any means. Bonar Law (later prime minister), persuading an English gathering to lend its support to the Ulster insurrection, proclaimed that the Opposition, to which he belonged, would "not be restrained by the bonds which would influence us in any ordinary political struggle." "We shall," he said, "use any means, whatever means seem to us likely to be most effective. I say now, with a full sense of the responsibility which attaches to my position, that if the attempt be made under present conditions, I can imagine no length of resistance to which Ulster will go in which I shall not be ready to support them." The acts and utterances of the Conservatives in the Ulster crisis were characterized by Winston Churchill (then a Liberal) as follows: The Tories "denounce all violence except their own. They uphold all law except the law they choose to break. They always welcome the application of force to others. . . . They . . . select from the Statute Book the laws they will obey and the laws they will resist." [48]

[48] See Herbert Asquith, *Fifty Years of the British Parliament* (1926), II, pp. 136--138, 147.

So also the French Royalists, who seek to restore to France the orderliness of absolute monarchy, advocate and practise disorder as a means for achieving that goal: they threaten armed resistance to the present government of France and commit acts of violence against private citizens who stand in their way.[49] Conservative journals in Great Britain and the United States have applauded not only the iron hand by which the Fascists govern Italy but also the course of illegal violence the Fascists pursued in getting themselves into control of government. Conservative economic groups sometimes resort to and widely condone violence as a cure for labor radicalism (as in the personal assaults and the destruction of property directed against members of the I.W.W. at Everett and Centralia, Washington, in 1916 and 1918); and they encourage, approve, or tolerate a lawless enforcement of law (as in the prosecution of Thomas Mooney in California).[50]

Thus it appears that not every publicist who advises respect for order and authority is opposed to violence or illegality as such. His attitudes on such a matter may be varied, colored by the circumstances of the moment. His opposition may be to sedition of one color, but not to sedition of all colors; he may condemn only the disorderly acts committed by other groups or committed for ends not his own. Indeed the doctrines of either violent rebellion or of government by violence are peculiar neither to conservatism nor to radicalism. They are rather characteristic of extremes of opinion, both to the right and the left. The Sinn Fein leaders—De Valera and Pearce—were not more ardent advocates of armed insurrection as a political weapon in Ireland than were Sir Edward Carson and Bonar Law. Mussolini and his admirers throughout the world have been, we shall now see, as explicit as Lenin and Trotsky in justifying both revolutionary violence and a governing authority dependent upon the "strong arm and sharp sword."

SELECT BIBLIOGRAPHY

ADVOCATES OF THE AUTHORITARIAN NATIONALIST STATE

Bernhardi, Friedrich, *Germany and the Next War* (New York, 1914), translation, by Allen H. Powles, of *Deutschland und der nächste Krieg* (Stuttgart and Berlin, 1912).

---

[49] See *supra*, p. 338.
[50] See Louis Adamic, *Dynamite: the Story of Class Violence in America* (1931), *passim;* The *Mooney-Billings Report* (1932), from the report of the "Wickersham Commission."

Bosanquet, Bernard, "The Duties of Citizenship," in *Aspects of the Social Problem* (London, 1895).

——————, *The Philosophical Theory of the State* (London, 1899).

——————, *Social and International Ideals* (London, 1917).

Cecil, Lord Hugh, *Conservatism* (London, 1912).

Giddings, Franklin H., *Democracy and Empire* (New York, 1900).

Goltz, Freiherr Colmar von der, *The Nation in Arms* (London, 1887, etc.), translation, by Philip A. Ashworth, of *Das Volk in Waffen* (Berlin, 1883, etc.).

Haeckel, Ernst, *The Riddle of the Universe* (London, 1900), translation, by Joseph McCabe, of *Die Welträtsel* (Leipsic, 1899, etc.)

——————, *Der Kampf um den Entwickelungsgedanken* (Berlin, 1905).

Keyserling, Count Hermann, *Europe,* translated by Maurice Samuel (New York, 1928).

Kidd, Benjamin, *Control of the Tropics* (New York, etc., 1898).

Lamprecht, Karl, *Krieg und Kultur* (Leipsic, 1914).

Lea, Homer, *The Valor of Ignorance* (New York and London, 1909).

——————, *The Day of the Saxon* (New York, 1912).

Pearson, Karl, *National Life from the Standpoint of Science* (London, 1901, 1905).

Pobiedonostsev, Constantine, *Reflections of a Russian Statesman,* translated by Robert Crozier Long (London, 1898).

Rönne, L. von, *Das Staatsrecht der preussischen Monarchie* (1856–1863; fourth ed., Leipsic, 1881–1884).

Rohrbach, Paul, *German World Policies* (New York, 1915), translation, by E. von Mach, of *Der deutsche Gedanke in der Welt* (Düsseldorf and Leipsic, 1913).

Scheler, Max F., *Der Genius des Krieges* (1915, third ed., Leipsic, 1917).

Schulze, Hermann, *Preussisches Staatsrecht* (1872–1877; second ed., Leipsic, 1888).

Seeley, J. R., *The Expansion of England* (London, etc., 1883).

Steinmetz, S. R., *Die Philosophie des Krieges* (Leipsic, 1907).

Treitschke, Heinrich von, *Freiheit und Königthum* (fourth ed., 1871) in Vol. III of his *Historische und politische Aufsätze,* 4 vols. (Leipsic, 1886–1897).

——————, *Politics,* 2 vols. (New York, 1916), translation, by Blanche Dugdale and Torben de Bille, of *Politik,* 2 vols. (Leipsic, 1897–1898).

Vaccaro, Michele Angelo, *Les Bases sociologiques du droit et de l'état* (Paris, 1898), translation, by J. Gaure, of *Le basi del diritto e dello stato* (Turin, 1893).

CRITICAL DISCUSSIONS

Davis, H. W. C., *The Political Thought of Heinrich von Treitschke* (London, 1914).

Delaisi, Francis, *Political Myths and Economic Realities* (New York, 1927), Ch. IV.

Gross, Leo, *Pazifismus und Imperialismus: eine kritische Untersuchung ihrer theoretischen Begründungen* (Leipsic and Vienna, 1931).

Handman, Max S., "The Sentiment of Nationalism," *Political Science Quarterly*, XXXVI (1921), 104–121.

Hausrath, Adolf, *Treitschke: His Doctrines of German Destiny and of International Relations, together with a Study of his Life and Work* (New York, 1914).

Hayes, Carlton, J. H., *Essays on Nationalism* (New York, 1926).

Hecker, Julius F., *Russian Sociology* (New York, 1915), Pt. I, Ch. II.

Hocking, William E., *Man and the State* (New Haven, 1926), Ch. V.

Le Fur, Louis, *Races, nationalités, états* (Paris, 1922).

Masaryk, Thomas G., *The Spirit of Russia*, 2 vols., translated by Eden and Cedar Paul (London and New York, 1919), Vol. II, Chs. XV–XVI.

Meinecke, Friedrich, *Die Idee der Staatsräson in der neueren Geschichte* (Munich and Berlin, 1924).

Michels, Robert, *Der Patriotismus: Prolegomena zu einer soziologischen Analyse* (Munich and Leipsic, 1929).

Mitscherlich, Waldemar, *Nationalismus, die Geschichte einer Idee* (second ed., Leipsic 1929; first published under title *Der Nationalismus West-Europas*, Leipsic, 1921).

Niebuhr, Reinhold, *Moral Man and Immoral Society* (New York, 1932).

Rose, J. Holland, *Nationality in Modern History* (New York, 1916).

Sorokin, Pitirim, *Contemporary Sociological Theories* (New York and London, 1928), Ch. VI.

Sumner, William Graham, *War and Other Essays* (New York, 1911), Ch. I.

Watson, John, *The State in Peace and War* (Glasgow, 1919).

Willoughby, Westel W., *Prussian Political Philosophy* (New York and London, 1918).

CHAPTER XVII

THE FASCISTS

ORIGINS

Most accounts of Fascism relate its advent to the manner of operation of parliamentary government in Italy during the sixty-odd years preceding the Fascist *coup d'état* of October 28, 1922. In 1861, the several states occupying the Italian peninsula were merged into a kingdom of Italy, King Victor Emmanuel of Piedmont becoming king of Italy and the Piedmont constitution (the "Statuto" of 1848, granted by his father) becoming the constitution of Italy. This constitution provided for parliamentary government of the English type. Although it did not in set terms make cabinet ministers responsible to the elective chamber, it was so interpreted by those who put the system into actual practice. The administrative system set up in the new kingdom was copied generally from that of France. Thus a country that since medieval times had been covered by mutually independent states—alike in having autocratic governments, but with varying political traditions—was first put under a system of responsible government, borrowed from a country of long experience with representative institutions, and then given a system of centralized administration and uniform local government, borrowed from a country that had been politically united and administratively centralized for several centuries. The multiple and unstable party situation, the strength of the traditions of localism, and the high degree of illiteracy among the people put extreme difficulties in the way of the normal operation of a liberal parliamentary system of government in Italy.

As to the measure in which these difficulties were overcome, there are wide differences of opinion.[1] The Fascists and their apologists mark exclusively the bad features—demagogy, bureaucracy, and electoral cor-

[1] For varying views on this question, cf. Benedetto Croce, *History of Italy, 1871–1915* (1929); Robert Michels, *Sozialismus und Fascismus in Italien* (1925), pp. 1–87; Gaetano Salvemini, *Il Risorgimento Italiano* (1925); Luigi Sturzo, *Italy and Fascismo* (1926), Ch. I; Luigi Villari, *Italy* (1929), Chs. VI, VII.

ruption in the government, the inconstancy of politicians, and the political apathy and ignorance of the people. There was rarely, it is maintained, any predominant political voice of the nation. The masses were more interested in private, local, and group affairs than in national questions, and they were generally unimpressed by such abstractions as "national government" and "popular rule." Parliaments and ministries were generally dominated by ambitious and skilful leaders, who, although not uninspired by ideals of national welfare, were able and willing to maintain themselves in power by methods of factional intrigue in parliament and of governmental pressure upon an indifferent electorate. Depretis, eight times premier between 1878 and 1887, employed methods of intimidation, patronage, and bribery in the manipulation of elections. Crispi set further precedents of dictatorship through despotic methods in the restraint of labor disorder and radical propaganda, imposing harsh punishment upon rioters and agitators and suppressing freedom of speech and association. Giolitti, leading political figure in the years immediately preceding the War, although generally liberal and democratic in his political aims, appears to have practised corrupt and forcible interference in elections more systematically and effectively than any of his predecessors. On the other hand, many observers, particularly the adverse critics of Fascism, maintain that parliamentarism in Italy, with all its faults, was not a failure: illiteracy was being gradually reduced and had been brought down to encouragingly low proportions in the early twentieth century; the number of persons participating in national elections was increasing, so that the proportions, in recent elections, were not substantially lower than in the United States; and in most regions of Italy electoral corruption was no more prevalent than in other countries. Thus, these observers maintain, Italy, after 1900, was making slow but steady progress towards actual democracy; and her parliamentary system was working well in administering the public finances and in promoting popular education and social justice.

The Fascist movement began in the critical period immediately after the World War, when chaotic conditions created formidable difficulties for any government.[2] Italy at this time exhibited in an exaggerated de-

---

[2] On post-war Italy and the beginnings of Fascism, see the following: Dino Grandi, *Le origini e la missione del Fascismo* (1922); Ivanoe Bonomi, *From Socialism to Fascism* (1924); Guglielmo Ferrero, *Four Years of Fascism* (1924), Pts. I, II; Johann W. Mannhardt, *Der Fascismus* (1925), pp. 145–214; Robert Michels, *Sozialismus und Fascismus*, pp. 189–250; Odon Por, *Fascism* (1923);

gree the characteristic features of post-war economic and social disorganization: gross profiteering, monetary inflation to meet the extraordinary costs of the war, strikes for higher wages to meet the resulting rise in the cost of living, serious deficits in the national budget, dissatisfaction among returning soldiers, widespread disappointment over the results of the war and the course of the peace negotiations, criticism of the government's apparent ineptitude in the face of these conditions, and a general distrust of established institutions and policies. Movements for reform or revolution pointed in various directions. The "Nationalists" were energetically renewing their pre-war attacks on parliamentarism and were demanding an authoritarian, aristocratic government, and an imperialist foreign policy for Italy. The Socialists were increasing in numbers, and there were radical movements among the working-men. There was also a new political group, the "People's Party" (*Popolari*), formed early in 1919, led by Don Luigi Sturzo, a Sicilian priest, and composed mainly of devout Catholics from among artisans and small landowners. This was in the nature of a Christian-democratic party, seeking to have the government apply principles of Christian benevolence in improving the economic and social lot of the common man and yet precluded, both by their own doctrine and by the political attitude of the Vatican, from affiliation with the too rationalistic Democrats, Conservatives (*Liberali*), and Socialists. The *Popolari* enjoyed a brief period of political prominence; in the elections of November, 1919, they became the second strongest party in the Chamber of Deputies, where at times during the next three years they held the balance of power. The Socialists gained an unprecedented success in the 1919 elections, their parliamentary membership being tripled so that they constituted the largest united party group in the Chamber (150-odd Socialists as against 250-odd Democrats and Conservatives, now split into many small factions). A year later the success of the Socialists was repeated in local elections, when they gained control of some 2,500 communes—nearly a fourth of the total number.

Meanwhile, propaganda by emissaries from the Russian Communists strengthened the radical movement among the workers. Bolshevism in

Giuseppe Prezzolini, *Fascism* (1926), Ch. I; Gaetano Salvemini, *The Fascist Dictatorship in Italy* (1927); Herbert W. Schneider, *Making the Fascist State* (1928), Chs. I and II; Count Carlo Sforza, *Makers of Modern Europe* (1930), Chs. XXVIII–XXXI and *European Dictatorships* (1931), Chs. I–II; Henry R. Spencer, *Government and Politics of Italy* (1932), Chs. III–IX; Luigi Villlari, *Italy*, Chs. IX, X.

Italy assumed principally the form of direct-actionism—a policy of local and general strikes to achieve independence of the regularly constituted government. In September, 1920, as a climax of a series of strikes, the workers secured possession, for a few weeks, of most of the factories in northern and central Italy. The tide soon turned, however. Moderate labor leaders negotiated a settlement, under governmental auspices, between employers and workers, whereby in return for promises of wage increases and a slight working-men's participation in management, the factories were returned to the owners. The promises brought only insignificant and very temporary benefits to the workers, and in 1922 wages began to be reduced again. The general economic conditions in Italy were highly unfavorable to the success of any insurrectionary working-men's movement. The strong economic position of the employers, the large proportions of small-property-owner groups in the population, the intensity of the middle-class fear of revolutionary proletarian action, the dissensions among the Socialists, made it apparent that no insurrection of a syndicalist or Bolshevist sort would prosper in Italy.

Although a proletarian revolution was escaped, the factors of social discontent and disorder remained strong, particularly in the hardships of unemployed and low-paid working-men; the willingness of large numbers of well-to-do landowners and business men to countenance extra-legal measures against strikers; and the restlessness among large sections of middle-class citizens, dissatisfied because the war had not brought about the anticipated elevation of their own and their nation's status. Late in 1920 there set in a period of disorderly conflict between radical working-men and their radical opponents, with many disorderly strikes, bloody riots, assaults, and destruction of property. The Fascists played a leading part in the violent action against the workers; and they and their eulogists claim that it was their force that delivered Italy from Bolshevism, although their leader, Benito Mussolini, had warmly applauded the workers' occupation of the factories in 1920.

Since early youth, Mussolini had been a revolutionary socialist.[3] His father, a blacksmith and innkeeper in a country village, was also an active socialist. Benito was trained to be a teacher but soon abandoned this profession and moved to Switzerland, partly, it appears, in order

---

[3] On the life of Mussolini, see Antonio Aniante, *Mussolini* (1932); Giuseppe Prezzolini, *Fascism*, Ch. II; Margherita Sarfatti, *Life of Benito Mussolini* (1925); Augusto Turati, *A Revolution and Its Leader* (1930); Benito Mussolini, *My Autobiography* (1928).

to find a freer field for the development of his radical views. While in Switzerland he earned a livelihood by various sorts of manual labor and took part in forming labor unions and promoting strikes. His activities brought him into conflicts with the public authorities, so that he was frequently forced to change his place of residence. His biographers record nearly a dozen terms of imprisonment—in Switzerland, Austria, and Italy. Returning finally to Italy in 1910, he entered whole-heartedly into the socialist movement, chiefly as a journalist. Meanwhile his doctrine had shifted from conventional Marxism to the idea of a socialist *coup d'état* by secret organizations of workers (in the manner advocated by Louis Blanqui in the mid-nineteenth century) and also to the syndicalist direct-actionism of Georges Sorel. He was at one with the Socialist party in vigorous opposition to the Tripolitan war of 1911 and served a term in prison for his anti-war agitation. In the following year he took part in the expulsion of Bissolati, right-wing leader, from the party; at this time he was made editor of *Avanti!*, official organ of the party, and the paper flourished under his editorship.

After the outbreak of the World War Mussolini at first opposed Italian participation. Soon, however, he turned to an advocacy of Italian intervention on the side of the Allies. In this pro-war attitude he appears to have been inspired, in part at least, by his idea that the effects of the war might dislodge the present wielders of power in Italy and promote the internationalist aims of revolutionary socialism. As the socialists were overwhelmingly opposed to his attitude and denounced him as bourgeois, he resigned his editorship of *Avanti!* in October, 1914; and in November, still expressing his firm belief in socialism, he was expelled from the party. "Do not think," he declared, "that in taking away my membership card you will be taking away my faith in the cause, or that you will prevent my still working for Socialism in revolution." [4] At once he founded a daily paper of his own, called *Popolo d'Italia*, devoted to propaganda for Italian intervention, and later for a vigorous participation, in the war. In September, 1915, he entered the army as a private and served until he was wounded in a bombing practice, in February, 1917. A few months later he reassumed active editorship of his paper; and he took a leading part in the activities of the bands that were conducting parades and noisy, some-

---

[4] *Mussolini as Revealed in His Political Speeches* (1923), p. 6.

times violent, demonstrations in order to force the government to adopt a more assertive war policy.

Fascism as an organized movement to control the policy of Italy took definite origin at Milan, on March 23, 1919, in a small meeting summoned by Mussolini. The meeting formed a *Fascio di Combattimento* ("Fighting Band") and adopted a program of vigorous action designed both to secure for Italy the fruits of her victorious part in the war and to set up certain changes in the domestic policy of the nation. Affiliated groups were soon organized in other localities in northern and central Italy. The original Milan meeting was made up largely of ex-soldiers, who were generally of radical political views but were now chiefly motivated by disappointment over their own low economic state as contrasted with that of the working-men, who had prospered at home during the war by exploiting the country's emergency to their own advantage but who were now yielding to the leadership of communist internationalists. The Fascist bands, however, soon drew their membership chiefly from other sections of the population: returning army officers; jobless, disillusioned, but adventurous, youth of petty bourgeois and landowning families; and others attracted by the promises of valiant action to put an end to labor disorders and secure justice for the soldiers and for Italy. Mussolini had prepared the program for the Milan meeting; and he was thenceforth the generally acknowledged leader of the Fascist movement.

The Fascists, during the first four years, displayed considerable vagueness and vacillation as to their objectives; and there were frequent dissensions among them on matters of strategy. Their unity of action was due chiefly to the eloquent, forceful, and skilful leadership of Mussolini. His own program, however, suffered many fluctuations. The platform he prepared for the original meeting in 1919 contained proposals for liberal and socialist reform: a national constituent assembly, universal suffrage, proportional representation, and the abolition of the Senate and of all titles of nobility; the eight-hour day, the nationalization of munitions plants, the confiscation of the revenues of the bishops and of the major portions of war profits; a capital levy, heavy inheritance taxation, a workers' management of the railways and—where practicable—of other industries.[5] During 1920, his program continued

---

[5] Carlo Avarna di Gualtieri, *Il Fascismo* (1925), pp. 15–18; Antonio Aniante, *Mussolini* (1932), pp. 166–167. Cf. H. W. Schneider, *Making the Fascist State*, pp. 58–59; Gaetano Salvemini, *Fascist Dictatorship in Italy*, p. 13.

generally along the same lines, although with some radical leftward shifts: in March he declared himself an anarchist; in September, as we have seen, he approved the workers' seizure of the factories.[6] In 1921, on the other hand, acceding to a proposal of Premier Giolitti, he had the Fascists take part in the parliamentary elections as one of the groups of a "constitutional bloc," opposing the Socialists and Popularists. Shifting again during the next few months he made several advances to these latter groups for a union between them and the Fascists in a coalition of representatives of "the masses." After the failure of this effort, he rapidly forsook his socialist sympathies and yielded entirely to his conservative allies. In November, 1921, the Fascists organized themselves as a political party, and soon a fusion of Fascists and Nationalists in the Chamber of Deputies was achieved.

The apparent objective of the Fascists was now to defeat "Bolshevism." The party membership came to consist principally of those who were opposed, whether for selfish or for idealistic reasons, to the aggressive claims of working-men and who were exasperated over what they regarded as the government's tolerant or timid attitude in the situation. Many industrial and landed proprietors welcomed the movement as a protection to their own economic interests and gave generous financial assistance. Thus Fascism became generally a nationalist, counter-revolutionary, anti-socialist movement. Meanwhile force and intimidation had come to be its principal means of action. Late in 1920 the Fascists had begun to form armed bands (*squadre*), and these bands carried on a two-year struggle by violence against radical working-men's groups and the agencies of communist propaganda. They smashed newspaper presses, broke up meetings, deported speakers, forced socialists and communists to give up membership on municipal councils, and committed numerous acts of personal assault and destruction of property.

By 1922 it was plain that the Fascists were ready to employ squadrism for more positive political ends. Their first formal program, drawn up in the original party congress at Rome, in 1921, declared that Fascism intended to replace the state if the latter showed itself unable to suppress disorder and prevent national disintegration. The government's attitude during this period of violence was one of official neutrality, with evidences, however, of an increasing tendency to lean

---

[6] Salvemini, *op. cit.* (Eng. ed., 1928), pp. 26 and 42, quoting from *Popolo d'Italia*, April 6 and Sept. 28, 1920.

upon or yield to the Fascists. The police (according to circumstantial accounts by spokesmen for the Fascists) frequently connived at, and in some instances were implicated in, the raids by Fascist bands; and officers of the regular army aided in organizing and training the bands and took part in their "march on Rome." [7] The government meekly accepted the aid of Fascist forces in suppressing the general-strike movement of August, 1922. There followed the familiar events of October· Mussolini's declaration of allegiance to the king; his assertions, however, in public speeches and in his *Popolo d'Italia*, that the Fascists would march to Rome unless Parliament were dissolved; the resignation of the Facta cabinet; the taking possession, by Fascists, of city halls, post offices, and railway stations; the gathering of the bands toward Rome; the king's refusal to attach his signature to the proclamation of martial law drawn up by Facta; the king's appointment of Mussolini as premier, with a coalition cabinet of Fascists, Nationalists, Liberals, members of the People's party, and a few without definite party affiliation.

The Fascists, with their Nationalist allies, dominated this cabinet. At the beginning the moderate groups in the Chamber followed the Fascist-Nationalist leadership because of their common opposition to socialists, communists, and others looked upon as factors of disorder. When it became clear that the Fascists meant to use the devices of autocracy and terrorism not only for suppressing proletarian disturbances but also for maintaining themselves in power, the moderate groups withdrew their support. The Fascists soon demonstrated that they were able to govern without that support. For a brief period Mussolini made some attempts to preserve the institutions and practices of parliamentary government. Always, however, he made it plain that he would ignore Parliament if it should withhold from him the extraordinary governmental powers he demanded. Meanwhile, outside opposition was being crushed, both by repressive governmental measures against public criticism of the new régime and by the violent acts of private Fascist bands. In January, 1925, Mussolini openly broke away from the constitutional system; and during the next few years he dictated the enactment of statutes giving legal forms to the Fascist policies. "Having created the Fascist party," he said, "I have always dominated it." [8]

---

[7] Adolfo Zerboglio, *Il Fascismo* (1922) pp. 5–6 and foot-note; Luigi Villari, *The Awakening of Italy*, pp. 175–180; *The Fascist Experiment*, p. 162; Giuseppe Prezzolini, *Fascism* (1926), p. 52.

[8] *My Autobiography* (1928), p. 296.

THE STRUCTURE AND POLICY OF THE FASCIST STATE

Italy, like Russia, is now a one-party state; and the National Fascist Party is, like the Russian Communist party, a close corporation, hierarchically organized.[9] Members are admitted only after tests as to their Fascist character and loyalty, and they must take an oath "to follow without question the orders of the *Duce*." Breach of party discipline is a cause for expulsion from the party, which means exclusion from political life. Party administration is in the hands of a National Directorate selected and presided over by the *Duce*. Provincial party officials are appointed and controlled by the central organization. About 400,000 of the party members are now organized into the Fascist militia, evolved out of the earlier *squadre;* some 50,000 of the latter are on permanent duty and, since 1928, have been coördinated with the regular armed forces of the nation.

Legislation of the Fascist régime has established a strict, centralized, governmental control of the economic life of the nation.[10] Fascist party pronouncements, in 1922, declared in favor of national corporations of local workers' syndicates, to be integrated into the national political structure. Subsequently a formal legal structure was worked out for them as well as for associations of employers and professional men. The laws (as they stand in 1933) provide for thirteen great associations: six federations each of employers and employees (Industry, Commerce, Agriculture, Sea and Air Transport, Land Transport and Inland Navigation, and Banking) and a single federation of "independent artists, artisans, and professional men." [11] The laws are vague as to the appointment of officials of the federations, but they appear to be selected by the Fascist party leaders. Wage agreements in each industry are fixed, in first instance, by negotiation between the proper employer

[9] The following supply excellent accounts, from varying points of view, of the organization, methods, and achievements of the Fascist régime: "Fascism: a New Challenge to the Spirit of 1776," *Survey Graphic,* Vol. LVII (March, 1927); Francesco L. Ferrari, *Le régime fasciste italien* (1928); "Fascist Rule in Italy," *Foreign Policy Reports,* Vol. VII, No. 3 (1931); "J.," "The Achievements of Fascism," *Foreign Affairs,* IV (1925–1926), 661–676; Johann W. Mannhardt, *Der Fascismus* (1925) pp. 215–385; Gaetano Salvemini, *The Fascist Dictatorship in Italy;* Herbert W. Schneider, *Making the Fascist State,* Chs. III–V; Herbert W. Schneider and Shepard B. Clough, *Making Fascists,* Chs. I, IV, VIII, XI; Henry R. Spencer, *Government and Politics of Italy,* Chs. XII–XXIII; Luigi Sturzo, *Italy and Faşcismo,* Chs. VI–IX; Luigi Villari, *Italy,* Chs. X–XVII.

[10] See Carmen Haider, *Capital and Labor under Fascism* (1930); Herbert W. Schneider, *Making the Fascist State,* Ch. IV, and Appendix, Pt. IV.

[11] Henry R. Spencer, *Government and Politics of Italy,* p. 258.

and labor organizations; failing agreement, a court of labor, composed of a judge and two official labor experts, decides the matter. Strikes and lockouts are forbidden. No employer or laborer is compelled to join these associations under Fascist auspices; but no others are "recognized," and employers and employees must pay contributions to the official federations, whether or not they join them. The government also authorizes the federations to make collective contracts binding on both members and non-members, in the industries to which the contracts apply.

Complete political centralization and absolutism have been achieved through laws and decrees, from 1923 to 1928. In November, 1926, all opposition parties were dissolved, and prison sentences were provided for those who tried to revive the parties or who carried on propaganda for their doctrines. Other laws or decrees have nullified all responsibility of the ministry to Parliament. The king remains formally the constitutional executive, but, by law of 1925, the premier —selected by the king without consulting parliamentary opinion and responsible only to the king—is made "Head of the Government," with authority to issue decrees having the full force of law. The other ministers are subordinates, not colleagues, of the premier.

The final steps in the destruction of the institutions of constitutional democracy were accomplished by the laws of February, March, and December, 1928. These laws abolish the old Chamber of Deputies and establish in its stead a new "corporative parliament." This body is composed of 400 members, who represent not local constituencies but official groups created by the government: namely, the thirteen federations already named and twenty-odd non-incorporated organizations, such as the National Association of State Employees, the Disabled Soldiers' Association, the Universities, and the National Association of Primary Schools. The Grand Council of Fascism (made fully a part of the government) fixes the quotas of representation, with reference to the relative importance of the functions for which the several organizations stand in the life of the nation. Each organization submits a list of candidates—generally twice the number to be selected—to the Council, which either selects the required number from the list or substitutes other nominations of its own. The list as finally approved by the Council is then submitted to the electorate for acceptance or rejection.[12]

---

[12] In the election of March 24, 1929, the vote on the list submitted by the Council was: "Yes"—8,519,558, "No"—135,761. See "Fascist Rule in Italy," p. 67.

The electorate is confined to Italian citizens, twenty-one years of age (or eighteen years for married citizens having children), of the following groups: those who pay syndicate dues or a certain amount in taxes; those who receive a regular payment from the state or from a province or commune; clergy of the Roman Catholic Church or of other churches recognized by the state. The law declares that the new parliamentary chamber is to "coöperate with the government"—that is, with the "Head of the Government" and the Grand Council of Fascism, which is also the "Grand Council of the National State" and "the supreme body which controls all the activities of the régime." The chamber has no power of initiative; it acts only on proposals submitted by the "Head" and may only discuss (this includes a nominal right to criticize) the proposals; it may not reject them. Control of government and of the Fascist party is made permanent by the provision for succession to the headship of government, which is also the headship of the party. The law provides that when the present incumbent dies or resigns, his successor is to be appointed by the king from a list of names submitted by the Grand Council. Thus power centers finally in a single person, who is both "leader of fascism" (*duce del fascismo*) and "head of the government" (*capo del governo*). He makes the appointments to superior positions in the party, selects the members of the Grand Council of Fascism (which nominates the candidates for the Chamber of Deputies), and ratifies or vetoes the governmental decisions of the Council.

Through all fluctuations in Fascist policy, certain objectives have constantly stood out, in profession and practice: the restoration of the power of the Italian nation externally and the establishment of vigor and efficiency in the domestic administration of economic and civic affairs. The most distinguished leaders of the former Nationalist party are now preëminent among the counselors of Mussolini; [13] and their assumption is that the prestige and influence of the state require an assertive foreign policy and a rigidly hierarchic organization of domestic government.

The Fascists, in pursuing these aims, recognize no individual liberties as sacred and rely chiefly upon the methods of moral intimidation, physical compulsion, and official censorship and propaganda. Both in their illegal activities before their seizure of formal power and in their subsequent governmental policy, they have dealt summarily and malev-

[13] E.g., Corradini, Rocco, Federzoni, Forges–Davanzati, Maraviglia.

olently with their opponents. In the first few years of their régime the Fascist government tolerated the kidnapings, beatings, and slayings inflicted by the private bands, sometimes in retaliation for outrages committed against Fascists, sometimes without any such provocation. Probably no country, in recent years, with the possible exception of tsarist and Soviet Russia, and Germany under Hitler, has explicitly adopted methods so repressive as those embodied in the Fascist laws and decrees of 1925 and 1926. These make it a crime, punishable by imprisonment, to criticize the government, to conduct propaganda for the doctrines of associations that have been dissolved by the government, and to spread false or "exaggerated" news abroad concerning internal conditions of the country; they empower the government to deprive anti-Fascist Italians abroad of their citizenship and property. For the trial of these crimes the laws establish a special tribunal—chosen by the *Duce* from officers of the army, navy, air force, or militia—employing the procedure of a court martial. There is also a rigid governmental control of all published opinions. The law requires every newspaper or other periodical to be operated under the control of a director approved by the government and limits the contributors to persons registered by the government-controlled syndicates of journalists. The government has vigorously prosecuted and suppressed socialist and liberal periodicals and has "fascistized" the more mildly critical journals (such as the famous *Corriere della Sera*), forcing the replacement of independent managers and editors by persons who will applaud, without serious qualifications, the Fascist rule.

The Fascists have adapted their religious and educational policies to the requirements of their system of government. Until 1921 Mussolini and the Fascists had been outspokenly anti-religious. Events, however, soon modified this attitude. The affiliation of strongly proclerical Nationalists with the Fascists had something to do with the change. Perhaps more important than this were the intellectual and emotional sympathies between Fascism and the Vatican in their common antipathy to liberalism, and also the Fascists' realization that the Church was a potential rival, which could be silenced or mollified not by conquest but only through conciliation and a division of authority. As a result of the "Vatican-Italian Accord" of February, 1929, the breach (since 1870) between Church and state has been ended and a cooperation established.[14] The Holy See now recognizes the validity of the

[14] See Vera A. Micheles, *The Lateran Accord, Foreign Policy Association, In-*

Kingdom of Italy under its Fascist auspices, and the government recognizes the temporal sovereignty of the Pope in the "City of the Vatican" (about 100 acres in extent) and assures certain judicial privileges to the clergy in Italy. The state allows religious freedom in the sense that it permits all cults to preach and practise their creeds, but it makes religious instruction in the Catholic faith compulsory for children of Catholic parents. The Holy See, on its side, prohibits all priests and members of Catholic religious orders from "joining or taking part in any political party" (which in effect prohibits their opposition to Fascism), but permits them to advocate popular support of Fascist candidates at the polls. Mussolini insists, however, that education, in so far as it has to do with the shaping of the character and ideals of the youth, must be a monopoly of the state.

The Government uses the elementary and secondary schools for Fascist propaganda; this use determines the selection of courses and textbooks and the appointment of teachers. The responsible spokesmen for Fascist educational policy represent the "building of character" as the primary object of education and the inculcation of the "national tradition"—which means the Italian tradition interpreted according to Fascist doctrine—as the primary factor in building character.[15] University professors are required to swear to maintain their loyalty to the Fascist régime and to inculcate the Fascist ideals in the minds of their students. The prescribed textbooks of the schools direct attention to the beauty and grandeur of Italy; the glory of her historic achievements in literature, art, music, industry, commerce, and war; and the valiant record of the Fascists, under Mussolini's skilful and heroic leadership, in delivering Italy from Bolshevism and in reinvigorating her political and economic institutions. Thus the Fascists, like the Russian Communists, regard it as an essential function of government to see that the people of the coming generations are inspired with the faith of the governing group.

FASCIST DOCTRINE

There are no Fascist manifestoes summarizing and rationalizing the aims and policies of Fascism. Whatever general hypotheses and proposi-

formation Service, Vol. V, No. 9 (July, 10, 1929); H. W. Schneider and S. B. Clough, *Making Fascists,* Ch. IV; Carlo Sforza, *Makers of Modern Europe,* Ch. XXXII; Henry R. Spencer, *Government and Politics of Italy,* Ch. XXI.

[15] See H. W. Schneider and S. B. Clough, *Making Fascists,* Ch. V; Giovanni Gentile, *Il Fascismo al Governo della Scuola* (1924).

tions the movement now contains were not given it by a theoretical
founder, in the way that Marx created or discovered and put together
the doctrines of nineteenth-century socialism, or Lenin the basic ideas
of Bolshevism. As a political leader, Mussolini has been as forceful,
popular, and inspiring as Lenin was in Russia; but he has little of the
latter's erudition, range of information, or dialectical skill. It has occasionally been said that Fascism has no doctrinal basis, that it is
wholly empirical and practical. Mussolini himself has often expressed
his disdain for abstract thinking and has exalted Fascism by contrasting its live reality to the sterile theory of other movements. "Fascism
is based on reality, Bolshevism is based on theory. . . . We want to
be definite and real. We want to come out of the cloud of discussion and
theory." "My program . . . is action, not talk." Alfredo Rocco has
said: "It is true that Fascism is, above all, action and sentiment and
that such it must continue to be. Were it otherwise, it could not keep
up that immense driving force, that renovating power which it now
possesses, and would merely be the solitary meditation of a chosen
few." [16]

Despite this emphasis upon immediate practical achievement, Fascism
does make certain theoretical assumptions and does formulate its general social ideals. It has constructive and comprehensive aims: a fundamental reorganization and invigoration of Italian life and, to that
end, a restoration of the strength and prestige of Italian governmental
authority. In pursuit of these aims it has displayed a striking combination of realism and mysticism. On the one hand, it disparages any political philosophy that would have action wait until a formulation of some
systematic program has been agreed upon among theorists and understood and approved by the populace. Thus Fascism is described and
widely applauded as empirical and pragmatic: acting first; theorizing,
when it does theorize, afterwards; deriving its creed from experience,
not from reasoning. The principles of structure and method it adopts
from time to time are those that prove themselves to be workable in
attaining its objects; they are, therefore, not fixed and are not necessarily consistent one with another. Although Fascism now admits theory,
it has a narrower place than schemes for translating theory into fact.
Fascist doctrine, their philosophers explain, is to be found, not primarily
in formal treatises, but rather in the deeds and proposals of men

[16] Rocco, *The Political Doctrine of Fascism* (1926), p. 10.

actively engaged in realizing the Fascist aims.[17] On the other hand, leading Fascists place great emphasis upon their myth and upon the fervor of Fascist devotion to it. Their myth is the state, or the nation—an independent entity, with a "real" will different from the fictitious popular will assumed in the democratic dogma. The national will is distinct from the wills of all the citizens and even of all governing officials, and somehow resides in an hereditary ruler; it is interpreted and formulated, however, in the decrees of self-perpetuating party "heads" and councils and is finally expressed in an assent accorded by officially approved representatives of the citizens. Gentile maintains that Fascism is a return to the Italian idealism of Mazzini and the Risorgimento period of the mid-nineteenth century. Its mood, under this view, is that of a great religious crusade; its goal is to make Italy and its government strong and illustrious; all its policies of economic and cultural regeneration are only means to that end.[18]

These assumptions and ideals of Fascism have been copiously phrased by Mussolini, in numerous addresses and interviews; and other leading Fascists have undertaken the task of supplying general and ordered explanations of their political aims. Most important among the Fascist theorists are the following: Alfredo Rocco, formerly professor of commercial law at the University of Padua, ardent Nationalist from before the days of Fascism, minister of justice from January, 1925, till July, 1932, and author of the most important political measures of the Fascists; Giovanni Gentile, a leading Hegelian philosopher in Italy, a Fascist only after 1922, minister of public instruction from 1922 to 1924, and author of the drastic educational reforms; Enrico Corradini, senator, chief theorist and propagandist of nationalism in the decade before Fascism; Luigi Federzoni, one of the founders of the Nationalist party, minister of colonies in the first Fascist cabinet, later minister of interior and minister of colonies, president of the Senate since 1929; Maurizio Maraviglia, formerly head of the Fascist propaganda bureau.[19]

"Fascism," says Rocco, "has a theory, which is an essential part of

[17] Gentile, *Che cosa è il Fascismo*, p. 47. Cf. *Ibid*, pp. 61–63.

[18] *Ibid.*, pp. 13–16. Cf. H. W. Schneider and S. B. Clough, *Making Fascists*, Ch. XI.

[19] For titles of the works of these and other Fascists theorists, see the list on pp. 494–495, *infra*. Roberto Forges-Davanzati, former editor of the Nationalist (later Fascist) *Idea Nazionale*, is also regarded as an able and authoritative exponent of Fascist doctrine. His expositions appear in periodicals to which I have not had access. For works of critical analysis of the Fascist doctrine, see particularly the titles (p. 495, *infra*) by Edwin von Beckerath, W. Y. Elliott, Jacob Marschak, and Herbert W. Schneider.

this historical phenomenon, and which is responsible in a great measure for the successes that have been achieved. To the existence of this ideal content of Fascism, to the truth of this Fascist logic we ascribe the fact that though we commit many errors of detail, we very seldom go astray on fundamentals. . . . Fascism, moreover, considered as action, is a typically Italian phenomenon and acquires a universal validity because of the existence of this coherent and organic doctrine. The originality of Fascism is due in great part to the autonomy of its theoretical principles." And Mussolini declares, in endorsing Rocco's pamphlet: "Fascism has a doctrine, or, if you will, a particular philosophy with regard to all the questions which beset the human mind today." [20]

Rocco (ignoring conceptions set forth over a century ago by the Counts de Maistre and de Bonald, and a half-century ago by von Treitschke) describes Fascism as "a new conception of civil life," "a powerful innovating movement," the beginning of a "new culture." [21] The novelty consists essentially in a repudiation of the assumptions, ideals, and methods of democracy, liberalism, and socialism. Liberalism and democracy, Rocco declares, look to the interests of individuals, socialism looks to the interests of an economic class; in none of these doctrines is there any conception of preëminent social or national ends or of obligations of present to future generations. "For Fascism, society is the end, individuals the means, and its whole life consists in using individuals as instruments for its ends." [22]

By "society," the Fascists mean, almost invariably, "nation"; and a nation, they explain, is based on persistent "biological" similarities that reveal themselves in unities of language, custom, and religion; differentiate the whole group from other national groups; and define the direction and limits of its development. Such a naturally coherent group has a life more continuous, permanent, and important than the lives of its members. The state is the organic structure of the nation; so that state-ism and nationalism embody essentially the same sort of appeals to the emotion and reason of the citizen. Fascism, the theorists continue, came on the scene as a movement against the anti-patriotism of the socialists, the individualism of liberals, and the too indifferent nationalism of the traditional political leaders. It stands for the ab-

[20] Rocco, *Political Doctrine of Fascism,* pp. 7, 10–11.
[21] *Ibid.*, pp. 23, 31.
[22] *Ibid.*, p. 19.

solute sovereignty, moral and legal, of the national state. The interests of the latter may sometimes harmonize, at other times conflict, with the interests of its living citizens, but they must always take precedence. A war for the preservation, expansion, or exaltation of a nation may be supremely justifiable, even though it may frustrate the special interests of every lesser group and destroy the lives of the nation's most worth-while citizens.[23]

Thus it is the explicit aim of Fascism to displace the enfeebling creeds of individual equality, freedom, and right, by its own orderly doctrine of an organic, hierarchically constituted nation, whose few virile and discerning citizens hold the multitude of commonplace individuals in subservience to the realization of destinies more important and permanent than their limited hopes and beliefs can contemplate. For the democratic slogan of "Liberty, Equality, and Fraternity," Fascists will substitute "three words of a higher, purer, and more noble significance—to wit—"Responsibility, Discipline, and Hierarchy," which encourage a man to employ all his faculties in an efficacious participation in the national life." [24]

At times the Fascist spokesmen explicitly renounce liberty as a Fascist ideal. Italy, they say, needs law, order, and efficiency rather than liberty. At other times they say that real liberty is possible only under a political system which rigidly enforces law, order, and efficiency. Moral or spiritual liberty is not an endowment of nature but something to be achieved under or received from a state that is both strong and progressive. If liberty is understood not as a right but as a duty, then there is no opposition between authority and freedom. Just as the private "self-realization" of an individual comes about only under the restraint and direction exercised by his rational and spiritual faculties over his physical instincts, so the development of the finer types of individuals in society is made possible by a supremacy of public law and order over all the degenerative activities of its average citizens. "Thus always," declares Gentile, "the maximum of liberty coincides with the maximum of State force." [25] Law and the state are the supreme manifestations of liberty. The citizen gains true personality and freedom not by safe-

[23] See especially, Rocco, *op. cit., passim;* Enrico Corradini, *L'Unità e la potenza delle nazioni* (1922, 1926), Pt. I, Chs. IV–V; Pt. II, Ch. VI. Also, Francesco Ercole, "Il carattere morale del nazionalismo," *Politica,* XI (1922), 193–218.
[24] Emilio Bodrero, "Mussolini and the Dictatorship of Italy," in Otto Forst-Battaglia, *Dictatorship on Trial,* p. 251.
[25] Gentile, *Che cosa è il Fascismo,* pp. 49–50.

guarding some private interest or by giving expression to some individual capacity but only by losing or merging himself in larger unities—his family, church, and finally, state. Fascism forces the individual to develop his personality in behalf of the nation, and restrains him from acting, even in "self-realization," in opposition to the state. Liberty must be defined in the phrase of Hobbes, as "subjection to law," and as a "concession by the state." The individual has rights in so far as the state confers them; and his will counts, in political decisions, only when it is "legitimate"—that is, when it "coincides with the will of the state." [26]

These basic ideas—that the nation is more important than any or all of its members and that the public interest must always predominate over any sort of private interest—determine the Fascist principles of governmental structure and policy. Political authority must be aristocratic and autocratic; it must represent not individuals but essential groups within the nation; and it must be centralized in its organization and indomitable in its action.

The constitution of a state is essentially aristocratic because only a minority of the nation has the capacity to perceive and give effect to the national interest.[27] Sovereignty, therefore, is not in the people but in the national state; and only the élite are competent to speak for the nation. Fascism indeed, although repudiating democracy's impossible dogma of the sovereignty of a multitude of human beings, does not, its spokesmen contend, try to isolate government from all influence by popular sentiment. It acknowledges an instinctive popular feeling for the national welfare; it does not persistently ignore the desires of the majority, and it affords appropriate means for the expression of popular opinion. But, however much it recognizes and utilizes this nationalistic devotion of the masses, it denies their capacity to guide and govern the nation.[28] The masses are incapable of any spontaneous expression of opinion or will. They are always subject to a few dominating spirits. The ability, in specific instances, to sacrifice private interest to the national welfare and to discover and pursue the right way to that end, are qualities possessed only by a few, peculiarly fitted by their

[26] *Che cosa è il Fascismo*, p. 34; Rocco, *Political Doctrine of Fascism*, pp. 20, 29.
[27] Mussolini, *Discorsi della rivoluzione* (1927), pp. 21–22; Rocco, *op. cit.*, pp. 21–22.
[28] Corrado Gini, "The Scientific Basis of Fascism," *Political Science Quarterly*, vol. XLII (1927), 115; *Mussolini as Revealed in His Political Speeches* (1923), p. 175.

inherited character and cultural training. Political aristocracy is, therefore, both reasonable and unavoidable. Government must be in the hands of those who, although they seek at all times to discover every possible identity between majority interest and opinion, on the one hand, and the higher interest and opinion of the nation, on the other, yet must be ready at any time to sacrifice the former to the latter where they cannot find this harmony. The effective participation of the rank and file in national life is to be realized not by their pronouncing judgment upon those who govern or by expressing assent or dissent to measures proposed by the latter but by their taking the places and fulfilling the tasks assigned to them by the supreme guardians of the nation. The essential qualification for political rulership is not an aptness in winning popular favor but an ability to inspire respect and exact obedience.

Thus the function of a national parliament is not to formulate and impose a popular will upon the active organs of government but to reveal to these organs the feelings and desires of nationally minded citizens, explain to the citizens generally the aims of Fascist policy, and to collaborate with the "Head of the Government" in other ways proposed by the latter.[29] This sort of popular expression and co-operation cannot be secured by any election based on territorial constituencies, for such a system allows local and special interests to obscure national interests. The nation is not a sum of individuals scattered over the national territory; it is a series or hierarchy of groups each of which forms an organic part of the whole national life and in each of which individuals function as organic parts. There is no such thing as a general will derived from a summing up of any number of individual wills and no such thing as a public opinion made up of private opinions.

Fascism describes itself as replacing the atomistic by the corporative conception of the national state. The state is constituted not of individuals but of groups of nationally minded and nationally acting individuals. Matter is composed not of simple entities but of complex groups of electrons and protons, and the important unities in an organism are not the cells but the organs. In the national organism the organs are the groups into which individuals fall naturally in performing useful economic and social functions. These occupational groups are essential and natural, but they must exist not for class competition

29 Rocco, "La trasformazione dello stato," *Politica*, XXVI, 36–47.

but for national coöperation. Every individual finds his proper place by joining with others who perform a similar type of activity of use to the whole nation. Each group should be organized in a way that enables it both to enter into agreements with the other groups in serving the national interest and also to give to its special function a representation in the corporate organization of the nation. Thus a national parliament must consist of representatives not of territorial regions but of industrial and professional associations. Every valid economic or social group must be a political group; if it has no useful function to perform in the organized political life of the nation, it should not be allowed to exist.

The national, collegially composed, deliberative body must act under the direction of a more narrowly constituted executive authority. For the primary requisites in the proper organization and functioning of political government are unity, force, and discipline. Accordingly, the national executive must maintain close control, through powers of appointment, removal, and direction, over all local governmental agencies and must itself be under a single controlling head. The state cannot have a plurality of highest rulers. The ultimate safeguard against dissent and discord in national action is to be found only in the judgment and energy of one man. The state—organic, not mechanistic, in its structure—must have a head to coördinate, direct, and regulate its activities. Political authority is, by its nature, concentrated and coercive. Throughout Mussolini's autobiography are his assertions of "my command", "my guidance", "my sense of balance and judgment", "my irresistible domination." [30]

The measures whereby the head of the state directs the life of the nation may vary according to circumstances; but under all conditions he must, by whatever means prove necessary, maintain the strength and prestige of government and the loyalty and subservience of the citizens; and censorship, espionage, and coercion may often be the best means to such ends.

Fascists generally, and Mussolini in particular, have been explicit in defense of "violence" as a means of achieving political aims. In part, the justification is stated in familiar terms. There are the "realistic" arguments: when two movements show themselves to be in irreconcilable opposition to one another the only way out is through physical conflict; and no philosophical doctrine, however spiritual or rationalistic,

[30] *My Autobiography*, pp. 98, 144, 162. etc.

can prevent the most powerful group from acquiring and exercising control over society.[31] The justification is sometimes conceived in more psychological terms. The ordinary man, it is said, is by nature self-centered and covetous, fickle and unadventurous, and without a sense of public values. He is aroused to diligent, heroic, public-spirited action only when he is prodded, restrained, or inspired by his valorous superiors. He must be made either to love and revere his government or to fear its fury. From all this it follows that brute force—to whatever extent a ruler finds it necessary—is a proper political means in guaranteeing the prestige and stability of his government and maintaining orderly and efficient action in the economic life of the nation. Thus a man who is unwilling or unable to be a ruthless despot is not fit to be the head of the state.

Fascist doctrine has at times justified violence, moreover, not only in formal execution of the will of the state but also in defiance of an existing government and in insurrection against its authority, when such revolutionary action is directed towards laudable national ends. We have seen that violence—in destroying property and maiming and killing people—played a major part in the movement through which the Fascists secured their predominance in Italy. In leading that movement Mussolini was applying to other proximate ends the revolutionary creed of his socialist days. He defended the illegal burnings and assaults as practically and morally necessary.[32] Following the suppression of the general strike in August, 1922, he said: "After having made use of it (violence) systematically for forty-eight hours, we got results which we should not have obtained in forty-eight years of sermons and propaganda. When, therefore, violence removes a gangrene of this sort, it is morally sacred and necessary." [33] The *coup d'état* of October, 1922, was clearly a usurpation of power by an armed minority, threatening violence against the constitutional authorities of the state. Mussolini has described it as such. Gentile, in academic phrases, has explained this revolutionary violence as follows: "The bludgeon of Fascist squadrism was intended to be, as it was, a force vindicating the state—when the central organs of the state misunderstood and renounced its constructive powers. It was, therefore, the necessary substi-

---

[31] Corrado Gini, "The Scientific Basis of Fascism," *Political Science Quarterly,* XLII (1927), 99–115; *Mussolini as Revealed in His Political Speeches* (1923), p. 175.
[32] *Discorsi del 1925,* p. 97; *Discorsi del 1928,* p. 101.
[33] *Mussolini as Revealed in His Political Speeches,* p. 147.

tute for the force of the state itself in a period of revolution when, according to the logic of all revolutions, the state was in crisis and its force was being gradually shifted from its fictitious, legal organs to its real organs—organs which, though at the time illegal, were moving towards legality." [34]

The Fascists discriminate between the disintegrating violence of revolutionary socialism and their own "holy" violence. Gentile declares: "As did Jesus, so, following him, men have always resorted to acts of violence when they have been convinced that such acts represent law or some other higher, universal interests." [35] Under this conception, violence is not to be exalted as the normal means of political action; it is for abnormal times and conditions, a surgical method for rehabilitating a diseased body politic. So Mussolini speaks of "violence within limits," of violence "sometimes moral," made so by the purposes for which it is used.[36] In other Fascist views, a sort of mystic virtue seems to be perceived in destroying and killing; and any predisposition against violence is to be taken as something ignominious, indicating and cultivating a lack of courage and energy. Thus the Fascists justify war not only as an unavoidable means in the inevitable competitions among the competent and civilized nations of the world but also as a culture for the virtues of resoluteness and audacity, in the decadence of which a nation becomes decadent. "We are charged," said Mussolini in 1925, "with having imposed upon our nation a war discipline. I admit it, and I glory in it." [37] If consideration be given to the whole Fascist theory and practice, the position appears to be this: whenever violence is inspired by lofty nationalist motives, it is to be regarded as normal, moral, useful, whether issuing from private or public agencies, whether or not applied in accordance with laws and settled usages, and whatever its form.

The economic ideas of Fascism are in full accord with its general

[34] *Che cosa è il Fascismo,* p. 51: "Il manganello dello squadrismo fascista voleva essere è fu la forza vindice dello Stato disconosciuto e denegato dagli stessi organi centrali de' suoi poteri constituiti. Fu cioè il surrogato necessario della forza medesima dello Stato in un periodo riviluzionario, quando, secondo la logica di tutte le rivoluzioni, lo Stato era in crisi e la sua forza gradualmente si spostava da' suoi organi fittizi e legali a' suoi organi reali e illegali ma tendenti alla legalità."

[35] *Ibid.,* p. 31.

[36] Mussolini, *Discorsi della rivoluzione,* p. 19; *Mussolini as Revealed in His Political Speeches,* pp. 146–147.

[37] In his address on the third anniversay of the March to Rome. See Mussolini, *Discorsi del 1925* (1926), p. 189; and cf. Enrico Corradini, *L'Unità e la potenza delle nazioni,* Pt. III, Ch. II.

social philosophy. The Fascists admit neither, on the one hand, the individualist's standard of private rights of property-owners nor, on the other hand, the socialist's criterion of the laborers' rights to the full product of their labor or the collectivist's ideal of a distribution of products according to the several needs of users. They consider all economic questions from the standpoint of national utility; the production and distribution of wealth are primarily matters of national, not individual, concern. Accordingly they reject both *laisser-faire* and public ownership as their dominant economic policy. The productive energies of the nation must be maintained at their highest possible point in order to supply the means for maintaining virile citizens and preserving the national strength. The nation must be economically as well as politically consolidated. Every individual and every group, in economic as well as in other pursuits, must be made an instrument in the advancement of the nation. For such ends, private ownership of property is a valuable means because economic self-interest is the most powerful incentive to productive activity. But this interest must be held in constant subordination to the national interest.[38] Fascism recognizes no unassailable private rights of property and admits no class interests of either laborers or employers. The nation is an organic corporate society in its economic as well as in its cultural, moral, and political life. Accordingly, the Fascist government holds itself free to intervene at any time and in any way—whether by aid, restraint, or direct management—whenever private initiative fails in serving the national security and prosperity.

· Fascism permits no appeal to any other loyalty—to individual conscience or reason, to an economic class, to international tribunals or a world proletariat. It believes that future wars are inevitable, and is skeptical and cynical in regard to projects for pacification through the consultations of international agencies. Italy must be treated as the absolute equal of the other great nations. She "will not tolerate insults." She accepts peace only when it is a Roman peace. "Nations are free only when they are fully masters of their own future."

Thus the whole ideology of Fascism is dominated by the dogmas of sovereign state and irresistible government. All particularistic interests of individuals must be suppressed by an omnipotent, hierarchical organization of the nation. A citizen's political obligations are more important than his rights. This is the Fascist "totalitarianism," which recognizes

---

[38] *Discorsi della rivoluzione*, pp. 128 ff.

no sphere of individual life as immune from political authority. The true Fascist, declares Gentile, is Fascist in his home, school, and workshop as well as in his politics.[39] The supreme task of a state is to guarantee the interests of the nation, by sacrifice of any conflicting individual or class interests and in defiance, if necessary, of the interests and opinions of whole generations of citizens. The state recognizes the will and welfare of the majority of its citizens only in so far as it can harmonize them with the higher interests of the nation. Infidelity to the state—in deed, word, or attitude—is rebellion, which is the most baleful of all human evils. "The public order must not be disturbed for any motives, and must be maintained at whatever cost." Fascism "proclaims the rights of the state, the preëminence of its authority, and the superiority of its ends." "No aspect of the social life escapes the wise discipline of Fascism." [40]

COMPARISONS AND APPRAISALS

The Fascist faith in the predominant, organic nation, its disparagement of democracy and liberalism, and its exaltation of aristocracy show, in a minor way, the influence of the doctrines of recent Italian sociologists—notably, Vilfredo Pareto; but the influence at this point comes more obviously and immediately from the Nationalists—Corradini, Federzoni, Rocco, and others—who had, before their identification with the Fascists, set forth in somewhat moderated form the monarchist-nationalist ideas of Barrès, Maurras, and other contemporary French royalists.[41] Exaltation of the state and insistence upon the supreme part it plays in the making of worthy individuals are part of the traditional "idealist" political philosophy; the two leading living Italian philosophers—Benedetto Croce and Giovanni Gentile—are of that school, and Gentile has made the step from idealism to absolutism. The advocacy of government by strong men, ruling through force and

---

[39] *Che cosa è il Fascismo,* p. 38.

[40] Mussolini, *La Nuova Politica,* II, 165; Rocco, *Political Doctrine of Fascism,* p. 26.

[41] See especially the following: Charles Benoist, "L'Esprit de Machiavel et les méthodes politiques," *Revue des deux mondes,* XXXV (1926), 375–400; Angelo Crespi, *Contemporary Thought of Italy* (1926); Giovanni Gentile, "The Philosophical Basis of Fascism," *Foreign Affairs,* VI (1928), 290–304; Aline Lion, *The Pedigree of Fascism* (1927); Harold J. Laski, "Machiavelli and the Present Time," *Quarterly Review,* CCXLIX (1927) 57–70; Johann Mannhardt, *Der Fascismus,* pp. 113–134; William K. Stewart, "The Mentors of Mussolini," *American Political Science Review,* XXII (1928), 843–869.

fear rather than through intellectual and moral suasion, is a contemporary application of ideas of Machiavelli, Hobbes, Treitschke, and Nietzsche. From Sorel comes the idea of violence as a means of destroying an existing social system and bringing on a new order of society; this phase of Sorel's theory had greater vogue in Italy than in France; and Mussolini, we have seen, accepted it in his youth and adhered to it—at least until his own accession to governmental power. Some phases of Fascist theory can be explained as applications, or misapplications, of the pragmatism of William James and of the mysticism of Henri Bergson, transmitted by various Italian writers. Through all the activities and utterances of Fascist leaders—notably, Mussolini, Gentile, and Rocco—there are evidences of a belief, sometimes acknowledged, more often concealed, in the practical value of visionary social ideals as means of securing devoted and energetic coöperation among the great masses of citizens. Thus, it is said, Mussolini, impressed by Sorel's idea of the energizing myth, grips the popular imagination by his myth of "greater Italy," stirring the people into a more persevering and orderly action and thereby realizing his more immediate and prosaic ends of a nation-wide prosperity.

Many of the critics of Fascism have described it as predominantly a movement of bourgeois resistance to socialist or liberal reforms in behalf of the common man. They point out that manufacturers, bankers, landowners, and merchants have given strong support to the movement. Its defense of private ownership, its denunciation of the disintegrating and degenerating effects of socialism, its vigorous action in maintaining order and suppressing strikes, its emphasis upon efficiency and orderliness as the tests of the validity of a social system— all this has gained for it powerful support from property-owners generally. It is sometimes suggested, therefore, that as Fascism finds it increasingly necessary to impose unwelcome restrictions upon the free action of property-owners, support from the latter may become less whole-hearted. For Fascism, we have seen, admits no limits to its right to regulate property in the public interest. It recognizes not only the productive value of self-interest but also the inevitable individual and group rivalries which self-interest creates, and holds that, since it cannot abolish, it must control these rivalries.

Many of those who regard Russian Communism as the most dangerous or contemptible of all political creeds, praise Fascism because of its efficient action in overcoming labor radicalism. Nevertheless, the two systems, although in some essential aspects antagonistic, have close spiritual affinities and in many respects their methods of government are the same. Both Fascists and Bolsheviks acquired their power by violence or by threats of violence, and both exalt compulsion as the supreme method of political action. They ridicule democracy and liberalism, regarding these creeds as superstitions of the ignorant or impractical ideals of the visionary. They recognize no individual liberties as immune from governmental destruction. They claim a monopoly in the use of the press and the schools as agencies of propaganda. They fear free discussion and suppress it ruthlessly. In both, there is an identification between political party and government. Both have had aggressive, courageous, skilful, public-spirited leaders, inspired by the ideal of saving their people or their country from the injustice or misrule of an old régime. Both justify their methods of coercion by the exalted aims they pursue: freedom, comfort, and enlightenment for the Russian masses; unity, power, and prestige for the Italian nation.

Much has been written of the similarities between the "corporative state" of Fascism and the group autonomies of syndicalism, guild socialism, and the medieval guild system.[42] Mussolini, in his socialist days, accepted the French syndicalist doctrine of the general strike, sabotage, and violence as means of a direct revolt against capitalism. In the World War he abandoned the anti-nationalism of syndicalism and rejected the weapon of the general strike, but he retained the idea of autonomous labor action as a weapon in an economic struggle and as late as 1920, we have seen, looked with favor upon the workers' forcible occupation of factories. As a political ruler he has discarded completely the anti-bourgeois as well as the anti-political aspects of syndicalism, and he has used the associations of employers or laborers only as agencies of an obligatory national coöperation. The Fascist government fixes the organization and composition of the industrial associations, selects their officers, and compels them to arbitrate industrial disputes, forbidding strikes and lock-outs. Its corporative state has little in common with Sorel's society of syndicates. Sorel spoke of an illegal working-class organization, developing outside the capitalist organization of society, to be used to destroy the latter and the state supporting it. Fascism seeks to strengthen capitalism and centralize authority. Obviously, therefore, Fascism has none of the anti-capitalism

[42] See Odon Por, *Guilds and Coöperatives in Italy* (1923); Edmondo Rossoni, *Le idee della ricostruzione: Discorsi sul sindacalismo Fascista* (1923).

and anti-state-ism of French syndicalism, none of the industrial autonomy of the guild-socialist system, none of the localism and craft independence of the medieval guilds. It is simply applying a system of nominal or very limited economic devolution to the maintenance of its hierarchic and absolutist political régime.

We have seen that dictatorships have arisen recently in several other European countries.[43] Most of them are like the Italian model in their ideals of extreme nationalism and in their reliance on violence and censorship as the means of suppressing political opposition or dissent. The "National Socialists" of Germany, who came into control of the government of the Reich early in 1933, have, in aims and tactics, approached most nearly the Italian model.[44]

The usual factors for the success of such a movement were present in Germany. There were, in the first place, the unsettled economic and political conditions: extreme economic distress; a restless nationalistic fervor aroused by resentment over the terms of the treaty of Versailles; the inability of the several groups supporting the Republic to unite in any working agreement; a growing belief in the incompetence of any sort of liberal leadership—or even of any reactionary leadership, acting within the limits of a constitution—to find a way out. Secondly, their leader, Adolf Hitler (who had served a brief term in prison, on conviction of high treason for his part in the reactionary "Putsch" of 1923 at Munich) was skilful in popular electioneering and impressive, at least to conservative interests, in his promises of valiant action against socialism and communism. The Nazis rose to power partly by means of the violent acts of their "storm troops" and partly by their adroit propaganda—with promises to destroy the Versailles treaty, secure military equality for Germany, end reparations, expel the Jews, suppress radical labor movements, and, at the same time, take vigorous steps to pare down inequalities of wealth. Thus their earlier appeals were addressed to all classes of the population, and their programs

[43] See *supra*, pp. 339–340.

[44] The official name of the group is *Nationalsozialistische deutsche Arbeiter Partei*, whence their designation—"Nazis." In the general election of 1929 the party elected twelve members to the *Reichstag;* in 1930 they won 107 seats and became the second largest party; and in July, 1932, casting 37 per cent of the popular vote and electing 230 members they became the largest party; in November, 1932, their vote fell off considerably, returning only 195 members; but the movement of domestic and international events during the next few months retrieved their loss for them.

contained varied mixtures of state socialism and a politically nourished private capitalism. Their membership included at first a considerable proportion of political radicals. Later they appeared to be controlled chiefly by large landowners, wealthy industrialists, retired army officers, and discontented and adventurous youth of the upper middle classes; although they continued to include a large number of proletarians with a *petit-bourgeois* view of society. Like the Italian Fascists, the Nazis, as they approached victory, became a party of extreme nationalism and conservative economic policy. Their accession to power was widely acclaimed by Italian newspapers as a sign of the collapse of another democracy and as a vindication of the Fascist creed of strong and autocratic action.

In rapid strokes the Nazis achieved a "totalitarian" state for Germany. Hitler was appointed chancellor on January twenty-ninth, with a cabinet of Nazis and members of the center and older nationalist groups. As this coalition appeared to be somewhat unstable in Parliament, he secured a dissolution of the *Reichstag* and the proclamation of an election for March fifth. In opening the campaign, he denounced the "crime of 1918" (i.e., the revolution establishing the Republic), and promised to destroy Marxism, communism, and class warfare; to fight the "parliamentary-democratic" system; to "find the way of reorganizing the new unity of the German nation"; to reawaken a popular veneration for the great national traditions; and to educate the youth in reverence for the old imperial army as the emblem of the nation's greatest achievements. Alfred Hugenberg, leader of the older Nationalist party (and for a short period Minister of Economics and Agriculture in the Hitler cabinet), announced that the Nazi-Nationalist coalition would cling to power whether or not they were endorsed by the voters at the election. On February twenty-eighth, President Hindenburg, in exercise of emergency powers conferred by the Weimar constitution, suspended the articles prohibiting arbitrary arrest and imprisonment and guaranteeing property rights, the sanctity of the home, the secrecy of private correspondence, and freedom of speech, assembly, and association.[45] The Nazis and their Nationalist allies carried the elec-

[45] See Art. 48 of the Weimar constitution, as follows: "The President, in the event that public security and order in the German nation should be considerably disturbed or endangered, may take all necessary measures to reëstablish such public security and order, and, if required, to intervene with the aid of armed power. To

tion by a slight majority; [46] and on March twenty-third, the new *Reichstag* granted blanket powers to the cabinet for a period of four years. The government soon dissolved the Communist, Socialist, and other opposition parties; suppressed opposition newspapers; imprisoned, or drove into exile, thousands of political suspects; excluded the Jews (as "non-Germans") from public office as well as from important sections of the cultural and industrial life of the nation; and brought the press, the radio, the schools, and the Protestant church into subservience to the Nazi ideology.[47]

There has been widespread praise of the dictatorships as régimes of "strong men who get things done," in regions where democracies have become "bankrupt" and public and private morale "debased" by the factiousness and incompetence of parliaments and politicians. A typical generalization is this: Where representative institutions and liberal governmental policies fail in vigor of will and action or permit the sacrifice of national to factional interests, then the people are ready to yield to the autocratic domination of any one who, however he gains his power and by whatever methods he rules, keeps order and makes government efficient and respected, at home and abroad. American eulogists have praised particularly the Italian dictatorship, characterizing it as a system which, although it is willing to modify both its theories and its methods as rapidly and as radically as changing conditions seem to require, yet is always a machine intended "to run, to function, to do, to accomplish." A former American ambassador to Italy has ascribed qualities of "super-statesmanship" to the driver of this political machine. Writing in 1928, he said: "In our time it may be shrewdly forecast that no man will exhibit dimensions of permanent greatness equal to those of Mussolini. . . . In terms of fundamental and permanent effect upon the largest number of human beings . . . the *Duce* is now the greatest figure of this sphere and time." [48]

this end he may provisionally abrogate, in whole or in part, the fundamental laws established in Articles 114, 115, 117, 118, 123, 124, 153."

[46] The Nazis received 44.1 per cent, and the Nationalists 8 per cent, of the total vote.

[47] For accounts of the Hitler régime, see the titles, pp. 495–6, *infra*. The triumph of German fascists aroused the hopes of smaller kindred groups in countries still under the régime of parliamentarism—particularly in Czechoslovakia and Austria. Sir Oswald Mosely, leader of the British fascists, declared that England (oldest of the parliamentary countries) would be the next to yield to fascism.

[48] Richard Washburn Child, "Foreword" to Mussolini, *My Autobiography*, pp. xi, xix. See also this further striking appreciation by Mr. Child: "He [Mussolini] likes cats—their independence, their decision, their sense of justice, and their appreciation of the sanctity of the individual."—*Ibid.*, p. xiv.

Other observers, less adulatory, have agreed that, judged by many of the familiar standards of political efficiency, the Fascist régime has been successful in Italy. It has, they say, maintained itself in power through difficult emergencies, improved the public finances, procured a more efficient operation of the public services, usefully exploited Italy's natural resources, carried out successfully vast projects of land reclamation and other public works, and greatly enlarged the facilities of popular education. It has at the same time stimulated private industrial activity and put an end to violent labor disputes. It has also established better working relations with the Church, strengthened the international position of Italy, satisfied national pride, made itself acceptable to the masses. Thus Fascism has given the Italian people what, according to Mussolini, they have most needed: roads, bridges, and drains; safety and security in homes and workshops; punctual trains; orderly industry; pride in the destiny of the Italian nation. Throughout its whole policy it has, by inspiring some and coercing others, created a new spiritual unity and vigor among the Italian people. The successes, these observers believe, have been due in considerable measure to the efficient organization of the Fascist party, the intensive and dominating leadership of Mussolini and his exaltation of Italy's historic mission.

These claims of Fascist competence have been challenged by several eminent Italians—notably, Professors Gaetano Salvemini and Silvio Trentin, ex-premier Francesco Nitti, and Count Carlo Sforza. These men point out that the labor disorders of 1919 and 1920 (when Mussolini was still a revolutionary extremist) were not so extensive or violent as to threaten any general political and economic breakdown; that the worst of the crisis was over by the end of 1920, before the Fascists entered upon the scene in any important way; and that a rehabilitation along the lines of pre-war political formulae could have brought a vigor and prosperity to Italy without any destruction of the moral and intellectual freedom of the people. They deny that the Fascists have improved the public finances; they maintain that the extraordinary expenses dependent upon the war were being rapidly reduced before the Fascists took control and that deficits in the national budget reappeared in 1925 and have been mounting rapidly. They cite statistics to show that under Fascist rule wages have been lowered in greater degree than the cost of living; and they argue that no real or permanent prosperity but only a temporary show of it is secured by the government's manipulation of prices and its suppression of information as to the actual extent of bankruptcy, unemployment, and destitution. They regard Mussolini as unscrupulous rather than pragmatic; as ambitious rather than heroic; a puppet of capitalists and militarists rather than a statesman or leader with ideals of his own. No one, they maintain, can well say whether Fascism is really popular with the masses, for these have no channels for the free expression of their views; if Fascism were popular with the people, it would not need to keep the country under a régime of constant espionage and repression.[49]

Many outside observers also, recognizing the practical achievements of Fascism, challenge, nevertheless, some of the claims made in its behalf and hold that its possibilities of evil consequences may outweigh its apparent or present benefits. At best, these critics say, a dictatorship is run as an elaborately organized house of correction, in which each inmate is assigned his task and vigilantly inspected as to the manner in which he discharges it. This is well enough for the delinquent and defective members of society but not for men of normal character and mentality and particularly not for superior men. A highly centralized and coercive direction of the public and cultural life of a nation destroys the possibility of the development of great learning, literature, and art. "A dictatorship," says Professor Albert Einstein (in a nineteen-word essay on "Science and Dictatorship"), "means muzzles all round, and consequently stultification. Science can flourish only in an atmosphere of free speech." [50] The Fascist policy, moreover, according to these observers, will not even succeed politically, in the long run. Its methods of control and appeal will evoke habits of popular response of too capricious a sort to be relied upon as supports for any constant public policy. Fascism, it is said, goes too far in ignoring the values of individual self-discipline; attributes too low a value to informed and voluntary compliance with law; depends too much upon methods of intimidation or control that enervate the minds and spirits of the citizens—all for the sake of a formal national unity and a vague national glory. According to this view, the advocates of Fascism have taken too little account of post-war experience in other countries whose

---

[49] Gaetano Salvemini, *The Fascist Dictatorship in Italy* (1927); Silvio Trentin, *L'aventure italienne: légendes et réalités* (1928); Francesco S. Nitti, *Bolshevism, Fascism and Democracy* (1927); Count Carlo Sforza, *Makers of Modern Europe* (1930), Ch. XXXVIII; *European Dictatorships* (1931), Chs. IV, V, XIV; "Italy and Fascism," *Foreign Affairs*, III (1924–1925), 358–370.

[50] In Otto Forst-Battaglia, ed., *Dictatorship on Trial*, p. 107.

currencies were stabilized, budgets balanced, public order maintained, and productive energies invigorated under the direction of parliamentary governments operating principally through traditional methods.[51] The commentators maintain, therefore, that the widely prevailing notion that democracy and parliamentarism have "gone to seed" is only a passing mood; and they cite the records of history—of French kings, Russian tsars, Turkish sultans, Chinese emperors—to show that absolutism itself is a fertile soil for political quackery and maladministration.

This skepticism of Fascism's survival value has been characteristically expressed in challenges made by two of Italy's foremost living scholars —a philosopher and a historian. "What does history teach?" asks Benedetto Croce; he answers: "that . . . régimes of force can survive only among decadent peoples; that they can figure only as temporary expedients in nations that are growing and in the ascendant; and that . . . repressions only produce more violent explosions of the forces they would restrain." [52] "What force had created," asserts Guglielmo Ferrero (ostensibly considering ancient Rome), "force destroyed. The child of the armies, the Roman Empire, was destroyed by the armies that had given it birth. And ancient civilization perished with the Empire when the latter found that its Government had become one of force alone, unsupported by any legal right." [53]

Force and fear are probably natural foundations of authority for those who, like the Fascists, regard national power and glory as ends in themselves and a strong state as more worthy than a just or benevolent state. All through Fascist literature runs the note of praise of Machiavelli's disparagement of weakness, indecision, and sentimentality as the greatest evils that can beset a nation. The policy of a national state, it is said, is subject to one fundamental law—the natural law of survival of the fittest. Accordingly, Fascism may be regarded as the supreme manifestation of a "pragmatic," "realistic" spirit, widely prevailing in political discussion to-day. Human reason and good will, it is said, cannot make programs of action for governments in dealing either with other governments or with their own citizens. A national government must always face the actualities of an existing situation, and opportu-

[51] See the editorial, "Fashions in Dictators," New York *Times*, February 12, 1926.
[52] Croce, "Has Liberalism a Future?" *New Republic*, XLII (1925), 257. Cf. also his article, "Of Liberty," *Foreign Affairs*, XI (1932), 1–7.
[53] Ferrero, in his essay on "Dictatorship in Ancient Rome," in Otto Forst-Battaglia, ed., *Dictatorship on Trial*, p. 33.

nism must determine its domestic and foreign policy. Talk and conference, sentiment and theory, must give way to the efficient action of strong men. Some of the Fascists, as we have seen, find an idealistic justification for this realism. Human life, Gentile constantly asserts, must not be conceived in egoistic and materialistic terms; social life is a realm of duties to be performed, not of rights to be vindicated; the citizen must be inspired or else compelled to take life seriously, to live a life of toil and sacrifice for an ideal more important than his own salvation.[54] But what is the ideal? The ideal of Fascism, declares Rocco, is a national state "well-ordered internally, aggressive, and bent on expansion."[55]

SELECT BIBLIOGRAPHY

BIBLIOGRAPHIES

Santangelo, Giulio, and Bracale, Carlo, *Guida Bibliografica del Fascismo* (Rome, 1928).

Schneider, Herbert W., *Making the Fascist State* (New York, 1928), pp. 365–385.

Spencer, Henry R., *Government and Politics of Italy* (New York, 1932), pp. 289–301.

HISTORY AND DESCRIPTION OF THE FASCIST RÉGIME IN ITALY

Aniante, Antonio, *Mussolini,* translated into the French by Juliette Bertrand (Paris, 1932).

Avarna di Gualtieri, Carlo, *Il Fascismo* (Turin, 1925).

Bonomi, Ivanoe, *From Socialism to Fascism: a Study of Contemporary Italy,* translated by John Murray (London, 1924).

Buell, Raymond Leslie, *Europe: a History of Ten Years* (New York, 1928), Ch. XVII.

Cambo, F., *Autour du Fascisme italien* (Paris, 1925).

Cantalupo, R., "Fascism in Italian History," *Foreign Affairs,* IV (1925–1926), pp. 61–71.

Farinacci, Roberto, *Un periodo aureo del partito nazionale fascista* (Foligno, 1927).

"Fascism: a New Challenge to the Spirit of 1776," *The Survey Graphic,* Vol. LVII (March, 1927).

Ferrari, Francesco Luigi, *Le Régime Fasciste Italien* (Paris, 1928).

Ferrero, Guglielmo, *Four Years of Fascism* (London, 1924); translation of *Da Fiuma a Roma* (Milan, 1923) by E. W. Dickes.

---

[54] *Che cosa è il Fascismo,* pp. 38–39, 43–44.
[55] *Political Doctrine of Fascism,* p. 28.

Forst-Battaglia, Otto, ed., *Dictatorship on Trial* (London and New York, 1930); translation by Huntley Paterson of *Prozess der Diktatur*, Zurich, 1930).

Haider, Carmen, *Capital and Labor under Fascism* (New York, 1930).

J., "The Achievements of Fascism," *Foreign Affairs*, IV (1925–1926), 661–676.

McGuire, Constantine E., ed., *Italy's International Economic Position* (New York, 1927).

Mannhardt, Johann W., *Der Fascismus* (Munich, 1925), 215–385.

Martin, William, "Mussolini's Ten Years of Power," *Current History*, XXXVII (1932), pp. 33–37.

Matteotti, Giacomo, *The Fascisti Exposed: a Year of Fascist Domination*, translated by E. W. Dickes (London, 1924).

Micheles, Vera A., *The Lateran Accord*, Foreign Policy Association, Information Service, Vol. V, No. 9 (July, 1929).

Prezzolini, Giuseppe, *Fascism*, translated by Kathleen Macmillan (New York and London, 1926).

Salvemini, Gaetano, *The Fascist Dictatorship in Italy* (New York, 1927).

——————, *Mussolini, Diplomate* (Paris, 1932).

——————, " 'The Corporative State' in Fascist Italy," *Nation and Athenæum*, XLIII (1928), 9–10.

——————, "The March on Rome: Revised Version," *Current History*, XXXVII (1932), 38–43.

——————, "The Problem of Italian Overpopulation," *Contemporary Review*, CXXXIV (1928), 708–715.

Schneider, Herbert W., *Making the Fascist State* (New York, 1928).

Schneider, Herbert W., and Clough, Shepard B., *Making Fascists* (Chicago, 1929).

Sforza, Count Carlo, *European Dictatorships* (New York, 1931).

——————, *Makers of Modern Europe* (Indianapolis, 1930).

Sillani, Tomaso, ed., *What is Fascism and Why?* (London, 1931).

Spencer, Henry R., *Government and Politics of Italy* (New York, 1932).

Sturzo, Luigi, *Italy and Fascismo* (London, 1926).

Survey of Fascism: the Year Book of the International Centre of Fascist Studies, Vol. I (London, 1928).

Trentin, Silvio, *L'aventure italienne: légendes et réalitiés* (Paris, 1928).

——————, *Les transformations récentes de droit public italien de la Charte de Charles-Albert à la création de l'état fasciste* (Paris, 1929).

Villari, Luigi, *The Awakening of Italy: the Fascista Regeneration* (New York and London, 1924).

——————, *The Fascist Experiment* (London, 1926).

——————, *Italy* (London and New York, 1929).

Zerboglio, Adolfo, *Il Fascismo* (Bologna, 1922).

FASCIST THEORISTS

Bottai, Giuseppe, *Il Fascismo e l'Italia Nuova* (Rome, 1923).

Corradini, Enrico, *L'unità e la potenza delle nazione* (Florence, 1922; second ed., 1926).

Ercole, Francesco, "Il carattere morale del nazionalismo," *Politica,* XI (1922), 193–218.

——————, "La morale del Fascismo," *Ibid.,* XXVIII (1927–1928), 5–37.

Federzoni, Luigi, *Presagi alla nazione* (Milan, 1924).

Gentile, Giovanni, *Che cosa è il Fascismo: discorsi e polemiche* (Florence, 1925).

——————, *Il Fascismo al governo della Scuola* (Palermo, 1924).

——————, "The Philosophical Basis of Fascism," *Foreign Affairs,* VI (1928), 290–304.

Gini, Corrado, "The Scientific Basis of Fascism," *Political Science Quarterly,* XLII (1927), 99–115.

Gorgolini, Pietro, *Il Fascismo nella vita italiana* (Turin, 1922).

——————, *The Fascist Movement in Italian Life,* translated by M. D. Petre (London, 1923).

——————, *La Revoluzione Fascista* (Turin, 1923).

——————, *Il Fascismo spiegato al Popolo* (Turin, 1931).

Grandi, Dino, *Le origini e la missione del Fascismo* (Bologna and Trieste, 1922).

Maraviglia, Maurizio, "Dalla rivoluzione alla collaborazione," *Politica,* IX (1921), 13–24.

——————, "Preludi Collaborazionisti," *Ibid.,* X (1921), 273–280.

Mussolini, Benito, *Discorsi politici* (Milan, 1921).

——————, *Discorsi del 1925, Discorsi del 1926* (Milan, 1927, 1928).

——————, *Discorsi della rivoluzione* (Milan, 1927).

——————, *La nuova politica dell'Italia* (addresses, 1922–1924, Milan, 1923–1926).

——————, *My Autobiography,* with a Foreword by Richard Washburn Child (New York, 1928).

——————, *Mussolini as Revealed in His Political Speeches* (November, 1914–August, 1923), selected, translated, and edited by Bernardo Quaranta di San Severino (London, New York, and Toronto, 1923).

——————, "The Political and Social Doctrine of Fascism" (a translation by Jane Soames, of an article contributed to Vol. XIV of *Enciclopedia Italiana*), in *Political Quarterly,* Vol. IV (July–Sept., 1933), 341–356.

Pennachio, Alberto, *The Corporative State* (New York, 1927).

Rocco, Alfredo, *The Political Doctrine of Fascism,* translated by Professor

Bigongiari, International Conciliation Bulletin, no. 223 (New York, 1926).

———, "La Trasformazione dello Stato," *Politica,* XXVI (1926), 28–49.

Rossoni, Edmondo, *Le Idee della ricostruzione: discorsi sul sindacalismo Fascista* (Florence, n.d.; addresses, 1922 and 1923).

Valli, Luigi, "La Nazione e l'idea liberale," *Politica,* XXIII (1925), 5–22.

CRITICAL EXPOSITION OF FASCIST DOCTRINE

Beckerath, Erwin von, "Idee und Wirklichkeit im Fascismus," *Schmoller's Jahrbuch für Gesetzgebung, Verwaltung und Volkswirtschaft* (1928), 201–218.

Benoist, Charles, "L'Esprit de Machiavel et les méthodes politiques," *Revue des deux mondes,* XXXV (1926), 375–400.

Elliott, W. Y., *The Pragmatic Revolt in Politics: Syndicalism, Fascism and the Constitutional State* (New York, 1928), Ch. XI.

Laski, Harold J., "Machiavelli and the Present Time," *Quarterly Review,* CCXLIX (1927), 57–70.

Lion, Aline, *The Pedigree of Fascism: a Popular Essay on the Western Philosophy of Politics* (London, 1927).

Marschak, Jacob, "Der Korporative und der hierarchische Gedanke im Fascismus," *Archiv für Sozialwissenschaft und Sozial-politik,* LII (1924), 695–728; LIII (1924–1925), 81–140.

Michels, Robert, *Sozialismus und Fascismus in Italien* (Munich, 1925), pp. 251–323.

Nitti, Francesco S., *Bolshevism, Fascism, and Democracy,* translated by Margaret M. Green (London, 1927).

Schmitt, Carl, "Wesen und Werden des Fascistischen Staates," *Schmoller's Jahrbuch für Gesetzgebung, Verwaltung und Volkswirtschaft,* LIII (1929), 107–113.

Schneider, Herbert W., *Making the Fascist State* (New York, 1928).

Schneider, Herbert W., and Clough, Shepard B., *Making Fascists* (Chicago, 1929).

Stewart, William K., "The Mentors of Mussolini," *American Political Science Review,* XXII (1928), 843–869.

Trentin, Silvio, *L'antidémocratie* (Paris, 1930).

THE HITLER MOVEMENT IN GERMANY

Armstrong, Hamilton Fish, *Hitler's Reich: the First Phase* (New York, 1933).

Hoover, Calvin B., *Germany Enters the Third Reich* (New York, 1933).

Fay, Sidney B., "The Nazi 'Totalitarian' State," *Current History* (August, 1933), pp. 610–618.

Kosok, Paul, *Modern Germany: a Study of Conflicting Loyalties* (Chicago, 1933).

Lasswell, Harold D., "The Psychology of Hitlerism," *Political Quarterly,* IV (July–Sept., 1933), 373–384.

Nordicus (pseud.), *Hitlerism: the Iron Fist in Germany* (New York, 1932).

Prittwitz, Friedrich W. von, "Germany in Transition," *Current History,* XXXVIII (July, 1933), 385–391.

Villard, Oswald Garrison, *The German Phoenix* (New York, 1933).

Wertheimer, Mildred S., "Forces Underlying the Nazi Revolution," *Foreign Policy Reports,* Vol. IX, No. 10 (July 19, 1933).

CHAPTER XVIII

THE PLURALISTS' ATTACK ON STATE SOVEREIGNTY

THE theories we have reviewed in the two immediately preceding chapters hold up the ideal of an absolute, morally supreme state; and they advocate "realistic"—i.e., physically coercive—means for assuring the realization of that ideal. They put loyalty to the national state above loyalty to individual conscience or to the claims of any group that is less or more than the nation. The state, they maintain, should under all conditions have the first claim upon the citizen's loyalty, and may rightfully enforce this allegiance when it is not willingly conceded. Some writers now attack this absolutist doctrine, contending that there are other essential associations on a parity with the state. Man's social nature, they maintain, finds expression in numerous groupings, pursuing various ends—religious, social, economic, professional, political; no one of the groups is superior, morally or practically, to the others.

These "pluralist" ideas have been set forth most fully by Dr. J. Neville Figgis, Harold J. Laski, and A. D. Lindsay in England, and, as a special legal theory (to be considered in the immediately following chapter), by Léon Duguit in France. Ernest Barker in England and Miss M. P. Follett in the United States have endorsed many of the pluralists' criticisms and proposals; and Miss Follett has given the most extended and discriminating discussion of the whole pluralist trend in theory and practice. All these writers show the influence, on the one hand, of earlier sociological and juristic discussions of the state's relation to economic and professional groups, and, on the other hand, of broader ethical ideas on the values of variety and freedom in self-expression. Their doctrines are also in close relation to certain economic and political transformations which society has undergone during the past half-century.

Most pluralists take as their main object of attack not the absolutist doctrines of Hegel, Treitschke, Bosanquet, and the Fascists but a doctrine of legal sovereignty, set forth most typically by writers who made no special claims in behalf of the moral or practical supremacy of the state. The pluralists discredit the notion that the state habitually exercises any sort of authority that can be properly designated as sovereign; argue that a general and explicitly acknowledged distribution of social authority among various groups within the nation would further the economic, moral, and intellectual well-being of man and society; and contend that in order to secure this general devolution of authority we must surrender "the whole conception of sovereignty" and particularly the unreal, "arid," and "unfruitful" conception of legal sovereignty.

THE STATE'S LEGAL SOVEREIGNTY

The doctrine of the legal sovereignty of the state is a distinctively modern doctrine. The classic theorists of ancient Greece, for example, although they greatly exalted the state, did not place it above law. Generally they ranked the authority of customary law, embodying the dictates of gods or human reason, higher than that of the decrees of any political rulers. Their writings, however, afford no support to the pluralist's ideal of a society in which the state is brought down to the level of other associations. To them the state was the supreme social institution; they recognized other forms of association as essential to the existence of men but regarded the position of the state as unique. The state, in Aristotle's words, was "the highest of all associations . . . which embraces all the rest." [1]

It is in the political situation of the Middle Ages that the pluralists find the historical model for their ideal of a society where authority within any given region is distributed among a number of rival associations. During the greater part of the Middle Ages the state was not the predominant organization of the community. Indeed the state, in the ancient Greek and Roman conception, hardly existed. Organized control over individuals in any territory was shared by various authorities—Roman Church, Holy Roman Emperor, king, feudal lord, chartered town, guild; these several authorities often competed with one another in their efforts to extend their spheres of control over the individual. What laws there were of a "civic"—i.e., secular and territorial—character were not, for the most part, national but rather customary, and varied often according to the boundaries of fiefs or

[1] Aristotle, *The Politics.*

towns.[2] During the eleventh to thirteenth centuries the Church's pretensions to a final authority in social life became extensive, asserting a right of control not only in all moral conduct and religious doctrine and ritual but also in matters of education and learning, trade and commerce, war and peace, in so far as any of these matters were of interest to the Church. Thus it has been said, speaking generally of the Middle Ages, that there was then "no feeling for the state; no common and uniform dependence on a central power; no omnicompetent sovereignty; no equal pressure of civil law; no abstract basis of association in formal and legal rules—or at any rate, so far as anything of the sort was present, it was a matter only for the church, and in no wise for the state." [3]

In the later Middle Ages various conditions combined to increase the power of the state at the expense of its rivals. Economic and social changes had created the need for relief from the confusion of overlapping and conflicting claims upon the allegiance of the indivdual, and had, at the same time, weakened the authority of the Roman Church as an agency of unity. Political authority now appeared again to be, as it had been in ancient Greece and Rome, the most likely instrumentality for securing social order and tranquillity. In several regions of Europe strong national monarchies were evolving, concurrently with the decline of medieval institutions and ideas. The doctrine of the state as a unique authority in determining the form and content of civil law was developed as a useful theoretical foundation upon which to explain the claims made in behalf of the political rights of national monarchs. To give a moral and rational justification for these claims it was necessary to destroy both the idea of an imperial or papal authority above the state and the notion that the authority of the monarch was in any way limited by rights of feudal lords, self-governing towns, and industrially autonomous guilds. This idea was implicit in the situation in fourteenth century France under Louis XI and was, at the same time, made explicit in several theoretical discussions, notably in a work by Pierre du Bois and in a few passages from Bartolus of Sassoferrato. Two centuries later, Jean Bodin, in his famous *De Republica*, defined the commonwealth, or state, as an "association of families and their common affairs, governed by a highest power (*suprema potestas*) and by

[2] See Ernest Barker, "Unity in the Middle Ages," Ch. IV in F. S. Marvin, ed., *The Unity of Western Civilization* (1915).

[3] *Ibid.*, p. 116, quoting from Ernst Troeltsch, *Die Soziallehren der christlichen Kirchen und Gruppen* (1911).

reason," and defined sovereignty (*maiestas*) as "highest power over citizens and subjects, unrestrained by laws (*legibus soluta*)." "The chief mark of sovereignty," he said further, "is the power to give law to all citizens, generally and singly." [4]

By virtue of Bodin's definitions, as well as of his discussion of the specific attributes of sovereignty, he has frequently been referred to as the "founder" of the doctrine of legal sovereignty. There are varying opinions, however, as to how far Bodin meant to extend the lawful powers of the sovereign by characterizing his power as *"legibus soluta."* It is clear that he did not mean that there were no limits to the right- ful authority of the ruler. He said explicitly that the sovereign is limited by "natural and divine laws" (*leges naturae et divinae*) and by "laws of the realm" (*leges imperii*). He gave specific examples of these legal restraints upon sovereignty: under the limitations of natural and divine law the sovereign could not violate private property or break contracts to which he was a party (unless, in the latter case, his sovereignty would be imperilled by holding to the contract); and "as to *imperii leges*," he said, "the prince [i.e., the repository of sovereign power] cannot abrogate or modify them, since they are attached to the very sovereignty with which he is clothed; such is the Salic law, which is the foundation of our monarchy."

How are these apparently contradictory positions of Bodin to be reconciled? Some commentators maintain that Bodin, in holding the sovereign to the limitations of natural and divine laws and laws of the realm, meant only to indicate moral restraints to sovereign authority— showing what the sovereign ought not to do.[5] Others contend that he held principally to the older doctrine of "really legal limitation upon the sovereign"; in the sense, for example, that if the sovereign trans- gressed laws of God, nature, or the realm, his act should be disregarded by the courts of the state.[6] Bodin was not thoroughly clear and con- sistent in the matter. Apparently he was, on the one hand, attempting

---

[4] These definitions are from Bk. I, Chs. I, VIII, and X of Bodin's *De Republica* (1586).

[5] See for example, F. J. Hearnshaw, "Bodin and the Genesis of the Doctrine of Sovereignty," in *Tudor Studies*, R. W. Seton-Watson, ed. (1924), pp. 109–132.

[6] See especially Max A. Shepard, "Sovereignty at the Crossroads: a Study of Bodin," *Political Science Quarterly*, XLV, (1930), 580–603; Charles H. McIlwain, *Growth of Political Thought in the West* (1932), pp. 386–388. Messrs Shepard and McIlwain, in these keen and authentic discussions of Bodin's doctrines, some- what exaggerate (in the present writer's opinion) the contrast between their own and the "typical" (e.g., W. A. Dunning's) interpretation of Bodin's conception of sovereignty.

to establish the doctrine that there were laws of an "ordinary" or "civil" character which became laws only by command of the political sovereign and which did not bind the sovereign himself, and, on the other hand, insisting upon the older idea that every political ruler is subject to customary laws which he cannot lawfully change. In other words, although the powers of the sovereign are not legally unlimited, there are no institutions, independent of the state, or ultimately independent of control by the state sovereign, to tell him what the laws that limit him are.

Later theorists went further, building up more specifically and clearly the content of our contemporary doctrine of legal sovereignty.[7] Thomas Hobbes in the seventeenth century, Rousseau and Blackstone in the eighteenth century, and the "analytical jurists" of the nineteenth and twentieth centuries, are generally regarded as having set forth the doctrine in its most typical form. Hobbes maintained that laws, properly speaking, are nothing but the commands of a political sovereign, so that there can be no legal limits to his sovereignty; so-called divine or natural laws have no politically legal significance, except to the extent adopted and in the manner interpreted by the political sovereign. Rousseau also maintained that sovereignty, which, in his theory, could rationally be held to reside only in the "body politic" or "general will" (a will, however, that must be general in its objects as well as in its origin), had no legal limitations: "the sovereign, being formed wholly of the individuals who compose it has, and can have, no interest contrary to theirs"; it is the "sole judge of what is important" for subjection to the general will and errs only when it legislates for particular interests and when "partial associations are formed at the expense of the great association." [8]

This doctrine of legal sovereignty as we have it to-day exists most typically in the form given it by nineteenth century jurists—most notably in John Austin's *The Province of Jurisprudence Determined.*[9] Austin held that laws in the political sense ("positive laws," that is, as distinguished from divine laws and from rules of custom and morality—such as "laws" of fashion, honor, honesty, decency) are simply

[7] On the history of the doctrine of sovereignty, see the following: George H. Sabine and Walter J. Shepard, "Translators' Introduction," in H. Krabbe, *The Modern Idea of the State* (1922); Harold J. Laski, *Grammar of Politics* (1925), pp. 44–55; Georg Jellinek, *Allgemeine Staatslehre* (second ed., 1905), pp. 421–460; Charles E. Merriam, *History of the Theory of Sovereignty since Rousseau* (1900).

[8] Rousseau, *The Social Contract*, Bk. I, Ch. VII; Bk. II, Chs. II, III, IV, VI.

[9] Published in Austin, *Lectures on Jurisprudence* (1861–1863), Lectures I–VI.

commands emanating directly or indirectly from a determinate legal sovereign in an independent political society. He defined "sovereign" and "independent political society" as follows: "If a determinate human superior, not in the habit of obedience to a like superior, receive habitual obedience from the bulk of a given society, that determinate superior is sovereign in that society and the society (including the sovereign) is a society political and independent." Every command of such a sovereign is law, and no other command is law.[10] This doctrine implies that in the structure of every independent political community it is possible to find a definite sovereign whose function it is to establish the law and whose position is above law: in every state there is some person or group of persons, some organ or collection of organs —the tsar of Russia (before 1917), the British king in Parliament, the American Congress and commonwealth legislatures in coöperatively amending the constitution of the United States—that has legally unlimited authority.

In applying this theory to the contemporary constitutional state, the analytical jurists make a discrimination between sovereignty, involving a power to make and change the fundamental law of the state, and ordinary governmental authority, supreme only within the limits prescribed by the fundamental law or constitution, which only the sovereign, not the government, can change. Thus in the United States the law-making powers of Congress are limited by the Constitution; but two thirds of each house of Congress, with the concurrence of the legislatures of three fourths of the States, can change the Constitution and so exercise sovereign or legally unlimited powers. Another distinction is made between legal and "political," or "physical," sovereignty. It is said that political sovereignty lies wherever actual power lies—the power that is ultimately obeyed. Thus the people generally may be considered to be politically sovereign, in the sense that, if they use the actual powers they possess, they can, in the long run, force the formally sovereign authority to follow their desires. The analytical jurists describe this as "a political, not a legal, fact." Their doctrine is concerned only with the law.

This theory of legal sovereignty is not a doctrine of physically, morally, rationally, or socially unlimited power. No "monist" or "analytical jurist" has maintained that the actual policy of the sovereign

---

[10] *Lectures on Jurisprudence,* especially Lecture VI. The quotations can be found on p. 226 of the fourth edition (1873).

organs of a state is not modified by popular opinion or that the powers of the organs are not limited by the possibilities of effective disobedience. Even Austin spoke of "principles or maxims . . . which the sovereign habitually observes" because of "the regard which is entertained for those principles or maxims by the bulk or most influential part of the community" or because of the sovereign's "perception of utility or from a belief of their conformity to the Divine will"; and he represents the sovereign as "obliged or restrained morally; by opinions and sentiments current in the given community." [11] Moreover, there is, in Austin's doctrine, no identification of sovereignty with might. He commented on the "capital error" of Hobbes, whose political treatises he admired generally, in inculcating "too absolutely" the obligation of submission to an existing government, and he characterized the proposition that "right is might," as either "a flat truism" or "highly false and absurd." [12] Hobbes, by an elaborate analysis of the basic springs of human action, invalidated all claims of moral right against a sovereign in power. Austin explicitly recognized the moral and religious duties of sovereigns to subjects.

This so-called monistic doctrine has no preference as to the structure of government, as between centralization or decentralization, and contains no presupposition as to the desirable or expedient scope of state activity. Nor does the doctrine in any way imply that to criticize, disobey, or resist state authority is irrational, unethical, anti-social, or even impractical. The analytical jurist holds merely that the state exists to enact and apply law; therefore the state cannot be subjected to limitations of the same character and authority as those which it is established to formulate and execute. He does not represent the state as irresponsible; he maintains only that it cannot be responsible to any authority of like character to itself. In brief, the state, as organization for law within a given territory, is legally superior to all other groups within that territory.

CRITICISMS AND PROPOSALS OF THE PLURALISTS

Despite the explicit qualifications made by all exponents of the doctrine of legal sovereignty, the pluralists consider it a pernicious or futile doctrine. "If we look at the facts," A. D. Lindsay has said, "it is clear

---

[11] *Lectures on Jurisprudence* (fourth ed.), I, 273.
[12] *Ibid.*, notes on pp. 287 ff. and 292 ff.

enough that the theory of the sovereign State has broken down." [13] "No political commonplace," said another writer, "has become more arid and unfruitful than the doctrine of the sovereign State." [14] And Harold J. Laski, most persistent and prolific in the attacks, argues that "it is impossible to make the legal theory of sovereignty valid for political philosophy," and that "it would be of lasting benefit to political science if the whole concept of sovereignty were surrendered." [15]

The pluralist charges the monists with the error of regarding all non-political associations created by the state as dependent for their continued existence upon the will of the state and as exercising only powers conceded by the state. He holds that other associations arise naturally and spontaneously and in their peculiar spheres act independently of state control. The state, therefore, cannot in any important sense be said to be sovereign in its relation to these independently originating and functioning associations.

Most of the pluralists acknowledge their indebtedness to a legal and historical theory of corporations set forth by Otto v. Gierke and F. W. Maitland in the last quarter of the nineteenth century. Briefly stated, the doctrine of Gierke and Maitland is that the permanent associations which arise naturally within any society possess personalities which are real, not hypothetical, fictitious, or created from without. Each association has a collective consciousness and will distinct from the consciousness and wills of its individual members. Each, moreover, is an original organ in the elaboration of law; each, that is, functioning prior to any concessions from the state, acts as one of the agencies through which common beliefs of a legal quality find their expression in the actual rules of law. The state's rôle in this legal elaboration is principal but not exclusive.[16] The primary interest of Gierke and Maitland was in establishing a basis for the recognition of the corporate privileges, obligations, and liabilities of these associations. They argued that the state should accept the common point of view that permanent associations have rights and duties as groups, whether or not the

---

[13] "The State in Recent Political Theory," *Political Quarterly*, I (1914), 136.

[14] "The Superstition of the State," London *Times, Literary Supplement*, XVII (July, 1918), 329.

[15] Laski, *Grammar of Politics* (1925), pp. 445, 55.

[16] For Gierke, see his *Das deutsche Genossenschaftsrecht* (1868–1913), *passim*. For Maitland, see his "Moral Personality and Legal Personality," a lecture delivered in 1903 and published in *The Collected Papers of F. W. Maitland*, H. A. L. Fisher, ed., III (1911), 304–320; and the *Introduction* to *Political Theories of the Middle Ages*—his translation of a section of Gierke's *Genossenschaftsrecht*.

state has accepted them as corporations. Just as the state is bound—morally and practically—to accept the sense of the community that individuals are subjects of rights and duties within themselves, not derived from the state, so the state is coming to feel the practical and moral necessity of recognizing the common opinion that groups which act in an integral way become right-and-duty-bearing units, regardless of whether the state has by some formal act endowed them with legal personality.

Other writers have given special attention to the position—considered historically, legally, and politically—of professional and economic groupings in society. J. Paul-Boncour's works have been notably influential among such writers.[17] The history of professional associations shows, he holds, that in all countries and ages such groups have arisen spontaneously; that in time they reach a position where they are able to devise and enforce the conditions under which the vocations for which they stand are pursued; and that the relations of such associations, to members as well as to outsiders, although originally contractual, tend to acquire an obligatory character. Paul-Boncour maintains also that the law of associations gives legal confirmation to this practical development. The law, by recognizing a free right of association and by according to the associations privileges which put them in position to interdict work except under conditions decreed by them, tends to make the associations obligatory in law as well as in fact—to make them "sovereign" rather than voluntary groups. He argues further that these developments are not accidental or avoidable but are inherent in the very nature of economic society; and the conditions that result accord with the true principles of popular government. The basic principle of popular sovereignty, he holds, is this: Since the protection of liberty is the sole end of social organization, the necessary limitations upon liberty can properly be made only through the coöperation, in the formation of laws, of all whose liberties are to be limited by the laws; only in this way is there a guarantee that the restrictions which law imposes are an exact reflection of the solidarity which necessitates the restriction. The right of the majority to act for all within any given association is justifiable only upon the assumption that the majority can and does normally act in the common interest of the members of the association. But the majority of an entire nation is not competent to act for the

[17] See his *Le fédéralisme économique* (second ed., Paris, 1901), especially pp. 1–16, 177–224, 369–423.

interests of all citizens in all things, because these interests are not common in all respects; and there is always the danger that the majority will act in behalf of some particular group. Therefore, besides a national sovereign deciding questions in cases affecting the common interest of the citizenry, there should be particular sovereigns to decide in matters where the special interest of some group is more important than the remoter interest of the nation. Only in that way can there be secured an application of the principle that in the creation of any obligatory rule only those should participate who are truly united by a community of the particular interests and rights with which the rule is concerned.

Various sociologists have criticized the traditional democratic structure on the ground of its inadequacy as the principal regulative factor in the complex industrial society of to-day; they have, like Paul-Boncour, sought to transfer from the state to the vocational group the function of economic control. Émile Durkheim, in particular, argued for the restoration of the ancient occupational association as a definitely recognized public institution. We have at present, he argues, no clear principles and no juridical sanctions through which to determine relations between employers and employees, between competing employers, and between employers or employees and the public. The state cannot establish these principles and sanctions. Economic life is too specialized to be reached by the state. The activities of any given occupation can be regulated only by a group near enough to that occupation to be acquainted with its functions and needs. The professional groups must, therefore, be reëstablished both as bases for political representation and as sources of economic regulation. Geographical divisions have lost their economic and social, and, therefore, their political, significance; they must be replaced by vocational divisions which will reflect more accurately the varieties of social interests.[18]

Other authors have argued in behalf of the rights of lesser associations generally against prevailing creeds of state omni-competence. The late Dr. J. Neville Figgis criticized the efforts of the modern political leader to invade the proper spheres of such essential social groups as churches, trade-unions, local communities, and the family; and he advocated a policy which would attribute to all such groups the character

---

[18] Émile Durkheim, *Le Suicide* (1897), pp. 434–450, and *De la division du travail social* (second ed., 1902), pp. i–xxxvi, "Quelques remarques sur les groupements professionels."

of public associations and accord them a large discretion and initiative in controlling their respective interests.[19] Ernest Barker, although rejecting the Gierke-Maitland conception of the "real personality" of groups, yet accepts the main tenet of their doctrine—namely, that these groups exist prior to any act of the state, each as a juristic person created by a common conviction among its members of its corporate character and function. He holds that this view necessitates a revision of general theory as to the nature of the state and its relation to the other associations. "We see the State less as an association of individuals in a common life; we see it more as an association of individuals, already united in various groups for a further and more embracing common purpose." [20] A. D. Lindsay declares that the corporate personalities in society are infinite in number, and that many of them, because they are more homogeneous and represent a closer community of interests, attract deeper loyalties than the state and, if permitted to act autonomously, prove themselves to be more effective agencies of social coordination.[21]

In order to prove that the doctrine of a sovereign state is practically untenable, Harold Laski and others often refer to actual instances of state impotence in the face of determined resistance by groups within the nation.[22] Laski pictures three great ecclesiastical groups in the nineteenth century successfully asserting extensive rights of self-control against the opposition of the British government. He also shows us the British Parliament, during the World War, not daring to enforce the anti-strike provisions of the Munitions Act against the defiant Welsh miners or to put into operation the Irish home-rule act against the rebellious Ulsterites; and he shows the railway brotherhoods in the United States (in 1916) forcing Congress, by threat of a strike, to enact an eight-hour day. Citing these and other familiar instances of effective pressure by private groups upon the highest organs of government, he asks what validity or importance there is in a doctrine that attributes sovereignty to an official authority which is compelled by unofficial groups to adopt policies to which it is opposed.

Laski assails also the moral validity of the doctrine that ascribes

---

[19] J. Neville Figgis, *Churches in the Modern State* (1913).
[20] Barker, *Political Thought in England from Herbert Spencer to the Present Day* (1915), pp. 175–183.
[21] Lindsay, "The State in Recent Political Theory," *Political Quarterly*, I (1914), 128–145.
[22] Laski, *Problem of Sovereignty* (1917), especially Ch. I and Appendix A.

sovereignty to the state.[23] Here he appeals to the claims both of individual conscience and of various group loyalties. The state, he says,
has no right to the allegiance of an individual save in so far as his
conscience gives assent. "The claim of authority upon myself is . . .
legitimate proportionately to the moral urgency of its appeal." "The
only State to which I owe allegiance is the State in which I discover
moral adequacy. . . . Our first duty is to be true to our conscience." [24]
The state, moreover, "is only one among many forms of human association." [25] It "does not exhaust the associative impulses of men."
Society "should be regarded as essentially federal in its nature." "The
group is real in the same sense that the state is real." "No association
can legislate for the whole of myself." [26] The state must compete with
churches, trade-unions, employers' associations, friendly societies, political parties, professional associations. In any instance of conflicting demands the state's preëminence over other associations depends upon
the superiority of its moral appeal in that instance. "We give to this
particular group [the state] no peculiar merit." [27]

The common feature of all these discussions of the essential functions of smaller groups is the idea that the state is confronted not
merely by unassociated individuals but also by other associations
evolving independently, eliciting individual loyalties, better adapted than
the state—because of their select membership, their special forms of
organization and action—for serving various social needs.

The pluralist doctrine is in part a rationalization of recent practical
movements that look in various ways towards a more decentralized
application of social control. There are, for example, the plans to give
greater recognition to vocational groups within the government service,
by enlarging the powers and responsibilities of associations of public
employees; the projects for reinvigorating local governing units by enlarging their functions and increasing their administrative autonomy;

[23] Laski, *Authority in the Modern State* (1919), especially Ch. I; *Foundations
of Sovereignty and Other Essays* (1921), especially the essay on "The Pluralistic
State," pp. 232–249; *A Grammar of Politics* (1925); *Politics* (1931). For an excellent critical examination of Laski's views, see W. Y. Elliott, *Pragmatic Revolt in
Politics,* Ch. V.
[24] *Grammar of Politics,* pp. 249, 289.
[25] *Authority in the Modern State,* p. 65.
[26] *Grammar of Politics,* pp. 29, 255, 256, 270.
[27] "The Personality of Associations," *Harvard Law Review,* XXIX (1915–1916),
pp. 404–426, at p. 426.

and the suggestions that the state, in reorganizing the control of industry so as to bring about a fairer distribution of wealth and broader opportunities of self-expression, should encourage private systems of joint-control, under state auspices, rather than establish a direct governmental administration or regulation of industrial enterprises.[28]

With a steadily expanding nationalization or municipalization of various economic and social services, political authorities have done little in the way of affording opportunities to governmental employees to exercise a responsible part in administering their services. In the absence of means within the governmental organization itself for self-expression and responsible action, the employees in many instances have created for themselves organs of collective action. In the later decades of the nineteenth century and the first decade of the twentieth century the movement for unionizing civil servants made rapid progress, generally against persistent governmental opposition. In Great Britain and France the national services became almost completely unionized and the local services extensively so; considerable progress was also made in other countries. Some headway was made by the unions in forcing the political heads to recognize and deal directly with them. There were scattered instances of a limited grant of powers of control accorded to the associations of public employees, their representatives being given a minority voice in determining certain questions of administrative policy. Recently several of the *syndicats* of public functionaries in France have assisted in devising schemes for consolidating offices and providing fairer and more practical systems of promotion and discipline. There is a widespread demand that public employees should be accorded the same rights of association and collective bargaining that employees in private enterprises have. Most proposals for state ownership now include, as we have seen, plans for a considerable devolution in the ordinary administration of the socialized industries. The principle is that a state-owned enterprise should be managed not by politically minded ministers but by boards selected by the groups particularly concerned in the efficient and equitable operation of the enterprise. This is not merely to permit governmental employees to defend their special interests but also to protect the public from the evils of bureaucracy, on the theory that useful innovation and flexibility in ad-

[28] See F. W. Coker, "Technique of the Pluralistic State," *American Political Science Review*, XV (1921), 186–213.

ministrative policy is more likely to come from persons actually performing the day-by-day work of the enterprise than from political heads
of departments.[29]

Another movement of reaction against the all-absorbing centralized
state has been in the direction of a greater localization of governmental
control. There are various projects for redefining existing areas of local
government in order to make them logical units of social feeling and
economic life and then devolving many existing governmental functions
upon these reconstructed districts. The aim is to preserve popular self-
government against control by a central government which, however
democratically constructed as to suffrage and the distribution of representation, is too far away from the mass of citizens to know their needs
and opinions.

It is principally, however, in the activities of groups outside the
formal structure of government that the pluralists discover the most
significant practical trends vindicating their doctrine: they refer to the
"self-regulating" activities of trade-unions, employers' associations, co-
operative producers' and consumers' societies; to the systems of "joint-
control" in private industry; and to the activities of private occupational and industrial groups in bringing pressure on governmental
decisions.

Most observers agree that vocational groups are taking an increasing
part, or at least an increasingly obvious part, in determining the action
of formal governing bodies. This appears in the lobbying activities
of associations of laborers, professional men, farmers, manufacturers,
traders, bankers, etc. Governments, indeed, often take the initiative
in securing the coöperation of these associations in formulating policies
of legislation or administration. The operation of systems of compulsory arbitration of industrial disputes, for example, is largely dependent upon the activities of workers and employers in the respective
associations. In various other ways the state recognizes the value of dealing with economic problems through agencies representing the organized groups immediately concerned.

Several European countries have recently made the attempt to co-
ordinate and regularize this sort of group activity, by setting up national economic councils jointly representing labor organizations; associations of industrial employers; chambers of commerce; professional
associations; farming, banking, and insurance groups; and consumers'

[29] Cf. *supra*, pp. 132–133; *infra*, p. 549.

societies.[30] It has been said that, in Germany, the revolution of 1918 was largely instigated, and that the setting up of the new republic was greatly influenced, by bodies fundamentally occupational in their composition—namely, the soldiers' and workers' councils. It was upon the demand of these bodies that provision was made in the Weimar constitution for a National Economic Council representing workers, employers, and "other interested groups proportionately to their economic and social importance." The constitution required that important social and economic measures proposed by the ministry be submitted to this council before introduction into the *Reichstag;* it gave to the council the right to introduce such measures on its own initiative and to have its proposals and views presented to the *Reichstag,* whether or not the ministry assents to them; it authorized Parliament to confer "powers of control and administration" upon the council. These constitutional provisions were never carried out. The "Provisional Economic Council," set up by ordinance in 1920, possessed only advisory powers and had no authority either to initiate legislation or to have its views presented to the *Reichstag* against the desires of the ministry. The constitutions of Jugoslavia and Poland provide in general terms for such councils; but nothing has been done in execution of the provisions.[31] In Czechoslovakia and France, bodies similar in their general composition and function to the German Provisional Economic Council have been set up by governmental decree.

The councils of Germany, France, and Czechoslovakia have supplied their governments with advice on measures elaborated by the ministries, relating to matters of taxation, social insurance, housing, conditions of labor, and to the regulation, protection, and encouragement of production and trade. The advice, however, is principally of an expert sort, not political: furnishing technical or empirical information where the ministries require such knowledge to aid them in pursuing

[30] See Lewis L. Lorwin, *Advisory Economic Councils* (1931); Elli Lindner, *Review of the Economic Councils in the Different Countries of the World,* prepared for the Economic Committee of the League of Nations (1932); Edith C. Bramhall, "The National Economic Council of France," *American Political Science Review,* XX (1926), 623; Herman Finer, *Representative Government and a Parliament of Industry: a Study of the German Federal Economic Council* (1923); Agnes Headlam-Morley, *The New Democratic Constitutions of Europe* (1928), Ch. XVI; E. Pendleton Herring, "Legalized Lobbying in Europe," *Current History,* XXXI (1930), 947–952; Karl von Siemens, "Germany's Business Parliament," *ibid.,* XX (1924), 994–998.

[31] Cf. the constitutions of Germany, Art. 165; Jugoslavia, Art. 44; Poland, Art. 68.

policies upon which they have already decided. It may be said generally that where vocational bodies take the initiative in pressing their
opinions upon government, they continue to do so, in these as in other
countries, extra-legally—by their lobbying activities and by the familiar
pressures they apply to the leaders of political parties.

The pluralist, as we have indicated, appears to regard all these
practical movements as implying a greater diversification in the formulation and execution of social policy than the theory of state sovereignty
can account for; and he approves the movements because they indicate
a respect for the independence and initiative of "spontaneous"
economic, professional, and local groupings that correspond to "natural"
unities of interest and function. None of the pluralists, however, follows
the anarchist or the pre-war syndicalist and makes these groups independent of the state. And this can be said generally also of the pluralists'
forerunners.

At no point did Maitland consider his doctrine of corporations in the
light of its relations to the doctrine of legal sovereignty. Gierke, although maintaining that both individuals and associations must be
recognized as having domains of free existence unassailable by the
state, yet maintained that the state is sovereign where general interests
demanding the exertion of power for their maintenance are concerned.
The state, he maintained, is distinguished from other social bodies
by its position above them; for the state alone there is no limit through
a higher collective existence; its will is the sovereign general will; the
state is the highest *Machtverband*.[32]

Paul-Boncour regards the state as the sole representative of general
interests and of national solidarity. Although he speaks of the other associations as auxiliary and even rival sovereignties, yet he places them
in such relations of subordination to the state as to leave the latter with
sovereignty of the traditional type. It is, he holds, the duty and prerogative of the state to determine, in general outlines, the constitutions of
the several associations, confine them within their respective spheres
of competence, and prevent them from using improper methods for accomplishing their ends. In particular, it is the state's duty to prevent
any one group from acting oppressively toward the public, toward other
groups, or toward its own members. Accordingly, the state must prohibit

[32] "Die Grundbegriffe des Staatsrechts und die neuesten Staatsrechtstheorien,"
Zeitschrift für die gesammte Staatswissenschaft, Vol. XXX (1874).

strikes in essential industries; it must intervene in the conflicts between groups in order to require arbitration; and it must even interfere in the internal affairs of a group if necessary to protect the members against abuse by a controlling faction.[33] Durkheim likewise ascribed to the state the function of laying down the general principles of economic control; he left to the several associations the function of diversifying, under state supervision, the application of the principles according to the varying conditions of the respective associations.

Dr. Figgis described the state as the "society of societies" and assigned to it a distinctive function and a superior authority as an agency of coördination and adjustment. One of the chief values in the several smaller groups consists in the fact that they foster loyalty to the state. "It is largely to regulate such groups and to insure that they do not outstep the bounds of justice that the coercive force of the State exists." [34] Ernest Barker insists that the pluralist trend in recent social development must not carry us too far. "The State," he says, "as a general and embracing scheme of life, must necessarily adjust the relations of associations to itself, to other associations, and to their own members—to itself, in order to maintain the integrity of its own scheme; to other associations, in order to preserve the equality of associations before the law; and to their own members, in order to preserve the individual from the possible tyranny of the group." "We see the State invited to retreat before the advance of the guild, the national group, the Church. Yet whatever rights such groups may claim or gain, the State will still remain a necessary adjusting force; and it is even possible that if groups are destined to gain new ground, the State will also gain, perhaps even more than it loses, because it will be forced to deal with ever graver and ever weightier problems of adjustment." [35] Miss Follett criticizes the pluralists' conception of the state as "competing" for the citizen's loyalty; and she explains so fully the state's unifying functions, and its direct contact with individuals, that she is hardly to be classed properly among the pluralists.

Laski's proposed scheme of economic institutions involves a considerable concentration of power in a single political organization over the several economic units.[36] He would have public employees participate in the management of public enterprises; and in each private

---

[33] *Le fédéralisme économique*, pp. 389–423.
[34] Figgis, *Churches in the Modern State*, p. 49.
[35] Barker, *Political Thought in England*, pp. 178–179, 183.
[36] *Grammar of Politics*, Ch. IX.

industry he would set up a council, representative equally of owners, workers, users, and the government, and empowered to issue orders as to wages, working conditions, hours, the stability of employment, and the settlement of labor disputes. However, he proposes state ownership of those industries which, because of their monopolistic nature and their indispensableness to the welfare of the community, are of a "public" character and so must "be operated for use and not for profit," with only as much devolution in controlling management as will not interfere with the community's right to set minimum standards of efficiency, decency, and fair play. Moreover, he would endow the national political parliament with the power not only of determining the policies of the public enterprises but also of defining basic standards for hours, conditions, and wages in private industry and fixing prices of the necessities of life.

Many of Laski's more general statements of political doctrine are in full accord with his program for a centralized control of economic policy. In his earliest book he said: "Legally no one can deny that there exists in every state some organ whose authority is unlimited"; and "that government is the most important of institutions few, except theocrats, could be found to deny." [37] In a more recent, and his most comprehensive, work he sanctions "the ultimate reserve power of the state"; recognizes the distinction of the state from all other associations, in the fact that it is "an association in which membership is compulsory"; defines the state as "the association to protect the interests of men as citizens," agrees that "to satisfy the common needs, it must control other associations to the degree that secures from them the service such needs require"; and concedes finally that "clearly a function of this kind . . . involves a preëminence over other functions." Again he says: "However much we may reduce the direct administrative capacity of the political State, the fact remains that once it is charged with the provision of services of which men stand in common need, it has their interest in trust to a degree with which no other body can, at least in a temporal sense, compete. Even if we abstract from the modern State the final control of international affairs, the civic area of internal matters that is left seems, in any casual glance, overwhelming." [38] Few, if any, of the Austinians, have seen in sovereignty anything more "overwhelming" than an "ultimate" authority perform-

[37] Laski, *Foundations of Sovereignty*, pp. 236, 237.
[38] *Grammar of Politics*, pp. 62, 69, 70, 75.

ing functions which, because they secure "common needs," involve "a preëminence over other social functions."

CONCLUSION

In general then it appears that when the pluralist sets forth his abstract theory, he denies the sovereign power of the state, or else characterizes the power as something that is properly only ultimate and reserved; but when he devises specific institutional arrangements, he assigns tasks to the state—in defining standards, laying down general policies and seeing that the standards and policies are observed—that obviously require the application of not an ultimate and reserved power but a very direct and constantly exercised one.

It is, of course, possible not merely to repudiate the theory of state-sovereignty, as Laski and the other pluralists attempt to do, but to construct a positive theory of social organization based upon the repudiation. The doctrines of the anarchists and the revolutionary syndicalists were founded on the hypothesis that social order, peace, and justice can be best maintained when there is no association vested with the special task of authoritative coördination among the manifold coöperating groups in society. Kropotkin held that no centralized, coercive authority over man is needed: if individuals are left free to associate themselves as they see fit, all will respect the interests of one another and act generally in response to natural impulses of sympathy and good will. Under that view social discord is due only to the perverting influence of the unnatural and unjust restrictions inherent in political authority and private property. The syndicalist doctrine also provided for completely self-determining industrial groups, each free from any organized control above it. The syndicalists and anarchists proposed social systems that afforded clear and consistent applications of the pluralist's creed of divided or discarded sovereignty. They argued that it is no more necessary for the state to assume police and military functions or set standards of economic policy and compel men to accept and pay for these services, than it is for the state to meddle compulsively with private morals and opinions. The pluralists, on the other hand, do not expunge from their theory the principle of either compulsory taxation or of a compulsory citizenship applied to persons by virtue of residence or birth; and most of them assign to the comprehensive and coercive political community very extensive duties in directing the economic and social life of the nation.

There is, moreover, the question of experience—whether the familiar schemes of "self-regulation" do, in their net practical effect, establish any real group autonomies or tend towards any actual diminution of the scope and significance of political authority. In the first place, if the workers are to be certain of any participation in actual control, they must be able to maintain strong and independent unions; and this seems to require considerable support from the state—as much, at least, as is accorded to the organized activities of private bankers, traders, and farmers. The state has to intervene to the extent of outlawing "yellow-dog" contracts, restricting the employers' use of armed guards, and affording full protection to the peaceful activities of strikers. Secondly, if any of these voluntary but legally protected arrangements between owners and workers secure any real self-government for all the parties immediately concerned, it then becomes necessary for the state to see that such coöperating groups do not exercise their autonomy in ways that contravene the interests of the community. For now the state will have to define the general ends that are to be served and the methods to be pursued in carrying out the voluntary agreements. Finally, after the "autonomous" groups are set up, the state, it is generally conceded, will have many economic duties to perform directly—in disseminating market information, controlling unemployment, checking the flow of capital into overdeveloped industries, stabilizing price levels, and so forth.[39]

It seems to be true not only that, as Mr. Laski says, man is a creature of competing loyalties and that the state cannot absorb them wholly but also that the loyalties of some men often conflict with the loyalties of others and that the different groups attracting these loyalties come into rivalries of interest and competence. So we need an organization that has the special function of adjusting and adjudicating such clashes as well as of caring for certain common interests. To recognize the indispensableness of such a common association is not to ignore the social values of the smaller groups; and to recognize the state's peculiarly comprehensive membership and its special right to use organized coercion as one of its means of action is to make no claim to moral absolutism for the state or to suggest any judgment as to the rightness or expediency of any particular system of economic organization or governmental policy.

[39] Cf. Sumner H. Slichter, *Modern Economic Society* (1931), Chs. **XXXI** and *passim*.

Perhaps the defects of the pluralists' analysis lie in part in their failure to make clear which of the specific functions assigned to the state by the monist they would deny to it, and in part in their underlying assumption that, if only an individual or group be released from state control, then we shall have a condition in which spontaneous action, self-expression, and initiative will enjoy free play. Experience hardly bears out this assumption. Many who raise the loudest outcry against state encroachment upon individual or group freedom are the most ardent supporters, or the most complacently tolerant, of other forms of social coercion. A. E. Zimmern has warned us that "those who talk of state-absolutism are ignoring the simple truth that there is no tyranny like the tyranny of near neighbors. The smaller the group the tighter the strangle-hold over your life and activities." [40] Every "lesser" or "voluntary" association does in fact habitually recognize the state's supreme authority whenever it needs an assertion of this authority to protect it from other groups that contest its freedom of action in a sphere it claims as its own.

The political monist accepts the state as an association intended to maintain the ascendancy of the social dispositions of men over individual and group selfishness; and suspects that the smaller groups —trade-unions, religious and professional associations—will fare better in their efforts to become centers of spontaneous, creative action when they all recognize the legal supremacy of the state. If the pluralists admit this or if they admit, as they all apparently do, that we have only one association in which membership is normally compulsory and that this association possesses rightly the power to define common interests and, in sustaining these interests, to exercise powers of coercion through the usual forms of law enforcement, then it does not seem to make much theoretical or practical difference whether or not there is agreement that these approved and admittedly unique attributes of the state can best be described by the term "sovereign." The significant fact appears to be that, however much we exalt individual or group freedom, we are faced at present with the prospect of a more varied and centralized political control, and that the net result of our practical efforts at devolution will not soon diminish greatly the scope or importance of state authority.

[40] Zimmern, "Political Thought," pp. 321–352 in Richard W. Livingstone, *The Legacy of Greece* (1921), p. 348.

SELECT BIBLIOGRAPHY

STATEMENTS OF THE PLURALIST DOCTRINE

Barker, Ernest, *Political Thought in England from Herbert Spencer to the Present Day* (London and New York, 1915), pp. 175–183.

Figgis, J. Neville, *Churches in the Modern State* (London and New York, 1913).

Follett, M. P., *The New State* (New York, 1918).

Gierke, Otto von, *Das deutsche Genossenschaftsrecht* (Berlin, 1869–1913).

——————, "Die Grundbegriffe, des Staatsrechts und die neuesten Staatsrechtstheorien," *Zeitschrift für die gesammte Staatswissenschaft*, Vol. XXX (1874).

Laski, Harold J., *The Problem of Sovereignty* (New Haven, 1917).

——————, *Authority in the Modern State* (New Haven, 1919).

——————, *Foundations of Sovereignty and Other Essays* (New York, 1921).

——————, *A Grammar of Politics* (New Haven, 1925).

——————, *Politics* (Philadelphia, 1931).

Lindsay, A. D., "The State in Recent Political Theory," *Political Quarterly,* I (1914), 128–145.

Maitland, F. W., *Introduction,* in Otto von Gierke, *Political Theories of the Middle Ages,* translated by F. W. Maitland (Cambridge, 1900).

——————, "Moral Personality and Legal Personality," in *Collected Papers,* edited by H. A. L. Fisher, III (Cambridge, 1911), 304–320.

Paul-Boncour, J., *Le fédéralisme économique* (second ed., Paris, 1901).

"The Superstition of the State," London *Times, Literary Supplement,* XVII (July, 1918), 329–330.

PLANS FOR AUTONOMOUS OR ADVISORY GROUPS WITHIN THE STATE

Bramhall, Edith C., "The National Economic Council of France," *American Political Science Review,* XX (1926), 623–630.

Brun, Charles, *Le régionalisme* (Paris, 1911).

Budon, Adrien, "L'association professionelle et le syndicat chez les fonctionnaires," *Revue politique et parlementaire,* CXI (1922), 104–118.

Buell, Raymond L., *Contemporary French Politics* (New York and London, 1920), Ch. XII.

Cole, G. D. H., *The Future of Local Government* (London, New York, 1921).

——————, *The Next Ten Years in British Social and Economic Policy* (London and New York, 1929).

Durkheim, Émile, *De la division du travail social* (second ed., Paris, 1902), pp. 1–36.

—————————, *Le suicide* (Paris, 1897).

Favareille, René, *Réforme administrative par l'autonomie et la responsabilité des fonctions* (Paris, 1919).

Finer, Herman, *Representative Government and a Parliament of Industry: a Study of the German Federal Economic Council* (London, 1923).

Gide, Charles, "Le conseil national économique," *Revue d'économie politique,* XLII (1928), 1049–1060.

Harmignie, Pierre, *L'état et ses agents: étude sur le syndicalisme administratif* (Louvain, 1911).

Headlam-Morley, Agnes, *The New Democratic Constitutions of Europe* (London, 1928), Ch. XVI.

Hemmeon, Joseph C., *The History of the British Post Office* (Cambridge, Mass., 1912), pp. 79–88.

Hennessy, Jean, *Régions de France, 1911–1916* (Paris, 1916).

—————————, *Réorganisation administrative de la France* (Paris, 1919).

Herring, E. Pendleton, "Legalized Lobbying in Europe," *Current History,* XXXI (1930), 947–952.

Laurin, T., *Les instituteurs et le syndicalisme* (Paris, 1908).

Lefas, Alexandre, *L'état et les fonctionnaires* (Paris, 1913).

Leroy, Maxime, *Syndicats et services publics* (Paris, 1909).

Lindner, Elli, *Review of the Economic Councils in the Different Countries of the World* (Geneva, 1932).

Lorwin, Lewis L., *Advisory Economic Councils* (Washington, 1931).

Moses, Robert, *The Civil Service of Great Britain* (New York, 1914), pp. 200–211.

Paul-Boncour, J., *Les syndicats des fonctionnaires* (Paris, 1906).

Siemens, Karl von, "Germany's Business Parliament," *Current History,* XX (1924), 994–998.

Zapp, Jean, "Le syndicalisme dans les services publics," *Revue politique et parlementaire,* CXI (1922), 119–126.

CRITICAL ANALYSES OF PLURALIST DOCTRINE

Elliott, William Y., *The Pragmatic Revolt in Politics* (New York, 1928), Chs. III and V.

Ellis, Ellen D., "The Pluralistic State," *American Political Science Review,* XIV (1920), 393–407.

Gettell, Raymond G., *History of Political Thought* (New York, 1924), Ch. XXIX.

Hocking, William E., *Man and the State* (New Haven, 1926), Chs. VII, IX–XIII, XXVI.

Hsiao, Kung-Chuan, *Political Pluralism: a Study in Contemporary Political Theory* (London and New York, 1927).

Sabine, George, "Pluralism, a Point of View," *American Political Science Review*, XVII (1923), 34–50.

Willoughby, Westel W., *The Ethical Basis of Political Authority* (New York, 1930), Ch. XXXIII.

CHAPTER XIX

LAW AND THE STATE

THE attempts to define theoretically the limits of state authority take three principal forms. There is, first, the theory that man has a definite sphere of private life in which—by virtue of universal principles of right, the nature of man or human society, or the laws of organic evolution—he is entitled to be free from direction or restraint by his government. Here fall the familiar doctrines of individualism we have already considered: the idea of natural rights to liberty of conscience, freedom of opinion, freedom of contract, etc.; the hypothesis that natural economic forces decree a policy of political *laisser-faire* in relation to private property; and the argument that biology, revealing throughout all organic life a beneficent evolution from lower to higher types of beings in an "unregulated" struggle for survival, condemns certain sorts of state activity. Secondly, there is the theory that within any normal community there are important and enduring social groups (e.g., churches and trade-unions) which are on a par with the state in their social and moral values and often also in their actual power and which, therefore, are not properly or effectively subject to the latter's dictation within their own proper spheres of action. This pluralist doctrine we have discussed in the immediately preceding chapter. Finally, there is the theory (appearing like the other two in widely varied and often mutually contradictory forms) that the state is in fact and by right limited by "law."

The discrimination between state decrees and laws higher than the state has been familiar in all ages of political speculation. Philosophers of ancient Greece discussed the question as to whether political justice and right was created by laws, or *vice-versa*. They also made the distinction between written, humanly decreed, laws—limited in application to the boundaries of particular communities and changing within any community with changing conditions—and unwritten, divinely or naturally appointed, laws—universal in application and immutable in time. Generally they held that the former ought to conform to the lat-

521

ter; and on this ground they contrasted "pure" with "perverted" forms of state: the former—royalty, aristocracy, and polity—ruling subject to the unwritten laws; the latter—tyranny, oligarchy, and ochlocracy (called democracy by some)—governing in defiance of these laws.

This ancient idea survives in the medieval and modern idea of "natural law"—a system of rules that are of a normative, not merely descriptive, sort and are yet distinct from both moral precepts and political decrees, although they are particularly applicable through the agency of the latter. Normally just and reasonable men, according to the natural-law theorists, understand these ideally just and reasonable rules, although the opinions of men particularly qualified, by native endowment, special training, or official position, may be needed to discover their correct applications in actual life. At all times we find varied and often conflicting opinions as to the practical consequences that follow from the supremely obligatory character of this universal law of "right reason." Did it (in medieval and early modern times) establish a lawful right of tyrannicide against an oppressive or usurping king? Did it, in seventeenth century England, invalidate a parliamentary enactment repugnant to it or at any time limit the king's prerogative? Does it now establish legal limits to the highest authorities of formal law in the United States—the bodies which collectively amend the Constitution? And more generally, do judges, in applying the "common law," exercise any legally creative function or perform only an act of expert legal discovery and announce an already existing law?

Questions as to the legal limits of the state, even when it acts through its highest organs, supply some of the most controversial issues of contemporary political theory. The contenders agree that orderly social life can exist only where there is a general recognition of an obligation to abide by laws. All agree that political agencies have indispensable and distinctive functions to perform in defining the specific content of these laws and in devising the modes of their execution. They sharply disagree, however, as to the essential character and force of the state's activity in declaring, "enacting," and carrying out law. The debate takes varied forms—now over principles of right, now over questions of fact. Is the general obligation to respect that law with which the state deals a duty owed principally to the state, or rather to some object of loyalty of higher authority than the state? Do any of the state's law-making or law-declaring organs—legislatures, courts, or constituent assemblies— ever actually decide what the law is or is to be, or do they normally only register and expedite legal conclusions already somewhat effectively reached in another manner? Among those who choose the latter alternatives in these two questions, there are varying ideas as to the sources, sanctions, contents, and practical effects of the law that is superior to all political authority.

THE ANALYTICAL CONCEPTION OF POSITIVE LAW

Most of the contemporary discussion of the relations of the state to law centers on questions concerning the theoretical correctness and moral and practical significance of what is called the "formal" or "analytical" theory of law—often described also as the "orthodox," "conventional," or "classical" theory. This theory, we have seen, using the word law in its positive sense, maintains that the laws with which the jurist or political scientist has to do are the commands of determinate political authorities. The positivist doctrine received its most precise and uncompromising formulations, first, in the writings of British utilitarians, notably Jeremy Bentham (in 1776) and John Austin (in the middle of the nineteenth century), and later in the works of jurists of the German Empire during the last quarter of the century. In each case there were practical reasons inducing the writers to emphasize the unique part which contemporary organs of the state play, and in their opinion should play, in fashioning the law of the day.

Juristic writing in the early nineteenth century (in Germany until after the middle of the century) was dominated generally by historical interpretations. The historical jurists, rejecting the prevailing natural-law doctrine of absolute, universal, and unalterable rules of law, put in its place a conception of laws determined by characteristics and experiences of a particular people.[1] These laws, they maintained, have their origin neither in a universal and unchanging human reason nor in the decisions of contemporary agencies of government, but in a national will or mind that reveals itself in the orderly practices of a national community. Judges, informed by legal history, find that law and make their decisions accordingly. Courts play the chief part in building up the essential features of the national law. Enacted law should be only a formal embodiment of historic law. A legislative body, if it confines itself to its

---

[1] Gustav von Hugo (1764–1844) is regarded as the founder of the historical school of jurisprudence, in Germany, and Friedrich Karl von Savigny (1799–1861) as its most influential exponent.

proper field, merely decides what customary rules of conduct need formal definition in order to secure their better observance. Its task is to clarify the existing law or indicate certain particular applications and sanctions for social rules already in force. Thus law in its most characteristic form is common law or "case law." And the ultimate sanctions of the law are not the penalties which either legislatures or courts lay down but the habits, opinions, and emotions of the body of people whose standards of right thereby reveal themselves and give enduring force to the sanctions of the formal statutes and judgments.

The utilitarians, we have seen, were legal reformers.[2] Conservatives of the day opposed their projected reforms, on the grounds either of universal right or of principles embodied in the customs and unwritten laws of the country. The reformers desired to show that there was no rational basis for regarding a political community as hampered, in its efforts to rectify social injustices and inconveniences, by either natural or traditional law. Although the community cannot rightly act contrary to the general welfare, its highest law-enacting agencies do possess a legally unlimited competence in adopting any measures they determine to be necessary to satisfy the needs of the living generation. The jurists of this school did not deny the rational, moral, and historical ingredients of law, but they held that these can be maintained by deliberate political action, particularly in preventing tradition from becoming a cloak for injustice or an impediment to practical improvement. In other words, they regarded law as an instrument of human welfare, a changing means for the constant end of human happiness. Laws are the rules which a community desires to support in the formal and coercive manner we generally describe as political. They follow social customs or popular opinions as to what is just or expedient, and their forms are influenced by previous legal action; but at any time the formal endorsement of existing legislative bodies or courts gives the rules their character as laws.

The object of the jurists of the earlier German empire was likewise to make the German state a free agent of law in meeting the needs of the time, unhampered by restraints supposedly embodied in vague notions as to what was demanded by rules of natural justice or by com-

[2] The legal doctrine of the utilitarians was set forth most succinctly by Jeremy Bentham (1748–1832) in his *Fragment on Government* (1776) and John Austin (1790–1859) in his *Province of Jurisprudence Determined*. For a fuller historical sketch of the analytical conception, see the immediately preceding chapter, pp. 501–503; and for the general ideas of the utilitarians, see *supra,* pp. 23–25.

mands of a mythically conceived national mind. As the utilitarians offered a legal theory to justify legislative intervention in removing injustices and anomalies from the traditional law, so the German jurists sought similarly to validate the powers asserted by the imperial government in its work of consolidating strongly the German nation.

The transition from historical to positivist conceptions of law in Germany appeared in the writings of Karl Friedrich von Gerber (1823–1891), during the decade preceding the formation of the empire. Von Gerber's earlier works were written directly under the influence of the historical school. His later position represented a sort of combination of historical and positivist conceptions.[3] German law, he held, is an expression of the German juridical consciousness, but the expression takes place through the deliberate acts of tribunals and officials of the existing state. Whatever the social origins of the norms of the laws, it is the sanctions applied by these active organs that transform the norms into legal rules. Law, as the jurist conceives it, has no meaning apart from a system of political agencies possessed of a power to rule.[4] Paul Laband (1838–1918), who wrote during the first decade of the empire and who was the most famous and influential of its teachers of constitutional law, stated the positivist conception in precise and unqualified terms.[5] The state must have an authority that has no legal limits; and legal questions constitute the sole materials for the juristic scholar. His task is to find, by precise and objective analysis of the commands of the legal sovereign, what the law is. Questions as to the moral rightness or the practical effectiveness of the law belong to scholars of other disciplines.

Georg Jellinek (1851–1911) accepted in general the juristic methods and categories of Gerber and Laband.[6] The state, he said, is "the corporate expression of an established people with an autonomous sovereignty," or "an autonomous corporation exercising territorial sover-

---

[3] See especially von Gerber, *Grundzüge eines Systems des deutschen Staatsrechts* (1865 and later eds.), pp. 19–69, 180–204 of the 1865 edition.

[4] Von Gerber, however, admitted limits of a juridical character to the competence of the state. The latter is sovereign in the sense that it is not subject to any organized control but also limited in the sense that it cannot lawfully act except for proper legal ends. If it seeks to control opinion or interfere with property, beyond what the necessities of public order and security require, it acts unlawfully.

[5] See Laband, *Das Staatsrecht des deutschen Reiches* (1876–1882, and later editions), *passim.* See especially the preface to the second ed. (1887) and, in the fourth ed. (1911), vol. IV, pp. 64–74.

[6] See Jellinek, *Allgemeine Staatslehre* (1900, and later editions), especially pp. 155–166, 324–360 (1905 ed.).

eignty"; and sovereignty is "the negation of every subjection or restraint of the state through an alien power." He admitted sociological and ethical conceptions into his "general political theory" by showing (somewhat in the Hegelian style) that the state is the supreme agency for realizing a great human moral ideal. He held, however, that this exalted task of the state justifies its legal absolutism. The true state recognizes its subservience to its great moral task and so voluntarily submits itself to law. It becomes thereby a *Rechtsstaat,* in which its action is under legal limits. But the limits are set only by the state itself. In other words, a political theorist recognizes that a juristic theory does not set forth the full nature of the state; for all political organs act under the impulsion of forces—cultural, intellectual, moral—which determine generally the actual life and character of a state, and, more significantly, influence the content and the effectiveness of the law. No strictly juristic doctrine undertakes to describe or account for these forces. The limits to the competence of the state are determined by philosophy, not by jurisprudence.[7]

Most of the later juristic writers have attempted to bring within their own field of study the broader analysis indicated by Jellinek as the task of the political or social philosopher. In other words, they have abandoned the effort to study law as a completely self-centered system, and they endeavor to show its place in the whole current of human life. It is impossible within the limits of a chapter to indicate at all adequately the scope and variety of these broader studies. We undertake here only brief sketches of several of the more distinctive discussions, in order to indicate their bearing on questions as to the relations between the state and law. For the purpose in hand we select, first, three influential jurists of Germany—Rudolf von Jhering (1818–1892), Rudolf Stammler (1856–), and Joseph Kohler (1849–1919)—who incorporated the positivist conception into their broad and somewhat original sociological and philosophical theories of law; and, secondly, Léon Duguit of France, H. Krabbe of Holland, and H. J. Laski of England, who explicitly controvert or belittle the significance of the positivist conception and adopt "realistic" or ethical criteria in its place.

---

[7] See also Albert Haenel, *Studien zum deutschen Staatsrechte* (1873–1883); *Deutsches Staatsrecht* (1892), pp. 108–119; and for an extensive account of the German imperial jurists, see Rupert Emerson, *State and Sovereignty in Modern Germany* (1928), Ch. II.

POSITIVE LAW IN RELATION TO SOCIAL PHILOSOPHY

Human institutions, von Jhering maintained, are to be explained by their purposes, not by their causes.[8] An end in view rather than an anterior event supplies the key to the ways of human behavior. "The stone does not fall in order to fall, but because it must fall, because its support is taken away; whilst the man who acts does so, not *because* of anything, but *in order* to attain to something. This purpose is as indispensable for the will as cause is for the stone. As there can be no motion of the stone without a cause, so can there be no movement of the will without a purpose. In the former case we speak of the *mechanical* law of causality, in the latter of the *psychological*." [9]

The purposes controlling human conduct may be individual or social. Many acts are determined by self-interest. Much of our organized social life is simply a means of bringing about, more or less artificially, a harmony among various self-seeking activities. However, the individual is also moved to action in many instances by an ethical purpose—a desire to help others. Thus various individuals may be made to serve a social end by appeals both to their self-interest, through rewards and penalties, and to a natural human sympathy and sense of social duty. Rewards and penalties operate more or less spontaneously in the life of trade, the fundamental principle of which is *"quid pro quo"*: differences in capacities and needs lead to a division of labor and to exchange, and these in turn lead to contracts and other mutual adjustments that promote the interests of all the parties. We find the conditions for a legal system of society only when individual egoism has been transformed into a social egoism—that is, where social ends (which have hitherto been unconsciously served by individual self-seeking) are desired in and for themselves.

The state, in which the organization of human purpose "attains its highest point," takes individual egoism into its service.[10] It acts through law. Von Jhering, like the utilitarians, regarded law as made for the masses of men. It is a means to an end, and the end is not the right of the individual but the interest of society. Thus the law recognizes property rights only in so far as the exercise of such rights promotes the social

---

[8] See especially von Jehring, *Der Zweck im Recht* (1877–1883, and later eds.), translated by Isaac Husik as *Law as a Means to an End* (1913); especially Chs. I–III and VIII.

[9] *Law as a Means to an End*, p. 2.

[10] *Ibid.*, p. 32.

welfare. When law fails to satisfy human needs it should, like other human institutions, be changed by deliberate human effort. Laws, then, are the rules which men in society apply through their political agencies, for the purpose of guaranteeing the conditions necessary for the life and welfare of society.

Under Stammler's doctrine, the principal task of the jurist is to find the criterion for "right" law—or "a methodical and well-founded judgment concerning the presence or absence of the quality of justice in a legal content." [11] For jurisprudence is a "telic," not a "natural," science (*Zweckwissenschaft*, not *Naturwissenschaft*). It is not concerned in the distinctions between true and false with regard to the ways in which objects, as we observe them, behave and arrange themselves in regular relations of time, space, and causality. It differentiates between the good and bad as a means to an assumed end. The criterion for such a judgment can be obtained not by generalizations from the observed experiences of men living under law but by a strict logical analysis of our conception of what we consider to be the end of law as we actually use the term. We understand by community a society in which each individual is neither wholly end nor wholly means—where no one treats his own end as so important that he can make all other individuals his tools and where no one considers his own end so unimportant that he is willing to be treated as a tool of others. The end of law is the perfect community, as the end of moral doctrine is the perfect individual. "Right" law is different not only from law as actually established in existing enactments and judicial decisions but also from what is demanded by the sense of right of a community or of any class within the community. Although ethics and just law can never be essentially in contradiction, they relate to different aspects of human behavior. Ethics has to do with character, jurisprudence with conduct; the former inculcates good motives, "purity of thought," "perfection of the inner life" and distinguishes between love and hatred, mercy and cruelty, honesty and dishonesty; the latter is indifferent to motives and is concerned with the execution of contracts and the prevention

---

[11] Stammler's general doctrines appear in his *Die Lehre von dem richtigen Rechte* (1902), translated by Isaac Husik as *The Theory of Justice* (1925); *Wirtschaft und Recht nach der materialistischen Geschichtsauffassung* (1896; fourth ed., 1921); "Wesen des Rechtes und der Rechtswissenschaft," in *Die Kultur der Gegenwart*, II. 8 (1906), i–lix; *Lehrbuch der Rechtsphilosophie* (1921, 3d ed. 1928). See the article by George H. Sabine, "Rudolf Stammler's Critical Philosophy of Law," *Cornell Law Quarterly*, XVIII (1933), 321–350.

of crimes and torts. Ethics operates through instinct and the regulation of intent; the law operates through physical rewards and penalties.[12]

The criterion for the appraisal of law, however, must be found in a philosophy of social life. Stammler's philosophy is idealistic in the sense that it rests on a conception of society as constantly in a process of development toward a goal conceivable by human reason. Justice is the end of the law not because each law has or even is intended to have that end but because, within any community governed by law, there is a general recognition of the fact that law ought generally to tend to that end. The jurist, therefore, is directly concerned with the good faith of law. He must show not simply what the law is in fact—what legislatures and courts have done, why they did it, or what they are likely to do because of the pressure of public opinion or the character and experience of the legislators or judges—but also what the law ought to be—what the legislature should enact, what the court ought to decide. Law being not only a command of a sovereign or a product of popular opinions or social conditions but essentially a social means to a social end, it is the function of the student of law to determine how adequately any given law serves its end. As for every other standard of right, the criterion for law must be a fundamental and "universally valid manner of judging," applying at all times and to all possible laws. The question then is "Under what universal conditions is the quality of objective justice present in a specific legal rule?" [13]

Stammler's formula for guiding the legislator or judge in discharging his task of following right law is "natural law with variable content" (*Naturrecht mit wechselndem Inhalte*). This is a universal standard, however, only as a formal measure of the law. The actual content of right law varies infinitely. The constant ideal of law is a community in which every individual demands consideration for himself and accords it to others. This means that no one is subject to the arbitrary control of another and that no one is excluded from the juristic community. Law binds the individual, regardless of his consent in any given instance, only because it is an inevitable means for maintaining the society that secures his freedom and because he participates in the society from which the law issues. Thus the nature of right law is determined by the end of law, which is not individual freedom, equality, happiness

---

[12] Stammler, *Theory of Justice,* Pt. I, Ch. II.
[13] *Ibid.,* p. 21.

or moral goodness, but the ideal of human society—namely, "a community of men willing freely." [14]

In Kohler's juristic system, law must first be discovered empirically. [15] What ought to be is to be found only in what has been. Human reason works itself out in history, but the nature of the realized reason is to be discovered by an analysis not of rational concepts but of the forms in which the concepts operate in the actual world. There is no such thing as an eternal and universal law. Law continually changes. Any legal institution—the family, slavery, private property—that has existed through long periods of history and played an effective part in determining the development of culture is legally proper for those periods, whether or not it conforms to certain *a priori* conceptions of right. Slavery cannot be said to be in itself wrong. At any given stage in the history of a given people it may be right—suiting the contemporary economic and social conditions and the prevailing intellectual and ethical ideas, yet showing an advance in the right direction over the institutions of an earlier stage. Law is the product of "the totality of human achievements" in knowledge, literature, art and religion. A "philosophy of law must set forth how at every stage of development definite legal institutions have embodied the cultural ideas then maintained." [16]

On the other hand, Kohler maintained that law must be studied not only as a vital part of a past or existing culture but also as a force assisting society towards its final goal. He agreed with Stammler in holding that a mere description of the law, as found in legal history or in an analysis of statutes and decisions, supplies very little understanding of the law. The juristic philosopher is as much concerned with the ideal as with the actual content of the law. For law is both the product of culture and a means for furthering it. Law, then, as an instrument of culture, must be appraised as good or bad according to the measure in which it both fits an existing culture and also helps that culture move towards the ideal of all culture—"the greatest possible development of human control over nature" or "the maximum of human knowledge and of human creative power." [17]

---

[14] *Theory of Justice*, p. 153.
[15] Kohler's general legal doctrine appears most fully in his *Lehrbuch der Rechtsphilosophie* (1909), translated by Adalbert Albrecht as *Philosophy of Law* (1914). See also among his numerous works: *Moderne Rechtsprobleme* (1907, second ed. 1913).
[16] *Moderne Rechtsprobleme* (1913 ed.), 1–15; and *Philosophy of Law, passim*.
[17] *Moderne Rechtsprobleme*, p. 2 and *passim*.

Although these three German theorists introduced philosophical and sociological standards of right law into their juristic systems, they left undisturbed the unique and important position of the state in defining and giving effect to the standards.

Von Jhering was emphatic in specifying state-enforcement as the distinctive mark of law.[18] There are, he said, three forms of "social imperatives," i.e., rules of conduct having the interest of society as their object; these are moral precepts, social conventions, and laws. The two former are realized by society independently of state action. Laws, although they may be laid down as a result of moral or conventional standards, are only those social rules that are backed by political action. Society takes the form of the state in respect to whatever indispensable rules it considers to be dependent upon coercion to secure their observance. And an absolute need of the state, demanded by the very purpose for which it exists, is the possession of a power superior to every other power within society. This predominance of the state does not indeed rest upon a mere preponderance of physical force; if it did, the state would be impotent against a majority and would always yield to an adverse popular opinion. The fact that it does not have so to yield is due not only to the better organization and technique of its force but also to its superior moral power—the stronger human impulses to action that come to its aid. The psychological supports of state power are: "insight into the necessity of political order; the sense of right and law; anxiety for the danger threatening persons and property in every disturbance of order; and fear of punishment." [19]

Nevertheless, "only those rules laid down by society deserve the name of law which have coercion, or since, as we have seen, the state possesses the monopoly of coercion, which have political coercion behind them; whereby it is implicitly said that only the rules which are provided by the state with this efficacy are rules of law; or that *the state is the only source of law.*" If other associations enjoy a certain autonomy, including a right to make legal rules for themselves, they do so only by express grant or tacit consent from the state. For the jurist, "coercion put in execution by the state forms the absolute criterion of law. . . . All rules which are realized in this way are law; all others, even though

[18] See especially *Law as a Means to an End*, Ch. III, Sec. 5; Ch. VIII, Secs. 1–10.
[19] *Ibid.*, p. 239.

they are actually followed in life ever so inviolably, are not laws; they become law only when there is added to them the external element of political coercion." [20]

Stammler gives only brief consideration to the function of the state in reference to right law.[21] On the one hand, he holds, the idea of law is logically prior to the idea of the state: we can define a legal order without reference to the state, and not *vice versa*. On the other hand, there must be, in any legal society, some one body with whom ultimate decision rests. Law is autocratic social regulation. The ideal content of law should guide the legislator or other official vested with the task of determining the formal law. It should also guide the judges or other interpreting executors of the law; but only in so far as the formal law leaves some leeway in the matter, for the administrators of law cannot disobey or transcend its formal directions. The only opportunity a judge has for utilizing "right" law in applying formal law is where the latter is silent or ambiguous or where it explicitly calls for an exercise of discretion in order to apply the proper legal principles.

Kohler is more explicit in this positivist position.[22] The supreme task of the state is to advance culture in all its forms, directly for the particular nation and indirectly for "all humanity." In promoting culture it shares its tasks with individuals; there are no hard and fast lines to define the division of functions here. It does, however, have practically a monopoly in realizing law. "The state must intervene wherever it is assumed that essential cultural tasks cannot be adequately accomplished by the activity of individuals." In discharging this task it has to make heavy demands upon the latter. It demands their lives—whenever the integrity, independence, honor, or "ideal possessions" of the nation are in danger. In realizing, administering, or "coercing" the culture of a nation, the state in Kohler's system has an exalted position no lower than Hegel assigned to it. The development of culture through unconscious custom is slow and weak. Only when political rulers and leaders conceive a clear vision of the destiny of a nation and take a vigorous initiative in promoting the realization of that destiny does the nation's cultural advancement become swift and sure.[23]

The distinctive feature of law, Kohler maintains, is its coercive character. "Law is the standard of conduct which, in consequence of the

---

[20] *Zweck im Recht* (fourth ed.), I, p. 249; *Law as a Means to an End*, p. 242.
[21] See particularly *Wirtschaft und Recht,* fourth ed., pp. 523 ff.
[22] Kohler, *Philosophy of Law,* Ch. III, and Ch. VIII, Secs. xxi–xxv.
[23] *Ibid.,* pp. 208–209, 241–242.

inner impulse which urges men toward a reasonable form of life, ema-
nates from the whole, and is forced upon the individual. It is distinguished from morals, customs, and religion as soon as the point is
reached at which compulsory standards are separated from those demands that involve merely social amenity." [24] The object of law, as a
coercive rule, is not merely that of protecting rights and securing a fair
distribution of the advantages of social life. Law is equally a guardian of
cultural values, and not every essential activity of the state is coercive
or restrictive. The state offers services, confers powers, as well as commands and forbids, but its distinctive feature is that all its activities
have the ultimate sanction of law—i.e., coercive regulation—behind
them to the extent that they need that sort of sanction.

THE LAW ABOVE THE STATE

Duguit, Krabbe, and Laski are repelled by these claims that any
action of the coercive state can establish the discrimination between
lawful and unlawful conduct. They and their followers variously describe the positivist conception of law as a pernicious untruth, a truism,
or a barren and futile truth. They argue that law is not really made
by any organized body of men. They concede that there are definite
agencies in society which issue commands or make decisions normally
obeyed by the bulk of the community. But they hold that not all of
these commands and decisions deserve to be regarded as laws. Some
other quality is essential to give the rules the real character of law.
Duguit describes his criterion as realistic and objective, in contradistinction to the metaphysical subjectivism of the positivist doctrines.
Krabbe and Laski hold generally to subjective explanations but find
the sources for their standards directly in the consciences of men rather
than in the decrees of any official agencies.

Law with Duguit is simply the name for the rules of conduct actually controlling men who live in society.[25] Its obligations arise not
from having been commanded, expressly or by implication, by any organized authority but solely and directly from the necessities of social
life. The obligations are based upon the fact that men live in society
and must so live in order to survive and that life in society requires a

[24] *Philosophy of Law,* p. 59.
[25] Duguit's theory is set forth chiefly in the following works: *L'état, le droit
objectif et la loi positive* (1901); especially pp. 1–19, 613–618; *Manuel du droit
constitutionnel* (second ed., 1911), especially pp. 49–51, 69–79.

certain manner of conduct. If the advantages of social life are to be maintained, certain rules must be observed; otherwise society disintegrates. Men are naturally conscious of these rules and are impelled by self-interest to obey them. They are instinctively aware or learn naturally from experience that they have common needs and desires which can be satisfied only by living together; that they have diverse capabilities as a consequence of which their several needs can be satisfied only by an exchange of services; that, in short, they live longer and suffer less in association with other men. These facts constitute social solidarity. The whole of law can be reduced to three general rules: respect all acts determined by the end of social solidarity; abstain from acts determined by any contrary ends; do everything possible to develop that solidarity.

Duguit recognized that these rules must have a guaranty, but held that the guaranty is neither organized coercion nor a social sense of right. The sanction for law is primarily psychological—resting in each individual's awareness of the social approval or reprobation of his conduct according to its conformity or non-conformity to the fundamental social rules as defined above. This awareness exists among normal individuals of any and every society, even where there are no organized bodies to formulate the rules and execute them through physical coercion. In every community acts done in harmony with the rules of law will be satisfactory to the mass of individuals. Understanding the need of social solidarity, men conceive and desire the rules of conduct which are its consequences. Laws in the fundamental sense are the rules of conduct which normal men know they must observe in order to preserve and promote the benefits derived from life in society.

Thus Duguit made a full and sharp discrimination between state authority and the authority of law. Both reflect facts; both apply to men living in society and give rise to commands sustained by sanctions which secure their habitual obedience. But the facts and sanctions are fundamentally different in the two cases. The state as such has no essential connection with law (*droit*); its authority has no legal (*juridique*) or moral justification. It is merely a body of men inhabiting a definite territory, in which the strong impose their will on the weak. The strength of the rulers may rest on a majority's physical weight of numbers or upon a minority's superiority in wealth or intellect. In any case, the sanctions for political commands are simply the physical penalties the rulers are in a position to apply to those who disobey.

Law is independent of, anterior to, above and more comprehensive than, the state. There are positive and negative limits of a jural sort to the state's competence: things a "legal sovereign" must or must not do, judged by the standard of the law. If the state, through either its statute-making bodies or its constitution-making organs, violates any of the rules of social solidarity, it acts unlawfully. The force of government is legitimate not in itself but only when employed to sustain law—that is, to guarantee coöperation towards social solidarity. The function of the state, in so far as it acts as an agency of law, is simply that of adapting an already existent rule of law to a given set of facts. Its constitutional or statutory acts (*lois*) are obligatory, from the standpoint of law, only if they embody rules that are in themselves imperative. Thus law is objective. The legal validity of any act of the state depends not upon its source but upon the end which it serves.[26]

Krabbe explains law according to the source from which it springs.[27] But the source is not, as in the classical theory, any sort of formally governing official, assembly, or tribunal; for law is objective in so far as the "will" of any number or body of persons is concerned. Law is the totality of rules, general or particular, written or unwritten, "which spring from men's feeling or sense of right." [28] Not that the law for any individual is determined by his own sense of right. For law is the rule of a community. And a community does not exist where each individual recognizes as law only the rules derived from his own sense of right. A community, since it exists for some social, i.e., common,

[26] Duguit agreed that in every actual application of law there must be some exercise of judgment on the question as to whether a given rule does or does not tend to promote the ends which give legal quality to the rule. The rule's consequences for social solidarity is never a matter about which there is such unanimity of opinion that authoritative pronouncements are never required. And in all Duguit's illustrations of the actual working out of his doctrine in political society, he pointed to definite governmental organs applying the *régle de droit* by issuing judgments and orders determined, as he explains, by their findings as to the objective ends thereby promoted. He devoted a volume to showing in detail how certain organs of government in France—council of state, administrative courts, ordinary courts—adjudge the determinations of certain other organs —administrative officers and even Parliament—to be unlawful on the ground of *ultra vires* or abuse of power, because directed to unlawful ends.

[27] See Krabbe, *Die moderne Staatsidee* (1919), translated by George H. Sabine and Walter J. Shepard, as *The Modern Idea of the State* (1922).

[28] *Modern Idea of the State*, p. 39, and more generally Ch. III, Secs. vii–viii:

end, postulates unity of legal rule; and this unity is achieved only in groups among whose members there is some substantial approach to common convictions as to what is right.

Unanimity in such convictions appears in no community; the lack of it is due not so much to diversity in standards of right as to variety in the opinions as to what sort of conduct conforms to the common standards. How then is the essential legal unity to be secured in a community where there is disagreement as to the measures for realizing the community's sense of right? It is secured in part by submitting to the commands of the enacted law—assuming, first, that the law-enacting authorities are so constituted as normally to reflect the sense of right of the majority of the people and, secondly, that the enactments are subject to modification in application by tribunals of the unwritten law. These tribunals are likewise obligated to attribute legal authority only to the majority's sense of right. "Since there cannot be a single rule except by recognizing the principle of the majority, the communal life, which controls our consciousness and makes the sense of right effective in us, carries with it the obligation to govern our conduct according to the rule approved by the majority." [29] Krabbe, however, adds a significant qualification to this general rule that legal obligation is dependent on the majority's sense of right. "If," he says, "the members of a community differ regarding the rules to be followed, those rules which are desired as rules of law by a majority possess a higher value—*assuming a qualitative equality of the members in their sense of right.*" [30] Thus law in Krabbe's conception appears to be what is demanded by the sense of right of the right-minded majority of the community.

In any case, law, according to Krabbe, is above, and in origin, independent of, the state. He emphatically rejected the idea of state sovereignty understood as "an extra-legal competence to issue commands." His theory "accepts no authority as valid except that of the law; . . . the sovereign disappears, as a source of law, from both legal and political theory." He agreed that ordinarily the legislative acts of a state must be accepted as lawful. He recognized that the rule of law, as he defined it, could not prevail unless normative force were given to the decisions of the persons selected to reflect the community's sense of right and also unless some independence of judgment

---

[29] *Modern Idea of the State*, p. 78.
[30] *Moderne Staatsidee*, p. 83.

in the matter were allowed to such persons. "For it is his [the representative's] own sense of right, and not the more or less conjectural convictions of the electors, which possesses the value needed to give a rule the quality of law." But how is the supremacy of law over the state to be maintained in the exceptional case where a legislative body enacts rules "which lack the quality of law either because the organization of the legislature is defective or because it mistakes what the people's sense of right demands?" There are two correctives. First, there is the ultimate moral "right of revolution." Secondly, there is the ever-acting modification of statutory by unwritten law. The majority's sense of right determines decisions by judges and juries. Both statutory and unwritten law, differing in their immediate origins, stand upon the same planes and have the same basis for their binding force; and either may modify the other. If the statutory law goes against the sense of right of the majority, unwritten law will soon bring it, in actual application, into the proper conformity. "No power on earth can control the action of the sense of right; and when it acts, a binding rule follows spontaneously." Where either statutes of legislatures or decrees of courts apply rules that do not come from the majority's sense of right, they are applying something other than law.[31]

Laski holds that the jurist is concerned not so much with identifying and analyzing law as in finding the test for its "validity."[32] "An adequate legal philosophy must not only explain the legal right of a government to obedience, but its ethical right as well." He indicates his own test largely in a criticism of the "classical" theory of sovereignty, which he identifies particularly with Hobbes and charges with maintaining that, because "the state must necessarily perform the chief part in coördinating social activities, and . . . cannot accept dictation from any other authority in performing that function," every decision of the state or of the government which speaks in its name exhibits this quality; the orderly citizen (according to this interpretation of the classical theory) must always acquiesce in the will of the government merely because it speaks the will of the state.[33] Conceding that order is "good," Laski controverts the holding he attributes to the classicists that "order is, and always must be, the highest good."

[31] *Modern Idea of the State*, pp. 47, 93, 102, 144–145.
[32] See Laski, "Law and the State," *Economica* (November, 1929), pp. 267–295; *Studies in Law and Politics* (1932), Ch. V: "The State in the New Social Order," Ch. XI: "Law and the State."
[33] "Law and the State," pp. 272. 278.

He discredits any juristic doctrine that does not leave room for the possibility that those who resisted King Charles I in 1642, the French monarchy in 1789, and the tsar of Russia in 1917, were, although deliberately risking disorder, yet keeping entirely within the ambit of law because they were pursuing ends which in the given circumstances were higher than peace and order. They were, according to Laski's position, defiant of the state but faithful to the law above the state.

The state, he says, is entitled to obedience to the extent that it is so organized as to represent adequately the interests of the individuals, territorial groups, and functional associations affected by its laws, and that it is actually devoting its powers to these interests. But who is to decide whether the state effectively renders and executes its decision with such interests in view? We have seen that Laski has a general theory of opposition to the claims of a single, comprehensive, territorial community to impose on "functional" associations within the community its ideas as to what a legal order demands. That is his pluralistic doctrine which we have already considered.[34] In several essays concerning the relation of the state to law, he presses chiefly the claims not of these other associations but of the several individual citizens to define the limits of their lawful obligations. The source of law, he here maintains, is neither the state nor any smaller group, but the individual, acting according to his conscience. "My own view is clear," he says, "that these questions can only be answered in terms of the judgment of individual citizens. They are the persons who feel the results of state action in their lives; they, therefore, are the only persons who are entitled to pronounce upon its quality. They make the law valid by consenting to it. They consent to it as it satisfies their desires. A good law, therefore, is a law which has, as its result, the maximum possible satisfaction of desire; and no law save a good law is, except in a formal sense, entitled to obedience as such." He characterizes his theory as an "attempt to recover the individual conscience as the only true source of a law which claims obedience from its subjects." The theory, he says again, "puts the source of law where it most truly belongs, in the individual consenting mind." [35]

In Laski's discussion of the morally binding force of international law, he seems to contradict his general assertions that the obligations of law rest only upon the several judgments of those to whom it is

---

[34] See *supra*, pp. 507–508, 513–516.
[35] "Law and the State," pp. 282, 283, 295.

addressed. He assails the position of those who contend that legal rules affecting international relations have the real force of law for any given state only in so far as that state consents to them. This, he declares, is as bad as "to allow the private citizen to be the judge of his own acts." There can be no orderly international community if each member-state is to be its own judge as to the validity of the law binding within that community, just as no municipal community can survive if each citizen-member is "to be the judge of his own actions." The state, therefore, "is bound in the rules it makes by the superior rules of the international community to which it belongs. It cannot make and unmake them any more than the individual can make or unmake the law of the state of which he is the subject." This argument by Laski is simply applying to international law the positivists' doctrine of municipal law. Indeed in another sentence of the same article he stated generally the moral and practical aspect of the positivists' doctrine, by saying: "I entirely agree with the view that the cases where men or associations oppose the will of the state should always be cases of last instance." [36]

CONCLUSION

There appears to be nothing essential in the juristic doctrines of Duguit, Krabbe, or Laski that is inconsistent with the theories either of the strictly analytical jurists (e.g., Austin and Laband) or of those who adhere to the analysts' definition, yet study broadly the social origins and consequences of the laws. Each group acknowledges the existence and significance of the normative rules the other calls laws. The anti-positivists recognize, explicitly or implicitly, that there are differences of great practical significance between politically supported rules and the rules enforced only by other forms of social pressure. The positivists recognize that law-enacting assemblies or deciding judges act under the impulsions and restraints of "opinions and sentiments current" in the community or in its "most influential part."

On the one hand, no juristic scholar makes the state a general arbiter of right and wrong. On the other hand, jurists of all schools now generally regard law as an instrument for the furtherance of human welfare. They consider not only what the laws are as they appear in constitutions, statutes, and judicial decisions but also what effects

[36] "Law and the State," pp. 273, 277, 279, 286, 289, 295.

they have produced in the past, how they operate to-day, and how they may be improved by deliberate human effort.[37] All recognize the varied social and psychological sources of the law. All agree that the convictions, beliefs, desires, and prejudices of various people, in and out of office, enter into the determination of the rules laid down by political organs. Statutes reflect the ideas and wishes of legislators or of persons whom the legislators like, respect, or fear. The statutes in their application may be substantially modified by the ideas and wishes of other officials—policemen, judges, jurors—or of private persons to whom these officials feel in some way subservient. Jurors, following their own or some common feeling that a formally forbidden act is morally worthy or socially desirable, fail to convict the violators of a statute. A trial magistrate often disposes of cases by some unformulated rule of right, punishing or freeing an accused person on the basis of discriminations which neither legislative enactments nor judicial precedents recognize but which evolve from his own convictions or prejudices or from his rough interpretation of some other opinion as to what is demanded by justice or expediency in the particular case. Higher judges, in applying rules of reason to the interpretation of statutes and precedents, follow the same course. They do lip service to the supremacy of the formal law and justify their interpretation on the ground that the legislators or earlier deciding judges must be assumed to have intended only reasonable ends in their enactments or decisions and that the latter must, therefore, be interpreted in that sense, even though their terms, understood in their usual meanings, would have a very different effect.

All the jurists are in general accord in their essential conceptions of political action. The inter-relations among individuals and groups in society are such, they agree, that an organization of unification and coördination is necessary; this organization, in order to fulfil adequately its essential functions, must be comprehensive and compulsive in membership and be equipped with a power to issue commands that

---

[37] Among contemporary writers Roscoe Pound has been the most explicit and elaborate in discussing these broad social aspects of law.

The general ideas in the paragraphs that follow fit easily, the present writer believes, into the general legal doctrines of most other recent and contemporary writers. See particularly the works of Benjamin R. Cardozo, Morris R. Cohen, John Dickinson, John Chipman Gray, William E. Hocking, A. D. Lindsay, Adolf Merkel, Richard Schmidt, and Westel W. Willoughby; listed *infra*, pp. 542–543. Among these writers Willoughby and Dickinson are the most explicit in reconciling sociological and ethical with positivist conceptions of law.

may be executed through the organized force of the community, in the form, for example, of constraint directed against the body of an individual or distraint of his property; and this organization must normally, within any given community, have a monopoly of that sort of power. All agree in calling this unique institution "the state."

The controversy over the relation of the state to law appears, then, to arise principally from the different senses in which the disputants use the term "law." No word in social theory is used with a greater variety of meanings. Some writers apply the term to rules of social conduct which everywhere men of normal intelligence and disposition understand and ordinarily obey independently of any pressure from the organs of political government. Others—notably certain anthropologists describing primitive societies—apply the term to any uniformity of social behavior. Still others consider that laws are the rules that have the stamp of some moral approval—a sense of right of the community, or of the majority or the right-minded part of the community; or laws are, for each individual, the dictates of his own conscience. Others again call laws the customs that have certain social consequences or tendencies—the "behavior patterns" that tend towards "social solidarity" or that "make possible the life of civilization." With others, laws are the rules that are backed by the comprehensive and compulsive social institution we call the state.

Obviously the state does not initiate the dictates of an individual's conscience, independently create uniformities of social behavior, influence alone the course of human culture, or fix the community's ethical creeds. It does, however, give its peculiar sanctions, directly or indirectly, to certain forms of behavior. A jurist of the positivist school does not call a rule "law" until a legislative body, court, or constitution-making body has acted; his critics either apply the term to some earlier stage of the rule or else withhold the term until they see how effectively, with what consequences, or with what correspondence to their own or some broader judgments of right, the rule is executed. All the jurists appear to agree essentially in their ideas as to the relations between any of the various social imperatives, on the one hand, and organized political authority, on the other hand. They have varying theories of the relations of the state to law only because some apply the term law to one type of imperative and others to another type.

SELECT BIBLIOGRAPHY

Austin, John, *The Province of Jurisprudence Determined,* in *Lectures on Jurisprudence* (London, 1861–1863), I–VI.

Cardozo, Benjamin N., *The Nature of the Judicial Process* (New Haven, 1921).

——————, *The Growth of the Law* (New Haven, 1924).

——————, *The Paradoxes of Legal Science* (New York, 1928).

Dickinson, John, "A Working Theory of Sovereignty," *Political Science Quarterly,* XLII (1927), 524–548; XLIII (1928), 32–63.

——————, "Social Order and Political Authority," *American Political Science Review,* XXIII (1929), 293–328, 593–632.

——————, "The Law Behind Law," *Columbia Law Review,* XXIX (1929), 113–146, 285–319.

Duguit, Léon, *L'état, le droit objectif et la loi positive* (Paris, 1901).

——————, *Manuel du droit constitutionnel* (second ed., Paris, 1911).

——————, *Transformations du droit public* (Paris, 1913).

Gray, John Chipman, *The Nature and Sources of the Law* (New York, 1909; second ed., 1921).

Jellinek, Georg, *Allgemeine Staatslehre* (Berlin, 1900 and later editions).

Jhering, Rudolf von, *Der Zweck im Recht,* 2 vols. (Leipsic, 1877–1883; fourth ed., 1904–1905).

——————, *Law as a Means to an End,* translated by Isaac Husik (Boston, 1913).

Kohler, Joseph, *Lehrbuch der Rechtsphilosophie* (Berlin, 1909, second ed., 1917).

——————, *Philosophy of Law,* translated by Adalbert Albrecht (Boston, 1914).

——————, *Moderne Rechtsprobleme* (Berlin, 1907, second ed., 1913).

Krabbe, H., *Die moderne Staatsidee* (The Hague, 1915, second ed., 1919).

——————, *The Modern Idea of the State,* translated by George H. Sabine and Walter J. Shepard (New York and London, 1922).

Laband, Paul, *Das Staatsrecht des deutschen Reiches,* 3 vols. (Tübingen, 1876–1882; fifth ed., 4 vols. 1911–1914).

Laski, Harold J., "Law and the State," *Economica* (November, 1929), pp. 267–295.

——————, *Studies in Law and Politics* (New Haven, 1932), especially Chs. V and XI.

Lindsay, A. D., "The State in Recent Political Theory," *Political Quarterly,* I (1914), 128–145.

Merkel, Adolf, *Über das Verhältnis des Rechtsphilosophie zur "positiven"*

Rechtswissenschaft und zum allgemeinen Teil derselben, in *Hinterlassene Fragmente und gesammelte Abhandlungen,* Pt. II (Strassburg, 1899), pp. 291–323.

Pound, Roscoe, *An Introduction to the Philosophy of Law* (New Haven, 1922).

——————, *Law and Morals* (Chapel Hill, 1924).

Schmidt, Richard, *Allgemeine Staatslehre* (Leipsic, 1901–1903).

Stammler, Rudolf, *Die Lehre von dem richtigen Rechte* (Berlin, 1902).

——————, *The Theory of Justice,* translated by Isaac Husik (New York, 1925).

——————, "Wesen des Rechtes und der Rechtswissenschaft," pp. i–lix in Vol. II. 8 (Berlin and Leipsic, 1906) of *Die Kultur der Gegenwart,* edited by P. Hinneberg.

——————, *Lehrbuch der Rechtsphilosophie* (Berlin, 1921; third ed., 1928).

——————, *Wirtschaft und Recht nach der materialistischen Geschichtsauffassung* (Leipsic, 1896; fourth ed., Berlin, 1921).

Willoughby, Westel W., *The Fundamental Concepts of Public Law* (New York, 1924).

——————, *The Nature of the State* (New York and London, 1896), Ch. VII.

HISTORICAL AND CRITICAL WORKS

Berolzheimer, Fritz, *The World's Legal Philosophies,* translated by Rachel S. Jastrow (Boston, 1912).

Binder, Julius, "Zur Lehre vom richtigen Recht," *Archiv für Rechtswissenschaft und Wirtschafts-philosophie,* XXII (1928), 116–140.

Borchard, Edwin M., *The Relation Between "State" and "Law"* (New Haven, 1927), reprinted from Vol. XXXVI of the *Yale Law Journal.*

Cohen, Morris R., *Law and the Social Order* (New York, 1933).

Eastwood, R. A., and Keeton, G. W., *The Austinian Theories of Law and Sovereignty* (London, 1929).

Emerson, Rupert, *State and Sovereignty in Modern Germany* (New Haven, 1928).

Fowler, Robert L., "The New Philosophies of Law," *Harvard Law Review,* XXVII (1913–1914), 718–735.

Hocking, William Ernest, *Present Status of the Philosophy of Law and of Rights* (New Haven and London, 1926).

MacIver, R. M., *The Modern State* (Oxford and London, 1926), Chs. VIII and XV.

Mattern, Johannes, *Concepts of State, Sovereignty and International Law:*

with Special Reference to the Juristic Conception of the State (Baltimore and Oxford, 1928).

Pound, Roscoe, "The Scope and Purpose of Sociological Jurisprudence," *Harvard Law Review*, XXIV (1911), 591–619; XXV (1911–1912), 140–168, 489–516.

——————, "The End of Law as Developed in Juristic Thought," *Ibid.*, XXVII (1913–1914), 605–628; XXX (1916–1917), 200–225.

Sabine, George H., "Rudolf Stammler's Critical Philosophy of Law," *Cornell Law Quarterly*, XVIII (1933), 321–350.

Sabine, George H., and Shepard, Walter J., "Translators' Introduction," in H. Krabbe, *The Modern Idea of the State* (New York and London, 1922).

CHAPTER XX

EMPIRICAL COLLECTIVISM

THE men that have been the most actively concerned in bringing about the increasing economic legislation of recent years are known by various names, such as Liberals, Liberal Democrats, Radicals, Popularists, Populists, Progressives. They present no organized "movement," hold allegiance to no theoretical founder, and have no compact set of theoretical dogmas. Their general objectives and the arguments in support of their proposals are set forth in books on Social Justice, Liberalism, Economic Liberalism, Economic Democracy, Industrial Democracy. A characteristic mark of all of them is to be found in their "collectivist" point of view. This appears, in the first place, in the location or range of their sympathy: they are interested in the welfare and freedom not of some select group but of ordinary men and particularly the many who appear to be unfairly dealt with under existing laws and customs. Their collectivism appears also in their conceptions of the social bases of the advantages which even the most highly endowed members of society enjoy. In modern industrial life, they argue, the functions of producton are so minutely subdivided that nothing can be done in the creation of wealth by the isolated efforts of individual capitalists or laborers; and after useful commodities have been fabricated, an individual's claims to them have actuality only in so far as the organized community endorses the claims, defining and protecting them as legal rights. Finally, they believe that an economic policy based upon a narrowly individualistic theory proves to be inefficient as well as unfair—inadequate for meeting the material needs of society. Production conducted for private profit proves strikingly incapable of preventing the forced liquidation of debtors in times of rapidly falling prices, or of avoiding the widespread sufferings that appear in economic crises. Even under normal conditions profit-making tends to destructive competition and oppressive monopolies; to overstimulation of buying, overcapitalization, and overproduction; to a depreciation of the quality of products and exhaustion of natural resources; and to an exploitation of wage-laborers and salaried brain-workers.[1]

Collectivism is as vague a word as individualism, but there is perhaps no better term to designate the sort of ideas that we consider in this chapter. The collectivist, as we use the term, rejects, on the one hand, the socialist doctrines of economic determinism, labor-created-value, and class-war; he recognizes that differences in wealth create divisions of the community into different and often opposing political groups, but discredits the doctrine of a clear-cut distinction of classes and a continual antagonism between them.[2] On the other hand, he believes that a creed of economic individualism gives too exalted a place to private ownership; for that creed disregards or inadequately recognizes wage-earners and the community as creators or conservers of value. He opposes the claims of owners of capital to an exclusive control over the management of industry and the distribution of its profits.[3] He undertakes to show the economic interdependence among all members of the community and seeks to find the proper adjustment of their relations to one another. Some writers have attempted to work out schemes for assigning to all essential factors in production their appropriate shares, in income as well as control. Owners should be duly rewarded for their thrift and risk; they should receive a "fair" rate of interest, varying with the degree of the risk, and should exercise a part in management sufficient to protect their risk; but others also, upon whose virtues and activities the amount and value of things produced also depend, must have their proper allotments of income and power: laborers, by hand or brain; consumers, whose demands determine the prosperity of an enterprise; and the community, and the state repre-

[1] For the various criticisms of economic individualism and its practical consequences, see the following: H. N. Brailsford, *After the Peace* (1920; rev. ed., 1922); J. A. Hobson, *Incentives in the New Industrial Order* (1922), Ch. I; C. F. G. Masterman, *England After War* (1923); Sir Leo Chiozza Money, *The Triumph of Nationalization* (1920), Ch. II; Viscount Alfred Milner, *Questions of the Hour* (1923); C. E. Montague, *Disenchantment* (1922); Walter Rathenau, *In Days to Come* (1921); R. H. Tawney, *The Acquisitive Society* (1921); Lester F. Ward, *Applied Sociology* (1906), Ch. II; Sidney and Beatrice Webb, *The Decay of Capitalist Civilization* (1923); Walter E. Weyl, *The New Democracy* (1912), Chs. I–X; W. W. Willoughby, *Social Justice* (1900), Ch. IX.

[2] See the following: L. T. Hobhouse, *Liberalism* (1911), pp. 167–174; J. A. Hobson, *Crisis of Liberalism* (1909), pp. 133–156; Ramsay Muir, *Liberalism and Industry* (1920), Ch. VII.

[3] On the general attitude to private capital, see Oliver Brett, *A Defence of Liberty* (1921); Ramsay Muir, *Liberalism and Industry*, Chs. V, VI, and VIII; J. M. Robertson, *The Meaning of Liberalism* (1912), Pt. III, Chs. V–VII; W. W. Willoughby, *Social Justice*, Ch. IV

senting it, from whom come those indispensable conditions of good order and legal security which capitalists and laborers, severally or in coöperation, cannot supply.

The specific proposals of this sort of collectivism are varied and tentative. It is generally admitted that no one policy as to the lines between private and public control can 'fit all cases: private competition may, under certain conditions, work efficiently and economically in retail trade and farming; under essentially the same conditions, it may not work well in the coal-mining and oil-extraction industries or in the development of water-power. No single or simple panacea is offered; and no sudden, sweeping, root-and-branch reconstruction of the present economic order is advocated. Existing methods are to be changed in an eclectic, piecemeal manner. The general point of view of this "empirical collectivism" can perhaps be illustrated sufficiently by indicating briefly certain typical proposals and the arguments in support of them, in reference to (1) public ownership, (2) labor legislation, (3) regulation of prices, (4) taxation, and (5) land policies.

(1) The collectivist whom we are describing makes a fetish of neither public nor private ownership.[4] He would have the issue determined in each particular case by the lessons of experience. He challenges the stock-in-trade arguments of conservatives against all proposals for new forms of governmental enterprise. He generally discredits the common criticism that public ownership supplies unusual opportunities and temptations for corruption or destroys the incentives to diligence and skilfulness in economic endeavor. A government, in the interest of the general safety and welfare, has to prescribe and enforce certain standards for the conduct of industry; its hand is in business inevitably; the character of its dealings with business, public or private, reflects the general moral and intellectual character of the citizenry. As to the contention that public ownership must fail practically because

---

[4] See the following; A. E. Davies, *The Case for Nationalization* (1920), Chs. I and II; Elliott Dodds, *Is Liberalism Dead?* (1921); J. A. Hobson, *Crisis of Liberalism*, pp. 114–132; Dexter M. Keezer and Stacy May, *Public Control of Business* (1930), Ch. VIII; C. F. G. Masterman, *The New Liberalism* (1920), Ch. V; Viscount Milner, *Questions of the Hour;* Leo Chiozza Money, *The Triumph of Nationalization*, Chs. VIII–IX, XIV; Ramsay Muir, *Liberalism and Industry*, Ch. XIII; W. W. Willoughby, *Social Justice*, pp. 95–106; Max Ried, *Organisation und Verwaltung öffentlichen Unternehmungen* (1914); Elmer Roberts, *Monarchical Socialism in Germany* (1913), Ch. I.

On the present scope of public ownership, see the following: Harry W. Laidler, *Public Ownership Throughout the World* (1918); Carl D. Thompson, *Public Ownership: a Survey of Public Enterprises* (1925).

it makes inoperative the incentives to competent activity which come only from a competitive pursuit of economic gains, the argument, the collectivist holds, is weakened by several conditions: competition in private industry is already greatly limited and the opportunities for men of talent narrowly restricted by the financial control exercised by a small number of individuals; the desire for economic gain is not the only incentive to energetic and skilful workmanship; and public ownership does not preclude gradations in rank and reward.

The profit-making motive must operate preëminently, if the peculiar virtues of private enterprise are to be fully effective. The collectivist, therefore, makes a positive case for public ownership where the special conditions under which a particular enterprise is likely to be carried on are such as not to call the profit-making motive into play, or as to compel or allow the motive to operate disadvantageously to the community. The examples are obvious. Now that we agree both that postal communication and certain opportunities for education, recreation, and artistic enjoyment must be open to all (and that these facilities cannot be made so generally available on any strictly profit-making basis), we agree also that government must conduct enterprises in those fields; their "public" nature is almost universally admitted. The collectivist goes further and holds that certain other businesses, capable of being conducted with great financial profit to the owners, should, nevertheless, in the public interest, be publicly owned and operated. For a private enterprise has to be conducted with a view to immediate profits; it cannot afford to forego present gains in the interest of greater productivity in the future; where a government can afford to safeguard these future needs, a private industry may have to be wasteful of natural resources in order to secure profits for existing shareholders. The pursuit of profits may in other ways work adversely to the general interests of consumers, since in many cases corporate combination has eliminated the competition that has been traditionally assumed to guarantee a price no higher than necessary for reasonable profits. Accordingly, the industries which the collectivist ordinarily proposes for nationalization fall generally within such categories as the following: those that must be conducted on a large scale and in which a natural tendency towards monopolistic control exists; those which show a high degree of wastefulness in their methods of operation; those in which the technique of production is already highly developed so that experimentation and invention are no longer the main factors in development; those whose uninterrupted operation is indispensable to the successful conduct of other vital industries or to the satisfaction of essential needs of the inhabitants generally. The railway, electric-power, and coal-mining industries have some or all of these marks: they supply utilities that affect daily the welfare of everybody; they condition the activity of most other basic enterprises of the community; and competition among a number of independent companies creates an uneconomic multiplication of plants, and, in the case of coal-mining, brings about a waste of natural resources.

This doctrine generally assumes that the greater part of industry is to be privately owned and operated, subject to whatever regulations are demonstrably necessary in order to secure just treatment for all who participate in the several industries and for the community as a whole. Whether the community can in a given industry attain these ends most effectively through rigid regulation or through public operation has to be determined specifically for that industry. Generally a proposal for public ownership is made only for a business that is already subject to an extensive governmental control, and the change from regulation to ownership does not constitute a radical transformation in the operation of the business. For if the doctrine of class-war is repudiated, confiscation must be rejected as both unjust and inexpedient; usually nationalization through purchase is proposed, to be carried out in somewhat the manner in which private property is taken for public use by exercise of the right of eminent domain. Taxation of incomes and inheritances can then be used to recapture in part the payments made to the former owners. The management of publicly owned enterprises is to be entrusted to commissions of long tenure, separate from the ordinary political organs, safeguarded against partisan political influence, and composed in part of experts and in part of representatives of active workers in the enterprise.[5] The distinction is not great between publicly owned enterprises managed by non-political, semi-autonomous, governmental commissions, and those privately owned enterprises whose rates and services are strictly regulated by government and whose dividends are also, as a result of the regulations, limited to conventional standards of a "fair return" on the investment; so that the shareholders exercise little control over the business.

(2) We have seen that even individualist doctrines now tolerate

[5] Cf. A. Emil Davies, *The Case for Nationalization*, Chs. VIII and XVI; and *supra*, pp. 132–133.

extensive regulation in behalf of the health and safety of working-men. Empirical collectivism keeps somewhat ahead of empirical individualism in this field and stands not only for regulation of ages, hours, and sanitary conditions but also for a more aggressive dealing with problems of unemployment and low wages.[6] It would set up public agencies to find employment and would maintain either governmental insurance or compulsory private insurance against the risks of unemployment. It also advocates governmental intervention for the establishment of minimum wage standards in industries where the conditions are such that neither the scarcity of workers nor the activity of labor unions' secures a wage sufficient to support a normal-sized working-man's family in healthy existence.

(3) Every political doctrine has place for some form of price control by the state.[7] Many publicists who call themselves individualists are advocates of a protective tariff, which is in intention and in fact a governmental regulation of prices. All opinions agree, moreover, that the state is under obligation to prevent violent fluctuations in general price levels, in so far as it can do so through its control of the credit and monetary structure of the nation; so governments intervene to fix the discount rates and reserve requirements of banks and also to inflate or deflate the non-metallic elements in the monetary circulation. There is also an indirect governmental control of prices, in the old and still operative restrictions upon combinations in restraint of trade. The more direct regulation of the charges by public utilities rests upon an equally old principle—that where owners devote their property to public use or operate their property "in a manner to make it of public consequence and affect the community at large," then government may determine what is a reasonable compensation for the services rendered by the owner in connection with such property.[8] As to

[6] For the individualist attitude to labor legislation, see *supra*, pp. 400–401; for the collectivist attitude, see the following: Eveline M. Burns, *Wages and the State* (1926); Ernst Freund, *Standards of American Legislation* (1917), Chs. I, III; L. T. Hobhouse, *Liberalism*, pp. 204–213; Jacob Hollander, *The Abolition of Poverty* (1914), *Economic Liberalism* (1925), Ch. V; Jeremiah W. Jenks, *Governmental Action for Social Welfare* (1910); Ramsay Muir, *Liberalism and Industry*, Chs. VIII–XI, XVI; B. Seebohm Rowntree, *Industrial Unrest: a Way Out* (1922) Walter E. Weyl, *The New Democracy*, Chs. XVII and XIX.

[7] For expert discussions of the functions of government in relation to prices, see John M. Clark, *Social Control of Business* (1926), Pt. III; Jacob Hollander, *Economic Liberalism*, Ch. II; Ernst Freund, *Police Power* (1904), Secs. 374–378, 658–662; Sumner H. Slichter, *Modern Economic Society* (1931), Chs. XII–XIX, XXI.

[8] See Munn v. Illinois, 94 U. S. 113 (1876).

what are the special conditions that make of a public nature some kinds of private property or some private callings, legal doctrine is not altogether clear. It is now partly a matter of tradition; government to-day regulates the rates of railroads as they formerly regulated the charges by hackmen, wagoners, and other common carriers. Another legal justification rests upon the doctrine of "natural" or "practical" monopoly: where physical or economic conditions make a business one which cannot be profitably or efficiently carried on except under a virtually monopolistic control and where competition as a regulative factor is impossible, then government may step in to prevent or minimize the effects of the monopoly and protect consumers from excessive charges. Still another justification has reference to the fact that the ordinary public utilities have been granted certain public privileges—such as the power of eminent domain or special rights in the public highways—so that special obligations can be imposed on them in return for the privileges.

(4) Many collectivists look upon taxation as a rational and prac-tical means for reducing extreme differences in wealth and for achiev-ing other desired economic changes.[9] Taxes are essentially payments which members of the community make for the benefits of community life. The burdens should therefore fall chiefly upon the industry and wealth that is due primarily to the growth and enterprise of the com-munity. In taxing real estate the collectivist would increase the rates upon the unimproved value of the land, lower the rates on houses and other improvements, and thus encourage the better use of the land. In taxing incomes, he would fix lower rates on earned income—salaries and wages—and higher rates on incomes from rents, profits, and in-terest. These proposals, he argues, do not ignore the fiscal purposes of taxation or subordinate them entirely to other social ends. He ac-knowledges that the main and immediate objects of taxation are to obtain income for governmental expenditures; and he recognizes the practical considerations that should determine the selection of taxes: a tax should be so adjusted as to hamper trade as little as possible; it should not, as a protective tariff generally does, impose upon the in-habitants generally a substantially larger final cost than the amount

---

[9] See the following: L. T. Hobhouse, *Liberalism*, pp. 193–204; J. A. Hobson, *Taxation in the New State* (1919); Jacob Hollander, *Economic Liberalism*, Ch. III; C. F. G. Masterman, *The New Liberalism*, Ch. IV; Ramsay Muir, *Liberalism and Industry*, Ch. XVII; J. M. Robertson, *The Meaning of Liberalism* (1912), Pt. I, Ch. III; Sumner H. Slichter, *Modern Economic Society*, Ch. XXVIII.

the governmental treasury receives; and it should not, as taxes on necessities frequently do, fall so generally out of any relation to ability to pay as unreasonably to lower productive efficiency or degrade standards of living for large numbers of taxpayers. Taxation, he maintains, must be considered in all its essential aspects—its net revenue-producing capacity, its final incidence, and its social effects. Generally he proposes heavily progressive taxation upon inherited wealth; he rejects the common argument that the existence of a wealthy, leisured minority is indispensable to the preservation and propagation of culture; and he is skeptical also of the common argument that the desire to accumulate large estates for the benefit of descendants is an indispensable stimulus to economic initiative and industry. He is willing, however, to meet this latter objection in part by fixing lower duties upon the portions of an estate that represent the legitimate earnings during the lifetime of the deceased. He advocates heavily progressive income taxation, beginning with nominal taxes upon incomes sufficient to provide a decent livelihood for a normal family, and rising gradually, with careful discrimination between earned and unearned incomes, to heavy taxes upon large or "excess" incomes. Such taxes, he argues, are not likely to discourage any activity of great social utility; for the great organizers of industry are inspired by other impulses than the desire for an unlimited accumulation of wealth.[10]

(5) The landlord owns the sites for homes, farms, factories, parks, and electric-power; and he can so administer his ownership as to contribute to insufficient production, crowded and unsanitary conditions of living in cities, oppressive terms of farm tenancy, low wages for agricultural laborers, and restrictions on industrial enterprise, especially where there is a relatively small number of available sites. We have seen that reformers in various camps have advocated a special taxation of bare land values, in order that an owner who improves his land or builds factories or well-constructed tenements will pay a substantially smaller percentage of his total investment than the owner who leaves his land idle or maintains dilapidated and unsanitary buildings on it.[11] In regions where land is "scarce," or where it is owned by a very small

[10] See L. T. Hobhouse, *Liberalism*, pp. 197–202. As to the taxation of industry, however, the collectivist recognizes the necessity of certain practical precautions, such as that new enterprises must be allowed a period within which they are permitted to enjoy unlimited profits, say until they have been able to build up adequate reserves. Cf. Ramsay Muir, *Liberalism and Industry*, Ch. XVII.

[11] Cf. *supra*, pp. 88 ff.

minority of the population, demands are often made for a more direct governmental intervention in behalf of rural and urban tenants, farm workers, or the general body of consumers.[12] Some contemporary governments have set up public authorities to establish fair rents, modify other oppressive leasehold conditions, and restrain the eviction of tenants at the caprice of landlords; some have created boards to fix minimum-wage standards for agricultural workers; some have authorized municipal authorities to acquire land by exercise of the right of eminent domain, in order to erect houses to be let at low rentals. In recent years the agricultural landowner has increasingly appealed for governmental intervention. Industrial developments have created a growing disparity between the declining prices of the farmer's staples and the advancing prices he has to pay for farm machinery, household goods, and other manufactured products; he is dependent upon governmental aid to save him from the disabilities of a pursuit that does not lend itself easily to organized self-protection. Thus the farmer in the United States secures from his government various forms of assistance: tariffs on imported farm products to protect him from foreign competition; excise taxes on manufactured substitutes for farm products, to protect him from domestic competitors; free advice and information on breeding and cultivation and on the extermination of plant and animal pests; and other governmental services in the way of support for coöperative marketing, the provision of credit facilities, and the stabilization of the prices of farm products.

There is no occasion here to review in further detail the scope of recent collectivist legislation.[13] In most countries the "legal" justification of the legislation is generally recognized. It is true that in the

---

[12] On tendencies in collectivist policy in relation to landowning in England, see the following: A. Emil Davies and Dorothy Evans, *Land Nationalisation: the Key to Social Reform* (1921); Elliott Dodds, *Liberalism in Action: a Record and a Policy* (1922), Chs. VI, VII; C. F. G. Masterman, *The New Liberalism,* Ch. VI; Viscount Alfred Milner, *Questions of the Hour;* Ramsay Muir, *Liberalism and Industry,* Chs. XIV and XV; Robert Murray, *The Land Question Solved* (1922).

[13] For descriptions of the scope and development of recent collectivist legislation, see Edward P. Cheyney, *Modern English Reform: from Individualism to Socialism* (1931); A. V. Dicey, *Law and Opinion in England in the Nineteenth Century* (second ed., 1914), lectures VII, VIII; Ernst Freund, *Standards of American Legislation,* Ch. I; Charles W. Pipkin, *The Idea of Social Justice: a Study of Legislation and Administration and the Labor Movement in England and France between 1900 and 1926* (1927); Elmer Roberts, *Monarchical Socialism in Germany,* Chs. II, V; Neil Skene Smith, *Economic Control* (1929), Pts. I, II.

United States the courts sometimes block the legislative attempts to set up new governmental limitations upon private economic activity, on the ground that they see no essential relation of the limitations to any legitimate end of government; they adjudge the legislation to be void as a violation of a constitutional injunction against depriving a person of liberty or property without due process of law. In the great majority of instances, however, these courts sustain the legislation; and the prevailing tendency of their decisions is to discern more readily the general welfare that invests with the saving quality of due process a limitation upon the privileges of private ownership. When the decisions do not, the obstacle is generally not in the constitution but in the judges who expound the constitution.[14] In some decisions, indeed, the American courts have enunciated a broad and positive collectivist doctrine, holding that the main consideration, in determining whether a government may regulate the services or prices of a private enterprise should be not the existence of a *de facto* or *de jure* monopoly or the possession of some special public privilege but rather the extent of the use of the commodity or service in question or its importance in relation to the comfort, prosperity, or security of the community.[15]

Many writers now insist that the latter is the only realistic criterion; for an intelligent community, whatever its traditional law may be, will not persistently tolerate business practices that result in inadequate supplies or excessive prices for the ordinary necessities and conveniences of life; it will put an end to the practices by whatever reasonable means appear to be necessary, whether by nationalization or regulation. Thus the question as to whether the coal-mining industry, for example, is to be subjected to additional control will be settled neither by theoretical arguments as to sources of value and the relative merits of socialism and individualism nor by technical arguments as to whether the industry falls within the traditional categories of natural monopolies or public utilities. It will be settled largely by the conduct of the operators and mine-workers themselves; if these groups persistently act on the assumption that their interests in the industry are, severally or jointly, superior to the interests of the community at large, their action will determine the question in favor of a more extended governmental control in some form.

[14] See Felix Frankfurter, *The Public and Its Government* (1930), Ch. II.
[15] See People *v.* Budd, 117 New York 1(1889); Brass *v.* North Dakota, 153 U.S. 391 (1894); Block *v.* Hirsh, and Marcus Brown Holding Co. *v.* Feldman, 256 U.S. 135 and 170 (1921).

The legislatures of most other countries are free from any substantive restraint in a constitutional requirement of due process. Indeed several of the post-war European constitutions make it not only the right but also the duty of their parliaments to intervene in economic affairs in order to see that the uses of property do not destroy decent standards of living or create social injustices of any sort. "The organization of economic life," the German constitution of 1919 provided, "must conform to the principles of justice, to the end that all may be guaranteed a decent standard of living." "Property imposes obligations. Its use by the owner shall at the same time serve the public good." "Labor shall be under the special protection of the Reich." [16] The Estonian constitution declares that "the economic organization must correspond with the principles of justice, the object of which is to secure conditions of living worthy of human beings"; and the constitution of Finland provides that "the labor power of citizens shall be under the special protection of the state." [17] Most of the constitutions contain provisions that empower or obligate the respective parliaments to promote these ends in specific ways, as by setting up schemes of social insurance, regulating trade in the necessities of life, confiscating royalties derived from natural resources, and taxing unearned increments of wealth.[18]

An actual individualist economy has now ceased to exist in the large industrial countries, even if law leaves private business generally unregulated. It has been shown that in the United States (in 1932), 200 corporations, out of a total of twenty-odd thousand, control more than half the total corporate wealth of the country.[19] The millions of the "owners" (stockholders) of the giant corporations have only a theoretical control. Their motives of individual initiative and responsibility do not enter far into the conduct of the business. A few thousand managers exercise the actual control.

Even the most conservative theorists and the most practical business men now generally agree that some sort of foresight and constructive planning is indispensable if evils of over-production, price instability,

[16] Arts. 151, 153, 157.
[17] Constitution of Estonia, Art. 25, and of Finland, Art. 6. See also the Constitution of Yugoslavia, Arts. 26, 37.
[18] See the following constitutions: Germany, Arts. 37, 155, 161; Austria, Art. 11; Poland, Art. 161; Finland, Art. 6. See also Agnes Headlam-Morley, *The New Democratic Constitutions of Europe* (1929), Ch. XV.
[19] Adolf A. Berle and Gardiner C. Means, *The Modern Corporation and Private Property* (1932).

unemployment, and the like are to be avoided; they agree also that the planning has to be coöperative and that it involves a considerable degree of collective restraint upon individual discretion. Business conditions do not automatically right themselves. In many instances, J. M. Keynes has pointed out, there is a "tendency of big enterprise to socialize itself," and the management of a large bank, railroad, or insurance company may consider the stability and reputation of the enterprise above unlimited profits for stockholders.[20] Many of the greater industries have to be variously socialized—in the interests either of owners or the public, and either by private agreements and benevolent concessions by the owners, in their dealings with one another and with their employees or customers, or by state action. Self-interest, a sense of public responsibility, the pressure of public opinion, the compulsions of formal law—all work together in bringing it about that a large and essential enterprise, whether owned by private shareholders or the state, is to a considerable degree administered in the interests of its customers or of the public generally. There is no important economic group that now holds in practice to any anti-interventionist conception of the proper sphere of state activity in the economic field. Organized wage-earners, chambers of commerce, professional societies, associations of manufacturers, traders, and farmers—all look extensively to their government for assistance, guidance, and compulsive intervention in their behalf. Whether they demand an old-age pension, a minimum wage, an enforcement of professional standards, an export debenture, an equalization fee, a restraint on peaceful picketing, a ship subsidy, or a protective tariff—they essentially repudiate any consistent theory of *laisser-faire.*

In 1933, a committee on "Social Trends" (appointed by President Hoover, in 1929, with no particular relation to the "depression") made its report, presenting a broad factual background for the collectivist trend of legislation in the United States.[21] It sets forth, with vast arrays of statistical and documentary evidence, the recent economic, cultural, and institutional development. It points to "the elements of instability in our social structure," particularly to the maladjustments due to "the unequal rates of change." Employment does not keep pace with increased production; the capacity to produce goods outdistances, there-

[20] *The End of Laissez-faire* (1926).
[21] *Recent Social Trends: Report of the President's Research Committee* 2 vols. (1932). See especially the "Review of Findings," I, xi–lxxv; and also Vol. II, Chs. XXV, XXIX.

fore, the capacity to consume them. New inventions and discoveries bring on other unsolved problems of public morals, education, and the law. The movement of political practice and doctrine lags generally behind the pace of social and economic change: "there is in our social organizations an institutional inertia, and in our social philosophies a tradition of rigidity." In indicating the probable direction of the changes in governmental policy—determined eventually by the economic changes —the committee points to the possibilities of an extensive and varied control by government.

It is conceivable that without any surrender of our belief in the merits of private property, individual enterprise and self-help, the American people will press toward a larger measure of public control to promote the common welfare. One possibility is a further extension of the list of public utilities to include coal mining and perhaps other industries. Progressive taxes may be graded at still steeper rates. An upper limit may be put upon inheritances. Public ownership may be extended . . . on the pleas of security owners who see no escape from heavy loss except through sale to the government. Small business men may succeed in getting drastic restrictions placed upon corporate enterprises. Farmers may demand and receive further special legislation to lighten their burdens. Labor organizations seem likely to push with vigor various plans for social insurance. And among the interests which will demand that government concern itself actively with their needs, large corporate enterprises will continue to occupy a prominent place.

. . . Our property rights remain, but they undergo a change. We continue to exercise an individual initiative, but that initiative has larger possibilities, affects others more intimately and therefore is subject to more public control.[22]

The world-wide depression, beginning in the autumn of 1929, brought on new and significant challenges or repudiations of the old theory of a self-adjusting industrial order. The numerous books that consider the background of this depression disagree at some points and agree at others, in their analyses of "causes"—war debts and reparations, political disturbances, overspeculation, tariff barriers, a general outdistancing of consuming or purchasing power by productive capacity. All agree that certain maladjustments, which came to a crisis in the depression, are fundamental and not temporary and that they need more than a mere tinkering with externals.[23] They hold that, in Sir Arthur

[22] *Recent Social Trends*, I, xxxiii.
[23] See especially, Sir Arthur Salter, *Recovery: the Second Effort* (1932); George

Salter's words, "the world's economic mechanism has lost its self-adjusting quality," or they deny that it ever had that quality. Business, they say, can no longer, if it ever could, be safely allowed to run "adrift"; and business men must be made to consider "social" as well as "business" needs and objectives. Generally the writers do not propose a very extensive reorganization of the machinery of government, any general program of public ownership, or a direct governmental fixing of prices, profits, and wages. Some offer proposals for a "managed currency," an extensive scheme of unemployment insurance under governmental auspices, a further redistribution of wealth through income and inheritance taxation, or a partial governmental ownership of such basic industries as the railways and coal-mining. They all submit "plans" for a "managed economy" and assign to the state an important part in management. The state must control credit expansion, regulate new capital investments and the application of new inventions, restore pre-war price-levels, set up and supervise "planning" bodies in large industries. Most of them regard these inevitable, and in some instances radical, extensions of governmental activity—by way of restraint, prohibition, guidance, aid, and direct service—as not actually a reversal of policy but only a strengthening or acceleration of processes already in operation for at least a century, beginning, say, with the English factory acts of 1802 or the American tariff act of 1789. Few informed critics now challenge the recent proposals on the ground merely of their collectivist tendency or deny to the state a unique responsibility in safeguarding the wealth and welfare of the community from the excesses of private competition.

Perhaps no observer could have predicted the rapid advances in collectivism actually achieved by the United States in 1933, in execution of the "new deal" for the common man advocated by President Franklin D. Roosevelt. Submitting to the president's vigorous leadership as well as to pressure from numerous private groups, Congress enacted a series of measures bringing the government at Washington into a direct and extensive control of hours of labor, wages, working conditions, prices, the rationing of production, the safeguarding of bank deposits, and the marketing of securities.[24] The control was to be exercised in coöpera-

Soule, *A Planned Society* (1932); Stuart Chase, *A New Deal* (1932); Wallace B. Donham, *Business Looks at the Unforeseen* (1932); Charles A. Beard, ed., *America Faces the Future* (1932).

[24] See Charles A. Beard and George H. E. Smith, *The Future Comes: a Study of the New Deal* (1933); Ernest K. Lindley, *The Roosevelt Revolution* (1933);

tion with private industry; and associations in the several industries were invited to propose their own regulatory codes; but the government had the final decision both as to the "truly representative" character of the "voluntary" associations and as to the acceptability of their codes; and it could in any instance impose a code of its own. The grants of power in this legislation were in most instances for limited periods; and the laws were especially intended by some of the sponsors, and widely approved popularly, as cures for the depression. It seems probable, however, that if they work passably well in the emergency, they will in many particulars became permanent parts of governmental policy. This was explicitly within the intention of some of the advocates of the legislation; and indeed the measures represent only more sudden advances in a current of practice and opinion already strongly in motion throughout the Western world.

It is not suggested, however, that those who have opposed the regulatory measures described in this chapter are any more individualistic, in their general attitude to governmental action, than those who have supported the measures. As the means of production and distribution change, the forms of social interdependence also change, creating new problems of comfort, convenience, decency, and order. The specific interferences with individual economic freedom have recently assumed somewhat new forms, and there may appear to have been a general movement from individualism to collectivism. But private property is itself a highly collectivistic institution, dependent for its existence upon very substantial restraints, rigorously applied by the organized force of the community, upon individual freedom. At any given period of time, therefore, the law intervenes, not only to protect individual owners in what are then regarded as proper uses of private property, but also to safeguard individuals and the community as a whole against oppressive and incompetent uses of property.

SELECT BIBLIOGRAPHY

Adams, Henry Carter, "Relation of the State to Industrial Activity," *Publications of American Economic Association*, Vol. I (1886–87).
Beard, Charles A., ed., *America Faces the Future* (New York, 1932).

Earle Looker, *The American Way: Franklin Roosevelt in Action* (1933); Franklin D. Roosevelt, *Looking Forward* (1933); Rexford G. Tugwell, *The Industrial Discipline* (1933).

————————, *The Economic Basis of Politics* (New York, 1922).

Beard, Charles A., and Smith, George H. E., *The Future Comes: a Study of the New Deal* (New York, 1933).

Berle, Adolf A., and Means, Gardiner C., *The Modern Corporation and Private Property* (New York, 1932).

Brailsford, H. N., *After the Peace* (London, 1920; New York, 1922).

Burns, C. Delisle, *Industry and Civilisation* (London and New York, 1925).

Burns, Eveline M., *Wages and the State: a Comparative Study of the Problems of State Wage Regulation* (London, 1926).

Chase, Stuart, *A New Deal* (New York, 1932).

Cheyney, Edward P., *Modern English Reform: from Individualism to Socialism* (New York, 1931).

Clark, John M., *Social Control of Business* (Chicago, 1926).

Croly, Herbert, *Progressive Democracy* (New York, 1914).

————————, *The Promise of American Life* (New York, 1909).

Davies, A. Emil, *The Case for Nationalization* (London, 1920).

Davies, A. Emil, and Evans, Dorothy, *Land Nationalisation: the Key to Social Reform* (London, 1921).

Deschanel, Paul, *L'organisation de la démocratie* (Paris, 1910).

Dicey, A. V., *Lectures on the Relation between Law and Public Opinion in England, during the Nineteenth Century* (second ed., London, 1914).

Dickinson, G. Lowes, *Justice and Liberty* (New York, 1908).

Donham, Wallace B., *Business Looks at the Unforeseen* (New York, 1932).

Dunbar, Charles F., "Reaction in Political Economy," *Quarterly Journal of Economics*, I (1886), 1–27.

Eliot, Charles W., *The Conflict between Individualism and Collectivism in a Democracy* (New York, 1910).

Fairchild, Henry P., *Profits or Prosperity* (New York, 1932).

Frankfurter, Felix, *The Public and its Government* (New Haven, 1930).

Frederick, J. George, *A Primer of "New Deal" Economics* (New York, 1933).

Frederick, J. George, ed., *The Swope Plan* (New York, 1931).

Freund, Ernst, *The Police Power* (Chicago, 1904).

————————, *Standards of American Legislation* (Chicago, 1917).

Gleason, Arthur H., *What the Workers Want: a Study of British Labor* (New York, 1920).

Goodnow, Frank J., *Social Reform and the Constitution* (New York, 1911).

Grandvilliers, Jean de, *Essai sur le libéralisme allemand* (Paris, 1914).

Hobhouse, Leonard T., *The Elements of Social Justice* (London, 1922).

————————, *Liberalism* (London and New York, 1911).

————————, *Social Evolution and Political Theory* (New York, 1913).

Hobson, J. A., *The Crisis of Liberalism: New Issues of Democracy* (London, 1909).

—————————, *The Evolution of Modern Capitalism* (London and New York, 1895; rev. ed., 1926).

—————————, *Incentives in the New Industrial Order* (London, 1922).

—————————, *Problems of a New World* (London, 1921).

—————————, *Taxation in the New State* (London, 1919).

Holcombe, Arthur N., *The New Party Politics* (New York, 1933).

Hollander, Jacob H., *The Abolition of Poverty* (Boston, 1914).

—————————, *American Citizenship and Economic Welfare* (Baltimore, 1919).

—————————, *Economic Liberalism* (New York, 1925).

Howe, Frederic C., *The City the Hope of Democracy* (New York, 1905).

Hutchins, B. L., and Harrison, A., *A History of Factory Legislation* (second ed., London, 1911).

Jenks, Jeremiah W., *Governmental Action for Social Welfare* (New York, 1910).

Keezer, Dexter M., and May, Stacy, *The Public Control of Business* (New York, 1930).

Keynes, John Maynard, *The End of Laissez-faire* (London, 1926).

Laidler, Harry W., *Public Ownership Throughout the World* (New York, 1918).

Liberal Land Committee, "The Land and the Nation" (London, 1925).

Liberal Conference, February, 1926, "Land Policy Proposals" (London, 1926).

Lindley, Ernest K., *The Roosevelt Revolution* (New York, 1933).

Lippmann, Walter, *Drift and Mastery* (New York, 1914).

Looker, Earle, *The American Way: Franklin Roosevelt in Action* (New York, 1933).

Masterman, C. F. G., *England after War* (New York, 1923).

—————————, *The New Liberalism* (London, 1920).

Milner, Viscount Alfred, *Questions of the Hour* (London, 1923).

Montague, C. E., *Disenchantment* (London, 1922).

Money, Sir Leo Chiozza, *The Triumph of Nationalization* (London and New York, 1920).

Muir, Ramsay, *Liberalism and Industry: Towards a Better Social Order* (London, 1920).

—————————, *Politics and Progress* (London, 1923).

Murray, Robert, *The Land Question Solved* (London, 1922).

Parsons, Frank, *The City for the People* (Philadelphia, 1901).

Pipkin, Charles W., *The Idea of Social Justice: a Study of Legislation and Administration and the Labor Movement in England and France between 1900 and 1926* (New York, 1927).

Rathenau, Walter, *In Days to Come,* translated from the German by Eden and Cedar Paul (London, 1921).

Recent Social Trends: Report of the President's Research Committee, 2 vols. (New York, 1932).

Reeves, William Pemder, *State Experiments in Australia and New Zealand,* 2 vols. (London, 1902; reprint, New York, 1925).

Ried, Max, *Organisation und Verwaltung öffentlicher Unternehmungen, mit Berücksichtigung Deutschlands, der Schweiz und insbesondere Österreichs* (Berlin, etc., 1914).

Roberts, Elmer, *Monarchical Socialism in Germany* (New York, 1913).

Robertson, J. M., *The Meaning of Liberalism* (London, 1912).

Roosevelt, Franklin D., *Looking Forward* (New York, 1933).

Roosevelt, Theodore, *Progressive Principles and Other Essays* (New York, 1913).

Rowntree, B. Seebohm, *Industrial Unrest: a Way Out* (London, 1922).

Salter, Sir Arthur, *Recovery: the Second Effort* (New York, 1932).

—————, *The Framework of an Ordered Society* (New York, 1933).

Slichter, Sumner H., *Modern Economic Society* (New York, 1931).

Smith, Neil Skene, *Economic Control* (London, 1929).

Soule, George, *A Planned Society* (New York, 1932).

Storey, Harold, *The Economics of Land Value* (London, 1913).

Tawney, R. H., *The Acquisitive Society* (London, 1921).

—————, *Equality* (New York, 1931).

Thompson, Carl D., *Public Ownership: a Survey of Public Enterprises, Municipal, State and Federal, in the United States and Elsewhere* (New York, 1925).

Tugwell, Rexford G., *The Industrial Discipline* (New York, 1933).

Wallas, Graham, *Our Social Heritage* (New Haven, 1921).

Ward, Lester F., *Applied Sociology: a Treatise on the Conscious Improvement of Society by Society* (Boston and New York, 1906).

—————, *Psychic Factors of Civilization* (Boston and New York, 1893).

Webb, Sidney, and Webb, Beatrice, *The Decay of Capitalist Civilization* (New York, 1923).

Weill, Georges, *Histoire du mouvement social en France de 1852 à 1924* (Paris, 1924).

Wells, H. G., *After Democracy* (London, 1932).

—————, *The Shape of Things to Come* (New York, 1933).

Weyl, Walter E., *The New Democracy* (New York, 1912).

Wilson, Woodrow, *The New Freedom* (New York and Garden City, 1913).

Willoughby, Westel W., *Social Justice* (New York, 1900).

INDEX

Proportional representation, 298, 299.

Proudhon, Pierre Joseph, 38, 45, 194-195, 198, 200.

Psychological doctrines, in post-war socialism, 133 ff.; in anarchism, 203, 204, 209, 216, 217; in guild socialism, 265-266; in anti-democratic theory, 313-315, 319-320; anti-democratic claims controverted, 359-361; in defense of private property, 403-404; in support of war, 450-451.

Public ownership, Marx on, 54-55; position of orthodox socialists, 73-74; Fabian socialists, 106; post-war moderate socialists, 132-133; Russian Communists, 157-158, 167-168; guild socialists, 281; in recent empirical collectivism, 547-550, 557; individualists' doctrine, 401 ff.

Race superiority, theory of, 319-325; refutation, 354-358.

Rappoport, Chas., 190.

Raskowski, 81.

Rathenau, Walter, 546, n. 1.

"Reason of State," Ch. XVI, *passim*.

Reckitt, 263, 267, n. 8, 271, n. 15, 273, n. 19, 274, n. 21.

Reclus, Élisée, 217.

Religion, in support of socialism, 19-21; in anarchist doctrines, 192, 203, 216-217, 223-224; in Russian Communism, 178-182; in Italian Fascism, 471-472; in the defense of war, 445.

Renan, 442, n. 22.

Renaudel, 127.

Renner, Karl, 130.

Renouvier, Charles, 385, n. 5, 412.

Representation, 170-171, 172-173, 295 ff.

Requa, Mark L., 406.

"Revisionist" socialists, 69, 107 ff.; theory of value, 108-109; theory of history, 109; conception of socialist evolution, 109-111; conception of class struggle, 110-111, 116; theory of revolution, 111-112, 116; ideas on democracy, 112-114, 118; nationalist doctrine, 116-118.

Revolution, Karl Marx on, 56-59; position of orthodox Marxians, 71-72; position of revisionist socialists, 111-112; in Russian communist doctrine,

163-167; in anarchist doctrine, 205, 214.

"Revolution of Institutions," 254.

Ricardo, David, 42-43, 45.

Ritchie, D. G., 415, n. 15.

Robertson, J. M., 546, n. 3, 551, n. 9.

Rocco, Alfredo, 473-478 (*passim*), 484, 492.

Roe, Gilbert, 366, n. 40.

Roosevelt, Franklin D., 558.

Roosevelt, Theodore, 366, n. 40, 368, 561.

Rossoni, 476, n. 23.

Rousseau, J. J., 292.

Rowntree, B. Seebohm, 550, n. 6.

Royalists, French, 336-339, 457.

Rubinow, I. M., 84.

Ruge, Arnold, 39.

Russell, Bertrand, 262, 405.

Russian autocracy under tsardom, 147-149, 151-154, 436-437.

Russian Communist Party, *see* "All-Union Communist Party" of Russia.

Russian Communists, historical background, 146 ff.; governmental régime, 157-160; criticism of capitalist system, 161-162; doctrine of revolution, 163-167; conception of the state, 168 ff.; dictatorship of the proletariat, 168-171, 173, 175, 184; attitude toward democracy, 162, 169-173, 183-184; system of soviets, 169-173, 175; rule by force, 168, 173-174, 176-177; attitude to religion, 178-182; cultural activities, 182-183; anarchist goal, 184; doctrine compared with Marxism, 162-166; with anarchism, 221-222; socialist criticism, 175-176; relation to Italian Fascism, 462-463, 466, 484-485.

Russian political doctrine under tsardom, 437-439.

Ryan, John A., 405.

Sabotage, 239-240.

Sadler, Wm. S., 335.

St. John, Vincent, 250, n. 35.

Saint-Mandé Programme, 114.

Saint-Simon, 18, 19.

Sait, Edward M., 377, 405.

Salter, Sir Arthur, 557-558.

Salter, F. R., 139, n. 27.

(6)